A. J. Monson

NOTABLE BRITISH TRIALS SERIES.

Madeleine Smith. Edited by A. Duncan Smith, Advocate.

Dr. Pritchard. Edited by William Roughead.

The Stauntons. Edited by J. B. Atlay, Barrister-at-Law.

Franz Muller. Edited by H. B. Irving.

The Annesley Case. Edited by Andrew Lang.

Lord Lovat. Edited by David N. Mackay.

Captain Porteous. Edited by William Roughead.

William Palmer. Edited by Geo. H. Knott, Barrister-at-Law.

Mrs. Maybrick. Edited by H. B. Irving.

Dr. Lamson. Edited by H. L. Adam.

Mary Blandy. Edited by William Roughead.

City of Glasgow Bank Directors. Edited by William Wallace, Advocate.

Deacon Brodie. Edited by William Roughead.

James Stewart. Edited by David N. Mackay.

A. J. Monson. Edited by J. W. More, Advocate.

Oscar Slater. Edited by William Roughead.

Eugene Marie Chantrelle. Edited by A. Duncan Smith, Advocate.

The Douglas Cause. Edited by A. Francis Steuart, Advocate.

Mrs. M'Lachlan. Edited by William Roughead.

Eugene Aram. Edited by Eric R. Watson, Barrister-at-Law.

J. A. Dickman. Edited by S. O. Rowan-Hamilton, Barrister-at-Law.

The Seddons. Edited by Filson Young.

Sir Roger Casement. Edited by Geo. H. Knott, Barrister-at-Law.

H. H. Crippen. Edited by Filson Young.

The Wainwrights. Edited by H. B. Irving.

Thurtell and Hunt. Edited by Eric R. Watson.

Burke and Hare. Edited by William Roughead.

IN PREPARATION.

Mary Queen of Scots. Edited by A. Francis Steuart.

Steinie Morrison. Edited by the Hon. H. Fletcher Moulton.

George Joseph Smith. Edited by Eric R. Watson.

Particulars may be had from the Publishers.

Wm. Hodge & Co., Ltd., Edinburgh and London.

Ardlamont House, Argyllshire.

Trial of

A. J. Monson

EDITED BY

John W. More, B.A.(Oxon)

Advocate

SECOND EDITION

EDINBURGH AND LONDON

WILLIAM HODGE & COMPANY, LTD.

PRINTED BY
WILLIAM HODGE AND COMPANY, LIMITED
GLASGOW AND EDINBURGH

PREFATORY NOTE TO FIRST EDITION.

In presenting this, the first published report of this notable trial, the Editor has the honour to acknowledge the help given him by the Right Honourable the Lord Justice-Clerk in revising the proofs of his Charge to the Jury. The Editor's thanks are also due to Sheriff J. Campbell Lorimer, K.C., who revised the proofs of the Solicitor-General's Address to the Jury, and to Sheriff John Wilson, K.C., who revised the proofs of Mr. Comrie Thomson's Address to the Jury. In preparing his report of the medical evidence for the Prosecution and the Defence the Editor received the greatest assistance from Emeritus Professor Sir Henry D. Littlejohn, M.D., Edinburgh, and Professor Matthew Hay, M.D., Aberdeen, respectively, which he gratefully acknowledges. The Editor's especial thanks are due to William Roughead, Esq., W.S., who put at his disposal his unique collection of matter relating to the trial. Help, in the shape of material for the preparation of this report, was also given by William Findlay, Esq., Advocate, and by William Blair, Esq., W.S., which the Editor has pleasure in acknowledging.

March, 1908.

CONTENTS.

FIFTH DAY—SATURDAY, 16TH DECEMBER, 1893.

Evidence for Prosecution—continued.

SIXTH DAY—MONDAY, 18TH DECEMBER, 1893.

Evidence for Prosecution— continued.

SEVENTH DAY—TUESDAY, 19TH DECEMBER, 1893.

Evidence for Prosecution—continued.

Evidence for Defence.

EIGHTH DAY—WEDNESDAY, 20TH DECEMBER, 1893.

Evidence for Defence—continued.

NINTH DAY—THURSDAY, 21ST DECEMBER, 1893.

Evidence for Defence—continued.

TENTH DAY—FRIDAY, 22ND DECEMBER, 1893.

LIST OF ILLUSTRATIONS.

ALFRED JOHN MONSON.

INTRODUCTION.

THE trial of Alfred John Monson on the double charge of attempting
to murder and of murdering Windsor Dudley Cecil Hambrough at
Ardlamont, Argyllshire, may be placed in the list of Scottish trials
as the most important which has taken place since that of Madeleine
Smith, nearly fifty years ago; and, as in the case of that trial, the
most abiding interest to students of criminology lies in the fact that
the verdict was that anomalous and peculiarly Scottish one of " not
proven," and that the mystery which was seen to enfold the case
from the first was not dispelled by any definite pronouncement by
the jury. Not only was the charge against the prisoner the most
serious which any man has to face at the hands of his fellow-men,
but also the circumstances of the alleged crime, the place where it
occurred, and the social position of the accused and of his alleged
victim were of such a kind as at once to arrest attention and to make
people look with interested eyes to the High Court of Justiciary in
Edinburgh, where, on 12th December, 1893, the prosecution and the
defence began their efforts, extending over ten long days, to get at
the heart of the mystery. But as day by day the evidence unfolded
itself, and as the rival theories upon which the Crown and the defence
were staking their respective cases came to be apparent, the interest
became deepened until, throughout the length and breadth of the
country, men were busy with the solution of the problems of the
case which soon came to be known, and has continued to be known,
as " The Ardlamont Mystery."

Round the question of how the boy Cecil Hambrough came by
death was woven, as the trial proceeded, a web of evidence the like
of which, in complexity and in diversity, has been surpassed in no
criminal trial in Scotland. In the attempt by the Crown to show to
the satisfaction of the jury that the accused man was guilty as libelled,
and in the attempt to refute this contention, the counsel on either
side brought forward the evidence of diverse and dissimilar witnesses,
from the unlettered testimony of ploughmen, grooms, domestic servants, and gamekeepers, to the expert evidence of surveyors, gunmakers, and medical men of great experience and high standing. The
motive which the Crown sought to prove in order to strengthen their
contention was the accused man's belief that by the death of Cecil
Hambrough he would be financially a gainer to a considerable extent,

Alfred John Monson.

and for the proving and disproving of this element of the case a tangle of financial enterprises in which the prisoner had been engaged for several years had to be unravelled by the evidence of actuaries, insurance officials, and financial men of many and varied hues. The case was further complicated by the evidence relating to the identity and disappearance of Scott, the alleged accomplice of the prisoner, that enigmatic figure which flitted across the stage at the most critical moment of the drama, coming from where no man knows and disappearing beyond the ken of men.

Although, undoubtedly, of all the evidence which was led during the trial, that which dealt most intimately with the young man's death is, from a sensational point of view, of most clamant interest, yet there are many eddies and backwashes of the stream of evidence which are well worthy the attention of those who have the taste for studying the *minutiae* of a great trial; and, looking at the case from a purely technical point of view, it is important on account of the legal points which came up for decision and which form an appendix to this report.

The uncontroversial facts of the case revealed during the progress of the trial are briefly these. In 1890 Mr. Monson was introduced to Major Hambrough, the father of Cecil Hambrough, by Mr. Tottenham, a London financier, and at Major Hambrough's request Mr. Monson undertook the custody and tuition of the boy Cecil, then seventeen years of age, till he should pass into the army, and for his services Mr. Monson was to be paid at the rate of £300 a year. At this time Major Hambrough was in a state of financial difficulty, and had mortgaged his life interest in certain family estates to an insurance company which had foreclosed, that is, had made itself owner of the interests mortgaged. Soon after taking up his duties as tutor to the boy Mr. Monson entered into negotiations with Major Hambrough with a view to relieving the Major's embarrassment, and these negotiations went on for some time. In 1892, however, for some reason a rupture occurred in the relations between Mr. Monson and the Major, who, from this time onward, used all his influence to induce his son to leave his tutor's house. In this he was unsuccessful, and Cecil continued to stay with Mr. Monson, most of his time being spent at a place in Yorkshire, where Monson was then residing.

In August, 1892, Mr. Monson was adjudicated bankrupt. In January, 1893, negotiations were entered into by him and Cecil with a view of raising money on the boy's expectancy in the Hambrough estates, but in February these broke down. Shortly after this Mr. Monson began to communicate with a firm of shooting agents in London in order to obtain the lease of a shooting in Scotland for the season, and in May a lease of Ardlamont House and shootings, in Argyllshire, was entered into in the names of Cecil Hambrough and Mr. Jerningham, a gentleman whom Mr. Monson represented as being Cecil's guardian and good for the rent. The rent was £450 for the season, half to be paid by 1st August, under the condition that if it

2

Introduction.

were not paid within a certain number of days thereafter the lease was to be void. Mr. Monson with his family went north to Ardlamont, and Cecil Hambrough joined them after finishing his training with the Yorks Militia, in which he held the rank of lieutenant. At this period and for some time before Mr. Monson and Cecil were being financed by Mr. Tottenham. In July Mr. Monson commenced to negotiate with Messrs. J. & F. Anderson, W.S., Edinburgh, agents for the proprietor of Ardlamont, for the purchase of the estate by Cecil Hambrough, but the price offered by Monson on behalf of Cecil was so inadequate that the agents would not consider it and the negotiations came to nothing. At the same time attempts were being made to effect an insurance over the life of Cecil Hambrough, and, after proposals to several insurance companies had been refused, owing to difficulties as to the insurable interest of those proposing the insurance, a proposal by Cecil Hambrough for insurance on his own life for £20,000, divided into two policies of £10,000 each, was accepted by the Mutual Life Assurance Company of New York, and the first premium, amounting to £194, was paid by Monson out of a cheque sent for another purpose by Tottenham. The policies were dated 4th August, and on 7th August Cecil Hambrough wrote to the manager of the Mutual Assurance Company, asking him to deliver them to Mr. or Mrs. Monson and saying that he had assigned them to Mrs. Monson for proper consideration, and that she would be the person to whom the insurance money would be payable in the event of his death. On the same day he wrote a letter to Mrs. Monson assigning the policies and saying, " I am willing that you should hold the policies as security for all monies due to you from me, and as security against all liabilities incurred by you on my behalf, and in the event of my death occurring before the repayment of these monies you will be the sole beneficiary of these policies."

On Tuesday, 8th August, the day after the above two letters were written. a man arrived at Ardlamont in company with Mr. Monson. Ardlamont is only accessible from Glasgow and the Clyde by water, and the nearest pier to the house is at Kames, about four and a half miles off. This man, who travelled from Greenock by the same steamer as Mr. Monson, and who was apparently not familiar with the locality, left the steamer at Tighnabruaich, a pier about six miles from Ardlamont, and proceeded in the direction of Ardlamont by road. Mr. Monson, who landed at Kames, drove back to meet him and brought him to the mansion-house, where he was introduced to the household as Scott, an engineer who had come to inspect the boilers of a yacht which Monson had purchased on behalf of Cecil. Scott took his meals with the family and was generally treated as a guest, although obviously not a gentleman in the social meaning of the word.

On the afternoon of Wednesday, 9th August, Monson and Scott went for a sail in a rowing boat, taking with them some of Mr. Monson's children. After dinner, at which Scott was present, the

3

Alfred John Monson.

three men, Monson, Hambrough, and Scott, went down to Ardlamont Bay to engage in fishing. Monson and Cecil got into a boat in which was the net used for the fishing and Scott stayed on the shore. The party returned to the house about midnight, Monson and Cecil with their clothes soaked, both having somehow been immersed in the sea, but otherwise in good spirits and apparently treating the mishap as a joke. This misadventure was the cause of the Crown formulating the charge of attempted murder—the first head of the indictment under which Monson found himself in the dock. About six o'clock on the following morning, Thursday, 10th August, Mrs. Monson, accompanied by the governess and the children, left the house to go by boat to Glasgow for the day, and shortly afterwards Monson, Cecil, and Scott went out to shoot, Monson and Cecil each carrying a gun. The morning was wet and stormy. From the windows of the schoolhouse, which stands on the road to the mansion-house at the south end of the wood in which Cecil Hambrough met his death, the three men were seen by the witness Dunn walking along the road for a little in the direction of Ardlamont House and then crossing a fence to get into the field on the right-hand side of the road. After walking for a short distance in the field together, the three men were seen to spread out and enter the wood on the west side of the field in extended order, as if to beat the wood for rabbits, Scott, the man who had no gun, being in the middle. After entering the wood they were lost to Mr. Dunn's view, and nothing of them was again seen till some time after, when Monson and Scott returned to the house from the north end of the wood, passing the stables and offices on the way and bringing with them the two guns. On reaching the house Mr. Monson told the butler that Mr. Hambrough had been killed. The butler, accompanied by Monson and some of the estate servants, who were called upon to give assistance, went to the place where the body lay at the north end of the wood. It was found, with a gunshot wound in the head, lying on its back with the head towards the north, on the top of a sunk fence which divided the margin of the wood from a plantation of young trees on the east. The sunk fence was about 4½ feet in height, and at the bottom of it was a ditch overgrown by rank grass and bracken. The body was lifted and carried to the house, where the wound was washed. The local doctor was called in who, having examined the wound and received from Monson a statement as to the death, certified it as accidental. After luncheon Scott said that he had business to attend to which required that he should leave Ardlamont in the afternoon, and was told by the doctor that it was unnecessary for him to remain. He left by the afternoon boat for Glasgow and was not heard of again. Cecil Hambrough's father and mother were telegraphed for, and stayed at Ardlamont for two days. After their departure the body was taken by Monson to Ventnor, Isle of Wight, and was there buried, Monson returning to Ardlamont after the funeral. No suspicion was aroused as to the manner in which Cecil Hambrough had met his death until two

Introduction.

officials of the Mutual Life Assurance Company came to Ardlamont on 23rd August to make inquiries concerning an application which had been made to the company for payment of the two insurance policies. They were taken by Monson to Inveraray to see the Procurator-Fiscal, and in consequence of what passed the Procurator-Fiscal began for the first time to look into the matter. The result of his inquiries was that he felt there was sufficient suspicion about the case to justify his putting the law in motion against Monson, and on 29th August Monson was arrested by the Chief Constable of Argyllshire. Orders were given for the exhumation of the body of Cecil Hambrough, and the examination following thereon resulted in a report by the medical officer of the Crown and the doctor who had been called in at the time of the death, upon which a great part of the trial turned. Efforts were made both by the Crown and by Monson's legal advisers to find the man Scott, but without success; not only were the utmost efforts of the police of the country unavailing, but also the advertisement which was widely made by Monson's law agent met with no response. Scott's connection with the matter yet remains the most inexplicable element of this mysterious case. Immediately after his arrest Mr. Monson called in the help of Mr. John Blair, W.S., of Messrs. Davidson & Syme, Edinburgh, who, in due course, retained Mr. Comrie Thomson, Mr. John Wilson, and Mr. William Findlay, advocates, to conduct the case for the defence. Nearly three months were spent by those engaged in the case in preparing for the trial, and it was not till 12th December that Monson stood at the bar before the Lord Justice-Clerk and a jury to answer the charges made against him. Such, in brief outline, are the main facts of the story, the elucidation of which occupied the greater part of the ten days spent over the trial.

Before the trial actually began an interesting formality was gone through by the macer of Court calling upon Scott, the missing man, to appear; upon his failing to do so, the judge passed sentence of outlawry against him.

As regards the first charge, namely, attempted murder by drowning late in the night of 9th August or early in the morning of the 10th, the theory of the Crown was that Monson took the boy out in a boat, in which he or Scott or both had previously cut a plug hole, and that when in deep water Monson removed the plug from the hole, with the result that the boat filled with water and sank, throwing them both into the sea, and that Monson, an expert swimmer, so attempted to drown the boy, who was unable to swim.

The defence explained the occurrence by saying that the hole was cut by Cecil himself for the purpose of emptying the boat of the water which accumulated during the course of fishing with the splash net, that Monson and the boy were thrown into the water by the boat capsizing through coming in contact with a rock, upon which Cecil clambered, and where he remained until Monson swam ashore and brought another boat to take him off. In his declaration on this

Alfred John Monson.

matter Monson said—" So far from attempting on that evening to take young Hambrough's life, I consider that I saved it."

As regards the second charge, namely, that Cecil Hambrough met his death at the hand of another, and that other the prisoner at the bar, the Crown's theory was that he was killed by a glancing shot from a 12-bore gun, loaded with amberite powder, fired from behind at a distance of about 9 feet to the south of where he was standing at the time; that he lay where he fell, and died from loss of blood. This 12-bore gun was admittedly the gun by which the fatal shot was fired and was not the gun which Cecil was in the habit of using. Monson at first stated that the boy was carrying a 20 bore gun, but subsequently stated that on the occasion of the accident he himself was carrying the boy's short 20-bore gun with which Cecil usually shot, the latter having taken his (Monson's) 12-bore that morning in order to try new amberite cartridges.

In working out this theory many elements were taken into consideration, such as the nature and direction of the wound, the position of the body when first seen by others than Monson and Scott, and the traces of blood on the ground. Stress was also laid upon the position in which a blood-stained cartridge wad and two small pieces of bone, proved to be pieces of the skull, were found in relation to the body. Marks of pellets in trees to the northward of where the body was found lying afforded the main clue upon which was based the Crown theory as to the direction of the fatal shot and the distance from the deceased at which it was fired. Elaborate experiments to test such points as the spread of shot, the relation between the distance from which a shot is fired, and the signs of discoloration and singeing in the object fired at, were explained in evidence and put to the jury as bearing out the theory that it was the prisoner's hand which had done Cecil Hambrough to death.

The defence, for their part, contended that the place where the body was seen by the butler and the others who went to carry it to the house was not the place where it was first found by Monson and Scott, and that they had lifted it from the ditch where it was lying and placed it upon the higher level of the sunk fence. That being so, they argued, the Crown theory as to the line of fire fell to the ground, and Mr. Comrie Thomson very pertinently pointed out in his address to the jury that the position of the body when seen by the witnesses, namely, lying on its back with the head pointing north, and upon which the Crown's case was largely founded, was utterly inconsistent with the theory that it had been shot from behind and from the south and that it lay where it fell.

As has been already indicated, the motive for the alleged crime assigned by the Crown was the prisoner's belief that by causing the death of Cecil Hambrough he would, through his wife—to whom the insurance policies over the boy's life purported to be assigned—reap the benefit of these policies, amounting to the large sum of £20,000. It was proved beyond doubt that the Monsons were literally penniless

6

Introduction.

at the time and entirely dependent upon such small doles as they were able to get from their friend Tottenham and others ; it was argued that Monson, in ignorance of the elementary rule of law in Scotland as in England, that a minor cannot make a valid assignment without the consent of his guardians, believed that the assignment of the policies was good ; and that the death of Cecil Hambrough was the coping-stone of a deeply laid scheme by which Monson sought to rehabilitate his broken-down financial condition.

The defence met this theory by arguing that the prisoner was well aware of the boy's incapacity to assign before attaining majority and of the impossibility of Mrs. Monson recovering anything under the policies if Cecil died before twenty-one. In explanation of the letters relating to the assignment, it was argued that they were to be read merely as a declaration of indebtedness by Cecil, which could be referred to when the boy came of age, so that the Monsons might secure repayment of the advances which they had undoubtedly made to both the boy and his father and get discharge of Monson's bill for board and education, towards which he had not received one penny from Major Hambrough during the long time the boy was a member of his household. The defence admitted that a claim had been made to the insurance company after Cecil Hambrough's death, but Mr. Tottenham, who made the claim on behalf of Mrs. Monson, admitted in the witness-box that in doing so he was trying to " bluff " the insurance company into paying the money, £4000 of which he was to receive, by agreement with Monson, as his share of the spoil. The defence summed up their position on the matter of motive by pointing out that Monson had everything to lose and nothing to gain by the death of the boy before he reached the age of twenty-one, and that if the prisoner wished by his death to gain pecuniary advantage he killed him some months too soon and chose the very worst time for doing the boy to death.

These theories for the prosecution and the defence, of which an outline has been given, were put to the jury by the Solicitor-General and by Mr. Comrie Thomson in speeches which were worthy of the importance of the case. That of the Solicitor-General was a model of skilful forensic oratory, marked by great sincerity and at the same time by that fairness which, it is hoped, will always remain a characteristic note in the speeches of the law officers of the Crown in Scotland. Mr. Comrie Thomson's address on behalf of the prisoner worthily upheld the high standard set by Lord President Inglis in his speech in defence of Madeleine Smith, the opening words of which, it is interesting to note, were quoted by Mr. Comrie Thomson. In urging upon the jury the necessity of bringing to the discharge of their duty an unprejudiced mind, Mr. Comrie Thomson referred in strong terms to the hostile attitude taken up by the press of the country towards the prisoner from the date of his arrest.

The Lord Justice-Clerk, in his careful and exhaustive charge to the jury, gave due prominence to the many doubts and difficulties

Alfred John Monson.

in the case which the prosecution had left unsolved, and then the jury retired to consider their verdict. On their return to Court the foreman announced that the verdict of the jury was " not proven " on both charges. The prisoner was released from the dock and passed quietly out of Court, and the great trial came to an end. The Ardlamont mystery was still a mystery, and so it is likely to remain for a long time to come.

An echo of the case was heard in May of the following year, when the mysterious Scott appeared in an Edinburgh music hall as part of a conjurer's equipment, and during his stay in Edinburgh petitioned the High Court of Justiciary to recall the sentences of outlawry against him, which was done, the Crown putting in no appearance against him.

The prisoner was placed at the bar, charged under the following indictment :—

ALFRED JOHN MONSON, prisoner in the Prison of Edinburgh, and EDWARD SWEENEY, *alias* DAVIS, *alias* SCOTT, some time residing at Ardlamont House, parish of Kilfinan, Argyllshire, you are indicted at the instance of the Right Honourable John Blair Balfour, Her Majesty's Advocate, and the charges against you are (1) that you, having formed the design of causing by drowning the death of Windsor Dudley Cecil Hambrough, some time residing at Ardlamont House aforesaid, now deceased, did, in execution thereof, bore, or caused to be bored, in the side of a boat, the property of Donald M'Kellar, boathirer, Tighnabruaich, Argyllshire, a hole, and having plugged or closed said hole, you did, on 9th August, 1893, induce the said Windsor Dudley Cecil Hambrough to embark along with you, Alfred John Monson, in the said boat, and on said date or on 10th August, 1893, you, Alfred John Monson, in execution of said design, did, in Ardlamont Bay, in the Firth of Clyde, while the said boat was in deep water, remove, or caused to be removed, the plug from said hole, and admit the water into, and did sink said boat, whereby the said Windsor Dudley Cecil Hambrough was thrown into the sea, and you, Alfred John Monson, and Edward Sweeney, *alias* Davis, *alias* Scott, did thus attempt to murder him; (2) that on 10th August, 1893, at a part of a wood situated about 360 yards or thereby in an easterly or north-easterly direction from Ardlamont House aforesaid, you, Alfred John Monson, and Edward Sweeney, *alias* Davis, *alias* Scott, did shoot the said Windsor Dudley Cecil Hambrough, and kill him, and did thus murder him; and you, Edward Sweeney, *alias* Davis, *alias* Scott, being conscious of your guilt in the premises, did abscond and flee from justice.

JOHN ALEX. REID, A.D.

8

THE TRIAL.

TUESDAY, 12th DECEMBER, 1893.

The Court met at Ten o'clock.

Judge—

THE LORD JUSTICE-CLERK (*Macdonald*).

Counsel for the Crown—

THE SOLICITOR-GENERAL (*Asher*).
R. U. STRACHAN, J. A. REID, and J. C. LORIMER, Esqs.,
Advocates-Depute.

Agent—

Mr. JOHN COWAN, W.S.

Counsel for the Panel—

J. COMRIE THOMSON, J. WILSON, and
W. FINDLAY, Esqs., *Advocates.*

Agent—

Mr. JOHN BLAIR, of Messrs. Davidson & Syme, W.S., Edinburgh

R. C. MALCOLM, Esq., *Advocate,* instructed by Messrs. CAR-
MICHAEL & MILLAR, W.S., watched the case for Major
Hambrough.

Alfred John Monson.

10

The Trial.

38. Letter, A. J. Monson to the manager, Liverpool and London and Globe Insurance Company, Liverpool, 26th July, 1893.

39. Copy letter, J. Wardle to A. J. Monson, 29th July, 1893.

40. Letter, A. J. Monson to J. Wardle, 29th July, 1893.

41. Letter, A. J. Monson to the manager, Liverpool and London and Globe Insurance Company, Liverpool, 31st July, 1893.

42. Letter, W. D. C. Hambrough to the manager, Liverpool and London and Globe Insurance Company, 31st July, 1893.

43. Copy letter, J. Wardle to A. J. Monson, 2nd August, 1893.

44. Proposal by Agnes Maud Monson to British Empire Mutual Life Assurance Company for £1000 on life of W. D. C. Hambrough, dated 15th November, 1892.

45. Letter, Agnes Maud Monson to secretary of said company, 10th December, 1892.

46. Letter, Agnes Maud Monson to secretary of said company, 12th December, 1892.

47-47A. Two proposals and declarations by W. D. C. Hambrough to the Scottish Amicable Life Assurance Society on his own life for £5000 each, both dated 13th May, 1891.

48. Letter, A. J. Monson to the secretary, Scottish Amicable Life Assurance Society, 13th May, 1891.

49. Letter, A. J. Monson to resident secretary of said society, 18th May, 1891.

50. Two reports by private friends relative to said proposals, dated respectively 18th and 20th May, 1891.

51. Proposal and declaration by W. D. C. Hambrough to said society for £2000 on his own life, 1892.

52. Letter, A. J. Monson to G. C. Maclean, 24th October, 1892.

53. Letter, A. M. Monson to C. F. Maclean, 13 St. Andrew Square, Edinburgh, 31st October, 1892.

54. Letter from A. J. Monson, commencing "I have some business to introduce," 6th March, 1891.

55. Letter from A. J. Monson, commencing "The object of paying off," 10th March, 1891.

56. Letter from D. A. Hambrough, commencing "You will wonder," 20th March.

57. Letter, A. J. Monson to J. O'Hagan, 30th March, 1891.

58. Letter, A. J. Monson to the Caledonian Insurance Company, 24th May, 1891.

59. Proposal by W. D. C. Hambrough to the Caledonian Insurance Company for £5000 on his own life, dated 25th May, 1891.

60. Letter, A. J. Monson to manager of said company, 13th July, 1891.

61. Proposal and declaration to the Reliance Mutual Life Assurance Society for £1000 on life of W. D. C. Hambrough, dated 27th July, 1893.

62. Letter, Agnes Maud Monson to H. Kidson, 31st October, 1892.

63. Copy letter, Herbert Kidson to Mrs. Monson, 4th November, 1892.

64. Proposal for loan of £2000 by Agnes Maud Monson to the Lancashire and Yorkshire Reversionary Interest Company, Limited, dated 5th November, 1892.

65. Copy letter, Herbert Kidson to Mrs. Monson, 7th November, 1892.

66. Copy letter, Herbert Kidson to Mrs. Monson, 8th November, 1892.

67. Letter, signed "Agnes Maud Monson, p. A. J. M.," to K. Kidson, 10th November, 1892.

68. Particulars of proposal referred to, and enclosed in the foregoing letter.

69. Copy letter, Herbert Kidson to Mrs. Monson, 11th November, 1892.

70. Letter, Maud Monson to Herbert Kidson, undated, commencing "I am so glad."

11

Alfred John Monson.

71. Assignment of judgment debt by Mrs. A. M. Monson to B. L. Tottenham, Esquire, dated 9th February, 1893.

72. Declaration by Mrs. A. M. Monson relating to said judgment debt, dated 9th February, 1893.

73. Declaration to A. J. Monson relating to said debt, dated 9th February, 1893.

74. Letter, signed W. D. C. Hambrough, dated 8/5/93.

75. Letter, A. J. Monson to B. L. Tottenham, undated, headed "Tuesday, North-Eastern Station Hotel, Harrogate."

76-87. Letters, A. J. Monson to B. L. Tottenham.

88. Holograph writing by A. J. Monson, undated, commencing "The two cheques are posted."

89-91. Letters, A. J. Monson to B. L. Tottenham.

92-94. Letters, Agnes Maud Monson to B. L. Tottenham.

95. I.O.U. for £25 by Agnes Maud Monson in favour of B. L. Tottenham, dated 6th September, 1893.

96-101. Letters, W. D. C. Hambrough to B. L. Tottenham.

102. Telegram, "Hambrough" to "Kempton, 8 Delahay Street, Westr., Ldn.," 13th May, 1893.

103. Letter, W. D. C. Hambrough to B. L. Tottenham, 14/5/93.

104. Telegram, "Hambrough" to "Tottenham, c/o Brown, 13 Clifford's Inn, Lon.," 15th May, 1893.

105. Telegram, "Hambrough" to "Tottenham, 8 Delahay St., Westminster, Lon.," 15th May, 1893.

106-112. Letters, W. D. C. Hambrough to B. L. Tottenham.

113. Telegram, "Hambrough" to "Tottenham, 8 Delahay St., Westminster, Lon.," 23rd June, 1893.

114. Letter, W. D. C. Hambrough to B. L. Tottenham, 28/6/93.

115-116. Letter, W. D. C. Hambrough to B. L. Tottenham, dated 9/7/93, with envelope bearing post-marks, "'Columba' steamer, 10th July, 1893," and "London, 11th July, 1893."

117-118. Letters, W. D. C. Hambrough to B. L. Tottenham.

119. Telegram, "Paton" to "Forty-eight, Edin.," 24th April, 1893.

120. Letter, Edward Paton & Son to J. & F. Anderson, W.S., 24th April, 1893.

121-122. Letters, J. & F. Anderson to E. Paton & Son, 24th and 25th April, 1893.

123. Letter, E. Paton & Son to J. & F. Anderson, W.S., 25th April, 1893.

124. Copy letter, J. & F. Anderson, W.S., to Mr. Jerningham, 26th April, 1893.

125. Letter, J. & F. Anderson to E. Paton & Son, 26th April, 1893.

126. Letter, E. Paton & Son to J. & F. Anderson, W.S., 27th April, 1893.

127. Letter, J. & F. Anderson, W.S., to E. Paton & Son, 28th April, 1893.

128. Telegram, "Forty-eight, Edinburgh," to "Shootings, London," 28th April, 1893.

129. Copy letter, J. & F. Anderson, W.S., to Mr. Jerningham, 1st May, 1893.

130-131. Letters, J. & F. Anderson, W.S., to E. Paton & Son, 1st and 3rd May, 1893.

132. Letter, A. J. Monson to J. & F. Anderson, W.S., May 8/93.

133. Copy letter, J. & F. Anderson, W.S., to A. J. Monson, 9th May, 1893.

134. Letter, A. J. Monson to J. & F. Anderson, W.S., 5/10/93.

135. Letter, Agnes Maud Monson to Paton & Son, 10th May, 1893.

136. Copy letter, J. & F. Anderson, W.S., to A. J. Monson, 11th May, 1893.

The Trial.

137. Letter, Edward Paton & Son to J. & F. Anderson, W.S., 11th May, 1893.

138. Letter, A. J. Monson to "F. & J." Anderson, W.S., May 12/93.

139. Letter, J. & F. Anderson to E. Paton & Son, 17th May, 1893.

140. Letter, Edward Paton & Son to J. & F. Anderson, W.S., 18th May, 1893.

141. Minute of let between William Hugh Murray, W.S., factor for Major John Henry Lamont of Lamont, and Windsor Dudley Cecil Hambrough and Adolphus Frederick James Jerningham, Esquires, of Ardlamont House and shootings, dated 9th and 13th May, 1893.

142-145. Letters, A. J. Monson to J. & F. Anderson, W.S.

146. Copy letter, J. & F. Anderson, W.S., to A. J. Monson, 22nd August, 1893.

147. Letter, A. J. Monson to J. & F. Anderson, undated, commencing "I will let Mr. Hambrough have your letter."

148. Letter, A. J. Monson to Hanna, Donald & Wilson, undated, commencing "I have just received a letter from Mr. Tottenham."

149. Letter, A. J. Monson to "Messrs. Donald," July 22/93.

150. Document, partly in pencil and partly in ink, signed "Hanna, Donald & Wilson."

151. Letter, A. M. Monson to Dugald Kerr, 26th July, 1893.

152. Letter, Agnes Maud Monson to "Manager, Royal Bank, Tighnabruaich," 7th August, 1893.

153. Letter, A. Dennistoun to "The Agent, Royal Bank of Scotland, Tighnabruaich," 10th August, 1893.

154. Letter, A. J. Monson to Dugald Kerr, undated, commencing "I have received your kind note this morning."

155. Letter, Agnes Maud Monson to "The Manager, Royal Bank, Tighnabruaich," 23rd August, 1893.

156. Certified Excerpt from Book, Royal Bank of Scotland, Tighnabruaich, of Account of "Mrs. Agnes M. Monson, Ardlamont House," to 30th August, 1893.

157. Debit note, for 2s. 6d., in account with said bank, dated 26th July, 1893.

158-160. Cheques on said bank drawn by A. M. Monson.

161. Debit note in account with said bank, 8th August, 1893.

162-163. Cheques on said bank drawn by A. M. Monson.

164. Debit note in account with said bank for £250, dated 11th August, 1893.

165-171. Cheques on said bank drawn by A. M. Monson

172. Debit note in account with said bank for 14s. 9d., dated 18th August, 1893.

173-175. Cheques on said bank drawn by A. M. Monson.

176. Letter, Agnes Maud Monson to manager, Royal Bank, Tighnabruaich, dated August 28/93.

177-178. Copy letters, Dugald Kerr to Mrs. Monson, 29th and 30th August, 1893.

179-180. Two letter-books of B. L. Tottenham.

181. Letter, W. D. C. Hambrough to D. A. Hambrough, 1st May, 1892.

182-183. Letters, D. A. Hambrough to W. D. C. Hambrough, 20th June and 18th November.

184. Letter, W. D. C. Hambrough to D. A. Hambrough, commencing "I should have answered."

185. Letter, D. A. Hambrough to A. J. Monson, 27th October, commencing "I have once more written."

186. Letter, W. D. C. Hambrough to Mrs. D. A. Hambrough, commencing "I am afraid you will think."

13

Alfred John Monson.

187-188. Copy telegrams, D. A. Hambrough to W. D. C. Hambrough, 13th and 14th September, 1892.

189. Telegram, W. D. C. Hambrough to D. A. Hambrough, 14th September, 1892.

190-194. Copy telegrams, D. A. Hambrough to W. D. C. Hambrough, 14th and 15th September, 2nd, 7th, and 8th November, 1892.

195. Money order receipt, payable at Harrogate to C. Hambrough.

196. Copy telegram, D. A. Hambrough to W. D. C. Hambrough, 8th November, 1892.

197. Telegram, W. D. C. Hambrough to D. A. Hambrough, 8th November, 1892.

198. Copy telegram, D. A. Hambrough to W. D. C. Hambrough, 12th November, 1892.

199. Telegram, W. D. C. Hambrough to D. A. Hambrough, 12th November, 1892.

200-201. Letters, A. J. Monson to D. A. Hambrough.

202. Office copy, receiving order against A. J. Monson, dated 11th August, 1892.

203. Certificate of adjudication in bankruptcy against A. J. Monson, 5th September, 1892.

204. Office copy, certificate of appointment of trustee of the property of A. J. Monson, 21st September, 1892.

205. Record book in bankruptcy of A. J. Monson.

206. Mortgage of life interest, D. A. Hambrough to Sir George Russell, Baronet; William Augustus Guy, Esq.; and the Hon. W. P. Manvers Chetwynd Talbot, 9th June, 1885.

207. Probate of the will and four codicils of John Hambrough, Esquire, 3rd March, 1863.

208. Letter, W. D. C. Hambrough to Hammond & Richards, 29/3/93.

209. Letter, A. J. Monson to the chairman of the directors of the Eagle Insurance Company, 11th April, 1893.

210-211. Letters, W. D. C. Hambrough to H. W. Richards, 23rd April and 8th May, 1893.

212. Letter, W. D. C. Hambrough to Hammond & Richards, 31st May, 1893.

213. Letter, A. J. Monson to Hammond & Richards, 31st July, 1893.

214. Copy letters, Hammond & Richards to A. J. Monson, 13th April and 3rd August, 1893.

215. Sealed copy, last will and testament of William Day of Eversley Garth, 18th May, 1892.

216. Sealed copy, letters of administration of the personal estate of the said William Day, 22nd May, 1882.

217. Sealed copy, last will and testament of William Buckley of Stairfoot, in the parish of Darfield and county of York, 6th April, 1854.

218. Letter of authority of Marianne Holdsworth and others to Messrs. Carter, Ramsden & Carter, solicitors, Leeds, dated 20th March, 1893.

219. Mortgage by Alfred John Monson and Agnes Maud, his wife, to the Lancashire and Yorkshire Reversionary Interest Company, Limited, 19th September, 1890.

220. Pawn tickets by Thomas James Brook, 21st November, 1892, for silver watch, to Mrs. J. Monson.

221. Pawn ticket by C. B. Vaughan, 16th February, 1891, to "Mr. Rutter."

222. Pawn ticket by C. B. Vaughan, 2nd July, 1893, to "Mrs. Morrison," Ardlamont House, Argyllshire.

223. Pawn ticket by Middleton & Pollard, 24th October, 1892, to "Alice Morrison."

224. Letter, "Mrs. Morrison" to Mr. Vaughan, 12th July, 1893.

14

The Trial.

225. Letter, Mrs. "John Monson" to Charles Cox, 22nd December, 1892.

226. Pawn ticket by Middleton & Pollard, 17th July, 1893, to "Agnes Morrison," Wooton House, Harrogate.

227. Cheque by W. A. West in favour of Edward Davis, 20th July, 1893.

228. I.O.U. for £10, 20/1/93, by Edward Davis.

229. Letter, E. Davis to G. Smith, 2nd July, 1893.

230. Diary for 1893 kept by A. J. Monson.

231. Letter by W. D. C. Hambrough to A. E. Sebright, 11th January, 1893.

232. Receipt by W. D. C. Hambrough in favour of A. E. Sebright, 10th January, 1893.

233. Letter, signed Geo. Hunt, to G. Smith, 1st August, 1893.

234. Letter, A. J. Monson to F. A. Law, undated, commencing "As I have previously told you."

235. Letter, A. J. Monson to F. A. Law, 6th July, 1893.

236. Letter, John Davis to G. Smith, 13th October, 1893.

237. Letter, A. J. Monson to Procurator-Fiscal, Inveraray, 26th August, 1893.

238. Medical report by Henry D. Littlejohn, Doctor of Medicine, and John Macmillan, M.B., dated 13th September, 1893.

239. Five photographs taken at Ventnor, marked A, B, C, D, and E.

240. Thirty-one pieces of cardboard, numbered 1 to 31 inclusive.

241. Four pencil drawings, numbered 1 to 4 inclusive.

Label No. 1. Jacket.
Label No. 2. Cartridge No. 6 shot, 12-bore.
Label No. 3. 18 Cartridges No. 6 shot, 20-bore.
Label No. 4. Pair knickerbockers.
Label No. 5. Jacket.
Label No. 6. Cap.
Label No. 7. 20-bore gun.
Label No. 8. 12-bore gun.
Label No. 9. Three amberite cartridges.
Label No. 10. Seven cartridges No. 5 shot and three cartridges No. 6 shot, 12-bore.
Label No. 11. Three cartridges No. 6 shot, 20-bore.
Label No. 12. Five cartridges No. 6 shot, 20-bore.
Label No. 13. Four pellets.
Label No. 14. Four metallic fragments.
Label No. 15. Four pellets No. 5 shot.
Label No. 16. Four pellets No. 6 shot.
Label No. 17. Pieces of bone.
Label No. 18. Skull.
Label No. 19. Rowan tree.
Label No. 20. Part of rowan tree.
Label No. 21. Part of beech tree.
Label No. 22. Part of lime tree.
Label No. 23. A rowlock.
Label No. 24. A knife.
Label No. 25. Part of a boat.

JOHN ALEX. REID, A.D.

LIST OF WITNESSES ANNEXED TO THE FOREGOING INDICTMENT.

1. James Brand, civil engineer, 109 Bath Street, Glasgow.
2. Frederick Gairdiner Holmes, civil engineer, 109 Bath Street, Glasgow.
3. David Wilson, apprentice engineer, 109 Bath Street, Glasgow.

Alfred John Monson.

4. James Wright, some time footman, Ardlamont House aforesaid, presently residing at Afton Lodge, Tarbolton, Ayr.

5-7. (5) Archibald Whyte, gardener; (6) Hugh Carmichael, ploughman; and (7) Jane Carmichael, his wife, all at Ardlamont.

8. John Steven, factor, The Camp, Ardlamont.

9-11. (9) Donald M'Intyre, gamekeeper; (10) George Lamont, gamekeeper; and (11) Stewart M'Nicol, joiner, all at Ardlamont.

12. James Dunn, watchmaker, School Road, Auchterarder.

13. Betsy Drummond Smitton, School Road, Auchterarder.

14. Flora M'Kinnon, some time cook, Ardlamont House, presently residing at Clydeview, Radnor Park, Dalmuir.

15. Jessie M'Leod, housemaid, Ardlamont House.

16. Alexandrina Shand, nurse, residing at Holly Bank, West Bay, Dunoon.

17. Mary Fraser, residing with Mrs. M'Lagan, 8 Corn Street, Glasgow.

18. Janet Guinea, some time kitchenmaid, Ardlamont House, now residing at Bloomlands, Inchinnan, Renfrew.

19. Edith May Hiron, presently residing at Holly Bank, West Bay, Dunoon.

20. Hugh Carmichael, groom, Ardlamont.

21. Donald M'Kellar, boat hirer, Tighnabruaich.

22. James Lyon, Kildavaig, Ardlamont.

23. John Douglas, gamekeeper, Portavadie, Kilfinan, Argyllshire.

24-25. (24) Duncan M'Calman, police constable, Tighnabruaich, and (25) Donald Campbell, police constable, Ardrishaig.

26. James M'Phee, some time boots, Tighnabruaich Hotel, Tighnabruaich, presently residing at 456 St. Vincent Street, Glasgow.

27. John M'Intyre, police constable, Colintraive.

28. James Rippie, Campbell's Land, High Street, Rothesay.

29. Frederick Harris, 22 Watergate, Rothesay.

30. John Tweedley, 76 Montague Street, Rothesay.

31. Colin Schroder, 27 Bridge End Street, Rothesay.

32. Alexander M'Bride, mason, Oaklea Villa, Kames.

33. Peter Galbraith, fisherman, Tighnabruaich.

34. James Ross, sergeant, Argyllshire Police, Lochgilphead.

35. David Stewart, criminal officer, Inveraray.

36-37. (36) James Donald and (37) Robert Hanna Donald, both engineers, residing at Riccartsbar, Paisley.

38-39. (38) John Graham M'Lean, manager, and (39) William Everard Herbert, resident secretary, both of the Mutual Life Insurance Company of New York, 54 Gordon Street, Glasgow.

40. Donald Carmichael Haldeman, manager, Mutual Life Insurance Company of New York, 17 and 18 Cornhill, London.

41-42. (41) James Graham Watson, manager, and (42) Henry Robertson Cockburn, secretary, both of the Scottish Provident Institution, 6 St. Andrew Square, Edinburgh.

43. William M. Wisely, agent of Scottish Provident Institution, 29 St. Vincent Place, Glasgow.

44. David Stewart, resident secretary, Liverpool and London and Globe Insurance Company, 30 George Square, Glasgow.

45. James Wardle, local manager, Liverpool and London and Globe Insurance Company, Leeds.

46. George Campbell M'Lean, secretary, The Scottish Amicable Life Assurance Society, 13 St. Andrew Square, Edinburgh.

47. George Viner, clerk, British Empire Mutual Life Assurance Company, 4 King William Street, London.

48. Neil Ballingall Gunn, secretary, Standard Life Assurance Company, 3 George Street, Edinburgh.

16

The Trial.

49. David Deuchar, manager, Caledonian Fire and Life Insurance Company, 19 George Street, Edinburgh.
50. Nicholas Thomas Wilkinson, clerk, Reliance Mutual Life Assurance Company, 71 King William Street, London.
51. Arthur Macdonald Blair, solicitor, 5 St. James Square, Manchester.
52. Herbert Kidson, secretary, Lancashire and Yorkshire Reversionary Interest Company, 5 St. James Square, Manchester.
53. William Lockhart, underwriter, 2 Change Alley, Cornhill, London.
54. Dugald Kerr, bank agent, Tighnabruaich.
55. Dudley Alfred Hambrough, 58 Edith Road, West Kensington, London.
56. Beresford Loftus Tottenham, financial agent, 8 Delahaye Street, London.
57. Godfrey William Hambleton, Doctor of Medicine, 23 York Street, Portman Square, London.
58. Henry Prince, solicitor, 9 Fleet Street, London.
59. Charles Whitbread Graham, solicitor, 6 New Square, Lincoln's Inn, London.
60. Arthur Toovey, solicitor, 18 Orchard Street, Portman Square, London.
61. Henry Weller Richards, solicitor, 16 Furnival's Inn, London.
62. Charles Robert Tennant, residing at 22 West Kensington Gardens, London.
63. James Hanks Loching, clerk, Messrs. C. F. Kemp, Ford & Co., 73 Lombard Street, London.
64. John Wortham, clerk, Record Department, Senior Registrar's Office, High Court of Justice in Bankruptcy, London.
65. Henry John Layton, clerk, Probate Registry, Somerset House, London.
66. Morris Natali Fuller, solicitor, 1 Church Court, Clement's Lane, London.
67. Harold Mark Carter, solicitor, 82 Albion Street, Leeds
68. Walter Ramsden, solicitor, 82 Albion Street, Leeds.
69. William Hugh Murray, Writer to the Signet, 48 Castle Street, Edinburgh.
70. Edward Lonsdale Paton, estate agent, 14 St. James Street, London.
71. Edward Arthur Butler, auctioneer and surveyor, 90 and 91 Queen Street, Cheapside, London.
72. Thomas James Brooks, pawnbroker, 79 Wardour Street, London.
73. Thomas Newstead, assistant pawnbroker, 39 Strand, London.
74. John Lewenden, assistant pawnbroker, 39 Strand, London.
75. William Thomas Middleton, pawnbroker, 143 Briggate, Leeds.
76. Clara Nelson, Trafalgar House, Gresham Road, Staines, Middlesex.
77. George Sweeney, hall porter, Westminster Palace Hotel, London.
78-79. (78) William Henry Keen and (79) Frances Thomson Keen, his wife, both residing at 35 Sutherland Street, Pimlico, London.
80-81. (80) Joseph Wiggins and (81) Emily Wiggins, his wife, both residing at 16 Avery Farm Road, Pimlico, London.
82. Sidney Russell, 86 Camberwell New Road, London.
83. Ambrose William King, 25 Beaconsfield Road, St. Margaret's, Twickenham.
84. Adolphus Frederick James Jerningham, Trafalgar House, Gresham Road, Staines, Middlesex.
85. Leslie Murray Robertson, 56 Hill Rise, Richmond.
86. George Smith, tailor, 8 and 9 High Street, Eton.
87. Henry Algernon West, Elmore, Ennerdale Road, Kew Gardens, Middlesex.
88. Arthur Edward Saunders Sebright, mortgage and insurance broker, 10 Portman Square, London.

c

17

Alfred John Monson.

89. Frederick Arthur Law, D Flat, 100 Addison Road, Kensington, London.

90. William Paynter Browne, solicitor, 22 Charing Cross, Whitehall, London.

91. Henry Arthur Hudson, District Probate Registry, York.

92. Alexander Houston, town-clerk, Ventnor.

93. John Gillet Livesey, Cromarty House, Ventnor.

94. Hugh Jeffrey, curator of the Ventnor Cemetery, Ventnor.

95. John Campbell Shairp, Sheriff-Substitute of Argyllshire, Inveraray.

96. John Campbell M'Lullich, Procurator-Fiscal of Argyllshire, Inveraray.

97. Thomas M'Naughton, Depute Procurator-Fiscal, Inveraray.

98. James Fraser, Chief Constable of Argyllshire, Lochgilphead.

99-100. (99) Thomas Greet, inspector, and (100) Thomas Brockwell, sergeant, both of Criminal Investigation Department, London.

101. Samuel James Porter, photographer, Maison Rouge, High Street, Ventnor.

102. James Macnaughton, gunmaker, 26 Hanover Street, Edinburgh.

103. William Cullen, jun., chemist, Nobel's Explosive Company, Stevenston, Ayrshire.

104. John Macmillan, Bachelor of Medicine, Tighnabruaich.

105. Henry Duncan Littlejohn, Doctor of Medicine, 22 Royal Circus, Edinburgh.

106. Patrick Heron Watson, Doctor of Medicine, 16 Charlotte Square, Edinburgh.

107. Joseph Bell, Doctor of Medicine, 2 Melville Crescent, Edinburgh.

108. John Macdonald Brown, Fellow of the Royal College of Surgeons, Edinburgh, 12 Cumin Place, Edinburgh.

109. John Rendall, Fellow of the Royal College of Surgeons, England, Forestside, Symington.

110. James T. Murray, artist, 3 Queen Street, Edinburgh.

[Of the above witnesses seventy-two were examined for the prosecution.]

INVENTORY OF DOCUMENTS, &C., PUT IN EVIDENCE FOR THE ACCUSED.

1-2. Two wooden models, numbered 1 and 2 respectively.

3-17. Fifteen wooden targets, marked Nos. 3 to 17 inclusive.

18. Copy mortgage to secure £5000 and interest, by D. A. Hambrough and W. D. C. Hambrough to A. J. Monson, dated 23rd May, 1891.

19. Deed of covenant and charge by D. A. Hambrough and W. D. C. Hambrough to A. J. Monson, dated 1st September, 1891.

20. Mortgage to secure £2600 by D. A. Hambrough to A. J. Monson, dated 17th September, 1891.

21. Agreement for sale of life interest in estates and policies, Sir George Russell, Bart., with R. C. Hanrott, dated 8th January 1892.

22. Mortgage to secure £3400 and interest, D. A. Hambrough to A. J. Monson, dated 1st December, 1891.

23-34. Twelve photographs, marked Nos. 23 to 34 inclusive.

35-36. Two pieces of cloth, marked Nos. 35 and 36 respectively.

37-39. Three dog skins, marked Nos. 37, 38, and 39.

40. One amberite cartridge No. 5 shot, 12-bore.

41-42. Two cartridges No. 6 shot, 20-bore, marked Nos. 41 and 42 respectively.

43. Part of an amberite cartridge case, No. 12-bore, with wad therein.

44. Part of a 20-bore cartridge with wad therein.

45. Letter, W. D. C. Hambrough to Hammond & Richards, 16 Furnival's

The Trial.

Inn, London, dated on or about 7th March, 1893, with reference to negotiations for the purchase of the father's life interest in the Hambrough estates.

46-48. Three letters, W. D. C. Hambrough to Hammond & Richards, dated respectively on or about 29th March, 23rd April, 31st May, 1893.

49. Letter, A. J. Monson to Hammond & Richards, dated 31st July, 1893.

50. Copy notice by Birdsall & Cross, Scarborough, agents for London and Yorkshire Bank, Limited, to W. H. Domville, D. A. Hambrough, and W. D. C. Hambrough, dated 13th November, 1891.

51-52. (51) Envelope and (52) letter, D. A. Hambrough to A. J. Monson, Ardlamont House, Tighnabruaich, Argyllshire, dated 27th August.

53. Letter card, Godfrey W. Hambleton to A. J. Monson, dated 17th July, 1893.

54-55. (54) Envelope and (55) letter, George Outram & Company to A. J. Monson, Ardlamont House, by Millhouse, Argyllshire.

56. Extract entry of birth from the Register of Births for the district of Winchester of a son of Dudley Albert Hambrough, extracted 26th July, 1893.

57. Proposal by Windsor Dudley Cecil Hambrough to the Scottish Provident Institution for insurance for £50,000, dated 20th July, 1893.

58. Proposal by D. A. Hambrough to be laid before the Prudential Assurance Company, Limited, with reference to loans, &c., dated 8th January, 1889.

59. Particulars of the security offered for a £50,000 mortgage.

60. Type-written list of " Existing policies of assurance," with surrender values noted in pencil.

61. Copy letter, A. J. Monson and D. A. Hambrough to Messrs. A. M'Laren and F. Urch, dated 2nd December, 1891.

62-63. Two letters, W. D. C. Hambrough, commencing " My dear Father," dated 22nd and 24th March respectively.

64. Letter, A. J. Monson to D. A. Hambrough, dated 24th March, 1892.

65. Letter, W. D. C. Hambrough, dated 25th March, commencing " My dearest Mother."

66. Letter, W. D. C. Hambrough, dated 28th March, commencing " My dear Father."

67-68. Two letters, A. J. Monson to Major Hambrough, dated 31st March, 1892, and 5th April, 1892, respectively.

69-70. Two letters, A. J. Monson to M. N. Fuller, dated 21st February, 1892, and 23rd May, 1892, respectively.

71. Letter, W. D. C. Hambrough, " Ardlamont House, Argyllshire," commencing " Dear Dr. Hambleton."

72. Letter, W. D. C. Hambrough, dated 27th April, 1893, commencing " Dear Lang."

73. Letter, W. D. C. Hambrough, " Ardlamont House, Argyllshire," commencing " My dearest Mother."

74. Letter, Carter, Ramsden & Carter to M. N. Fuller, dated 16th March, 1892.

75-76. Two letters, A. J. Monson to Major Hambrough, dated 29th March, 1892, and 10th April, 1892, respectively.

77. Instructions to counsel to settle originating summons re John Hambrough, deceased.

78. Opinion thereon by Dr. Serrell, dated 11th March, 1893.

79. Statement of annual income and expenditure in respect of Hambrough estates.

80. Declaration by James Dunn, watchmaker, Newcastle-on-Tyne, presently residing at Auchterarder, made before William Laurence Young, J.P., for the county of Perth, on 29th August, 1893.

81-89. Nine letters, W. D. C. Hambrough to A. J. Monson, dated 10th, 13th, 15th, 16th, 23rd, 25th, 27th, 29th May, and 1st September respectively.

19

Alfred John Monson.

90-91. Two letters, D. A. Hambrough, commencing "Dear Monson," both undated.

92-98. Seven cheques drawn by D. A. Hambrough upon the London and Yorkshire Bank, Scarborough, payable to Junior Carlton Club or bearer, dated respectively 16th, 20th, 23rd, 24th, 25th, 28th, and 29th July, all in 1891.

99-104. Six letters, W. D. C. Hambrough, commencing "Dear Mrs. Monson," dated Thursday, Wednesday, Thursday, Wednesday, Friday, and 20th April, 1893, respectively.

105. Letter, W. D. C. Hambrough, dated 7th July, 1893, from Ardlamont House, Argyllshire, commencing "Dear Massey."

106-142. Thirty-seven letters [not referred to in evidence].

143. Book containing twenty-four cheques upon Mrs. Monson's account with the London and Yorkshire Bank, Limited, Scarborough, and two deposit slips.

144. Book containing thirty-six cheques upon Mrs. Monson's account with the London and Yorkshire Bank, Limited, Scarborough, and two deposit slips.

145. Book containing twenty-three cheques upon Mrs. Monson's account with the London and Yorkshire Bank, Limited.

146. Letter, A. Toovey, London, to Faithfull & Owen, London, dated 4th December, 1893.

147. Telegram, D. A. Hambrough to A. J. Monson, dated —— August, 1893.

148. Birch twig.

149. Elm branch.

150. Larch branch.

151. Plane branch.

152. Plane branch.

153. Mountain ash twig.

154. Mountain ash twig.

155. Birch twig.

156. Ash branch.

157. Plane branch.

158. Pellets.

159. Bound volume of newspapers.

160-161. Letter, "Glen" to Messrs. Davidson & Syme, and envelope bearing Edinburgh post-mark "Sp. 10. 93."

162. Letter, "Mrs. Elizabeth Scott" to Messrs. Davidson & Syme, dated 29th October, 1893.

163. Copy correspondence between Messrs. Davidson & Syme, W.S., and the Crown agent.

164-192. Twenty-eight letters and one telegram from the Crown agent to Messrs. Davidson & Syme, forming the principal letters and telegram embraced in the copy correspondence, No. 163.

193. Piece of human skin.

194. Projection of gunshot experiments.

195. Letter, dated 25th July, 1890, commencing "My dear Monson" and signed "T."

196. Letter, dated 20th July, 1890 (or 20th July, 1893), commencing "My dear Monson" and signed "M. T."

197. Letter, dated 13th May, 1893, commencing "My dear Cecil" and signed "M. Tottenham."

198. Telegram, bearing post-mark 18th August, 1893, commencing "Monson, Millhouse," and ending "Tottenham, Central Hotel."

199. Letter, dated 26/5/93, commencing "Dear Monson," and signed "Cecil Hambrough."

200. Letter, dated Corsey, Friday, commencing "My dear Monson," and signed "Stafford Jerningham."

20

The Trial.

201. Telegram, 26th August, 1893, commencing "Monson, Ardlamont House, Millhouse," and ending "Fiscal."

202. Letter, dated 30th September, 1893, commencing "Dear Tottenham," and signed "A. J. Monson."

203. Copy correspondence between the Scottish Provident Institution and A. J. Monson, and between the Glasgow branch of said Institution and the head office in Edinburgh.

All the Productions in the List of Productions annexed to the Indictment.

The following witnesses were examined for the defence :—

1. Harold Mark Carter, solicitor, Leeds.
2. Godfrey William Hambleton, physician, 23 York Street, Portman Square, London.
3. Edith May Hiron, Holly Bank, West Bay, Dunoon.
4. W. F. E. Massey, Poole Hall, Nantwich, Cheshire.
5. John MacEwen, innkeeper, Kames.
6. John M'Callum, general merchant, Kames.
7. Matthew Hay, Doctor of Medicine, Professor of Medical Logic and Jurisprudence in the University of Aberdeen.
8. William Gordon Woodrow Sanders, Bachelor of Medicine and Master of Surgery, assistant to the Professor of Clinical Medicine in the University of Edinburgh.
9. Arthur Logan Turner, Fellow of the Royal College of Surgeons, 19 Rutland Street, Edinburgh.
10. J. Hume Paterson, 7 Lauriston Lane, Edinburgh.
11. James M. Bain, photographer, 60 Summers Street, Aberdeen.
12. Tom Speedy, shooting agent, Edinburgh.
13. Arthur Edwards Saunders Sebright, 10 Portman Square, London.
14. Edward Lang, gunmaker, 10 Pall Mall, London.
15. G. G. André, Clyde Mills Company, Sandbank, by Greenock.
16. Philip R. Day, 3 Bath Street, Dewsbury.
17. J. Basil Walters, 3 Selby Road, Annerly, Surrey.
18. William Donald, engineer, Paisley.
19. Robert Hanna Donald, engineer, Paisley.
20. G. H. Tillard, retired colonel, Wayside, Harrow.
21. John W. Brodie Innes, advocate, Edinburgh.
22. John Blair, Writer to the Signet, Edinburgh.

The CLERK OF COURT (Crole) called the diet of Her Majesty's Advocate against Alfred John Monson and Edward Sweeney, *alias* Davis, *alias* Scott. Edward Sweeney, *alias* Davis, *alias* Scott failed to appear, and the macer proceeded to the hall, called his name, and returned to Court.

The CLERK OF COURT—Any answer, macer?

The MACER—No answer.

The SOLICITOR-GENERAL—I move your Lordship for sentence of outlawry against Edward Sweeney, *alias* Davis, *alias* Scott.

Sentence of outlawry was formally pronounced.

The LORD JUSTICE-CLERK—Alfred John Monson, you have already pleaded not guilty to this indictment. Do you adhere to that plea?

The PRISONER—I do, my Lord.

Alfred John Monson.

The following jury, after ballot, was empanelled:—

Thomas Kerr, farmer, Oatridge, Uphall.
Adam Brown, builder, Penicuik.
Alexander Binnie, baker, Pencaitland.
Thomas Forrest Tweedie, draper, Rankeillor Street, Edinburgh.
James M. Kerr, provision merchant, Great Flemington Street, Queensferry Road, Edinburgh.
James Black, grocer, West Bow, Edinburgh.
Daniel Robertson, grocer, Juniper Green.
John Ranken, plumber, 19 Union Street, Edinburgh.
Lennox Blyth, baker, Albert Street, Leith Walk, Edinburgh.
James Gordon, Engine Street, Bathgate.
William Mitchell, coal merchant, 141 St. Leonard's Street, Edinburgh.
Thomas Neilans, farmer, Huntlaw, Pencaitland.
Thomas Wilson, commercial traveller, Trafalgar Lane, Edinburgh.
William Lawrie King, commercial traveller, 34 Castle Street, Edinburgh.
William Nicolson Thomson, architect, 91 Albany Street, Edinburgh.

The CLERK OF COURT then read the charges against the prisoner as set forth in the foregoing indictment.

The LORD JUSTICE-CLERK, addressing the jury, said—Gentlemen of the jury, you have been balloted for to try this case. I am afraid that, from the long list of witnesses, you will see that it is impossible to close the trial to-day. It will therefore be necessary for you to be kept in confinement during the period of the trial. If any of you wish to communicate with any one, in order to get such comforts as you may require, as you will not be able to return to your homes, the Clerk of Court will give an opportunity of making communications at the adjournment. You can send a note or telegram now if any of you live at a distance.

Evidence for the Prosecution.

1. JAMES BRAND, examined by the SOLICITOR-GENERAL—I am a civil engineer and land surveyor, of the firm of Colledge & Brand, Glasgow. On 4th October last I went to Ardlamont, in Argyllshire, for the purpose of making a survey, and, as a result of my survey, prepared plans. The plan produced (No. 5/6) shows two pieces of the Ordnance Survey map joined together; it shows Ardlamont House and offices, the surrounding ground, and Ardlamont Bay. Between the young plantation and the old plantation, 1231 on the plan, there is a sunk fence or retaining wall. This I have shown on the large plan to the right of the sheet. Near the top of the sheet there is the word " Offices," that is, coach-house, joiner's yard, &c. Immediately to the south of Ardlamont House there is a grass field, and to the left of that a bank covered with wood.

At Ardlamont I met certain persons, who pointed out certain points on the ground—James Dunn pointed out to me the places marked A, B, C, D, E, F, and G on the plan. A is the scullery

22

Evidence for Prosecution.

James Brand

window of the schoolhouse; B is where Dunn saw Monson, Scott, and Hambrough before the accident pick up a rabbit after firing a shot; C is the kitchen window in the front of the schoolhouse; D is the corner of the junction of two roads, where Dunn saw Monson, Scott, and Hambrough cross the fence on the east side of the road. That is the easiest place to cross the fence at. E is the point to which the three men walked together, and where they separated; F is the direction in which Monson and Scott went; G is the direction in which Mr. Hambrough went. With the help of Dunn, Constable Macintyre, and my apprentice Wilson, I rehearsed what Dunn had told me of the routes taken by Monson, Scott, and Hambrough on the morning of 10th August, and was able to fix the point G.

The *locus* of the accident on 10th August is indicated by the letters J, K, L, M, O, on the smaller section of the plan, which is not large enough to allow of my marking these points. The points are accurately marked out on the larger section of the plan. These points were pointed out to me by the Depute Fiscal, and afterwards confirmed by Archibald Whyte. J marks the spot where Mr. Hambrough's head was when he was found dead; K is a rowan tree, and is marked from actual survey; L is a branch of a beech tree; and M is the stem of a lime tree. The branches of the lime and of the beech tree overlapped at the point L. At P there is a little footpath running down parallel with the wood. Q indicates the gamekeeper Lamont's house. Hugh Carmichael pointed out the place indicated by the letter S as the point where he saw Monson and Scott walking down to the mansion-house. U is the front door of the mansion-house; there are a number of steps leading up to it. V is the gate at the end of the avenue leading to the mansion-house. B to U is the avenue leading to the house. The distance from A to B as the crow flies is 120 yards; from B to D, measuring along the road, the distance is 155 yards; from D, where the three men crossed the fence, to E, where they began to separate, the distance is 23 yards. G, the point where Mr. Hambrough was lost sight of by Dunn, is 78 yards from D. From G to K, the rowan tree near which Mr. Hambrough's body was found, the distance is 392 yards along the sunk fence. The distance from the point J, where Mr. Hambrough's head was lying, to the rowan tree K, is 6 feet 6 inches. From K to L—that is, to the branch of the beech tree—the distance is 13 feet 9 inches; from K to M—that is, from the rowan tree to the stem of the lime tree—the distance is 16 feet 3 inches. To mark the parts of the rowan tree which were broken off by pellets, I took little pieces of paper and tied them on the branches underneath the breaks. I then took their levels, and found that No. 1 branch was 4 feet 8 inches above the ground, No 2 was 6 feet 2 inches, No. 3 was 5 feet 4 inches, and No. 4 was 5 feet 10 inches. I then took the beech tree, and found a pellet mark on a branch 8 feet 8 inches above the ground; and on the lime tree I found a pellet mark 7 feet 8 inches and another 6 feet 8 inches above the ground. To a person entering

23

Alfred John Monson.

James Brand

the wood on the right of the plan—that is, the old plantation—at
the south near the schoolhouse, it would present the appearance
principally of a birch wood, with some trees of considerable age. At
the south end of the wood there is practically no undergrowth, and
the trunks of the trees are fairly large. Between the top of the
sunk fence and the wood there is a level plateau, and then it slopes
down to the level of the wood. In some places the level of the wood
is practically the same as the level of the top of the sunk fence.
On the top of the fence there is fairly good sward turf, which seems
to have been put on at one time as a coping. Walking through the
wood from the schoolhouse you would have the sunk fence on your
right. From my own observation I should say that F and G,
indicated by Mr. Dunn, were the points where persons would be
out of sight of any one looking out of the kitchen window of the
schoolhouse. Near the place where the body was found the large
trees are not so numerous, and there is a great deal of undergrowth
and some whin bushes 10 feet high. The head was found about 3
feet from the sunk fence; some of the people present when I was
making my survey lay down on the ground to show the position in
which they found the body. I should describe the place as comparatively level; there is no brushwood immediately at the place. The
place was not visible from the schoolhouse, the growth of whin would
be enough to obscure the view. Going to it from the schoolhouse a
person would have to make his way through clumps of whins and
bramble bushes. There was a particular line where one could get
more easily through the whins than at any other point. I got a
person to stand at the place where the body was found, and placed
myself at the opening coming through the wood, and from there I
could see the rowan tree, the beech tree, and the lime tree. They
were practically in a line, one behind the other, and the pellet marks
which I had indicated with pieces of paper were in a line. There
was a good deal of undergrowth to the west and south-west of where
the body was found. The point where Hambrough's head was
found was a little lower than the top of the sunk fence. The ground
along the top of the sunk fence I found fairly good to walk on.
The sections of different parts of the wall which I prepared, and
which are produced, show that the top of the wall was comparatively
smooth; there are one or two places near the schoolhouse where a
person walking along it would have to diverge a little to get round
a tree. For a little bit the ground upon the top inward from the
retaining wall is comparatively free from trees, and a person walking
along there could see into the young wood at the bottom of the sunk
fence. The young wood—that is, the wood to the right of the sunk
fence—is very thick, principally pine. It is open for about 6 or 8 feet
back from the retaining wall, gradually sloping up from the ditch.
The rowan tree (shown No. 19) was uprooted under my superin-
tendence and brought to Edinburgh; I also superintended the cutting
down of the portions of the beech and lime trees. The distance from

24

Evidence for Prosecution.

James Brand

Ardlamont House to the place where Hambrough's body was found I found on measurement to be 360 yards, as the crow flies. The body lay east by a little north.

You mentioned a point in the wood where a person can come through the whins by a natural route; I am not sure whether I asked you the distance that point was from the point where Mr. Hambrough's head was found?—It was 15 feet.

Mr. COMRIE THOMSON—That is important.

Examination continued—I have been at Ardlamont on a number of occasions, and have looked at the coast near Ardlamont. The place marked "Ardlamont Bay" on the Ordnance sheet represents low water—that is, there will be water there at all states of the tide. On the Survey sheet there are rocks represented on the foreshore—that is, the shore which is covered at high water. I found a boulder on the foreshore of Ardlamont Bay to the west of the wash-house, but I have not been able to find any rocks in Ardlamont Bay below low-water mark, although I went there for the purpose of finding such rocks. I was there only last week, and both at high water and at low water was unable to see any rocks. One day at low water it was blowing half a gale from the southward directly on to shore, and had there been any rocks I would have been able to see the waves breaking on them. Immediately to the left of W there is a ridge of rock, about 115 yards from high-water mark, which the Government must have found when making a survey, but it could not have been any height, for I did not see it; I imagine that it had been covered up with sand. Immediately to the north of these rocks there are some which come up to high-water mark. The beach is sandy, with small stones, shelving gently down to the water. There is a drystone dyke running north-east up into an arable field. Archibald Whyte pointed out to me that as the place where the rowlock was found; it was a reef of rock going up to high-water mark, a little to the west of this place.

Cross-examined by Mr. COMRIE THOMSON—My visit was made two months, less six days, after the date of the accident. My information as to the points marked on the plan at the south end of the wood depended entirely upon Dunn; the gist of it is that the three men entered the wood, as men would do who were going to shoot the wood, in a line, Mr. Hambrough keeping to the right-hand or east side, Monson and Scott towards the other side, and the last that was seen of them, according to Dunn, was that they were proceeding through the wood in that order. My information as to the part of the wood where the body is alleged to have been found depended entirely upon that of the Depute Fiscal and Whyte, the gardener; and of these Whyte alone had personal knowledge. The Fiscal told me where the body had been found, after prosecuting his inquiries for two months. When I speak of where the head was I mean where Whyte said to me that he had found the head lying. No suggestion was made to me

25

Alfred John Monson.

James Brand

that the body had been found by the first persons who saw it lying
at the east side of the sunk fence.

So that if it be true that the dead man fell, and was found lying
on the other side of the sunk fence, your calculation with relation
to the rowan tree, the beech tree, the lime tree, and the direction of
the pellets would fall to be discredited?—Yes, if that is the case.

So that the whole of your calculations depend upon your having
been accurately informed as to the place where the man was shot?
If he was shot a little way from that, and stumbled forward or
stumbled sideways, or fell, or if he had been lifted from the place
where he originally fell to the place pointed out to you, then, in any
case, your calculations would necessarily fail or would disappear?—
That is so. I believe it was Mr. M'Naughton, the Depute Fiscal,
who lay down and showed me where the body was found. I made my
calculations with regard to the man standing erect, in imagination.

You have put the feet in the place where the head was lying?
—I am not going to assume that.

Have you made your calculation on the footing that the man's
feet were standing where the head was lying?—I am not going to
assume where his feet were; I took my directions from where his
head lay.

You put the man's feet in the place where Hambrough's head
was said to be?—I believe that it so. Letter J (where the head was)
is 3 feet from the edge of the sunk fence. All my measurements were
taken 3 feet from the edge of the sunk fence. Three feet from the fence
the ground is comparatively smooth and easy walking. On the top
of the stones of which the dyke is built it is also smooth; it is a path,
not a paved street. The dyke is a drystone dyke covered with sods,
and opposite to where I laid the man's head some of the sods were
slightly loose; by slightly loose I mean that the roots of the grass
had not entirely given way. I did not find the sods movable when
walking along. I don't think it necessary to any one accustomed to
country walking to walk along the dyke with particular care to prevent
stumbling—it is not a paved street, nor a macadamised road. Neither
of my attendants pointed out a place where there was a conspicuous
hole or trap in which a foot would be apt to trip; the Fiscal said
nothing about that. One would naturally, walking along the cover,
with the young wood on the one side and the older wood on the other,
keep pretty much on the line of the dyke, especially for sporting
purposes. Where the head was lying there are brambles, blackberries,
and whin, and some other soft underwood. In the centre of the plantation the ground is open. Supposing I found myself in the extreme
north of the plantation, and wanted to go to the mansion-house, I
would find myself on a road leading to the offices and continuing on
to the mansion-house. The lower gate is below 1231 on the plan,
and there is another a little further up the avenue to the north of E,
the point where Dunn saw the three separate. In order to get to that

Evidence for Prosecution.

you would have to go through the thick undergrowth that is between J and V—that is between the place where the body lay and the gate on the avenue leading to the mansion-house—or else go along the top of the dyke in a southerly direction, and then strike nearly due west. In giving the height of the retaining wall I took it from the ditch immediately below. You can get across the ditch and on to the rising ground on the other side without much exertion; the width of the ditch is about 2 feet. The rowan tree was cut on 5th October. I looked all round for other trees with pellet marks in them, but did not find any.

Did you examine any other trees except the rowan, the beech, and the lime trees to see whether they had been peppered with pellets? —Yes, I looked at the trees round about this place, and found no pellets in them.

You will be astonished to find that there is scarcely a tree in the wood that is not peppered with pellets?—Yes, I shall. I looked to see if there were any other trees to uproot. It was upon my assumption as to the place where the man had been shot that I looked at the trees. I made no examination of the trees except those that were of importance in this inquiry if the place where the man was shot was accurately described to me; it would have taken me a year to have gone over all the trees. There might have been a good many pellets found in the trees with people shooting winged game; I was informed that this was a favourite cover for Ardlamont. The authorities did not lay before me that this was a wood very much shot in; nor was I aware that Mr. Hambrough had shot frequently, almost daily there, especially shooting wood pigeons.

How many pellets did you find altogether in the trees you selected?—I did not take note of them, but, to the best of my recollection, there were six in the rowan tree, three or four, I think, in the lime tree, and one in the beech tree.

What did you do with the pellets?—The pellets were not in the trees; the branches only were marked. I did not get any pellets. What I saw were little holes, which I took to be marks of shot and marks where the pellets grazed the trunk with long lines. I cannot say whether all the marks of pellets were of the same age, because every tree would show a different result. So far as colour goes, some of the marks looked fresh and some of them looked old, but in my opinion colour is no test, because the rowan tree is a much softer wood, and will darken very much more quickly than beech will do. In the same tree, I admit, the shot marks of yesterday will be different from those of a month ago. I saw differences in the marks on different trees, but not in the same tree. I looked specially for differences among the pellet marks in the same tree. Those in the rowan tree were all well browned. The grass on the east side of the retaining wall was rather rank; I would not say it was long, but the blades, owing to the damp soil, were inclined to be broad and coarse.

27

Alfred John Monson.

James Brand

What was the nature of your inspection of the bay of Ardlamont outside the foreshore?—The weather was so boisterous that I could not have gone outside. I did not go out in a boat; a boat would not have lived. I was there two days, 5th and 6th October, and went over the whole of Ardlamont Bay from Craigmore Point to Corra Point. At that time I was going round the district; I wanted to see the general nature of the coast, and my attention was not then directed to rocks in the bay. I was sent down on another day to see if I could find a certain rock, and, with the exception of getting to rocks I was able to wade out to, my investigation consisted in standing upon the shore and looking out at high and low water for breakers. At Craigmore and Corra and on the Lochfyne side of Corra the water broke on shore, but I did not see any broken water outside. Either at low or high water there were no rocks, so far as I could judge, except on the foreshore. The place where the rowlock was found is not shown on the plan; it was at a point measuring from the extreme end spoken of, 230 feet in a south-west direction. I found at the place in the wood shown to me by the Fiscal and Whyte traces of a good many people having been there; it was beaten down.

Re-examined by the SOLICITOR-GENERAL—I had no difficulty in finding in the rowan tree, the beech, and the lime the places marked with pellets. There were some marks which I discarded, as there were doubts about them. I had no doubt about the beech and the lime. In looking round the place I saw one pellet mark on a pine tree which I had my doubts about; it was a little to the east of the lime tree, very much in the same direction. The marks were on the twigs in all cases with the exception of the beech tree; it was thicker than the others, and the mark represented more of a scar or furrow. The dyke was almost plumb to the east. When you come near the dyke from the west it does not present the appearance of a wall; it is covered with sods, and the ground comes up to it. Walking along the top there is nothing to suggest a wall, except that at some points the stones crop up. If there had been a hole or trap on the top of the wall along the place where my sections were taken I would have drawn it on them. There is no hole within 12 feet of the point where the body was found. On the east side at the bottom of the sunk fence there was longish grass, and the soil was of a very damp character.

2. JAMES WRIGHT—I went as butler to Ardlamont on 9th August last, arriving just before lunch. When I went to Ardlamont I found I was the only man-servant in the house. There were living in the house at the time Mr. and Mrs. Monson and family, Mr. Scott, and Mr. Hambrough. I waited at table at lunch on the day of my arrival. The servants in the house were the cook, housemaid, nurse, kitchenmaid, and governess. I did not see the party go out after lunch, and I cannot call to mind when I saw the gentlemen again.

Evidence for Prosecution.

James Wright

I was not out with any of them in the afternoon. I waited at dinner that night; Mr. and Mrs. Monson, Mr. Hambrough, Mr. Scott, and Miss Hiron, the governess, were present at dinner at eight o'clock. There was nothing unusual about Mr. Scott; he was just like the rest of the party. After dinner one of the gentlemen said they were going out fishing. I don't know when they went out; I missed them from the house, and so knew they were out. I was told to sit up, and did so. One of them—Mr. Hambrough, I thought at the time—came back about one o'clock on the morning of the 10th and asked for a lamp; he said the boat was sunk, and they had had to swim ashore. It was dark at the time; the gentleman was in the passage when he spoke. From the sound made by the person's boots I knew they were wet. I cannot say who it was that came back. As nearly as I can say the time was about one o'clock. I did not hear the gentlemen come in, but I heard them about half an hour afterwards in the smoking-room. I saw them all about the house, and I went into Mr. Monson's and Mr. Hambrough's bedrooms for their clothes. I found the clothes which they had been wearing. They were wet, as if they had been all under water. I took them into the kitchen. I do not remember if I took away any other clothes besides Mr. Monson's and Mr. Hambrough's. After going to bed about two o'clock, I heard the three men in the smoking-room. I got up about seven o'clock. Mr. Monson, Mr. Hambrough, and Mr. Scott were up before me, and I saw Mr. Hambrough in the dining-room. He asked me for a glass of milk and a biscuit. I did not see Monson or Scott at that time; I don't know where they were. I know they were up, because I was in their bedrooms and they were not there. I don't know where Mr. Hambrough went after taking the milk and biscuit. I did not see him in the house. I saw Monson and Scott come in, but I don't know at what time. I had not seen Monson and Scott that morning before I gave Hambrough the milk and biscuit, and I heard no mention of going out shooting. After doing that, the next time I saw Monson and Scott they were together, and that was probably about nine o'clock. I saw them standing at the dining-room door. I don't know by what door they entered. Scott was carrying rabbits, and he said that they had fallen to Mr. Hambrough's gun. Neither of them had guns in their hands at the time. Monson said Mr. Hambrough had shot himself, and when I asked had he shot himself in the arm, he said no, it was in the head, and he was quite dead. I asked him where the body was, and he said in the wood. I went out to look in the shrubbery. I could not find him, and ran back and told Monson, whom I had left with Scott at the door of the dining-room. He said, " Come, and I will show you." I passed out with him by a door at the back of the house, past the stables at the back of the house. As I was passing the stables I saw Whyte, the gardener, and Hugh Carmichael, the coachman. They were at the offices. Monson spoke to them, but I don't know what he said. We went straight along the main path. We

Alfred John Monson.

James Wright

were in the wood, and Monson guided me by a footpath to the body. I do not remember Scott being with us. The body was lying on the top of the dyke by the side of the ditch. There is no fence. The body was lying with the head inclined on the left shoulder, the right arm straight by the side, and the left arm across the breast. The left arm was nearest the drystone wall. I suppose the wall would be about 2 feet from the body. I saw no gun lying near. Monson said, I think, " What should we do? " I said, " We had better send for a doctor." The coachman was sent to fetch him. Whyte and I, and perhaps Carmichael, rolled the body in a rug. When we rolled the body in the rug I saw a wound about the size of a half-crown behind the right ear. There was blood on the ground where the head was lying. There was a cart near at the time, and it came along the field from the direction of the gamekeeper's house. The body was carried to the field, and the cart took it back to the house, past the offices. It was put in a bedroom, and I took part in dressing it. This would be about ten o'clock. I was not present when the doctor came. Mrs. Monson was in Glasgow. She had left that morning with Miss Hiron and the children. I did not see her go away. I don't think there was any one at the house that afternoon except Monson and Scott. Monson and Scott were together in the morning. Scott went away about two, I think. I don't think that I had heard anything about Scott going away before that, and no explanation was given to me. Scott told me he would be going away in the forenoon.

By the LORD JUSTICE-CLERK—Scott told you he was going away in the course of the forenoon, or what did he say?—He told me in the forenoon, after the body was brought in.

Examination continued—Scott was taken away in a trap. I think it was Mr. Steven's, the factor; he was going about that forenoon. When Scott told us he was going away we stopped the trap to inquire, and he said he had business which took him away. He said he was leaving his address at the Central Station Hotel, Glasgow. This was about two o'clock. Scott and Monson had been together all day up to that time. The doctor came about luncheon time. I think all who were at luncheon were Monson, Scott, the doctor, and the factor. Mrs. Monson came back some time in the evening. Scott slept in the room beside Mr. Hambrough's. Both bedrooms are beside the smoking-room, one on one side and one on the other. I think Mr. Tottenham came the following day, and Mr. Donald and three other gentlemen, whose names I don't know. Tottenham remained till next morning. Major and Mrs. Hambrough came and went away before the body was taken away. They came on the Saturday, I think. Mr. Monson went away with the body. Major and Mrs. Hambrough had dinner in the dining-room, but I think Mrs. Monson had hers in her bedroom the first day. Shooting began again at Ardlamont a few days after. Monson came back

Evidence for Prosecution.

James Wright

after he had taken the body away. I was in Ardlamont when he was apprehended, and remained at Ardlamont till 12th Steptember, when I left because I was told that I was not required.

Have you seen Scott since the occasion you mentioned?—No.

Have you been shown a photograph by Inspector Stewart and Inspector Grant?

[Mr. COMRIE THOMSON objected to the question, on the ground that the photograph was not among the productions.

The SOLICITOR-GENERAL—I propose to ask the witness whether he has been shown a photograph by two witnesses named on the Crown list. I am prepared to prove that the photograph had not been discovered by the Crown at the time the indictment was served, and therefore could not have been made a production. I do not propose to show the photograph to the witness. I contend that it is competent to ask him if he has seen a photograph in the hands of a particular officer and whether he recognised it. The defence can suffer no hardship, as, the names of the witnesses in whose hands the photograph was seen being given, they can see the photograph for themselves, and make what use they like of it in cross-examination.

Mr. COMRIE THOMSON—The question divides itself into two parts —first, " Did you see a photograph in the hands of certain officers? " To that I have no objection, except in so far as it is merely put to lead up to the second question, "Do you recognise it? Who is it?" To that I object. The photograph is not on the table of the Court, and cannot competently be put upon it. Therefore I have not got it, and cannot see it, and am deprived of the use of it in cross-examination, and prevented from showing it to other witnesses.

The LORD JUSTICE-CLERK—I have no hesitation in holding that no question can be asked about a photograph which cannot be produced. A photograph would have been a perfectly proper production to be made in this case, and if produced, it could have been used for any competent purpose; but this is a photograph which it is admitted cannot now be produced. It is one of the advantages of our law that a person accused of a crime is entitled to notice of the articles produced against him, and certainly if a photograph is to be founded upon as part of the prosecutor's case, that photograph ought to be given notice of. It would be a singular thing to introduce a photograph into a case simply because it could be proved that the prosecutor did not recover it in sufficient time to produce it. It is not maintained that he can now produce it. That he should be allowed to lead evidence as to what is practically the contents of an article which he cannot be allowed to produce in evidence—that is to say, a likeness, shown by a photograph—is out of the question. It would be to place the defence under every disadvantage as regards preparation of the case and cross-examination at the trial.]

Examination resumed—There was a cap beside the body when I saw it, but whether it was lying on the ground or was on the head

Alfred John Monson.

James Wright

I cannot say. [Shown label No. 6.] I identify the cap. I had never seen Scott before I went to Ardlamont. His age would be about twenty-eight or thirty, his height 5 feet 9 or 10 inches. His complexion was rather sallow. He was rather thin and rather delicate looking. He had a very slight moustache, rather dark in colour. From what I saw I should have thought he was a tradesman of some kind. Whilst he was at Ardlamont he appeared to be treated just as an ordinary visitor.

Cross-examined by Mr. Comrie Thomson—The party at luncheon on the 9th—Mr. Monson, Mr. Hambrough, Scott, and Mrs. Monson—appeared to be on perfectly good terms, speaking quite frankly and openly. Dinner was about eight, and the conversation was general. I do not remember hearing one of the gentlemen saying during dinner that they were going out to fish that night. It was after dinner that I first knew they were going out, and that I was to sit up for them. I could not be certain what hour it was when one of them came back for the lamp. He seemed to be in a hurry to get away with the lamp, and he took the lamp that was burning in the smoking-room.

Do you remember what it was he said exactly; whether it was that they had had to swim ashore, or that one of them had to swim ashore? He said the boat had sunk and they had had to swim ashore. About half an hour after that the three of them returned. There were two suits left dripping wet, and I removed them. The persons whose clothes had been wet put on dry suits and then came down to the smoking-room, where I heard them all talking in a friendly way. They were all in good spirits, and I heard them laughing. I don't know whether they were treating the ducking as a kind of joke. I don't know whether Mrs. Monson and Miss Hiron and the children went away by the early boat, and I don't remember if I saw them about the house that day. I did not see Mr. Hambrough start after he had his breakfast. When Monson came in after the accident and told me Mr. Hambrough was shot he seemed excited, sorry, and vexed. He told me where the body was, but I was not familiar with the place, and came back and said I had not found it. Monson said it was in the woods, and I went out with him and he took me to it. The way I went was by the back avenue and the road by the offices, and up a rough path by the end of the wood to the place. I came back the same way. The cart with the body came to the house by the same road after it got out of the field. When I saw the body the head was about 2 feet from the front of the wall, but I did not measure the distance. There was blood oozing from the wound. When I was with Monson at the body he still seemed excited and vexed. He said, "What shall we do?" And then it was suggested to send for the doctor, who came before luncheon, which was a little before two. Steven came with the cart for the body. He had been there all the time. He stayed to luncheon.   Scott wanted to catch the bus, but it did not run, and he went by a later boat than he intended. I heard him say that he intended to go by an earlier boat, and he went by a later one. When Scott left he said his address would be the Central Station Hotel. Mr. Tottenham and Mr. Donald were evidently expected.   Mrs. Monson returned before dinner, but was too distressed to come downstairs. I do not know whether the gentlemen shot on the 12th and 13th. I do not know if there was any shooting before the funeral.

3. ARCHIBALD WHYTE, examined by the SOLICITOR-GENERAL—I am gardener at Ardlamont.   Mr. Monson came in the month of May. I supplied the family with vegetables, and was in the habit of seeing them. On the morning of 10th August, when I was down at the shore, I heard some shots coming from the direction of the plantation east from the house. It would be about seven o'clock. It was a coarse morning, thunder and lightning and rain. I heard more than one shot. My house is at the offices. After having been at work for some time at the shore I went back to the garden.   I was standing in the arch of the building leading into my house when I saw Monson coming up from the house. Carmichael was with me at the time, and Wright was with Monson. Monson said to me, " Young Hambrough's shot himself ; see and find something and bring him up to the house." I went and found a rug, which I took with me to the plantation, Monson leading the way. The body was lying upon the grass on the top of the old dyke. I looked at the body and saw that it was dead. It was lying on its back turned a little to the left side. There was no gun near the body, and Monson was not carrying a gun when I first saw him. I saw a wound on the back of the head, and there was a good pool of blood under the head on the ground ; a small hole in the ground was full of blood. That was all the blood I saw on the ground. The head was nearest to the rowan seedling, which I knew. We had taken a rug with us. There were other people who were helping. The people present were— Steven, the factor, Stewart, Carmichael, the elder Carmichael, the ploughman, and James Lyon, who had his cart. After placing the rug under Hambrough's feet we drew it up below the body. It was lifted and placed in the cart and taken up to the house, round about by the offices and the end of the wood. When we got the body to the house we undressed it.   [Shown labels Nos. 4, 5, and 6.]   I identify these clothes. The only blood I noticed on the clothes when they were taken off was a little about the collar ; that, along with the blood at the head, was all the blood I saw. I don't remember if there was any blood on the rug when we took the body out of it. Monson wasn't present when we put the body in the rug. I don't know what became of him ; he went away after pointing out where the body was. We put the body in a bed, and later in the day dressed it. During the forenoon I went back to the place where the body was found, because I had heard that the body had been found

Alfred John Monson.

A. Whyte

in the ditch. That would be, perhaps, an hour and a half after I had taken the body away from there. On going back I saw quite well where the head had been. The blood was quite visible. Having heard the rumour, I examined the ditch. The ditch was grown over with grass and ferns. There was no appearance of blood anywhere in the ditch. Mr. Hambrough was a tall man. I think he would be pretty nearly 6 feet. He was also stout. The brackens and grass there were of such a kind as to have shown traces of the fall of a man of that height and weight into the ditch. There was not the slightest appearance in the ditch of any heavy body having fallen into it. I looked specially for that. In looking about the place I found two small pieces of bone. [Shown label No. 17.] They are both there. I found them 6 or 9 inches from the head, between the head and the ditch on the grass on the top of the wall. They were lying about 6 or 9 inches from the wall and on the same level as the head. In the larger of the pieces of bone there were three pellets. I showed them to M'Nicol, the joiner, and then buried them in the pool of blood, which we covered with a sod off the dyke. I went back to the garden for about twenty minutes, and then returned to the place, because I had noticed a track of grass and earth tramped down going back from the body and wondered what it was. I went back alone this time, and saw a track leading west from the body and then going south into the bushes. It was a rainy morning, and the grass was wet. I first of all followed a track on the top of the dyke southwards for about 20 paces. It was the track of one man, and appeared to go southwards in the ·direction of the schoolhouse. Having followed the trail back along the top of the dyke I returned to where I first found the body. I then went back to the track leading west from the body. I followed the track and found the two trails join. The place where they joined would be about 15 or 17 paces back from the body. The point where they joined into one was south from the body. The ground between the point where the two trails joined into one and the place where the body was lying was covered by grass and ferns. There were bushes growing on the ground between the body and the place where the two trails joined. I went through the bushes along this trail. There was only room for one person going through the bushes. There is one portion of the bushes which it is more easy to get through than the rest, and when I got through I saw a track split into two. There was room for two people beside it. I followed the centre trail for about 10 or 12 paces. It seemed to go on. I followed the other track for 40 or 50 paces, and it also appeared to go on. The track next Ardlamont House went in a west-south-west direction, and the other was a little more to the south. Both tracks led down to near the schoolhouse. I had no difficulty in following them. I saw the grass bruised down and the trail of footsteps. It was between ten and eleven o'clock in the forenoon that I saw the tracks through the bushes. M'Nicol had been with me there in the earlier part of

Evidence for Prosecution.

the day, and I mentioned the tracks to him some time that day. At the time when the body was lifted, or at any time, no one had been near the place where I found those trails through the bushes. On the forenoon of the same day I found a wad on the ground about 2 feet from the head. I noticed blood upon it. I dropped it carelessly. I searched for it frequently, but could not find it. I searched afterwards for the two pieces of bone. I found the piece with the pellets in it—the piece which has been shown. I was with John M'Intyre, the policeman, when he found the smaller piece. I had put a sod on the top of it, and it was found not far off. My house is considerably nearer the spot where the body was found than Monson's house.

On the morning of the 10th I heard something about the boating accident the night before. I went to M'Nicol and told him about it, and we went and saw the two boats lying on the shore below high water. One of the boats was M'Nicol's and the other was M'Kellar's, who is a boat-hirer at Tighnabruaich. Monson had hired the boat from him, and used it sometimes for fishing purposes. I had seen it out in the bay, but I can't say who was in it. When I went down to the shore there was a net near the boat. M'Kellar's boat was lying bottom up, and there was a jacket under it. [Shown label No. 1.] I identify that jacket. There was a pipe with tobacco in one of the pockets. I noticed there was a hole in the boat, but not a round hole, such as a plug hole. It was in the wrong place for a plug hole, and was too large, and did not seem to have been cut in the usual way. It seemed to have been cut with a knife. [Shown label No. 25.] That is a cross-section of a rowing boat from keel to gunwale. The hole was towards the stern, and more in the side than in the bottom.

By the LORD JUSTICE-CLERK—It was on the edge of the fourth plank counting from the keel.

Examination resumed—When I was at the boat Monson came down about three, and said that the night before the boat had upset, and that he had got young Hambrough on to a rock. He said he remembered walking across the old dyke, and made a sign to the place where he had crossed the old dyke. The place was about 400 or 500 feet above the shore from where the boat was. I found the rowlock of the boat on the shore on 8th or 9th October. It was found on rock 18 paces below high-water mark. The depth at high water was 3 feet 9 inches. I afterwards pointed out the place to Mr. Brand. While we were talking it began to rain, and Monson and I took shelter in the washing-house. When in the washing-house Monson said it was all settled about the purchase of Ardlamont by Hambrough, except as to seeing Major Hambrough. Referring to the accident of that morning, he said it was a great pity, and that, but for Scott coming up behind, the body might have lain long enough before being found. He said nothing about having lifted the body

35

Alfred John Monson.

from the ditch. I first noticed the pellet marks on the rowan tree on the Tuesday or Wednesday after Hambrough's funeral. I saw the twigs of the rowan tree hanging down and some of the branches peeled, but I was not certain at the time what was the cause. When Dr. Littlejohn came my attention was drawn to the fact that an opinion could be formed as to the direction of the shot from the injury done to the branches. I saw Mr. Macnaughton and Dr. Littlejohn at Ardlamont, and pointed out the place where the body was found. At first a piece of turf marked the spot where the head was found, and when the turf was removed a small cairn of stones was put down. They were afterwards displaced, but I cannot say when.

Cross-examined by Mr. Comrie Thomson—I saw Monson and the butler at the offices, and followed them past the office through the planting, which was the only way to the body. After the body was brought through the park it was taken past the offices back to the house. When I went to the body past the offices I went by the path that runs north of the plantation, and Monson and the footman went the same way. I didn't see Monson and Scott going down to the house.

On that occasion was any search made in the ditch or in the neighbourhood of the ditch?—Yes, I searched.

On the first occasion, was any examination made by you of the ditch at the back of the body?—No.

And no one else that you saw examined it?—No.

Nor the neighbourhood of the ditch?—No. Steven, the factor, came up before the body was removed. There was about a kitchen bowlful of blood in the pool beneath the head. I saw no other blood.

You said before that you had seen blood on the collar of Hambrough's coat. [Shown label No. 5.] Do you see it now?— No, I don't see it now. The blood was oozing very slowly from the wound. I can't tell you who it was that first put it into my mind that the body was found in the first place on the other side of the fence. I must have heard it among the working classes.

Who do you mean by the working classes?—I heard it rumoured in the dead man's room.

You heard it rumoured amongst those who were round the body when it was being dressed?—Yes. There had been rain at six o'clock in the morning, and it continued pretty well all day. There was no water in the ditch below the dyke. It was overgrown with ferns, bracken, and grass. On the bank adjoining the ditch on the east side there was long, soft, fine grass like pasture grass, not rank grass. If blood had escaped to the same quantity as I saw it had escaped upon the jacket, I think I would have seen it, but it would depend upon the quantity. If two men had leaped from the dyke into the ditch I would have expected to see the grass broken down.

I went back from the garden to look for a trail, because I had seen a track under the body. I went back to please my own

Evidence for Prosecution.

A. Whyte

curiosity. I mentioned the trail I had found for the first time that day. I did not tell the Procurator-Fiscal about these trails. The trails went through long ferns and grass. I would not call them brackens. The track there would have required more than one person passing up and down to make it. It led in the direction of the nursery. Near the body it broke into two branches. Walking along the top of the drystone dyke would not be as easy as walking along a turnpike road, but I don't know of any holes or places where one might trip; when I was on the top of the dyke I did not find it slippery with the rain.

What became of the three pellets you found in the bone of the skull?—I don't know; there were two in it when I handed it over.

There were three at first?—Yes, there were three when I delivered it.

When were there two?—Some time after. I don't know that now there are no pellets in the bone. I delivered it to Constable M'Intyre and some time after I saw it in the hands of Constable Campbell, and there were two pellets in it. I have not seen it since. [Shown label No. 17.] I see a graze on the bone, but no pellets. I cannot say why I threw the wad away which I found. I showed it to Lamont, the keeper. The plantation had been shot in frequently during the previous weeks, while Monson and Hambrough were there. I found the jacket [label No. 1] under one of the seats of M'Kellar's boat. The hole in the boat was such that a common cork would fill it up. It appeared to me to be made by a knife or some other tool, and not by an auger.

Re-examined by the SOLICITOR-GENERAL—I never saw a plug hole like this one in a boat before. I saw three tracks from the body, and they appeared to be freshly made. There was one track along the top of the dyke, made by one person. When I went through the bushes and found the track split into two, each of which was the track of more than one person. I followed the trail nearest the mansion-house for 40 or 50 paces, and it appeared to be the trail of one human being. I did not follow the track nearer the dyke so far, only about 12 paces; it also appeared to be the trail of one human being, likewise the trail along the dyke backwards, which I followed about 20 paces. The place which I referred to as being marked by a number of people walking was from the body back to where the trail split into two. With regard to the track which I followed for 40 or 50 feet—the one nearest the mansion-house—it was going in a west-south-west direction from the point where the two split. While I was following it back I was going in the direction of the lower edge of the plantation towards the schoolhouse. In following back the middle trail for 12 feet I was going south, which is also in the direction of the schoolhouse. The trail along the top of the dyke led straight to the body.

By the LORD JUSTICE-CLERK—I examined the marks on the rowan

37

Alfred John Monson.

tree on Tuesday or Wednesday, and the beech tree some time after that.

4. STEWART M'NICOL, Ardlamont estate joiner, examined by the SOLICITOR-GENERAL—On the day before 9th August Mr. Monson came about ten o'clock to the estate offices, where I was working, accompanied by a man whom I took at the time to be one of the shooting gentlemen. I found out afterwards that he was Mr. Scott. He was 5 feet 8 or 9 inches in height, slightly built, with a dark complexion and a small dark moustache. Monson asked the loan of my boat for two nights. My boat lay at Ardlamont Ferry. I knew that they had a boat of M'Kellar's, which Mr. Hambrough was in the habit of using. Monson said his own was not extra safe. I agreed to let him have my boat for two nights. When I went to the ferry at twelve o'clock the same day the boat had been taken away. My boat was a 15-feet keel boat, sharp at both ends, and had a plug hole near the stern. The plug was a cork.

On the morning of the 10th I was informed of the accident to Mr. Hambrough. Carmichael came to me, because they wanted a board to carry the body. I went to the spot. I went straight to the west. I was working about half a mile east of the young plantation. The body was lying in a rug on the top of the dyke. It had been put in a rug before I saw it. Lyon's cart was there at the time. I went with the body to the house, and was present when it was undressed. Hambrough was a heavy, tall, and pretty stout man. There was a little blood on the collar of his jacket, on the right side. We found blood in the rug after we lifted the body out. When we took it out I saw a wound on the right side of the head, at the back, behind the right ear. It was from there that the blood was coming. It was still flowing when we dressed the body. There was some oozing out of the wound. When I went to the body while it was lying on the dyke Monson was not there, and I did not see him at all that morning till after we had undressed the body. I went to the workshop for a stretching-board, and saw Monson and Scott coming out of the front door. That morning, as I was returning to my work, I re-visited the place where I first saw the body. Whyte was with me, and we saw blood on the top of the dyke where the head had been; Whyte picked up two small pieces of bone, in one of which three pellets were sticking. The pieces of bone were found on the top of the dyke 6 or 9 inches from the place where the head had lain, in an easterly direction towards the young plantation. Whyte placed them on the top of the dyke and covered them up.

While we were undressing the body somebody had said that it had been found in the ditch, so on this visit to the place I jumped into the young plantation and walked alongside the ditch for 10 or 12 yards back from the rowan tree, but saw no marks of blood, nor any marks of a body having fallen into it. I found a track, as if the grass had been trodden down, going to the south-west of the

Evidence for Prosecution.

rowan tree. There was also a track from the body going south in the direction of the schoolhouse, and this I traced back about 9 yards. At the point where I left it, it seemed to be going on through the bushes. I cannot say whether it appeared to be recent, but the grass seemed to be freshly broken down. I know that it wasn't made by anybody lifting the body, because I was present when it was taken to the cart, and nobody went near the place.

About three in the afternoon I went down to my boat, accompanied by Whyte, who had told me there had been an accident to the boat. I found my boat lying on the beach, and also the one belonging to M'Kellar, which was turned upside down. They were lying about 70 yards below high-water mark. Both of them were rowing boats, and M'Kellar's was fitted with rowlocks, but there were neither rowlocks nor oars in it. In M'Kellar's boat we found a jacket, with a pipe in the pocket. [Shown label No. 1.] There was a hole in the boat. It was in the fourth or fifth plank from the keel. The hole is about an inch in diameter. It seems to have been made with a knife. If I had been making the hole I would have done it with an auger. The wood was soft yellow pine. The hole could be made in ten minutes or a quarter of an hour at the most. I have been about boats all my life, and never saw a plug hole like that before. A plug hole is generally made smooth round the edges, so that you can get a cork firmly into it. It would not be easy to get a plug firmly into that hole. When I was working at the boat Monson and Lamont came down. Monson said to me that he remembered coming over a stone wall about 500 yards to the west on the previous night. That was on the 10th. On the following Monday I found a knife below high-water mark in Ardlamont Bay. It was lying near where the boat was found, and was quite fit to make the hole.

My attention was directed to the marks on the rowan tree about three weeks after that. Constable M'Intyre drew my attention to them. They were pellet marks, and appeared discoloured. The direction of the marks was a little upwards.

By the LORD JUSTICE-CLERK—That is ambiguous. It is going downwards in one direction and upwards in another. Looking in which direction?—From the direction in which the body lay.

Towards the trees?—Yes.

By the SOLICITOR-GENERAL—Rising horizontally a little upwards as you went from the body?—Yes. I helped to cut down the rowan tree and the branches of beech and lime.

Cross-examined by Mr. COMRIE THOMSON—I remember that on two occasions previously Monson asked the loan of my boat to go out fishing. At that season of the year splash fishing is carried on at night. On the first occasion Hambrough took Douglas, the keeper, with him. When Monson asked for the boat for two nights he did not say that Douglas was to go with him on the 10th. He gave as his reason for wishing my boat that his own was a bit of a crank.

Alfred John Monson.

S. M'Nicol

It is almost necessary to have a plug in a boat in which there is a splash net. So far as I know, M'Kellar's boat had no plug. The hole in the section shown could be plugged with a cork. When I saw the boats on the 10th M'Kellar's was capsized, and underneath one of the seats I found a jacket. The boats were tied together by a rope. I never saw Mr. Hambrough with the knife which was found.

I should describe the top of the dyke where the body was found as uneven ground, composed of grass and turf, and with the stones of the dyke cropping up through the grass. The hole where the blood lay was sufficiently big to admit the toe of a man's boot. Care would have to be taken in walking along the dyke, more especially on the day in question, as there had been heavy rain. After the body was taken to the house, Carmichael, the ploughman, washed the blood off the face with soap and water. I don't know whether it was the last witness or Whyte who suggested that the body might have been in the ditch; the suggestion didn't come from me anyway. The stuff growing in the ditch was grass and fern, not rough, big bracken, and nothing like fine pasture grass. On the back as it rises from the east towards the young plantation there was grass of the same kind, rank stuff. I found no blood there. The blood was only oozing from the wound when the body was being removed. There was some blood on the coat; just a little about the collar. I think that the impression made by a man falling in the grass would last a good time. The track went from the body westwards; I did not say that I saw a track going southwards. The only track I saw went from the body westwards, and then turned to the south in the direction of the schoolhouse. I followed it about 9 yards. No branch of it turned towards the north. The track had been trampled down pretty much; it might have been trampled down for days; two or three persons going over it once would not have caused it. It was a formed path that had been several times used.

Re-examined by the SOLICITOR-GENERAL—The track led from the body west and then south. About two yards from where the body lay it went south. I followed the track westwards from the body about 2 yards, and then about 9 yards southwards. The track kept at pretty nearly the same distance from the dyke. It might be 2 or 3 yards back from the dyke in a southerly direction towards the schoolhouse.

My boat, as compared with M'Kellar's, is pretty nearly the same length, but broader. If two men and a net were in the boat it would not draw over a foot of water. There are rocks in the bay about 70 yards from the dyke, but I do not think there are rocks 200 or 300 yards from the shore on which a boat could have upset, and on which a man might get. I have never seen any rocks there. The rocks I mentioned are seen at low water. The place where I was told the rowlock was found was pretty close to a rock. I found, at about 10 paces from the rock, between it and the shore, that the water was 3 feet 9 inches deep at high water of

Evidence for Prosecution.

ordinary tide. The depth of the water outside the rock would be about 4 feet 6 inches.

5. HUGH CARMICHAEL, ploughman, Ardlamont, corroborated the evidence of the last three witnesses as to the finding and disposal of Mr. Hambrough's body.

Examined by the SOLICITOR-GENERAL—I saw Mr. Monson on the morning of the 10th going down towards Ardlamont House. He was carrying two guns—one in each hand—and was accompanied by a gentleman whom I didn't know. This gentleman was carrying a rabbit in his right hand. I saw Monson and the gentleman again about ten minutes afterwards, and he told me Hambrough had shot himself. Monson had no gun with him. I pointed out the place where the body was found to the Depute Procurator-Fiscal. Dr. Littlejohn was there at the time, but I do not remember having seen Mr. Macnaughton, gunmaker, at Ardlamont. The last time I pointed out the place was to Mr. Baxter; on that occasion there were three gentlemen present.

Cross-examined by Mr. COMRIE THOMSON—On the morning of the accident I saw that Monson was distressed, but, of course, I did not care to look at him. After the body was taken to the room I sponged the blood off the face with soap and water. Four or five weeks later Whyte told me that he had seen a kind of a track, but he did not say that he had discovered it, or a way into the wood, or anything of that kind. I am unable to say whether there were any marks in the ditch or young plantation.

6. JOHN STEVEN, factor at Ardlamont, examined by the SOLICITOR-GENERAL—I live at the Camp, about three-quarters of a mile from Ardlamont mansion-house, and was at Ardlamont when Monson came about the end of May. I remember meeting Monson and another man about eleven o'clock on 9th August, the day before Mr. Hambrough's death. Monson introduced his companion to me as Mr. Scott, and told me they were going to the ferry to launch M'Nicol's boat, and take it round to Ardlamont Bay. He explained that the boat he had hired from M'Kellar in Tighnabruaich was not, in his opinion, safe when nets were in it. Monson made no reference to the purpose of Scott's visit at that time, but on the afternoon of the following day, the day of the accident, he spoke to me about Scott in connection with the boilers of the yacht. He said that Mr. Hambrough had thought it advisable to have an independent man to examine the yacht on his behalf, and Scott, I understood, was the independent man.

By the LORD JUSTICE-CLERK—To see that the boilers were all right? That was what Scott was said to have come for.

Examination continued—I walked to the ferry with them and helped them to launch M'Nicol's boat, which they rowed round in the direction of Ardlamont. That was all that I saw of Scott that

Alfred John Monson.

John Steven

day. On the following day I had occasion to be at Ardlamont offices about a quarter to seven, and I stayed there till a little before nine o'clock, when I went down past the schoolhouse towards my home. I was at the offices when Whyte told me of the death. That was a little before nine o'clock. I suggested to Lyon, to whom I had been talking, and who had a cart, that he should take it down as it might be of use. I went down through the wood to where the body was; when I got to it there was no one there. Whyte followed me. The body was lying in a rug on the ground. [Here witness corroborated the evidence of previous witnesses as to the position and appearance of the body.] Along with the others I lifted the body on to the cart. I took the short cut through the wood to the mansion-house. Up to that time I had not been near Monson to speak to him, and when I got to the mansion-house I inquired for him and found him and Scott in the smoking-room. I said, " This is a terrible job ! " Scott answered, " It is a terrible job ! " I do not recollect that Monson said anything. He had given no instructions as to what was to be done with the body, and I asked him where it was to be put. He asked if we were bringing the body to the house, and I said we were, and that it would be there presently. I said, " Where shall we put it ? " He said, " I don't know." I asked, " Where is his bedroom ? " He said, " Next door." I said, " We had better put it there," and he said, " All right." I asked Scott if he had had a gun, and he said no, that he was carrying the rabbits. He said that Monson and Mr. Hambrough had guns, but that he was no sportsman, and that he thought it best to leave firearms alone. I do not remember Monson making any remark when Scott said that. I went to the smoking-room to ask Monson about dressing the body, and found that he and Scott had left the room. After looking through the house for them, I went outside and saw them walking about together about 50 yards from the house. I asked Monson what should be done about the dressing of the body, and he told me to do just what I thought proper. After going back to the bedroom and seeing what was being done there, I went to my own house, and returned again to the mansion-house about eleven o'clock. I saw Mr. Monson, and went up with him to the place where the body had been found. As we were going there, Monson told me that Mr. Hambrough had shot himself, and then he began to describe the positions in which they were in the wood. Hambrough, he said, was walking on the top of the wall, Scott was in the middle, and he was behind. He said he heard a shot from a short distance from the underwood at the end nearest the offices. He walked on to the end of the wood, and then, having got up there, he turned up to the corner to the side of the wall at the end of the wood. I mean the end nearest the offices. Then he walked along the end of the wall near the wood. He then cried, " Hulloa,

42

Evidence for Prosecution.

John Steven

Hambrough, where are you? What have you got? " and, hearing no answer, he walked back to the end of the wall where Hambrough should have come along, and a short distance down he said he was horrified to find Hambrough lying shot.   Scott came in behind him, and they met at the body.   He pointed to two places immediately opposite where the body was lying when I saw it down in the new plantation.   I mean on the east side of the ditch.   He pointed to two places, and after he did that he said, " To tell you the truth, Mr. Steven, I don't know where we lifted him from, but we lifted him."   The places he pointed to were just immediately below the wall, a little below where the body had been lying.   I saw no traces of blood at either of the places to which he pointed, nor any marks of a man having fallen at that place.   The brackens were standing in their natural condition—not broken down at all. I found that a turf had been placed at the spot where I had found the body, which showed that somebody had been there in the interval.

Monson and I left the place together, and he remarked that it was a strange coincidence that he had been nearly drowned the night before.   He said that when out fishing they had struck a rock, and the boat had upset, and he had got either an anchor rope or net round him, and was nearly drowned, but that Mr. Hambrough and he got on to a rock, and he struck out for shore. He made no reference whatever to anybody else than Mr. Hambrough and himself being in the boat or on the shore at the time the boat upset.   I knew that Hambrough could not swim; he had himself told me so.   Monson described himself as a good swimmer, and was proud of his explcits in the water.   On the day of the accident, when Dr. Macmillan came, about twelve o'clock, I introduced him to Monson.   Monson showed no inclination to go to the body.   At that time I did not examine the pockets of Mr. Hambrough's jacket; I felt cartridges in the pocket from the outside only.   After the examination of the body by the doctor I went up again to see Monson; it was not shortly afterwards that he first said anything about Scott going away.   Just before luncheon Monson told me that Scott was going away by the 1.55 boat, and, hearing that he had not ordered a trap, I went and told the groom to bring the trap round to the front door.   Then I was asked up for luncheon, at which the doctor, Monson, Scott, and myself were present.   From Scott's appearance, I could not judge what kind of employment he followed; he might have been anything.   Had he been described as a clerk, I would have believed it from his appearance.   He was invited to luncheon just as one of the party.

On the day of the accident Monson gave me a letter to read about insurances on Mr. Hambrough's life.   It was from the Scottish Provident, and was a letter accepting an insurance, on which, however, the premium had not been paid.   I do not remember

Alfred John Monson.

John Steven

Monson having said anything to me that day about any insurance on Mr. Hambrough's life which had been completed. I do not think that he made any reference to the fact of two insurances of £10,000 each having been completed on Hambrough's life. The impression left on my mind was that Hambrough's life had not been insured, or that insurance had not been completed on that policy. Monson made no reference to any other policy.

[The Court adjourned at six o'clock, to resume at ten o'clock the following day.

The LORD JUSTICE-CLERK, in intimating the adjournment to the jury, said it was hardly necessary for him, as a matter of duty, to ask them not to form any views about the case at all meanwhile. They had heard little of the case, and they were a long way off from hearing what would be brought forward on the part of the prisoner. He would ask them rather to use their time out of Court by taking such relaxation among themselves as would the better fit them for these protracted sittings than by discussing the trial.

The jury were housed in the Waterloo Hotel.]

Second Day—Wednesday, 13th December, 1893.

JOHN STEVEN, examination resumed—After luncheon Monson, the doctor, and myself walked up to the place where the body was found. There was no one else with us except one of Monson's little children. Dr. Macmillan had not been there before, and he asked where the body was lying. I saw that Monson was excited, so I pointed out the two places which he had shown me. They were just opposite to where the body was lying in the ditch in the lower plantation. The ditch is not on the same level, and the plantation is about 3 feet from the bottom of the ditch. When Dr. Macmillan asked the question I don't recollect Monson making any reply. Dr. Macmillan looked at the place I pointed out, but he did not go down. I pointed out to him where I had found the body. I don't think that I told Dr. Macmillan that Monson had told me about the places.

I accompanied Monson to Ventnor with Mr. Hambrough's body on the Monday after the occurrence. I don't remember when was the next time that I visited the place where the body was found, and I do not think that I was ever there again with Monson. The day on which Mr. Blair was at Ardlamont was the first occasion on which I heard Monson speak about killing a rabbit on the day of the accident. On that occasion Mr. Blair and Monson went to the wood; I was a little behind them, and overtook them when they reached the spot where the rabbit was found. On the night, I think, when Monson was under police surveillance in the house, Monson told me that on the morning of the death he went over to the keeper's for the 20-bore gun which Mr. Hambrough was in the habit of using, and he left Hambrough and Scott in the house, intending to find them when he came back from the keeper's, and when he came back he found they had gone out, but that Mr. Hambrough had lifted his (Monson's) gun, the 12-bore one, and taken it with him. Mr. Hambrough, Monson said, kept the 12-bore gun all morning, while Monson kept the gun he got from the keeper, that is, the 20-bore gun. Monson said he fired one shot and killed a rabbit, which he left lying, intending to pick it up on his way home, but he did not come back that way. The rabbit was lying at the foot of a hedge past the end of the wood to the west of the house. That is a different wood from that in which the death occurred. Supposing they had shot down the plantation referred to, and were going to return by the road, they would

45

Alfred John Monson.

John Steven

have had to cross the field before they got near the school; they would get on to the road which goes up past the schoolhouse. The rabbit I refer to was lying 100 yards south of the end of the wood. [Shown No. 5/6.] It is not shown in this plan, which ends with the wood. If they were going round by the schoolhouse to go into the other wood they would require to cross the field; but I understand they went round the hill.

On the day I was at the *locus* with Monson and Mr. Blair— the third Saturday after the accident—I saw pellet marks in the rowan tree, a few to the north of where Mr. Hambrough's head had lain. I saw some twigs broken as if by a pellet. Mr. Monson, Mr. Blair, and I saw that. I stretched over and drew the branches over to examine them, and saw the pellet marks quite plainly. They came in a horizontal direction.

By the LORD JUSTICE-CLERK—Could you see the branches of the rowan tree if you were standing with your feet at the place where the body was?—Yes.

By the SOLICITOR-GENERAL—So far as I can recollect, Monson said to me that Scott went to the body by the way Hambrough had gone. I saw Mr. Macnaughton, gunmaker, Edinburgh, at Ardlamont, and I was with him when the place where the body was found was pointed out to him by Whyte.

Cross-examined by Mr. COMRIE THOMSON—I do not remember how long it was after the Monsons came down that Mr. Hambrough joined them at Ardlamont. It was more than a month, but before the end of June. He was there some time before I knew. I often saw Mr. Hambrough and Monson together, and they seemed to be on the best of terms. I discovered that Hambrough was fond of fishing, for he consulted me about flies, and he told me that they were going to fish with a splash net; Mr. Hambrough had hired a boat for the purpose from M'Kellar at Tighnabruaich. I met Monson and Scott on 9th August near Ardlamont avenue, and went to the ferry to help them with M'Nicol's boat.

When I first saw the body it had already been handled, for a rug had been put underneath and folded over it. The position in which I found the body was therefore, so far as I know, a different one from that in which it had originally been. There was blood oozing gently out of the wound. I stooped down and lifted the head, and in doing so I perceived a very strong smell of whisky. When I returned to the house and saw Monson in the smoking-room he seemed to feel very vexed; I noticed that he was affected; he was crying. He seemed to be too distressed to give any particular directions about what should be done with the body; he left it all to me. The body was in the bedroom before I left, and the men were attending to it. I accompanied Dr. Macmillan, who arrived about twelve o'clock, to the room. I saw Carmichael sponging the face and wound with soap and water. The doctor then proceeded to examine the wound. He said there was no smell of singeing,

Evidence for Prosecution.

John Steven

and asked me to come forward and see whether I could detect any smell, but I could not. I saw no pellets about the head or neck. The wound was very small, and I formed the opinion that the muzzle of the gun must have been near—I should say, within the length of the barrel from the head at the farthest—otherwise the wound would have been more spread. I formed that opinion at the moment, and I retain it still. The doctor said the wound would have missed being fatal if it had been an inch or half an inch to one side.

I was informed that Scott was going away by the 1.55 boat, but in further conversation Monson said that Scott was to wait for a later boat about 2.40. When Scott was leaving, Monson, at the steps, said to Scott, " It is a pity you can't wait." The doctor was in the dining-room when Scott went away. Monson and the doctor spoke about Scott going away, and the doctor thought there was no need for Scott waiting, as he was confident that his report would satisfy the authorities as to how the accident occurred. Monson said that in England there would have had to be a coroner's inquest, and the doctor said that in Scotland they were particular, too; but then, he added, his report would satisfy the authorities, and so Scott went away. At the place where I first saw the body there was a hole on the top of the dyke, in which a man's foot might very well catch. The hole was very near the body. On the second occasion on which I visited the spot a stone had been put in the hole. The grass on the top of the dyke becomes glossy with the wet. The ditch runs along the bottom of the wall, and is irregular.

Kindly repeat as exactly as you can what Monson said to you as to where he found the body?—When Monson and I went up the first time to the place where the accident occurred he looked down into the plantation and pointed to different places, and said— " We lifted him, but from where I really don't know "; and when I pointed out the place where the body was found, he looked rather surprised at that being the spot. He seemed to be confused and shocked at what had happened.

Assuming that Mr. Hambrough was shot and fell on the ditch side, would it not have been a decent thing to have lifted the body from the ditch and laid it upon the surface of the dyke?—Yes; it would have been a natural thing to do. The wood to the south-west of where the accident is said to have happened is thick, but it is possible to get through it. Any one going once through it might leave a trail or a track, or he might not. I found the remains of a rabbit at the place where Monson said that he had shot it; that was not in a plantation at all, but in a field.

On 17th October Mr. Tom Speedie, the sporting editor, came to Ardlamont and made an investigation in the wood. I accompanied him on his rounds, and saw him take several branches from trees, because there were pellet marks and pellets in them. [Shown Nos.

47

Alfred John Monson.

148-157 of defence productions.] These are the branches which Speedie took away. The trees from which the greater number of these branches were taken were within gunshot of where Mr. Hambrough was walking on the top of the dyke. I saw a good many other trees all over the wood marked by pellets. Wood pigeons are very common in that wood, and in shooting wood pigeons it is invariably the case that the trees get pellets into them. Since Mr. Speedie left I have examined the wood several times, and have found branches marked by pellets. Monson did not say why, after getting the 20-bore gun from the gamekeeper on the morning of the accident, he kept it. He said that Mr. Hambrough had left the house with the 12-bore gun, and that they were trying some new powder, but I did not at the time catch its name. I now know that it was amberite powder, but I thought at the time that Monson said " Hambrough powder." He did not say who was using the new powder; he said " they were trying a new powder."

Re-examined by the SOLICITOR-GENERAL—When Monson told me what had happened he did not say whether Mr. Hambrough was alive or dead when he or Scott came up to him. I do not remember asking anything about it. Monson did not suggest that he died in their presence, but I remember him saying that he tried to rouse him, and cried to him, but got no answer. My impression from the conversation I had with Monson was that Mr. Hambrough was shot dead. It would have been natural to leave the body lying where it fell until the circumstances were looked into, but if he had fallen into the ditch it would have been more natural to lift him out of it. I saw no traces of any one having been in the ditch, or of any one having been lifted out of it. I had never seen a case of a wound like this one; I had never seen a gunshot wound before, and my data for forming an opinion on the distance of the muzzle from the head were just the narrow compass of the wound. I have been accustomed to shooting an average amount. I did not myself measure the height of the marks on the rowan tree, but I saw generally that they were horizontal, and rather higher up than my own height. I have shot wood pigeons, and they are generally shot higher than 6 feet from the ground. The place which I referred to where there was a stone out of the dyke was about half-way between where the head was and the foot of the rowan tree, further north from the body.

7. JAMES DUNN, examined by the SOLICITOR-GENERAL—I am a watchmaker at Newcastle, and in the month of August last was spending a holiday at Ardlamont, occupying a part of the schoolhouse along with my half-sister. While there I often saw Mr. Hambrough and Mr. Monson, and was quite familiar with their appearance. I remember Mr. Hambrough's death, and on the morning on which it happened I was in the schoolhouse. About nine o'clock I saw Mr. Hambrough, Monson, and a stranger on the road near the house— that is the road which passes the west side of the schoolhouse going

Evidence for Prosecution.

north. I was at the pantry window, which looks south. I saw Hambrough jump over the wall and pick up a rabbit, which he handed to the third person, whom I did not know. They went past the gable, out of my sight, and I then changed my position to the front window of the schoolhouse. I saw them cross the turnpike road and jump over the wire fence into the plantation. The three walked a short way together, and then Hambrough struck off by himself to the right, Monson and the other man keeping to the left. I do not know the distance at which I finally lost sight of them, but I pointed out to Mr. Brand the places where I first saw them, where they crossed the fence, and the direction in which they went respectively along the wood. I also pointed out the place at which I lost sight of them. Some time after they had disappeared I heard a shot, which seemed to come from the north.

Cross-examined by Mr. COMRIE THOMSON—Before the morning in question I had occasionally seen Mr. Hambrough and Monson walking together through the wood, each with his gun.

If these three men on the morning in question continued to walk in the same direction in which they were going when you lost sight of them, could they have met?—No; if they kept in the same direction. It was about three minutes after I lost sight of them that I heard the shot.

8. GEORGE LAMONT, examined by the SOLICITOR-GENERAL—I have been second gamekeeper at Ardlamont for eighteen months. It was my duty to attend Mr. Hambrough and Mr. Monson when they went out, and was available whenever wanted. On the morning of the 10th I first saw Monson at seven o'clock. He came to my house at the offices to tell me to go to M'Intyre, the head keeper, with a message that he was wanted at ten o'clock, as the gentlemen were going out. I am in the habit of keeping the guns for the purpose of cleaning them, and Mr. Monson asked me for Mr. Hambrough's 20-bore gun, saying that Mr. Hambrough wanted it. [Shown label No. 7.] That is the 20-bore gun which Mr. Hambrough had been using. I went off for the head keeper, who lives two miles away from the mansion-house, and got back about half-past ten. On my way down I heard of the death. I did not know till then that any one had been out shooting that morning; I had heard nothing of it. When I got back to the house I saw Monson, and he said to M'Intyre in my presence that Mr. Hambrough fell, his gun went off, and he shot himself. He did not tell us how the body lay. He said he had heard a shot, and had cried out asking what he had got; there was no answer, and on going forward they found Mr. Hambrough dead.

Did he say who went forward?—No; he said " they went forward." Some time after I found that they were Scott and himself. I went down with Whyte to where the body had been. Whyte lifted a turf on the top of the dyke, and I saw below it two pieces of bone and a little bit of skin. There was blood below the turf. [Shown

E

Alfred John Monson.

G. Lamont

label No. 17.] These are the pieces of bone. It was about twelve o'clock when I went first to the place. I know the rowan tree which was near the body. I saw that some of the branches about my own height from the ground were broken, and hanging down, but I did not examine them closely at the time. I saw the gun wad which Whyte picked up just beside the turf. There was blood on one side of it. It was thrown away carelessly. I went down to the mansion-house early in the afternoon, because Monson had told me earlier in the day that some friends of Mr. Hambrough were coming for the shooting, and he wanted to stop them at some of the piers, as he did not know their addresses. I went down to offer my assistance in stopping them, but Monson said he would go himself. I don't know if Scott had left by this time; I did not see him. The 12-bore gun [shown label No. 8] was the one which Monson was in the habit of using. This and the 20-bore gun were the only guns they had. There was also an estate gun, which they had used before the 20-bore gun was got, but since then I had used it. After the death, I saw the two guns lying on the sofa in the smoking-room when I went over to offer my assistance. I took them away to clean, and Monson saw me doing so, but made no remark. There were no cartridges in either gun.

I had been in the habit of going out splash-net fishing with Mr. Hambrough, who had hired M'Kellar's boat a few weeks before his death. The last occasion on which I was out fishing in M'Kellar's boat with Mr. Hambrough was on the evening of the 8th; John Douglas, an under-keeper, was with us. On the night of the 8th I did not see any plug hole in M'Kellar's boat; I noticed nothing wrong with the boat. Mr. Hambrough made no complaint to me about M'Kellar's boat, nor did he ever say to me that a plug hole was required, or ever speak about making one. I found M'Kellar's boat quite safe for two. On the 10th, when I was returning back after having taken the message to M'Intyre, I saw two boats down by the shore. I recognised M'Kellar's, but did not know the other. I knew that it had been arranged for two parties to be out on the night of Thursday, 10th. Late on the afternoon of the 10th I went down to the boats, and on the road down met Monson, and we both went down together. M'Nicol and Whyte were then getting the boat pulled up. I saw a hole in M'Kellar's boat. [Shown label No. 25.] That is a bit of the boat containing the hole; there is a spar across the section, put there to save the planks. That occasion was the first time I had seen the hole. It was not in the usual place for a plug hole; it was too far up, and it was not smooth and round, as if it had been cut with the usual instrument. A jacket had been found in M'Kellar's boat, but it was not in the boat when I went down. [Shown label No. 1.] This was the jacket found, and I had seen Hambrough wearing it. Monson saw the jacket, and was surprised that it should have remained in the boat. The oars and the rowlocks were amissing from the boat.

Evidence for Prosecution.

G. Lamont

I went back that night to the place where the body was found. I looked again carefully at the ditch, but saw no appearance of anybody having fallen into it. I remember a police officer being placed near the rowan tree to prevent any one from interfering with it. I examined the tree again after Monson was arrested, and formed the opinion that the breaking of the twigs had been caused by shot. Monson did not speak to me about Scott till after I was examined by the Fiscal before Monson was arrested. This would be about a fortnight after the death. I asked Monson about the position they were in in the wood, and for the first time he mentioned that Scott came in the centre. Monson told me that Scott was an engineer, and that he had come about something connected with the yacht, the "Alert," I was shown the place where one of the rowlocks was found by Archie Whyte. It was a little bit from the rocks, north-west of Ardlamont Bay, beyond the dyke. To come into contact with the rock a boat would have to come close inshore. The tide comes out by the rock, and leaves it dry. When the tide is well up the depth of water above the top of the rock would be about my height. It is not a place for splash-net fishing. There are boulders of rock about three or four feet high lying all along the shore, but there is no rock, so far as I know, out below low water with which a boat could come in contact and upset. M'Kellar's boat, with two men and a net in it, would draw about a foot of water.

Cross-examined by Mr. COMRIE THOMSON—M'Nicol had been at the place where the body was found before my first visit. I did not know till afterwards that they had been looking in the ditch for any traces.

Did you make a search?—Yes; on my first visit.

Did you go into the ditch?—No.

Then you made no search?—I looked over the top of the wall.

M'Nicol and Whyte were able to go down and search the ditch, and no trace was left of them having been there. Why do you express surprise that there should be no trace if the dead man had fallen there when no trace was left of the two men groping about?—Well, the ferns were growing strong, and if a dead body was thrown in it could not have been brought out without some smashing of ferns.

Do you think there would be smashing of ferns if Whyte and M'Nicol were there?—They could jump. I cannot say how often I was out in the boat with Hambrough, but it was more than twice, and after dark. It was not till after the accident that my attention was drawn as to whether there was a plug hole in the boat or not. Most of these boats have plug holes, but not the lighter ones. M'Nicol's had a plug hole, but it was a heavier one. The net brings a lot of water into the boat after having been used for splash-net fishing. [Shown label No. 25.]

Did you notice anything like that loose spar?—I cannot say anything of a spar.

Alfred John Monson.

G. Lamont

And you do not know by whose ingenuity it has been tied here?— No.

Does it look like a spar belonging to the boat at all?—Yes.

It is not like any of these other spars?—No; it is a part which comes in contact with the feet, and the varnish gets rubbed off. I knew nothing about the spar until now. The jacket, when I saw it, was lying over one of the seats; the boat had already been moved when I first saw it. Monson expressed surprise that the jacket had remained in the boat, the boat having capsized. Mr. Hambrough never rowed the boat when I was in it. M'Kellar's boat would not have had enough water to take it across the place where the rowlock was found.

You have said there would be 6 feet, and that the boat with two men in it would draw 1 foot. In that case anything between half-tide and full tide would give water enough to float the boat over that place?—No; it would not float over the rock where the rowlock was found. There was perhaps $3\frac{1}{2}$ feet over the rock. I cannot say minutely. I have looked for rocks, but only from shore, never from a boat. I say there are no rocks there, because I have seen fishing boats sailing there.

And they know how to steer?—Yes.

They keep out of the way. I suppose fishermen will know better than you whether there are rocks there?—Yes. Monson said to me on the 10th, with reference to this plug hole in M'Kellar's boat, that Mr. Hambrough made the plug hole in the boat. He did not say that Mr. Hambrough had made it with his own knife. The hole I saw had the appearance of having been made recently with a knife.

Rabbits and pigeons were the only things that would be shot in the plantation. The place where Mr. Hambrough met with his death was a favourite spot for sport. I remember one occasion on which Mr. Hambrough gave me a rook rifle to clean which he had been using. The stock was broken, and he said that he had fallen on the rocks and had broken the stock. When I was out with him when he was shooting I used to relieve him of his gun when he was crossing dykes or fences. I know nothing about the 20-bore gun after I had given it to Monson early on the morning of the 10th. When I saw Monson in the smoking-room after the death he seemed very much excited and distressed; he was scarcely able to speak. Nothing was said at the time about the guns. I was not surprised to find the guns unloaded; it is usual to draw the cartridges from breech-loaders on going indoors. I was not Mr. Hambrough's regular attendant when he was out shooting, because I had the pheasants to attend to. Monson and he frequently went out without any keeper. They were both keen on wood pigeons, which were very plentiful in the plantation where the accident happened. The wad I found was a 12-bore cartridge wad. I opened one of the cartridges which I saw Monson use for the 20-bore gun, and I am satisfied that the wad I saw on

52

Evidence for Prosecution.

the dyke was not one of these. The 12-bore wads are much thicker. I have also seen one of the amberite cartridges for the 12-bore gun.

I believe you first stated—I don't blame you for it—that you first thought it was a 20-bore gun that Hambrough had been shot with?—Yes. I had some conversation with Monson, when he said that Mr. Hambrough had a 12-bore gun out that morning, and wanted to try the amberite cartridges.

If that statement be true, of course you were under a misapprehension about the matter as to the 20-bore gun?—Yes.

You assumed that Mr. Hambrough would be carrying the 20-bore gun?—Yes.

You have been with Monson when he shot with the 20-bore gun sometimes—Yes. I have never seen a 20-bore amberite cartridge. [Shown label No. 2.] The wad in that 12-bore cartridge is similar to the one I found. I have seen pellets and marks of pellets in some other trees besides that rowan tree.

Re-examined by the SOLICITOR-GENERAL—When Monson came to me in the morning about the 20-bore gun, he said nothing about changing guns with Hambrough. I took the guns from the smoking-room after the accident without being told to do so. The right hammer of the 20-bore gun was down and locked; the left was at full cock. There were no cartridges in the gun. I did not notice how the hammers of the 12-bore gun were. It was about a fortnight after he had been examined by the Fiscal that Monson first spoke to me about a change of guns. When I was being examined by the Fiscal, he told me to get the 20-bore gun and an amberite cartridge, and bring them to him, so I went to Monson and asked for them, who discovered the mistake he had made, and said that when he came down with the 20-bore gun that morning Hambrough had out the 12-bore gun on the front lawn to try the amberite cartridges. I had heard nothing of this before.

The rocks on which the rowlock was found had a bare space at high water in an ordinary tide of about 50 paces. There are stones, but it is a sloping beach down to high water. There was no great necessity for a plug hole in M'Kellar's boat, because, being a light boat, it could easily be tilted over and emptied of water.

Re-cross-examined by Mr. COMRIE THOMSON—But it was a much easier way to take out the water by a plug hole than by tilting the boat?—Yes.

At the time when Monson spoke to you about the guns, that was the first time you had been conversing on the subject?—Yes.

There was no charge against Monson at that time?—No. I was merely telling him what I had stated to the Fiscal.

After you had been with the Fiscal, and made a statement, the Fiscal told you to bring a gun and some cartridges, and it was then that Monson explained to you that you were under a misapprehension?—Yes.

Alfred John Monson.

9. JOHN DOUGLAS, examined by the SOLICITOR-GENERAL—I am gamekeeper on the Ardlamont estate, and have lived there for twenty-three or twenty-four years. I attended Mr. Hambrough when he went fishing, and looked after the boat and the ret. When I went sea-fishing with Mr. Hambrough we used M'Kellar's boat, and I did not know of any plug hole in it till after the death. Mr. Hambrough never spoke to me of the necessity of a plug hole in the boat, which I had always found quite safe for fishing with two men and a net in it. I remember on 4th August examining the boat to see that it was all right; there was no plug hole in it then, and the same night Mr. Hambrough, Hugh Carmichael, and I went out fishing. The last time I was out in M'Kellar's boat was on the Tuesday before Hambrough's death. The boat was going just as usual. [Shown label No. 25.] I identify that as part of the boat, and I see the hole; this hole I first saw on the Thursday night after Mr. Hambrough's death. The boat was then hauled up on the beach. I have been accustomed to boats all my life, but I have never seen a plug hole in the same part of a boat as this one is. The flooring came across the four timbers to save the planks, which form the inside of the boat, and to cut the hole one would have to remove one of these planks.

I had an appointment with Mr. Hambrough on Thursday afternoon, and it was when going down to the mansion-house that I heard of his death. My house is about two hours' walk from the mansion-house. George Lamont took me to the place where the body was found, and he told me that it was said that the body had been in the ditch. I looked at the ditch to see traces of a body having been there, but saw none. When I went down to the boats I saw the fishing net, and I noticed that there were small sticks sticking in it; there might have been seaweed. From what I saw sticking in the net I formed the opinion that it had been in the water not far from shore. There is a burn leading out from the garden, and the refuse is carried out to the shore by it. The stuff sticking to the net seemed to be stuff of that kind. I have fished Ardlamont Bay for twenty-three or twenty-four years, and during all that time I never saw a rock in Ardlamont Bay below low-water mark. On the north side of the burn there is a rock pretty close inshore against which a boat might come; there is another near the dyke on the north side of the bay, and a third on the other side of the dyke. This last is not a spot where one would put down a net for fishing, it is a rock upon the foreshore between high and low-water mark. The rock at the foot of the burn is a big boulder 5 or 6 feet high lying on the foreshore. I never saw any rock below low-water in Ardlamont Bay which would be dangerous to a boat.

Cross-examined by Mr. COMRIE THOMSON—The coast is rather a rough one. The best place for fishing is in the bay. If I wanted

Evidence for Prosecution.

to fish I would never think of starting from the rocks at the extreme end of the bay and going south by east to the centre of the bay; I would go out further east at the corner of the bay. At the other horn of the bay there is Craigmore, a rock island; I agree that on both sides of Ardlamont Bay the coast is rocky. [Shown label No. 24.] Mr. Hambrough carried a knife of that construction, but whether his knife was like that or not I could not say; his knife was attached to a chain.

Re-examined by the SOLICITOR-GENERAL—I think that Hambrough had a ring through his knife attached to a chain from his pocket; there is no ring upon this knife.

10. DONALD M'KELLAR, examined by the SOLICITOR-GENERAL— I am a boat-hirer, Tighnabruaich, and in June last I let a boat for three months to young Mr. Hambrough. There was no plug hole in the boat when it was got from me; there was no necessity for a plug hole. I heard of Mr. Hambrough's death soon after it occurred, and on a Sunday I went over to Ardlamont to have a look at my boat, which I found lying on the beach. [Shown label No. 25.] The plug hole is not in the usual place; it is too high up and too far away from the keel. It has not been made with an auger, which cuts a clean, round hole, which can be easily filled with a cork and made watertight all round. I should say from the look of it that the plug hole was cut with a knife, and to make it in that place the guard board would have to be removed. If the guard board were replaced then the hole would not be visible from the inside of the boat, and it would be below water mark if the boat was floating with some person in it. I examined my boat on the day I went to see it, but saw no mark of damage which would have indicated that it had been on a rock.

Cross-examined by Mr. COMRIE THOMSON—I do not know from experience that a boat like that might go against a rock with sufficient force to throw an inexperienced man standing in it into the sea and yet no mark of damage be left on the boat.

But an inexperienced man standing in a boat like that, and suddenly the boat bumping against a rock, would be very apt to be thrown out?—It is not often the case.

But that might happen and yet your boat show no trace of damage, and all the more so if the rock was covered with seaweed? —That would help to prevent any damage from being visible.

11. ALEXANDRINA SHAND, examined by the SOLICITOR-GENERAL —I went to Ardlamont as nursemaid on 10th June, and stayed until Mr. Hambrough's death. I was engaged through a Glasgow registry office. On the afternoon of 9th August, a little after three o'clock, I took the children for a walk on the beach, and saw Scott and Monson sailing in a boat in the bay. It was a varnished boat. Mrs. Monson and Mr. Hambrough were walking on the cliffs below

55

Alfred John Monson.

A. Shand

Ardlamont Point. After taking some of the children out for a sail for about twenty minutes, Scott and Monson continued rowing about for three-quarters of an hour. I saw Monson walking along the road to the mansion-house after leaving the boat; Scott, meanwhile, remained sitting in the boat, and after about twenty minutes he took off his shoes and stockings, and came out of the boat and began to pull it ashore. I then returned to the house and saw Monson returning in the direction of the boat.

I do not know the hour at which Mrs. Monson left for Glasgow on the morning of Mr. Hambrough's death, but she came to my room about half-past five o'clock in the morning and said that she and the two elder children were going to Glasgow. That was the first definite information I got of their going to Glasgow, but I was aware that they intended going there some time soon.

Cross-examined by Mr. Comrie Thomson—I knew that one of those days Mrs. Monson and some of the children were going to Glasgow. I had prepared a list of things for the nursery which they were to get in Glasgow. Mrs. Monson and Mr. Hambrough were in sight at the time when the children were walking on the beach; they could see the whole proceedings as they were on the higher ground on the top of the cliff looking right down to the bay. Monson, Scott, and the children could have seen Mrs. Monson and Mr. Hambrough if they liked to look.

12. John Tweedley, examined by the Solicitor-General— I am a herring buyer at Rothesay and buy fish from trawlers. My boat lies on the Rothesay coast opposite Ardlamont. On 9th August I was out with my boat for the purpose of buying fish from the trawlers, and proceeding right to Ardlamont Bay went on shore a little to the south for my evening meal. I went up the south side of the burn to get some water, and there I saw two boats, in one of which there was a net. I arrived in the bay about sunset, nine o'clock, and about ten o'clock I started out again to go to some drift-net boats to the west. As I was leaving I heard voices coming from the direction of Ardlamont House. I also heard a sound as if a boat were being drawn on the shore, some distance off. Within an hour after leaving the shore I heard two screams from a north-western direction. After the screams I heard a voice answering from the shore, but I was too far out to hear what was said.

Cross-examined by Mr. Comrie Thomson—The screams did not appear to come from any one in distress; had I thought so I would have gone to help. I thought that the noise was from the trawlers, who always make a lot of noise when they are at work. When I landed for my supper I went and looked at the two boats; the tide was flowing and one of the boats was just beginning to float; it was bumping on the shore. The water was round the other boat, but it was not yet afloat or bumping. At the time when I heard

Evidence for Prosecution.

J. Tweedley

the shouts there was a southerly sea coming in. When boats are left to bump in that way with a flowing tide it would be apt to knock the plug out of the bottom. A little bit south of where I saw the boats lying there are some rocks visible at all states of the tide. The beach is rocky all along, the rocks extending southward and onward to Ardlamont Point. That neighbourhood is a dangerous place in the dark to any one unacquainted with it. It is quite possible that two Englishmen went out there in the evening to fish with a splash net and that the boat bumped against a rock.

Re-examined by the SOLICITOR-GENERAL—Do you know any rock outside in the bay below high-water mark?—I never came in contact with any rock there.

13. PETER GALBRAITH, examined by Mr. STRACHAN—I have been fisherman and ferryman at Tighnabruaich for eighteen years and a half, and am well acquainted with Ardlamont Bay. I know of no rocks in the bay below low-water mark, but there are various boulders along the foreshore, most of which are covered at high water. At half-tide they are all dry. There is one rock to the north of the dyke that runs into the sea about 30 yards, which becomes an island at high water. Last Saturday I examined the depth of the water between this rock and the shore at high tide, and made it about 4½ feet. There is no rock whatever of that depth in the vicinity against which a man might come and capsize a boat and have to swim 200 or 300 yards to reach the shore. I should say that the farthest a man would have to swim to reach the shore would be 10 yards.

By the LORD JUSTICE-CLERK—Would you say that if a man swam 10 yards he would be within his depth?—I would say that.

Examination continued—I was out fishing in Ardlamont Bay with my brother on the night of the 9th. We saw a great many trawlers there, and coming home to Tighnabruaich we tacked into within 100 yards of the shore near the dyke. This would be about half-past twelve; we saw a couple of trawlers with their lights burning at anchor right opposite the place. There was plenty of noise; fishermen are in the habit of crying to one another. I heard no noise in the direction of the dyke. When we passed Ardlamont Bay about twelve o'clock I should say that the state of the tide was about an hour and a half off ebb-water; it was high water about eleven o'clock. There would be very little water between the rock and the shore at that time, probably about a foot and a half. There was no moon, but it was not a dark night.

Whyte pointed out to me where the rowlock was found; at high water there would be 3½ feet of water at the place. I see no reason why a boat should be launched to take ashore a person who had come in close contact with a rock and had got on to it. I could get ashore without swimming.

Alfred John Monson.

P. Galbraith

CROSS-EXAMINED by Mr. COMRIE THOMSON—Suppose a person wanted to swim ashore at high tide, not being acquainted with the shore and on a moonless but clear night, as you have described, do you think if he were a good swimmer he might naturally swim along till he saw a place to land without rocks?—I think any man thrown into the water would make for the nearest point.

But suppose the man was confident of his powers as a swimmer?— I could not say what some men would do, but it is quite possible. My calculation that the water was 3½ feet deep at the place where the rowlock was found was arrived at by an approximate guess. It is quite possible that two men out there with a very slight acquaintance with the bay, on a dark night, might bring a boat upon a boulder, but there is no danger of them getting drowned.

But suppose that one of them was standing in the stern working a splash net, and the boat suddenly bumped against a boulder, do you not think it very natural that he should tumble over into the water?—He would tumble into the boat instead of tumbling out.

Are you sure?—He might stumble over, but it is into the boat he goes if the boat struck in the fore part.

But if the boat struck sideways, he might tumble over sideways? —He would tumble to the opposite side of the boat.

And would probably go over?—He might.

That is all I want. A man standing up in the stern of a boat, with a splash net, without experience, and the boat coming against a rock, is more likely to go over the side of the boat than anything else?—Oh, yes.

14. JAMES M'PHEE, boots at the hotel, Tighnabruaich, examined by the SOLICITOR-GENERAL—I knew Monson by sight. It was my duty to attend the steamers when they arrived at Tighnabruaich. I waited for the steamer which arrived from Glasgow about five o'clock on the afternoon of 8th August. A man came off the steamer with whom I put myself in communication. He appeared to have lost his friends, and did not know where he was going. He gave the porter in charge of the pier his black bag to take down to the end of the pier. I followed after him, thinking he was going to a hotel. He still maintained he had missed his friend. Previous to that he had forgotten his coat, and he went on board the boat to fetch it off. He said he expected to have a friend and a conveyance meeting him. The porter inquired at me would I take him along. I said I did not mind. I suggested that his friend might wait further on, and I took him along to Auchanlochan in the hotel trap. The man said he was a complete stranger to the neighbourhood. I inquired at the man in charge of Auchanlochan Pier if any one had come off. He said no. I suggested to the gentleman I was driving that we should go on to the next pier, Kames. While we were going along I asked him, in case he did not see his friend, did he know where I was to take him to? He took out a piece of paper on which was the telegraphic address

58

Evidence for Prosecution.

of Ardlamont House. I then took him towards Kames Pier. As you approach Kames Pier there is a hill. I stopped at the head of the hill. There was a machine approaching. Monson was in it. I passed the remark to the gentleman I was driving, " That is the gentleman you are looking for." As they came up Monson appeared to be acquainted with the man with me, for he smiled a little. The man in the trap with me seemed displeased, and said, " Where do you think you are going now? " Monson replied, " I was coming along to pick you up," and then the man in my trap got out and took his place in Monson's trap. The stranger was 5 feet 8 or 9 inches in height, about thirty-five years of age, with a nervous, delicate appearance, and a very slight moustache. I saw him leaving from Tighnabruaich on the day of Mr. Hambrough's death. He never told me his name.

Cross-examined by Mr. COMRIE THOMSON—Kames is the nearest pier to Ardlamont, and the natural pier for persons going there.

Does all that you have been telling us amount to this, that the man you spoke to—we will call him Scott—came out at Tighnabruaich, two piers sooner than he should have done, and that when Monson arrived at the proper pier—Kames—he drove back to meet Scott?—Yes. I don't know the name of the boat by which Scott left Tighnabruaich; it was about five o'clock, and he was at the pier just like an ordinary passenger. I acted on the advice of Mr. Macnaughton, the Deputy Procurator-Fiscal, and gave no information to the agent of the accused.

15. HUGH CARMICHAEL, examined by the SOLICITOR-GENERAL— My father is a farm servant at Ardlamont, and I was engaged to be groom to Mr. Monson. On the evening of 8th August I went with the trap to meet Mr. Monson at the steamer at Kames. Mr. Monson took the reins and drove towards Tighnabruaich, away from the direction of Ardlamont. We met a trap driven by M'Phee coming towards us; in it was a man named Scott. Scott got into our trap, and Monson drove back to Ardlamont. On the afternoon of the day after Mr. Hambrough's death I drove Scott to Tighnabruaich, and at the pier I saw Constable M'Calman, to whom I pointed out Scott.

Cross-examined by Mr. COMRIE THOMSON—I heard of Mr. Hambrough's death about a quarter to nine on the morning of 10th August. I saw Monson at the house that morning about nine o'clock; he seemed to be mostly crying. I was ordered to get some one to take something up to carry the body in. Some one brought a cart, and I was told to go for the doctor. Some time during the summer I saw about a dozen cattle in the wood in which Mr. Hambrough was killed; they were close to the fence along the road leading to Ardlamont. I was ordered by Mr. Steven to put them out. They could not have been very long in the wood, because I had seen them shortly before in the field. They travelled through the plantation about half-way down. I thought that this had occurred some time before the accident

59

Alfred John Monson.

to Mr. Hambrough, but when I was asking about it I was told by
Mr. Lyon that it was after the accident; I thought he said that it was
in the month of May or June, and I believed him, as I remember that
I met him at the time I was going to put the cattle out of the wood.
Lyon is a witness for the Crown.

16. JAMES LYON, examined by the SOLICITOR-GENERAL—I know
the last witness Carmichael, and I know the wood where Hambrough's
death occurred. Once in the end of September or beginning of
October I saw six cattle belonging to Mr. Proctor, Point Farm, in
the wood, but I do not remember whether Carmichael was with me
at the time. Carmichael spoke to me about the cattle to-day, but
I cannot remember what passed between us. I took Mr. Hambrough's
body in my cart to the mansion-house.

Cross-examined by Mr. COMRIE THOMSON—No one else except
Carmichael has spoken to me to-day or yesterday on the subject of the
cattle. I cannot positively say how many cattle I saw—there were
about half a dozen. Carmichael says that he saw me at the time I
saw the cattle, but I don't remember. I did not see cattle to the
number of ten in May or June in that wood. I saw the body just
before it was lifted from the spot where it was found. I saw a path
going to the west apparently trodden down by a lot of people.

17. JAMES DONALD, examined by the SOLICITOR-GENERAL—I am a
partner of the firm of Hannah, Donald & Wilson, engineers and ship-
builders, Paisley. In the end of July my firm was corresponding
with Mr. Monson with regard to the purchase of a steam yacht, the
"Alert." On 22nd July I received this letter from Monson—" I
have talked the matter over with Mr. Hambrough. We have decided
to purchase your boat. I think the price £1200 is very high. However, as Mr. Hambrough is willing to buy her, I will forward you a
cheque for that amount. I have probably to pay a cheque to
the agents for the purchase of the Ardlamont estate by
Mr. Hambrough, therefore I shall not be able to forward you a
cheque before 10th August." I wrote Monson accepting his offer,
agreeing for payment being made on 10th August. The yacht was
lying at Kames at that time, and the arrangement was that we were
to get two days' notice if Mr. Hambrough or Mr. Monson wished the
use of the boat. On each occasion when it was used it was returned
to its moorings at my yard. The price has never been paid. On 8th
August I was on one of the South-Western Railway's boats, going
from Princes Pier to Kames. I went down with Monson in the same
compartment to Greenock, and after we were at Innellan I met him
on board the boat. He was talking to another man whom he described
to me as a person from the estate office who was going to see Mr.
Hambrough. I did not understand him, as I had never heard the
estate office mentioned. When we passed Tighnabruaich Monson
asked me if I had seen the fellow going ashore. I told him that I

60

Evidence for Prosecution.

had not. Monson looked for him at Kames Pier, and I saw Monson's trap going away in the direction of Tighnabruaich. This person looked to me to be a respectable man of about thirty-three years of age; 5 feet 8 inches in height. He was slightly built, with a sallow complexion, and had a slight moustache.

Cross-examined by Mr. COMRIE THOMSON—Monson said to me that the man had come down at Hambrough's request; he did not mention his name. Monson and this man had not been in each other's company during the whole trip, because when we were coming to Kames he asked, " Where is that fellow? " He assumed that he must have got off at the wrong pier. The man was not with Monson in the railway carriage. I remember in July meeting Monson and Hambrough on one of the South-Western steamers; Monson introduced me to Mr. Hambrough. On that occasion Hambrough and Monson each had a gun, Monson an air gun, Hambrough a rook rifle. Hambrough was explaining to those around him how an accident took place when he was carrying a gun. He said he was holding it about 18 inches from the muzzle, that it had gone off, and that he had had a narrow escape, the charge having gone close past his head. He said he had been carrying his gun in his usual way.

Re-examined by the SOLICITOR-GENERAL—Hambrough said he was holding the gun by the barrel, with the stock near the ground, the barrel being in the air. He said that was how he generally carried his gun.

18. JESSIE M'LEOD, examined by the SOLICITOR-GENERAL—I was housemaid at Ardlamont during the Monson's stay there; I am at Ardlamont still, but not in Mrs. Monson's employment. Until Wright, the butler, came I waited at table. I remember Monson coming home on 8th August, the Tuesday before Mr. Hambrough's death, and some person, whose name I was told was Scott, coming with him. As instructed by Mrs. Monson, I prepared a room for Scott; it was in the sunk flat, and similar to Mr. Hambrough's. As far as I could judge, he was treated as a gentleman would be who stayed in the house. He looked like a gentleman, and was well dressed. It was my duty to attend to the bedrooms, and on the morning of Mr. Hambrough's death I attended to the bedrooms of Mr. Monson, Mr. Hambrough, and Mr. Scott; they had all been occupied. The same morning I saw some wet clothes hanging in the kitchen and drawing-room.

Cross-examined by Mr. COMRIE THOMSON—Monson and Hambrough seemed to be on friendly terms; they were always shooting together. Mr. Hambrough was fond of shooting. On the morning of the accident I saw Mr. Monson; he seemed to be much distressed.

ARCHIBALD WHYTE recalled—Since I was examined yesterday I have had an opportunity of seeing Mr. Macnaughton with his

61

Alfred John Monson.

hat on. I recognise him as the person whom I saw at Ardlamont, and to whom I pointed out the place where the body was. I only saw him with his hat on on that occasion.

HUGH CARMICHAEL recalled—Since I was examined yesterday I have had an opportunity of looking at Mr. Macnaughton with his hat on. I think that I recognise him as the person to whom I pointed out at Ardlamont the place where the body was.

19. JAMES MACNAUGHTON, examined by the SOLICITOR-GENERAL —I am a gunmaker in Edinburgh. I have been in this business for twenty-nine years, and have had experience of firearms of different kinds. On 23rd September I was shown a skull by Dr. Littlejohn and Dr. Macdonald Brown. [The Lord Justice-Clerk then directed that the witness should be taken into an adjoining room to see the skull.] Witness on returning said—I have seen the label No. 18 attached to a skull. That is the skull shown to me by Dr Littlejohn and Dr. Macdonald Brown. My attention was directed to a part of the skull which appeared to have been injured. The effects of the injury to the skull were pointed out to me by the doctor. [Shown No. 239.] These are five photographs of the skull. One of them shows that the middle part of the right ear is away. The skull appeared to be injured chiefly immediately behind the ear. There were the appearances of pellets round the outside break in the skull, channelling it out in a circle just as if it had been cut by pellets entering.

I was at Ardlamont on 26th September, and was taken to the place where Hambrough's body was found. Wright, the Ardlamont butler, Mr. Steven, two constables, the Fiscal, his deputy, and several of the estate officials were there. On a later occasion I visited the place along with Whyte and Carmichael; they pointed out to me the place where the body was found. It was the same place as was previously shown to me. I examined the place carefully. I was told that the head of the body was lying towards the rowan tree and the feet down the course of the wall, as it were. My attention was specially directed to the rowan tree, which was situated in a line very nearly north of where the top of the head had lain, and about 6 feet 1 inch distant. I saw seven or eight marks about the branches and twigs of the tree which suggested to my mind injury from pellets. There were many more marks through the leaves, which might, however, have been caused by insects, and these I leave out of account. I do not put too much stress on perforated leaves. Taking everything I saw about the rowan tree into account, I am quite decided that the main injuries were caused by pellets. The injuries which were caused by pellets were scars and furrows on the branches and broken twigs; they presented the appearance of which I am familiar as the effect of shooting through such a tree. In order to ascertain the diameter

62

Evidence for Prosecution.

of the passage of the shot through the tree I made very careful measurements from one or two pellet marks which could be got opposing one another, whether they were quite lateral or not, or whether they were vertical or not. I took them if they were opposing one another on the opposite side on the injured part of the tree.

The SOLICITOR-GENERAL—What measurements did you find with regard to that? [Witness looked among his notes, but was unable to find his figures; witness offered to give the figures from memory, but the Solicitor-General pointed out to him that he would have to find the figures, and requested him to get them as soon as he could. Meantime, another witness was called.]

20. SAMUEL JAMES PORTER, examined by the SOLICITOR-GENERAL—I am a photographer in Ventnor, and in September last I was requested to take certain photographs of a skull by the Procurator-Fiscal. [Shown No. 239.] I took five photographs, which accurately represent the skull.

21. HENRY ARTHUR HUDSON, district registrar of the Probate Registry of York, examined by Mr. STRACHAN—I have the original will of William Buckley of Stairfoot in my hand. The will is dated 11th September, 1853, and there is a codicil dated 4th April, 1854. I have also a sealed copy [No. 217] certified by me as registrar.

22. JAMES T. MURRAY, examined by Mr. STRACHAN—I am an artist in Edinburgh. The four pencil drawings [No. 241] now shown me were made by me under the supervision and direction of Dr. Macdonald Brown, and are correct.

Cross-examined—I understood that it was Mr. Hambrough's skull I was drawing, but I had no personal knowledge.

23. HUGH JEFFREY, examined by the SOLICITOR-GENERAL—I am curator of the Ventnor Cemetery, and was in charge of the cemetery when the body of Mr. Hambrough was buried on 17th August. I was not at the funeral, but was at the cemetery the day before it took place, and saw Mr. Monson there; he explained to me that Mr. Hambrough had been out shooting with a fellow-officer, and that while getting over a wall 4 feet high he either struck the gun, or fell with his head on it, that it went off and blew out his brains, killing him in an instant. He said that Mr. Hambrough had been staying with him at the time. The body was exhumed on 4th September, and I was present when it was taken out of the coffin in the mortuary.

Cross-examined by Mr. COMRIE THOMSON—My conversation with Monson took place in the cemetery at Ventnor on 16th August; no one else was present. It was the only conversation which I had with Monson. I have not read much in the papers about this case.

Alfred John Monson.

Hugh Jeffrey

Have you always avoided reading paragraphs headed " The Ardlamont Mystery "?—I do not read a daily paper; I get *Lloyd's Weekly*. The coffin was brought on the 15th, but I did not see the name on the name-plate until the 16th. I have known Mr. Hambrough's father for years; he has the rank of Major. I had no idea that his son was going into the army, and it was not till I saw the name-plate on the coffin that I knew he was in the army. I believe Monson said to me that some of Hambrough's fellow-officers had been coming for the Twelfth. He said nothing about the date of their arrival; he only said they were coming for a day's shooting. I did not know who the man was who had been with Mr. Hambrough at the time of the accident. When Monson said that they were going out for a day's shooting I assumed that he meant himself and Mr. Hambrough. I have told you all the conversation we had about the occurrence.

By the LORD JUSTICE-CLERK (at Mr. COMRIE THOMSON'S request) —Was that the account given in *Lloyd's Weekly?*—I did not see it. I have not seen anything about it there at all.

24. JOHN WORTHAM, Clerk of the Record Department, Senior Registrar's Office, High Court of Justice in Bankruptcy, London, produced a file of adjudication in the bankruptcy of Alfred John Monson, also copies of the receiving order and appointment of trustee in bankruptcy on the estate, and stated that the bankrupt was still undischarged.

25. HENRY JOHN LAYTON, clerk, Probate Registry, Somerset House, London, produced the last will and testament of the personal estate of William Day of Eversey, Garth.

Cross-examined by Mr. COMRIE THOMSON—These documents only show the gross value of the personal estate, £2544; there is nothing to show the net value nor the value of the real property.

26. J. CAMPBELL SHAIRP, Sheriff-Substitute of Argyllshire, Inveraray, examined by Mr. STRACHAN—I remember 30th August, the day on which Monson was arrested. On that day a search was made, under my direction, at Ardlamont House for papers, and in the course of my search I found the papers numbered 20 and 61, both, I think, in the smoking-room. [Shown Nos. 220, 221, 222, 223, and 226.] These are five pawn tickets, and were all found at Ardlamont. I think they were found in the bureau in the smoking-room. [Shown No. 230.] That is a diary found in a bag said to belong to Monson. The bag was found in the Royal Hotel, Tighnabruaich, on 30th August, and contained, besides the diary, some visiting cards and a letter addressed to Monson.

[Mr. COMRIE THOMSON—Before my friend goes further, I have no objection to the diary being put in, but I have an objection to its being received as evidence.

Evidence for Prosecution.

J. C. Shairp

The LORD JUSTICE-CLERK—Everything regarding the documents remains open. It is only being proved that these documents have been discovered in particular places.]

Examination continued—When the search was being made that day, did you see Mrs. Monson?—I did.

Did you ask her about any documents?——

[Mr. COMRIE THOMSON objected to this question.

The LORD JUSTICE-CLERK—I have doubts about that being a competent question.]

Examination continued—I saw a small bundle of documents in a sliding drawer in the wardrobe in Mrs. Monson's room. I glanced at them, but did not take possession of them. There were two letters, but I cannot say what their contents were. I cannot explain why I did not take possession of the letters without saying what Mrs. Monson said to me.

By the LORD JUSTICE-CLERK—In consequence of what she said you did not think it necessary to take possession of them?—I did not.

Mr. STRACHAN—Did you ascertain what the letters were?

[Mr. COMRIE THOMSON—Are the letters here?

Mr. STRACHAN—No.

Mr. COMRIE THOMSON—Then I object to that question.]

Cross-examined by Mr. COMRIE THOMSON—I took, as magistrate, two declarations from the prisoner. One is dated 31st August, the day on which the accused was apprehended, and in it the charge is confined to one of murder. The second was taken on 30th October, and has reference to a charge of attempted murder. On both occasions when the declarations were taken the prisoner's law agent was in attendance, and the prisoner acted under his advice.

In the case of the second declaration, was it dictated by the accused word for word until the last question, which was put by yourself?—From memory I cannot say yes or no to that; but much the larger part of the declaration was dictated word for word, and the declaration itself shows where the dictation stops.

JAMES MACNAUGHTON, recalled and examined by the SOLICITOR-GENERAL—I have got my notes now. On a rowan tree I saw certain marks which, in my opinion, had been caused by pellets. I took measurements to ascertain the breadth of the spread of the charge as it was going through the rowan tree. I took the first measurement from a groove in a branch on the one side to a broken twig on the other; both of these marks I was satisfied were caused by pellets. The space between these two points I found to be 20 inches. I took another measurement directly across the tree, in a different line from the one already taken; both measurements were slightly diagonal. In the second measurement I measured between a grooved branch on the one side to a grooved branch directly opposite, and found the distance to be 17 inches. These measurements, in my

F

Alfred John Monson.

James Macnaughton

opinion, accurately gave the diameter of the passage of the shot. The spaces I measured were fully 6 feet above the ground, about the middle of the spaces.

Besides the rowan tree there were two trees noticeable as being struck by shot—a lime tree, which grew nearest to the rowan, and further on a beech tree. The stem of the lime tree was nearer to the rowan than the beech tree. The branches of the lime tree were pretty well spread over the ditch and mingling with the branches of the beech tree, which projected very much from the stem.

Would the impact of the pellets with the rowan tree—supposing the shot passed through the branches of the tree—have an effect on the dispersion of the pellets?—I think very much, indeed.

By the LORD JUSTICE-CLERK—Do you mean that the shot would be diverted in some direction or other?—It would simply spread.

Examination continued—Would the first thing it struck give fairly well the dispersion of the shot?—At the rowan tree it spread a little wider than I should have expected to find it. I saw marks of pellets on the lime and beech trees. Any shot reaching the lime or the beech from the body would go through the rowan tree. I now turn my attention to the lime tree, and I find that my measurements give 15 inches as the distance between two pellets on a branch of the tree; the distance between extreme pellet marks taken laterally was nearly 20 inches, and the distance between the highest and the lowest pellet marks on the lime tree was 26 inches.

By the LORD JUSTICE-CLERK—The first measurement is not a measurement between extreme points. With regard to the beech tree, we took the beech branches and the lime branches to make our measurement; they were so situated that a shot going through would strike both the beech and the lime. In order to ascertain the width of the spread between the lime and the beech I took both into account.

Examination continued—I took the extreme pellet mark on the lime tree and the extreme pellet mark on the beech tree, and found that the distance between them was 41 inches very nearly horizontally.

Before going to Ardlamont I made some experiments with a 12-bore gun with the view of judging as to the distance traversed by a charge as estimated by the spread of the shot. In comparing these experiments with the spread of the shot in the rowan tree, I had to allow a little for the difference of guns. The new gun with which I shot before going to Ardlamont was a good gun, the muzzle in good order, and a very close pattern. On shooting with the actual gun from Ardlamont I came nearer to what the size of the shot was that pierced the rowan tree. Making my calculation at Ardlamont, I formed my opinion as to the distance from the rowan tree at which the gun had been fired from what shooting I had seen before and from the natural spread of the shot. The spread of shot in the beech and lime branches gives no indication at all, because of

66

Evidence for Prosecution.

James Macnaughton

the deflection in going through the rowan tree; when a shot strikes an object it is deflected in a way which one can hardly calculate. In making my calculation I went entirely by the rowan tree, and I concluded that the shot could not have been fired under 20 feet from the rowan tree. The deflection caused by contact with the rowan tree disturbed the spread of the injuries to the beech and the lime, but it aided me in ascertaining the direction of the shot, and I thought that was of great use, because in looking through the injured portion of the rowan tree to the centre of the spread of the shot in the lime and beech trees, and walking backwards, I could not help thinking of the line of fire. If it was one shot which injured these three trees then I was in the line. I went backward in a line as determined by the injuries to the three trees. Further, I placed a tape-line exactly in a line through the centre of the rowan tree to the centre of the shots in the beech and the lime branches, and carried it backwards to the distance from which I thought the shot had been fired, judging from the spread on the rowan tree. When I got to that distance I found myself at a point in the brushwood rather behind the whin bush, which was about breast-high. I had the sheriff officer from Inveraray with me at the time; he was about the same height as Mr. Hambrough. I asked him to stand with his feet where it was said that Hambrough's feet lay, and I stood at the point in the brushwood of which I have spoken, and put a gun which I had with me to my shoulder, pointing it to the centre of the injury to the rowan tree. I could not see it, because the officer's head interrupted my aim at that point; it was in the direction of the line of fire from the point where I was standing to the centre of the injuries in the rowan, the lime, and the beech. The ground sloped gently down from where the officer was standing to my feet; I might be about a foot or so lower than the officer. I was standing 22 feet from the rowan tree. In pointing the gun to the centre of the injury it would be slightly inclined upwards. I found that the injury to the lime and beech trees behind the rowan tree was a good piece higher than the injury to the rowan, and the difference in vertical height would be accounted for by the difference in the level of the ground where I was standing as compared with where the officer was standing. The pellet marks on the rowan tree were mostly grooved and furrowed, and this fact gave me an indication of the direction of the shot, more especially when two shot marks were in one branch. They were then parallel, and I found the grooves and furrows to be mostly horizontal, with a slight upward inclination. After this examination I came to the conclusion that the point from which the shot, which had injured the rowan, lime, and beech trees, had been fired was the opening in the brushwood I speak of behind the whin bush. At the opening there is a good deal of rank grass, broken whin, and other scrubby bushes, and if one wanted to get away out from the side of the ditch to the southward this would have been the opening one would have made for; it was the most natural way

Alfred John Monson.

out, except along the top of the wall. If I were coming from the south end of the wood I would for choice go along the top of the dyke, but if I were not using the top of the dyke the opening would be the next best way by which to approach the place where the body lay.

I was told that there was a suggestion that the body had been found in the ditch on the lower side of the retaining wall. I looked at the ditch and the level of the ground there. Assuming that the pellet marks in the rowan, lime, and beech trees were the marks of the shot which killed Mr. Hambrough, it is my opinion that by no possibility could the shot have been fired from the ditch, nor from the top of the wall immediately above the ditch. If the shot had come from the ditch and hit the trees I should have expected that it would have been very nearly vertical.

[Shown labels Nos. 7 and 8.] These are the Ardlamont guns; one a 20-bore and the other a 12-bore gun. I have experimented with both of them. I have examined the muzzle of the 20-bore gun, which I found a little bit worn. This would incline to make the shooting irregular and to scatter the shot. In experimenting with both I did not find any appreciable difference between the spread of the shot from either on the average shooting. That would be in consequence of the worn state of the 20-bore gun, I expect. I got specimens of cartridges, said to have been found at Ardlamont, and have examined them. I got the guns from the sheriff-officer at Inveraray, and the cartridges from Dr. Littlejohn. [Shown Nos. 2 and 3.] I examined the powder in these cartridges, and found that they contained three kinds—black powder, Schultze, and amberite. The sizes of the shot were Nos. 5 and 6. I opened the cartridges, weighed the charges, took notice of the thickness of the wadding, and filled them again. I made trial cartridges exactly the same, and restored the old loads to the old cases, and they are all here in Court.

By the LORD JUSTICE-CLERK—The object of my experiment was to make trial cartridges exactly corresponding to the old ones. I took care that the cartridges I made were in all respects exactly the same as those I got; of that I am positive. I found one of the old cartridges with No. 5 shot in it.

Examination continued—I know that there was one cartridge with No. 5 shot that was for the 12-bore gun, but I do not know whether or not there were more of the proportion of the respective guns. I made shooting experiments with both guns.

By the LORD JUSTICE-CLERK—I ascertained the contents as regards powder, shot, and wads of each cartridge handed to me by Dr. Littlejohn, and having done that I replaced the powder, shot, and wads; but the cartridges now are not in the same state as they were before; it would be impossible to make them so. I restored them to Dr. Littlejohn, who gave me a receipt for them.

Examination continued—I made a set of experiments with the guns and with the different kinds of shot used in each gun—one set

68

Evidence for Prosecution.

James Macnaughton

with black powder, another with Schultze, and a third with amberite. The amberite I fired only out of a 12-bore gun, and the black out of both. That was after I had been at Ardlamont and determined what, in my opinion, was the line of fire. I took the line of fire from the point 22 feet from the rowan tree, and determined the distance by the experiments with my own gun. [Shown No. 240.] These are four sets of cardboard diagrams. [Witness at this point explained his series of experiments, illustrating by means of the cardboard diagrams produced the various results obtained, in the scattering of pellets and discoloration, by variations of distance, powder, and size of shot.] I made these experiments down at my private range by the Water of Leith in presence of Drs. Heron Watson, Joseph Bell, and Littlejohn. Measurements were taken from the muzzle of the gun. Speaking generally, I did not find any appreciable difference in the pattern on the cardboard according as I used No. 5 or No. 6 shot, and with regard to the two guns, I found a very slight difference in favour of the 20-bore as regards concentration. Between the various powders there is no difference at those near ranges with regard to concentration; there may be a little difference, however, in regard to the scorching. Scorching would soonest disappear with the nitro powders, that is, with the Schultze and the amberite. All these experiments were done with the Ardlamont guns. Up to nearly 3 feet smoke or singeing is present with all the powders.

[Mr. COMRIE THOMSON objected to the use of the word scorching.]

Up to 3 feet there is discoloration, which I attribute to scorching. In no case did my experiments disclose discoloration, attributable to scorching, at a greater distance than 3 feet. I was shown the skull [label No. 18] and the photographs attached to the label [No. 239]. I examined carefully the injury to the skull as well as the photographs, and I attribute the injury to the skull to its having been shot at. The photographs show a man shot at. Comparing my experimental diagrams with the injuries shown on the skull and the photographs, I conclude that the shot was fired at a distance of 9 feet from the head. I saw where the body of Mr. Hambrough had been lying; according to my measurements, it was 6 feet 1 inch from the root of the rowan tree, measuring from the head. Supposing that the man was found lying, and that he was shot at from behind, I should expect him to have been standing some 5 feet further from the rowan tree. It depends upon his height, and Hambrough was about 6 feet. I think that, as a shot has a pushing as well as a penetrating effect, it would, coming from behind, make him fall forward; if he were a man of 6 feet he might fall his own length. Adding his own length to the 6 feet 1 inch which I found his head to be from the rowan tree, that would place his feet 12 feet 1 inch from the rowan tree. Adding the 9 feet, the distance from which I suppose the shot to have been fired, to the 12 feet 1 inch, that would make a distance of 21 feet 1 inch. When I was on the ground at

Alfred John Monson.

James Macnaughton

Ardlamont I made up my mind as to a point 22 feet from the rowan tree. That was the place where I was standing, and my shooting experiments confirmed the view which I had formed at Ardlamont as to the point from which the shot had been fired.

If a man were carrying his gun in his hand, how far off do you think he would hold the muzzle?—Keeping control of the trigger at the same time he could only hold it at a very short distance off; a very long-armed man might keep the muzzle 5 or 6 inches from his head. Apart from having his finger on the trigger-guard, he could hold it the length of his arm; he could hold the gun by the muzzle. Judging from my experiments, the result of a shot fired within 3 feet would have been that a hole about $1\frac{1}{4}$ inches would have been driven through the skull, if not along the side of it. If fair on the skull, a hole of $1\frac{1}{4}$ inches would have been driven through the skull, and the shot going like a ball in at that distance would go through the head and shatter the skull at the other side. At this distance, I have been shown by my experiments, there are no stray pellets. Judging from my experiments and the injuries to the head which I saw, I am unable to see the possibility of the wound having been self-inflicted, accidental or otherwise.

The witness Whyte pointed out to me the place where he had found two pieces of bone. [Shown label No. 17.] The place where these two pieces of bone were found was about 8 inches from where the head had been, a little to the right. Whyte also pointed out to me the place where the cap had been found; it was just a foot further on, nearer the rowan tree, due north of where the body lay. He was unable to point out to me the tracks which he had seen on the ground after Mr. Hambrough's death, but he walked over the ground where the tracks had been. He pointed out where the track along the top of the wall had been, and another leading from where the body had lain, down to the opening in the cover I have spoken of, past that for a few yards, and then diverging to the right.

By the LORD JUSTICE-CLERK—He pointed these tracks out to me as things he had observed at the time; he merely indicated what he had formerly seen. The one track, namely, that which led from where the body had lain to the opening in the cover, came up alongside of the place at which it appeared to me that the shot had been fired.

[The Court adjourned.]

Third Day—Thursday, 14th December, 1893.

JAMES MACNAUGHTON, cross-examined by Mr. COMRIE THOMSON —My first visit to Ardlamont was on 26th September, my second on 27th November. I got my information as to the position of the body from the estate servants, Whyte and Carmichael. My evidence and the conclusions at which I arrived depend upon the accuracy of the statements made by these two men in regard to the position of the body and of the trees.

In fact all your evidence, except in regard to the cardboard experiments?—No; the most important part of my evidence was based on deductions from my examination of the skull and the photographs of the head. I first saw the skull on 23rd September.

I admit that a part of my evidence would be misleading if I have been misinformed as to the position of the body when the shot was fired, so far as this, that there would be no connection between the trees and the body. I did not see the scalp nor that portion of the ear that remained. I have no surgical or anatomical knowledge; my evidence is that of a gunmaker. My evidence is given on the theory that the feet of the body were 6 feet from the place where it was pointed out to me that the head was lying, and that when the fatal shot was fired Mr. Hambrough was standing erect. If he had been stumbling or inclining his head at the time, my evidence would be modified to a certain extent. I took the grooved marks upon the skull to be made by individual scattered pellets. [Shown label No. 18.] This is a facsimile of a skull. The dark part, representing the fissures going out, is the opening out of the fracture from the main wound, caused by the impact of the main body of the shot; the fissures caused by the pellets are on the rear edge of the wound. Others are caused by the large bone behind the ear being forced forward by the impact of the solid shot. I attribute the ragged appearance of the edge of what may be called the principal fracture to the presence of pellets; I understand that these pellets are produced. It is my opinion that the pellets found in the brain were the cause of the irregular appearance of the edges of the fracture. I understand that there were four pellets and fragments found in the head. I attribute the beginning of the fracture to the action of the four pellets. In a cartridge there are, roughly, from 250 to 300 pellets. I do not say that all this mass of shot struck this man's head behind, because the shot was a glancing shot. In my evidence I

71

Alfred John Monson.

have made allowance for the deflection of the shot caused by contact with the hard skull of a man. In my calculation I have taken deflection into account in this way, that had there been no deflection from the hard skull, and no help to deflection from the greasy nature of the scalp, the shot in the rowan tree would have been smaller in the scattering than it is. I think that a portion of the shot struck the head at an angle, and the rest of it flew off past the ear. I should roughly describe the angle as being from the left rear—I could not say how many degrees; it struck on the right side of the head from the left rear.

By the LORD JUSTICE-CLERK—The left rear of the head would be the left side, and that was the direction the gun was pointing, catching upon the head to the extent of nearly missing it on the right.

Cross-examination continued—Yesterday I put it as my theory that the distance from the muzzle of the gun to the head of the deceased was about 9 feet. The experiments with the cardboard at 9 feet were made with the gun fair on the flat surface. To that extent they differ from actual circumstances in the case; they want obliquity. I see that in my specimens there is considerable scattering outside the circumference of the wound. I saw nothing of this upon the skull, but at the time I saw it that would be impossible, and even if none had been seen upon the skull when the body was fresh that would not have influenced my opinion. My reason for saying this is, that if you look at the left-hand side of the diagram, upon which you see scattering, and turn it to the side, you will find that there is an almost entire absence of scattered pellets there.

By the LORD JUSTICE-CLERK—There are four wads in a cartridge, and they take a line for themselves away from the shot. But, as a rule, the heavy wad behind the shot travels in the line of the shot for some distance, and it will be found impinging on the ragged edge made by the shot in the diagram, showing that it followed the body of the shot very closely. At two or three yards I should expect the wad to strike. I heard a witness state to Mr. Baxter on the last occasion when I visited Ardlamont, that a bit of wad with blood upon it was found close to where the body was.

Cross-examination continued—And if it be the case that the wad went into the main wound, would that not suggest to you that the distance between the muzzle of the gun and the wound was not a serious one?—Not in the case of the thick wad.

You told us, I think, that the thick wad generally followed directly. If the wad was found with blood on it near the body, is it not likely that the shot was fired within a comparatively short distance, the blood having come from the wad entering the wound? —I think not, because the wad was found too near the body. My answer depends to some extent upon the spot where the wad was

72

Evidence for Prosecution.

James Macnaughton

found in relation to the body, and that depends upon Whyte's statement. I have to point out that the thick wad would follow the line of the shot a much further distance than counsel has in his mind.

I did not measure the height of the pellet marks in the rowan tree; I put up my hand and bent down the branches to my face; I did not treat them from a surveyor's point of view. I cannot tell the direction of each pellet. I examined one other tree besides the rowan, beech, and lime. It was a tree about 20 yards from the rowan tree; I am not sure what kind it was; it was a hardwood tree. I saw shot fired into it. I examined all the trees, foliage, branches, and trunks of trees that were the least in the direction of my assumed line of fire or about the rowan tree. I examined no other trees; I confined my investigation very much to the line of fire which I thought corresponded with the position of the rowan tree. In forming an opinion as to the scatter at the rowan tree I left out the marks upon the leaves, so far as measurement was concerned; that is, so far as concerned the lateral and vertical extension of the scatter. I did this in case the marks upon the leaves might have been caused by insects; it is the case that some insects in their operations upon leaves leave marks very like pellet marks. I considered what was the probable age of the pellet marks which I saw upon the rowan tree, but, not having any data to go by, I was unable to come to any definite conclusion, except that they were not fresh. I assumed very much for the purpose of my calculations that they had been made upon 10th August.

The words " scorching " and " discoloration " are not identical in meaning—the one is the cause and the other the effect; " scorching " is the cause of the " discoloration," more particularly in the case of nitro powder. In every case in which amberite cartridges were used there was scorching up to 3 feet. Beyond 3 feet we might have got a little scorching for an inch or two, but there were no diagrams made at inches. At 3 feet there would be no stray pellets, and so if I found a wound in which there were no stray pellets I would assume that the distance had been 3 feet or less.

Would the fact of a charge entering the skull at an aperture of $1\frac{1}{4}$ inches suit your account of the scatter of the shot in your experiment at 9 feet?—I don't think that the shot struck the skull in a mass at all.

And if it struck in a mass it would not suit your 9-feet experiment?—If it struck it square it would not; neither would it suit if it struck at an angle. Not having the power to cut down the branches of the tree I could not ascertain whether there were any pellets embedded in the branches. If I had found pellet marks on the other side of the rowan tree or adjacent trees, that would not have made the line of fire different, because when I examined

Alfred John Monson.

James Macnaughton

the rowan tree I did not look so much to the surface injury to the tree for giving the direction as to the grooved marks in branches. Looking along these grooves led me to look straight to the pellet marks in the lime tree and the beech tree. You could not get a spot in the rowan tree to represent the centre of dispersion of the shot, but you might imagine one, and to do so you would have to get broken branches or twigs on either side as equally as possible.

You stop at a certain distance on the one side, and at a certain distance on the other, and the mean is the centre of dispersion?—So far on each side as the groove would take you.

But suppose that the grooves are found upon the other side of the tree or upon an adjacent tree, that would, of course, alter the position of your centre of dispersion?—Not as regards the rowan tree if grooves were found upon an adjacent tree.

But suppose there was some shot?—I cannot suppose that there was any shot beyond my measurement. I looked at the rowan tree and saw nothing alongside. Pellets were bound to go into the air if they did not catch the branches, but they could not go on either side, because the tree was too broad.

But suppose a considerable deflection from the head, would that not modify your view that the line of fire was straight to the rowan tree from the place where the head was?—It did modify my view, and I gave effect to it. At first, in making my experiments, I made use of both barrels of both guns to see if there was any appreciable difference in the shooting of the two; then for the sake of uniformity, and to get good diagrams, I did the rest of the shooting with the right barrel of each. I noticed that the pull of all the triggers was on the heavy side, but I only tested the pull with my fingers. I was quite prepared to test them accurately if I had found them easy in fingering, but they were not. There was not a noticeable difference in the two triggers of the 20-bore gun. I should be quite prepared to hear that the pull of the right barrel was $5\frac{1}{2}$ lbs. and the pull of the left barrel $5\frac{3}{4}$ lbs. As regards the 12-bore gun, I should be quite prepared to find that the pull of the right barrel was $5\frac{1}{2}$ lbs. and of the left barrel $4\frac{3}{4}$ lbs. I noticed that there was a rebounding lock on the 20-bore gun and not on the other. Both guns have cylinder barrels.

Re-examined by the SOLICITOR-GENERAL—The measurement from the spot pointed out to me as where the head had lain to the rowan tree was taken, not along the ground, but by a tape held horizontally from the stem to the barrel. From what I saw in my examination of the wound in the skull, my opinion is that the head was nearly missed. I was led to this opinion by the direction from which the shot had come—from the left rear, as I put it before—and from the shape of the wound, as seen in the photographs, and also, I may add, from the glancing having occurred. I saw from the photographs that part of the ear had been cut off. That had some effect in forming my opinion as to the line of the shot. Sup-

Scene of Mr. Cecil Hambrough's Death.

Evidence for Prosecution.

posing that the whole shot had struck the head at 9 feet, and taking it at the same angle as that at which it is, the shot would have been more to the left and better into the head, making a larger wound. If four pellets were found in the wound, that would indicate that there had been scattered pellets, and that yet there had been strength enough for the pellets to go through the skull. In the case of a glancing shot, only part of the body of the shot would strike the head, while the rest of the shot would fly in its own direction. The portion of the charge which struck the head would be deflected. All my experiments with the cardboard were made at right angles to the cardboard. On three occasions I fired oblique shots into a cadaver in presence of the three doctors whom I mentioned yesterday. Some of the shots had the obliquity corresponding to the assumed obliquity in this case. I did not see the results; that was for the doctors to see. If it was an oblique shot, the wad would follow the shot; it ought to go that way. If only a part of the charge struck the head, the wad, being a flat disc, might curl on to the wound, even though it hit it with its edge. There were no other trees near to where the body was lying with pellet marks similar to those on the rowan tree. There was a tree 20 yards from the rowan with grooves from the size of my little finger downwards in the branches.

Re-cross-examined by Mr. Comrie Thomson—The experiments with the dead body were made in the mortuary in Edinburgh. I cannot give you the dates, as I took no note of them. I do not think that any one representing the accused was present. I fired the shots in the presence of three doctors. I fired at three bodies. I have no note in my note-book of the distance from which the shots were fired; the doctors were responsible for the distance and the angles at which the shots were fired. I have heard that photographs were taken, but I have not seen them, nor did I look at the bodies to see the results of the shots. The hard-wood tree I referred to was about 20 yards east by south from the rowan tree. It was as much south as to be straight across the ditch from the opening in the furze; that would be a good many yards, certainly more than 6 feet south of the rowan tree.

By the Lord Justice-Clerk—I saw a number of twigs hanging down broken by shots on the rowan tree. The leaves on the broken twigs were quite fresh, this year's growth.

27. Dr. Henry Duncan Littlejohn, examined by the Solicitor-General—I am surgeon of police and lecturer on medical jurisprudence at the Surgeons' Hall, Edinburgh. At the request of the Crown Agent I went to Ventnor, in the Isle of Wight, in the beginning of September, for the purpose of making an examination of the late Mr. Hambrough. The body was disinterred. The Depute Procurator-Fiscal of Argyllshire was there, and also my colleague, Dr. Macmillan, Tighnabruaich, who had seen the body after death,

Alfred John Monson.

Dr, Henry D. Littlejohn

and who knew the deceased in life. When the body was disinterred a *post-mortem* examination was made. Dr. Sanders was present on behalf of the prisoner. Our examination resulted in our making the following report:—

"13th September, 1893.

" We hereby certify, upon soul and conscience, that on Monday, 4th September, 1893, at Ventnor, we assisted at the exhumation of a body by directions of the Procurator-Fiscal of Argyllshire, and subsequently made a *post-mortem* examination. The body was enclosed in a coffin, the plate on which bore—' Windsor Dudley Cecil Hambrough, Lieutenant 3rd Battalion West Yorkshire Regiment. Died from gun accident at Ardlamont, Argyllshire, 10th August, 1893, aged twenty years.'

" On this and the inner metallic shell being opened, the body of a tall, well-proportioned young man was disclosed fully dressed for the grave. The features were somewhat swollen, but admitted of ready identification by the Depute Procurator-Fiscal of Argyllshire, Mr. M'Naughton, and by one of our number, Dr. Macmillan, Tighnabruaich, as that of Windsor Dudley Cecil Hambrough. Decomposition was making slow progress, and the body generally was well preserved. The cuticle, or outer skin, everywhere separated with facility. On removing the wrappings, some pieces of cloth were found loosely applied to the lower part of the right side of the head, and, on these being lifted off, a wound was exposed involving the skin, subjacent tissues, and the bone. Before this wound was further examined two photographs were taken, to which we refer. They are marked on the back respectively A and B, and are initialed by us. This wound was of a triangular shape, the base of the triangle being towards the face, while the apex was situated about an inch below and slightly in advance of the occipital protuberance. Its extreme length was 3½ inches. At its base it had a width of 2½ inches. At its middle it measured 2 inches, whence it tapered off posteriorly. The right ear was mutilated—a portion of its external surface being awanting, leaving a lacerated surface measuring from above downwards 1½ inches, and leaving the upper part of the ear and its lobe below intact. The superior and inferior extremities of this wound had elongated pieces of skin attached. These are specially visible in photograph B, where a piece of white paper placed under the ear shows the extent and character of the mutilation. The wound was now carefully examined—its edges were somewhat thickened, and posteriorly exhibited a distinctly bevelled and pretty regular surface. Anteriorly towards the ear the edges were irregular, and from its upper part a portion of skin 1 inch long and ¼ inch broad hung down. On no part of the edges or surface was there any appearance of blackening, as if from gunpowder or scorching; but four minute specks, apparently metallic, were found adhering to the edges. These were removed and preserved. The entire scalp was well covered with hair, but this,

76

Evidence for Prosecution.

Dr. Henry D. Littlejohn

owing to advancing decomposition, was easily detached, and it was observed that, on removing the cloths from the wound, and also during the minute examination of the wound, portions of the hair in its vicinity came away in the fingers. The whole of the hair was now removed from the scalp on the right side, which was carefully inspected, with the result that no wound or aperture, such as might be produced by shot of any kind, was seen. Immediately in front of the right ear, and about its middle, the skin exhibited a laceration fully a quarter of an inch long, from above downwards, which communicated with the larger wound behind the ear. The scalp was now dissected from off the right side of the head, when the skull presented a localised shattered appearance, stretching from below the occipital protuberance directly forwards in direction of the ear. Photograph C was now taken. Over a space of an irregular shape, and measuring 2 inches from before backwards, and fully 1 inch at its greatest breadth, the bone was awanting. Here the brain was exposed, and two pieces of loose bone were observed on its surface, and removed; the larger of these presented its internal surface uppermost. Immediately above this aperture a portion of the right temporal bone, measuring 2 inches square, was found detached and kept in position by the pericranium (or investing membrane of the skull). This piece of bone could be raised like a lid from behind forwards. Photograph D represents it in this raised position. Another portion of bone which admitted of being easily detached lay in position in front of the aperture, and consisted of the squama and a portion of the zygoma of the right temporal bone. It measured roughly 2 inches long and 1 inch broad. On passing the finger into the aperture several pieces of bone could be felt, and the base of the temporal bone (petrous portion) was found to be much shattered. Anteriorly a considerable portion of the brain was wanting; behind, though much softened, it could be felt *in situ*. It was now considered advisable to remove a portion of skull from the left side to enable us to ascertain the condition of the skull, membranes, and brain opposite to the injury, and also to secure any foreign bodies that might be lodged there. On this being done, the cranium, membrane, and brain were found uninjured. The brain was much softened, and the convolutions were only faintly seen. The cerebral substance of the left side was removed *en masse* and submitted to a minute examination, when four metallic masses of irregular shape and resembling shot were removed and preserved. The falx cerebri (or membrane which hangs down from the vertex between the hemispheres of the brain) was intact, and the tentorium cerebelli (which lies between the cerebrum and lesser brain or cerebellum) was similarly uninjured. The structure of this lesser brain was much softened. The surface of the entire cranium was now carefully examined by removing the investing membrane, when various lines of fracture (fissures) were observed stretching upwards to the vertex, forwards into the parietal bone, in front and above, and lastly, forwards in a zig-zag manner into the

77

Alfred John Monson.

Dr. Henry D. Littlejohn

temporal fossa, crossing that depression, and reaching the frontal bone
1 inch above the orbit. The rest of the body was uninjured. All
the important internal organs presented to the eye a healthy appearance. All the cavities of the heart were empty, and their internal
lining showed no staining. The great vessels were empty, and generally throughout the body there was an absence of blood. The stomach
was empty—when opened, no particular odour was observed.

" From the foregoing examination we are of opinion that the
deceased died from shock, the result of a gunshot injury of the skull
and brain, and of subsequent loss of blood.

" HENRY D. LITTLEJOHN, M.D.

" JOHN MACMILLAN, M.B., C.M."

Examination continued—The complete absence of blood
showed that extensive hæmorrhage had occurred. [Shown No. 239.]
Three photographs were taken by a photographer under my direction
at Ventnor. Nothing was done to the wound until the first photograph A was taken. Observing the peculiar character of the mutilation of the ear, I thought it important that this should be brought
out. I therefore introduced a piece of white paper under the ear
showing the mutilation. The second photograph B was then taken
with the piece of paper introduced behind the ear. It also was
taken before the *post-mortem* examination. The photograph shows
the exact part of the ear that was absent with absolute accuracy.
About an inch and a half out of the centre of the external flap of the
ear was entirely awanting. This injury lay exactly in the line of the
level of the wound. When I say in my report that the edges of
the wound posteriorly exhibited a distinctly bevelled and pretty
regular surface, I mean that it had the appearance of having been
scooped out. I may mention that before touching the wound we
subjected it to careful examination with a lens in order, if possible,
to determine any blackening, any scorching, or any foreign particle.
Four minute particles were seen, which at first looked like four
small pieces of coal. These were preserved and are produced.
After we had carefully examined the wound, we took the whole right
side of the scalp and brought it down, exposing the injury to the bone.
This was photographed before any one of us touched the wound at all.
Photograph C shows the result. In the aperture which I have
described we saw two loose pieces of bone of considerable size lying,
one of them the size of a florin, the other the size of a shilling. These
were preserved. We found a large portion of the skull, about 2
inches square, fractured but still attached by its interior surface to
the skull, and finding that it could be elevated we elevated it and put
a small piece of stone behind it to keep it in an elevated position,
and then called upon the photographer to take another photograph,
which is photograph D. I have another skull here so cut as to show
the portions of the skull which were removed. [Shown label No. 18.]
We thought it desirable to remove the uninjured portion of the skull

78

Evidence for Prosecution.

Dr. Henry D. Littlejohn

shown to allow us to examine carefully the injury to the skull and the brain itself on the opposite side without disturbing it in any way, by finger or otherwise. On removing that portion of the skull we found that the left side of the head was uninjured. We examined the membrane, which hangs like a curtain between the two hemispheres to prevent one pressing against the other when the head is moved, and we all agreed that it presented not the slightest trace of injury. We then took out the left side of the brain by itself, and we subjected it to a most careful examination for any foreign particles, but found none. We now proceeded to examine the right side of the brain, and there we found four pellets, which are productions in this case. What I have in my hand is a skull without the superficial covering, the pericranium. At the *post-mortem* examination we removed the pericranium from the skull, and found an aperture corresponding to the blackened portion of this skull which I hold. From that there spread out a number of fissures, and these, being traced at the *post-mortem* examination, we found extended forward as shown by the black lines on this skull. In the other room I have seen and identified the skull which we examined.

[Mr. COMRIE THOMSON—I would consider it a favour if the Solicitor-General will allow this artificial skull to remain and allow me to put it into the hands of my medical men, because it is better that we should work upon one thing.

The SOLICITOR-GENERAL—Certainly.]

Examination continued—We did not make a detailed examination of the bones; the time at our disposal was not sufficient to enable us to do that. When I brought the skull to Edinburgh I handed it to Dr. Macdonald Brown for detailed anatomical examination. I also handed six detached pieces of bone to Dr. Macdonald Brown; they were put in a small bottle. I gave them to Dr. Macdonald Brown to enable him to see what relation they bore to the skull. [Shown No. 17.] This is the box which I received from the Depute Fiscal, and I recognise the two bones it contains. I opened the box on 11th October. After examining the two bones I handed them to Dr. Macdonald Brown. The hæmorrhage referred to in my report came from a large vein in the brain called the lateral sinus. It runs transversely, and is marked on the inside of this preparation. When we examined the skull in question we found this vein much injured, and it was the hæmorrhage from this vein which caused death. I have no doubt whatever that it was a gunshot injury which caused the injuries to the head.

In ascertaining how an injury has been caused, there are certain matters familiar to doctors as aids to the determination of the question. In the first place, the direction of the wound is most important. In this case the direction was from behind forward, and this I conclude from the triangular shape of the wound in front presenting this comparatively smooth, bevelled appearance, gradually passing

79

Alfred John Monson.

Dr. Henry D. Littlejohn

on and producing a larger amount of laceration; and, finally, we have this condition of the ear, which, in my opinion, settles the question of the direction of the wound. The characteristics of the wound which I found in the skull were such as a wound from behind forward would lead me to expect. It appeared to me from the small number of pellets which we found in the brain that it was only the outside of the charge which inflicted the injuries we have described in the report. The effects would have been quite different if the wound had been from the side; the skull would have been entirely broken up and the whole of the charge would have been found in the cavity of the skull itself. The membrane dividing the hemispheres of the brain could not possibly have been intact as we found it. If the shot had been from below upwards we would have found the skull in a shattered condition. The direction of the wound, as we found it, is quite inconsistent with its being inflicted from below upwards or from the front backwards.

The distance from which the shot is fired is also an aid to a doctor in determining how a wound has been inflicted. I was present when a number of experiments were made by Mr. Macnaughton for the purpose of assisting the doctors in the determination of the distance from the head at which the shot had been fired. I recognise two series of experiments made by Mr. Macnaughton in my presence. I took a detailed note of the conditions under which the experiments were made. We found that at any distance under 3 feet the injuries were dissimilar from what we found in the case of the deceased. I therefore would be inclined to place the possible distance between 3 feet and 15 feet. In all the experiments we made the wounds at 9 feet present the closest similarity to the injuries we found on the deceased's head. Any distance under 3 feet would be inconsistent with what was found on the skull; the injuries were something frightful under 3 feet, the head was blown to pieces. We made four experiments on the cadaver, firing to the best of our ability in the direction towards the head which the wounds on Mr. Hambrough's head would lead us to expect as to the shot. From these experiments we found that whenever we got beyond 4 feet the injuries assumed a remarkable similarity to the injuries found on the head of the deceased; at less than 4 feet we found such a shattering of the head as rendered it quite unlike the comparatively limited shattering in the case of Mr. Hambrough.

The position in which the dead body is found is all-important in determining how death occurred. I had no assistance as to that in the present case, except that my colleague, Dr. Macmillan, when I visited and examined the ground, described to me the position of the body.

The position of the weapon with regard to the dead body is also very important in determining how the death occurred. If a gun had been found beside the deceased, and had gone off when beside him, the wound would not, I have no hesitation in saying,

80

Evidence for Prosecution.

Dr. Henry D. Littlejohn

have been of the kind I found on Mr. Hambrough; I would have expected far more extensive shattering than in the case of the deceased, and possibly blackening or even singeing of the hair.

On 12th September, a week or so after the *post-mortem* examination, I went to the place where I was told that the death had occurred. Two of the witnesses I see here, Whyte and Carmichael, arranged a person in the position which they said was the position of the body when they were called to see it. I examined very carefully the place at which the head was, and I saw a circular staining of the grass and turf generally at that place. We removed portions of the stained grass, which I submitted to chemical examination, with the result that there can be no doubt that that staining was due to blood. We thought there had been a considerable quantity of blood; the stain was perfectly distinct. The body was described and shown as lying with the right side of the head uppermost and the limbs disposed diagonally in a direction from the rowan tree towards the thicket. I looked at the rowan tree which was near the head, and observed on it certain wounds, and also on two trees beyond. I am not an expert in shot marks on trees, but so far as I could make out these wounds appeared to have been produced by pellets. These injuries I recognised on the trees subsequently brought to Edinburgh in the Crown Office. I saw several grooves in the wood, which showed a transverse grooving, and, so far as I could make out, the line of these grooves was exactly in a line with the line of the body. I was informed that two pieces of bone had been found a little way from the head, and these were sent me for examination; I found that there were three distinct metallic fragments driven, so to speak, into the tissue of the bone. I was also informed that a portion of a cartridge was found nearer the rowan tree than the body. Having seen the place where the head was lying, the rowan tree, the pieces of bone, and the wad, I formed the opinion that the shot had been fired from behind, and slightly to the right side.

By the LORD JUSTICE-CLERK—Do you mean a little to the right of the line drawn?—I should have said a little to the left of the line drawn from the rowan tree, in the direction of the bushes. That line, in my opinion, would correspond with a line through the injury to the head passing away by the back of the head.

By the SOLICITOR-GENERAL—Could the injuries have been caused accidentally by the deceased?—I think it is impossible.

Cross-examined by Mr. COMRIE THOMSON—I remember in my individual professional experience of two cases of homicidal shooting with a shot gun which were brought to trial. I have also seen many cases of accidental shooting; they happen every year in the shooting season. In this country homicide by a shot gun is a comparatively rare thing. As regards my report, I say that the features of the face were very much swollen; knowing nothing of this gentleman in life, I can only say what struck me as a person accustomed to look at dead bodies in every stage of decomposition. I do not doubt that

Alfred John Monson.

Dr. Henry D. Littlejohn

the features were easily recognisable. I cannot say that his flesh was much swollen by decomposition, or else I believe that the identification could not have been so readily made. There were one or two wrappings on the wound, but nothing tight—nothing to prevent swelling. He was a young man, with a thick neck, well-proportioned and muscular, and I have not the slightest doubt that a very slight amount of swelling would give rise to the opinion that it was due to decomposition. There was nothing unusual about the skull; it was such a skull as I would expect such a well-developed young man might possess. It was not unusually thick; it was a well-developed skull. I measured the apex of the wound. I have not given the measurements, but I have done better; I have given a photograph, which can be measured. I did not take measurements at the time on the body. I did not think it necessary, having the photograph. I measured the middle and base of the wound, but not the apex. My report says that the apex was situated about an inch below and slightly to the advance of the occipital protuberance. I only measured the distance roughly; I do not think this particular measurement is all-important in determining the leading question in this case. I define the words of the report, " slightly in advance," as about a quarter of an inch.

Can you tell me the measurement of the skull—how far the apex of the wound was in advance of the occipital protuberance?—I make it out to be about three-quarters of an inch.

Was it not about an inch?—It might be. The occipital protuberance is the protuberance on the back of the head upon which when one falls the injury is received. It is a somewhat marked prominence about the centre of the back of the head. I do not know about Dr. Macmillan's report on the day of the accident; I understand that Dr. Macmillan made a very hasty examination. I deny that the flesh wound was 1½ inches wide. I do not think that the difference between the 1½ inches given in Dr. Macmillan's report as the width of the wound and the 2½ inches given as the width in my report might be accounted for by the process of decomposition. I do not know what method of measurement Dr. Macmillan adopted. The right ear was mutilated, and a piece of the external surface was wanting. The shot had apparently gone through the ear, carrying a portion of it away. You will see from the photograph exactly what I mean by the external surface. The shot seems to have gone through a portion of the flap of the ear, between the lobe and the upper part, carrying it away. The shot was scattering at the time, and I have no doubt the chief body of the shot may have passed through that portion of the ear. My idea is that the impact of the mass of the shot caused the wound, and that it then deflected, passing through the ear and on into space. There were only four pellets found altogether, all having entered the brain through the aperture. I examined the skull both before and after the skin and

82

Evidence for Prosecution.

Dr. Henry D. Littlejohn

hair were removed, and saw no trace of any appearance of pellets there. There were no stray pellets outside the brain. Undoubtedly the mass of the shot must have come against the head with a pretty smart blow. There was only one aperture made, but there was fracturing of adjacent portions of the skull. That was the effect of the impact and the explosive force of the shot as it passed onwards.

You say further, " The wound was now carefully examined; its edges were somewhat thickened, and posteriorly exhibited a distinctly bevelled and pretty regular surface." Now, is that not to some extent an indication that the shot had been fired from no great distance ?—It depends upon what you mean by no great distance.

Take the fact as you give it, that " the edges exhibited a pretty regular surface," does that not suggest that the distance cannot have been great ?—It indicates that the shot had not begun to spread until the time of impact. That is demonstrated in one of the cardboard experiments, in which the edges are seen to become irregular; the regularity of the surface shows that the shot had not begun to spread. I distinguish blackening and scorching in this way: blackening is the discoloration due to carbon which has not been consumed, scorching is burning from explosive gases. I am not sure that blackening would be rubbed off easily. The blackening on the head would not be washed off so easily with soap and water as you might imagine, because the fragments of carbon are driven with great force into the substance of the skin. I am aware that there is a great difference between the blackening caused by nitrous powder, such as amberite, and that caused by common black powder; I have seen blackening from amberite, but there is no scorching.

Immediately in front of the right ear and about its middle the skin exhibited laceration; this was due, in my opinion, to the progress of the shot from the wound to the zygoma (a small piece of bone connecting the face with the cranium); this was broken off and propelled by the shot. The area of the skull which received the first impact was an irregular space measuring 2 inches from the front backwards; it is fully an inch at the greatest breadth. The four metallic masses taken from the skull look like pellets, but they are not rounded to the extent that pellets are rounded; they were found on the right side of the brain. The tentorium cerebelli, that is the membrane which passes down to the lower brain and prevents it moving upwards on a sudden movement of the body, was uninjured. There was very little blood from the wound, undoubtedly due to decomposition having set in. Generally speaking, gunshot wounds do not leave much blood, because of the smashing of the arteries, but in this case we had laceration of a most important vein, and the presumption is that there was profuse hæmorrhage. The description by those who saw the body immediately after death of the blood oozing slowly describes excellently well the hæmorrhage in this case.

Alfred John Monson.

Dr. Henry D. Littlejohn

Because this sinus was injured, you think that the bleeding here would be profuse?—Yes; I have no doubt it was.

A flow?—A flow and oozing. I examined the body generally for any bruises of the limbs; I examined the hands. We made a careful external examination of the body, with the view of making the *post-mortem* examination as complete as possible. The stomach and its contents were most carefully examined, in order to obviate the possibility of the suspicion that alcohol was still present in the stomach. It is pretty certain that the odour of alcohol would disappear after twenty-five days' decomposition. I noticed in the experiments a little interval of skin between the wound and the ear. It was still intact, but some solid matter had passed behind it. It was ridged up. I noticed that in the experiments at the 9-feet distance there was considerable scattering; but, so far as the man's head was concerned, there was no trace of it except on the ear and in certain pieces of bone being dislodged and carried forward. Whyte and Carmichael were present when I made my calculations. I assumed that the deceased was standing up, and that he was about 6 feet in height. I considered that he fell slightly forward and on his left side. It was not suggested to me that he was lying on his back, but slightly on his side. I admit that it is all conjecture as to the position of the man at the time; he might have been stooping to pick up something, or might have stumbled. In my calculations I put his feet 4 or 5 feet away from where his head was. When a man falls he does not spread his limbs out, but he doubles up, and the man who lay in the position of the deceased when I was at Ardlamont lay in this doubled-up position, with his legs drawn up. I put the man in the position which, from my experience, I thought best. The man would fall in a heap. It must be borne in mind also that death would not be instantaneous; there might be some spasmodic or convulsive movement, which might also alter the position of the limbs.

You are not aware that when deer are shot behind the head they generally make a bound forward?—I am not a sportsman. All my researches have relation chiefly to human beings, and we find that in human beings shot in the heart there is that involuntary spring, but not in the case of wounds of the head. If it be the case that the body was lying, not on the dyke, but in the ditch, or on the ground on the other side of the ditch, that would undoubtedly neutralise all the deductions that had been drawn from the shot in the trees. My conclusions, I admit, depend very much upon whether it be true that the place pointed out to me as the place where Mr. Hambrough fell was really the place where he was shot, and also upon the position of the weapon. All the experiments with the cardboard were made point blank. The experiments made upon the cadaver were made under my direction. [Shown Nos. 1 and 2 of defence productions.] These are two wooden models of heads with wound marks on them.

84

Evidence for Prosecution.

Dr. Henry D. Littlejohn

Do these fairly represent the position of the wound on the man's head?—No; both of them are about a quarter of an inch too high. Otherwise they are something like it. [Shown No. 23.] This is a photograph of three horses' heads.

That is a photograph of an elongated wound, Dr. Littlejohn. Can you tell me how the shot was fired?—We can make no conclusion from a wound on a horse's head; it has, however, the general characteristics, in so far as it shows a triangle like the wound in question; the wound is elongated and less broad at one extremity than at the other, but there is an enormous difference between this and the wound in question. I have got with me one photograph of an experiment upon the cadaver, but there is none as a production. I am here to give you a particular account of each experiment that was submitted to the Crown. We have mentioned in our precognitions what we found.

Re-examined by the SOLICITOR-GENERAL—With regard to the exact position of Mr. Hambrough's feet before he was shot, there might be a certain amount of conjecture; there is undoubtedly no conjecture as regards the wound having been inflicted from behind forward. Assuming that Mr. Hambrough's head was where it was said to have been, and that the blood which I saw on the ground was discharged from the head, and looking to the nature of the wound, my inference would be that he would be found in the position which was assumed by the person under the direction of Whyte and Carmichael when I visited the *locus*. Looking to the nature of the wound, if he had been shot elsewhere in the neighbourhood I should have expected that there would be blood found there.

By the LORD JUSTICE-CLERK—If he had been shot not at the spot pointed out?—There would have been evidence of hæmorrhage; the effect of the shot would be to fell him at once; he would fall all of a heap. I would expect blood to be lying where his head was lying; his limbs might move, but not his head. He was lying slightly on his left shoulder.

Can you inform me how long there would be life after the shot? I think from ten minutes to a quarter of an hour, but in regard to this matter I cannot express a confident opinion. The shock must have been most severe.

Re-examination continued—When I was at Ardlamont in September I myself saw the bloodstain where the head had been; it was most marked—a circular mark of a dark colour. I employed myself for some time in looking about the immediate neighbourhood, and also in the ditch, and on either side of where the body was found, but I could discover no evidence of blood. If the two pieces of bone labelled No. 17 were found where I was told they were found, and if they belonged to the skull, then the question as to the place where the shot was fired is, in my opinion, settled; the body must have been shot at the place where it was found. I handed the two pieces

Alfred John Monson.

Dr. Henry D. Littlejohn

of bone to Dr. Macdonald Brown for the purpose of having the detached pieces of bone placed in the skull. I assisted Dr. Macdonald Brown in the first instance in fitting them, and we ultimately managed to fit them into the aperture, for which there was no other piece of bone recoverable by us, and, by a certain anatomical peculiarity presented by the large fragment, we proved indisputably to our minds that it occupied a certain position in the skull; it proved that these two pieces of bone were parts of Hambrough's skull. The fact that there was no blood found upon the clothes of the deceased, except a small speck on the collar of the coat, would point to his having been shot where he was found; the hands and clothes of a person lifting the body would have been exposed to damage by blood. Undoubtedly I should have expected to find blood upon the persons who lifted him. The loose portion of bone driven forward into the ear, to which I referred in cross-examination, is to my mind conclusive as regards the direction of the wound as being inflicted from behind. This is one of the strongest points in the case. With regard to the direction of the wound in the head, there were two well-defined points—the wound of entry and the portion of the ear carried away. The direction of the shot was a little above the horizontal, a little inclined upwards. In the flap of the ear there was a laceration in the direction of the line of shot. This wound was caused either by the passage forward of pellets or by the piece of bone which was detached by the force of the charge behind. I identify label No. 14 of the productions as four metallic particles found by Dr. Macmillan and myself adhering to the margins of the wound on the head. They were adhering to the external surface of the flesh wound. I identify label No. 13 as the four pellets removed by us from the brain; they are more or less disfigured by coming in contact with such a hard substance as bone. We found the pellets in the substance of the right side of the brain. They were all on the right side of the brain, and therefore I think that their disfigurement was caused by violent impact with the bone, and that leaving the bone they simply lodged where they were found, not being carried into the brain with such force as to pass out again, or even to pass to the left side. The four metallic fragments labelled No. 14 were found on the immediate surface of the flesh wound. As we were going over the flesh wound very carefully with a powerful lens we found these small black particles. At first I took them to be coal, but on removing them and carefully examining them they proved also to be fragments of lead. There were four of them, and that would indicate that the skull showed marks of being hit by four separate pellets. My own opinion is that the shot did not spread until it received violent impact on the bone, but this shows the breaking up of the pellets on striking the bone, and I believe these small particles glanced off the pellets, which impinged with such force on the bone as to drive

86

in the aperture which I have described. In short, the aperture was undoubtedly made by these pellets.

[Shown No. 23 of defence productions.] I entirely fail to draw any useful deductions from these photographs of horses' heads. [Shown No. 2 of defence productions.] The proportions of the wooden bust shown me are most faulty, and not exactly the same as a human head. The substance of this model is very different from the cranium. We made experiments with pasteboard, and we lined the pasteboard with clay, to represent as closely as possible the condition of matter in the human skull, but that is not such a solid mass as this, which is liable to split in all directions. It is my opinion that the difference as regards the solidity of a block like that and the human head displaces the reliability of an experiment based upon it. The block shows the ear and the mutilation of the ear. The figure here is solid, and does not represent the position of the human ear. Anatomically, it is not correctly placed.

By the LORD JUSTICE-CLERK—Suppose people had lifted young Hambrough without bringing the head in contact with their clothes, lifted him from the place about 3 or 4 feet down up to this place where he was said to have been found, would you have expected to find a flow of blood between the place they lifted him from and the place he was laid down?—I would. In death by shock the blood remains fluid and the head naturally falls, and in lifting such a heavy man as Mr. Hambrough the head would fall.

That is to say, if the head was not leaning against a person?—If that were so, the blood would have been evident on their clothes.

But if they got him up with his head hanging down?—The flow would have been more impetuous, and the passage would have been marked or littered with blood. It would have needed two very strong men to have lifted Hambrough.

28. Dr. MACMILLAN, examined by the SOLICITOR-GENERAL—I am a Bachelor of Medicine and a Master of Surgery, and have been in general practice in Tighnabruaich since 1884. I was attending Mr. Monson's family professionally at Ardlamont, and I made the acquaintance of Mr. Hambrough. On 10th August, about ten o'clock in the morning, the Ardlamont coachman came to me saying that I was to go to Ardlamont, as Mr. Hambrough had shot himself. I arrived at Ardlamont about half-past eleven, and saw Mr. Steven and Mr. Monson. Mr. Steven took me to the room where Mr. Hambrough lay. I found the body lying on the bed, quite dead. On the right side of the head I found a wound involving the scalp and the bone. The wound was smooth behind and jagged and irregular in front, a little wider in front than at the back. I inspected the wound, and felt with my finger that there was a hole in the skull. I had already been told by Mr. Steven what had occurred, and from my examination I had no doubt that it was a gunshot wound. I

Alfred John Monson.

Dr. Macmillan

fancied the charge would be in the head, because I thought that a charge fired at that near distance would have gone more directly, and that the charge would be in the head. I was shown the jacket produced. [Label No. 5.] There was a little blood upon the collar on the right side. The marking is not nearly so visible now, but I see some of it. That was the only article of clothing I saw. I have never before in practice seen a gunshot wound in the head. There was a lot of blood soaking the dressings and the pillow on which the head was lying. I examined the wound to see if there was any blackening or singeing, but could find traces of neither. From the appearance of the body, I formed the impression that about three hours had elapsed since the time of death. After making my examination, I bound up the head, cleaned away the blood, and helped to dress the body. I then went upstairs with Mr. Steven and saw Mr. Monson, who took me into the dining-room to have luncheon. A little after, Mr. Steven was also brought in for luncheon. Mr. Monson was present at luncheon, and another gentleman, who was introduced by Monson as Mr. Scott. He looked like a clerk. At luncheon Scott said that he had an important appointment that day in Glasgow which he must attend to. He was wanting to catch the two o'clock boat, and as there was very little time to catch it I said, unless his business was very urgent, he could get a steamer at quarter to three or another at quarter to five. At luncheon the subject of the death and how it occurred was pretty much avoided, but Mr. Monson remarked that had it happened in England there would have been a coroner's inquest, and he supposed there would be nothing of that kind in Scotland. I said that there would be a private inquiry, when the Procurator-Fiscal would make his own report upon the occurrence, and as this had been an accident there would probably not be a *post-mortem* examination. In a casual way I asked Scott if he had been shooting while he was down, and he said, '' No ; firearms are best left alone.'' After luncheon, I asked Monson to give me a more particular account of what happened. We went into another room, and I took some notes in Monson's presence—having in view the fact that the Procurator-Fiscal would have to make a report.

Monson said the name of the deceased was Windsor Cecil Dudley Hambrough, and that his own name was Alfred John Monson ; that he was no relation of the deceased ; and then I asked him as to the course of events. He said both had gone shooting rabbits with Mr. Scott. They had gone shooting in the wood to the south-east of Ardlamont House, at the south end of it, Mr. Hambrough taking the right or east side along the turf bank, Mr. Monson the left, and Scott walking in the middle carrying the rabbits. When near the end of the wood he heard a shot fired, and called out, ' Have you shot anything? '' but he got no response ; and shortly afterwards Mr. Scott, he said, came up, and they turned back together. They had not gone very far along the turf wall until they found Mr. Hambrough's body

88

Evidence for Prosecution.

lying in the ditch. There was no sign of life in the body. The gun was close beside it.

Did Monson say whether Scott and he went to the body together, or whether they met at the body?—He said that he had gone up to the end of the wood, and Scott presently came up to him, and that they came back together from the end of the wood. He said that he must have been 50 yards off when he heard the shot. After having that interview, I asked Scott to come into the room. He told me the same story as Monson. After this interview I saw Scott drive away from Ardlamont House. After lunch, I went to the place where the body was said to have been found that day. Mr. Steven and Mr. Monson, who had his little boy with him, went with me then. When we got to the place Mr. Steven said that when the body was found it was lying either there, pointing to a place in the ditch about 6 or 7 feet south from the rowan tree, or there, pointing to another place 4 feet further south, but not quite in the ditch. Monson corroborated him. There was no blood to be seen, and my attention was not called to any place where there was blood. At that time I was standing on the top of the west wall, looking down. It would be about two or three o'clock. There was no appearance of blood, or of the ground having been disturbed, and I said to Mr. Steven, " It does not appear to have been there, or even there, because the grass does not seem to have been disturbed." Mr. Monson said he was not quite sure of the exact spot. At that time I had not been told that the body had been found on the higher level, on the top of the dyke. After that I went to the offices to get my trap. Monson accompanied me, and in the course of our conversation he said it was very curious that he had had a very narrow escape from drowning the night before. He said he and Hambrough had gone spla h fishing, and when about a mile from shore the plug went out of the boat, and they saw it filling, and turned and made for the shore as fast as they were able, and when half-way into the shore the boat came on a sunken rock and capsized, throwing them both into the water. Mr. Hambrough scrambled on to the rock first, and Mr. Monson, being entangled with some ropes, was longer of getting on. But when he got on to the rock, being an expert swimmer, and Hambrough not being able to swim, he swam to the shore. He had not gone very far before he was able to touch the ground with his feet, and he brought out the second boat and rescued Hambrough. At the offic s I got my trap and returned home. Monson gave m e a telegram to despatch for him. It was to acquaint Major Hambrough f his son's death. It was sent off from Tighnabruaich.

On the evening of Friday, 11th August, I got a message from the police constable asking me to go to Ardlamont to re-dress the head. I understood the message to have come from Monson. On

Alfred John Monson.

Dr. Macmillan

the evening of the 12th Monson called upon me. He said he wanted me to re-dress the head, so as to make it as presentable as possible in view of Mrs. Hambrough's expected arrival at twelve o'clock. I went to Ardlamont, and was taken downstairs by Mr. Tottenham. I had not seen him before. He was not at Ardlamont on Thursday, the 10th. I did not re-dress the body. I thought it better that Mrs. Hambrough should not see the body, as decomposition was commencing. I put a clean covering over the old dressing. Monson did not accompany me to the bedroom either on the 10th or on the 12th.

On Monday, 14th August, I received a visit from two gentlemen of the name of Herbert and M'Lean. They gave me their cards, and I found they were connected with a New York insurance company. They brought me a schedule for the purpose of having it filled up. This is only important with regard to the 14th question and answer, which is—" (A) State the remote cause of death ; if from disease, give the predisposing cause, date of the first appearance of its symptoms, its history, and the symptoms present during its progress." My answer was—" Gunshot injury to brain." " (B) State immediate cause of death." My answer was—" A gunshot." " (C) If from any cause other than disease, state the medical and other facts connected therewith." My answer was—" He had been accidentally shot by his own gun through the occipital bone, the charge entering the brain in a compact mass through an opening 1 inch in diameter. See explanatory note." The explanatory note is in substance what I had learnt from Monson and Scott with regard to the occurrence. In this note I arrived at the following conclusions :—" It seems to me highly probable that deceased was going along carrying a short-barrelled 20-bore gun, with his finger on the trigger, when he stumbled, and, putting out his hands to break the fall, raised the muzzle, lowered the breech, and pushed back the trigger, with the results I have described. The injury was caused by the discharge of the gun while his finger was on the trigger."

On 15th August I got a communication from the Procurator-Fiscal, asking me to send him a report, which I sent him as requested. The following is the report :—" Windsor Dudley Cecil Hambrough, deceased. On the 10th August, 1893, I was asked to go to see Mr. Hambrough, who, it was said, had been shot dead. I arrived at Ardlamont House about 11.30 a.m., and found deceased, whom I identified, lying in a room on the ground floor. The body was still warm, but *rigor mortis* was commencing in the limbs, showing that death must have taken place about three hours previously.

" I found the bed much soiled with blood, which was oozing out of a wound in the head. This wound was a large, ragged one.

Evidence for Prosecution.

Dr. Macmillan

about $3\frac{1}{2}$ by $1\frac{1}{2}$ inches on the scalp, extending upwards and forwards from the right side of the occipital protuberance to near the back of the right ear, part of which had been carried away. About the centre of the scalp wound there was an irregular opening about 1 inch in diameter, right through the occipital bone into the brain. The bone had been carried into the substance of the brain. The wound was exactly what I would expect to find from a charge of small shot fired from a distance of perhaps 12 inches. The shot had not time to spread, as there were no separate pellet marks. I would expect blackening of the edges of the wound from the powder, but afterwards ascertained from Mr. Monson that they had been trying amberite, a nitro powder. That explains the absence of blackening. The skin or hair was not burned. Mr. John Steven, factor, Ardlamont, informed me that he and three others removed the body from the scene of the fatality, where he found it. When he saw deceased first, he was lying in the ditch beside a turf wall. His gun, lying beside, but not grasped by deceased, as described by Mr. Monson, was not seen by witness. Mr. Alfred John Monson, Ardlamont House, informed me that he and deceased had gone rabbit shooting together, witness taking the west and deceased the east side of the strip of wood. Mr. Scott walking between and behind them to carry game. When last he saw deceased in life he was walking along the top of the turf wall. When nearly through the wood, he heard Hambrough's gun go off, and called out, ' Have you killed anything?' He got no answer. Mr. Scott came forward at the same time, and together they turned to the place from which the shot sounded. They had not gone more than a dozen yards along the turf dyke until they found the body beside the wall in the ditch, quite dead, and a gun beside it, but not grasped.

" Mr. Edward Scott, engineer on the ' Alert,' informed me he was walking about 20 yards behind the deceased, but in the wood, and separated by the thick growth of a nursery of forest tree plants. He heard the shot when near the end of the wood, and called, ' Have you killed anything?' but got no answer. On coming up to Mr. Monson, they together turned to see what had become of Mr. Hambrough, and found him as already described. The keeper Lamont, who cleaned the guns, says that one trigger was full cock and the other down, but as Mr. Monson had removed the cartridge cases he could not tell if the cap of the empty one had been struck by the hammer. My object in making this inquiry was to be certain that the amberite had not exploded spontaneously.

" The information above given makes it probable that the deceased was going along the wall with the gun—a short 20-bore—under his arm and his finger on the trigger, when his foot caught on something, and he plunged forward, put down his hands to save himself, thus lowering the breech, raising the muzzle, and pressing the trigger, with the result described in the first part of this report.

Alfred John Monson.

Dr. Macmillan

" Given upon soul and conscience at Tighnabruaich, this 16th day of August, 1893, by

(Signed)   " JOHN MACMILLAN, M.B., C.M."

That report is dated 16th August, 1893. I afterwards made an additional report as follows :—" Windsor Dudley Cecil Hambrough, deceased. To the report on above of 16th August I now wish to make the following addenda. I implicitly accepted the statement of witnesses Monson and Scott that the injuries to Hambrough were due to an accidental shot from his own gun, a short-barrelled 20-bore boy's weapon, charged with amberite. The apparently entire absence of motive made the bent of my inquiry not so much how could this injury most likely be produced, as how could deceased have done it accidentally. It now transpires there were no amberite cartridges for this diameter of gun, and that I too hastily came to the conclusion or theory advanced at the end of my former report. Having handled and tried the gun now in the possession of the Procurator-Fiscal, I am convinced the injuries were not caused in the way I thought possible.

" Given on soul and conscience at Tighnabruaich, this 25th day of August, 1893, by

(Signed)   " JOHN MACMILLAN, M.B., C.M."

Examination continued—Both Monson and Scott told me that the injuries were caused by Mr. Hambrough's own gun. They did not describe the gun, but I afterwards understood that Hambrough's own gun was a 20-bore boy's weapon. On 25th August I wrote to the Mutual Life Insurance Company, New York, the following letter :—" Windsor Cecil Dudley Hambrough, deceased. Dear Sir, —Since sending you report on the above, facts have come to my knowledge which make it certain that the injuries were not caused in the way or with the weapon I then thought them to have been. I therefore now ask that that report be hereby cancelled."

Between your original report to the Procurator-Fiscal and your original report to the insurance company and your second report and second letter you changed your opinion?—I did.

Take your own way to explain the grounds on which your change of opinion rested?—In the first place I founded my opinion on the statements of Monson and Scott, and I found after some of the statements were communicated that I had been told untruths about parts of the matter, and that therefore it might be all an untrue story. If I had been told when I was on the ground that the body had been lifted from the ditch and placed upon the top of the bank, my view of the matter after I was there the first day would probably have been affected thereby.

I accompanied Dr. Littlejohn to Ventnor for the purpose of making a *post-mortem* examination, and was present when the coffin was opened and the body removed for examination. I was present with Dr. Littlejohn at the *post-mortem* examination. As a result of

92

Evidence for Prosecution.

Dr. Macmillan

the examination I found that the charge had not entered the head. My experience is that of a country medical practitioner. Before this occasion I had seen a pistol shot on the finger and a gunshot wound through the ankle; nothing else except small pellet wounds. My knowledge of such matters is more educational than practical. I am not a sportsman. As a result of the *post-mortem* examination, my opinion was that the wound could not have been caused accidentally. I had determined the direction of the wound before the *post-mortem*. I was certain all along that the shot was from behind, and the *post-mortem* confirmed me.

Tell us on what grounds you now think that the injury could not be accidental, as you originally supposed?—I have since taken guns of different lengths and tried them in every possible position and way, and found it absolutely impossible to produce a wound of this kind. I passed through London on my way to Ventnor on 3rd September, and gave Inspector Greet and Sergeant Brockwell, of the Criminal Investigation Department, a description of Scott, the same as I had previously given to the authorities.

Cross-examined by Mr. COMRIE THOMSON—In my second report I stated as a ground for wishing my first report altered that I had implicitly accepted the statements of Monson and Scott to the effect that the injuries to Hambrough were caused by an accidental shot from his own gun, which was a short-barrelled 20-bore boy's gun charged with amberite. This was one important reason for my altering my opinion at that time; it set me thinking of the facts of the case. The effects which I set forth in the first report were in no way modified either by finding that I had misapprehended Monson's statement or by my being set a-thinking that the wound was of the character and dimensions which I set forth in the first report. It remained true that the wound was of the dimensions mentioned— that it extended upwards and forwards from the right side of the occipital protuberance to near the back of the right ear. My opinion formed at my first examination, that about the centre of the wound there was an irregular opening about an inch in diameter right through the occipital bone, was confirmed by my fuller examination of the body. That does not affect the result arrived at in my first report. The breadth of the wound, as stated in my first report, was about 1½ inches. In the joint report made after the *post-mortem* examination the breadth of the wound is put at 2½ inches. The change is accounted for by the swelling due to the *post-mortem* processes drawing the scalp open. The measurement in my first report is a rough one, but it is tolerably correct.

You state that the wound was "exactly what I should expect to find from a charge of small shot fired at a distance of 12 inches." What was there which led you in any way to modify your opinion?— That opinion was founded on the article on gunshot wounds in Taylor's "Medical Jurisprudence." I have, however, since made experiments

93

Alfred John Monson.

Dr. Macmillan

myself which make me certain that my opinion was not correct. I
know that Taylor's works are of very high authority. What led me
to alter my opinion was the fact that the wound was not so extensive
nor was the destruction of bone so great as it would have been had the
shot been fired at a short distance. At 12 inches I should expect the
head to be blown to bits. I do not expect that at 12 inches a shot
would be much deflected. If you hit the head at that distance there
would be bound to be a great deal of smashing of bone whatever the
angle. I made experiments on sheep heads. I tried to get a wound
resembling that on Mr. Hambrough's head by letting the shot touch
the head as little as possible. At the near range the head was all
smashed up. [Shown No. 23 of defence productions.] I see the
flesh wound in the photograph, but I do not see the smash of bone;
I can hardly speak as to a photograph. I have witnessed the results
of experiments upon the cadaver in Edinburgh. I have descriptions
of the direction of the gun from those who carried out the experiments,
one of whom was Mr. Macnaughton. I found that in every case,
whatever angle he fired at, the substance fired at was blown away.
The shot fired at the near range resulted in a complete smash. Mr.
Macnaughton did not mention whether it was fired point-blank. The
idea of firing at angles is one with which I am not familiar by actual
measurement.

Is it upon the results of experiments made by you upon sheep,
and of experiments reported to you in the way you have mentioned
by Mr. Macnaughton, that you maintain now that Taylor's work,
which you had been brought up to believe, is inaccurate?—Not with
sheep heads only, but on a good many cards as well.

Were the cards fired at from an angle?—No, straight. At the
time I wrote this first report it was my opinion that the injury had
been caused before the shot began to scatter much. I did not see
any pellets whatever until at the *post-mortem* examination; I saw the
trace of pellets very distinctly on the ear.

So there had been no scattering, so far as you could judge, at the
time of the impact of the shot?—There must have been some scattering, looking to the injury to the ear.

I understood you to say that your view was that the shot struck
the place where the wound was, and that it then projected through
the flap of the ear, carrying away a portion?—My notion at the time
of my first report was that a small portion of the shot had carried
away a part of the ear, and that the bulk of the shot had gone
into the head. I am now of opinion that only a small part of the
shot had struck, the rest of it having gone past. I do not know
how many pellets would be required to produce the wound and the
fissures above the wound. It was a severe blow which made the
wound and all the cracks on the skull; I do not know if these
results could be produced by two or three stray pellets. The skull
was an ordinary one; having no experience of skulls, I do not know

94

Evidence for Prosecution.

Dr. Macmillan

whether it was thicker than most men's at twenty years of age. It is still my opinion that the shot had not time to spread, as there were no separate pellet marks.

It was not explained to me before I saw the body that a sponge and soap and water had been applied to the face and to the wound. I fancy that soap and water would take off blackening. In my experiments made with amberite powder there was usually scorching up to 12 inches, but not always. My change of opinion and alteration in my report was founded, in the first place, upon the fact that I was informed that there were no amberite cartridges for the 20-bore gun. Even if I had misunderstood the opinion that I gave, and if, in fact, the gun which did the mischief was a 12-bore gun, I think that still I would have written this additional report, because I had begun to think over the medical part, and I had before me the mistake of taking moral instead of medical evidence. The moral consideration was that I did not credit that a man like Monson could be guilty of so dreadful an act as killing his friend. I began to think over the character of the wound, its position, direction, &c., and I took a gun, and tried it in every direction to see if I could get it into a similar position. This was on 25th August, the day I met the Procurator-Fiscal. The Fiscal brought me my report and this gun. " Now," he said, " that is your report, and there is the gun with which Hambrough is said to have been shot. How do you reconcile it? " The gun was the 12-bore, and I took it and tried it in every direction. Even with a very much shorter gun I could not have produced such an injury. I asked the Fiscal to be allowed to withdraw the report, but he said I could not; he said, however, that I might make an addition. The report of 16th August is the report that I modified by that of 25th August.

In your experiments with the gun did you retain command of the trigger with your hand?—Yes; I tried in every way I thought possible. All my experiments were made on the footing that command of the trigger was retained. My experiments were directed to the impossibility of a gun being so directed accidentally that the charge would enter the head in the way it did. I admit that it could have been done suicidally. An ordinary man could not hold his gun so that the charge would enter the head in the way it entered Mr. Hambrough's. I could not put my hand into the required position. I have taken into account the case of a man making a violent stumble and the gun falling out of his hands and going off, but I have not experimented that way. Supposing a man were to stumble and fall, his gun would need to fall the required distance and to go off the required way, and that, I think, is improbable, though not impossible. On the top of the dyke it is very fair walking; it is not so rough as an ordinary hill and not so smooth as an arable field. There are holes in it, and stones sticking up in it. There is not any more care required in carrying a gun

95

Alfred John Monson.

along the dyke than when walking on an ordinary moor. There are no deep holes in it. I have read Mr. Steven's evidence, and in some respects I do not agree with his description of the wall. For example, I should not regard it as a place where one was likely to stumble. A sportsman out with his gun has not, as a rule, the main road to walk on.

[Witness was then shown a number of photographs showing men in various positions, with guns pointed at their heads.] Artificial erections would be required to hold the gun in the positions shown. These positions do not appear to me to be reasonable probabilities; they could not be accidental. They are suicidal and would require some one to pull the trigger. If a man got into that position the shot would go through the head and come out about the bridge of the nose. Suppose a gun were discharged at an angle towards the head, the shot would go through the head and come out at the left eye.

Re-examined by the SOLICITOR-GENERAL—At the time when you made your first report you say—" The entire absence of motive prevented me inquiring, not so much as to how the injury was most likely produced, as to how it could possibly have been accidental "? —That is my position. I was me ical attendant to the family at Ardlamont before this case. I had no suspicion in my mind before I went to see the body on 10th August. I thought all concerned were above suspicion. At the time of making my report to the insurance company it was my opinion that the whole charge entered the brain in a compact mass. I am now thoroughly satisfied that it is impossible to fire a charge 12 inches from the head with the result of the whole charge entering the head and producing the wound I saw at Ventnor. Since getting the additional information as to the extent of the charge entering the brain, I am satisfied that my opinion should be modified. On further consideration of the experiments which I made, I find that tremendous smashing of all the bones in the head would be the result of a shot fired 12 inches from the head at such an angle to the head as to cause the whole charge entering the head in a compact mass. In this case I found no smashing, but a wound behind the right ear; all the smashing of bone was to the front of the opening.

29. Dr. MACDONALD BROWN, examined by the SOLICITOR-GENERAL—I am a member of the Royal College of Surgeons and Lecturer on Anatomy in the Surgeons' Hall, Edinburgh. I have devoted special study to anatomy. Dr. Littlejohn handed a skull to me, which I have identified as the skull in question. The brain had been removed from the skull by sawing off one-half of the skull cap from the sound side. On the left side there was a considerable smashing of the skull at the lower back part. I prepared a model of the skull. I got six detached fragments of the bones from Dr.

Evidence for Prosecution.

Dr. M. Brown

Littlejohn, and afterwards two other fragments. I placed the first lot in position in the skull by fitting the fragments one into the other. I found the six pieces fit so well together as to form the opinion that they were parts of the skull in question. The two small bones I received later I was able to fit into position in one of two small openings which were still left of the original opening after the other pieces had been fitted. I found a part of the temporal bone awanting. A considerable piece was destroyed, and the second small piece of bone not only had the characteristics of the temporal bone, but it partially fitted the gap. I was satisfied that it was the smaller part of the temporal bone which had been displaced. I found certain fissures of the bone appearing on the skull. I marked the lines on the model skull. The fissures seemed to run forward. The part of the temporal bone which was awanting lies at the inside of what is called the external ear. It had been torn off by a force inside the skull, on the same side as the little hole. From my examination of the skull I formed an opinion as to the direction of the wound which had injured the skull. I was satisfied that it came from behind. [Shown No. 241.] I caused these drawings of the skull to be done. No. 1 is a typical skull; No. 3 represents the skull with the slight exception of a small fragment, which was not quite firmly in position. Otherwise, that is a drawing of the original skull as I got it, No. 2, with the fragments taken away. They were movable fragments, but in position. Having removed these two fragments, the skull presented an aperture which was enormously large.

By the LORD JUSTICE-CLERK—The two fragments were already separated, but held slightly in their position by soft structures.

Examination continued—They were movable some little distance, but in order to take them out altogether I had to destroy certain parts of the skin attached to them. There were a considerable number of small fractures at the base of the skull. I got permission from Dr. Littlejohn to have these parts removed, and I caused the artist to make the drawing [No. 4] in order that the fissuring on the base of the skull might be seen.

I have five reasons for believing that the shot was from behind. Firstly, the position of the original aperture and the character of its posterior border. The posterior border shows certain rounded markings. Not only does it show this, but it is a very thin border, and is thin at the expense of the inner table of the skull. Such a condition would be accounted for by the impact of shot pellets there. The marks I regard as the marks of the shot pellets. My second ground is that fragment No. 2 has evidently been displaced from within or from behind, certainly from within. That is, in front of the original aperture. On removing this fragment its edges were distinctly bevelled at the expense of the outer table of the skull. That bevelling was such as to show that it was split

H

Alfred John Monson.

Dr. M. Brown

off from within the skull. My third reason was that on examining the inside of the base of the skull there was a distinct grooving of the petrous part of the temporal bone. The petrous bone is an external bone between the ear and the aperture. That is a popular way of describing it. It is as nearly as possible opposite the entrance of the ear into the head. Its condition showed that the displacing force was from behind forward. My fourth reason is the direction of the fissures in the skull, most of which have a distinct direction forwards, although some of them passed upwards. From their direction I would expect that the blow would be from behind. The fifth point was that, on examining the skin wound, I was surprised to find a small point of bone piercing it from behind, and, without dislodging or attempting to dislodge this piece of bone, I slightly detached the soft part of the ear, and found that a small piece of the temporal bone had been fractured off and driven through the skin of the back of the ear, that is to say, the skin of the ear passage on its back part.

All these five appearances indicate force from behind, and they are not consistent with any other theory. I believe that the line of the pellets was as nearly as possible horizontal, assuming that the wound was caused by pellets. This conclusion I deduce from the following facts :—First, from the furrowing of the temporal bone just spoken of, and secondly, from the position of fragment No. 2, as compared with the aperture in the front; a shot coming from behind, as nearly as possible horizontal, would naturally, if it dislodged anything at all, dislodge a piece of bone on the same horizontal plane. That fragment practically indicates that the shot came from behind forward and also indicates the line in which the shot would pass. A third reason with regard to the line of the shot was the presence of the small specular bone which pierced the posterior wall of the skin of the ear in its passage. This is a guide to the line of the shot, because a line drawn from the position of that small piece of bone passed almost through the centre of the original aperture behind.

As the result of my examination, I was satisfied that all the various pieces of bone handed to me by Dr. Littlejohn formed parts of Mr. Hambrough's skull; that the shot which injured the skull came from behind; that the line of that shot was as nearly as possible horizontal.

I made a series of measurements of the exact position of the original aperture. It was 2 inches broad by $1\frac{1}{2}$ inches high. It lay obliquely. I have four other separate measurements. One is from the middle of the upper margin to the inside of the saggital suture, $5\frac{1}{4}$ inches. Horizontally from the occipital to the nearest point of the posterior margin measured $1\frac{5}{8}$ inches. From the lowest point of the aperture to the foramen magnum was $1\frac{1}{4}$ inches. These measurements localised the original opening of the skull.

98

Evidence for Prosecution.

Dr. M. Brown

Cross-examined by Mr. COMRIE THOMSON—When I say that there was "considerable smashing," I mean that the bone was broken up into bits. The petrous part of the temporal bone, a very hard part of that bone, was injured. There was also an injury across the base of the skull.

Was that caused by the impact of the shot in a mass or by individual pellets?—I am here as an anatomist, not as an expert in gunshot wounds.

Your answer is a justifiable one, but I want to know whether in your judgment this mischief was caused by individual pellets or by the impact of the shot in a compact mass?—I really have not considered that.

It would have been of some advantage for perfect accuracy as to the direction of the shot to have seen the fresh wound?—It would.

You are aware that the medical gentlemen who made the *post-mortem* examination described the wound as extending upwards and forwards from the right side of the occipital protuberance to near the back of the right ear?—I have not seen the report. I had a skull given to me, and I have described carefully what I found upon that skull.

Re-examined by the SOLICITOR-GENERAL—I had nothing but the skull and the pieces of bone, and I had to consider whether these pieces of bone belonged to the skull, and if they did, what was their proper place in the skull. I had to consider, assuming that these pieces of bone had been displaced by force, what was the direction from which they were forced off, and I believe that it was from behind. I have not applied my mind to anything but the anatomical aspect of the question.

30. Dr. PATRICK HERON WATSON, examined by the SOLICITOR-GENERAL—I am a Fellow of the Royal College of Surgeons, and practise in Edinburgh. I have practised as a surgeon for about forty years, and served during the Crimean War as an army surgeon, during which time I had special experience in gunshot wounds. [Shown No. 238.] I have read this report by Dr. Littlejohn and Dr. Macmillan, and have also seen and examined Mr. Hambrough's skull. I have also seen three photographs of the skull, and was present at certain experiments made by Mr. Macnaughton, the gunmaker. [Shown Nos. 7 and 8.] These are the guns with which Mr. Macnaughton shot at the cardboards. The *post-mortem* examination indicates that Mr. Hambrough died from the effects of loss of blood. The *post-mortem* examination would not indicate the shock; it would indicate loss of blood. The wound, in my opinion, must have been the result of a shot fired by the hand of another; it could not have been fired by Mr. Hambrough himself either designedly or accidentally. My opinion is based upon the situation and the direction of the wound. The direc-

99

Alfred John Monson.

Dr. Patrick H. Watson

tion, as shown by the skull and the photographs [No. 239], was from behind forwards. The commencement of the wound in the soft part is a little behind the point at which the impact occurred in the occipital region; the injury to the blood-vessel which caused loss of blood is a little further forward, near the lateral sinus. In looking at the photograph I noticed a distinct grooving at the soft parts before the surface of the bone is reached. That is the narrowest part of the wound; further forward it becomes wider, and evidently reaches its greatest width at the point where the flap of the ear has been cut off. Looking at the bone, the point of impact is a comparatively limited-sized aperture, and you have in front of that the line of fissuring taking place in a different direction. You have more especially one portion of the bone at the root of the zygoma which has been completely broken off, and in a direction which implies that separation began behind, and went forward. These various points satisfy me that the wound was from behind forward. The direction of the wound is the result of a glancing shot, a shot not fairly perpendicular upon the surface on which it impinged. In my view the line of passage past the head is nearly transverse, with a slight inclination from below upwards. The fact which led me to the view that that was the line of the shot was that if you draw a line thr ugh the middle of it it indicates the line in which the shot arrived in contact. As regards the distance from the head of the barrel of the gun which caused the injury, my opinion is that a distance of 9 feet from the muzzle of the gun is that most likely to correspond with the effects of this injury, but that is a matter upon which I do not express an absolutely certain opinion. I think I may say, however, that the distance could not be less than 4 feet, and, on the other hand, it was not likely to be greater than 10 or 11 feet; I do not think it would be as much as 12 feet. If it were less than 4 feet the injury inflicted on the bones of the skull would have been much greater than what I found; if it were beyond 11 or 12 feet the scatterings of the shot would produce a pattern, that is to say, there would be pellet wounds forming a circumferential band round the main injury, and the pellets would even, to some extent, go beyond. In all probability the coat would have been perforated by pellets. I saw the coat after the time of the accident, and there were no marks of pellets upon it at all. It is my view that the shot was fired at a distance of something like 9 feet from the head, and that the direction was slightly upwards and horizontal. If a man were shot in this way he would drop instantly. Assuming that he was found lying with his head in a pool of blood, and with two pieces of bone, which were bits of the skull, lying near to the right side of the head, I should assume that the man dropped where he was shot, and bled to death where he lay. If he had been moved from where he fell after some minutes to another place I would expect to find a pool of blood at each place.

Suppose he fell, and was lifted up and placed in another place, would you expect to find blood on his clothes, unless his head was

100

Evidence for Prosecution.

Dr. Patrick H. Watson

held so that the blood would fall on the ground?—I should, and if he were carried head downwards, so as to keep it clear of his clothes, I should expect to find blood on the ground. Supposing the shot to have been fired at a distance of 9 feet I should not expect to find any singeing; it is difficult to say absolutely at what distance one would find singeing, but I should not trust singeing in connection with this matter except at a distance of not more than 6 inches. Supposing that a glancing shot had been fired at a distance within the limits which I have mentioned, 2 or 3 feet from the head, the skull would have been shattered completely; if it was fairly right on it would probably have gone right through the skull. If, however, it had come as a glancing shot it would have broken it up more.

Is the injury you found in the skull consistent with a shot fired at a distance of not more than 2 or 3 feet?—It is not; it is consistent with being more probably at a distance of 9 feet.

Cross-examined by Mr. Comrie Thomson—I will grant that to some extent we have been in the region of conjecture in the evidence I have led; I did not see the man shot. The weapons which caused the injuries in the Crimean War were rifles; the wounds I saw in hospital were rifle bullet wounds fired at a distance, not at close quarters.

My sources of information in this case were doctors' medical reports and the cardboards. The shots were fired point blank at the cardboard. In the wound there is a certain upward direction, not very much; the slight obliquity might depend upon nothing more than the position of the head. The point where scattering of shot commences depends upon the charge and the formation of the gun— a smooth bore carries much more continuously. These guns produced are cylinder guns; scattering with these guns with an ordinary cartridge containing 250 to 300 pellets begins at the very moment when the charge leaves the gun; perceptible scattering begins at about 6 feet from the gun. With a well-made gun it is perceptible at 3 feet according to the cardboard experiments, and at 9 feet it is very perceptible. It was pointed out to me that no stray pellets were found in any part of this man's head except those which had entered by the aperture, so that there is no sign of scattering so far as the head and the neck and adjacent parts of the body are concerned. There was considerable smashing of the skull, but not so considerable as it would have been had the shot been fired from a distance of 2 to 4 feet. The bone was broken into bits at the original point of contact, where the bone was apparently driven in, and other parts were broken off attached to the soft parts. The destruction of the substance of the skull caused by the shot depended to some extent on the obliquity of the impact. There was only a small spot of blood on the coat.

Do you not think that if a body within half or three-quarters of an hour of death had been handled by being wrapped in a rug, lifted into a waggon, and carted about a furlong, there would be a considerable amount of blood to be found in the cart, on the rug, and on the

Alfred John Monson.

clothes?—Well, in half an hour there would be very little blood left to run out. I should, however, have expected to find some blood on the rug, or the clothes, or the coat.

I understand that Mr. Hambrough fell in the way which is commonly called the drop—that is, he went down with his head on one side. He would be lying on his face or on his side, but I should not expect him to lie on his back. If a man carrying a loaded gun stumbles, and the gun goes off, the contents of the gun would enter the body exactly on the line at which the loaded barrel was presented to it.

There is considerable variety in gunshot injuries; my experience of such injuries is limited to accidental or suicidal gunshot wounds. My only knowledge as to scorching with amberite powder is derived from the cardboards which I saw. The blackening and scorching produced by black powder is very different from any such effects produced by amberite powder. The data on which I proceed in fixing the 9 feet are, in the first place, that the shot was a glancing one; that would admit of the pellets, which were beginning to scatter, injuring the soft parts, and at the same time being followed up by the mass, so that the one would run into the other. In the second place, the degree of breaking up in the skull at 1, 2, 3, or 4 feet would produce too great an effect.

31. Dr. JOSEPH BELL, examined by the SOLICITOR-GENERAL—I am a Doctor of Medicine and a Fellow of the Royal College of Surgeons, Edinburgh, and have been in practice in Edinburgh as a surgeon for many years. I had an opportunity of seeing and examining the report of the *post-mortem* examination in this case by Dr. Littlejohn and Dr. Macmillan. I also saw and examined the skull of the late Mr. Hambrough, and the photographs taken at Ventnor. I was present at the experiments made by Mr. Macnaughton with the two Ardlamont guns and I have seen and examined the cardboard targets showing the result of these experiments. I was also present when experiments were made upon cardboard heads lined with clay, and upon one or more occasions when experiments were made upon the cadaver. From the information given me, I have formed the opinion that Mr. Hambrough died in consequence of a gunshot wound, and I have not been able to make out any way by which the injury could have been done either designedly or accidentally by Mr. Hambrough himself. I have no doubt whatever that the wound was inflicted from behind in a direction almost horizontal, but slightly upwards. As regards the distance of the muzzle of the gun from the head when the shot was fired, I have considered the experiments made very carefully, and have arrived at the conclusion that the most probable distance is about 6 to 9 feet. Had the wound been inflicted at a less distance, the skull must have been much more smashed up; had the wound been inflicted at a greater distance, the body of the shot would have been

Evidence for Prosecution.

Dr. J. Bell

scattered by the time of impact, and would not have inflicted the deep-grooved wound in the bone which we find has been inflicted.

The effect of such a shot upon the person receiving it would be to make him fall down immediately, unable to move; he would probably have died directly. The inference which I should draw from being told that the body was found with the head lying in a pool of blood, and that two small pieces of the skull were found lying near, is that he had died in his tracks; he would have crumpled up and fallen down. If he had been shot at a particular place, and had lain there for two or three minutes, and then had been lifted by two persons to a different place, I think that there would certainly have been blood at the place where he first fell; unless he had been carried with his head downwards there would have been blood on his clothes, and if his head had been downwards the blood would probably have dropped upon the ground or upon the clothes of the persons carrying him. As the result of my examination of the case, my opinion is that this wound must have been inflicted by a gun in the hand of another than the deceased.

Cross-examined by Mr. COMRIE THOMSON—I have not visited the scene of the accident. If a man carrying a gun makes a bad stumble, and in falling throws the gun away from him behind, there are certainly infinite possibilities as to how he could have shot himself; I have not been able to formulate any idea of how it could be done for myself.

You will, I think, allow that there is room for conjecture?—If you could get a gun to go off about 3 or 4 feet from the patient, then, I think, certainly it could be done.

Your difficulty, therefore, lies mainly in this, that you do not see your way to get the gun nearer to him than 6 feet?—Well, I believe it could go 4 feet; I think myself it would be 6, 7, or 8 feet. but I could imagine it was as near as about 4 feet. I cannot imagine it any nearer. The cardboard experiments were made point blank; I forget whether there was visible scattering at 3 feet. I think there was one shot at 2 feet which began to scatter. The scattering went on increasing from foot to foot, and at 9 feet it was very considerable.

It is an element, I suppose, of considerable importance that no stray pellets were found in this man's head?—Four, I think, were found all entering by the aperture. The fact that no pellets or traces of pellets were found in any part of the head or neck, except those entering by the aperture, is of importance with reference to what one knows of scattering. The amount of destruction of the substance of the skull would depend upon the directness of the obliquity of the impact. My theory as to the way the man would fall upon receiving the shot is that he would drop down crumpled up, that there would be finally one or two convulsive movements, and then the man would fall altogether on his face or

103

Alfred John Monson.

on his back, one way or the other. The body of the shot went right through the bone *en balle*; having struck, four pellets appear to have entered the aperture, and the rest to have gone into space.

Re-examined by the SOLICITOR-GENERAL—The shot struck *en balle*, but probably only one-half struck the head. The force would depend upon the distance and the direction. Striking *en balle*, as it did, if it had been within 2 or 3 feet, it would have forced the bones from within outwards, shattering them to a greater extent, and probably no bone in the head would have escaped. My opinion of the injury rests on the fact that the shot struck *en balle*.

By the LORD JUSTICE-CLERK—The whole of the charge flying *en balle* probably did not strike the head. Taking the shot as a bullet $1\frac{1}{2}$ inches in diameter, probably one-half struck the head; a considerable part probably did not touch the head at all.

32. JOHN GRAHAM M'LEAN, examined by the SOLICITOR-GENERAL —I am district manager of the Mutual Life Insurance Company of New York. On Wednesday, 2nd August, I had a visit from Mr. Monson at my office in Glasgow. He said he was trustee and guardian of Mr. Hambrough, a young gentleman who was coming into a fortune of £200,000, that Mr. Hambrough was about to purchase the Ardlamont estate, that Mrs. Monson was to advance £20,000 to secure the purchase of Ardlamont, and that he wanted to effect an insurance on Mr. Hambrough's life to cover the advance. Monson asked for terms for a £20,000 insurance, and I told him that I should have to write to London before I could give him a quotation. He said that he was staying at Ardlamont, but was to be in Glasgow all day, so I asked him to call again in the afternoon, saying that we would have a doctor present, so that if anything came of the negotiations Mr. Hambrough could be examined. He came back to my office about half-past two accompanied by Mr. Hambrough. My secretary and I were in the room with them. Monson said that, on thinking matters over, he would like to take out a whole-life policy. A doctor was in attendance, and he examined Mr. Hambrough. I wrote out a proposal for the insurance of Mr. Hambrough's life for £20,000, to be contained in two policies for £10,000 each, which was signed by Mr. Hambrough in my presence. With a policy for that amount we require a second medical examination, and this I arranged to be made on Friday, 4th August, at Ardlamont. On that day I went to Ardlamont along with Dr. Broadfoot, of Greenock, and the second examination was carried through. When I was at Ardlamont, Monson said that he would like the transaction carried through by 8th August, as he was going to complete the purchase of the Ardlamont estate, and would like to know if Mr. Hambrough was accepted by that date. He said that he was going to Edinburgh to see the solicitors about the purchase of the estate. On the morning of 8th August he called

104

Evidence for Prosecution.

J. G. M'Lean

at my office in Glasgow. I met him as he was coming out of my office, and saw him off to Edinburgh by the ten o'clock train. He said that he would come back in the afternoon to pay the premium. He came back to my office about half-past two, and paid the premium by a cheque for £194 3s. 4d. on the Tighnabruaich branch of the Royal Bank, signed by Mrs. Monson. [Shown No. 162.] In exchange for the cheque I handed to him two temporary policies for £10,000 each, provisional policies issued subject to the approval of the Home Office. He said that Hambrough preferred to pay the premium half-yearly, as the burden would not be so heavy as if he paid it yearly. [Shown No. 9.] That is the medical report with reference to the insurance—[Shown No. 10]—and those are the usual certificates of friends, which are signed by A. Houston and E. M. Hiron.

I first heard of Mr. Hambrough's death through the press on 10th or 11th August. On Monday, 14th August, I went to Tighnabruaich, accompanied by my secretary, taking with me a form of certificate which has to be filled up when a person insured in our office dies. Our office requires this certificate to be filled up by the doctor who attended the deceased, and at Tighnabruaich we saw Dr. Macmillan, who said that he could not fill up the certificate at the time, but that he would forward it to us along with an explanatory letter, which he did. Before seeing Dr. Macmillan, I had seen Mr. Monson on board the steamer at Kames Pier on our way to Tighnabruaich. When we arrived at Tighnabruaich we found that the funeral of Mr. Hambrough was taking place. After the body was on the steamer, seeing Monson on the steamer, I went on board and spoke to him. I asked him why he had not sent us word of the death. He said that he had telegraphed, and when I told him that we had not received any telegram he said that it must have gone amissing, as had two or three other wires of his. We sailed from Kames to Tighnabruaich, and at the pierhead I saw Dr. Macmillan, with whom I asked an interview. I went ashore and saw the doctor. Monson said that he was leaving Glasgow the same night by the Midland train at half-past nine. I said I would go and see him in Glasgow, as he looked very depressed, and he said, " Very well, very glad to see you." I saw him at half-past eight at St. Enoch's Hotel in Glasgow, and during our conversation I asked him how Mr. Hambrough's death had occurred. He said he could not tell ; all he knew was that the three had started out in the morning to shoot rabbits, Hambrough on one side, he on the other, and Scott in the middle. They were to meet at a point, at which he and Scott arrived, but Hambrough was not there. They retraced their steps, and found Mr. Hambrough lying dead, but Monson did not say to me what sort of a place the body was lying in. All that Mr. Monson said about claiming the insurance money was to ask how he would go about the claim. I said that

Alfred John Monson.

J. G. M'Lean

when the funeral was over we would arrange that. On the following Monday, 21st August, I saw Monson again at our office, when he called to talk over the claim. Mr. Tottenham was with him. I told him that we should require evidence of the death before we could discuss it; we had the doctor's certificate already, but still required evidence of the death from the Fiscal. I said that our head manager was in Scotland on a holiday, and that I thought the best thing to do would be to ask him to meet with Monson, and I would wire for him to come. I did this, and got an answer back from our manager saying that he could meet Monson next day at twelve o'clock. Tottenham and Monson agreed to come to my office on that day to see the manager. On Tuesday Tottenham called, but Monson did not.

I was instructed by the general manager to go to Inveraray to get evidence, which I did on Wednesday, 23rd August, accompanied by Mr. Herbert. At Tighnabruaich we were joined by Monson and Tottenham, and they accompanied us to Inveraray. At Inveraray I went to see the Fiscal; Monson was not present. The following day, Thursday, 24th August, I saw Monson at Glasgow, and he told me he was looking for Scott. Nothing else passed that day. On Tuesday, 29th August, Monson telegraphed for Mr. Herbert and me on important business, and we went to Ardlamont. We asked what he wanted to see us about, but we do not know yet what it was. The police were there by that time. He said, in reference to Scott, that a telegram had come that night to the effect that they thought they had him. He said nothing more about Scott on that occasion. On Thursday, 24th August, when Monson was in my office, I asked him if he knew anything about Scott, and he said that all he knew was that he came from Stockton-on-Tees, and that it was Mr. Hambrough who employed him.

[Shown No. 13.] This is a letter addressed by W. D. C. Hambrough to the manager of the Mutual Insurance Company, and delivered to me by Monson on the day he paid the premium to me. It is as follows:—"August 7, 1893. Dear Sir,—Will you kindly deliver my two insurance policies of £10,000 each to Mr. and Mrs. Monson, as I have assigned the policies to Agnes Maud Monson for proper considerations received? Mrs. Monson will therefore be the person to whom the insurance is payable in the event of my death. Kindly acknowledge receipt of this notice, and oblige, yours truly, W. D. C. Hambrough." [Shown No. 14.] I know that document, but I could not swear to the actual date on which it came into my possession; it must have been on 21st, 22nd, or 24th August. Its own date is difficult to make out; it is either 7th or 9th August, 1893. It was left at my office either by Mr. Monson or by Mr. Tottenham. I shall explain the way it came into my possession—Herbert Tottenham, Monson, and myself were in my room in my office in Glasgow, and this document was handed to Herbert, who handed it to me. I was called out of the room for

106

Evidence for Prosecution.

a little to see some one, and when I came back I took this document and put it, along with other papers bearing on the subject, into the safe. I did not read it at the time. I handed it over to the Crown, along with all the papers in my possession bearing on the case. The letter is as follows:—" The Royal Route Steamer ' Iona,' August 7, 1893. Dear Mrs. Monson,—If you will pay the premiums on the two policies of assurance on my life of £10,000 each with the Mutual Life Insurance Company of New York, I am willing that you should hold the policies as security for all moneys due to you from me, and as security against all liabilities incurred by you on my behalf; and in the event of my death occurring before the repayment of these moneys you will be the sole beneficiary of these policies, and I have given notice to the Mutual Insurance Company of New York that you are the person to whom the insurance is payable, and they have accepted my notice.—Yours sincerely, (signed) W. D. C. Hambrough. To Mrs. Agnes Maud Monson, Ardlamont." I do not know whose handwriting the letter is in.

[Shown No. 17.] This is a letter from Dr. Macmillan, addressed to Mr. Herbert, secretary, and dated 20th August, 1893. It was not opened till Monday, 28th August, as Mr. Herbert was from home at the time. In this letter Dr. Macmillan asks that his report in regard to Mr. Hambrough's death should be cancelled in consequence of facts which had come to his knowledge.

Cross-examined by Mr. COMRIE THOMSON—It was at my second interview with Mr. Monson that I first saw Mr. Hambrough; he did not hear all that passed between me and Monson. Monson said that he would give me the particulars of the proposal while Hambrough was being examined by the doctor; the examination took place in another room. I read over the clauses of the proposal to Mr. Hambrough and asked him to look it over; having done so, he signed it. No reference was made by Monson in Hambrough's presence to arrangements which required to be effected regarding the Hambrough estates. On this occasion he did not say to me that when young Hambrough came of age he would probably have to insure his life for £50,000 in order to take over his father's insurances. On the day on which he was paying the premium Monson said that young Hambrough would increase his insurances, but he did not give the reason. No reference was made by Monson or by Tottenham to Major Hambrough or to his position with regard to his estates. The Eagle Insurance Company was not mentioned. At my second meeting with Monson, the one at which I first saw Mr. Hambrough, I advised that the policies should be taken out in Hambrough's own name, and that they should afterwards be properly assigned to Mrs. Monson. I knew that the young man did not come of age till the following year, and that the assignation was not of any good without the consent of his guardians.

Did Monson know that also?—I do not know.

Did the conversation proceed on the footing that both you

Alfred John Monson.

J. G. M'Lean

and he were aware that the assignation by young Hambrough without the consent of his father would be of no avail?—I knew that, but Monson did not know, so far as I gathered from his conversation. I did not assume that every one would know that a minor could not assign without consent. The cheque was on the Royal Bank, Tighnabruaich, and I received it on 8th August. Till the cheque was honoured the risk was not on. In the provisional policy there is this clause, " Subject to such terms of said company's policies." These terms include what I have mentioned, that the premium must be paid before the risk is on. [Shown No. 14.] That letter is in pencil, and is written upon the steamer " Iona's " writing paper; it bears to be the copy of a letter. I do not know by whom it is written. I never saw the principal. After the death, it was Tottenham who was the more eager about getting payment of the contents of the policy.

Do you remember on Tuesday, 29th August, at Ardlamont, telling Monson that he could not claim the amount?—Yes. Did he say he was quite satisfied that he could not?—He did. The exact words that he used were that he knew that he could not finger a penny.

Re-examined by the SOLICITOR-GENERAL—This conversation took place on the occasion on which I went to Ardlamont and found the police there. Monson told me at my early interview with him that he wanted the insurance transaction completed by 8th August, on which date he was going to Edinburgh to finish the transaction with the solicitors, and he wanted to know by that time whether Hambrough would be accepted. He told me that it was Mr. Hambrough who was going to buy Ardlamont, and that Mr. Hambrough was to pay for it, Mrs. Monson advancing £20,000 to secure the purchase. He told us that Mrs. Monson would get the policies to secure the advances she had made. There was no particular reason for there being two policies; life policies are sometimes divided. Monson's first proposal was that the policy should be in name of Mrs. Monson, not of Hambrough. The cheque passed through our London bank on the 8th, and was cashed; we got the money all right, and retained it. It was at St. Enoch's Hotel, Glasgow, when on his way south to the funeral, that Monson first spoke to me about claiming the insurance. At the first meeting of all which I had with Monson, when the insurance was proposed, Monson was alone. I did not see Hambrough at all that day in Glasgow, except when he came to my office in the afternoon with Monson, and signed the proposal. He just signed the proposal without saying anything.

By Mr. COMRIE THOMSON—It may have been upon my proposal that the sum was divided into two policies, but I cannot exactly say. Everything was done quite openly, and in Hambrough's presence.

The Court adjourned.

Fourth Day—Friday, 15th December, 1893.

33. DAVID STEWART, resident secretary in Glasgow of the Liverpool, London, and Globe Insurance Company, examined by Mr. REID—I received a letter from our assistant manager in Liverpool, dated 20th July, 1893, relating to a proposal for insurance upon the life of Mr. W. D. C. Hambrough, amounting to £50,000. On 25th July Monson called at my office. He wished to have Hambrough examined by our medical referee. He said he was anxious to get away by two o'clock, and he wished to have the examination over by that time. I accordingly arranged to go to Dr. Finlayson, Woodside Place, at twelve o'clock. About that hour Monson came back to my office. Hambrough was with him, and I drove with them to Dr. Finlayson's house. [Shown No. 32.] That is the proposal. It is for £50,000, and is signed by Agnes Maud Monson. I forwarded the proposal along with the medical report to the head office in Liverpool on 25th July. I had no conversation with Monson as to the object of the insurance. I had no conversation with Hambrough. That was the only time I saw him. Monson called again on 2nd August to ascertain if I had heard if the proposal had been accepted. I told him that the information would not come to me, and that he had better telegraph to the head office. The proposal had been negotiated through Mr. Wardle, our Leeds agent, and the intimation as to the acceptance or declinature would go to the Leeds office. Mr. Monson that day had wired to our Liverpool office asking if they would accept the proposal, and asking a reply by wire. The reply came to Glasgow, and I opened it. It conveyed the information that the proposal had been declined. That was on 2nd August. I handed the telegram to Monson, as it was a reply to his telegram. He looked a little disappointed, as any one would do in such circumstances. He did not say anything except " It is a pity."

Cross-examined by Mr. COMRIE THOMSON—[Shown No. 31]— This is a proposal by Monson to our company for £15,000 on the life of Hambrough, on the margin of which there is this statement as to the insurable interest—" He has undertaken, on his coming of age, to repay loans to himself and to his father to the extent of about £50,000." [Shown No. 32.] This is a proposal, apparently, for £50,000 by Mrs. Monson on Hambrough's life, in the body of which there is this declaration as to the amount of her

Alfred John Monson.

interest—" I hereby declare that I have an interest in the life of the said Windsor Dudley Cecil Hambrough to the extent of £50,000." Mr. Wardle is our Leeds secretary.

Mr. COMRIE THOMSON—I shall read you a letter [No. 41] signed A. J. Monson—" July 31st, 1893, Ardlamont House, Argyllshire. Dear Sir,—I received a letter from Mr. Wardle to-day, saying that you require further particulars of Mrs. Monson's interest in the life of Mr. Cecil Hambrough. I had, however, then written a letter to you saying that the policy for £50,000 was *not* now required, as we have arranged to secure Mrs. Monson's liability under the agreement by other means which are less costly. We shall, however, require a policy for £26,000, and this will have to be increased to £52,000 next year, when he attains twenty-one. Thus you will require to know that the extent of Mrs. Monson's interest in Mr. Cecil Hambrough's life amounts to £26,000. Mr. Wardle seemed to think that a minor could not incur a liability beyond that for maintenance, education, and necessaries—this, however, does not concern us. A minor can undertake to make certain payments on his attaining his majority, if he should so long live. There would obviously be an interest in the life of the minor in such an undertaking. This is the position in the present case. Mrs. Monson incurs liabilities on behalf of the minor, and makes him advances and provides him with education extending over four years. Mr. Cecil Hambrough, in consideration therefor, gives her an undertaking in writing whereby he agrees to pay her the sum of £26,000 on attaining twenty-one, and since he succeeds to estates under the will of his great-grandfather to the value of £200,000 or thereabouts, there can be no question as to whether Mrs. Monson has not an interest in his life to the extent mentioned, and it cannot concern you to enter into the details of how the £26,000 is made up, so long as you have evidence of the fact. I therefore enclose a letter by Mr. Cecil Hambrough, which I assume will be sufficient evidence.—Yours truly, A. J. Monson. To the Manager of the Liverpool, London, and Globe Insurance Company."

I now show you a letter [No. 42]—" Ardlamont House, 31st July, 1893. Dear Sir,—I am requested by Mrs. Agnes Maud Monson to write to inform you that she has an interest in my life to the extent of £26,000. I have given her an undertaking to pay her this sum on my attaining twenty-one, if I should live until then.—Yours truly, (signed) W. D. C. Hambrough."

WITNESS—I did not receive this letter; it went direct to the Liverpool office. I never saw either of these letters.

34. JAMES WARDLE, examined by the SOLICITOR-GENERAL—I am manager at Leeds of the Liverpool, London, and Globe Insurance Company. [Shown No. 31.] This is a proposal on the life of Mr. Hambrough for £15,000 made by Monson, and dated 28th May, 1892. It was necessary to state the interest.

Evidence for Prosecution.

[Witness at this point described the proposal in the same terms as the last witness, David Stewart.]

[Shown No. 32.] This is a proposal for £50,000 on the life of Mr. Hambrough in the name of Agnes Maud Monson. In this case also it was necessary to state the interest. In this proposal there is no statement of the interest; it was suggested that the interest should be detailed in a separate document, because there is only a small space there. [Shown No. 38.] That is a letter from Mr. Monson to the manager stating the interest—"Ardlamont House, Argyllshire, 26th July, 1893. Dear Sir,—I am instructed by Mr. Wardle, of your Leeds office, to send you particulars of Mrs. Monson's interest in the life of Mr. Cecil Hambrough. Therefore I beg to inform you that the insurance is to cover advances made by request of Mr. Cecil Hambrough, and for his maintenance, &c., extending over four years; also to cover liabilities incurred under an agreement with the Hambrough estates." [Shown No. 39.] That is my reply to Monson, dated 29th July, 1893—" Dear Monson,—I have a letter from Liverpool this morning acknowledging receipt yesterday of a letter from you, dated 26th inst., containing, in respect of the full title of Mrs. Monson's interest in Hambrough's life, a notification that 'the insurance is to cover advances made at the request of Mr. C. Hambrough, and for his maintenance, extending over four years; also to cover liabilities incurred under the agreement in connection with the Hambrough estates.' This information is really nothing further than you gave me in the first instance, and, as I said in the letter I wrote you from Liverpool, is not nearly sufficient. It is far too vague for our directors to say whether Mrs. Monson has a legal insurable interest in Mr. Hambrough's life, particularly seeing that he is a minor, and I shall be glad if you can arrange to send to Liverpool by return of post details as to the advances, the amount for maintenance, and the nature and extent of the liabilities incurred by Mrs. Monson in the agreement aforesaid.—With kind regards, yours very truly, J. Wardle, local manager." I sent a copy of this letter to Scotland, and in reply received the letter from Monson, No. 41, dated 31st July, 1893. [Witness here read letter No. 41, which had been read by Mr. Comrie Thomson in cross-examining the previous witness, David Stewart.]

That letter speaks of an agreement between Hambrough and Mrs. Monson?—I never saw any such agreement. In my letter of 29th July I had said that the general statement of interest was not sufficient to enable me to proceed upon it. In this letter of 31st July Monson further states that they would require a policy for £26,000, which would have to be increased to £52,000 when Hambrough attained his majority, and that Mrs. Monson's interest amounted to £26,000. Monson enclosed in that letter a letter signed by Hambrough, with the remark that he presumed it would be taken as sufficient evidence of Mrs. Monson's interest. That letter is No. 42. [Witness here read letter No. 42, which had been read by Mr. Comrie Thomson in cross-examining the last witness, David Stewart.] The proposal, as

111

Alfred John Monson.

reduced from £50,000 to £26,000, and all the evidence of interest was put before our directors, with the result that we declined the proposal, because we were not satisfied as to the insurability of the interest even for the reduced sum of £26,000. Subsequently, we got a proposal for making the insurance £15,000, which was not proceeded with. I informed Monson that it must go off for the moment. The reason for not proceeding with this proposal was Monson's financial difficulties.

Cross-examined by Mr. COMRIE THOMSON—There were two proposals which did not proceed beyond medical examination. One of the proposals was in name of Agnes Maud Monson. I was aware that Monson had been adjudicated a bankrupt. I had more than one personal interview with Monson; I saw him in Leeds one day in July on his way from London to Glasgow.

Can you tell me whether the information given by Monson verbally and in writing amounted to this, that there were two objects in effecting the insurances—the one to cover advances made at Cecil Hambrough's request for his education and maintenance, and the other to cover liabilities incurred under an agreement in connection with the Hambrough estates. Were these two objects throughout represented to be the objects he desired the insurances effected for? —Yes.

Were you informed that an agreement had been, or was to be, immediately entered into whereby, when he came of age, Cecil Hambrough was to purchase for a large sum of money his father's life interest in the estate?—We were told that an arrangement was to be made, when he came of age, which would involve his finding the money. I knew that there was no money in the family, and that Major Hambrough, the father, had disposed of his life interest to the Eagle Insurance Company.

You knew that Monson had entered into an agreement to buy the interest from the insurance company for a sum amounting to between £40,000 and £50,000?—I know he had entered into an agreement, although he did not tell me the amount of money to be paid. That was before he was adjudicated bankrupt.

Re-examined by the SOLICITOR-GENERAL—Monson only told me in general conversation that he was going to take over Major Hambrough's interest; he never showed me any documents to show that he intended to purchase Major Hambrough's interest.

35. WILLIAM M. WISELY, examined by the SOLICITOR-GENERAL— I am secretary of the Glasgow branch of the Scottish Provident Institution, the head offices of which are in Edinburgh. [Shown No. 18.] This is a letter received at the head office on 11th July relating to an insurance on the life of another; it does not mention the name. I was informed later on that the proposal came from Mr. Monson. I was instructed by the head office to make inquiries, and, the proposal being a large one, I went down to Ardlamont on 19th July and saw

112

Evidence for Prosecution.

W. M. Wisely

Monson and Hambrough, with whom I discussed what the insurance was to be and its extent. Monson told me that the insurance was to be on Hambrough's life, and that it was to cover advances made to Mr. Hambrough. I understood at first that Monson was in some way a guardian of Mr. Hambrough, but at another meeting I was told by Monson that he was no longer a guardian. I communicated to the head office what passed at that meeting at Ardlamont. It is all contained in my letter. I understood Monson to have said something about being trustee for Hambrough; I cannot recollect his exact words. When I asked him afterwards at a subsequent meeting, he told me he was no longer a trustee. As a result of my interview with Monson at Ardlamont, I understood somehow or other that he was trustee of Mr. Hambrough; I had no possible source of information on that subject, except my verbal communications with Mr. Monson. He said to me that, with the advances in connection with the Hambrough estates and with the father, he would be a loser in the event of Cecil Hambrough's death to the extent of £49,000. The result of my interview was a proposal for £50,000. We had already sent him an " own-life " proposal form, but this proposal on the life of another required another form, and I arranged with him when I returned home to send him the appropriate form, which he got and filled up. The date was 21st July, 1893, and the amount was £50,000. The proposed insurance was by Mrs. Monson on the life of Windsor Dudley Cecil Hambrough. On our proposal forms there is a printed question to the effect—" State here or on the back of the proposal the nature of the interest in the life proposed to be insured." The answer given to that was—" To cover advances made and liabilities in connection with the Hambrough estates."

In a policy of this nature, before it is completed we require to be satisfied of the genuineness of the interest. It is also a practice to require reports from private friends with regard to the history and habits of the person proposing to be insured; in this case we got reports from six friends, one of them signed " E. M. Hiron." At the very first I had a meeting with Monson, and told him he would require to show the company the interest which he had in the life of the insured; it was at this meeting that he referred to his being the loser to the extent of £49,000 in the event of Hambrough's death. One of the six friends, a Mr. Houston, of Ventnor, Isle of Wight, gave a report with which we were not quite satisfied, and I said to Monson that it was strange that he should have replied in that way. Monson seemed surprised when I said that. All the explanation that he offered was that Mr. Houston must be making some mistake, that he must have written in reference to an uncle instead of the nephew. He said that it was probably our fault for writing the name Mr. Windsor D. C. Hambrough, the uncle being generally known as Mr. Windsor Hambrough, and the nephew as Mr. Cecil Hambrough. This conversation took place in Glasgow. As to his and Mrs. Monson's insurable interest, he said that we would be satisfied by his

Alfred John Monson.

solicitors; he did not say when. Our office was prepared to accept the proposal on condition that it was satisfied as to Mrs. Monson's insurable interest. That condition was not fulfilled, and the insurance was not completed. I had no conversation with Mr. Hambrough on the subject of the insurance, but a considerable part of my conversation with Monson took place in his presence.

[Shown No. 29.] This is a letter from Monson, dated 3rd August, 1893, by which the proposal for insurance on Mr. Hambrough's life was reduced from £50,000 to £10,000. We never got any evidence of the insurable interest to the extent of that reduced sum, and a policy was never considered even for that reduced extent. [Shown No. 30.] That is a letter written by me to Monson on 9th August, which ended the matter so far as our office is concerned.

Cross-examined by Mr. COMRIE THOMSON—On 9th August I wrote a letter to Monson stating that " we are willing to accept the £10,000 proposal for one year at £1 16s. 3d. per cent., subject to the statement by Mr. Hambrough as to the pecuniary interest Mrs. Monson has in his life being satisfactory, and which we have still to receive." That was the one thing necessary, and the payment of the first premium would have completed the transaction. On 9th August, the day before this young man's death, the position of matters with our office was that the contract was on the eve of completion; we were prepared to accept the £10,000 proposal, and had communicated the fact to Monson. By complying with the condition as to satisfying us with regard to Mrs. Monson's pecuniary interest and paying the first premium Mr. Hambrough's life might have been insured at once for £10,000. The death occurred before my letter to Monson on 9th August was received by him.

Look at the letter you wrote after your visit to Ardlamont on 19th July, 1893; do you see there that A. J. Monson seems to have stated to you that he was a trustee on the estate, not of Cecil, but of Dudley Hambrough? You understood that Monson was trustee for Dudley Hambrough, the father, Major Hambrough?—I understood that Monson was trustee somehow in connection with the estate of either the father or the son; I was dissatisfied as to the evidence. Monson did not tell me that he had purchased as trustee for Major Hambrough his life interest in the estates, but in some way or other he said that he was a trustee on the estate of Dudley, and through advances to Dudley he was a loser to the extent of some £49,000. He told me that Cecil Hambrough's father's life was not insurable, as his life interest was in the hands of his creditors. I understood that Cecil Hambrough was coming into some property on attaining his majority in May next year, but Monson did not specify what the property was; I was not so much concerned with that as I was to be satisfied if there were an insurable interest. Mr. Hambrough was present at my interview with Monson; there was perfect frankness, and Monson and Hambrough seemed to be on friendly terms.

I refer you to your letter dated 1st September, 1893; glance over

114

Evidence for Prosecution.

W. M. Wisely

it. Did you explain to the head office that much of the suspicion which appeared in the papers would be cleared up if all the circumstances of which you were aware were fully known?—I was of opinion that young Mr. Hambrough knew that the insurance was for the benefit of Mr. and Mrs. Monson; none of the arrangements had been hidden from Hambrough, but were spoken of quite openly. I believed that the Monsons would be losers financially by young Hambrough's death. [Shown No. 21.] The name of one of two intimate friends is E. M. Hiron, Ardlamont House; the letter is written apparently in Mrs. Monson's handwriting, and the name is in the same hand. After the name I see two words written in pencil; they are " butler here."

Who did that?—The words were written either in our Glasgow office or in the Edinburgh office. They were not written by Mrs. Monson; it is false to say that the E. M. Hiron so described in the proposal is a butler. Mr. Monson's reason for the proposed policy being in his wife's name was that she had a separate estate. He did not tell me that he had been adjudicated a bankrupt. He seemed to know quite well that young Hambrough being a minor could not assign a policy on his own life. £10,000 is my limit; the rule is that I do not take a bigger risk on my own shoulders; but there may be re-insurance. Monson told me that the young man had been living with him and his wife for some time, and that he was somehow or other under his charge.

Re-examined by the SOLICITOR-GENERAL—Would you be kind enough to tell us what you mean when you say that this insurance for £10,000 was on the eve of completion?—We were prepared to accept the £10,000 proposal if sufficient proof of interest were given us; if this were given the risk would have been on the moment the premium was paid, but I did not know whether such interest existed or whether it could be proved. I was at one time of opinion that certain impressions of suspicion would be removed if facts known to me of what had passed were disclosed. The reports in the papers after the death were suspicious, but I thought that the suspicion would be removed if what I had been led to understand and what others did not know were disclosed.

What had you been led to understand, what class of facts?— What had passed in course of conversation, for example, that Mrs. Monson had an interest to the extent of £10,000 in Hambrough's life, supposing that to be true. I did not know at that time that there were separate insurances to the extent of £20,000; I knew of other insurances, but not the amount. Monson seemed to understand from the first that the policy taken on Hambrough's life could not be assigned by him, being a minor.

What did he say which leads you to make that statement?—I do not know that he said anything. Monson's first proposal was that Mrs. Monson should in her own name insure the life of Cecil Hambrough. Hambrough could not have insured his own life without

115

Alfred John Monson.

W. M. Wisely

his father's consent, but in course of conversation Monson said that the father's consent could be got. Monson said that the insurance was being taken out by Agnes Maud Monson, who had a separate estate, as a protection against Mr. Hambrough's death before he attained the age of twenty-one. I somehow understood that the advances to Mr. Hambrough were not necessarily all Mrs. Monson's, but that some had been made by Monson; I did not know at the time that Monson was an undischarged bankrupt. They wrote from the head office to ask whether Monson said he was a trustee to the father, the grandfather, or the son, but I could not say. I had no information with regard to the relations between Monson and the Hambrough estates and the advances made by him, except what I derived from my conversation with Monson on 19th July. As a result of what passed, my view was that Monson was a trustee on the estate of Mr. Windsor Hambrough, and that through advances on the estate and to Mr. Cecil Hambrough Monson was a loser to the extent of some £49,000. Cecil Hambrough was present for a considerable time during our conversation, and I understand he heard the conversation which gave me the impression which I have just explained. I understood Monson to say that Cecil Hambrough was the only child of his father till last year, when another son was born. All my knowledge of the subject was derived from what Monson told me that day. At that time I was led to understand from something that Monson said that the trustees were considering, and had almost fixed on, the purchase of Ardlamont estate for Cecil Hambrough.

Re-cross-examined by Mr. COMRIE THOMSON—[Shown No. 57.] This proposal was written on the wrong form; the name of the person proposed for the insurance is Cecil Dudley Hambrough, and it is signed by him. This proposal was not entertained by us. The proposal that was entertained was one by Mrs. Monson.

Does that not recall to you the fact that the question of Cecil's being a minor and his incapacity of assigning was in your mind, and was therefore made the subject of conversation between you and Monson?—Yes; the reason for its having escaped my mind was that that first form was thrown aside. In the proposal signed by Cecil in answer to the question, "How many children have they?" there are five children certified. My letter was written on 19th July; this proposal was signed on the following day, and it shows that I was quite under a misapprehension as to the members of Hambrough's family. It was stated to me by Monson that Cecil Hambrough had insured this year at the ordinary rates for £2000 with the British Empire.

Re-examined by the SOLICITOR-GENERAL—No. 19 is a letter written by Mr. Monson; the first words in it are—" I enclose the form of proposal duly filled up and signed by Cecil Hambrough." The proposal form was not enclosed, and I arrived at Ardlamont on 19th July before the letter was posted. After I was at Ardlamont the letter

Evidence for Prosecution.

came into my possession, and formed one of the documents between my office and Monson relating to the insurance.

By the LORD JUSTICE-CLERK—The letter was not completed by the time I got to Ardlamont.

By the SOLICITOR-GENERAL—The letter was posted after I left Ardlamont. In conversation with Mr. Monson at Ardlamont I discovered that the proposal Cecil filled up was not the proper one. The document containing the reference came into my possession on 20th or 21st July; the date of my conversation with Monson was 19th July.

By the LORD JUSTICE-CLERK—When I went to Ardlamont it was the erroneous proposal which I saw, and I went away without the letter and the first proposal. I intimated that there must be a proposal in stated form, and on getting back to Glasgow on 19th July I despatched the proper form.

36. JAMES HANKS LOCHING, examined by the SOLICITOR-GENERAL—I am clerk to C. F. Kemp, Ford & Co., chartered accountants, 73 Lombard Street, London, the firm which attended to matters connected with the bankruptcy of Mr. Monson, the official date of which was 24th August, 1892. Mr. C. R. Tennant, a partner of the firm, was appointed trustee and instructed me to take charge of the details connected with the bankruptcy. We went through the state of affairs made up by the bankrupt and found the amount of recoverable assets to be about £25 5s. This asset was the only asset we could discover, and consisted of a claim by Monson upon a certain gentleman for tutoring his son. The liabilities amounted in all to £2300, and consisted of claims of small amounts, debts for food supplied for household purposes, &c., and two money loans. Monson had a bank account in the County, with half a crown to his credit in it. Monson gave us his assistance as to information about his estate. The present state of affairs is that the bankruptcy remains where it was.

Cross-examined by Mr. COMRIE THOMSON—At the first meeting of creditors the list of proofs, that is, claims subject to affidavit, amounted to £417, and that amount was admitted by the Court. The statement was made up by the bankrupt himself, and brings out an apparent surplus of £600 of assets; the liabilities are stated at £48,654. The claim of £43,827, made by the Eagle Insurance Company is part of the liabilities. It was put down by the bankrupt himself as a contingent liability; I do not recollect it having been claimed by the company, and I cannot say whether they claim or not. The amount of liabilities, including this claim of £43,000, is £48,000, and the assets are £3557 3s. 2d. The surplus is shown by putting down £2900 of the assets to rank for dividend, and there is a surplus of £626 put down in the statement. The bankrupt said he had a claim against the Hambrough estates, but it was not set down in his state of affairs; so far as I can recollect,

117

Alfred John Monson.

it was an understanding that he should be paid, when young Hambrough came of age, for his board and education. So far as I can recollect, Monson told me that he had advanced some money to Hambrough's father, but I do not know the amount; it might have been a couple of thousands, but I cannot say for certain. It has not been recovered.

Re-examined by the SOLICITOR-GENERAL—No advance to Major Hambrough was put down as an asset in the statement. The amount of the assets set down by the bankrupt is £3625, made out, in the statement, as being the money that fully secured creditors would receive; we found that we could not realise anything of that; we considered it a mere paper entry. The liability to the Eagle Insurance Company is put down by the bankrupt as being only a contingent claim; it is not stated as a debt in bringing out the balance which he represents in his statement of affairs.

37. WALTER RAMSDEN, examined by the SOLICITOR-GENERAL— I am a partner of the firm of Carter, Ramsden & Carter, solicitors, Leeds. I was at one time solicitor to Mrs. Monson and to the Day family, of which she is a member. The Day family were interested in the estate of their maternal grandfather, Mr. Buckley, under his will. Mrs. Monson's share in the estate of her grandfather amounts to £910, which only comes into her enjoyment on the death of her mother, Mrs. Day, and may be increased by the death of any of Mrs. Monson's brothers and sisters. While I was acting as solicitor for Mrs. Monson I ascertained that her interests had been mortgaged to the extent of £760. Whilst acting as agent and endeavouring to effect a further loan on Mrs. Monson's interests, I found that the interests of her brothers and sisters were also mortgaged, and endeavoured to consolidate the mortgages of the different members of the family in order to reduce the interest and raise additional capital for the family generally. Looking to the amount of the estate and the amount of the mortgages, so far as Mrs. Monson was concerned, I found no margin for a loan unless the others assisted her. So far as individual instructions were concerned they were given to me by Mr. Monson, although relating to Mrs. Monson and the Day family.

Cross-examined by Mr. COMRIE THOMSON—My partner, Mr. Carter, was the person who attended solely to the transactions between Mr. Monson and Mr. Hambrough. He is here.

38. ARTHUR MACDONALD BLAIR, examined by the SOLICITOR-GENERAL—I am solicitor to the Lancashire and Yorkshire Reversionary Interest Company, and in 1890 I carried through a reversionary mortgage for £600, partially or wholly to Mrs. Monson, on the death of her mother, on her interest in her grandfather's estate. My recollection is that Mrs. Monson's interest would have an ultimate value of about £900, which was liable to be increased by

118

Evidence for Prosecution.

A. M. Blair

the death of some of her brothers or sisters during her mother's lifetime. It was contingent on her surviving her mother, so we insured Mrs. Monson's life against her mother's. [Shown No. 219.] That is a copy of the mortgage deed. The £600 was advanced; there was a good deal of difficulty in getting the interest, and it has ceased to be paid since September, 1892. The amount due on the mortgage at September last was £64 11s. 1d. The parties to the mortgage were Mr. and Mrs. Monson, Mrs. Day, and the company. I acted as solicitor for the company in a suit which they brought to recover the amount of £64 11s. 1d. due as interest. Mrs. Day was the only defendant, and we selected her because she was substantial and good for the money. The verdict was for the defendant, and we have been unable to recover anything from Mrs. Day under the mortgage.

Cross-examined by Mr. COMRIE THOMSON—The mortgage purports to assign the whole reversion of Mrs. Monson's interests in her grandfather's estate; it does not include her whole separate estate wherever situated. She may have other separate estate, but I do not know.

Re-examined—Mrs. Monson, as one of the assigning parties, is bound by the mortgage if she had any other separate estate that would be liable to the company for the mortgage, but as yet we have not discovered any separate estate from which we expect payment.

39. HERBERT KIDSON, examined by the SOLICITOR-GENERAL— I am secretary of the Lancashire and Yorkshire Reversionary Interest Company, Manchester. In September, 1890, a mortgage was entered into between our company and Mr. and Mrs. Monson and Mrs. Day for £600, the security offered being a contingent reversion, payable on the death of Mrs. Day, of the value of about £900. To borrow on a contingent reversion is more expensive than to borrow upon estate in enjoyment or in possession.

Cross-examined by Mr. COMRIE THOMSON—[Shown No. 62 of Crown productions.] In October, 1892, I got a letter from Mrs. Monson, in which she says that her husband was laid up in bed, and that she was writing on his behalf. She goes on to make a statement about a young gentleman living with them who comes into £200,000 when he comes of age in eighteen months, and says that his father, having got through all his life interest, and having heavily mortgaged the same, has had an absolute foreclosure made against him. She then goes on to state that her husband has got an opinion to the effect that the law provides that if a minor arranges with a person to supply him with the means to obtain the necessaries of life suitable to his position, the minor can enter into a contract to secure the repayment of any money employed to obtain such means, and that such a contract is binding, although the contractor be a minor. Then she asks our company, in these circum-

119

Alfred John Monson.

stances, to make an advance of £500 a year for eighteen months, until the minor comes of age, saying that she will refer us to solicitors for the title, &c. I answered this letter on 4th November, 1892, saying that our directors were willing to entertain the proposal on being satisfied as to security, and subject to the practicability of the scheme. I enclosed a proposal form. On 7th November I wrote, saying that we were unable to do this business, because we were advised by our solicitor that, as it was a minor's contract, it required the father's consent.

Re-examined by the SOLICITOR-GENERAL—I am not aware that my company took the opinion of counsel as to whether the authority of the Court of Chancery could be got for such a transaction; I do not think that it went that length. Mr. and Mrs. Monson sent me a document purporting to be an application for the authority of the Court of Chancery, but they never told me that they had actually applied to the Court of Chancery.

40. THOMAS JAMES BROOKS, examined by Mr. STRACHAN—I am a pawnbroker, 79 Wardour Street, London. [Shown Nos. 220 and 225.] No. 220 is a pawn ticket issued by me in favour of Mrs. J. Monson, and dated 21st November, 1892; the amount advanced was 12s. It was a renewal of a previous ticket which was granted on 21st November, 1891. No. 225 is a letter from Mrs. John Monson, enclosing 3s. for renewal of a previous ticket.

41. THOMAS NEWSTEAD, examined by Mr. STRACHAN—I am an assistant pawnbroker, 39 Strand, London. No. 222 is a pawn ticket for £8 advanced on some articles of jewellery to Mrs. Morrison, Ardlamont House, Argyllshire, on 2nd July, 1893. It was a renewal of a previous ticket. No. 224 is a letter to Mr. Vaughan from Mrs. Morrison, Ardlamont House, Argyllshire, enclosing £1 12s. 2d. for a renewal of a ticket dated 12th July, 1893. No. 221 is another ticket, dated 16th September, 1891, in favour of Mr. Rutter, for twelve knives and forks and two spoons, on which 10s. had been advanced. These articles were never redeemed, and were sold; I do not know who Mr. Rutter is.

42. JOHN LEWENDEN, examined by Mr. STRACHAN—I am an assistant pawnbroker, 39 Strand, London. The pawn ticket No. 221 is in my handwriting.

43. WILLIAM THOMAS MIDDLETON, examined by Mr. STRACHAN—I am a pawnbroker, 143 Briggate, Leeds. No. 223 is a pawn ticket granted by me in favour of Alice Morrison, Barr Street, Harrogate, dated 24th October, 1892, for two gold dress rings; the amount advanced was 10s. No. 226 is a pawn ticket in favour of Agnes Morrison, Woodlands House, Harrogate, for £4 advanced on two silver cups and some other articles. These articles were pawned on 5th July, 1892, and the ticket was renewed on 17th January, 1893, and again on 17th July, 1893.

Evidence for Prosecution.

44. BERESFORD LOFTUS TOTTENHAM, examined by the SOLICITOR-GENERAL—I am thirty-four years of age, and was at one time a lieutenant in the 10th Hussars. I afterwards served in the Turkish army under Baker Pasha, and also during the Cretan insurrection. At present I am a financial agent carrying on business under the name of Kempton & Co., 8 Delahaye Street, London. Four years ago I was introduced to Monson by a mutual friend, but had no business transactions with him at first. My acquaintance with Monson continued down to the date of his arrest. No. 77 is a fragment of a letter from Mr. Monson received by me; the first line is a broken sentence—" We can only just manage on the £40, because Hambrough wants £10 out of it." I cannot tell the date of this letter. No. 78 is a letter from Monson to me, dated Riseley Hall, Monday, and commences—" We have been in an awful fix to get the cheque cashed." That would be just before they left Riseley Hall to go to Ardlamont about the end of June. No. 80 is a letter from Monson to me, dated Ardlamont, 20th May; it commences—" I hope you posted the £25 on Saturday or to-day. I was bound to make a payment of £15 for coal a very short time before that." No. 89 is a letter from Monson to me, undated, commencing—" We are to settle re Ardlamont to-morrow." So far as the letters produced are from me, there are copies of them in my letter-book. With regard to the other letters shown to me, both Mr. and Mrs. Monson's letters are in the handwriting of the person they profess to be written by. [Witness was shown a number of letters and telegrams, which he identified as correspondence between himself and the Monsons and Hambrough.]

The correspondence I have referred to begins in 1893, but before that, on 9th January, 1893, Mrs. Monson had recovered judgment against Cecil Hambrough for £800 for board and lodging and education. The case was undefended, and I was asked by Mrs. Monson to purchase the judgment, which I did on 9th February, 1893, giving her £200 or £220 for it. Shortly after that an arrangement was made with Cecil Hambrough, whereby I was to make him a regular allowance of £5 a week for the present. The arrangement was made through Monson, but Cecil Hambrough himself spoke to me about it. This arrangement was made owing to Monson's difficulties and his inability to support Mr. Hambrough in the way he had been doing. At that time, so far as I am aware, Monson had no means of livelihood at all of his own, except what he could earn as an army tutor. He was living at Riseley Hall, near Ripley, Yorkshire, and his only other pupil about that time was a Mr. Swinburne. In the beginning of 1893 there was no pupil there at all except Cecil; I do not know when Mr. Swinburne came, but I think it was about that time. When the Monsons left for Ardlamont I did the necessary financing to enable them to get there. You may take it that the letters shown are applications for

Alfred John Monson.

B. L. Tottenham

money, and that when they were made I sent money. So far as I know, except for the money I sent, the Monsons had no means of carrying on an establishment. I first became aware of the suggestion about the purchase of Ardlamont on the occasion of my first visit there in July. Monson, Hambrough, and I had a discussion about it; I thought that the discussion related to a part purchase. The estate was to be bought by Mrs. Monson in trust for Cecil, but, so far as I am aware, Mrs. Monson had no available means at that time. There is a letter from Monson to me, dated 23rd May. [Shown No. 81.] It reads—"The Lancashire and Yorkshire Reversion Company are bothering for their interest due from Mrs. M. on her reversion. The amount of loan is £600 at 8 per cent. per annum. Can you arrange to send them a line and ask them if they will give you a fortnight to arrange the transfer? The address is H. Kidson, secretary, St. James Square, Manchester." That sum was due by Mrs. Monson on a mortgage granted over her separate estate. There is another letter from Monson to me, which reads—"There are swarms of rabbits and sea birds, but I have not a gun yet. Uncle is taking care of two. Can you manage to send a cheque to get them out?" That means that the guns were in pawn. I did not relieve them.

There is another letter, as follows:—"Please ask Stocks to draw up a form of contract for Mrs. Monson to sign to the following effect:—Whereas Mrs. Monson has entered into contract for the purchase of certain estates; and whereas it is agreed that the said purchase is to be made by Mrs. Monson on behalf of W. D. C. H., as the said Mrs. M. does hereby admit; and then Mrs. Monson must covenant to convey the said contract, with all benefits thereunder, to W. D. C. H. on his attaining his majority." Stocks is a solicitor in my employment. At page 46 of my letter-book I see a letter from me to Monson, dated 24th July—"Yours to hand. You seem to have made a good bargain *re* Ardlamont. Cecil had better write me a letter requesting me to pay £250 deposit." That refers to the purchase of Ardlamont, and the bargain was that Monson was negotiating for the purchase of the estate for the matter of £50,000, and I meant in my letter to say that I thought he had got an offer of the estate at a good price. The letter on page 48 is undated, and is probably the letter to which mine of 24th July is an answer —"Ardlamont House, Argyllshire. Dear Tot,—I have just returned home, and have seen the agents to-day and fully discussed the question of the purchase here. The existing mortgage on the property is £37,000 at 4 per cent. The interest has always been paid regularly. The mortgagees are an insurance company, and the Lamonts having policies with them they do not wish to disturb the investment. I was asked to make an offer. I therefore said I thought £45,000 a good price, as I was sure the rentals would have to be reduced, &c. They would not, or pretended not, to consider

122

Evidence for Prosecution.

B. L. Tottenham

such an offer. However, they eventually agreed to accept £48,000. They say they only do this because Major Lamont is so anxious to be rid of the property before he starts for India, and their instructions from him are to close with the best offer they can get, and it appears they have spent a lot of money in advertising and trying to sell, but they never had a single offer. They are willing to accept £250 as a deposit, on the contract being signed by Mrs. Monson, to be limited to June, 1894. The contract is now being drawn, and will be ready in the course of a week or so. They have a power of attorney to act for Major Lamont, and the contract will be drawn in their name as attorney. I have told C. that the price is £50,000 —£1000 each for division; thus he will have to raise £13,000 to enable him to complete next year." I took that as an intimation that an agreement had been entered into for the purchase. The deposit of £250, which, as I suggested in my letter of 24th July, Hambrough should ask me to make, was to be a deposit towards the price of Ardlamont. Hambrough did write me a letter about the deposit, but I do not see it here, and I understand that it has not been recovered.

Looking at page 32 of my letter-book, I see that on 28th July I wrote—" Enclosed please find cheque for £10. Very glad to hear from M. that medical examinations are going on so satisfactory. The cheque for deposit re Ardlamont you will receive on Monday morning." Following on this I wrote—" My dear Cecil,—Enclosed you will find a cheque for £250, to enable you to pay deposit for the purchase of Ardlamont estate. I have dated the cheque 10th, because, as you know, I have an awful lot of irons in the fire, and the oof don't always turn up exactly when expected." By " oof " I mean money. There is an undated letter from Monson to me— " Dear Tot,—We are to settle re Ardlamont to-morrow (Tuesday) morning at Edinburgh. I will ask the contract to be dated 10th August, and we shall have to hand it over to-morrow, so that the date in cheque and contract will be the same. Have you forgotten about the policy?—I am only waiting your instructions. It is ready to take up when you want it." The date of this letter would be about 7th August. When I sent the cheque for £250 I sent it, as stated in my letter, to be applied to paying a deposit for Ardlamont. After I had sent the cheque I thought I was parting with a large sum of money without any very sufficient proof of what the position of the negotiations were, and so I called on my solicitor, Mr. Gordon, and he wrote a letter to the bank requesting them not to pay the cheque. The cheque was on my account in the Bank of England. When the cheque was presented at the Bank of England it was refused. It had been paid at the Royal Bank of Scotland, Tighnabruaich, who are suing me for it. On page 23 of my letter-book I find a letter from Cecil Hambrough

Alfred John Monson.

to me—" Thanks very much for cheque for £250; do you think you could manage £10?"

I knew that the rent of Ardlamont is £450, payable half-yearly, one half-year's rent being payable on 1st August. In talking over the purchase of the estate with Mr. Monson, it was in contemplation that the purchase should supersede the necessity for paying the rent, that the rent would not be charged if a purchase were effected.

On 10th August I received a telegram from Monson—" Cecil had serious gun accident. Come up at once." I went to Ardlamont, arriving there on the 12th, and got an account from Monson of how the mishap had occurred. He told me that he and Cecil and Scott had been out shooting in the wood, that he heard a shot and called out—" What have you got?" Getting no answer, he went in the direction of the shot, and found Cecil lying alongside the ditch with the gun beside him. The morning on which I arrived at Ardlamont Monson and I had a conversation about insurances, and he told me that he had insurances for £8000, I think. Afterwards he said the amount was £10,000, and afterwards £20,000. I had been out of pocket by advancing money to the establishment for some time, and I said to Monson that I wished I had never heard the name of Hambrough, or something to that effect, and Monson said that it would be all right for me, and that he would make up what I should have got from Hambrough out of these policies if they were paid. I asked him what sort of assignments he had of the policies, and on the morning of the 13th he showed me a copy of the assignment. No. 14 is a copy of the assignment in my own handwriting; the original was in Hambrough's writing, and I made a copy on board the steamer " Iona " on my way to Glasgow with Monson, who was taking the body to Ventnor. After the funeral we had an interview with the manager of the New York Insurance Company in Glasgow, with the object of arranging about the payment of the policies. I left the copy of the letter (No. 14) with Mr. M'Lean, the manager of the insurance company, by mistake.

By the LORD JUSTICE-CLERK—I got the paper I made the copy of the letter upon on board the steamer " Iona." Monson had the principal with him, and, having shown it to me, I made this copy upon the steamer. The paper bears the heading " Royal Route Steamer ' Iona.' "

Examination continued—I do not know what became of the principal from which this copy is taken. On page 54 of the print of documents there is a letter in which Monson says—" I have arranged with Mr. Tottenham to have the cheque for £250 paid on presentation any day after Monday. He says it would be necessary for him to call at the Bank of England to verify the signature as a matter of form and authorise payment. Mr. Tottenham says he will not be in London before Monday." There was no necessity for my calling at the bank to verify my signature, and no such

124

Evidence for Prosecution.

arrangement was made. I disputed my liability on the cheque. At the bottom of page 53 of the print there is a letter from Monson to a man named Dugald Kerr—" I received your kind note, also a wire, as to cheque. It is only a matter of proof of signature. Before receiving your letter there was a cheque drawn for the cost of the carriage of the coffin to Ventnor, £36 12s., and one to Major Hambrough for £10. I will pay in £1000 on my return." So far as I know, Monson had no means of paying in £1000, nor the means of raising such a sum.

What was the total amount of your advances to Cecil Hambrough from the time you began financing him until his death?—Well, I suppose about £300, not including the amount of the cheque, which would bring it up to £550.

Cross-examined by Mr. COMRIE THOMSON—Before the time I have been talking about I had met Major Hambrough, Cecil's father. I was introduced to him about the middle of 1890 by Mr. Rutter, a financial agent. I discovered that the Major's life interest in his estates were mortgaged to the Eagle Insurance Office. I found that he was anxious to transfer the mortgages at a lower rate of interest and get some more money on the security. I ultimately proceeded to negotiate a financial arrangement in connection with Major Hambrough's estates, and made myself acquainted with the state of his affairs. I attempted to get further policies on his life, and in that connection I was introduced by Mr. Rutter to a Dr. Hambleton, who arranged with me that an effort should be made to get the Major into such a state of health that the insurance office would accept him. I agreed to find the money for the purpose. I did so, giving the Major £7 a week and the doctor £3. I got an equitable mortgage as a security for that. The Major had nothing whatever. The Major subsequently gave me a mortgage over his assets for £1000 and another for £1500. They are not paid yet. These mortgages represented money advanced by me to him with a bonus. The £1500 was for money advanced, and the £1000 was a general security to cover future advances. The £1000 was to some extent for commission. There were also promissory notes as collateral security to the mortgage. The Major also gave me power of attorney, but that was nothing. In consequence of my transactions with Major Hambrough I was out of pocket to the extent of about £1000. I was first introduced to Monson about three or four years ago. That was in 1890. I was only introduced to him casually at that time, and later on found that he required my assistance with regard to some colliery property in Yorkshire in which he said his wife had an interest. It was through me that Monson and young Hambrough were brought together. Major Hambrough expressed to me a desire that Cecil should be got on in order to prepare him to get into the army; he said that he was unable to educate him himself, and that

125

Alfred John Monson.

B. L. Tottenham

the boy's mother was desirous of getting him into the Guards. I spoke to Monson on the subject, and he agreed to take the boy and educate him until he should either go into the army or come of age. The terms agreed on were that the Major deferred payment until the boy came of age. The next time he was in town I introduced Monson to Major Hambrough and his son, and they fixed the terms upon which Monson was to take charge of the boy and conduct his tuition.

[Shown No. 104.] That is a letter in Cecil Hambrough's handwriting, dated 20th April, 1893, signed by him, and addressed to Mrs. Monson. It contains these words—" Tottenham has consented to find the money as soon as we have decided to take it," and then a little further on, " I had a talk with Tottenham last night. He has quite made up his mind to do what I asked him to do; so Monson and myself are going up by the night train to Scotland to-morrow." That was on the occasion of their going to Ardlamont. The two statements of fact with reference to myself are quite true; I had already arranged to give Cecil Hambrough £5 a week, and the arrangement referred to in this letter is that I agreed to increase the allowance to £10 a week, the understanding being that I was to be paid on his coming of age. The arrangement was not put into writing. At the time the Ardlamont lease was entered into I had arranged to provide funds sufficient to enable Mr. Hambrough to meet the expenses of travelling from Yorkshire to Argyllshire. I had said that I would supply him with money to a reasonable amount until he attained his majority, but no definite amount was necessary. I reckoned that the cash payments necessary to carry on an establishment like that would not be very large. At this time there was no talk of the purchase of Ardlamont; ultimately it was talked of, and I was willing to provide a deposit. I was prepared to go the length of £1000 in the way of an advance to Cecil in the interval between that time and his coming of age. My arrangement with him was £10 a week, but, of course, if there had been anything special outside that I should have gratified him, so far as my own means would allow. I had no more than Cecil's word that he would repay me. He had agreed to give me what money was owing me by his father and certain sums in consideration of my having kept him going; I calculated that the amount he would repay me when he came of age would be, in all, about £4000. As a security for the advances to both the father and the son I proposed that a policy for about £5000 in the Reliance Office should be effected on Cecil's life.

In the letter from Monson asking for the £250 cheque read by the Solicitor-General, £50,000 is the sum mentioned as the price of the estate, and it is explained that a certain amount of the price would rest with the insurance companies.

It was between five and six o'clock in the evening of 10th

Evidence for Prosecution.

B. L. Tottenham

August that I received the telegram which first intimated to me the accident to Mr. Hambrough. It was about eleven o'clock in the morning of the same day that I made the stoppage of the £250 cheque. On 9th August I wrote the following letter to Mr. Jones:—" 8 Delahaye Street. Dear Mr. Jones,—I really don't know why I should have made any mystery to-day. The matter is very simple. You are aware I am financing young Mr. Hambrough. Well, I have promised to cover for him a £250 cheque which he has given on account of the rent of his Scotch shooting. Thus you understand why I am pushed, and why I am open to pay for accommodation. I have deferred the matter till to-morrow evening to avoid (if possible) a visit to Edwards & Co. Thus, if you can pull through something during the day I shall be in your debt to an extent that only a good matter of business will wipe out.— Yours very truly, M. Tottenham." At the time of writing that letter I was not in easy command of money. As I have mentioned, I consulted Mr. Gordon, and was not quite satisfied with the arrangement that was being made; this was one of my reasons for proceeding to stop the cheque; if I had been flush of money I would have been able to chance it. Then shortly after this I got a telegram announcing the death of Hambrough. A cheque was sent off upon 3rd August, post-dated the 10th, and receipt was acknowledged by a letter dated 7th August. I was at Ardlamont a fortnight before the accident. I had talked over financial arrangements with Cecil, and also about the insurance policy.

Between 1890 and the time we are speaking of I had been endeavouring to arrange an increased loan for the Major. The policies on his life were at a high rate of premium, and I wished to get him into such a state of health that the company would take him at a lower rate. We proposed to drop the existing policies and to receive the surrender values, which would amount to about £5000 or £6000, and then insure at a lower rate for a larger amount. The benefit of that scheme would have been that the Major would have paid off the Eagle Insurance Company and would have had a surplus left for himself. I was unable to carry through that scheme, because the Major could not pass the medicals. Monson then tried it but failed. I am aware that Mrs. Monson made certain deposits in the Eagle Deposit Company, that there were negotiations prior to the time when the Eagle Company foreclosed, and that the Eagle Company ultimately foreclosed, and the foreclosure was made absolute. I dropped the scheme at that time. To my personal knowledge Mr. Monson was negotiating for a purchase of Major Hambrough's life interest from the company. It was arranged that the purchase from the Eagle Company was to be in name of Mrs. Monson, and it was in connection with that that certain deposits were to be made. But Monson was in the same difficulty as I had been—the Major's was not an insurable life. I

127

Alfred John Monson.

B. L. Tottenham

know that Monson started another scheme, namely, of insuring Cecil's life instead of his father's, but I do not know the details. It was an important element that after the young man came of age the father and son would terminate the entail, and in that way the land would be held by the son in fee-simple. In the letter of 30th May Monson says—" I have thought over carefully what you said in your letter about the disentailing of Pipewell Hall estate. Of course, by this means Cecil would personally be debarred from any interest whatever in the Pipewell estate, but if we carried out the proposed scheme to purchase Dudley's life interest from the Eagle for Cecil, he (Cecil) would, of course, have his father's life interest in the Pipewell estate, as well as the other life interests." Pipewell estate was the estate in which the Major was interested. The scheme was that the son was to get his father's life interest in the estate.

On 13th May, 1893, I wrote to Cecil—" Herewith cheque for £40, just to go on with. I conclude the moving job can be financed on that, and until the next week am short, as have to keep a balance at the Bank of England, or they give you notice to close the account. Next week a further remittance shall be sent. I have made the cheque payable to you for facility in cashing, but naturally I don't debit you with this ' oof,' but look on it as a payment made on the general account of the show." This shows that the Monson establishment was in difficulties, and the cheque for £40 was in addition to the weekly allowance I was making. The statement in my letter to Mr. Jones to the effect that I was financing young Hambrough is true. I know Mr. Jerningham; he is not a financial agent, he has no profession, but is living in expectation of succeeding to a considerable property. No. 97 is a letter from Cecil Hambrough to me—" I have to go to town to-morrow to see Richards with Jerningham." Richards is the solicitor of the Eagle Insurance Company. The letter continues— " I should be much obliged if you could post me a cheque on receipt of this, to the Metropole, as the journey will clear me clean out of cash. I have heard from Richards. He says his directors will be quite agreeable to the proposal. You may be sure I shall never forget your having helped me when I come of age." I was aware that Jerningham was assisting in carrying out this arrangement; he was acting as a friend of Cecil's. Monson, Cecil, and I on the one side, and Major Hambrough, Mr. Prince, and Dr. Hambleton on the other side, were trying to get the contract for the purchase of Major Hambrough's life interest in the estates and the insurance; there were two parties competing for the contract. Mr. Prince is Major Hambrough's solicitor. The price asked was about £40,000. The arrangement involved as part of it the re-insurance of the father's life or the insurance of the son's for about £50,000, but it was found that Major Hambrough's health was such that no com-

128

Evidence for Prosecution.

B. L. Tottenham

pany would insure it. If we had got the contract I was willing to pay the deposit and the money.

Letter No. 90 from Monson to me contains this passage—'' He (that is, Cecil) would be in possession when he came of age of an income of £2700 from Ardlamont, £4300 from Hambrough, making an annual income of £7000, with a further contingency of £1000, besides £1000 from the shooting of Ardlamont.'' This was the prospect if the contract with reference to the Hambrough estates and the purchase of Ardlamont were carried out.

And it was of vital and essential importance that the young man should survive twenty-one years of age?—Yes. On 8th August I wrote to Cecil—'' Your two notes to hand. I consider it very important that you should call upon the Reliance Company as soon as possible, otherwise the case will be crabbed.'' In the insurance world '' crabbed '' means spoilt. I wished Cecil to insure his life for £5000 with the Reliance Company to cover advances made by me to him and to his father. That insurance was not carried out. A proposal was made to me that Monson and Hambrough should go to Africa, and I wrote a letter pointing out that they must find themselves in Port Natal at a certain time in order that Cecil might sign any necessary deeds connected with his coming of age that might be sent out to him.

In the course of these interviews and negotiations which you had with Monson are you aware that he was quite alive to the fact that a minor could not legally assign a policy of assurance without the consent of his guardian?—I think anybody knows that; I have no doubt Monson did. There was some reference to the matter on the morning of my arrival at Ardlamont after Hambrough's death, but it is such a long time ago that I do not remember what the conversation was; I gave an account of it in my precognition.

I am afraid the Crown will not let me see your precognition. Was something said about Mrs. Monson making a proposal for an insurance upon the life of Cecil—that the proposal be made by Mrs. Monson, and that the policy be made out in her favour?—No; Monson seemed to be under the impression that the assignment he had from Cecil would not operate. After the funeral I made the claim for the insurance on behalf of Mrs. Monson.

Why did you do that, having been told by Monson that the assignment was not good? I had arranged with Monson that if I could get the money paid I was to get my £4000 out of it. I thought I might possibly get the money paid by '' bluffing '' the insurance office.

Re-examined by the SOLICITOR-GENERAL—The collieries in which Mrs. Monson was interested were the Mount Osborne Collieries in Yorkshire. They had been held by Mr. Day, Mrs. Monson's father. They were mortgaged, and Mrs. Monson asked me to go to Yorkshire and see if I could find out any way of raising money. I did

K

Alfred John Monson.

B. L. Tottenham

so, and endeavoured to arrange with the mortgagees terms on which they would release these collieries, but I was unsuccessful, and they are still held by the mortgagees. Consequently they are not available as a means of raising money.

I cannot tell the exact date when Cecil Hambrough went to stay with the Monsons; I did not make the arrangements. At that time Monson was staying at a place called Woodlands, near Harrogate. I introduced Monson to Hambrough in 1891, about the month of August. My financing of Cecil began in 1893. I cannot say from what source Cecil Hambrough got his finances between the autumn of 1891 and the time when I began to finance him in 1893. I was not in any way connected with the raising of a sum of money by Monson upon a mortgage by Major Hambrough. I was aware that the Eagle Insurance Company had foreclosed and become the absolute owners of Major Hambrough's life interest; the only way of acquiring it was by purchasing from them. So far as I am personally concerned, the last attempt to purchase Major Hambrough's life interest from the Eagle Insurance Company was shortly after I had introduced Monson to Cecil Hambrough; after that attempt I abandoned the project. I was aware two or three months before Cecil's death that the Eagle Company had decided to transfer the life interest to the friends of Major Hambrough, and not to Mr. Monson.

I heard of the purchase of the yacht on my visit to Ardlamont before the death, when we had a talk about it. Assuming that Monson bought the yacht himself for £1200, I cannot say where the money would come from. After the death I had a conversation at Ardlamont with Monson as to the assignation of the insurance policy, and Monson showed me a document purporting to be an assignation. He did not give me any reason why he had taken that assignation from Hambrough if he thought that a minor could not make an assignation. This document and others were looked up, and were taken with us when Monson and I went to the insurance office in Glasgow for the purpose of fortifying our claim against the company; they were used for that purpose in Monson's presence. Anything of the nature of financing Major Hambrough which I engaged in was shortly after I introduced Monson to him in 1891. The securities which I held for advances made to Major Hambrough were mortgages by him—one for £1500 and one for £1000; they were in my favour. I did not hold any mortgages purporting to be granted by Major Hambrough to Monson.

Re-cross-examined by Mr. COMRIE THOMSON—My proposal when the negotiations for the purchase of the yacht were on was that Cecil should pay for it when he came of age. I arranged with Mr. Donald, jun., in the train one day going to Glasgow, that the boat should be purchased by Mr. Cecil Hambrough, and that payment should be made when he came of age, and that that being so,

Evidence for Prosecution.

we could give £1150 for the boat. We should not have given so much if it had been a cash payment. I explained that Cecil was not in a position to find so large a sum of money, but that he would be in a year, and I was willing to make a payment to account. I know nothing about what arrangement had been come to between Monson and Cecil Hambrough as regards the purchase of the yacht. I do not remember Monson saying to me that he understood that Major Hambrough would be willing to give his consent to his son's assignation of the policy.

Did Mr. Monson explain that he had a letter from Dr. Hamble-ton on 17th July which led him to believe that Major Hambrough would give his consent?—I do remember something of that kind; Monson may have shown me a letter from Dr. Hambleton. I under-stood some months before Mr. Hambrough's death that the Eagle Insurance Company was not going to give the purchase of Major Hambrough's life interest to Monson. With reference to the insur-ance company and the payment of the money, I wish to explain that I think a wrong impression has been conveyed. What I meant was simply this, that I, differing from Monson, considered the assign-ment to Mrs. Monson perfectly good; that I believed that I would be able to get the company to pay. There was no idea that I should " rush " them, or do them out of the money in any way.

By the LORD JUSTICE-CLERK—I told Monson that I thought that under Scots law the assignment was good; he was under a contrary impression.

45. WILLIAM HUGH MURRAY, W.S., examined by the SOLICITOR-GENERAL—I am a partner of the firm of J. & F. Anderson, W.S., Edinburgh. My firm were agents for Major John Lamont, the proprietor of Ardlamont, which was let for last season to Mr. Hambrough and Mr. Jerningham at a rent of £450, payable on 1st August. The property was for some time for sale at the price of £85,000. On 8th August I had a meeting with Mr. Monson with regard to the purchase of Ardlamont; this was the only meeting I had with him. I had no direct correspondence with him about the purchase; there was correspondence through Messrs. Paton. [Shown letters Nos. 119 to 147.] Anything that passed in writing between me and Mr. Monson came within the correspondence shown to me. [Counsel at this point read letter No. 90, already put to last witness, B. L. Tottenham.] I received no communication on 24th July, 1893, in the nature of an offer from Monson with regard to the Ardlamont property, nor did he ever, in writing, say to me that he thought £45,000 was a good price for the property. At no time prior or subsequent to 24th July, 1893, did I accept, or agree to accept, £48,000 as the price of the property, nor did I ever say that I would be willing to accept £250 as a deposit on a contract signed by Mrs. Monson; no contract was ever in course

131

Alfred John Monson.

W. H. Murray

of being printed ready for execution. I was the member of the firm who had charge of the matter. On 8th August Monson called on me in Edinburgh; he was alone. My recollection of what took place is that he seemed to have a considerable knowledge of the estate and buildings, and that he said that if we came to terms a deposit would be made. I do not think that anything was said about the sum to be deposited, but the impression on my mind is that it would have been one of some thousands. Referring to the question of price, he said that his commission from Mr. Hambrough was to suggest not more than £60,000, and I said that my price was £85,000, and that, seeing the difference was so great, there was no use saying anything more about it. There was no agreement to purchase at the time; £48,000 as the price was quite out of the question; and I also considered £60,000 out of the question. I have since sold the property for £70,000. In the course of our interview Monson said that he would find the deposit and secure himself by insuring Mr. Hambrough's life; but the settlement was not to take place till Mr. Hambrough had come of age. In the ordinary course the year's rent would become due on 1st August, and the lease would fall if the rent was not paid within five days of 1st August. My interview with Monson was on 8th August; I had abstained from demanding payment of the rent in view of the expected interview. I got a telegram acquainting me with the death of young Hambrough. I waited till the funeral was over before writing to Monson about the rent. I have never got the rent; an action against Mr. Jerningham for recovery of the rent has been dropped.

Cross-examined by Mr. COMRIE THOMSON—Mrs. Monson was not a party to the lease.

I refer you to the letter which the Solicitor-General read. He did not read this part of it—" The limit of time for the completion of the contract would have to be fixed for 1st June, 1894, when Mr. Hambrough would have attained his majority. We have gone fully into the details of rental, &c., but we have had no particulars supplied of the outgoings in the various farms. I do not know whether Mr. Steven is at liberty to supply these, but perhaps you will kindly inform us as to this."—I quite realised that the proposal involved that there would be a deposit, and a postponement of the time when the balance of the price would be paid. There were some mortgages on the property—something like £30,000.

In a letter Monson says that there are mortgages on the property amounting to £37,000. Your price was £85,000. Mr. Monson's statement is that he understands the mortgages will not be disturbed, and that you will accept £48,000. If you add £48,000 to £37,000, you get £85,000. Now, you see his statement is that the mortgages which are to be allowed to remain amount to £37,000; he would have made quite an accurate state-

132

Evidence for Prosecution.

ment had he said £30,000 or £31,000. He then proposes that £48,000 should be paid. These figures bring the amount up to your price, £85,000, so that the only mistake is that made between the £37,000 and the £31,000. Do you see?—Yes.

Re-examined by the Solicitor-General—I am unable to reconcile Mr. Comrie Thomson's construction of the letter with what passed between Monson and me. I certainly never agreed to accept £48,000 or any other sum from Monson at any time for the estate of Ardlamont. I never agreed to accept a deposit of £250 from Monson. I never arranged any contract between my client and Monson.

By the Lord Justice-Clerk—If I got £48,000 and £37,000 together, I would have got the price I was wanting. I have never heard any suggestion such as that mentioned in Monson's letter to Tottenham that "they agreed to accept £48,000. They say they only do this because Major Lamont is so anxious to get rid of the property before he starts for India." If a gentleman comes to my office for an interview such as is alleged here, it would be noted at the time by whoever saw him. It was quite well known in the office that I was in charge of this transaction. Monson only came to me once—on 8th August. Such a deposit as £250 towards the price of this property would be of no account at all.

46. Dugald Kerr, examined by the Solicitor-General—I am agent for the Royal Bank of Scotland at Tighnabruaich. In July, 1893, a bank account was opened at the Tighnabruaich branch in name of Agnes Maud Monson. [Shown No. 151.] That is a letter which I received from Mrs. Monson which led to the opening of the account. Enclosed were two cheques, one for £5 and one for £10. I sent a 2s. 6d. cheque book, as requested by Mrs. Monson. On 7th August I received the following letter:—"Ardlamont House, 7th August. Dear Sir,—I shall be much obliged if you will place the two enclosed cheques for £250 and £50 to my credit. The cheque for £250 is dated the 10th in consequence of Mr. Monson's agent having instructions to remit £250 by the 10th, but as the cheque cannot now arrive at the Bank of England before the 10th, Mr. Monson told me to pay it in now." The £250 cheque was drawn by B. L. Tottenham through the Royal Bank of Scotland on the Bank of England, and was payable to Mr. Cecil Hambrough. It is endorsed by Mr. Hambrough. I sent on the cheque to our own offices in London, and debited them with the amount. No. 162 is a cheque by A. M. Monson in account with the Royal Bank, dated Tighnabruaich, 8th August, 1893, payable to J. G. M'Lean, Esq., or bearer, and the sum is £194 3s. 4d. It is endorsed J. G. M'Lean and D. C. Haldeman, and is crossed by the Bank of England to the account of the Mutual Insurance Company, New York. This cheque, having gone through

133

Alfred John Monson.

the Bank of England, would have passed on in the ordinary course to Tighnabruaich. It came there on 10th August, and was honoured and placed to the credit of Mrs. Monson's account. Apart from the £250, Mrs. Monson's account would have stood on 10th August with something like £57 at its credit, so that to the extent of £137 the cheque was paid out of Tottenham's money. In consequence of Tottenham's cheque being dishonoured, I received a letter from the Royal Bank, London.

By the LORD JUSTICE-CLERK—Orders not to pay was the reason given for dishonouring the cheque?—Yes.

Examination continued—Then I received letter No. 154 from Mr. Monson, stating that £1000 would be paid in to the account, but I never got this money. And he mentioned in that letter that two cheques had been passed upon the account for £36 10s. and for £10. I honoured these cheques, notwithstanding the return of the London one, but relying upon Tottenham's cheque, which I believed would be paid, because of what Monson said in his letter that it was merely a matter of proof of signature. [Shown No. 115.] This is a letter received by me from Mrs. Monson, dated 23rd August, 1893, in which she says that she had arranged with Mr. Tottenham to have the £250 cheque cashed any day after Monday; that Mr. Tottenham would have to call at the Bank of England to verify the signature as a matter of form; and that he would not be in London before Monday. On 28th August I received letter No. 176 from Mrs. Monson; it is in these terms—'' Dear Sir,—I enclose a policy of assurance received to-day on the life of the late Cecil Hambrough. The policy is for £10,000, and the company have arranged for the payment to be made at Glasgow, when the policy will have to be handed over, and a receipt given in the usual manner. The settlement will probably take place in a week or so. I will intimate the day as soon as I hear. The money can be paid into a bank at Glasgow, and the policy sent there. The policy is to cover money paid on behalf of the late Mr. Cecil Hambrough, but I regret to say I lose a considerable sum of money by his death, owing to there having been delay in taking out a further policy to cover guarantees given on his behalf in connection with same liabilities of his father. Curiously, the acceptance for the further policy only arrived on the very day of his death, and was therefore useless. It seems difficult to realise that, without a moment's warning, one should lose a dear friend just when we were in the height of enjoyment. It has been a great shock to us, and he was such a favourite with every one.'' With that letter I got a policy of insurance for £10,000 upon Cecil Hambrough's life. I acknowledged receipt of the letter, and retained the policy for the purpose of sending it to Glasgow at the proper time. I handed the policy over to the Procurator-Fiscal for the purposes of this case. I also sent Tottenham's cheque to London. I have never got payment of that cheque. Altogether, we have

Evidence for Prosecution.

advanced against Mrs. Monson's cheque the sum of £245 17s. 9d., which is the balance now standing at the debit of her account. She has never paid up that overdraft, and we must now seek payment from Tottenham.

Cross-examined by Mr. COMRIE THOMSON—The account opened on 26th July, and between that date and 8th August there had been only £25 paid into it in three sums of £10, £5, and £10. It was intimated to me that the account was to be regarded as a house-keeping account. On 8th August I received a letter from Mrs. Monson, dated the previous day, enclosing the cheque for £250, payable in London on 10th August.

Why, when the cheque was only payable in London on the 10th, did you place it to the credit of Mrs. Monson on the 8th?—You do at times come across post-dated cheques, and the same thing does happen.

This cheque, payable in London on the 10th, was put to Mrs. Monson's credit on the 8th. The regular course would have been to put it to credit on the 11th or 12th. You see, it is payable in London, and if you had waited until the proper time you would have been in receipt of the letter from London forbidding you to give credit. Have you any explanation?—We do at times get cheques in course of business post-dated. The cheque was returned to me from London in a letter dated 10th August from the Bank of England, giving me orders not to pay. The date of the cheque for £194 was 8th August. If that cheque had been passed in the usual way into the payee's account in Glasgow on the afternoon of 8th August, it would have been sent down to Tighnabruaich on the following day.

And if you had not put the £250 to Mrs. Monson's credit prior to the 10th, there would not have been enough to meet that £194 cheque?—No, not enough; just £50 odds.

Now, assuming that the state of knowledge of the Monsons was that this cheque for £250 could not be put to their credit before the 11th, and that the £194 cheque could not be met before the £250 had been put to their credit on the 11th, does it not suggest to you that they could not have had in anticipation the £194 being paid on the morning of the 10th?—Yes.

In a letter dated 7th August, 1893, Mrs. Monson says—'' I would be much obliged if you will place the two enclosed cheques for £250 and £50 to my credit.'' When a cheque is sent to a banker with a request to place it to the customer's credit, what does the banker understand that to mean? To put it to the credit of the current account?—A cheque may be handed to a banker for collec-tion or to place to credit, allowing the cheque to go on and to be met at the other end in the ordinary way. I entered the £250 cheque to Mrs. Monson's credit at her request; if I had not done so I should consider that I had been going against the instructions sent me. From the terms of Mrs. Monson's letter of 7th August I thought

Alfred John Monson.

the cheque would have been met in the ordinary way when presented at the Bank of England. The £250 cheque was crossed on the Bank of England. Having placed the £250 to the credit of the account as instructed by the customer I would have honoured a cheque to the amount of £194 drawn on her.

The Court adjourned.

Fifth Day—Saturday, 16th December, 1893.

[The LORD JUSTICE-CLERK, on taking his seat, said—Before proceedings of the Court go on I wish to say that since this trial began I have received several letters, some signed, some anonymous, in reference to the case. I do not read such letters, and I wish it to be known publicly that the writing of such letters to a judge in this Court when trying a case is not only reprehensible, but may subject the person doing it to severe punishment for contempt of Court.]

47. CHARLES WHITHEAD GRAHAM, examined by the SOLICITOR-GENERAL—I am a member of the firm of Lawrence Graham & Graham, London, which acted as solicitors to the trustees of the late Mr. John Hambrough, great-grandfather of the late Mr. Cecil Hambrough. Major Hambrough, under the late John Hambrough's will, was tenant for life of an estate at Ventnor, Isle of Wight, and of Stanmore, Staines, Middlesex. The estates were settled, after the death of Major Hambrough, on his eldest son, as tenant-in-tail, which means that the eldest son will come into the property as tenant-in-tail, and if he did nothing to bar the entail his eldest son would follow as tenant-in-tail on attaining his majority, and so on. It usually has happened that the tenant for life and the tenant-in-tail bar the entail and re-settle the estates. On the entail being barred the eldest son would be absolutely entitled, subject to his father's life interest. During Major Hambrough's life the whole income belonged to him, and the eldest son, Mr. Cecil Hambrough, would have had simply the reversion. If he had lived to be twenty-one and then predeceased his father he would have been entitled to nothing unless he had disentailed, which he could only do with the consent of his father. Without the consent of his father he could disentail to the extent of barring his own issue, but not his collaterals, that is, his brothers and sisters. Accordingly, if he attained majority and predeceased his father and left no issue, the next younger brother would become heir-of-entail. Cecil Hambrough could not during his minority effectually grant any mortgage over his prospective interests, and, according to English law, such a document would be of no validity whatever.

The annual value of the Ventnor estate, in the Isle of Wight, is about £1300, and that of the estate in Middlesex about £1900, without the brick royalties, which vary in value from about £400 to £700. In addition to the Ventnor and Middlesex estates there are

Alfred John Monson.

C. W. Graham

certain securities which stood in the trustees' name, subject to the same settlement; these are the proceeds of the sale of some of the settled land, amounting to about £23,000, invested in railway debenture stock, and producing about £780 to £800. The total gross income from these estates and securities amounts to about £3980. Major Dudley Hambrough had also a prospective interest in the estate of Pipewell Hall in Northamptonshire, subject to his uncle, Mr. Oscar Hambrough's life and his dying without issue, in which event Major Hambrough would become tenant for life and Mr. Cecil Hambrough would have an interest similar to that which I have described with reference to the other entailed estates. The rental of the Pipewell Hall estate, is, I am told, between £2000 and £3000 a year, but it did not come under my administration, and I cannot speak with certainty.

As solicitors for the trustees we would be the persons to receive notice of any mortgages connected with the Hambrough estates, and in 1885 we received a notice of a mortgage with the Eagle Office on the whole of Major Hambrough's life interest. In the event of the payments not being made it is competent for the mortgagee to foreclose, in which event he would become absolute owner of the tenant's life interest. I know that the Eagle Office did foreclose, though they gave us no formal notice of their doing so. Major Hambrough had power to appoint a jointure of £400 to his wife after his death and £5000 to his younger children, and we received notice that he would exercise both of these powers. Major Hambrough has not, to my knowledge, been adjudicated a bankrupt, though a receiving order was made against him, which is the first step in effecting a bankruptcy, according to English procedure. After the Eagle Company had foreclosed Major Hambrough's mortgage over his life interest, any sale of the interest thereafter would be made by the Eagle Company, no consent of Major Hambrough being necessary.

We had notice of a mortgage executed by Major Hambrough and his son Cecil in favour of Alfred John Monson; all the particulars about it which we received were that it affected all the settled estates. It was executed in September, 1891. Early in 1892, so far as I can remember, we got notice with reference to the depositing of this mortgage with the London and Yorkshire Bank as a security on an advance of £550 made by the bank to Mr. Monson.

Cross-examined by Mr. COMRIE THOMSON—I have no means of verifying the date of this notice. [Shown No. 50 of defence productions.] That is a copy of the notice, and it bears to have been received by the trustees on 14th November, 1891. I see now that my impression that the date was in 1892 was wrong. If Cecil Hambrough had survived his majority and his father he would have entered into possession of the estates as heir-of-entail in possession. If Cecil had attained his majority and his father were still alive it would

138

Evidence for Prosecution.

C. W. Graham

have been in the power of the father and son, without getting the consent of anybody, absolutely to terminate the entail. If Cecil survived his majority and his father were still alive he would have had an expectancy upon which he could have got an advance; it would be in the ordinary course of business that whoever made the advance would ask that he should insure his life against the chance of his dying before his father. I am aware that Major Hambrough mortgaged his whole life interest in the estate to the Eagle Company, and that the Eagle Company, upon the foreclosure becoming absolute, were in the position of uncontrolled proprietors of the life interest. They could sell it. The £5000 I have mentioned was a sum upon which, under John Hambrough's will, the Major had power of appointment to his younger children. Therefore that £5000 was practically a provision made by him for the younger children, the eldest son, Cecil, taking under the entail; and that provision did not come into effect so long as Major Hambrough was alive, it did not affect his life interest. The whole annual value of the settled estates was £3980. The income was derived as follows:—Ventnor estates, £1300; Middlesex estates, £1900; and income for securities in the trustees' name, £780. There are the brick royalties besides. I put them at £700 or £800.

By the LORD JUSTICE-CLERK—That makes the total income £4680.

Examination continued—I do not know of a policy being effected on the life of Major Hambrough against the life of his brother Oscar when the mortgage to the Eagle Company was granted. I have no knowledge of a policy for £7000 against the issue of Oscar. I have never seen a mortgage by Major Hambrough and Cecil securing £5000 to Monson. [Shown No. 19.] I got notice of a mortgage, but the one now shown does not agree with the notice. I should say that the capitalised value of £4680 would be about twenty-five years' purchase.

Re-examined by the SOLICITOR-GENERAL—The notice of the mortgage for £5000 by Major Hambrough was sent to me on 1st September, 1891; it was sent by the London and Yorkshire Bank, who were the creditors, the mortgage being received in security of an advance to Mr. Monson. The only person who could lodge it would be Mr. Monson. [Shown No. 18.] This purports to be a copy of a mortgage, dated 23rd May, 1891, for £5000 by Major Hambrough to Mr. Monson; I have no doubt that notice of this mortgage was made to the trustees. [Shown No. 20.] This is an original mortgage, dated 17th September, 1891, by Major Hambrough to Mr. Monson, for £2600. I received no notice of it. [Shown No. 22.] This is an original mortgage, dated 1st December, 1891, by Major Hambrough to Mr. Monson, for £3400, and of this I got no notice.

Re-cross-examined by Mr. COMRIE THOMSON—In the value of £4680, which I gave as the income of the Hambrough estates, I have

Alfred John Monson.

not included the proceeds of the income of the Pipewell estate, in which Major Hambrough had a reversionary interest contingent upon Oscar Hambrough not having any issue. Oscar Hambrough is between sixty and seventy years of age. It would be quite competent for Dudley to insure against Oscar's issue, and, assuming that he has insured for £7000, then upon Oscar's life interest failing by his death Major Hambrough would get the estate or the £7000. [Shown No. 22.] The mortgage of December, 1891, includes security subjects which are not included in the mortgage to the Eagle Company, amounting, so far as I know, to £2900.

Are you aware that the £550 advanced to Monson by the bank has been paid, and the mortgage delivered?—No; if a mortgage has been delivered it does not necessarily follow that the advance has been paid.

Re-examined by the SOLICITOR-GENERAL—It was not necessary in this case that notice should be given to the mortgagee after foreclosure, because the trustees had already received notice that the Eagle Company had gone into possession. They had not altogether foreclosed the mortgage or claim, but they had already taken possession of the estates, so that as far as the trustees were concerned, they knew that the rents were payable to the Eagle Office. After foreclosure by the Eagle Office a mortgage by a life tenant other than the Eagle would be of no value at all, and a mortgage by the tenant-in-tail being a minor would also be worthless.

48. MAJOR DUDLEY HAMBROUGH, examined by the SOLICITOR-GENERAL—I am forty-four years of age. I reside at Hexham-on-Sea, and, when in London, at the Junior Carlton Club. I am a grandson of the deceased John Hambrough, of Ventnor. Under his will, as successor of my father, I succeeded to a life-rent interest in the Ventnor estate. My father died in 1862. I came of age in 1870, and came into possession of the life interest. My family consisted of two sons and three daughters, the eldest of the family being Cecil, who was twenty in May last. My affairs became embarrassed in 1885, and in that year, or in 1886, I granted a mortgage to the Eagle Insurance Company upon my life interest in the Hambrough estate. Under that, of course, I had to pay interest half-yearly. The interest got into arrear, and the mortgage was foreclosed in February, 1891, or about that time. The gross income of the estate of which I was tenant for life was £5000 a year. I have a prospective interest in the Pipewell estate, Northampton, at present in possession of Mr. Oscar Hambrough. The income of that estate is £1500. My interest is contingent on my surviving Oscar, my uncle, and his dying without issue. My uncle's age is fifty-nine. He is a widower and has no family. In the autumn of 1889 I made the acquaintance of Mr. Tottenham, financial agent, in London. Certain financial transactions took place between him and me. He made me a weekly

Evidence for Prosecution.

Major D. Hambrough

allowance. He had no power of attorney to act. I first became acquainted with Alfred John Monson in May or June, 1890. I was introduced to him by Mr. Tottenham. At that time my son Cecil would be about seventeen years of age. He was introduced to me as an army tutor. At that time I was in financial difficulties. The introduction to Monson was made with a view to my son going to him to be trained for the army. Monson agreed to educate him for the army, payment to be made as soon as my financial affairs were arranged. An arrangement was made by which Monson was to be paid at the rate of £300 a year. Some time in autumn, 1891, my son went to reside with Monson. Tottenham having failed to get the estates from the Eagle Company with a view to reducing the interest by transferring them to some other company or individual, Monson said that he thought he could carry it through. I think this would be about May, 1891. My arrangements with Monson were verbal; there was no writing. These negotiations with Monson began in May, 1891, and went on till some time last year. During that time Monson, with my consent and approval, virtually took charge of my affairs. In the beginning of 1892 I put an end to the negotiations with the Eagle Company, so far as Monson was concerned, and placed my affairs in the hands of Mr. Fuller, my solicitor, and, apart from some private negotiations with Monson in May, 1892, from the beginning of 1892 onwards my affairs have been in the hands of Mr. Fuller and Mr. Prince respectively. My reason for displacing Monson was that I distrusted him; I was not at all satisfied with the way in which he was conducting the business; I thought that he was acting in his own interest.

Did you wish your boy to continue to be with him?—No.

When did you desire that your boy should be removed?—The first time was in January, 1892. I tried by letters, both to Monson and to Cecil, to try to get him removed, but did not succeed.

There was one particular money transaction which excited suspicion in my mind with regard to Monson. I got notice from the bank that they had made an advance to Monson on documents of mine which he held, including the mortgage, but Monson did not inform me that he had got money on it; and when I spoke to him about it he told me it would be all right. I understood that he would refund the money to the bank. All that I got of this money from him were small sums—sovereigns and half-sovereigns, no other money. After this I made an effort to get my son to leave Monson and to return to me. I found that Monson had undoubtedly acquired an influence over my son. I met Cecil occasionally and told him repeatedly of my desire that he should leave Monson and return to his family until I had other plans for him. He was always very friendly to me and the other members of the family, and was very much attached to his mother. I found Monson's influence operating against my advice to the boy, and had often great difficulty in getting

141

Alfred John Monson.

him to meet me when I desired him to do so in London. Mr. Fuller, my solicitor, was endeavouring, with my approval, to make other arrangements for Cecil. After this had gone on for some time there were some arrangements in progress to settle my affairs with the Eagle Company, conducted first by Mr. Fuller, and then by Mr. Prince. We were anxious that Monson should have nothing to do with my interest in the estate. I mistrusted Monson, and the arrangements between him and me were of such a character as to show him that quite distinctly. I was aware that there were negotiations with the Eagle Insurance Company for the purpose of obtaining a transfer of the mortgage from the company to Dr. Hambleton. These negotiations were carried on by my solicitor with my approval and consent. I ascertained that the company had given its consent to the arrangement, and early this year I learnt that under it Monson would have nothing to do with my interest in the estate. This arrangement has not taken complete legal form; the contract has not been signed, but Dr. Hambleton holds a letter agreeing to it, and the arrangements were progressing for the completion of the contract at the time of my son's death.

After I was first introduced to Monson, and during the time he was endeavouring to arrange my financial affairs, I granted him three documents, mortgages and bills. I had confidence in him at that time, and these documents were first given to me by him for signature; I had no separate advice. As far as I can recollect, these three documents were, first, a bill for £5000 signed by my son and myself in May, 1891. The second was a mortgage for £3000 given at the end of August or the beginning of September of the same year signed by myself alone. The reason for granting this was that Monson said that the bill for £5000 was far too large an amount, that he could do nothing with it, and he asked me if I would give him one for a lesser sum. I understood that the £5000 bill had not been negotiated, and at Monson's request I gave him the additional smaller amount; I never got back the original bills. The third document was a mortgage for £2600, also granted in September, 1891. There was no explanation of why it was wanted; Monson asked me to sign it, and I did so. The full amount of the documents which I granted to Monson was £10,600. I was getting some money from him from time to time; in all, apart from my son's expenses, I must have got something less than £200. [Shown No. 18.] This is a copy of a mortgage for £5000, dated 23rd May, 1891. I do not remember giving a mortgage on that date. [Shown No. 19.] This is a copy of a mortgage for £5000, dated 1st September, 1891, and purporting to be granted by me and my son. The signature at the end of the document is "Dudley Albert Hambrough."

Is that your signature? Do you sign your signature at full length?—No; I sign it "D. A. Hambrough." This is not in the form of my usual signature. My son's signature in this mort-

Evidence for Prosecution.

Major D. Hambrough

gage is at full length. I was in the habit of receiving letters from my son and of seeing his writing frequently. I should not recognise this signature as his writing; in my opinion it is not my son's signature.

[Shown No. 20.] This is the mortgage for £2600 which I granted, signing my name " D. A. Hambrough." [Shown No. 22.] That is a mortgage for £3400, dated 1st December, and bearing to be granted by me; the signature of my name is written in full, and I say that it was not written by me. When I became suspicious of Monson, and wished to make other arrangements for my son, I certainly contemplated that Monson should be paid for what he had expended on my son. Mrs. Hambrough shared in my desire that Cecil should leave the Monson establishment; she suffered in health in consequence of her anxiety about the matter.

The first I heard about my son's death was by a telegram from Dr. Hambleton—" Monson wired Cecil had serious gun accident, and that you are to go on at once." I started at once with Mrs. Hambrough for Scotland, wiring to Monson to have a telegram at Newcastle to let me know how Cecil was and the nature of the wound, but at Newcastle there was no wire. At Glasgow in the hotel I learnt for the first time from an evening paper the fact of Cecil's death. Before seeing the paper I got a wire from Monson in reply to one which I had sent asking for particulars; Monson's telegram said, " Prepare for the worst; come on at once." We arrived in Glasgow too late for us to start for Tignabruaich, but left next morning. Monson met us at Greenock, and when I asked him how the thing happened he told me that Cecil had been getting over a dyke, and had fallen and shot himself. He said that Mrs. Monson was going to Glasgow on business early in the morning, and that Cecil got up to see her off, and that after doing so he went down to the shore to tell the men at the yacht to get up steam. While they were doing this Cecil had taken his gun and gone for a stroll.

Did Monson say where he himself was, or what he had done?—He said that he was out for a walk before breakfast in the meadow, and that he heard a shot.

Did he say that he had been out shooting with Cecil, or whether he had not?—I understood him to say distinctly that Cecil was the only one who had a gun. I arrived at Ardlamont on Saturday, 12th August, and on Sunday morning Monson took me and my wife to see the place where my son had died. We went to the wood, and Monson pointed out the place where the body was found; it was in the ditch, but there was no appearance whatever of a body having lain there, and I made the remark to my wife at the time that I could not see where a heavy body had lain in the ditch. Monson said that my son had been accompanied by a man named Scott. I asked Monson about this man, and he told me that Scott had been so affected by the occurrence that he could not remain in the house, and had

143

Alfred John Monson.

Major D. Hambrough

returned to Glasgow. He said that he was an engineer who lived in Glasgow, and that I could see him there on my way back to England. On Monday morning Mrs. Hambrough and I left Ardlamont, Monson seeing us off at the boat, and coming on to Glasgow on Monday night. I was still anxious to see Scott, and I told Monson that I had made inquiries at the boots and waiters in the hotel about Scott, but could hear nothing of him.

By the LORD JUSTICE-CLERK—Was that at the Central Hotel?—No; at the North British.

Examination continued—When I told Monson about my inquiries after Scott, he said—" I have made a mistake as to where he lives; he is still at Tighnabruaich." I did not succeed in seeing Scott.

I heard that Dr. Macmillan had been called in after the shooting occurrence, and expressed a desire to see him. Monson told me that he had arranged for the doctor to meet me, and when I got to Ardlamont I asked if I could see him and was told by Monson that the doctor had got tired of waiting and had left. I was told that I could see the doctor at Tighnabruaich on my way back, but I never saw him. I arrived at Ventnor, Isle of Wight, on Wednesday afternoon, and my son's funeral took place there in St. Catherine's Churchyard on the Thursday. Monson paid all the expenses in connection with the funeral and made all the arrangements. At Ventnor he spoke to me about an insurance on Cecil's life; he said that he had papers for a policy with the Scottish Provident, and that a policy for £50,000 would have been carried out if my son had lived. He did not tell me that two policies for £10,000 each had been carried out a few days before my son's death. The only completed insurance which he spoke of was a small one of £400, the policy for which was held by Mrs. Monson, but he said that the premium had not been paid. After the funeral I went to London; Monson travelled up with me. Since parting with him in London I have not met him and have had no further communication with him.

[At this stage witness identified a number of letters and telegrams which passed between him and his son and Monson.]

[Shown No. 96.] That is a letter from my son Cecil to me, dated 1st May, 1892. It reads as follows:—" My dear Father,—I did not see Monson until nearly ten o'clock on Friday, and when I asked him about going to Retford he told me that he had received a letter from the colonel of the Yorkshire Militia saying that I was gazetted, and wanting me to join as soon as possible. Mr. Monson said there was nothing for it but for me to join them now, and to get a transfer next year into the Hants Regiment. He went with me to York to get me measured for my uniform, which is to be ready by Monday. I got your wire when I came back from York last night."

There is also a letter from me to Cecil, dated 20th June, in which I say—" My dear Cecil,—Your training with the Yorks Militia

Evidence for Prosecution.

Major D. Hambrough

will now be over in a few days. I am writing to tell you that it is our wish that you should join us here, and not return to Riseley. On no consideration whatever can I permit you to continue your studies under Mr. Monson. Your mother and I have our own very good reason for our decision in this respect, one of which is the gross and unpardonable deception which was practised upon us with regard to your joining the Yorkshire Regiment. We have made our own arrangements as regards you until you are of age; though, of course, we shall be anxious and willing to meet your wishes so far as lies in our power and our duties as your guardians will permit. I am arranging an allowance for your education and maintenance, which will enable us to give you everything necessary for your comfort, not, of course, permitting of extravagance.''

Explain what is referred to as '' the gross and unpardonable deception '' about the Yorkshire Militia Regiment?—I had arranged for my son to go into the Hampshire Regiment, and I told Monson this, saying that I supposed he had done nothing further with regard to the Yorks Regiment, and he said that he had done nothing since I had told him that I wished Cecil to join the Hants Regiment. Monson said that the London tailor would not make the boy's uniform and that he must go to York for it. I allowed him to go to York on the understanding that he would be with me again on a Saturday so as to go down to Winchester with me on the following Monday. On the Saturday I got a letter from Monson informing me that Cecil had joined the Yorks Regiment of Militia. I had special reasons for wishing my boy to go into the Hants Militia; he was a Hampshire man and knew the officers of the regiment, and I had consulted influential friends and had arranged everything.

The SOLICITOR-GENERAL then read the following letter from witness to Cecil Hambrough, dated 18th November, 1892:—'' I am much surprised and deeply grieved that you should take no notice of my letters and telegrams. You left us to go to Yorkshire, on your word of honour to return in a few days. That you have absolutely ignored, and injured yourself very much more than you have injured us. Any who may advance you money do so in direct opposition to the last Act of Parliament, which renders them liable to imprisonment, and any solicitor who may act in the matter is liable to be struck off the rolls, if not imprisoned, as a party to the act. After your most unjustifiable conduct, which I am certain is not of your own thought or desire, I have no choice whatever, much as it is painful to me, but to say that I shall put the criminal law in force against any one and every one who may take part in obtaining money for you. You know that I have made arrangements to adequately provide for your education and maintenance, and to do everything to place you in the position you hold as my son. It is matter of deep regret that you compel me to write in such terms, but you leave me no alternative, and if you do not at once return I shall apply to the

Alfred John Monson.

Major D. Hambrough

Court and prosecute any one who in any way aids or abets you in opposition to my repeated wishes.—Your affectionate but deeply grieved father, D. A. Hambrough.'' To what do you refer when you say, '' Your conduct, which I am certain is not of your own thought or desire?''—To his staying away and taking no notice of my telegrams and letters; I thought he was being influenced by the people he was with. In reply to my letter I got a reply from Cecil in which he says, '' I do not understand what you have further found out against Mr. Monson; but after he has done everything for me that he possibly could I think that it would be extremely mean of me to come away as you propose.'' On 27th October I wrote to Monson as follows:—'' Dear Sir,—I have once more written to my son requiring his presence in town, and will thank you to see that my wishes are obeyed. He only returned to you on the strict understanding and solemn promise on his part that he would return to us on the following Monday or Tuesday. I have good reason to know that he is in a very delicate state of health, and the climate with you is the worst possible for his complaint. His life is a valuable one to us, and I cannot allow him to run any risk. I have on more than one occasion given you notice of my intention to remove him, and not being of age he cannot choose for himself even if so inclined. But I am sure that it is not his wish to run counter to his parents. I have seen your letter to Fowler, and note what you say respecting his studies. He will continue them if so inclined, but certainly not with you.'' I sent a number of telegrams to Cecil between September and November urging him to return home. [Shown No. 102.] That is a receipt for money sent to Cecil by telegram to enable him to come to London. I sent this telegram to Cecil—'' You are killing mother and causing untold trouble, cannot explain conduct, did you receive money, wire receipt, reply.'' That was with reference to the money sent by telegram. I got a wire in answer to mine—'' Just got back, writing.—Hambrough.'' It seems to have been handed in at Burton Leonard. Some time this year I wrote to Monson asking him if he could tell me where my son was, as I had not seen him for a long time. I got this letter from Monson—'' 8 Delahaye Street, Westminster. Sir,—In reply to your letter I beg to say that I am not your son's keeper. I have not seen him for ten days or more. So far as I know, he is staying at Riseley Hall.'' Riseley Hall was Monson's house; this letter is dated from Tottenham Chambers. In reply to a letter I wrote him wishing my son to return to me I got the following reply from Monson:—'' 27/7/92, Primrose Club, 4 Park Place, St. James. Dear Hambrough,—I hereby give you notice that I am not custodian of your son, as you seem to suggest in your letter. Your son is perfectly at liberty to go when and where he pleases, as far as I am concerned.'' From that time onward it was most certainly my wish that my son should

146

Evidence for Prosecution.

Major D. Hambrough

leave Monson. In this letter there was also a reference to my proceedings in bankruptcy. I never was adjudicated a bankrupt, though there was a receiving order taken out against me.

Cross-examined by Mr. WILSON—When I granted the mortgage in 1885 to the Eagle Insurance Company I had to get policies on my own life for something like £42,000 made over to me. That was to secure the collateral security of the insurance company. The mortgage I granted in 1885 for £37,000 was not for an amount which I had borrowed in 1885, but was made up of sums of money which I had borrowed from time to time over many years. In 1870, when I came of age, I succeeded to the life interests referred to in this case. After granting the mortgage for £37,000 to the Eagle Insurance Company I got a further loan of £2500; that was in 1886. After that my credit was exhausted, and I was unable to borrow any more money at that time, without getting my life insured for an additional sum.

I was not adjudicated a bankrupt; an arrangement was come to by which I was to pay 20s. in the £1 and a dividend of 4s. 3d. in the £1. So far as I know, that was all that my creditors got. This was after the sale of the Steephill Castle property. Before I went to Tottenham Messrs. Kyne & Hammond were acting for me; they tried to raise an advance to pay off the Eagle Company, but they did not succeed. So far as I know, they were not going to surrender the insurance policies; they wanted further policies. It was after this that I went to Tottenham, who said that he could effect a re-insurance. At that time I was insured for £42,000, and what I wanted was an additional insurance for £6000. Tottenham endeavoured to get me into such a state as would enable me to pass a medical examination for a new policy. He gave me an allowance of £7 per week. At this time Dr. Hambleton attended me. I do not know whether Tottenham paid Dr. Hambleton anything; he was to be paid, but I have not paid him anything. Dr. Hambleton did not stay in the hotel where I was kept by Tottenham, nor did he live with me at the sea-coast when I went there for my health.

Tottenham failed to effect any new loan. I was practically penniless, and it was about this time that I met Monson. The first time I met him I had a talk with him about my son. I heard that Monson had been successful as an army tutor, and he showed me some testimonials which, I thought, were satisfactory. I did not know any of the men he had coached, and I made inquiries as regards his family; I was quite satisfied with his testimonials. The arrangement with Monson was that he was to keep and educate my son and prepare him for the army, and that he should receive board at the rate of £300 a year, when my financial arrangements were made.

Have your financial arrangements ever been completed?—They have not.

147

Alfred John Monson.

Major D. Hambrough

And Mr. Monson has not got anything?—No. I did not find it hopeless to effect a re-insurance on my life; I have not managed it yet, but I am not trying at the present time. When Tottenham failed to give me any further advances I had some conversation with Monson about his making some. Monson did not continue making me a weekly allowance. The first sum I had from Monson was a cheque for £25, which he sent to pay for my two daughters going to Germany, and he also gave me a cheque for £15 for travelling expenses, making £40 in all. Monson gave me a cheque for £120 to open an account with the London and Yorkshire Bank. I sent the cheque to the bank. [Shown Nos. 92 to 98.] These cheques were signed by me, and I got money for them; they were all drawn in July, 1891, and are made payable chiefly to bearer or at the Junior Carlton Club, London. I had permission to draw all these cheques but one; they were all paid by Monson. I was told not to draw any more. [Shown No. 91.] This is a letter from me to Monson, written from the Midland Grand Hotel—" I am so anxious about them at home that I have asked Tottenham to lend me a small sum. If you will enclose a Post Office order I shall be most grateful." I suppose that was an advance of £1 he was giving me; he occasionally gave me sovereigns, and I have had cheques for £2 or £3 from him. For these small sums I gave no receipt. In 1892 I had a bankruptcy petition against me; it has not been paid off yet.

Did Monson not pay £200?—There was something settled; the amount I do not know.

He paid off the bankruptcy petition?—It has not been cleared off yet; I am being sued at present. I do not know that Monson employed a Mr. Hardcastle, of Leeds, in connection with the proposed increased loans in order to pay off the Eagle Company, nor do I know that Mr. Hardcastle, in trying to get the loan, said that he would require valuations of all the securities. I do not know that Monson had to pay £300 to Mr. Hardcastle.

To be frank, do you not know that Monson incurred heavy accounts for legal and valuation expenses in connection with this? —I am not aware of it at all; I did not pay anything myself.

And Mr. Monson paid everything that there was to pay?—I do not know. After the Eagle Company foreclosed they became proprietors of my life interest. I have not got it back, though we are at present in negotiations with them. At the time when I found that I should have to purchase back my life interest, Monson proceeded as my agent to try to get a contract with the Eagle Company. I understood that he was to pay a certain deposit down and that I was to have a contract open for completion for a certain number of months, but subsequently he wrote and told me that he was acting entirely on his own account. The sum I heard of as being the amount of the deposit was £600. When Monson

148

Evidence for Prosecution.

wrote claiming to have a contract on his own account I left the matter in the hands of Mr. Fuller, my solicitor. I gave Monson a letter disclaiming his agency for me and saying that he was purchasing on his own account. This was done at the suggestion of Mr. Carter, who was acting as my solicitor. The letter was drawn by Mr. Carter and Mr. Monson, who told me that unless I did that they could not carry out the business on account of my bankruptcy proceedings.

Was it true that Monson was not your agent in the transaction? —Certainly he was not. I did not write the letter, but I signed it; I was advised as to it, and trusted Mr. Monson. I very much doubt about the education which Cecil got from Monson from 1890 onwards. I do not know that Cecil passed an examination creditably with 80 per cent. marks; he never told me about it. There was one tutor employed by Mr. Monson, Mr. Cowan, but not for my son. Subsequently I knew of a Mr. Cornell, B.A. I do not know what pupils Monson had.

In 1893 I was trying to carry through an arrangement with the Eagle Company apart from Monson, Dr. Hambleton acting as my nominee. He has no authority from me, he is not my agent; he is merely a friend. He is not my adviser; Mr. Prince is my adviser. I learnt quite accidentally that, at the time I was negotiating to get the contract from the Eagle Insurance Company for myself, Cecil was trying to get them to give the contract to his nominee. This came out through a communication that Mr. Prince had through Mr. Richards, the solicitor of the Eagle Company. Immediately on hearing this I went up to London and called upon Sir George Russell, the chairman of the company, and put the matter plainly before him, that my boy was being ill-advised in the matter, and that he was in the hands of people who were not acting in his interest, and that I was anxious that the contract should be in my name or in Dr. Hambleton's.

In 1892 I was told by Dr. Hambleton that Monson had made a proposal to him to the effect that Cecil's life should be insured for £50,000 or £60,000, and that the existing policies held by the Eagle Company on my life should be surrendered, and that the surrender money, something like £9000, should be secured and my life interest purchased back from the Eagle Insurance Company. I refused to have anything to do with Monson in the matter. Dr. Hambleton told me in the beginning of this year that under the proposed arrangement I was to get a certain allowance per week. [Shown No. 53 of defence productions.] I recognise this letter as in Dr. Hambleton's handwriting. It is to Monson, and is dated 17th July, 1893. Dr. Hambleton did not tell me what was written to Monson in that letter.

I think you said that your understanding and belief was that Cecil was being kept by Mr. Monson against his own desire?—I did not say so; I think that he was influenced by Monson to separate himself from me.

Alfred John Monson.

Major D. Hambrough

When do you say that that was done?—I say it had been for the last eighteen months or longer. [Shown Nos. 62, 63, 66 of defence productions.] These are letters written by Cecil to me in 1892. In the first of them, on 22nd March, my son writes—" My dear Father, —I received your letter this morning. I cannot very well come to town immediately, as Mr. Monson is away. I am afraid he would not like me going away just now, as it is in the middle of the term, because it would interfere with my work so much. He wants me to go in for my exam. in June. Mr. Cornell says if I work hard I shall have a very good chance of getting through, but that I have no time to lose. He also says I am getting on fairly well now, so you see it would be a pity to waste my time. I am glad you have made it up with Mr. Monson. I am sure he is doing his best. I believe he meant to have sent you some money last week, only he was disappointed in getting it. He expects to get it to-day, or at the latest to-morrow, so I believe."

The next letter is written from Riseley Hall, Yorkshire, on 24th March. It says—" I cannot see any good in coming to town. I could not do any good, and should only be an extra expense to you, and, goodness knows, money is scarce enough, and I should think it likely to remain so for the next two years. Mr. Monson says he does not see what good it would do. I should only be losing valuable time, and every day is of consequence to me now, if I am ever to pass this exam. Besides which, my going away would upset everything Rawstone would think, if I had a holiday in the middle of the term, that he ought to have one likewise. Mr. Monson has been good enough to provide me with pocket-money for the last year, and you can hardly wonder that I am grateful for it." The next letter is dated 28th March, 1892. It says—" My dear Father,—I am truly sorry if I have added to your troubles, and can only say that I had no intention of doing so. I think you greatly mistake Mr. Monson's intentions. I am sure he has not misrepresented things to me, and I cannot see what nefarious ends he has in view. He has always been straightforward to me. How has he attempted to defraud you? He has only tried to save the estates from being sold by the Eagle. If it had not been for him Hanrott would have bought them. I can assure you I mean no disrespect to you whatever. I am only doing what I am sure is for the best. I would sooner not leave my studies now, but in the holidays I should very much like to come and see you. The Eagle, as you are aware of, have foreclosed, and have got the foreclosure made good by the Court of Chancery, so it is impossible to upset it. Mr. Monson is going to pay off so as to cut off the entail when I come of age. If he does not succeed, and it passes into other hands, even when I come of age I do not see what could be done. I do not see how anything can be done at all except through him, so I think it is bad policy, if nothing else, to quarrel with him. I shall never forget how good both you and my mother have been

Evidence for Prosecution.

Major D. Hambrough

to me. I am sure this grieves me very much. But you know I must have an education; I cannot go about utterly ignorant all my life.''

Did not these letters satisfy you that Cecil himself thought it was best for him and you that he should stay and work with Monson? —I do not think that he was the one to judge; I think his father was. [Shown No. 65 of defence productions.] This is a letter from Cecil to his mother, dated 25th March, 1892. The letter states that he would rather not accept the invitation home just then, as he was most anxious to go on with his studies, and it would be unfair to Mr. Monson to leave in the middle of a term, and particularly when he had just engaged an expensive tutor. Besides, he had all he wanted there, and was quite happy and content. Mr. Monson was entering him for a militia regiment. He was old enough to understand his position perfectly well. He quite understood that when he came of age he would have to cut off the entail so as to pay his father's debts, which, of course, he would do. He could not do anything until he was twenty-one, and he was sorry he could not do what his mother asked him. He had quite made up his mind to work hard for his exam. [Shown No. 99 of defence productions.] This is a letter written by Cecil from the Depot Barracks, York, to Mrs. Monson, in which he says that he had had a letter from Colonel Hayes, asking whether he would remain at York or be transferred to Winchester. It was my desire that he should go to Winchester; I did not know that Cecil took the view that he should stay at York. He left me for the purpose of getting his uniform at York and of then going to Winchester.

Who was it who paid for your son's military outfit and other expenses?—That could have been arranged for, but no one has been paid as yet.

Who paid your son's mess bill and other expenses?—He managed out of his pay. [Shown letter No. 100 of defence productions.] This is a letter from Cecil to Mrs. Monson, written from York Barracks—'' Dear Mrs. Monson,—Thanks very much for your letter. After I wrote to you last night I had a wire from Carter—he is at Scarborough—saying that he would do his best in the business. He also said he was writing to-day, so I suppose I shall get his letter to-morrow morning. I had a letter from my mother this morning, saying that if I did not come immediately my father would arrive in York either to-night or to-morrow morning; but as he has not come yet, I suppose he will not come to-night now, and I think I shall go by the 10.15 train from York to Harrogate in the morning, as it would be so unpleasant if he comes here. Every one would know about it.'' I intimated that I was going to York, but I never went there.

Did these letters satisfy you that your son did not want you?— They were dictated to him.

In York Barracks?—All the letters were written under influence.

Alfred John Monson.

Major D. Hambrough

Even in York Barracks?—It just showed the influence he was under. I had provided for putting my son into a militia regiment, and in order to provide for him I had made arrangements with my solicitors, Fuller & Prince, for a second insurance. I had arranged to get money by order of the Court. I think the arrangements involved an insurance on my son's life, but I am not exactly sure what they were. I wrote in one of my letters to my son the following passage:—" I have at last obtained my insurance in a leading office. I am accepted as a first-class life, so that in a few days I hope to be able to get your mother everything she requires, and to replace her in the position to which she is entitled." My life had been accepted by the Scottish Imperial; the amount of the policy was not mentioned. I did not effect the insurance because a question arose afterwards as to my past history, and after a time I forgot the matter.

Were you told that without an insurance on your life nothing could be done about the transfer of the mortgage?—At that time I wanted an insurance to raise money to pay off the mortgage.

Does it come to this, that you were told by the insurance company that unless you satisfied them as to your past history they would not give you the insurance policy?—They wanted me to be re-examined, but I did not go.

You have not been passed by them in recent years, since 1886?—Yes; I was passed only last year by the Scottish Imperial. The policy was not taken up, because I went to another office on the same day, and one of the doctors saw something wrong with me, and it happened that the doctor of the Liverpool, London, and Globe Company, who had examined me half an hour before, was present, and they then refused.

I sent my son a telegram on 2nd November, 1892, saying—" All business blocked through you. Come at once. Your presence is absolutely necessary." Prince wanted him to come and reside in the family, to see if he was friendly with the family. The business referred to was the business of getting the transfer of the mortgage. It is not the case that I was telegraphing for my son in order to get him back to me for the purpose of insuring his life; I wanted to have him at home again. If Prince had found that Cecil was not hostile to his own family he would have found money for him until he came of age. This had nothing to do with the transfer from the Eagle.

Look at the mortgage. [Shown No. 19 of defence productions.] I find your name signed full out; is that your signature?—It is not my ordinary signature.

You say that it is a forged signature?—I say that it is not my ordinary signature.

You have signed a lot of deeds in your life, and it may be your signature?—I do not recognise it. I do not remember signing any document on that date; I never sign a document in full. [Shown cheque included in No. 143 of defence productions.] This is a cheque

152

Evidence for Prosecution.

for £18, dated 7th July, 1891, drawn by Mrs. Monson upon her account and payable to Dudley Albert Hambrough; on the back there is an endorsation, " Dudley Albert Hambrough." I do not write that kind of " A." I do not recollect writing my name on that cheque.

Is that your signature or not?—It is very like my signature. [Shown cheque included in No. 143 of defence productions.] This is a cheque drawn by Mrs. Monson upon her banker and payable to Major D. A. Hambrough. It is also endorsed, Dudley Albert Hambrough. The " A " is not like mine. It may be my signature, so far as I can see. I do not know where it was cashed. I was not in the habit of putting any cheques through a bank; I generally got the cash through tradesmen.

[Shown No. 19 of defence productions.] I have no recollection of having signed a mortgage for £5000; I do not think that I may have signed it. Mr. Fuller was acting as my solicitor in the beginning of 1892. In reply to a letter which I instructed Mr. Fuller to write to Monson asking him for a statement of the charges he had upon my property, Mr. Fuller got the following letter from Monson and read it to me. It is as follows :—" Sir,—In reply to your letter, dated 19th February, 1892, I have to say that, firstly, as to an account of all disbursements I have made on behalf of Mr. Hambrough, I beg to say that there is in such respect a large sum due to me. I don't now make any claim whatever on your client for the repayment of the money so due. Secondly—As to the two bills you have mentioned, I have never received any bill from your client for £5000, but I hold one for £3000, which I have not made use of, because, if I were to do so Mr. Hambrough would be subject to a criminal prosecution. Thirdly—I have never received an account for charges executed on property to the extent of £3000, which was not his property, but I have received one for £5000. I addressed one for £2600 to your client Mr. James, but he has not returned it, as promised on several occasions. Fourthly—As to the money due to me for maintenance, clothing, and education, there is a large sum of money due to me in this respect, but I don't now make any claim whatever against your client in regard to that.

" I beg to inform you that there is a large sum due to me on account of board at 89 Jermyn Street, and that he must in future pay all such accounts himself, and, in the event of his not doing so, he will have to be evicted from the rooms he now occupies. In consequence of the course of action your client has been foolish enough to take, I must withdraw my guarantee for the payment for his rooms. It may be as well to remark that it has only recently come to my knowledge that Major Hambrough is an undischarged bankrupt, and that, therefore, the money obtained has been fraudulently obtained.

" I beg to inform you in consequence of the withdrawal of my guarantee that Messrs. Edwards & Co., of Chancery Lane, will at

Alfred John Monson.

once take a receiving order against Major Hambrough unless the sum of £198 is paid to them by Tuesday next. The result of this receiving order will be most disastrous to your client, and it will be your duty to inform him that he will be called upon to account to the receiver for his infringement of the Bankruptcy Act by incurring other debts while an undischarged bankrupt. The explanation given to me by Hambrough is that he did not know that he was an undischarged bankrupt, but, of course, such an explanation will not be accepted by the Court, and therefore it will be advisable for you to discharge the numerous debts he has again incurred, otherwise he will undoubtedly be prosecuted criminally by some creditors who I know are by no means kindly disposed to him." That letter is dated 21st February, 1892.

Did Mr. Fuller read it to you?—He did. Mr. Monson said in the letter that he had a mortgage for £5000 granted by me, and at the time I said that I had not signed a £5000 mortgage. I left the matter in Mr. Fuller's hands; I do not know what he did.

It comes to this, no steps were in fact taken to challenge the deed Monson said he held for £5000?—I do not know what Mr. Fuller did. I got a letter or document sent to me from the bank in Scarborough intimating that Monson had borrowed a sum of money upon the £5000 mortgage. I thought this referred to the £5000 bill. I spoke to Monson, and he satisfied me. I trusted in him at that time. It is most certainly not the case that at that time I was living in apartments in Jermyn Street, London, and that Monson was paying the rent. [Shown No. 181.] This is a letter to me from Cecil, dated 1st May, 1892. It says—" I hope you like your new rooms, but it must be very disagreeable for you going without any luggage. Mr. Monson wired to say he would let you have £5, but he discovered afterwards he had wired to Brooke Street instead of Baker Street. He has got the bill all ready, but I believe he forgot to enclose it to you." After leaving Jermyn Street, I went to Baker Street; I had been wiring to Monson for money, but I forgot whether I got the £5 or not. Cecil sent no money to his mother at that time; the only time he sent any was in the early part of this year [Shown No. 186.] This is a letter from Cecil in which he says—" My dearest Mother,— I am afraid that you will think me very rude for not having answered your letter before, but I have been expecting some money every day, and was hoping to send some. I enclose £5. It is not very much, but it may be of use to you. I am hoping to be able to send you some more shortly." My son had no allowance from Monson, so far as I am aware, but I believe he had been introduced to moneylenders.

At Glasgow, on my way to Ardlamont, I sent a telegram to Monson asking for money. I left home in a great hurry, and had not sufficient money to go on with. I got £10 from Monson; he also paid the whole of the funeral expenses, railway fares, and hotel

Evidence for Prosecution.

expenses at Ventnor. I think that his expenses in connection with the funeral were considerable. I asked Monson to send an account of his expenses to Mr. Prince.

Had Prince any money of yours?—No. When I arrived at Ardlamont on the Saturday Monson gave me an account of the accident, and it was then that I got to understand that my son had been out shooting alone.

You would be distressed at the time, and you might quite well have misunderstood?—My memory is very clear. I arrived on Saturday and left on Monday. It was not till afterwards that I learned that Monson and Cecil and Scott had all been out together; I found out that I had been mistaken.

Re-examined by the SOLICITOR-GENERAL—In every case of signing cheques I signed " D. A. Hambrough." All the letters I wrote were signed " D. A. Hambrough." I have been shown a number of cheques drawn by myself on a bank account. The explanation of the variations in the form of my signature on cheques is that I endorsed the cheques in exactly the same form as the name to which the cheque is payable, but there is no reason of that kind in the deed to lead me to alter my signature.

As regards the bankruptcy proceedings which I mentioned as having been got rid of somehow, I understood that Monson had settled the matter, but I am being sued now.

As regards the deposit paid in connection with the Eagle transference, Monson at first, in the early part of 1892, told me that he had paid a deposit of £600; it was extended, however, till it amounted to £3000. I was not aware of Cecil's name being used in favour of the contract being got by Monson. Monson did not tell me that my son was opposed to my carrying the matter through in the way I approved.

In February, 1892, my affairs were being withdrawn from the control of Mr. Monson, and were being put into the hands of Mr. Fuller. I think that Monson did not wish me to go into Mr. Fuller's hands, and when I did the proceedings point to the Eagle contract being transferred to some person other than Monson.

Re-cross-examined by Mr. WILSON—Do you mean that you endorsed a cheque with your full name, and that you would not sign a deed which commenced with your full name, Dudley Albert Hambrough, in full? Look at the deed; it bears to be granted both on the outside and on the inside to Dudley Albert Hambrough. Does that not suggest to you that you would put your name throughout just as you do in cheques?

WITNESS—Yes; I admit that it would be reasonable to sign a deed with one's full name.

[The SOLICITOR-GENERAL explained that No. 20 of defence productions, the mortgage taken in the name of Dudley Albert Hambrough, was signed D. A. Hambrough.]

155

Alfred John Monson.

Major D. Hambrough

By the LORD JUSTICE-CLERK—Was there any occasion on which you did not sign your name as D. A. Hambrough except in the case of a document, where it was specially required by the person making the cheque payable in a particular name?—My regular signature was D. A. Hambrough.

49. MORRIS NATALI FULLER, examined by the SOLICITOR-GENERAL —I am a member of a firm of solicitors in St. Clement's Lane, London. I was consulted by Major Hambrough in February, 1892. The first thing I had to do as representing him was to write to Mr. Monson for particulars of the disbursements he had made on behalf of Major Hambrough and his son. I wrote Monson, and got a letter, in which he said—" I have endeavoured to explain matters to you, so that you will understand the responsibility you are incurring by taking up Major Hambrough's affairs."

For what purpose was that letter written?—Hambrough was an undischarged bankrupt, and I presume the letter was written to prevent me taking up the business. That was the impression I formed. The letter did not deter us from taking up his affairs. In consequence of that letter I made a search, and the Official Receiver told me that Hambrough had never been a bankrupt. Shortly after that there was a meeting in my office with Monson. Hambrough may have been there. We had a number of meetings.

Major Hambrough consulted me about getting Cecil from the Monsons. Cecil was present at our discussion, but I did not succeed in getting him to leave Monson. He was distinctly under his influence. From my investigations it did not appear to me to be favourable to Major Hambrough's interest or to Cecil's that he should remain with the Monsons, and I told the boy so. Acting for Major Hambrough, I had negotiations with Monson regarding the purchase of the estate, Monson sent a draft agreement for the purchase, but I did not approve of it because, in the first place, Monson would not agree to the price at which he would resell the estate to the father on the son coming of age; and, secondly, because Monson would not agree to act on behalf of Major Hambrough; he insisted on acting as principal. If the transaction had been carried out exactly on that line, the effect would have been to make Monson absolute owner of Major Hambrough's life interest, and we should, of course, have had to deal with Monson. When the boy came of age, Monson and the boy would be in such a position that Monson could do what he liked. I would not consent to that arrangement on behalf of Major Hambrough, and consequently the negotiations fell through. At this time the Eagle had foreclosed upon the mortgage. My suggestion was that the estate should be bought, and resold when the boy came of age, with a certain fixed profit to himself, a certain amount being charged upon the estate for that being done. From my conversation with the boy I formed the idea that he thought

156

Evidence for Prosecution.

M. N. Fuller

the effect of his leaving Monson would be that he would grow short of money. I thought he was very uncomfortable in his mind. I acted for Major Hambrough until the end of 1892. Throughout the whole of the time I acted, the arrangement, so far as Major Hambrough was concerned, was one by which Monson would have been excluded from the absolute ownership of the life interests. Monson would not agree to resell at a certain fixed profit, and if he had had his way he would have been left absolute master of the situation. During the negotiations he professed to be acting as Major Hambrough's friend, but I did not think so, though, of course, we were acting professionally; he had his own solicitor. It would not have been in Major Hambrough's interest to have completed the transaction on the lines proposed unless Monson had agreed to resell at a definite price, which he would not do, and, accordingly, I could not advise Major Hambrough to accept Monson's terms. I wrote to the Eagle Company, giving them notice that the negotiations had fallen through, and not to sell to Monson direct. I understood that if Monson had done what was suggested it would have been in the interests of the Major himself, but Monson would not bind himself, and gave as his reason that he had to borrow money to carry through this large transaction. He could not exactly say how much it would cost him, and therefore he could not say what profit would be got if the matter were carried through.

Cross-examined by Mr. COMRIE THOMSON—It was Mr. James, a mining engineer, who introduced me to Major Hambrough. The relation of solicitor and client subsisted between myself and Major Hambrough for about nine months, ending in September or October, when the negotiations fell through. Major Hambrough had no money except what he got from Monson. I knew that Monson was keeping and educating young Hambrough, and I admit that, to start with, he had a perfectly legitimate interest in trying to get into an arrangement whereby he would be repaid for his outlays when young Hambrough came of age. I inquired as to whether it was the case that Major Hambrough was an undischarged bankrupt, and found that there had been no adjudication, but that he had made a composition with his creditors; he was to have paid four shillings in the pound; I do not know if he has paid anything; I did not go into that.

[Shown No. 70 of defence productions.] I got the following letter from Monson:—" 23rd May, 1892. First Avenue Hotel, Holborn. Dear Sir,—I am instructed, in the event of Mr. D. A. Hambrough passing the medical examination to-day for insurance, to hand to you my cheque for £250 within a week from to-day. I also undertake to make him an allowance of £50 per month until his son comes of age." A vital part of the arrangement was what would happen when young Hambrough came of age. I got a letter from Messrs. Carter, Ramsden & Carter, solicitors, dated 16th

157

Alfred John Monson.

M. N. Fuller

March, 1892, as follows:—" Your letter received. My client is quite willing to regard Major Hambrough in the light of a purchaser of the estates, although under no obligation to do so, and considers the present time premature for discussing the terms of the purchase; and we may say that the terms contained in your letter are in nowise applicable, as past transactions cannot be allowed to enter into this proposal, which must be regarded solely in the light and relationship of vendor and purchaser. Our client is willing, prior to entering into this arrangement with Major Hambrough, to pay him a sum of money in consideration of his coming up for examination for insurance. Mr. Monson is unwilling to see Major Hambrough left unprovided for for the short intervening period between now and his son coming of age, and therefore proposes this arrangement. If your client is unwilling to enter into such an agreement as we propose, then please say so, and we will do without him, and he will understand that the matter between him and our client ceases, and we are specially instructed to say so." In the month of April there were several meetings between Major Hambrough, Dr. Hambleton, Mr. Monson, and myself in the First Avenue Hotel. At the first meeting we came to no arrangement, but on the following day we arrived at the heads of an agreement. They were sent to me by Messrs. Carter, but the agreement fell through. About 15th March I wrote a letter, to which the letter just read is an answer. This letter repeats the expression of willingness on the part of Monson to enter into an agreement with Major Hambrough to pay him a sum of money in consideration of his coming up for medical examination, and states that he is unwilling to see him left unprovided for in the interval before his son came of age.

What sort of establishment did Major Hambrough have in London; did he have a house, for instance?—No; he lived in lodgings. I knew that Monson had given Major Hambrough money to enable him to send his daughter to Germany. The Hambrough establishment consisted of the Major, his wife, and a little boy; they lived in lodgings, moving about a good deal from one place to another. At that time I know that Major Hambrough had not a penny except what Monson gave him.

Did it strike you as a strange thing that a lad, eighteen years of age, should prefer to go on with his education, living in a comfortable house, rather than come to the kind of life that his father was, unfortunately, obliged to live?—No. I met Cecil at my office on two occasions, I think; he came with his father. His father asked him in my presence to come and live with him, and as the negotiations for Monson purchasing the estate had fallen through, I advised Cecil to leave Monson and go up to his father.

What advantage was he to get in giving up a comfortable home and education, and on the eve of his examination, and coming up to London?—I cannot say.

Evidence for Prosecution.

M. N. Fuller

You thought, in the abstract, that a son should do what his father told him?—Yes; in the case of some fathers. In the telegram dated 2nd November, 1892, already referred to, I cannot say what the business was which was blocked by Cecil's absence, nor can I say why his presence with his parents was absolutely necessary. In the telegram dated 8th November—" You are causing great inconvenience; come to-morrow first train, or I fetch you "—the inconvenience which Cecil was causing by his absence was that the Major could not carry on some negotiations connected with insurance; it was very likely that he wanted to get his son's life insured. Part of the scheme before I ceased to be Major Hambrough's solicitor was that the young man's life should be insured for £50,000 or £60,000.

Can you explain any importance attached to his absence and to his causing great inconvenience, except the desire to have the young man up in London for the purpose of insurance?—It might be a dodge to get him up.

If it was a true statement, you think it must have been to get him for insurance, but you cannot be sure that it was a true story?—We were anxious to get him up. It was better for the Major and better for the boy. I ceased to be Major Hambrough's agent some time about November, 1892. At that time the project of Monson becoming the purchaser of the Major's life interest had come to an end.

The Court adjourned.

Sixth Day—Monday, 18th December, 1893.

50. HENRY PRINCE, examined by the SOLICITOR-GENERAL—I am a partner of the firm of Hutchins & Tunbridge, solicitors, London and Brighton. On 19th November, 1892, I was consulted professionally by Major Hambrough. I had an interview with Mr. Richards, representative of the Eagle Company, with the object of ascertaining from him what was the real position of affairs as regards the mortgages on the Hambrough estates. I ascertained that the Eagle Company had two mortgages, and that as mortgagees they had obtained absolute foreclosure against Major Hambrough's life interest. That had the effect of making them absolute owners of the life interest just as if they had been purchasers. I had negotiations with the Eagle Company with regard to obtaining a transfer. The object was to arrange to pay over to the Eagle Company the amount due to them, or the amount to which they were entitled, so as to lead them to give a transfer of their interests in the estates. I proposed to take a transfer to a mortgagee client of my own, but before that was done Mr. Richards wanted to enter into a definite contract. I was prepared to enter into a definite contract with a third party, Dr. Hambleton. I understood there was a competing application. I ultimately made the contract on 6th April of this present year. Certain information I got from Mr. Richards satisfied me that what I was doing was in the interest of the Major and his family, and that there was no ulterior object in what I was doing. Mr. Monson's name was mentioned in connection with the competing application, and Mr. Jerningham was mentioned as his nominee. Dr. Hambleton had no personal interest whatever in the matter. I think that the date by which it was expected that the contract should be completed was 1st August, 1893, but I am not clear about that. The contract was not completed by that date, the reason being that the contract was entered into subject to a formal contract being prepared and executed by the parties interested. There was nothing, except the delay by the solicitor of the Eagle office in sending the draft contract to me, that prevented the contract from being completed. I wrote for it several times. In so far as Cecil Hambrough's interests were concerned, they would have all been conserved under the arrangement I projected. The policies on Major Hambrough's life amounted to £40,000 in round figures, but more with the bonuses; under the proposed arrangement these policies were to be maintained, so as to

160

Evidence for Prosecution.

become available for Cecil's benefit on Major Hambrough's death. In the meantime, I offered that if Cecil came back to his family I would provide him with an efficient military tutor and make him an adequate allowance till he came of age, and also that I would place a hunter at his disposal. It was quite a voluntary act on the part of the Eagle Insurance Company to enter into the arrangement at all; they could have stood upon their absolute right to remain owners of the life interest during Major Hambrough's life if they wished. Whilst these matters were pending I heard of Cecil Hambrough's death.

Cross-examined by Mr. COMRIE THOMSON—Dr. Hambleton did not come along with Major Hambrough in the first instance, but later on he did. Dr. Hambleton was acting as a friend of Major Hambrough; I cannot say how far he acted as an adviser. He took an interest in Major Hambrough's affairs and communicated with me on the subject. I was not aware during this period that Hambrough was being financed by Monson; I did not inquire how he was living; I certainly did not know that Monson was keeping him. In the spring or summer of this year I understood from Dr. Hambleton that a suggestion had been made to him by Monson or on Monson's behalf that Cecil's life should be insured for £60,000 or £70,000, and that the existing policies on the Major's life should be surrendered. I did not approve of this proposal; I objected to surrender existing policies. [Counsel proposed to read a letter from Dr. Hambleton to Monson, dated 17th July, 1893.

The LORD JUSTICE-CLERK—I do not think the letter should be put to the witness, but questions suggested by it may be put to him.]

Cross-examination resumed—Hambleton frequently came about my office, but I cannot recollect his having mentioned to me anything about Cecil being insured for £60,000; I think that I mentioned that it might be necessary to insure him for £10,000 or £15,000. I cannot recollect anybody having spoken to me about the £60,000 other than Dr. Hambleton, who just mentioned it.

By the LORD JUSTICE-CLERK—Hambleton did inform me that the £60,000 had been suggested; he mentioned it as being a counter proposal. I was told that dissent had been expressed in Cecil's name as regards my proposed arrangements in this case. Mr. Richards mentioned to me that he had letters in the main favouring the arrangements. The letter from Hambrough to Richards referred to by counsel was not communicated to me.

Mr. COMRIE THOMSON—I have also a letter from Richards to Monson, and I want to know whether this correctly represents the view that Hambleton and Richards put before you—" It is unnecessary for the directors to go into any dealings between yourself and Mr. Hambrough "?

M

Alfred John Monson.

The LORD JUSTICE-CLERK—You must put the question on your own information. This is not a letter that the witness knows anything about as a letter.

Cross-examination continued—I think that Richards mentioned to me about April, 1893, that the negotiations with Jerningham were postponed until August. He said that his client had decided to give the preference to us, and that we could have till 1st August to carry this out, and that after then Mr. Jerningham's propositions would have to stand by. There was a date mentioned some time about 1st August, but I cannot say the correct date. The proposed arrangement was never carried out.

Re-examined by the SOLICITOR-GENERAL—I concluded the proposal for an arrangement with Mr. Richards on 6th April. Jerningham was to have nothing to do with the arrangement in the event of its being carried out. I was not only willing, but anxious, to carry it out. I understood from Mr. Richards that he would only consider Mr. Jerningham's proposal in the event of our not completing what was arranged.

My main objection to the proposed insurance of Cecil's life for £60,000, mentioned in cross-examination, was that to reinsure the Major the premium would be extremely high owing to his age, whereas the premiums on the existing policies were extremely low; and then the policies were of great value, having been in existence for twenty years. Their surrender value would have amounted to £10,000 or £13,000 in ready money, and their surrender would have involved a sacrifice of £2000 a year. There was no arrangement whatever about insuring Cecil's life as part of our arrangement; all that was said was that it might be necessary in certain eventualities. I knew that Monson's financial position was extremely low.

Re-cross-examined by Mr. COMRIE THOMSON—If Cecil's life had been insured, the premium of insurance would have been probably as low as were the original policies on the life of Major Hambrough.

51. HENRY WELLER RICHARDS, examined by the SOLICITOR-GENERAL—I am a solicitor in London, and partner of the firm of Hammond & Richards, Furnival's Inn. We are solicitors to the Eagle Insurance Company. They advanced a sum of £37,000 in 1885 for the mortgage of Dudley Albert Hambrough's interest under the Steephill will. In consequence of the interest not being paid they foreclosed in 1889 or 1890, and the foreclosure was made absolute in 1891. In the end of 1891 negotiations were opened with the Eagle Company by a Mr. Hanrott, solicitor, on behalf of Mr. Monson, for the purpose of acquiring the mortgage. There was an arrangement made which involved the payment of a deposit of £400. Monson did not make the deposit, and Hanrott made a deposit to get the contract in his own name in consequence of Monson's failure to pay. The transaction fell through, because

Evidence for Prosecution.

H. W. Richards

the purchase money was not forthcoming. There was a further £200 paid for an extension of time. The transaction fell through in July, 1892. Both the deposits were made by Hanrott, who had the contract in his own name, and made the deposits in his own name. In February, 1893, Mr. Prince entered on negotiations with me on behalf of Major Hambrough about the purchase of the Eagle mortgage, and on 29th March the directors agreed to sell to Mr. Prince for Major Hambrough. Prior to this I had been receiving applications from Cecil Hambrough in conjunction with Jerningham and Monson, and when the directors decided to give the contract to Prince they had the other applications before them. The decision of the board was communicated to Mr. Prince on behalf of Major Hambrough immediately afterwards. It was contemplated that the transaction would be carried through by 1st August. There was some delay in sending the draft contract to Mr. Prince, owing to pressure of work on our part; this delay and nothing else was what caused the arrangement to be broken off. From the end of March onwards, so far as the Eagle Company was concerned, it was arranged that Major Hambrough's friend should have the contract on the completion of the arrangement. We were having repeated applications from Cecil Hambrough, Jerningham, and Monson, acting, apparently, in association. [Shown No. 209.] This is a letter from Monson to the Eagle Company, in which he says—" A great mistake has been made in giving the contract for the purchase of the estates to Dr. Hambleton." I wrote to Monson on 13th April—" Having informed Major Hambrough's solicitor that the Eagle Company are prepared to sell to him, the transaction must go on; but if your views as to Dr. Hambleton's position are correct, then the transaction is postponed till August." The transaction, in point of fact, was not completed by 1st August, but this was entirely due to pressure of business on my part. The contract was still subsisting at 1st August.

[Shown No. 210.] This is a letter from Cecil Hambrough to me, dated 23rd April, in which he asks me to enter into a provisional contract with Mr. Jerningham, to take effect in August. I refused to agree to anything of this kind. [Shown No. 213.] On 31st July Monson wrote to me—" I understand from a letter from Dr. Hambleton that nothing has been done by them in regard to the purchase of the Hambrough life estates; therefore I assume your clients will be open to negotiations otherwise for the sale, as the time mentioned was in August. The proposal by Mr. Cecil Hambrough for Mr. Jerningham to purchase on his behalf cannot now be proceeded with, but Mrs. Monson would be quite willing to enter into a contract for the purchase, provided the time for completion is June, 1894. Mrs. Monson would pay a deposit of 5 per cent. upon the agreed-on purchase money. Cecil Hambrough is staying here with us. I do not see it concerns your clients what arrangements Mrs. Monson may enter into with Cecil Hambrough, so long as you are satisfied there is a

Alfred John Monson.

H. W. Richards

bona fide purchase for your clients and a substantial deposit made."
A deposit of 5 per cent. upon the purchase price of the mortgage
would amount to nearly £2000. In reply to this letter I wrote to
Monson on 3rd August as follows:- -" So far as we are aware, the
arrangements are still going on with Dr. Hambleton, but they have
rested with us, for we have been very much pressed with other matters,
and have not yet submitted the draft contract. We should, however,
be doing so in the course of a few days." I did not entertain at all
the proposal in Monson's letter that the contract should be taken in
Mrs. Monson's name. After this I had no further correspondence
with Mr. Monson.

Cross-examined by Mr. COMRIE THOMSON—I knew that Hanrott
was acting on behalf of Monson, and I was informed that subsequently proceedings were taken by Monson against Hanrott to prevent
him from acting in the matter on his own account. Jerningham was
acting along with Monson and Cecil Hambrough; Hambleton, Major
Hambrough, and myself were acting together, each side competing
for the contract. [Shown No. 208.] I received this letter, dated
29th March, 1893. The letter was in the following terms:—" The
question appears to be as to whether the directors will accept Mr.
Jerningham's offer, or that of Mr. Prince. I hope, however, that
the directors will take my position into their consideration and accept
Mr. Jerningham's offer, and that they will distinguish what a very great
difference there is between the *bona fides* of the two offers. The one
made by Jerningham, with a deposit of £5000, is a substantial offer
made by a gentleman of considerable position, and one from which I
shall benefit; while the other, made through Mr. Prince, with a
small deposit, is merely a speculation in the name of a person of no
position whatever, and with a view to making money out of me when
I come of age, ostensibly for the benefit of my father, but really for
the benefit of others. If the directors accepted the offer made by
Mr. Prince I should absolutely be deprived of any further interest in
the estate to which I am the tenant entail, because, when I come of
age, I should have either to disentail or take the consequences, which
might be very serious. My father has had the benefit of his life
estate, besides which he has recently charged the estate with an
annuity of £400 per annum to my mother, which has been already
mortgaged with a policy on her life; he has also charged the
estate with £5000 for the benefit of my sisters and brother, and thus
I am left quite unprovided for, and made to suffer the consequences.—
I am, yours truly, W. D. C. Hambrough." Up to 6th April the
Eagle Insurance Company had decided to give Dr. Hambleton the
offer to purchase the property comprised in the Hambrough security
on his paying a deposit of £200, and agreeing to complete the purchase on 1st August.

You were referred to a passage in a letter dated 11th April,
written by A. J. Monson to a board of directors of the Eagle Insurance

Evidence for Prosecution.

Company. I presume it was laid before you as solicitor?—It was, and I was instructed to reply to it.

Mr. COMRIE THOMSON—As it is important that the jury should hear the whole of it, I shall read it—"In the matter of the Hambrough estates it has come to my knowledge that certain untrue statements concerning myself have been made to your co-directors, originating, as I am informed, from Mr. Dudley A. Hambrough, and since these false statements appear to have been believed and circulated to my prejudice, I think it is my duty to at once place before you an accurate account of my transactions in this matter. My first transaction with Mr. Dudley Hambrough was on the 2nd November, 1889, when, in writing, he asked me to lend him £100 upon the charge of his reversion to the Pipewell estate, and from that date up to 1891 Dudley Hambrough obtained from time to time considerable advances of money from me without ever disclosing that he was bankrupt, and he obtained an advance upon certain representations which were not true, and giving me charges on his life estate. During the whole of the year 1891 Hambrough had no possible means of existence except what was thus derived. I made him a weekly allowance for the maintenance of his wife and children. I advanced money to enable his daughters to be sent to a school in Germany. I took Cecil Hambrough to reside with me, and engaged a tutor at a cost of £200 per annum to prepare him for the army. Apart from these advances, I paid large sums of money to save Dudley Hambrough from the possibility of criminal prosecution. In one case he actually drew several cheques on my bank, cashing them at the Junior Carlton Club, and it was only at great personal sacrifice that I was able to take up these cheques and save him from a criminal prosecution. Up to December, 1891, Dudley Hambrough owed me nearly £4000. It was only after communicating with your solicitors that I found out that he was bankrupt, and that your company had obtained orders of foreclosure against him. The only means of recovering my money appeared to be by entering into a contract to purchase the life estates. I was, however, not in the position to pay down the deposit required, but I was introduced to a solicitor, Mr. Hanrott, with the view to his finding the deposit and carrying out the purchase for me. Mr. Hanrott communicated with your solicitor on my behalf, and a contract was drawn up for the sale of your securities to myself; but without ever receiving intimation until afterwards, my name was removed from the contract, and that of Mr. Hanrott inserted instead. This involved me in litigation with Mr. Hanrott until I obtained an order from Mr. Justice Chitty for the surrender of the contract to me, upon my conveying to Mr. Hanrott the deposit. This action cost me upwards of £100 in cash out of my pocket. I had in the meantime completed a mortgage upon my interest in certain colliery property, and therefore I was able to pay the deposit. I found the security to be a most difficult one to deal with, which necessitated my applying

165

Alfred John Monson.

for a further deposit; and, apart from the deposits, I incurred very heavy expenses in endeavouring to complete the purchase. In fact, I absolutely spent upwards of £1000 after entering into the contract. Not one single farthing of the money owing to me from Dudley Hambrough has ever been repaid, and thus I lost upwards of £5000, money actually out of pocket. Mr. Cecil Hambrough has continued to reside with me. He has passed his first examination for the army, and I have obtained him a commission in the 3rd West Yorks Regiment. He has now an allowance of £5 a week, a considerable part of which he sends to his mother, and therefore I am indirectly supporting the family at the present moment. I ask, in justice to myself, that this letter should be read at the meeting of your co-directors.'' Then comes the passage that the Solicitor-General read.

WITNESS—The letter came before the board, and I answered it. The position of affairs was that Monson had been informed that if Dr. Hambleton would not complete the contract by the beginning of August, Jerningham might then open negotiations. I was not informed that Hambleton was willing to enter into an arrangement with Monson, part of which was that Cecil's life should be insured. I told Monson by 1st August that it was my intention to send the contract to Hanrott for revisal.

Re-examined by the SOLICITOR-GENERAL—No transaction entered into between the Eagle Company and any other person would in any way affect Cecil's right to the fee of the estate; it would affect nothing except Major Hambrough's life interest. Supposing that any one on Cecil's behalf had succeeded in purchasing the father's life interest in Cecil's name, the estate could not have been disposed of during Major Hambrough's lifetime; the entail could not be barred until after his death.

52. ADOLPHUS FREDERICK JAMES JERNINGHAM, examined by the SOLICITOR-GENERAL—I reside at Trafalgar House, Gresham Road, Staines, Middlesex. I first made Monson's acquaintance in the early part of last year, with reference to some pecuniary advances I wanted. My name was associated with a project for the purchase of Major Hambrough's life interest in certain estates. I had not means at my disposal sufficient to enable me to purchase, but I was asked by Monson to enter into the project as a kind of trustee for young Hambrough. Nothing was ever said about remuneration. The proposal was first broached in April, and after that it appears that there were other proposals, and in consequence of these being still in force, it was proposed by Monson to allow the project with which I was associated to stand over till the following August. I believe I was asked a question about it in May last, but between May and August I heard nothing whatever about it. I heard in April that the directors had decided to give the contract to Major Hambrough's friends.

Evidence for Prosecution.

A. F. J. Jerningham

Monson was in the habit of getting financial assistance from Tottenham, and it was this which really created the relations between Monson and me. [Shown No. 141.] That is the lease of Ardlamont. This is the second occasion on which I have seen it, the first being when I came to Edinburgh a week ago to-day in response to being summoned as a witness. I was not at Riseley Hall in May, 1893; I have not been there since March of this year. I arrived on Saturday, the 11th, and left on the following Tuesday. I had no footman of the name of Lillie in my employment in May, 1893; I had no footman at all in 1893.

The SOLICITOR-GENERAL intimated that he was about to ask witness a question concerning witness's signature to the lease.

Mr. COMRIE THOMSON objected, and the objection was sustained.

Cross-examined by Mr. COMRIE THOMSON—What is your occupation?—I am a civil engineer.

Where do you conduct your business?—I do not practise; I have not practised since 1876. I have private means derived from house property in London. I do not know exactly what it yields, it comes from my marriage settlement; I have nothing except what I got through my marriage. I cannot tell you what my income is. There was a change in my expectations on account of an opinion of counsel that was obtained; I was under the expectation of succeeding to a position of some distinction, but the opinion of counsel was that my expectation was not a good one. I did not accept counsel's opinion, and I maintain that my expectation is a good one.

I saw Cecil Hambrough for the first time in March of this year, and at that time the question was whether my offer or that of Mr. Prince was to be accepted. I knew that there was a competing offer, but I knew nothing of Mr. Prince. The only explanation that I gave to Cecil Hambrough was that what was being done was what Mr. Monson said from time to time should go on. Cecil knew very little about business, and only went by what Mr. Monson told him. On 29th March Monson wrote to the solicitors of the Eagle Company—" I understand that the proposal of Mr. Jerningham's purchase is to be placed before your directors to-morrow." That was in consequence of a visit I paid along with Monson to Mr. Richard's office in Furnival's Inn. Cecil was anxious to know the result, and I told him. It was Mr. Monson who suggested my name to the Eagle Company as trustee. I know Mr. Gordon and Mr. Nutting, the solicitors, and Mr. Nutting accompanied me on my visit to Mr. Richards. Mr. Nutting was introduced to me by Mr. Gordon, who, as far as I was aware, was Monson's solicitor. I was advised to have a separate solicitor, and Nutting was the man employed.

I know the firm of Messrs. Edward Paton & Son; they are well-known people in St. James'; they let shooting estates. [Shown No. 124.] This is a letter from J. & F. Anderson, W.S., to myself, dated 26th April, 1893:—" Dear Sir,—Messrs. E. Paton & Sons, estate

167

Alfred John Monson.

A. F. J. Jerningham

and shooting agents, 14 St. James' Street, London, S.W., wish to take Ardlamont House and shootings at a rent of £450, on behalf of Mr. Cecil Hambrough, of Trafalgar House, Staines, who, they state, wishes to rent it for a year with a view to purchase, and explaining that Mr. Hambrough will fall into a large fortune in the course of next year. They inform us that you are Mr. Hambrough's trustee and guardian, and refer us to you with regard to him. We shall be glad if you would say whether Mr. Hambrough will make a good and sufficient tenant. We note that Messrs. Paton observe that you are his guardian and trustee. This requires us to ask the question whether Mr. Hambrough is of age and is capable of entering into a binding contract. We could not let the place to a minor." I believe that I got that letter, but I have no recollection of replying to it.

Re-examined by the SOLICITOR-GENERAL—As far as I know, Cecil Hambrough's regular place of residence at that time was with Monson at Riseley Hall. I was asked by Monson to be Cecil Hambrough's trustee and guardian, but nothing was settled; I never heard that I was appointed.

On 1st May did you receive a letter from Messrs. J. & F. Anderson to the following effect:—" Dear Sir,—We had your telegram informing us that you were undertaking to pay the rent for Ardlamont, we therefore write that that matter is closed." Did you ever telegraph to Messrs. Anderson undertaking to pay the rent?— I have no recollection of that whatever, for the simple reason that I was never asked to pay the rent. I do not know that I ever got a letter of which this is a copy; I had nothing whatever to do with the taking of Ardlamont.

53. ARTHUR LOOVEY, examined by the SOLICITOR-GENERAL—I am a solicitor, Portman Square, London, and two years ago I was employed by the Yorkshire Banking Company to recover a sum of money from Mr. Monson, a claim for £700 in respect of an overdraft on his bank account. In security for this overdraft several deeds and a mortgage from an insurance company had been deposited. The mortgage was one by Major and Cecil Hambrough securing repayment of £5000 in consideration of £4000 advanced by Monson to the father and son; the date was 23rd May, 1891. Monson had overdrawn from the Yorkshire Banking Company to the extent to £540, and on being asked for further security had deposited this mortgage and got a further overdraft. On 27th August, 1891, I got judgment against him for £670 17s. 1d. and £8 costs, in all, £678 17s. 1d., and we got execution in Yorkshire, at Riseley Hall and at Harrogate. We obtained chiefly personal effects, realising £10 gross, and a little furniture at Harrogate, realising £15 gross. The Sheriff's fees amounted to £10 14s., leaving a balance of £14 odds.

168

Evidence for Prosecution.

A. Loovey

On 13th December, 1892, I was employed by another country firm, for whom I acted as London agent, to obtain judgment against Cecil Hambrough for £800. The writ was at the suit of Agnes Maud Monson, wife of Alfred John Monson, against Windsor Dudley Cecil Hambrough, to recover £800 for money lent and payments made at his request by plaintiff. I obtained judgment by default for £800 on 9th January, 1893, with £5 6s. costs.

Cross-examined by Mr. WILSON—The judgment against Monson was taken in August, 1891. At that time I did not know that Mr. Monson subsequently filed a petition in bankruptcy; I know now. The only claim against Monson with which I was connected appears to have been before his bankruptcy. I did not know that as regards the judgment for £800 against Cecil Hambrough there was an arrangement between him and Mrs. Monson; I got no letter from Cecil nor from my country agent about any such arrangement. My only information was to raise the suit. At the commission in London I was not asked to produce the mortgage for £5000 by Major Hambrough and Cecil in favour of Monson. I have it with me now, and am willing to put it into the custody of the Court.

54. DAVID DEUCHAR, examined by the SOLICITOR-GENERAL—I am an actuary in Edinburgh and am the manager of the Caledonian Fire and Life Insurance Company. I have been asked to make certain calculations with reference to the capital value of the late Mr. Cecil Hambrough's estate on his attaining his majority, and certain data have been supplied to me for that purpose. I was asked to assume the rental of the Ventnor estate to be £1300, of the Middlesex estate £1900, and the investments £780, making the value of the Hambrough estates in all £3980. I was asked to assume that the rental was burdened with a charge of £5000, and also to see what it would be without that charge. I was told that Major Hambrough's age was forty-four, and that Cecil Hambrough was between twenty and twenty-one. It was quite possible for Cecil Hambrough to realise his prospective interest; there are companies who deal with transactions of that kind. Assuming that Major Hambrough was tenant for life as heir of entail of the Hambrough estates yielding £3980, and is at present forty-four years of age, and assuming that his son, who was the next heir of entail, survived his father, he could have sold his interest when he came of age. He would have got only £18,560 for the sale, and to get this he would have had to sell absolutely the whole capital of the estate. I made a similar calculation in regard to some estates called the Pipewell Hall estates. Assuming the rental at £2000, the selling price of Cecil Hambrough's interest in these estates when he came of age would be £7380. There were two intervening lives. I regard the above sums as the full market value of the interests calculated on an ordinary actuarial basis.

Cross-examined by Mr. COMRIE THOMSON—The lending of money

Alfred John Monson.

on reversion with further security by way of life policy is quite a usual form of business, and done by perfectly respectable offices. In addition to the subjects mentioned as forming part of the estate, certain brickfields were referred to which gave a rental in royalties of from £400 to £700 a year. This rental, however, I was told, was to be set against possible expenses and commissions, and therefore they were thrown out of the calculations. It was not explained to me that the Middlesex property was what is called an improving feuing estate. It was not explained to me that there was a Metropolitan debenture stock representing the value of the heirlooms. I was not told, with reference to the Pipewell succession, that an insurance against issue had been effected, the premiums of which were fully paid, nor was I told that there was an insurance of life against life upon it for £7000. In arriving at the two sums, £18,560 and £7380, I did not take into consideration the termination of the entail by consent of Major and Cecil Hambrough, and therefore the enjoyment of the whole lands in fee simple. My calculation does not involve the possibility of those two persons barring the entail; of course, that would make a very considerable difference.

Re-examined by the SOLICITOR-GENERAL—In my calculations I assumed the total gross rental to be £5980 a year; this included £780 of income from securities. I took a larger value for the securities than if the income had been from land, because I understood that they were first-class securities. Of course, I made a calculation of taxes, expenses of management, repairs, and that sort of thing. I made a deduction in respect of the policy which would have to be effected, and, of course, if the policy had already been effected that deduction in respect of so much of the insurance money would have required to be cancelled. The insurance which I took into account would have to be an insurance of Cecil Hambrough's life against the two lives of his father and mother. The calculation I have given is based upon the assumption that Cecil Hambrough had simply to sell at his own hand. The value of his interest on coming of age, if he acted in concert with his father, excluding Pipewell, would be £45,551. In regard to Pipewell, as there are two intervening lives, it would require to be dealt with in a different way; I should say that the value is £7380, making a total of £52,931.

Re-cross-examined by Mr. COMRIE THOMSON—It was not explained to me that a portion of the Middlesex subject was sold last year at £400 an acre, nor was it explained that there were developable minerals and timber on the Pipewell estate; assuming these to be facts, they would enter into the calculations of the value.

55. WILLIAM HENRY KEEN, examined by the SOLICITOR-GENERAL —I am a messenger in the Crown Agent's Department at the Colonial Office, and I occupy a house at 35 Sutherland Street, Pimlico, London, part of which I let. I have resided there since June, 1890. In

Evidence for Prosecution.

W. H. Keen

November, 1891, a family of the name of Davis took four rooms in my house, and came to live there. The family consisted of Mr. Davis, his wife, one daughter, and two sons, Edward and George. Edward Davis was spoken of as " Ted." About nine weeks after they came they gave up one of their rooms. I was away from the house every day from a quarter to eight till six in the evening. It was not till the beginning of August of this year that I learnt what Ted's occupation was; he told me that he went to race meetings and went about with gentlemen to put money on horses. He was in my house in London in the beginning of August last.

Do you remember meeting him any day in the early part of August?—On 7th August I met him outside the door of my house, and he told me he was going north. After that I saw Ted Davis at the Post Office in Broad Sanctuary, Westminster, but I do not remember the date. So far as I know, he was resident in my house after 7th August, but I did not see him.

Ted Davis was about twenty-nine or thirty years of age, 5 feet 9 or 10 inches in height, of slim build, sallow complexion, with light blue eyes and dark hair. He had no moustache. I believe that he suffered from asthma. I do not remember seeing or hearing of him after the beginning of September. I saw nothing of him about my house after 7th August, but I believe he was there. It was after the first week of September that I learnt that he was no longer living in my house, and since then he has never, to my knowledge, been in my house. The rest of the Davis family left on 30th October, but I do not know where they went to. The family always went by the name of Davis, but letters came addressed to the name of " Sweeney," which were handed to the Davises, who accepted them as for themselves. I have taken in letters addressed to " Mr. E. Sweeney "; I cannot say whether I took in any letters addressed to that name about the beginning of September. I cannot say that I remember taking any letters coming addressed to that name upon thin tissue paper bearing the Edinburgh post-mark. Nobody of the name of George Hunt lived at 35 Sutherland Street, Pimlico, during last year.

Cross-examined by Mr. COMRIE THOMSON—This man Ted Davis was, to the best of my knowledge, clean-shaved; he had neither whiskers, moustache, nor beard. All my knowledge of the letters addressed to Sweeney is that the Davises told me that letters coming to my house addressed to that name were to be handed to them. They seemed decent enough people; they always behaved all right till just before they left, when there was a quarrel with my wife. The last time I saw Ted Davis to speak to was on 7th August. I saw him afterwards. On 7th August he did not mention any race meeting. I knew that he was in the way of going to race meetings; he had told me so. I cannot tell how long after this it would be till I saw him again at the Post Office at Broad Sanctuary; it was not the

Alfred John Monson.

next day; I believe it may have been a Saturday afternoon when I was coming home from business at the office. I cannot recollect how near I was to him; I passed him going up the steps leading to the Post Office. We did not speak; why we did not I cannot say. I should say that he was staying at my house at the time; he stayed there until the beginning of September.

Re-examined by the SOLICITOR-GENERAL—I don't suppose that I saw him a dozen times during the whole time he lived with us; there were weeks at a time during which I did not see him.

56. Mrs. KEEN, examined by the SOLICITOR-GENERAL—I am the wife of the last witness and reside with him at 35 Sutherland Street, Pimlico. Ted Davis lived with us nearly two years, along with his father and mother. The family left our house in October of this year. Ted Davis was about twenty-nine or thirty years of age, about 5 feet 8 or 9 inches in height, and of thin build, with a long face and sallow complexion, dark blue eyes, and dark hair. He had no moustache. He ceased to live at my house on 7th August, but he was in the house at the end of the same week, on the Friday or Saturday. Letters used to come to the house addressed, I think, to " G. Sweeney, Esq."; such letters came every morning and were given to Ted's parents. When they took the rooms we understood he was a nephew, but this was a mistake; he and his brother George were sons of Mr. and Mrs. Davis; there was also a daughter. It was the mother who said that letters addressed to " Sweeney " were to be given to them; this was always done. I do not recollect what month these letters began to come, but it was during fine summer weather. The daily arrival of a letter addressed to Sweeney continued, I believe, until the month of August. It suddenly stopped. According to the best of my recollection no letter came after Bank Holiday, 7th August. The letters bore the Edinburgh post-mark. I cannot remember the date on which Ted Davis left the house, but I remember his box being taken away. Wiggins took down the box for Davis and put it in a trap. I do not know which member of the Davis family it was who was going away, but I did not see Ted after that. When the Davis family left their luggage went in a van. Wiggins was a lodger in the house; he carried down the boxes at the request of Mrs. Davis.

Cross-examined by Mr. COMRIE THOMSON—There were two sons of the name of Davis, Edward and George. The letters came addressed to " G. Sweeney," that is, George. So far as I saw, no letters came to Edward. I do not know whether George Davis got the letters addressed to " G. Sweeney." The only letters I saw addressed to " Sweeney " were to " G. Sweeney "; they were letters bearing the Edinburgh post-mark and came during the last London season. I cannot describe the handwriting; I cannot say whether it was like a woman's or a man's.

172

Evidence for Prosecution.

George Davis left our house some time before his parents; I do not remember if he left before the Bank Holiday on 7th August. I believe George was in the house then. When he left the letters to " G. Sweeney " stopped. The last time I saw Ted Davis was, I believe, the Saturday after the Bank Holiday. I saw him at the door, passing out of the house. It was daylight at the time. My husband was not with me. I cannot tell you when it was that the boxes were taken away in the small trap. They were travelling boxes and belonged to the Davis family, but to which of them I do not know.

Re-examined by the SOLICITOR-GENERAL—George Davis used to be away from the house all day and only came back at night to sleep. I do not know when he ceased to sleep in our house, but it was some time before old Mr. and Mrs. Davis went away; it was months before the final leaving that George stopped coming back to sleep. He had some employment at the Westminster Palace Hotel, and I believe that he slept there. He had been employed there at the time when he slept at our house; I cannot say why he made the change of sleeping place.

I know of no person of the name of Hunt residing at our house during this year. A letter came to our house addressed to " George Hunt, Esq."; I do not know for whom it was intended; it was returned, I believe, " address unknown." I cannot say when that was. The letter from Edinburgh to " G. Sweeney, Esq.," arrived daily.

57. JOSEPH WIGGINS, examined by the SOLICITOR-GENERAL—I live at 16 Avery Farm Road, Pimlico, London. During this year, from 30th July to 20th September, I resided at 35 Sutherland Street. In the same house were living a family called Davis. On the morning of 5th September I carried some boxes belonging to one of the Davis family downstairs to a little spring cart. I did not see any of the Davis family go away with the cart.

Cross-examined by Mr. COMRIE THOMSON—There was no address on the boxes. I was afterwards asked by Mr. Davis to go and identify them, but I never went, and I do not know where they live. I have seen George Davis, but I never saw the other one; I do not know his name; I do not know to whom the boxes belonged.

58. Mrs. WIGGINS, examined by the SOLICITOR-GENERAL—I am the wife of the last witness. I was living at 35 Sutherland Street in August and September of this year. I only saw Ted Davis once; that was on 5th August. Telegrams used to come for him about three times a day; I used to hear the telegraph boy's knock at the door. I did not know that Davis sometimes bore the name of Sweeney, but Mrs. Davis once told me that if a telegram should come to her in the name of " Sweeney " I was to take it in.

Cross-examined by Mr. COMRIE THOMSON—Ted had no moustache.

173

Alfred John Monson.

Mrs. KEEN, recalled, in reply to the LORD JUSTICE-CLERK—I frequently saw telegrams coming to the house last summer; they were addressed to "Davis." They came very rarely more than once a day; I do not remember any addressed to "Sweeney."

Mr. COMRIE THOMSON—I would like your lordship to ask witness whether the post-mark on certain letters was not "Helensburgh" instead of "Edinburgh." This is in consequence of information I have received since luncheon.

By the LORD JUSTICE-CLERK—Are you quite sure that the post-mark was "Edinburgh" and not "Helensburgh"?—"Edinburgh," my lord.

59. GEORGE SMITH, examined by the SOLICITOR-GENERAL—I am a tailor at Eton. On 1st or 2nd July a man named Edward Davis was introduced to me by Mr. Sidney Russell, and gave me an order for £11 worth of clothes. The address given was 35 Sutherland Street, Pimlico. I got a further order for clothes from him by letter. On 18th July he called and paid for the clothes which he had ordered on his first visit to me and gave me the order for clothes mentioned in the letter. The value of the order was about £23 9s. I waited upon him at Anderton's Hotel, Fleet Street, to fit on the clothes. I sent half of the clothes about 26th or 27th July to 35 Sutherland Street, and the other half on 4th August. I got a letter with reference to clothes for George Hunt; I was to supply clothes to a person of that name at Eton. George Hunt told me to send the clothes to 35 Sutherland Street. I never saw any one of that name at Sutherland Street; I met George Hunt in Haxell's Hotel and fitted him on there.

Who had introduced him?—Edward Davis or Sweeney.

You say Davis or Sweeney. How do you associate the name of Sweeney with this man?—I have only heard since that his name is Sweeney. He introduced Hunt to me. I made the clothes, and they were sent to 35 Sutherland Street. I have been paid for the clothes by Hunt.

What does Hunt look like?—May I be allowed to explain? Since I have been here I have found out that Hunt is George Sweeney; since I have been here, not before.

When did you get the introduction?—When Davis called on me to pay his clothes he told me he would send a friend of his, Mr. Hunt, to get some clothes. He did not bring Hunt for some time.

[George Sweeney was at this stage brought into Court and shown to witness.]

By the LORD JUSTICE-CLERK—Look at that man; have you seen him before?—I first saw him on 22nd July at Eton. He was alone and said that Davis had sent him. I had heard before from Edward Davis that such a person was coming to me.

Examination continued—The man whom I have seen gave an

174

Evidence for Prosecution.

order in the name of George Hunt. I accepted the order and made the clothes, and sent them to 35 Sutherland Street. I got a letter from Hunt, saying—" Clothes to hand. Glad to say they fit very well. I shall not be going North for fully a week, so when ready please forward." I do not know what that refers to. He might have told me he was going on a holiday. I might have only sent half of the clothes, and he wanted the other half. Until I came to Edinburgh —until I was in the same room as the person I was shown just now— I knew him as George Hunt. I was introduced to him by the inspector of police, who said, " I will introduce you to Davis' brother "; but before I had the opportunity of being introduced I could see who the man was; I knew him already. In October I was requested by the police to render my account to Davis at 35 Sutherland Street, which I did the day after the police called. The account amounted to £23 9s. My account was rendered to Edward Davis. In appearance he was about 5 feet 8 inches in height, and about thirty-five or thirty-six years of age. His face was long and sallow, and his hair dark brown. I am under the impression that he had no moustache, but I cannot swear; if he had one, it would be very slight indeed, but I am not clear about that. His cheeks were sunken, and he had a cough. I asked him if he was going to the seaside for his holidays. He said, " I am very bad; in all probability I shall go South."

Cross-examined by Mr. COMRIE THOMSON—The only persons I knew in this matter were Edward Davis, George Hunt, and Russell. Russell introduced Davis to me, and Davis introduced Hunt. I found out that Hunt is George Sweeney or George Davis. It was on 18th July that Edward Davis said to me that he proposed to go South for his health. I called at Anderton's Hotel on 23rd or 24th July to try the clothes on, and since then I have not seen Edward Davis.

60. FRANCIS ARTHUR LAW, examined by the SOLICITOR-GENERAL— I reside at 100 Addison Road, Kensington. I do not follow any profession. I know Alfred John Monson. I was introduced to him in May, 1890, by a man called Whitelaw, a turf commission agent, and known in business as Cameron & Company. I met Monson casually in the Hotel Metropole on 30th June, and he spoke about getting a place in Scotland called Ardlamont. He asked me to dine with him that night at the Westminster Palace Hotel, where he was staying. He mentioned that he expected a bookmaker named Davis to pay him £250 of a bet which he had won on the previous day. After luncheon, two men came into the smoke-room. The man Sidney Russell was introduced to me as Davis. [Shown Sidney Russell.] That was one of the men; I had never seen him before, and Monson told me he was Mr. Davis, of the Victoria Club. Monson seemed to know him, and introduced us. He told me if I wanted to do anything that day he was all right. He did not say exactly to what figure

175

Alfred John Monson.

F. A. Law

it was safe to do business, but he was betting in twenty-fives himself. Monson said that Davis was a safe man. The other man was about 5 feet 9 inches in height, with a sallow complexion and slight moustache, thin, and decidedly delicate-looking.

I was introduced by Monson to another man called Robertson. Monson made some bets with Davis, *alias* Russell. Monson and the rest left the smoke-room of the hotel together, leaving me behind. Just before leaving, Monson said—" I forgot to go to the bank about getting a cheque cashed, and I have got no money; can you change it for me? " I asked him the amount, and said that I had not the amount about me. I pulled out the gold I had about me and said, " Help yourself! " which he did, taking three sovereigns and leaving me a couple of sovereigns. He said that he would repay me next day at the Metropole. Next day, 1st July, I went to the Metropole, after meeting Russell, accompanied by his sallow friend, in the Grand Hotel. Monson did not call, as he had promised, to repay the £3. I wrote to Monson about the man Russell, saying that he had not settled his account on the Monday, and at the same time asked Monson to send the money he had borrowed. I have never received payment of the £3 either from Davis or from Monson. The person who accompanied Davis, *alias* Russell, was with him all the time; I saw the two making bets together. On 1st July they were again together in the Grand Hotel.

Cross-examined by Mr. COMRIE THOMSON—I found Monson in the buffet of the Metropole; he was just leaving a young gentleman. He told me he was waiting for Russell, whom he called Davis. The sallow man came in along with Russell. Monson and the sallow man did not appear to have much conversation together; the conversation was mostly with Russell. I did not see Monson with Davis and the sallow man in the Grand Hotel buffet. Monson invited me to go north and visit him; I intended to be in the West of Scotland myself. I do not know whether he asked two or three other friends also.

61. LESLIE MURRAY ROBERTSON, examined by the SOLICITOR-GENERAL—I am in the wine and spirit trade, and reside at Richmond. I have known Alfred John Monson about two and a half or three years I met him first at my solicitors, P. J. Gordon & Sons, and I have been in the habit of meeting him since. I knew a man of the name of Sidney Russell for about eighteen months. He is a bookmaker. I knew a sallow man who used to be with Russell a good deal. His name was Edward Davis. He was about thirty-two years of age, and about 5 feet 9 inches in height. He was thin, but well built. His complexion was sallow and his hair brownish. I do not think that he had a moustache. I have only seen him about eight or a dozen times altogether. I was in the Hotel Metropole in the end of June on the occasion when Law,

176

Evidence for Prosecution.

Monson, and Russell were there; the sallow man was also there. Russell occasionally took bets for Davis; Davis and he used to bet together. Sometimes the one acted as principal and the other as clerk, and sometimes it was the other way round; they appeared to be associated in the betting business. The association between them did not begin until May last. It was Monson who introduced me to the sallow man. On one or two occasions I have seen Monson in company with Russell and Davis at the Hotel Metropole.

In July last I cashed a cheque for Davis, given by Mr. West. I was down in Richmond at the time, and Davis asked me to get the cheque cashed for him, and I said I would. He and Monson came down next morning, and I handed over the money. Davis was not with me at the bank; he came down by train, and I met him somewhere a little after ten. The man who gave me the cheque was the man whom I knew as Edward Davis, the sallow man who accompanied Russell. Davis was in the habit of frequenting various places; I have seen him at the Mitre in Chancery Lane, in the Grand Hotel, and in the Hotel Metropole. I heard Monson say at the Metropole that he had taken a place in Scotland, and I heard him talking about it afterwards. Monson said that the place he had taken was sixty miles from a railway station, and when I asked him how he could get to it he said, "Oh, we've got a yacht." I expressed surprise at his being able to take a place in Scotland while he was in the Bankruptcy Court. I last saw Davis in July in the Strand. He has not, to my knowledge, been seen in his usual haunts from that time till now. Russell is going on just as before. When I made a bet with Davis or Russell they were frequently together; it was immaterial which of them I looked to for payment of my money. I had the impression that Davis was the more substantial man of the two, but I had no accurate means of knowing. I have known Russell sometimes call himself Davis, but Davis never, to my knowledge, called himself Russell.

If Russell was calling himself Davis, how was he distinguished from the real Ted Davis?—There is no Ted Davis.

Then Edward Davis?—They were different-looking men altogether. A number of bookmakers on the course always go by the same name; I don't know for what reason. I have not heard Monson say that he was in the habit of pawning things. Ascot is in June, but I don't know when the Alexandra Park Meeting is; I rather think that it is after Ascot. I do not know if Monson was at the Alexandra Park Meeting. I only saw him the first two days at Ascot, and I understood that he had been winning money, but he told me the week after Ascot that he had not had a good week. I have no idea at all why Davis is not in his old haunts. I have not heard of his death; all I know is that I have not seen him or heard of him since July last.

N

Alfred John Monson.

Cross-examined by Mr. COMRIE THOMSON—I had not seen Monson in Davis' company prior to June last. I have never, to my knowledge, seen them alone together. Monson seemed to be acquainted with Davis in the same way as with half a dozen betting men. Monson was most profuse in asking people to come and visit him at Ardlamont. He asked two solicitors in one office, and a head clerk. I heard him ask a Mr. Law, and he also asked myself. I knew a young man named Cecil Hambrough, and that he was living with Monson at Ardlamont. I have heard Monson speak of him. He referred to him in most affectionate terms. I did not know that any one was financing Monson, but I understood that Tottenham was finding money till Hambrough came of age. I understood that Hambrough was to come into a lot of money when he came of age, and that he was being financed by Jerningham, a financial agent.

62. HENRY ALGERNON WEST, examined by the SOLICITOR-GENERAL—I reside at Richmond. I have no profession. I have known Sidney Russell for about a year. He introduced me to Edward Davis. I don't know what was the relation between Russell and Davis, but they appeared to be friendly. I have made bets with Russell, but not with Davis. So far as I knew, the two did not appear to be associated in business. I remember winning a bet of £50 on a horse called "Cabin Boy" about 20th July last, which Russell had made for me. Russell and Davis had been betting on the same horse, and they each won £50, making £150 in all for the three. Davis seemed to be very pleased at that success. Knowing that he had won, I lent him £10, taking an I O U from him. I saw him write it. In appearance Davis was about 5 feet 10 inches in height, rather sallow, with bluish eyes, and not a very large moustache. He did not seem to be in very good health. I saw him twice in Fleet Street after giving him the £10; on both occasions Russell was with him. I have not seen him since, and I have never got my £10. I do not know why he has become invisible. I asked Russell once or twice where Davis was, as I was anxious to get my money, and he told me Davis was ill at Brighton.

Cross-examined by Mr. COMRIE THOMSON—I never saw Monson in company with Davis. Russell also told me that Davis was at Blackpool. He seemed to be a delicate man. His moustache was quite perceptible.

63. AMBROSE WILLIAM KING, examined by the SOLICITOR-GENERAL—I am a solicitor's clerk, and live at Twickenham. I know Monson, having met him several times in the office of Mr. Brown, solicitor, Clifford, in whose employment I was at one time. I also saw Monson in Tottenham's office. I am not in the employment of any solicitor at present, but do solicitors' work for persons who

Evidence for Prosecution.

A. W. King

employ me. I have known Sidney Russell for twelve years, but I have never been employed by him. He was in the habit of calling at my office. I am employed by my late firm, and I also represent two or three loan offices; I did not act for Tottenham. Russell introduced me to Edward Davis in March last, and from that time forward I knew him. He was about thirty-three or thirty-four years of age, 5 feet 10 inches in height, rather broad shouldered, of thin build, with a sallow complexion, dark hair, grey eyes, and a small moustache. I first met him with Russell in the Mitre public-house, Chancery Lane. After that I was in the habit of meeting Davis with Sidney Russell; they went often to race meetings together, in connection with the betting business; they appeared to be associated somehow. Mr. Brown, my late employer, did not have a great deal of solicitors' business for betting people. Sidney Russell often came to his office to see me, but not on business.

I remember meeting Monson one day as I was going up Chancery Lane last June. He asked me if I had seen anything of Ted Davis. I said, " Yes, I have; I believe he has just gone up the lane." Monson said, " Come and have a drink," and I went with him and had a drink. When Monson spoke of Ted Davis I understood him to mean the man whom I had seen with Russell.

I read of Cecil Hambrough's death in the papers; it occurred upon 10th August. The first time that I saw Davis after this event was about 15th or 16th August. I saw him at the house of Mr. Russell in Camberwell New Road. Mrs. Russell came into the room where Russell and I were and said, " Here's Ted Davis come in." He entered the room, spoke to Mr. Russell, and then sat down on the couch. He looked extremely ill. He remained in the house for some time, and then went out with Russell. I did not know anything about a registered letter which came from Scotland for Davis. The arrival of a registered letter was, however, discussed in my presence in August in London. I heard a Mr. Robertson say, " Have you seen Davis? There is a registered letter for him." That was about the end of July or the first week of August. I have not seen Ted Davis since he went out with Russell a few days after the death at Ardlamont. I have not heard it suggested that he is dead; he has just disappeared. I know of no reason why I should not have seen him. Davis was never an associate of mine.

Cross-examined by Mr. COMRIE THOMSON—Mr. Brown was solicitor for Mr. Tottenham. I have seen young Hambrough at Brown's office, and also Mr. and Mrs. Monson. The only occasion on which I have seen Monson and Davis in company was that day I met them in Chancery Lane; Russell was not there. The conversation on that occasion was entirely about racing matters. I thought I saw Davis go up the lane, and I went into his office and found him having a glass of beer.

Alfred John Monson.

64. THOMAS BROCKWELL, examined by the SOLICITOR-GENERAL—
I am a sergeant in the Criminal Investigation Department in Scotland Yard, London, and was instructed on 2nd September last to make inquiry in London with regard to a person of the name of Scott, who was supposed to have been at Ardlamont. On the following day I got a description of the person wanted from Dr. Macmillan, who was in London, and Inspector Greet, of the Investigation Department, was associated with me in the work that was begun. We made inquiries with a view to finding out the person wanted. The first information I got was after 20th September. The person who appeared most closely to resemble the description I got was Edward Davis, now known as Sweeney, who resided at 35 Sutherland Street, Pimlico. I formed the opinion that Edward Davis appeared to be the man wanted after 20th September. I made the inquiries at 35 Sutherland Street, and I found he was not there. I could not discover where he had gone to. I found that a member of the family was employed at Westminster Palace Hotel, and I applied to him. I got no information from him; he refused to give any. I discovered the associates of Edward Davis, but was unable to find out from them where he was. A description of him was circulated in the Metropolitan police stations, the first occasion being on 12th September. The description was as follows:—" A man, aged about thirty; height, about 5 feet 10 inches; slim build, pale complexion, steel-grey eyes, dark hair and moustache, hair rather frizzy, in delicate health." We got the description in the first instance from Dr. Macmillan and Constable M'Calman, of the Argyllshire Police, who had seen Scott at Ardlamont. M'Calman had come to London for the purpose of assisting in the discovery and identification of Scott. The bills produced no result. The first circulation among the Metropolitan Police was on 12th September. The first bill was posted on 6th November. The man was first described as Edward Davis. In the second bill he was described as Davis, *alias* Sweeney, *alias* Scott. All the police methods for discovering persons wanted were resorted to, without success. We had instructions to offer a reward for the discovery of this person. We issued the offer of reward on 1st December. The amount was £200. It produced no result.

65. SIDNEY RUSSELL, examined by the SOLICITOR-GENERAL—I am a bookmaker and commission agent. I have known the prisoner Alfred John Monson since the beginning of June of this year. I have known a man named Edward Davis for about two years; among his friends he was known as " Ted " Davis, and he lived at 35 Sutherland Street, Pimlico. He made a book occasionally, and sometimes he backed horses. He and I were a good deal associated in betting business; sometimes he clerked for me, and sometimes we put money together and backed horses. I have seen Monson and

Evidence for Prosecution.

Sidney Russell

Davis together about a dozen times—at the Grand Buffet, Charing Cross, at the Ship in Parliament Street, and at the Mitre in Chancery Lane. They met for the purpose of betting. During the eighteen months that I knew Davis I was in the habit of seeing him two or three times a week, and sometimes we went to race meetings together. I remember being at the Hotel Metropole one day in the end of June, when Mr. Monson and Mr. Law were there. Ted Davis was there that day. I know Smith, a tailor; he has made some clothes for me. I introduced Edward Davis to him, and he employed him. I did not introduce George Davis to him. I did not know George Davis. I saw a notice of the death at Ardlamont in the newspapers.

Do you remember meeting Ted Davis shortly after that?—I met him on 16th or 17th August at my house the day when Mr. King was there.

Davis came to my house on 16th or 17th August; before that I had not seen him since 25th July at Goodwood. This was a longer interval than usually elapsed without my seeing him; I was in the habit of seeing him two or three times a week. On 16th or 17th August he was at my house for about a quarter of an hour; I have not seen him since, and have not the slightest idea where he is. I do not know whether he is dead or alive; all that I know about him is that he has disappeared. I did not know of any George Hunt, 35 Sutherland Street.

Cross-examined by Mr. COMRIE THOMSON—Those who represent the accused here have been at me several times trying to find out where Davis is. I knew Edward Davis pretty well; he had a very kind disposition. I should say that he would be one of the last men in the world to do a cruel action; I don't believe he would hurt a fly intentionally.

Re-examined by the SOLICITOR-GENERAL—I frequently betted under the name of Davis. It is not an uncommon thing for a man in London to take an assumed name; Davis betted under his own name; he made a book occasionally, and sometimes backed horses. I think that he had some capital, about a thousand or two, which I think he won by backing horses. He had been engaged in bookmaking about two years; I have not an idea what he did before that. I only made his acquaintance when he began bookmaking.

66. Constable M'CALMAN, examined by the SOLICITOR-GENERAL —I am a constable in the Argyllshire Police, and was stationed at Tighnabruaich. I heard of Mr. Hambrough's death at two o'clock on the day on which it happened—10th August. I heard of it at Tighnabruaich Pier, and while there I saw a man named Edward Scott; he was waiting for the steamer from Ardrishaig. I spoke to him, and asked him if he would stay for the inquiry; he said he could not wait, and on my asking him for an address which would

Alfred John Monson.

find him in the future, he told me his address was the Central Station Hotel, Glasgow. The boat then came in, and he went away. I then went to Ardlamont, where I saw Monson, and asked him who the man was whom I had seen go away. Monson said that he was an engineer; that he did not know the man, who had been engaged by Mr. Hambrough, and had come to look after the yacht.

After seeing Monson, I went to the place where the body was said to have been found, accompanied by Archibald Whyte. I looked at the ditch to see if there were any marks of the body having lain there. I did not see any such marks in the ditch. I saw the place where the blood was upon the ground; it was about 2 feet from the edge of the ditch. I did not see Monson again that day. I saw him next morning at the pier, where he was waiting for some friends. I spoke to him, and asked him to give me a statement in connection with the occurrence. He agreed to do so. I saw him go away in the morning, but he returned by the eleven o'clock boat. [Shown No. 3.] That is the document which he gave me; I handed it to the Procurator-Fiscal.

After 11th August I had nothing to do in the matter till 27th August, when I applied to Monson for Scott's address. I went to Ardlamont on the 27th in consequence of a telegram which I received from the Fiscal on the 26th. He told me that he did not know the address. I asked him to write down anything that he knew about Scott, to be forwarded to the Procurator-Fiscal. [Shown No. 4.] That is what he gave me; I handed it to the Fiscal.

The first statement which I got from Monson was on 11th August; it reads as follows:—" I, Alfred John Monson, of Ardlamont House, gentleman, aged thirty-two, say with reference to the sudden death of Windsor Dudley Cecil Hambrough, that about 6.30 a.m. on the morning of 10th August I went out shooting in company with Mr. Hambrough and Mr. Scott. Mr. Hambrough was in perfect health and spirits. I and Hambrough alone had guns. I shot three rabbits, which Mr. Scott was carrying. When we entered the cover by the house Hambrough took the right side, walking on the top of the sunk fence. I was walking on the left side, and Scott was following behind. Just as we got to the end of the cover I heard a shot fired. I waited a minute or so, and then called out and asked what he had shot. There was no reply. I walked towards the corner of the cover in the direction of the shot in company with Mr. Scott. I called ' Hambrough! ' several times, and there was no reply. I then saw Hambrough lying at the bottom of the sunk fence on his left side, with his gun beside him. We lifted him up, and he was quite dead. I then called out to the men at the stables. Three or four men came, and Mr. Hambrough was conveyed to the house. I think the time would be 7.30 a.m."

The statement which he gave me on 27th August with reference to Scott is as follows:—" Ardlamont House, 27th August. I am

182

Evidence for Prosecution.

informed that Edward Scott started business as an engineer in Glasgow, and that he failed; that he was afterwards working in connection with yachts; and that he was well known in Greenock. When we entered the wood in which the accident happened, I remember seeing a man watching us. I am told that he mentioned to some one here that he saw us in the wood. I have ascertained that his name was Smeaton, and that his luggage was taken away by Mr. M'Ewan, and that he has Smeaton's address." I got that statement from Monson on 27th August, and posted it to the Procurator-Fiscal. I was in London for thirteen weeks, and during that time I was associated with the London police in endeavouring to find Scott, but in spite of everything being done that could be suggested for the purpose of finding him, the search failed.

Cross-examined by Mr. Comrie Thomson—The steamer by which Scott went away left Tighnabruaich at three o'clock. I was aware that Dr. Macmillan had examined the body, and Scott told me that he had spoken to the doctor, but did not tell me what he had said. I made an attempt to detain him, suggesting that he should stay till the inquiry was finished. I repeatedly told him to stay, but made no physical attempt to detain him. I made no attempt to have the man stopped at Glasgow. I told the Fiscal that Scott had left Ardlamont, but, so far as I know, he made no attempt to stop him. It was four o'clock in the afternoon of the 10th when I went to look at the place where the body was found. I saw no disturbance in the ditch or on the top of the dyke, except some traces of blood on the dyke. I saw no marks to indicate that any one had been lying in the ditch, or on the bank rising from the ditch to the east. I believe that Whyte had been walking in the ditch in the morning; I did not know that Whyte, Lamont, and Stevenson and others had been there. Whyte told me some days ago that he had been there.

Re-examined by the Solicitor-General—I looked specially to see whether there was any trace of a man's body having lain in the ditch. If there had been a body in the ditch I think I should have seen the marks. The only marks I saw in the ditch were like marks made by one man walking.

Dr. Littlejohn (recalled), examined by the Solicitor-General—In my report of the *post-mortem* examination of the body of Mr. Hambrough I say—" At no part of the edges or surface of the wound was there any appearance of blackening as if from gunpowder, but four minute specks, apparently metallic, were found adhering to the edges." I weighed these specks on two occasions. On the first occasion I was alone, and I found them to weigh 0·8 of a grain. They were weighed again on 23rd November at Edinburgh University in the presence of myself and certain experts for the defence. The process of weighing was carried out more accurately on this occasion. The balance I had used at the first weighing turned about a 10th of a

Alfred John Monson.

grain; the balance now used turned about a 1000th of a grain. We found that the weight of the four fragments was 0·9 of a grain.

In my report the following passage occurs :—" The cerebral substance was removed *en masse* and submitted to a minute examination, when four metallic masses of irregular shape were removed and preserved." I weighed these masses with great care, and found their weight to be 7 grains and a little over that, according to the grosser balance which I at first employed. They were again weighed on 23rd November in presence of the experts for the defence already referred to.

[Shown No. 15.] That phial contains four No. 5 pellets, purchased in Mr. Macnaughton's shop. Their weight was found to be 8·165 grains, according to the fine balance. [Shown No. 16.] That phial contains four No. 6 pellets, also purchased at Mr. Macnaughton's shop. They weighed 6·878 grains. I got from Stewart, the sheriff officer at Inveraray, two guns and a parcel of cartridges. I handed the cartridges to Mr. Macnaughton on 20th November, and, on getting them back from him, I handed them, by direction of the Crown, to Messrs. Davidson & Syme, the prisoner's agents, just as I had got them from Mr. Macnaughton, with this exception, that Mr. Macnaughton pointed out that he had taken down certain cartridges in order carefully to measure their contents. He said that he had replaced the contents. I handed the guns also to Mr. Macnaughton, and got them back from him; I then handed them to Messrs. Davidson & Syme, by direction of the Crown. We again made the weighings, to which I have referred, in presence of Mr. Macnaughton, and Mr. Macnaughton, in my presence, took from two cartridges, one No. 5 and the other No. 6, four pellets and weighed them, after which they were returned to their proper cartridges in my presence. I am bound to state that there was some discrepancy in the weight of some of them, as compared with the specimens I bought in Mr. Macnaughton's shop, but it was comparatively slight. The No. 5 pellets weighed 7·5 of a grain, and the No. 6 6·5; this was with the balance with which I was formerly working.

JAMES MACNAUGHTON (recalled), examined by the SOLICITOR-GENERAL—I identify the cartridges shown me [labels Nos. 2 and 3] as being all the cartridges handed to me by Dr. Littlejohn. After I was done with them I gave them back and got a receipt. I opened up certain cartridges for the purpose of examining them and making up cartridges of an exactly similar description. These I carefully reloaded, except as to the turning-in of the cartridge cases, which cannot be done very neatly. In my former evidence I meant to say that all but one of the 12-bore amberite cartridges were loaded with No. 6 shot. There were three in all, two of them loaded with No. 6, and one with No. 5.

The Court adjourned.

Seventh Day—Tuesday, 19th December, 1893.

67. Inspector GREET, Criminal Investigation Department, Scotland Yard, London, examined by the SOLICITOR-GENERAL—I was put in charge of this case with the view of finding Scott. All the ordinary police methods for ascertaining his whereabouts were adopted. When Constable M'Calman came to London he was placed under my orders. He worked in the Metropolitan District, and also made inquiries in the county. A bill giving a description of Scott was issued on 6th November, and a second bill offering a reward of £200 was issued on 1st December. I found out that the Davis family were residing at Sutherland Street on 1st November. About that time I discovered a brother of Edward Davis, George Davis, who is a witness in this case. He told me nothing to enable me to find Edward Davis. On 28th November, I got a photograph of Edward Davis, which was sent to Scotland after the indictment was served.

68. Constable DONALD CAMPBELL, examined by the SOLICITOR-GENERAL—I am in the Argyllshire Police, and am stationed at Ardrishaig. I was at Ardlamont House on 30th August, and made a search in the room pointed out to me as the one which Mr. Hambrough occupied. [Shown label No. 1.] I found that jacket hanging on the top of the door of the press in the room; in the pocket I found nineteen cartridges, which I took. [Shown labels Nos. 2 and 3.] These are the cartridges; eighteen of them were for a 20-bore gun and one for a 12-bore, which was along with the rest, and not in a separate pocket. The shot in them is No. 6. There were no other cartridges in the room in which I found the jacket, but there was a number in the smoking-room. I took the jacket and cartridges in a parcel to Inveraray on 30th August. That was the day on which Monson was apprehended. I went back to Ardlamont to get the cartridges which were in the smoking-room, and found a large number of each kind, of which I took specimens and tied them up in bundles. [Shown labels No. 9, 10, 11, and 12.] These are bundles of the cartridges which I selected.

I was sent to Ardlamont to watch the place where Mr. Hambrough's body was found, to see that nothing was interfered with; John M'Intyre, another officer, was sent with me. One of us was always on the spot. We remained there till 5th October. [Shown label No. 17.] These are two pieces of bone which were given to me by Constable M'Intyre, and which I handed to the Procurator-Fiscal. I was present when the rowan tree was uprooted and when the

185

Alfred John Monson.

branches of the lime and beech trees were cut down. I took possession of M'Kellar's boat at Ardlamont on 10th September. I found a rowlock on the beach at Ardlamont on 9th October. Whyte, the gardener, pointed it out to me, and I took possession of it. It was lying to the west of Ardlamont Bay, north-west of the dyke, on sharp ridges of rocks which run up to high water. A knife was handed to me by Stewart M'Nicol; I handed it over to Stewart at Inveraray.

Cross-examined by Mr. COMRIE THOMSON—Monson was taken away on the morning of 30th August. That was before I took possession of the jacket, and he was not present to give any explanation about it or about the cartridges. I was not aware that the Deputy Fiscal, when he was there, had directed Monson to put aside the jacket, and also any cartridges which he found. I was not aware that Hambrough's clothes had been brushed and put aside after his death. I have no knowledge who put these cartridges into the jacket. The cartridges were all pink except one. I know nothing about this jacket, except that Whyte showed it to me, nor do I know anything about the knife, except that M'Nicol gave it to me. When I got the pieces of bone there were pellets in the larger piece. There is lead there yet; I cannot say that there are pellets, but there is lead.

Re-examined by the SOLICITOR-GENERAL—I found the jacket hanging on the inside of the door of the press. I saw nothing to indicate that the clothes had been brushed and folded and put aside. The coat was hanging by the tag, and a pair of knickerbockers was hanging by the waist amongst other clothes. They were not folded, simply hanging.

69. Constable JOHN M'INTYRE, examined by the SOLICITOR-GENERAL—I am in the Argyllshire Police, and on 2nd September I was sent to Ardlamont to watch the place where Mr. Hambrough's body was found. Campbell was there before me, and during the five weeks I was there one of us was always at the place. I was there when the two pieces of bone were found. Whyte was also there. The first piece was found on 27th September on the spot where the blood lay. It was given to me, and I gave it to Campbell. Three days after the second piece was found by Whyte, who gave it to me, and I gave it to Campbell.

Cross-examined by Mr. COMRIE THOMSON—Campbell and I were more than three weeks doing nothing but watching the place before we discovered both of these pieces of bone. Whyte was sometimes with us, two or three times a week; he came to talk with me. Hugh Carmichael, the groom, was also present when the first piece of bone was found; it was Whyte who first noticed it. We made further search to see if there was anything of the same kind at that time, but found nothing till three days afterwards. The second piece of bone was found two or three inches further south than the first.

Evidence for Prosecution.

Can you account for not seeing it when you found the first piece of bone?—The rain came on. It was my hand that found the second piece; Whyte was with me, but nobody else. There were pellets in it when I first found it.

Where are they now?—I have not looked.

Take a look; they are not there now, are they?—No; they are not here now. I do not know where they are now. The pellets were in the piece of bone when I handed it to Campbell.

Re-examined by the SOLICITOR-GENERAL—On 27th September Whyte was sent to search for the pieces of bone, and I searched along with him. Whyte took me to the place where they were found; just where the blood was.

70. DAVID STEWART, examined by the SOLICITOR-GENERAL—I am a criminal officer at Inveraray and bar officer in Inveraray Sheriff Court. I first went to Ardlamont on 12th September, and was shown the place where the body was said to have been found by Carmichael and Whyte. Dr. Littlejohn and the photographer were also present. On 26th September I was again at the place along with Mr. Macnaughton, the gunmaker. Mr. Macnaughton, in the course of his examination asked me to stand in particular places. I stood, as he told me, at the place where Mr. Hambrough's feet had lain; this would correspond with the place where the feet of a man would be whose head lay at the spot pointed out. On a previous visit I had seen where the head had lain—the mark was still there. I was looking over the dyke towards the rowan tree. From where I was standing I could not see any mark in the rowan tree; I was too far off. The lime and the beech were forward from me, a bit from the rowan tree. I looked at certain marks on the rowan tree along with the rest. From where I was standing they were in a line with the rowan, lime, and beech trees. I am 5 feet 10 inches in height.

[Shown labels Nos. 1, 2, 3, 4, 7, and 8.] These are the shooting jacket, knickerbockers, cartridges, and the two guns handed to me by Constable Campbell and Sergeant Ross. I took them with me to the production room at Inveraray and locked them up. I gave them to Dr. Littlejohn in Edinburgh on 4th October in the same condition as I got them. [Shown label No. 6.] I got that cap at Ardlamont House on 12th September. To the best of my recollection it was Wright, the butler, who gave it over to me. [Shown labels Nos. 19, 20, 21, and 22.] The rowan tree and the branches of the lime and beech trees were put into my custody by Constable Campbell; I took them to Edinburgh on 26th September. [Shown label No. 25.] That section of the boat came into my possession at the same time as the rowan tree and branches. [Shown label No. 23.] That rowlock was given to me by Campbell.

Cross-examined by Mr. COMRIE THOMSON—On 26th September, when I was at the place where the body was found, I was asked to

Alfred John Monson.

David Stewart

put myself where Mr. Macnaughton and Dr. Littlejohn suggested. I saw a mark where the head was said to have been lying. I did not measure about 6 feet or so, as representing the place where the feet should be. I did not say that I saw for myself marks of blood where the head was. I saw, the first time I was at the place, two stones, and was told that one represented the head and the other the feet. Somebody had lain down, and then put a stone to mark the place. I think it was the Depute Fiscal. I stood on the same line as where the feet were, and that was on a line between where the head was and the rowan tree. I was not standing exactly on the top of the dyke. The head lay nearer the ditch than the feet, which were 3 feet 6 inches from the ditch edge of the dyke, while the head lay 2 feet 6 inches from the edge.

Re-examined by the SOLICITOR-GENERAL—I stood in the position shown to me as where the feet were found. Whyte and Carmichael were there, and they showed as exactly as possible how the body was lying. A stone was placed to show where the feet were and another to show where the head lay. That was about 6 feet nearer than the rowan tree.

By the LORD JUSTICE-CLERK—I made no measurements.

71. JAMES ROSS, examined by the SOLICITOR-GENERAL—I am a sergeant in the Argyllshire Police. [Shown label No. 7.] I took possession of that 20-bore gun on 30th August; I was at Ardlamont on that day, and was in charge of Monson when he was brought to Inveraray. When I got there I handed the gun over to the bar officer, Stewart.

72. JAMES FRASER, examined by the SOLICITOR-GENERAL—I am chief constable of Argyllshire. I arrested Monson on the road between Ardlamont and Tighnabruaich. I was informed that a person named Scott had been at Ardlamont at the time of Mr. Hambrough's death. I heard of Greenock, Gourock, Paisley, and Glasgow as being places with which Scott was said to be associated. I tried to find traces of him, but failed. In none of these localities was there any engineer of the name of Scott answering to the description of the man said to have been at Ardlamont. I was also in communication with the London police, but could find no trace of him.

Cross-examined by Mr. COMRIE THOMSON—I began my search for Scott on 28th or 29th August. I was informed that on the 10th he had gone to Glasgow on his way south. I confined my search to Greenock, Gourock, Glasgow, and Paisley.

73. JOHN CAMPBELL M'LULLICH, examined by the SOLICITOR-GENERAL—I am Procurator-Fiscal of Argyllshire. On 22nd August I got a telegram from Monson saying that he was coming next day to Inveraray to see me. At that time there was no suspicion con-

188

Evidence for Prosecution.

nected with Mr Hambrough's death; I had got Dr Macmillan's report, in which he attributed it to an accident. On the 23rd I met Monson, who came from Ardlamont by the " Lord of the Isles." He told me there were two friends behind him on the boat—insurance men—who wanted to see me. I said that I did not know what insurance people had got to do with it. Monson walked with me to my office. He told me that Hambrough was using a 20-bore gun, which he had had for years, and that they were using amberite cartridges.

I had a deposition from my deputy that there was no insurance on Mr. Hambrough's life, and I said to Monson that I understood his life was not insured. Monson stated that Major Hambrough had insured his son's life, but that he had not been aware of it; he said that the amount was £15,000. Nothing more passed about the insurance. This conversation took place as Monson and I were walking up to my office, and when we got there Mr. M'Lean and Mr. Herbert, of the New York Insurance Office, came to the door and handed in their cards. I at once took them into another room. The result of my conversation with them was that I understood the amount of the insurance to be £20,000. Monson's statement about the insurance took me very much by surprise.

I said to Monson that the first thing for him to do was to send the 20-bore gun and the amberite cartridges by next day's boat. I accompanied him part of the way back to the pier; the whole of my interview with him took perhaps fifteen to twenty minutes. I ascertained the object of the insurance men's visit to me; they told me that the company required a certificate in a case of sudden death where there had been any investigation—a certificate by some person that death was accidental.

By the LORD JUSTICE-CLERK—I asked them if Monson had any interest, and they said that he or his wife had an interest.

Examination continued—From this communication your view of the matter materially changed?—Yes; at once. It was in consequence of this that I asked that the gun should be sent to me. I am quite certain that Monson said that it was a 20-bore gun which Mr. Hambrough was using, for I had never seen a 20-bore gun, having always been accustomed to a 12-bore, and I wondered at the time what kind of a gun it would be. When I asked him to send the 20-bore gun and amberite cartridges the next day he said that he would certainly do so by the mid-day boat. Next day, having thought the matter over, I came to the conclusion that I should go to Ardlamont, which I did. Before going on board the steamer for Tighnabruaich I inquired if any parcel had come for me, but found that none had come. I stayed at Tighnabruaich, and made my inquiries there. I examined Lamont, the gamekeeper, and told him that Monson had not kept his promise about sending the gun and cartridges. I told him to go and get the 20-bore gun and amberite

189

Alfred John Monson.

J. C. M'Lullich

cartridges; he went and brought back a 12-bore gun, but no amberite cartridges. From that time forward I proceeded with my inquiries. Monson called on me at the Tighnabruaich Hotel the same evening, but I said that I did not wish to see him, and declined to converse with him. [Shown No. 237.] That letter came to me by post from Monson. It is dated—"Ardlamont House, Argyllshire, August 26, 1893," and says—"Dear Sir,—Referring to what passed when I saw you at Tighnabruaich, I think it right to inform you that this morning my keeper told me that he had heard that a gentleman who was staying at the schoolhouse facing the southern end of the wood in which the accident happened saw the three of us, Mr. Hambrough, Scott, and myself, enter the wood. If this be so, no doubt he would corroborate what I have told you as to our relative positions as we went through the wood. This gentleman's name is Smeaton, but his address I cannot give; he has left the schoolhouse, and the schoolmistress from whom he had taken the house has not returned. She is expected back next week. On Thursday I went to Glasgow to make inquiry concerning Scott, but failed to trace him, as already explained. I had nothing to do with the engaging of him, and know nothing of him. He came here the day before the accident happened, and left the day on which it happened, between two and three o'clock. Not having traced him, I instructed an advertisement for him to be inserted in the *Glasgow Herald*. I have also instructed Messrs. Davidson & Syme, of Edinburgh, to endeavour to find him. I do not think I can do more, but if there is anything you can suggest I shall be glad to aid you if I can in any way.—I am, yours truly, (Signed) "A. J. MONSON."

Cross-examined by Mr. COMRIE THOMSON—As Procurator-Fiscal I was told to get up this case for the Crown, and I have been present during the previous days of the trial. There was some one else who accompanied Monson to Inveraray on the day I have mentioned. I was not introduced to him, but I know now it was Tottenham. He was with the insurance agents and came in at the same time, but I did not admit him. He was at the door of the room, but I took the two insurance agents out and left Tottenham at the door. I did not want him to hear any conversation that passed between the insurance agents and myself. My deputy was present with Monson and me. I did not know that my deputy was in the room in which Tottenham was. My deputy was not present when the conversation between Monson and me occurred. I made no note of what Monson said to me, but I think my deputy took a jotting in passing.

At Tighnabruaich Lamont said to me that, on the occasion of the accident, Mr. Hambrough had been using his 20-bore gun, and then he came back to me after he had been at Ardlamont and said that Monson told him that he had exchanged guns with Mr. Hambrough, who used the 12-bore gun. I have ascertained that, in

Evidence for Prosecution.

J. C. M'Lullich

point of fact, there were no amberite cartridges in existence for the 20-bore gun. There must have been a mistake somewhere.

About the policy, I am sure that Monson did not say, " I think his father would get the benefit of the insurance." What he said exactly was this—I asked him what the insurance company wanted with me, as there was no question of insurance in the matter, and Monson said—" I believe his father, without his knowledge, has insured his life." I then asked him the sum, and he said " £15,000."

May Monson not have said that, without his father's knowledge, he had insured the young man's life, but that he believed the father would get the benefit of it?—No.

Are you prepared to swear that that may not have been the statement and that you may not have made a mistake?—No. The Depute Fiscal was not present, so far as I know, when Monson made that statement. I made no jotting at the time; I was walking up the street of Inveraray at the time.

I think you will admit, as a man of the world and a man of sense, that you may have misapprehended the statement, and that it may have been as I put it?—That is so.

Re-examined by the SOLICITOR-GENERAL—The statement about the insurance was made while Monson and I were walking from the pier to my office; there was no one else present. That was the first intimation I had that Cecil Hambrough's life was insured. I have not the slightest doubt that the words which I have spoken to were used by Monson. In the course of the day I heard the amount of the insurance from the insurance people. It was not until I was precognoscing the witness Lamont that my suspicions were aroused. No suggestion had been made by anybody about the exchange of guns. Lamont had told me nothing about it, and it was not till I had sent him to fetch the 20-bore gun and he came back with the 12-bore, which he said he had got from Monson, that that suggestion was made.

74. GEORGE SWEENEY, examined by the SOLICITOR-GENERAL—I am twenty-five years of age and am a hall porter at the Westminster Palace Hotel, London. I am a son of Edward Sweeney, who lived at 35 Sutherland Street under the name of Davis, for the purpose of taking in correspondence for my brother Edward, who was a bookmaker. He was at Sutherland Street for two years, and during that time my brother lived there carrying on the business of a bookmaker. My brother Edward was twenty-seven years of age, about 5 feet 9 or 10 inches, I suppose, in height, of very thin build, with sloping shoulders, hair of a dark colour, blue eyes, and pale complexion. Any one seeing him would say that he was in consumption. He was very white and his face was very thin, quite hollow. In fact, he had been very ill for years. I have had communications

191

Alfred John Monson.

George Sweeney

about him during the last two or three months from officials of the London police. I had no information to give them. I ceased to know where my brother was about the middle of September. He called on me at the hotel and told me he was going to Bournemouth. He has disappeared from the knowledge of his family, but we imagine that he has taken a voyage to Australia for the benefit of his health, and that he left about the middle of September. He had mentioned that he thought he would take a voyage to Australia, as he had taken one before and had been much the better of it. I think that it was in November that I was first communicated with by the police about this case. I have seen about the case in the papers. We are not quite certain that my brother has gone to Australia, but that is our impression.

Is there any reason why his family should know whether he has gone to Australia or not?—Well, he was a very melancholy young fellow, owing to his being always ill, and he did not wish to tell us about his illness, because it upset his mother very much and worried her, and that is the reason why he has not written to us. We think that he is away on a voyage, but we are not certain about that. He was on affectionate terms with his family.

I ask you, if he was on affectionate terms with his family, can you give me any explanation why, if he went to Australia, his family should not know of it?—Well, my impression is that he does not wish his mother to know how he is. He was very ill, indeed, when I last saw him. I do not know at all whether he wishes or does not wish his mother to know that he has gone to Australia. His mother is very anxious about him. It is his absence without her knowing where he is which causes her anxiety. I will just explain. On the last occasion when he went to Australia, nearly three years ago, he was advised by the doctor to take a voyage to save his life. He said to me, " I shall not write, George, unless I am better. If I am better I will write." I did not have a letter from him for about two months after he had gone. I knew where he was then; I don't know now. Neither I, nor, so far as I know, any other member of his family knows whether he has gone to Australia or not. I do not know where he is, and none of the family know where he is. I saw him last about the middle of September. My father moved from Sutherland Street on 12th October. The police asked me two days after where he had gone, but I did not know at that time and could not tell them; I was not asked again. Afterwards, I was going home to my father's new address every evening, so that if the police had wanted to find out they could easily have followed me to the new address. My father is now living at 41 Osborne Terrace. He is one of the witnesses here for the defence. I was in Scotland at the end of August or beginning of September; I do not remember being asked by the police whether I had been in Scotland. I refused to tell them where I had spent my holidays. I did not leave my work at the Westminster Palace

192

Evidence for Prosecution.

George Sweeney

Hotel till 19th August, and I started my holiday on the 20th; I did not see how my holiday had anything to do with what occurred on the 10th. I was not in Scotland before 22nd August; I went to see my friends.

Have you relations in Helensburgh?—I decline to answer.

By the LORD JUSTICE-CLERK—You cannot decline to answer; you must answer.

Examination continued—I have friends in Helensburgh. My brother Edward was not there; he has not been there this year. I am quite certain if he had been there I should have heard; my friends would have told me about it. No one is attending to my brother's bookmaking business during his absence; so far as I know, he has made no arrangements in regard to that.

Have you or your family taken any steps to find out where he is?—Well, we have had no idea where to look for him.

That is not the question. Have you taken any steps to discover where he is?—Well, we have written to friends asking if they had seen him, but none of them appear to have seen anything of him. We began to make inquiries as soon as we heard he was being inquired for. [Shown No. 233.] That is a letter to Smith in my writing; it is signed by " George Hunt." It was signed in that way just as a joke. That was all, simply fun, nothing more. I paid for the clothes as soon as they came home.

This joke is not quite perceptible at first sight. Can you explain why you should order clothes in the name of " George Hunt "?— Simply the idea was that I was being introduced not as a brother. I was introduced to Smith by my brother Edward; at least, he told Smith that he would send a friend down, and I went down. That was about the middle of July, I think. I said to my brother, " Don't introduce me as a brother; introduce me as a friend and as Mr. Hunt." It was my proposal; I did not mean anything by it; it was a little idea of my own. As soon as the clothes came home I paid for them. The bill was fifteen guineas, and the tailor said, " Well, Mr. Hunt, you are before your time." I said that I always liked to pay up to date if possible, and Mr. Smith said, " We always give three months' credit; I will take off a shilling in the pound and take £15." My brother and I were very affectionate indeed; I thought a great deal of my brother. He has been a cause of great anxiety to me on account of his illness. He is one of the best fellows in the world.

But can you account for his adding to that natural anxiety by not writing to say where he is?—Simply because he does not wish to worry his mother.

Can you explain why, if a man is ill and his family are attached to him, it should relieve their anxiety to disappear and not tell where he is?—Well, he thinks we know that he is taking a voyage on the sea for his health. In the beginning of August I contemplated going to Scotland; I expected to get away from the hotel earlier than I

o

Alfred John Monson.

George Sweeney

managed, I expected to get away on the 10th or 12th. I don't think that it was at one time intended that my brother should go to Scotland with me; it may have been mentioned, but I don't think so. The order I gave for clothes had nothing to do with my intended visit to Scotland; I mentioned in my letter to the tailor that he need not hurry until the end of the week. I wrote and told him that I was going away for a holiday, and that he might let me have the clothes early. I then wrote him that I was not going away for a week afterwards, so that he need not hurry.

Observe, your letter says, " Clothes to hand. I am glad to tell you that they fit very well. I will not be going north for fully a week, so when ready, please forward." You must have been getting some additional clothes?—I believe there was another suit to come.

Had that other suit anything to do with the visit to Scotland?— Not that I remember. The letter I wrote to the tailor was in part acknowledgment of the clothes I received, and I just mentioned that I was not going north for a week. The words, " When the clothes are ready, please forward," means that the tailor was to send the other suit when it was made. These were the clothes I got upon the introduction of my brother; I ordered them under the name of George Hunt. My brother did not go north with me; I went alone. When I wrote to the tailor I expected to be going north on 1st August, but I could not get away till the 19th.

When you wrote the letter on 1st August to the tailor about the clothes coming to you in the name of George Hunt, you then expected to go north about a week after that—I might have expected to do so, but was detained at the hotel. [Shown No. 236.] I do not recognise the handwriting of this letter; it is not the writing of any of my family. I know my father's handwriting. I have not seen to whom it is addressed.

It is dated 13th October, 1893, and says, " Dear Sir,—In answer to yours, William Davis is at the present time out of town. He instructed me if you should write, would I kindly answer your letter. Being not well in health he has been ordered by his medical attendant to the seaside, consequently it will be quite a month before he will return home." Assume from me that that letter was written in reply to a letter which Smith, the tailor, sent to 35 Sutherland Street; would that at all aid you in saying who the writer of the letter was?—No. My father's name is Edward Sweeney. I suppose that when he lived under the name of Davis he would be called Edward Davis, but I don't believe that he ever called himself Edward Davis on letters or anything of that sort. He lived at 35 Sutherland Street for three years under the name of Mr. Davis; the people in the house always called him Mr. Davis. On 13th October, 1893, there was no other male person bearing the name of Davis living at 35 Sutherland Street except my father. I was not living there and my brother Edward had left.

194

Evidence for Prosecution.

George Sweeney

Look at that letter again, and assume that it was written from 35 Sutherland Street in answer to a letter sent there by Smith, the tailor, to Mr. Davis. Can you suggest any writer of that letter except your father?—I know my father's writing very well, and I can swear that this is not his; he would not sign "John Davis." My brother left no instructions, so far as I know, with reference to letters coming for him during his absence. No letters or telegrams have come for him since he left; he was in the habit of receiving a great deal of correspondence in connection with the racing business, and I believed that he had written to his clients stating that he was very ill and had suspended business for a time. When he came to see me in the middle of September he said that he had written to several of his clients to say that he was very ill and was going away for a holiday. I believe that all letters and telegrams to 35 Sutherland Street stopped at the time my brother disappeared; I was not living there then. When telegrams came to the house they were addressed to Davis, and letters to Mr. E. Davis or to E. Davis, Esq. There were some also in the name of Sweeney.

I read you the letter No. 236 again. On 13th October was there any Mr. Davis, who usually resided at 35 Sutherland Street, out of town except your brother, so far as you know?—I am quite certain the letter refers to my brother; he might have told some one else to write that letter, but I have no idea at all who it might be; I know that the writing is not my father's.

Can you give any explanation of the person writing in reference to your brother on 13th October that it would be quite a month before he would return home?—Possibly it may be one of his friends.

If he had gone to Australia he would not be back in a month, would he?—I am only assuming that he might have taken a voyage to Australia.

In October was there any expectation amongst his family that he might be back in a month?—We were not certain as to the time he might take. We thought he had gone to the seaside in consequence of his ill-health.

How do you reconcile that with what you have told me?—Simply from the conversation that took place between my brother and myself. I understood that he was going to the seaside, and if he did not feel any better he would take a voyage for his health to Australia. If he got better at the seaside, he might have been back in a month. The letter referred to is not in my brother's handwriting, nor is it in the handwriting of my sister, who stayed with my parents at Sutherland Street. Assuming that the letter reached 35 Sutherland Street in October, addressed to "Mr. G. Davis," and opened by one of my family there, I cannot explain why a reply should have been sent in the name of John Davis in a writing which I never saw.

By the LORD JUSTICE-CLERK—A letter came every day addressed

Alfred John Monson.

"G. Sweeney," and written on thin white tissue paper. That was from Middleberg, in Holland. It was a betting price list for my brother's business, and was sent regularly every morning during the racing season. I believe that the firm in Holland were written to about it. I have wired over to Holland for one of the bills, so that I can show the Court of what the paper consists.

Cross-examined by Mr. Comrie Thomson—This charge against my brother has been a source of great distress to my father and mother; when I came from home they were both in bed and very ill indeed. My father was cited here as a witness, but on Saturday I got a telegram from him saying that he thought it would be impossible for him to come, as he was very ill in bed. I was applied to by the advisers of the prisoner. I gave them just the same information as I gave to the police authorities. I did not believe it was my brother, and I do not believe so now. He was a very gentle, kind, young fellow; I do not believe he could hurt any one if he tried. I saw him last in September in the Westminster Palace Hotel. He was going about then quite openly. He seemed in fairly good spirits, only the young fellow was very ill indeed; his cough was very bad. My position in the hotel is in the hall, where people are constantly coming and going in great numbers. The hotel is very much frequented by Scotch people. My brother came there and saw me quite openly in September, and spoke to me for about half an hour. His intention in going to Australia was to get the benefit of the sea voyage; he took the same voyage three years ago, and it did him a deal of good. He had been in very bad health throughout this year, and I believe the young man was dying when I saw him last. His farewell of his mother might possibly have been regarded by both of them as a final farewell, and it would have upset his mother greatly. I am sure that he wanted to avoid this pain. I never heard of my father signing himself as "John Davis." I never saw Sidney Russell until he came here in connection with this case. I know that such a man was associated with my brother in betting transactions; I believe they were very much associated. I know that Russell said yesterday in the witness-box that he sometimes took the name of Davis. I should not be at all surprised if the letter signed "John Davis" with reference to my brother Edward was written by Sidney Russell. I knew very little about my brother Edward's friends; I was working at the hotel from nine in the morning till eight at night, and so had no chance of knowing them.

Re-examined by the Solicitor-General—I do not know where Sidney Russell lived; it was not at 35 Sutherland Street.

75. Alexander Houston, examined by the Solicitor-General—I am town-clerk of Ventnor, and manage the Hambrough estates in Ventnor. I was present at Cecil Hambrough's funeral. I saw the accused and spoke to him. On the day he arrived at Ventnor

Evidence for Prosecution.

I asked Monson if any policies had been effected on the life of young Hambrough, and he said none. I had been referred to as a friend in connection with certain proposed insurances; I received three references. [Shown No. 10.] That is a friendly certificate by me; it is the certificate of a friend on a form bearing the name of the Mutual Life Insurance Company regarding Cecil Hambrough. It is signed by me, and bears the date 3rd August, 1893.

Cross-examined by Mr. COMRIE THOMSON—So far as I knew, Monson's statement, that no insurances had been effected over the life of Cecil Hambrough, was quite true.

76. JOHN GILLET LIVESEY, examined by the SOLICITOR-GENERAL —I reside at Ventnor, and was acquainted with Cecil Hambrough for the greater part of his life. I saw Monson at Ventnor when he came for the funeral, and I was present at a conversation about insurances with Mr. Houston. Mr. Houston said to Monson—" I suppose none of these policies were completed? " Monson answered that, unfortunately, none of them were. I was present when the body was exhumed.

Cross-examined by Mr. COMRIE THOMSON—I could not tell if Monson spoke the truth when he made that statement about the insurances; I knew nothing about it, and had no reason to think about it one way or the other.

The Clerk of Justiciary (Mr. Crole) then read the declarations of the prisoner as follows:—
Judicial declaration, dated 31st August, 1893. At Inveraray, the 31st day of August, 1893. In presence of John Campbell Shairp, Esquire, advocate, Sheriff-Substitute of Argyllshire:

Compeared a prisoner, and the charge against him having been read over and explained to him, and he having been judicially admonished, Mr. Dugald M'Lachlan, writer, Lochgilphead, and Mr. Thomas Lindsay Clark, law agent, Edinburgh, agents for the prisoner, being present, and being thereafter examined thereanent— *Declares* : My name is Alfred John Monson. I am thirty-three years of age, and I am married. I have no profession, and at present reside at Ardlamont House, Argyllshire. I have to say that I am not guilty of the charge made against me, nor was I with Mr. Hambrough, nor within sight of him, when the accident happened. Therefore I cannot explain how it happened. Under the advice of my law agent, I decline to make any further declaration at present. All which I declare to be truth.

(Signed)   ALFRED JOHN MONSON.
(,,   )   J. C. SHAIRP.

J. C. MACLULLICH,
THOS. M'NAUGHTON,
JOHN CAMPBELL,
DAVID STEWART,
} Witnesses.

Alfred John Monson.

Judicial declaration, dated 30th October, 1893. At Kilmun, Argyllshire, the 30th day of October, 1893. In presence of John Campbell Shairp, Esquire, advocate, Sheriff-Substitute of Argyllshire:

Compeared a prisoner, and the charge against him having been read over and explained to him, and he having been judicially admonished (John Blair, Esq., Writer to the Signet, Edinburgh, agent for the prisoner, being present), and being thereafter examined thereanent—*Declares:* My name is Alfred John Monson. I am thirty-three years of age, married, and I lately resided at Ardlamont House, Argyllshire. After dinner on the evening of August the 9th Cecil Hambrough, who was living in family with me at Ardlamont House, stated that he was going out fishing, and asked me to go with him. I agreed to do so, though I did not care for the kind of fishing intended, which was fishing with a splash net. Hambrough had hired from a man at Kames or Tighnabruaich a small boat, which he had used on previous occasions for the same purpose. In this boat he and I started. We had on board a considerable length of net, probably about 300 yards, the width being about 14 feet. The nets were piled up in the boat, and were in themselves a considerable load. Hambrough took off his coat and rowed, while I busied myself preparing the nets. I did not steer the boat; there was, in fact, no rudder. While occupied with the nets, suddenly there was a bump, and the boat tilted, and I fell over the side. At the same time the boat capsized, and for a minute or two I was entangled in the nets. Immediately on getting clear I called out for Hambrough, and then saw him sitting on the rock laughing. The boat had struck the side of this rock and tilted over, which, with the load, and piled up as it was with nets, she would easily do. Hambrough, I knew, could not swim, so I told him to wait while I swam ashore and fetched another boat which was there. The sea was a little rough, and the night was dark. The distance I had to swim would be between 200 and 300 yards. As I was working with the other boat to get her off I observed Scott, a man who was staying in the house at the time, coming down, and called out to him to run to the house and fetch a lamp, as I could not find the plug or the plug hole in the boat. The tide, I understood, was then rising, so I deemed it wiser not to wait until Scott returned, and, accordingly, pushed off the boat. I knew that, although the plug might be out, there would be time without danger to row to where Hambrough was and back. I pulled off and picked up Hambrough. I told him that I thought the plug was out, but there was then only about 2 inches of water in the boat, and we decided to pull out and pick up the other boat and nets, which were floating about 20 yards or so away. I got out and made fast a line to the capsized boat, and we then hauled the nets in and proceeded to row ashore, but made no progress. Eventually we discovered that the anchor had fallen out of the capsized boat and

198

Evidence for Prosecution.

was securely fastened aground. We then got released and rowed ashore. There we found Scott, who had in the meantime come down with a lamp. By the time we landed the boat we were in was nearly full of water. We made fast the boats and went to the house. We all went into the smoking-room, and a man-servant brought whisky and water. I immediately went off to bed, leaving Scott and Hambrough together.

Both their rooms were near the smoking-room on the same floor. I do not know whether the plug was in the boat we first went out in; neither of us looked to see. The plug hole in that boat, however, was a homely affair. Hambrough complained that it had no plug hole, and that in consequence it was a bother to empty her after he had been out splash fishing, during which a lot of water gathered, and, accordingly, he himself cut a plug hole in the boat. I have no further answer to give to the charge now made against me. It is not true. On the contrary, so far from attempting on that evening to take young Hambrough's life, I consider that I saved it. The foregoing statement up to this point has been dictated by me word for word. Question put by the Sheriff-Substitute—"Is Scott, to whom you have referred, really called Davis, and do you know him?" Answer—"I have already said that I have no further answer to give to this charge." Question by the Sheriff-Substitute—"Were the nets used that night at all?" Answer—"I have no further answer to give." All which I declare to be truth.

(Signed)   ALFRED JOHN MONSON.
(,,)   J. C. SHAIRP.

J. C. MACLULLICH,
JAMES FRASER,   } Witnesses.
JOHN CAMPBELL,

The SOLICITOR-GENERAL—That is the case for the prosecution, my lord.

Evidence for the Defence.

1. HAROLD MARK CARTER, examined by Mr. COMRIE THOMSON—I am a partner of the firm of Carter, Ramsden & Carter, solicitors, Leeds. Early in January, 1892, the prisoner Monson instructed me in the matter of his contemplated purchase of the Hambrough estates. He informed me that Dudley Hambrough was the life tenant of certain estates in the Isle of Wight, in Middlesex, and elsewhere. The Hambrough estates comprise the ground rents of Ventnor, valued at £471 7s.; rack rents in the Isle of Wight, £459; and agricultural rents, £399. A rack rent is the best annual value that can be obtained from a property where there are buildings, or it is the best annual value of land where no previous premium has

Alfred John Monson.

H. M. Carter

been paid. The next subject is agricultural estate in Middlesex, valued at £1337 2s. 6d., and there are various properties, including ground rents, rack rents, and cottages near Southwold, producing £521 odds. Brick royalties are not included in that, only the minimum surface rents of the brick fields and other properties.

By the LORD JUSTICE-CLERK—That is the rent paid apart from the royalties.

Examination continued—The minimum rent produced out of brick royalties is £700 per annum. The next item is represented by investments, the result of the sale of some part of the estate, and valued at about £27,000; the original investment price was £23,000, but the investment has improved in value; it yields £731. That gives a total rental, including produce of investments, of £4618. There would be a deduction of about £150 for drainage charges. There is also a deduction caused by incumbrances, which leaves £4468. Before I got the final result I deducted an annuity secured to the North British Life Office of £800 per annum, which represents a loan of about £11,000 to Dudley Hambrough. That makes it £3635. The preferable annuity and the deduction for drainage come together to £975, which gives £3558. I should not say that the £150 is quite accurate; it is approximate. Deducting from that net income interest at 4½ per cent. on £40,000 and insurance premiums, £192, the surplus income would be £942; that is of all, excluding the Pipewell estates. At the time of my receiving instructions from Monson my understanding of his pecuniary position was that he was not a man of very great means, but I did not know of any great difficulty in carrying through the transaction, more particularly as no great amount of capital was required. I was satisfied that the proposed purchase was a *bona fide* one, and its attractions recommended it to me.

What were the attractions?—In the first place, we were satisfied as to Mr. Monson's intentions and the object he had in view, and we thought that, although the estate was at present bringing in a limited income, it might be considerably increased by a sale of certain of the properties, particularly of Southwold, and their re-investment in funds and railway stocks. Considering that the object Monson had in view was to disentail the estates to benefit both the life tenant and the tenant-in-tail, it was very essential that the legal estate should be in the hands of those friendly to such an arrangement. Their assent to disentail would be necessary to give it effect. The life tenant was Major Hambrough, the tenant-in-tail was Cecil, and their consents were necessary to the disentail, the consent of the latter not being available until he was twenty-one. The name of Hanrott was mentioned in connection with this matter at the time. Our first instructions were in regard to some difficulty in regard to the contract. The Eagle Company expressed their willingness to sell at a certain price, and to enter into a contract of sale on the

Evidence for Defence.

H. M. Carter

basis of certain deposits. A very limited time was given to Mr. Monson to pay this deposit, and he was not able to do so. His then solicitor, Mr. Hanrott, concluded the purchase in his own name and virtually appropriated the contract, and repudiated any obligation to Monson when Monson proposed to take it over from him. We then took legal proceedings against Hanrott, and the upshot was that in January, 1892, a judge of the High Court of Justice vested the contract in Monson. We found it would be impossible to complete this contract without the assistance of Mr. Hanrott, and it became necessary to make some friendly arrangement with him. The result was that Monson allowed Hanrott to identify himself with it to the extent of one-fourth, Monson having the remaining three-fourths. Upon that settlement Monson paid £300 as his proportion of the deposit, and it was arranged that the purchase should be completed in Monson's name, Monson giving a declaration to Hanrott as to the latter's one-fourth share.

I first saw Cecil Hambrough in the latter part of February or beginning of March, 1892. He called with Mr. Monson at my office, and the matter was fully discussed in his hearing. Cecil expressed the hope that we would be able to carry the matter through, as it was of the utmost importance to him that the estate should be in friendly hands. Cecil and Monson seemed to be quite in accord. In discussing the course to be adopted at the disentail, it was agreed by both Monson and Cecil that a provision should be made for Major Hambrough. Major Hambrough's pecuniary position was discussed, and it was suggested that upon the disentail being effected, instead of paying him a sum of money tied up, so that he could not anticipate it, a sum should be settled upon the Major and his wife for life, and that the remainder should be divided amongst the children. Cecil acquiesced in that, and Monson undertook to do his part. Neither at that time nor at any other did I ever see any apparent restraint put upon Cecil by Monson as to his returning to his parents. So far as I know, Cecil was a perfectly free agent in the matter.

After the arrangement that the purchase should be completed in Monson's name, I proceeded to negotiate the mortgage of the estates with Spencer & Clarkson, Keighley, Yorkshire. We handed them the particulars, and they referred the matter to their clients; they agreed to lend £40,000 at 4½ per cent. That proposed arrangement involved in a more or less large degree new insurances on Major Hambrough's life. We wished, if possible, to sell or surrender the whole of the old insurances, but, if that could not be done for the full amount, it was necessary we should effect new insurances for £7000. The purchase price consisted of the Eagle Company's arrangement, the loan, interest, &c.; it amounted to £43,620 3s. In the meantime the negotiations for the sale of the policies were proceeding. During the first six months of 1892 we negotiated for the substitution of new policies for the old ones being

Alfred John Monson.

H. M. Carter

carried out by Monson. He carried that out by himself; we had nothing to do with it. The new policies were all proposed to be on Major Hambrough's life. For some time Spencer & Clarkson endeavoured to secure insurances, but did not succeed. The obstacle was Major Hambrough's bad health. Some people thought it was temporary and might be cured, but the doctors took a much more serious view of it. The matter proceeded almost to a conclusion, the conveyance was prepared by counsel, but at the last moment Spencer & Clarkson declined to conclude the negotiations by reason of the failure to conclude new insurances on Major Hambrough's life.

We then opened negotiations with Messrs. Slight & Butler to sell the policies; an agreement was actually entered into and signed by both parties, subject to Mr. Monson's completion of the purchase, but it fell through. In order to produce money to effect new policies it was necessary for us to sell the old policies, but this could not be done.

The next negotiations were with Mr. Hardcastle, a Leeds accountant. That was early in August, 1892. Monson told me that Mr. Hardcastle had recovered judgment against him for negotiating a loan; I did not know at the time that he had instructions to negotiate. We therefore, upon the failure of the previous negotiations, called upon Hardcastle to complete the loan, and he assured us that it would be done. He said that the National Life Company would lend £46,000 upon the Hambrough estates, provided that they had an opportunity of insuring Cecil Hambrough's life for £17,000. I was informed a day or two later by Mr. Hardcastle that the National had accepted Mr. Cecil Hambrough's life for £17,000. That was at a rate which would be a little more than the premium on the £7000 life against life policy which it was proposed to surrender. In August, during the course of these negotiations, Monson was adjudicated bankrupt. It was then decided that Mr. Hardcastle should complete the purchase in his own name as trustee, and then sell the estates at his own price and plus his commission to the representatives of Mr. Monson. We had previously entered into an agreement, approved of by Hardcastle's solicitors, to secure to Monson, or to his wife, or to his creditors the benefit of the contract. Monson and his wife and Hanrott were to have the right to purchase the estate from him on the terms set forth in the agreement, Hanrott's share being still limited to one-fourth. The negotiations with the National fell through because it was discovered that particulars sent to the company were inaccurate. When accurate particulars were produced they found that the income was not enough to warrant the advance. On 16th August I had an interview with Mr. Richards in connection with these proposals. We informed him that Hardcastle was virtually a trustee, and that, really, to benefit Monson. I explained to him that it would ulti-

202

Evidence for Defence.

H. M. Carter

mately benefit Monson or his creditors and Hanrott, with an ultimate saving to young Hambrough. This last arrangement seemed
to have died a natural death, when we got a telegram from Hanrott
saying that if we could find £35,000 at 4 per cent. he could find the
rest. He stipulated that the purchase should be in his own name,
but said that he would give Mrs. Monson a right to acquire a third
share at the cost price. We received a letter from Mrs. Monson assent-
ing to this. We then arranged for the loan of £35,000 with
solicitors in Leeds, but Mr. Hanrott could not perform his part of
the negotiations, and it fell through.

In January, 1893, I went to London at Mr. Monson's request,
and was introduced to Mr. Sebright. I found that he had arranged
with Mr. Cecil Hambrough to purchase the estates for him as trustee.
No mention was made of new insurances in this connection. Mr.
Sebright mentioned that his remuneration would be the surrender
value of Major Hambrough's life policy. We told him he could not
claim this, and that we could not recognise it. He said that he
was prepared to rely on Cecil's word, as he had trusted him before,
having made advances to him on his note of hand. Mr. Richards,
of the Eagle Company, informed me on 11th January that their
interest in the estates was an offer to a firm of solicitors on Major
Hambrough's behalf, and he said he would take the first definite
offer. Mr. Jones, who acted for Mr. Sebright, and I had some
interviews with him, the result of which was that the arrangement
fell through because no definite proposal was made.

That brings us to Mr. Monson's direct relationship with Major
Hambrough. When I was first instructed by Mr. Monson in this
matter he informed me that he had lost large sums to Major Hambrough during the two previous years, and that he had paid off and
taken charges on the estate to secure his advances. He told me he
did not know at the time he made those advances that the Eagle
Company had foreclosed. I had seen Major Hambrough and Monson
together many times; they seemed to understand each other perfectly, and up to a certain time they were perfectly in accord. As
regards the Major's maintenance until the disentail, when I was first
introduced to Major Hambrough he and Monson were working the
matter together, and I understood that the arrangement between
them was that Monson should maintain the Major until Cecil came of
age, and that the Major, in return, should present himself for insurance. At that time it seemed clearly understood that Monson should
buy the estates. The original instructions which Monson had given
to Hanrott were that he should effect a transfer of the mortgages,
and Major Hambrough gave Monson a retainer, as Monson had given
Hanrott a retainer.

Until a day early in February, 1892, Major Hambrough always
expressed himself as hoping that Monson would be able to effect a
purchase. He was very anxious that the estate should be in friendly

203

Alfred John Monson.

H. M. Carter

hands until it was disentailed; he said that this was very essential. When we settled with Hanrott he suggested that the retainer he had received to effect the transfers for Monson on behalf of Major Hambrough might still be alleged to be in force, and he therefore wished some direction from Hambrough that Monson was purchasing these estates for himself. I saw Major Hambrough after this in Monson's presence, and he consented to write at once to Hanrott to the effect that he had no actual and personal interest in the purchase, and that Monson was purchasing the estate as for himself.

About this time Major Hambrough got to know three or four people in London, who assured him that they could find a much larger sum of money. From this time Major Hambrough's manner to Monson and myself changed. He required that a formal agreement should be entered into, that he should be maintained until disentailment took place, and he also required a sum to be paid down before he would come up for reinsurance. Down to this time I had frequently seen Monson advancing sums of money to Major Hambrough for which no receipt was taken. Monson also helped Major Hambrough in getting one or two bankruptcy petitions against him withdrawn. I frequently saw the Major in company with several of the persons who were in my mind. When we were negotiating with Mr. Richards we received information that they themselves intended to purchase the estates on behalf of Major Hambrough. We had continuous relations with Mr. Fuller during March and April. On 16th March, 1892, we received a letter from Monson that he had arranged with Major Hambrough to come up for insurance on our paying £50, and, on that being done, Mr. Fuller wrote to say that Monson had agreed to sell the estates. The Major wanted a sum paid down before he would come up for insurance. He wanted to be paid for it. He wanted a sum of money, and then his solicitor tendered an agreement stating that the estates had been bought for Major Hambrough without any provision being made for Monson's deposit or advance or anything else. Several meetings took place between Fuller, Hambrough, Monson, and myself, and agreements were entered into on several occasions, but these were broken. At last an agreement was entered into, the preliminaries of which were signed, to the effect that Monson should pay a certain sum down, should arrange certain debts of Hambrough's which were pressing, and should sell the estates at a certain price within two months, and, if Hambrough was unable to purchase the estates, then Monson was to give him 50 per cent. on the amount he might receive. Dr. Hambleton appeared about this stage in place of Major Hambrough's other friend who had disappeared. The Doctor was the Major's constant companion. Dr. Hambleton intimated to Monson and me that Major Hambrough would not sign the agreement. We prepared a formal agreement, and sent it to the solicitor, Fuller. Hambleton called a little later and said that Hambrough would not sign it.

Evidence for Defence.

H. M. Carter

Dr. Hambleton wished to negotiate terms of purchase for Hambrough if possible. We told him that we would sell only in the relation of vendor and purchaser. Dr. Hambleton assured me that Hambrough had friends behind him. Accordingly a letter was drafted for Mr. Monson to sign, containing an offer of sale. Monson wrote the letter offering to sell the estate to Hambrough at a price to be agreed on, and we insisted that the relation of vendor and purchaser should be maintained. That letter was handed to Dr. Hambleton for Major Hambrough. Upon receiving this letter Dr. Hambleton arranged a meeting with Hambrough and his agent, Fuller. I saw Hanrott, and agreed upon the price, which was fixed at £60,000. The meeting took place on 11th April, 1892, at the First Avenue Hotel. There were present Major Hambrough, Fuller, Dr. Hambleton, Monson, and myself. It was a very protracted meeting. We did not arrive at an arrangement about the price at the first meeting, but at a second meeting on the following day we did. A final offer was made by me on Monson's instructions. It was that Monson agreed to sell the estates for £60,000, giving Hambrough a certain time to complete the purchase; and he also agreed that if Hambrough could not effect the purchase, which was extremely probable, that whatever sum should be paid to him on the disentailment as representing the value of the life estate, he would give Hambrough one-half, and in the meantime would maintain him until the disentailment, and arrange his most pressing debts. It was part of the arrangement that Hambrough should give up every application for insurance. I prepared a form of agreement in these terms, and sent it to Fuller, but got a reply that his client would not agree to the draft. Some time after Monson handed to me a form of agreement that Fuller asked him to sign.

It would be useful if you would summarise to us exactly Monson's relation to Major Hambrough in this transaction?—Monson was simply providing for Major Hambrough's maintenance until the disentail; he would not permit the Major to regard him as an agent in the purchase, because that would have imposed very onerous liabilities upon Monson; he would have put himself under covenant to repay the mortgage while Hambrough had enjoyed the life interest. The original idea was that if Monson could purchase the estate as second mortgagee, he might get any surplus money that might be over from the first mortgage, and might save money, because he might be able to effect a loan on the estate at $3\frac{1}{2}$ or 4 per cent.

By the LORD JUSTICE-CLERK—He might have paid off the first mortgage and raised money on better terms; he might pay less interest and also have an increment in value.

Examination continued—The stipulated interest to the Eagle was 6 per cent., to be reduced to 5 per cent. if paid punctually. It was believed that if Monson paid off the first mortgage he might be able to raise the same amount of money at 3 or $3\frac{1}{2}$ per cent. The

Alfred John Monson.

H. M. Carter

insurance of Cecil's life was an important element in the negotiation with regard to the disentail. If the National had lent £17,000 on Cecil's life, and he had died, the disentail would have been deferred. If the loan had stood until Major Hambrough's death, and if the interest had fallen into arrear, a provision was made under this policy to reduce the £46,000 by £17,000.

Monson mentioned to me at this time that he was taking a doctor to see Major Hambrough when the negotiations fell through. Shortly after he informed me that he had had Major Hambrough examined by a doctor, and that he had arranged an insurance for about £42,000 with the Amicable. Spencer M. Clarkson agreed to advance the premium by way of loan to Monson. The insurance company, after reconsideration, thought they ought to have further medical examination, and Major Hambrough would not come forward. The question was revived again in another office for the same amount, but it was discovered that the office was not sufficiently substantial in Spencer & Clarkson's opinion.

At that time it became absolutely necessary that the insurance should be made in order to complete this matter, and a meeting was held at which it was agreed that, under the advice of the doctor, who advised that the Major's complaint was only intermittent, he should go to the country and take exercise instead of loitering about London. It was necessary to provide funds, and Monson advanced £25 towards personal expenses, and guaranteed a further £25 to be paid on Major Hambrough's return. He also agreed to pay £250 to Fuller to reimburse him for the loans that Fuller had made to Major Hambrough. That was £300 altogether. That agreement was committed to writing by me, and was signed. Major Hambrough also assented, and Mr. Hanrott, too. The Major and Dr. Hambleton went into the country. He was examined when he came back by five doctors, and the result was not satisfactory. They would not pass him as an ordinary life. They might have considered a loaded policy.

That brings us down to the month of June. Fuller had been making very extravagant demands for money upon Monson, who thought it necessary to have a proper understanding, so he asked me to meet Fuller on 9th June, which I did. Fuller wanted £400 for Major Hambrough's maintenance, and said that until the assertion of Monson's agency in this purchase could be proved, he should not draw any more money whatever. On 14th June I got a letter from Mr. Fuller, enclosing a copy letter from Mr. Richards, of the Eagle Company, directing him not to complete the contract with Monson. Richards also got notice that Fuller intended to call in question the legality of the foreclosure.

During the six months I came across Major Hambrough I should say that for the greater part of the time he was living entirely on Monson. In 1891-92 I was constantly shown letters from the Major

Evidence for Defence.

H. M. Carter

begging for money. I have even seen Monson handing money to Major Hambrough from time to time. On 29th June, 1892, I got a letter from Cecil Hambrough; that was at the time when the first negotiations had fallen through. I received the letter, directed from Depôt Barracks, desiring me to do my utmost to complete the purchase, both for Monson's sake and his own. In consequence of that letter, we were more disposed to enter into further negotiations that were opened up by Mr. Hardcastle. When the purchase proposed by Monson was first entertained I went to Southwold and made an estimate of what would be the value of the property, along with the valuator and solicitor to the mortgagees. It was ascertained to be worth £138,000, excluding the Pipewell estate. Taking into consideration the brick lands at Southwold, and having before us as an example a sale in the immediate neighbourhood which realised £400 an acre, and remembering, that to put such a large quantity of land into the market might water the price, we put it at £250 an acre. Subsequent to this valuation I consulted certain actuaries in London, in order to ascertain what would be Mr. Monson's prospective interest in the property, what Cecil Hambrough's, and what provision would be made for Major Hambrough. It was conceivable that Major Hambrough would not consent to this arrangement. We called in actuaries for the purpose of ascertaining what would be the relative value of the life interests and of the estate-tail, and we supposed, for this purpose, that those estates had been sold for £135,000. Taking that sum as invested at the rate of 3 per cent., we found that, taking Major Hambrough's life at forty-four and the Lieutenant's at twenty-one, and considering also that £5000 might be advanced to the children and would have to be taken out of the £135,000, and also considering the jointure that was then pending, we found that the life tenant's share was roughly £67,000, and that the entail share was also roughly £67,000, there being a difference of only £500. Therefore, whatever might be found to be the actual value of the estate, on realisation it made no difference if invested at 3 per cent. It would then divide equally. From these negotiations I gathered that Monson was prepared to protect the interests of Major Hambrough and Cecil all through. When this calculation was made, it was not taken into consideration that the Major was a bad life. By the agreement, which was signed in preliminary form, there would be left a sum of £22,000 for Monson, after paying off all incumbrances, and Monson agreed to pay half of that sum to the Major. That would leave about £11,000 to Monson, not too much considering the indebtedness and obligations undertaken by him. Cecil had said that he would settle a sum upon the Major out of his £67,000. The whole arrangement commended itself to us on many grounds as being reasonable and in the interests of all parties.

Now, is it an arrangement that could be carried through if,

Alfred John Monson.

H. M. Carter

failing new policies on the Major's life, you got policies on Cecil's life, and bought the Major's life interest?—That was not in our instructions at all, but it is a possible thing. A thing it would do would be to increase the charges on the rental for two years, with the year preceding Cecil's coming of age. Of course, he would have to maintain the old policies for one year. Under the circumstances, it was quite a feasible suggestion to insure Cecil's life alone, either for the whole amount, dropping the Major's policies the year afterwards, or for the difference between the existing policies and the others, seeing that the Major's was not an insurable life.

Cross-examined by the SOLICITOR-GENERAL—I began to act in this matter about 10th January, 1892, and I acted till some time in September. The matter was revived for a week or so in January of this year. I had to deal with the purchase of Major Hambrough's life interest, which had been mortgaged to the Eagle Company, and which the company had foreclosed. To effect the purchase the purchaser did not necessarily require money; Major Hambrough's interest was not mortgaged up to its full value on the terms of the present mortgage; by a readjustment of interest there would be a small margin.

Did you know what available capital Monson would invest in this transaction?—He had small sums of £600 or £700, and nothing caused us to make inquiries; he appeared to have reasonable command of a small amount of money; I believe there were occasions on which sums of £600 or £700 were paid over. I cannot say what available capital, if any, was in his hands for investment in this transaction. When capital was required he found it; for example, he paid a deposit of £300 and a further deposit of £150, and in another transaction he found about £225.

When did he find the first deposit?—He paid Hanrott £300 on account of a £400 deposit.

I understood you to say that Monson was unable to pay that?— That is so. That was between the end of December, 1891, and in January, 1892, before he came to us; we ascertained in connection with the same transaction that a deposit had been payable which he had been unable to pay. That deposit was payable, I think, by the first week or two of January, 1892, and the amount was £400. Monson deposited the £400 a day or two after the date on which it was payable. I am not sure where he got the money. He told me afterwards that he had borrowed £600 from a bank in London; the deposit came out of that, I have no doubt. I knew that in security for that £600 he had lodged one of Major Hambrough's mortgages. Monson did not take up the position of a trustee for Major Hambrough's life interest; he acted absolutely in his own name. If he had succeeded in buying the mortgaged interests he would have been master of the situation during the Major's life; neither father nor son could have taken the slightest benefit from the estate, except

Evidence for Defence.

H. M. Carter

upon such terms as Monson dictated, had there not been a special agreement entered into. Those advising Major Hambrough broke away from the arrangement because they would not consent to an absolute purchase by Monson.

Supposing that Monson had purchased the interest, and that both father and son had survived Cecil's majority, then neither father nor son could have taken anything without Monson's consent?—On disentail—no.

Suppose Monson did not buy the life interest, and Cecil came of age, Cecil could do nothing without his father's consent?—No; so long as the Major had a life interest. I have met Monson very often. This is the only matter in which I have had personally to do with him. He had solicitors, Messrs. Gordon & Nutting, of Lincoln's Inn, and there was no reason, so far as I know, for his coming to me in this connection. I saw my way to carry through this transaction if Major Hambrough and his friends had been agreeable. If my plan had been adopted and carried through, it would not have involved any insurance on Cecil's life at all. If the mode suggested by the National Life Company, already mentioned, had been adopted, the only insurance would have been for £17,000, but I cannot offer any suggestion as to how that figure was arrived at.

What was the interest or difference which, theoretically, would have been protected if the £17,000 insurance had been effected?—It would have brought the £46,000 proposed mortgage into an easier compass in the event of Cecil dying before he came of age, and the disentail of the estates taking place. They proposed that insurance in order to reduce the amount. There was no suggestion of an insurance of £50,000 on Cecil's life in my proposed arrangement. If such a suggestion had been made to me, or had occurred to me before we gave the matter up, we should have considered it as feasible as carrying through the proposed arrangement by means of a reinsurance of Major Hambrough's life; but it was never suggested. There was a distinct proposal for the loan of some money, over £400, I think, to the London and Globe Insurance Company. Major Hambrough was then examined by five doctors, and rejected at the ordinary premium. We asked Mr. Wardle about getting him taken at some different premium, but he advised us that it would encumber the estate more than it could afford. In my negotiations with Monson I discovered no interest in him in connection with Cecil Hambrough or Major Hambrough apart from this projected purchase of the life interest for a large insurance. As we arranged the scheme at first we did propose to sell or surrender all the policies on Major Hambrough's life; that would have assisted us very materially, and would have carried us through with £7000 of ready money and reinsurance. This proposal was made by Monson simultaneously with the suggestion of the reinsurance of Major Hambrough's life, and it would have had the effect of substituting for policies got at a

P

Alfred John Monson.

H. M. Carter

low premium earlier in his life new policies at a higher rate. That had the advantage that we could reduce the first mortgage. The first mortgagees agreed to reduce their loan. The first proposal was £40,000 at 4½ per cent. If we had obtained the policies and increased them by £7000, the mortgage would have remained, so that we should have got a further advance on the Pipewell estate. We could have got £6000 or £7000 by surrendering these policies. We would have increased the premiums, but I have reduced the interest on the mortgages. I admit that a proper comprehension of the effect on all parties of the purchase of Major Hambrough's life interest and the character of the title taken in Monson, and the respective rights of parties when Cecil came of age, would require careful consideration by a person without legal knowledge before he could understand it. Cecil Hambrough's age when I was seeing him in connection with this matter was nineteen or twenty. He understood perfectly well the significance of these transactions and the objects in view.

Did you ever see him take a different line from that adopted by Monson?—No, never. In discussing the projected financial operations we did not go into details; a client necessarily trusts the details to his solicitor. I think that Monson understood the details, and stood out for an absolute purchase in his own name, as originally arranged with Major Hambrough. He never departed from it.

And it broke down in consequence?—Not in consequence. It broke down in recent years owing to Major Hambrough's health.

Was it not because Major Hambrough's advisers would not allow him to sign the deed which Monson submitted?—He presented himself on several occasions notwithstanding that.

Was not the cause of the breakdown of this proposed arrangement that Major Hambrough's advisers would not allow him to sign the deeds which Monson submitted? —He did sign a preliminary agreement in one case, but he never signed a formal agreement, and I believe that was with the advice of his solicitors. Yet, on the occasion when Monson saw him, he did present himself before a doctor. He was examined in all by five doctors when Monson paid him the £50 and entered into those obligations which I have described. Monson paid the £50 in two sums of £25 about 11th April, 1892. The £250 was to be paid in the event of the purchase being completed. We advanced Monson one of the £25; I do not know where he got the other. I think we had about £1000 or £1200 paid into our hands on Monson's behalf, and we paid the greater part of that out. He got the £1100 from a London bank, and we got about £600 of it. The other £500 came from himself. The whole of it, with the exception of one item of £222, was paid into our hands by him, and we do not know where he got it. The £222 was from the sale of some shares. During the time we acted for Monson we paid £25 to Major Hambrough for him.

Evidence for Defence.

H. M. Carter

You said that you had seen Monson giving Major Hambrough sums of money—what sort of sums?—£5 and £1. I did not state as a fact that Monson paid off certain second mortgages for Major Hambrough; I said that I was instructed so. I have no personal knowledge of the matter except that one of the deeds came into our hands, one second mortgage. I think it is produced by the Crown. It refers to £3400, and is dated December. [Shown No. 22.] That is the document. It is a mortgage granted by Major Hambrough directly in favour of Monson.

Well, what do you mean by saying that Monson had advanced money in paying off a second mortgage on behalf of Major Hambrough?—I did not state it as a fact; the only knowledge that I had at all was that on 10th or 11th January, 1892, Mr. Monson made a statement to us that Major Hambrough had incurred considerable liabilities to him, that he had made advances on mortgages, and also that he had taken transfers. All the evidence which Monson ever put before us of payments of money by him on behalf of Major Hambrough was in letters from Monson to us. I do not think that we ever saw anything in writing in the way of acknowledgment by Major Hambrough. As regards the bankruptcy proceedings against Major Hambrough to which I have referred, a petition was presented by some creditor against Major Hambrough, and Monson, recognising that his interests and the Major's were identical, arranged with the petitioning creditor to withhold or withdraw the petition, and Major Hambrough was quite satisfied. I did not act as agent for either in making that arrangement. This statement which I am making is based upon a conversation between Monson and the Major; I never saw any document legally instructing the fact that Monson paid money on behalf of Major Hambrough to relieve these bankruptcy proceedings. In 1891 and 1892 Major Hambrough obtained small loans from Monson, and owed money for lodgings, and on one occasion he was threatened with distress. If the proposed transaction had been carried through Monson would have had an interest of £11,000. If that had come about Monson would, in exchange, in the first place, have covered advances to Major Hambrough of perhaps £3000 or £4000; he would have made himself responsible for the £40,000 mortgage, and would have had all the trouble as well as all the expense of the negotiations. Besides, he would have taken the estate into his own hands, out of the hands of strangers. It is impossible to fix the amount of advances of money by Monson that would be put into the transaction. Under the most favourable computation he would not have got more than £11,000.

Re-examined by Mr. Comrie Thomson—Cecil would, however, get a good deal—about £67,000. That would have been the result of the arrangement. It was represented to me that Monson had an interest in his father's and mother's marriage settlement, amount-

211

Alfred John Monson.

ing, I think, to £2000. I was not aware that he sold the expectancy; it was a marketable commodity.

Did the agreements of which you have been speaking in each instance provide against what my learned friend has called " Monson being the sole master of the situation "?—In every case.

Did any of them fail to be carried out on account of Monson proposing that he should be left master of the situation?—No; the agreements expressly provided that the money was to be divided between Major Hambrough and Monson. In each of these attempted agreements Cecil's interests were not safeguarded; it was unnecessary. Immediately on his coming of age he would have the reversion, and he would raise money upon it, and make it certain by insuring his own life against his father's. He could have raised a considerable sum immediately on his coming of age, notwithstanding that his father was alive. The father had the power to protect the son's interest, as nothing could be done without his consent.

I am aware that Monson lived for some time at Harrogate, and afterwards at Riseley Hall, near Ripley. These places are within half an hour's railway journey from Leeds, where my business is. Leeds is the nearest town. My firm had acted for Mrs. Day's family in part. It is within my knowledge that Monson paid Hanrott sums of £3000, £150, £75, and £30. The payments by Monson of £1 and £5 to Major Hambrough were very frequent.

By the LORD JUSTICE-CLERK—Cecil Hambrough was in my office with Monson on several occasions, at meetings, to see how things were going on. In the first place, we explained to him the mode in which we intended to carry the arrangement through, and he expressed his extreme desire that we should be able to do so. We did not think it desirable to see him alone on such a matter; it did not occur to us. He was a man of twenty, and not young for his age. It did not occur to us that in a large transaction like this he should have some one to advise him separate from the adviser of other people. There was simply a proposal by Monson to obtain a mortgage to protect his own money, and there was no need for Cecil to be consulted in the matter at all.

But he came to discuss it. Why did he come to discuss it if he had no interest in it at all?—He wished to get the estates out of the hands of the Eagle Insurance, or to prevent them being sold to strangers. Monson was his best friend, and he wanted him to be identified with the matter very much. Taking him as his best friend or guardian, or in any other capacity, it was to his interest to see a large sum of money placed in his hands. He was only brought to our office to express the wish that this should go on.

2. Dr. HAMBLETON, examined by Mr. WILSON—I am a physician and specialist in consumption, and reside at 23 York Street, Port-

Evidence for Defence.

Dr. Hambleton

man Square, London. I think I first made Mr. Monson's acquaintance in 1882 or 1883 through a hospital comrade, to whom he had done a kindness. I was subsequently introduced to Mr. Tottenham, who, I understood, was an ex-captain of the Guards. On 30th December, 1889, I think, Mr. Tottenham told me that it was desired that Major Hambrough should be got into condition to pass a medical examination with a view to insurance. I attended Major Hambrough for a considerable time professionally, and he was examined for a life insurance policy. I cannot say whether he was passed. At that time I was attending professionally to Major Hambrough, and I was a friend. I was aware of the scheme that was proposed, under which there was to be a purchase of Major Hambrough's life interest from the Eagle Insurance Company. Mr. Monson was acting, I always thought, as Major Hambrough's representative after Mr. Tottenham. The negotiations involved in that scheme were not completed. In 1893 a new proposal, involving the insurance of Cecil's life, was submitted to me by Monson, as representing Major Hambrough. The proposal was made by word of mouth at the Westminster Palace Hotel some time in the end of June of this year. There was no one else present. The proposal was that the son should purchase the life interest in the estates, that the son's life should be insured for about £60,000, and that a trustee should be appointed, for the purpose, I assume, of receiving the income on behalf of Major Hambrough and of Cecil. There was no trustee nominated by Monson at that time. He did not name Mr. Jerningham at any time, and I did not know that his name had been submitted as a party who would act as trustee. There was no arrangement that Monson would nominate some person. I considered that proposal, but I did not think it might form the basis of an arrangement; it would have had to be absolutely altered. [Shown No. 53 of defence productions.] That letter is in my handwriting; it is addressed to Mr. Monson, and is as follows:—" Seaforth, Sussex, 17th July, 1893. Dear Monson,—I shall be down here for another week on account of my little boy. The suggestion you make can be made the basis of an arrangement if Cecil can pass life assurance for the required amount. If the figures we have are correct, and I believe they are, as things look better than they did, it will be all the better. Cecil told you I had expected to have heard from you. Now, the question is, can Cecil pass the insurance? If you are satisfied on that, then arrange to come up to town with him so that we may know for a certainty that a good office will give a policy. Will you agree to this? Please let me know immediately.—Very truly yours, GODFREY W. HAMBLETON."

That letter was written for the purpose of getting a further communication as to the life proposal submitted in June, 1893, by Mr. Monson. This proposal could have been the basis for a life insurance for the required amount, which I understood to be about

213

Alfred John Monson.

£60,000. In my mind there was some difficulty about getting Cecil insured, because the proposal was for a large amount and also because I knew that Cecil had been postponed or refused before, in 1891, by the Reliance Company. I only knew about that through a letter from Major Hambrough. That proposal was for £2000 to justify the granting of an allowance for the boy's education and maintenance.

It was my idea that Cecil should come up to London. My reason for wanting him to come up to London was not in order to get him passed by an insurance company, but that he might have an interview with Mr. Prince about the suggestions that had been made. I knew that Cecil did not want to see Mr. Prince. [Shown No. 71 of defence productions.] That is an undated letter from Ardlamont House, signed W. D. C. Hambrough, which I received, I think, before 17th July. He says—" Dear Hambleton,—I shall not be in town just yet. I am quite willing to come to any arrangement with my father, except through Mr. Prince.'' Notwithstanding that letter I wrote the letter of 17th July to get him to come to town to see Mr. Prince. I did not say in that letter what my object was; if I had done so, probably Cecil would not have come. I think that if Major Hambrough had given his consent to Mr. Monson's proposal and Cecil's life had been insured for £60,000 the matter could have been arranged, but it was not the right thing to do either in the interest of Cecil or of Major Hambrough. The objectionable feature from Cecil's point of view was that whereas a certain amount of the estate would be cut off to pay off the liabilities on the estate, and would have been covered by insurance on Cecil's life, that insurance would have gone on Cecil's issue; Cecil would have himself paid off certain liabilities on the estate, and would not have been repaid, except through his issue. He would have paid off the mortgages. Whether he paid them off or not, the mortgages were there.

My view as to getting rid of the mortgages was that there should be a re-settlement of the estate, that certain funds should be realised, that the policies in existence should be a first charge on the resettled estate, so that in the ordinary course of events, when Cecil came into the estates, he lost nothing. That scheme provided for Cecil's maintenance in the meantime, because it would be a second condition that a sum would be allowed for Cecil's maintenance during his father's lifetime. It could not be effected till Cecil came of age. It comes to this, that although I wrote to Mr. Monson that this proposal might be a basis of arrangement, my own view was that my own scheme was the better one. I had no further communication with Monson after writing that letter. I was surprised that Monson proceeded to try to get Cecil's life insured after receiving my letter of 17th July.

Cross-examined by the SOLICITOR-GENERAL—I had no connection with the business part of the arrangement. I was trying to help

214

Evidence for Defence.

my friend Major Hambrough; I had no personal interest present or prospective in the matter. My name was only used as trustee for Hambrough.

I heard of the arrangement proposed in the letter of 17th July about the end of June; at this time an effort was being made to get Cecil out of Monson's hands. Negotiations were made with Cecil, and I had seen him previously. I had told him that certain friends were quite prepared to arrange a transfer of the mortgage to allow him a sufficient income—about £500 a year—and allow his father an income, and the condition was that he should be placed under the control of another tutor. That would be about February, 1893. It was from Mr. Prince that I got the information that enabled me to make that statement. Cecil received my statement by saying that Mr. Monson had been very kind to him; he did not seem to see why he should leave nor why that should be a condition of the arrangement. I explained to him that, in view of certain facts, no arrangement could be come to unless he left Monson and went to another tutor. The result of the interview was that Cecil said that in view of all things he believed Mr. Monson had acted the part of a good friend, that he was indebted to him for his education, and that he was sure that he would advise that such a transference should take place. After that I had some communication with Cecil in the end of June so as to ascertain whether he would consent to the proposal. As regards the particular mode of carrying out the arrangement, that was in the hands of Mr. Prince, and I was most anxious in the month of July that Cecil should come to town to enter into communication with Mr. Prince, so that he might see that it was a straightforward, *bona fide* transaction.

In that letter of 17th July you suggested that Monson and Cecil should come to town together?—Certainly. I wished to induce Mr. Monson to come to our view. So far as I know, they did not come to town. I had no communication of any kind with Cecil or Monson after this letter until I heard of Cecil's death.

Re-examined by Mr. Wilson—I very rarely keep my letters; as a rule I destroy them.

Have you had more than one talk with Cecil in which he referred to Mr. Monson's kindness to him?—Only one. I believe I have told you all that he said at that time about what Monson had done for him and his indebtedness to him. From what he said I gathered that he was on perfectly good terms with Monson, and that he felt grateful to him for what he had done.

3. EDITH MARY HIRON, examined by Mr. COMRIE THOMSON—I am twenty-two years of age, and entered Mr. Monson's family as governess about four and a half years ago. I obtained the situation through an advertisement in the *Guardian*. When I entered their service they were at a place in Surrey. Afterwards they

Alfred John Monson.

Edith M. Hiron

moved about a little, living sometimes at Harrogate, sometimes at other places in Yorkshire, on the coast. I remember Cecil Hambrough coming to live with them at Woodlands. He remained from that time onwards as a member of the household. After he had been with them a little I left them and went home, but returned in about six months. Mrs. Monson wrote asking me to come back. When I returned Cecil Hambrough was away for a holiday, but he came back shortly afterwards. I returned on 7th March, about two and a half years ago, and have remained with the Monsons ever since. I was with them during their residence at Ardlamont, and have been living with Mrs. Monson since then.

What were the relations between Mr. Monson and Cecil Hambrough during the time of your stay in the house?—They were on the best of terms. That was the case during the whole time that I lived in the family.

Have you heard Hambrough say anything as to his liking to stay with Monson?—Yes; I have. He said he would much rather be with him than go home, as his parents were living in lodgings. I remember the man Scott coming to Ardlamont. That was on Tuesday, 8th August. I first saw him about eight or half-past eight o'clock that evening at dinner. The dinner party consisted of Mr. and Mrs. Monson, myself, and Scott. Cecil Hambrough was out fishing that evening. He had been out most of the day. I had not seen him part of the day in the boat with the children, but I knew they were there. There was a nurse who looked after the younger children, and she asked my permission to go down to the boat with the children, and I gave it. I remember the children took down Cecil Hambrough's luncheon to the boat after they had their own, and stayed with him a portion of the afternoon. I remember Hambrough came into the dining-room that day for tea, and again left about six o'clock to go out. He said Douglas—that is the little boy—would be with him, and he stated that he would not be back for dinner. It was the habit of the house that evening clothes were put on for dinner except when they were going out fishing. Scott did not put on evening clothes, but he was decently dressed. He looked a very delicate fellow, and he was very quiet. Mrs. Monson and myself remarked that after dinner. Scott did not join us in the drawing-room after dinner. I do not remember if Mr. Monson did. Scott went down to the smoking-room, I think. I should not have called him a gentleman.

Did you gather from what you saw whether he was on terms of friendship with Mr. Monson?—I thought he was not, from the way they acted to each other. I do not remember hearing anything of Scott until he arrived, and I understood he had come on some business. I did not know anything more definite about him at that time. I saw him at breakfast next morning, the Wednesday morning. I think I spoke to him, but not more than saying

216

Evidence for Defence.

Edith M. Hiron

" Good morning." I next saw him about ten minutes to one on the Wednesday. Hambrough was late in getting up for breakfast that morning. He did not appear till about eleven o'clock. That forenoon I went down to the beach to get the children to lunch. They were down there with their father and Scott. I am aware that Monson and Scott had been round that morning to bring a second boat from the ferry. I met Scott again at luncheon. At luncheon Mr. Monson asked his two little girls to go out in the boat along with him and Scott. The little boy asked if he might go also, but I did not want him to go, and told him to wait until he was asked. When the boat was launched the children went out along with Scott and Mr. Monson, and the nurse remained on the beach while they were out. I was in the house that afternoon when the children were down at the boat. I knew that Cecil and Mrs. Monson had been walking on the high ground above the bay. It is an open place, where they can see the sea. The company at dinner was the same as the night before, with the addition of Hambrough. At the dinner hour something was said about fishing in the bay, but I don't remember much about it. I think a message came from the keeper, M'Intyre. I understood that some of the gentlemen were going out to fish. That was spoken about openly at dinner. I do not remember if the dinner was a little later than usual that night. When Mrs. Monson and I went to the drawing-room the gentlemen remained in the dining-room for about half an hour. I afterwards heard some of them leaving the house. They went downstairs to the smoking-room, and they would go out by a door there to the beach. I do not know of my own knowledge whether the whole three went out, but I think they did. I heard some one come back afterwards. I heard a man's voice. I was in Mrs. Monson's bedroom at the time. I did not hear what the man said. I heard afterwards that Scott had come back for a light. I heard nothing further that night. I went to bed and heard nothing until next morning. Mrs. Monson and I rose very early that morning, as we were going to Glasgow by an early boat. We went to Kames Pier. The boat left at seven o'clock. That involved our rising at five o'clock and leaving the house at six. It was at this time that I first heard of the boat accident. It was spoken of as a serious matter. Mrs. Monson said that it was very dangerous, as Mr. Hambrough could not swim.

It had been arranged some days before that Mrs. Monson and I, with some of the children, should go to Glasgow on the 10th. There was a lot of shopping to do, and the children had to get their hair cut. It was desirable that the children should be made smart before the 12th, when visitors were expected. It was left open whether we should go on the Tuesday, Wednesday, or Thursday. We came back to Tighnabruaich about seven o'clock. Monson came on board the steamer there, and came on to Kames, which is ten minutes' sail from Tighnabruaich.

Alfred John Monson.

Edith M. Hiron

When did he first speak about what had happened that day?—After we left Kames for Ardlamont.

What did he say?—That Hambrough had met with an accident.

Tell us exactly what passed.   Did Mrs. Monson say anything?—She said, "Is it serious?" Mr. Monson said, "He is dead."

Was anything more said?—I don't remember. The news distressed me very much. Cecil Hambrough very often spoke to me about Mr. Monson's kindness.   I remember when we were at Riseley Hall in the month of March of his making a remark to me when we were walking apart one Sunday afternoon with regard to Mr. Monson. He said he would never forget Mr. Monson's kindness to him, and that no other man would have done for him what Mr. Monson had done.   He also said that Mr. Monson had kept him all that time without payment, and that he would pay him back when he came of age.   I remember filling up a form in a proposal for insurance, as a friend of Mr. Monson, and answering questions. I signed it with my own signature.

It is not the case that you ever represented yourself as a butler?—No.

A letter which you received was addressed to "E. Hiron, Esq."?—Yes; I showed it to Mrs. Monson, and we had a laugh over it.   I remember Mr. Hambrough's father, accompanied by his mother, coming to Ardlamont on the Saturday after the death.   They stayed till Monday.   I remember standing aside while Mrs. Monson met the Major and conversed with him.   He took Mrs. Monson by the hand, and told her he was very sorry for all that had passed before the death.

Cross-examined by the SOLICITOR-GENERAL—Scott arrived on the Tuesday night.   Monson, I fancy, came with him, but I did not see him.   I was told so; I do not now by whom.   Monson went from home on the Monday, and returned before dinner time on the Tuesday, accompanied by Scott.   No one told me where he had been. It was on Wednesday that I first learnt about Scott.   I met him at breakfast, after which Mr. Monson and he went out to bathe.   They appeared together at luncheon, and went out together afterwards.   I only saw Scott at meals.   He went out on the Wednesday after tea to shoot with Mr. Monson, at half-past five.

I know that when gentlemen go fishing it is usual for a gillie or keeper to go with them.   I do not know why there was no keeper with them that night; I heard nothing said amongst them which would explain that fact.   I cannot remember at what hour the gentlemen went out to fish; I do not remember if the butler was instructed to sit up for them.   I can give no idea of the time when I heard the sounds of some of the gentlemen in the house.   I do not think that I heard that night that it was Scott who came to the house for a lamp; I have no idea when I heard it or who told me.

Evidence for Defence.

Edith M. Hiron

By the LORD JUSTICE-CLERK—I have just the impression on my mind that I was told.

Cross-examination continued—I did not hear of any occurrence with the boat that night; I heard about it some time next day, I cannot say when. I think Mrs. Monson told me on the way to Glasgow. I do not remember Mr. Monson saying anything about it in the morning.

You said that Scott and Monson were not on terms of friendship. Explain that to me?—I should not have thought they were friends; they did not appear to be; they did not seem on friendly terms. I heard that Scott was an engineer, but I cannot remember who told me.

Did you understand that he was a person in the same social position as Mr. Monson or not?—I did not understand anything about it. From what I heard or saw of him I did not form any opinion about him at the time. I heard Scott speak, and should think that he was a Londoner; he dropped his "h's."

Re-examined by Mr. COMRIE THOMSON—Mr. Monson was quite civil to Scott, but his general behaviour suggested to me that they were not friends. I do not know that two men only go out in a boat for splash-net fishing, and the keeper generally does not go. I know that a keeper is in attendance at the start, but as to his being in the boat I have no knowledge.

By the LORD JUSTICE-CLERK—There was a steam yacht, the "Alert"; it lay, I think, at Kames. I do not think that it was brought round to the bay while Scott was there; I do not remember that.

4. W. F. E. MASSEY, examined by Mr. COMRIE THOMSON—I hold a commission as lieutenant in the 3rd West Yorkshire Militia, and I first met Cecil Hambrough at the training at York in 1892. He mentioned Monson's name to me, and spoke of him in very friendly terms. This year, at the second training, Hambrough maintained the same tone with regard to Monson. It came to my knowledge that there seemed to be a coolness between Cecil and his father. Cecil was a keen fisherman. He asked me during last training to come down to visit him at Ardlamont before the 12th. Previous to going to Ardlamont I had seen Monson once; that was in London about July, 1892. He stayed in the same hotel with me, and Hambrough introduced me to him. I arrived at Ardlamont on the morning of 11th August. I first heard of the accident on board the steamer; the first of our party to hear of it was Lieutenant Strangeways. Mr. Monson and Mr. Donald came on board the steamer at Gourock, and Mr. Monson told me about the accident; he had come from Ardlamont that morning. A Captain White, of my regiment, was there also. Our first intention when we heard of the accident was not to go on to Ardlamont, but the steamer was already started

Alfred John Monson.

W. F. Massey

and we could not turn back. We had some talk about it, and we resolved to proceed. When we got to Ardlamont we resolved to wait till after the funeral. A Mr. Manfield arrived at Ardlamont on the day that the body was removed; he had taken a gun in the shooting. He had no previous acquaintance with Mr. Monson, so far as I know.

By the LORD JUSTICE-CLERK—He paid a sum to board and have his shooting at Ardlamont.

Examination continued—Before the funeral Monson seemed to be sincerely sorry and distressed about the loss of his young friend. There was no shooting on the Ardlamont estate between the death and Mr. Monson's return from Ventnor. It was ten days after the accident before there was any shooting; up to that time there was not a gun fired by any of us. My attention was drawn to a statement in the newspapers that there was shooting, but that statement is false.

Cross-examined by the SOLICITOR-GENERAL—We did not all travel to Ardlamont together. Captain White and I travelled together and arrived at Ardlamont on the morning of the 11th. The time for our arrival had been fixed about a fortnight before. Captain White got a letter about it and told me. If Hambrough had been alive he would have been shooting on the 11th. Manfield arrived on the day the body was conveyed to the steamer. We remained at Ardlamont during Monson's absence. We began to shoot when he returned.

I had gone to visit Cecil Hambrough, and I and the other two gentlemen just waited on till Monson's return; we had formed no idea of what we were going to do. When Monson came back it was decided that we were to stay on and shoot. I do not think that there was any decision with regard to that before Monson went away. I forget how long we stayed. We began to shoot the day after Monson's return. We went out shooting till the second week in September. Monson accompanied us when we went out shooting. I was at Ardlamont when he was apprehended on 30th August. I think we shot one day after the 30th. The shooting was stopped, because we learned it was not paid for. The landlord stopped it, and that put an end to our visit to the house.

Re-examined by Mr. COMRIE THOMSON—Major Hambrough, when at Ardlamont, said, with reference to the question whether we should stay on, that there was no reason why the sad event should stop the shooting. We did not shoot until after Mr. Monson had returned from Ventnor. Mr. Monson shot several times after that. On the day Monson was apprehended I went to Inveraray in the steam launch, and stayed there two days. I remained at Ardlamont about a week after that. I was not examined by the Fiscal, but I was examined by Monson's agents. We considered it only decent to allow an interval to elapse between the death and our resumption of shooting.

220

Evidence for Defence.

5. JOHN M'EWAN, examined by Mr. COMRIE THOMSON—I am innkeeper and also piermaster at Kames. I knew Mr. Hambrough, and I
know Mr. Monson; I frequently met them both together and separately;
they seemed to be on splendid terms. I was at Ardlamont on 8th
August, and I remember seeing M'Intyre, the gamekeeper. I heard
shots fired as I came along, as if coming from the plantation where
the accident happened. On my return to Kames I met Mr. Hambrough carrying a gun; that was about two o'clock in the afternoon.
He said he was practising at the rabbits for the 12th. I lent Mr.
Hambrough a splash-net 160 or 170 yards long and 3 or 4 yards
wide. I have weighed it, and found that dry it weighs ¾ cwt., and
wet 1 cwt. 3 lbs. In fishing the net is paid out over the stern of the
boat by a man standing there. If the water be a little rough or the
boat gives a lurch, with the net in the stern in the hands of an
inexperienced man, it is quite probable that the boat may capsize.
I saw Monson three hours after the accident, and his demeanour
struck me as that of a man very sorry for what had occurred. I
saw no signs of anything but profound and sincere grief. I do not
remember, when I was at Ardlamont, seeing a gun, but I remember
seeing the amberite cartridges. They were lying on a table in the
smoking room, and I lifted one of them which, as far as I can
remember, was slate in colour, with " Amberite " printed on the
outside. It was 12-bore. Mr. Monson explained to me how the
thing happened; he said that Hambrough was carrying a gun he had
got the loan of from Mrs. Campbell Lamont, a 12-bore gun.

Cross-examined by the SOLICITOR-GENERAL—I do not remember
Monson saying anything on that occasion about having a 12-bore
gun of his own. In splash-net fishing when we are paying out the
net we would never be further from the shore than half the length
of the net. I supplied beer, whisky, wine, and aerated waters to
the extent of £37 or £38 to the Monson family when they were at
Ardlamont. This sum Monson still owes me, and he also owes me
pier dues.

Re-examined by Mr. COMRIE THOMSON—There may be reefs at
each side of Ardlamont Bay, but I cannot describe that part of the
shore, as I never go far from home to fish. I cannot speak to the
configuration of Ardlamont Bay.

6. JOHN M'CALLUM, examined by Mr. COMRIE THOMSON—I am
a general merchant at Kames and Tighnabruaich. I know Mr.
Monson. On 2nd August he came to my shop and bought some
amberite cartridges. He got 100 charged with No. 5 shot for a
12-bore gun. I never sold him any cartridges for a 20-bore.
On 25th August I supplied him with 500 amberite cartridges charged
with No. 5 and No. 6 shot, all for a 12-bore gun. I never supplied
him with any No. 6 cartridges except on 25th August. These were
the only occasions on which I supplied him with cartridges. They

221

Alfred John Monson.

were all amberite cartridges, with a slate-coloured covering, the word " amberite " being marked across.

Cross-examined by the SOLICITOR GENERAL—The only sale of cartridges was to Mr. Monson.   I have a bill against him for £43, which has not been paid.

The Court adjourned.

Eighth Day—Wednesday, 20th December, 1893.

7. Professor MATTHEW HAY, examined by Mr. COMRIE THOMSON—
I am thirty-seven years of age, and am a Doctor of Medicine of Edinburgh University and Professor of Medical Logic and Jurisprudence in the University of Aberdeen. I am also police surgeon and medical officer of health for the city of Aberdeen. I have examined, along with Dr. Gordon Saunders, all the productions bearing on the mode of Lieutenant Hambrough's death at Ardlamont.

I visited Ardlamont on 14th September along with Dr. Saunders. Under the guidance of Mr. Steven, we carefully examined the *locus* where it was said that Hambrough had been found. Along with Mr. Speedy we made a series of shooting experiments upon targets, models of men's heads, and also upon animals' skins and freshly killed horses. While making these experiments we used the two guns which are produced. We used amberite cartridges and No. 5 shot; we used Schultze cartridges and No. 6 shot; and some experiments were also made with another gun similar to, but not the same as, the No. 12 gun with black powder cartridges. We also weighed the pellets found in Hambrough's head, and compared their weight with the pellets in the cartridges that came from the same place as the cartridges used by Monson on the day of the death. We also arranged, and had photographed, several attitudes of a person supposed to be accidentally shooting himself in the manner in which it is maintained for the defence that Hambrough shot himself.

I was not present at the exhumation and *post-mortem* examination, but I have read the reports of Dr. Littlejohn and Dr. Saunders. I have been associated with Dr. Saunders in every other part of the investigation. We carefully examined the pellet marks on the rowan and other trees. I found ten marks, I think, upon the rowan tree, and at least eight marks on the lime tree, and three on the beech tree. There might have been more, but I am quite clear about those numbers. I am quite certain we saw more than six marks on the rowan tree. We accepted as marks those which showed grooving or furrowing. The others consisted of breaks of twigs, and these breaks were distinguished from breaks due to mere pressure by the absence of tissue at the places where they were broken. We were satisfied we could distinguish between them. We certainly considered that an observation of the whole of the pellet marks was of importance in this case, as affecting the distance at which the shot was fired and the direction in which it was fired.

We found one mark at an elevation of 8 feet 8 inches on the beech, and two at a higher elevation than that, one being 20 inches at least above 8 feet 8 inches. There is not the slightest doubt

Alfred John Monson.

Prof. M. Hay

about these three. One of the three contained a pellet. The 8 feet 8 inches is above the highest level of the top of the dyke. The pellets on the beech tree were upon the twigs of one branch and the twigs of another.

I formed an opinion with reference to the probable age of the pellet marks, that they were at least two or three months old. Certain of the pellet marks on the rowan tree and also on the lime tree showed considerable signs of vital reaction, that is, healing. In the case of the rowan tree there were at least two of these pellet marks which showed this very distinctly, the scars having become completely healed over by fresh growth from the bark, forming elevations with small depressions in the middle, such as you see in small wounds on the bark, a swelling so as to cover up practically the whole of the wound.

By the LORD JUSTICE-CLERK—They showed such healing as you observe where small branches have been cut off or initials have been cut in the bark. The cut fills up by and by.

Examination continued—What is your opinion with reference to certain of those pellet marks and any alleged connection between them and the death of Cecil Hambrough?—Well, being of opinion that they are more than two or three months old, and as we visited the place only five weeks after the death, I believe that they have no connection with his death. But on the hypothesis that they were produced by the shot causing Hambrough's death, we carefully examined the position of the pellet marks. The area of the pellet marks which we observed in the rowan tree was 43 inches in a horizontal direction by 25 inches vertically. I am aware that 17 by 20 inches has been given as the area, so that my area is considerably larger. I state the area which I actually saw. Supposing no interference by an interposed head between the muzzle of the gun and the rowan tree, my calculations from my experiments with 12 and 20-bore guns show that a spread of 17 by 20 inches—that is, the spread detailed by the Crown witnesses—represents a distance of fire of about 30 feet. I have calculated that, not from an experiment made at 30 feet, but from experiments made at 10 and 20 feet, and making allowance for the amount of spread that would take place if the distance were 10 feet more. It is quite easy to make the calculation, because the spread increases directly as the distance. With my own measurements of the spread of the rowan tree, namely, 25 inches by 43 inches, the distance of fire would be about 50 or 60 feet. The interposition of a head against which the shot had struck, and from which it had glanced, would unquestionably affect any inference as to the distance of fire by shortening the distance, that is, the head would produce dispersion of the shot, or greater dispersion than would have occurred had the head not interposed.

By the LORD JUSTICE-CLERK—That would bring the actual firing point nearer.

224

Evidence for Defence.

Prof. M. Hay

Examination continued—The effect would be perfectly incalculable unless you knew what resistance the head would offer and the angle at which the shot was fired, and a number of physical quantities which I understand are absolutely unknown in this case.

Then do you consider that any deduction to the effect that the distance was about 22 feet from the head is worthless?—Absolutely worthless. It might, I should say, have been any distance between 50 or 60 feet and 2 or 3 feet; you cannot fix it at any particular point. It depends upon the amount of dispersion caused by the interposition of a hard body.

By the LORD JUSTICE-CLERK—If the shot had been fired at 50 or 60 feet from the rowan tree, and there had been no interposition of head, or if the head had been in no way affected through being touched by it, then the spread would, of course, have been such as I have observed; but if the shot had been fired at a nearer distance, and the head had come more in the way of the shot, more dispersion would have been produced, and perhaps with the same amount of spread as the pellets in the rowan tree. If a shot were fired within 1 or 2 feet of the rowan tree it is quite evident that the head would shut out of view a very large space. I am satisfied that the head was not squarely hit, but that it was a glancing shot, not striking full on the head, but the side of the head, and to a certain extent being dispersed.

Examination continued—In regard to the direction of the shot, I am not satisfied that the direction of the shot which made the marks on the rowan, lime, and beech trees corresponds with the line drawn through the centre of the marks on the rowan tree alone. The line of fire may have been such as has been indicated for the Crown; but when I examined these trees as a whole, along with Dr. Saunders, we formed the opinion that the line of fire came from a point nearer the edge of the dyke than the line indicated by the marks in the rowan tree alone—a point more to the east than the point given by the Crown. If the line through the trees as a whole were carried back it would have touched the edge of the dyke at a point 11 feet from the rowan tree. Perhaps I may explain the grounds on which I give that opinion. We took that to be the line in regard to our examination of the trees because of the direction of the group of marks upon the rowan tree in conjunction with those upon the lime and beech trees. I am of opinion that a shot in this line would have caused the pellet marks in the lime and beech trees, as well as in the rowan trees; not by being fired directly through both trees, but by the shot passing obliquely between the rowan tree on the left and the beech and lime trees on the right. That is, looking northwards, the spread of the shot to the left would have caught the right side of the rowan tree as it passed it, and further on the spread on the right would have caught the beech and lime trees as it passed them. If the shot to any extent touched the head the shot would not only have

Q

225

Alfred John Monson.

Prof. M. Hay

been dispersed, but the line of fire would also have been deflected. If it had taken place with a shot fired from the gap in the whins, and Hambrough had been walking towards the rowan tree, then the shot would have been deflected after it struck Hambrough's head towards the right, that is to say, towards the young plantation, to a greater or less extent.

It would not be proper in localising the place of fire to assume that the line of fire was straight and undeflected from the point of fire to the pellet marks. I understand that it comes to this, that the Crown's inferences—Mr. Macnaughton's inferences—are drawn as if no head had been interposed between the shot and the trees, except in so far as to make a certain allowance for increased dispersion. Assuming that the Crown witnesses have drawn their inferences as if no head were interposed, to that extent they would have been erroneous. It would be impossible to calculate as to what the amount of dispersion would be.

On the assumption that Hambrough was walking towards the rowan tree at the time that he was shot from behind, how was he likely to have fallen?—Forwards; because the body, when a person is walking, is lightly inclined forwards, and if the body had not been disturbed after the fall it would have been found lying on its face, with the head to the rowan tree. If he had been standing, when shot, with his face to the rowan tree, he might have fallen forwards or backwards, but the greater probability is that he would have fallen backwards. In that case his feet would have been towards the rowan tree and his head towards the whins. It was explained to me by Mr. Steven that the body was found lying on its back, with its head towards the rowan tree and the feet towards the gap in the whins. The left arm was therefore towards the dyke and the right arm towards the plantation.

Can you reconcile that position with his having been shot from the gap in the whins if the body had not been moved?—No.

Was the body likely to have moved itself after being shot?—No. The wound was probably immediately mortal. If it had fallen towards the rowan tree upon its face, then the body must have been turned over on one side or the other so as to put it on its back. If it had fallen backwards, the body would have had to be turned right round and the head put where the feet were. In the former case the distance the head would have been moved in the turning of the body would have been to the extent of the width of the shoulders, or about a couple of feet, and to that extent the head would have been shifted from the line of fire. That would have interfered with the reliability of the deduction from his position as to the line of fire.

By the LORD JUSTICE-CLERK—That is on the assumption that the body fell exactly as explained to me, and was then turned over to the one side or the other.

226

Evidence for Defence.

Prof. M. Hay

Examination continued—If the body had not been moved after it fell, and was found lying on its back, with the head towards the rowan tree, and assuming that it was shot from behind, the inference is that the shot came from the direction of the rowan tree rather than from the whins. Assuming that the body had been moved after it fell, I should not be very much surprised that the gardener and others had not observed traces of blood apart from the quantity under the head. Supposing the grass at the place was long and quite wet, and the flow of blood from the head had been gradual, I would not be surprised that blood was not very observable. The bleeding from a gunshot wound is generally slow.

I would not be surprised if I was informed that the deceased first fell in or near the ditch, and was moved by the accused and another man to the top of the dyke, and that no traces of blood were observed in or about the ditch. When I was at Ardlamont I examined the immediate neighbourhood carefully. It would have been quite possible for any one jumping from the top of the dyke into the young plantation to have cleared the ditch completely, and the brackens immediately around, and to have landed wholly on the grass. The brackens were confined to the side of the wall; beyond that there was grass. There is a track by the south side of the wall across the dyke from the old to the young plantation, and, of course, the grass and brackens in that track are beaten down, so that if Lieutenant Hambrough fell at that place there would be no very obvious mark of pressure on the grass or brackens.

Supposing that two men lifted the body from the side of the ditch to the top of the dyke, they would naturally take very considerable care about soiling their clothes when carrying the body. Between them it would be possible and practicable to carry the body without soiling their clothes.

Taking the situation into account, I think it quite possible that the deceased could have been shot somewhere about the ditch, and that his body could have afterwards been transferred to the top of the dyke. This opinion would not be materially affected by the fact that a blood-stained wad and two pieces of bone were found on the dyke 2 feet from the head, because the two pieces of bone and the wad might have dropped from the head in the course of being carried, or might have been pressed out of the wound in the course of an examination by a person after the death. I have seen the pieces of bone. One piece came from a portion of the temporal bone, and was about $\frac{3}{4}$ inch from the surface of the skull; that would be more than 1 inch from the surface of the head when the soft parts were on. I think that it is more likely to have fallen or to have been drawn out of the wound by the finger of a person examining the wound than to have been blown out. I do not think that the four pellets found inside the head would have blown the pieces of bone out.

Alfred John Monson.

Prof. M. Hay

I examined very carefully the whins and other undergrowth near to where the body was found. The path on the top of the dyke just as you approach the clump of trees is bounded on the right by the edge of the dyke, and on the left by the whins and other undergrowth extending a considerable distance towards the south, and at that point is very narrow—not more than 18 inches wide—and as you pass the clump of whins where the gap is, then you come upon the open pieces of green sloping sward, and it was upon that that I understand the body was found by Mr. Steven, who informed me that the head was about 3 feet or so from the edge of the dyke, and the feet about 4 feet from the edge. The suggestion that Hambrough fell where he was shot apparently involves this, that he must have been walking or standing at a distance of 4 or 5 feet from the edge of the dyke. In order to reach that position he must have swerved round the whins when leaving the path on the dyke. If that is so, the probability is that he would be walking with the left side of his head towards the gap, so that unless he had turned his head to the right or altered the direction of his walk, any shot fired at him from the gap would have entered the left side, and could not have made the injury found in the skull.

The path along the top of the dyke was rather rough, with here and there projecting pieces of turf, sometimes a stone from the wall beneath, and occasionally holes. Quite close to where I was told the deceased's body was found there was a distinctly large hole, almost a kind of trap to one's foot, in the ground; it was a place where a man might readily have stumbled, especially if he was not watching the ground as he walked along, if his eyes were directed to the search for game, or anything of that sort. The morning of the occurrence was a wet morning, and that would tend to his slipping on the grass if he went off the rough path of the dyke; the ground there slopes up, and the grass would be very wet.

I have examined the injured skull very carefully. In my opinion the direction of the shot which caused the injury was from behind forwards and somewhat upwards. I calculated that, assuming the head to have been erect at the time of the shot, the line of shot formed an angle with the horizontal of 10 to 20 degrees. I made this calculation working from the skull and regarding the hole in the back part of the skull to the right as indicating the part where the shot struck; and then, drawing a line from that to the middle of the gap in the ear—as if the ear had been attached to the skull—that gives a line which would form an angle of about 10 degrees with the horizontal. If, on the other hand, I work it out from the description given in the report by Dr. Littlejohn and Dr. Macmillan of the dead body and the photographs, it comes nearer to 20 degrees than to 10. Taking the head erect and the angle of the line of shot at 20 degrees, the distance from the body at which the line of shot would have touched the ground if extended backwards would be 15 or 16

228

Evidence for Defence.

Prof. M. Hay

feet for a man of the height of deceased. Assuming the shot to have been fired by a second person, both persons standing erect on level ground, it follows that the head of the deceased required to be bent forward to an angle of 10 to 20 degrees in order to permit of the calculated line of shot. The supposed line could have been obtained also by an assailant being on a lower level than the deceased, the head of the deceased still remaining erect. In order to get the line of fire, assuming the distance to be 9 feet, the supposed assailant would have to be placed about 4 feet lower than deceased; that is, supposing the head of deceased to be erect.

After careful examination of the skull and photographs, I consider that the injury to the deceased's head was such, in respect of the position of the injury and the line of fire, that it could have been inflicted by a gun held in the deceased's own hand. There are many, almost innumerable, positions permitting of the gun being held in the deceased's own hand when the shot was fired. I, along with Dr. Saunders, photographed a few of such attitudes, using a 12-bore gun, of exactly the same make and length as the one produced, except in the case of one of the photographs submitted. The photographs are Nos. 23 to 34 of the defence productions. In certain of the cases photographed it is assumed that the gun went off by being caught in the thicket or whins. In Nos. 23, 24, 27, and 28 it is assumed that the trigger was pulled by being caught in a bush or twig or undergrowth, the butt being at a distance of 20 or 22 inches from the level of the ground. That is the reason why in the photographs the butt of the gun is supported on a stool. It was necessary in taking the photographs that the gun should be supported by something; a person could not have held the muzzle for the time necessary to take the photograph. Mr. Hambrough's gun may have been momentarily supported by a bush. Nos. 25 and 26 of the photographs proceed on the footing of the butt end of the gun coming against the ground and being caught in the thicket, or being caught at a lower level than in the other photographs.

It would have been possible for the deceased to have shot himself in jumping from the dyke near the ditch into the young plantation. Nos. 29 and 30 bear upon such a possibility. No. 29 represents the gun upon the shoulder, apparently preparatory to jumping from the wall, the gun being held with the butt end backwards, the muzzle forwards, and the hammer downwards. No. 30 shows the attitude in which the deceased might have fallen after jumping from the wall, with the gun then pointing to the back of the head.

By the LORD JUSTICE-CLERK—No. 30 represents a man not in the act of jumping through the air, but how he would have fallen on reaching the ground. In this case the gun is caught on the edge of the wall. In the photograph, to represent the edge of the dyke we have put a stool upon a chair and brought it up to a height of

Alfred John Monson.

Prof. M. Hay

4 feet. The gun does not leave the man's hand in this case; it is caught on the edge of the dyke, and the hammer is brought down.

Examination continued—I do not say that one of the attitudes shown in the photographs was the one in the present case—they are only possible attitudes. In one of the attitudes shown in the photographs the gun is retained in the right hand by the barrel, with the butt behind and the muzzle towards the head. No. 31 shows an attitude corresponding to the leading attitude of the other photographs, but photographed from behind. In all the photographs a straight stick is inserted in the barrel and is carried forward to the supposed position of the wound in the head in order to show the line of shot. It was quite possible, however, judging from past experience of gun accidents, for the deceased to have been shot by his own gun accidentally, and still the gun not to be at the moment in his hand. When a man slips or falls he is apt to throw his gun away to avoid accidents, but he may shoot himself in so doing. That has happened in my own experience of cases.

I have studied most carefully the question of the probable distance at which the gun was fired, and for that purpose I have studied the medical reports on the deceased's body by Dr. Littlejohn and Dr. Macmillan, and the photographs which accompany the report. In my opinion the distance may have been anything between a few inches and 3 or 4 feet, but not exceeding 4 feet. I arrived at this opinion from an examination of the medical reports and of the skull, and also from certain gun experiments made with the guns produced, which were fired at wooden and cardboard targets, at wooden dummy heads, animal skins, freshly killed horses, and so on.

What do you regard as the extreme distance at which the deceased could possibly have been shot by his own gun whilst still holding the muzzle end of it in his own hand?—No measurements have been given in the medical reports by Dr. Littlejohn and Dr. Macmillan of the length of the deceased's arm. Mr. Hambrough's height is stated at 5 feet 11 inches, and, working on that height, I think the extreme distance would have been about 2 feet 8 inches or 2 feet 10 inches—that is, holding the gun just at the muzzle. It practically comes to this, that in my opinion the shot which killed the deceased was delivered within arm's length. The distance between the muzzle and the seat of the injury in the photographs is in some 2 feet, in others 1½ feet, and in some 1 foot. The characteristics in the injury which led me to the opinion I have expressed as to the distance were the condition of the edges of the wound at its entering point, that is to say, at its posterior part. I shall enumerate them. They are, first, the condition of the edges of the entering part. Secondly, the size and appearance of the wound in the scalp, the ear, and the skull; and, in the third place, the absence of separate pellet marks around the wound.

As regards the first of these characteristics, namely, the con-

230

Evidence for Defence.

Prof. M. Hay

dition of the edges of the entering part of the wound, it is stated by Dr. Littlejohn and Dr. Macmillan that the wound at its posterior part or entering part had—to use their own words—a pretty regular surface, and the photographs confirm that statement. From that I infer that the distance of fire was not more than about 3 feet or so, and from my experiments with guns this inference is confirmed. In my experiments it is shown that when you go beyond 2 feet or thereby the edge of the wound begins to get distinctly ragged on account of the action of the spreading shot. That is my first point, that the admitted regularity of the edge of the wound where the shot entered shows that the muzzle of the gun could not have been more than 2½ feet or so away.

Referring next to Dr. Littlejohn's and Dr. Macmillan's joint report as regards the second characteristic, I think the statement was that the wound was triangular in shape, with its apex pointing backwards and downwards, and that the wound was 3½ inches long by 2½ inches broad at its base, that is, the part behind the ear, and 2 inches broad at the middle. Dr. Macmillan's report of 16th August gives the same shape of the wound. He states that the length of it was 3½ inches, the same as given in the joint report, but that the width was 1½ inches, which I take to have been the width of the wound at its middle at that date.

By the LORD JUSTICE-CLERK—The width is at right angles to the direction of the shot.

Examination continued—Putrefying action would quite easily account for the difference of width in the reports, the joint examination of the deceased's body having been made some three weeks later than Dr. Macmillan's examination. Putrefaction helps to make the wound gape, on account of the formation of gases beneath the skin and the infusion of a certain amount of serum. The two measurements are perfectly reconcilable. It is just the amount of expansion that I should expect to find. From this I deduce that the probable width of the wound immediately after the accident would be the 1½ inches given by Dr. Macmillan. That I take to be the average width of the wound about the middle, as there is no qualification in Dr. Macmillan's report. The probable width of the wound at its commencement posteriorly must have been less, because it is a triangular wound, and in the joint report it is distinctly stated that it tapers off posteriorly, and, accordingly, the width near the apex across the entering wound in the scalp must have been under 1½ inches. The photograph confirms the fact of its tapering posteriorly. In comparing a wound in a human body with a hole in a target, whether of cardboard or of wood, allowances must undoubtedly be made for the peculiar character of the tissues of the body. The living skin is elastic and retractile, and so also are the muscles beneath it. This would have a considerable effect upon any wound made in the body. Physiologically, the tissues remain alive for a

231

Alfred John Monson.

Prof. M. Hay

time after a man has ceased to breathe. The muscles may remain alive for three hours after death. The effect of this retraction of the skin and the subjacent muscular tissues upon the wound made in such issues is that it causes it to gape. In a wound made in the situation of the wound found in the head of the deceased gaping would occur. It is very difficult to say to what extent, but I might put it this way—if a simple cut had been made behind the ear of the deceased extending for $3\frac{1}{2}$ inches backwards in the direction of the wound found in the head and made down to the bone, there would have been gaping to probably the extent of 1 inch from mere retraction of the parts; and if a strip of tissue had been excised from the part, say, 1 inch broad, it would have left a wound which would have been larger than the piece of excised tissue on account of this gaping. The muscles of the neck at their insertion into the neck would affect the size of the wound. They contract and pull the edges of the wound apart and would tend to increase both its length and width, though not to any material extent the length.

These conclusions as to what I call vital retraction are based upon experiments made on freshly killed horses, and are also the subject of everyday surgical experience. Taking the wound as having been $1\frac{1}{2}$ inches wide at its middle immediately after death, and allowing for vital retraction, I consider that the width of the strip of skin and tissues destroyed might not have been more than 1 inch. It would have been somewhat less at its posterior extremity. My inference from this, as regards the diameter of the shot as it struck the head, is that it must have been such as would have produced an opening of about 1 inch in diameter in a non-retractile tissue. My examination of the wound in the skull confirmed these conclusions. On the skull, towards the back of the head, there is a highly fractured area. That I take to be the part where the shot struck. From that highly fractured area fractures run in various directions over the right side of the skull. I found on measurement that this area was about $1\frac{1}{8}$ to $1\frac{1}{4}$ inches in diameter. That area corresponds to the wound shown in the scalp. I should describe that area as the area of the greatest impact of the shot so far as the skull is concerned. In its dimensions that area affords the diameter of the impacting shot. I take it that the diameter of the shot as it struck this part of the skull could not have exceeded $1\frac{1}{8}$ or $1\frac{1}{4}$ inches. It probably was less, because one finds that when a shot strikes a bone, especially at an oblique angle, the injury produced at the point of impact extends rather beyond the actual surface of impact, owing to the brittle character of the skull. I shall illustrate what I mean. If you fire a bullet through a pane of glass you find, as a rule, that the hole is bigger than the shot itself, and a shot striking a bone may carry away a portion of the bone beyond the area of actual impact. From this I infer that the diameter of the shot as it struck the skull at this point must have been less than the diameter of this wound; that is

232

Evidence for Defence.

Prof. M. Hay

to say, it may have been 1 inch or thereby. As the narrowest part of the area is 1⅛ inches, it is fair to assume that the diameter of the impacting shot may have been less.

By the LORD JUSTICE-CLERK—I mean that the diameter of the shot as a solid body was probably less than the actual hole in the skull; roughly, I think it is fair to put it about 1 inch.

Examination continued—In view of this aspect of the case, I have made certain experiments on horses' skulls at various angles. These experiments show that a shot when fired at an oblique angle to the bone of the skull causes a greater width of fracture than when it is fired at a right angle. At a right angle there is much less splintering of the bone because of the greater force of the impact. When a shot strikes against a body perpendicularly the force of the impact is greater, so far as the effects are concerned, than when it strikes at an oblique angle. This is partly owing to the slipping against the bone, which produces a certain amount of waste of force. I have made experiments on horses' heads, and am satisfied with regard to that matter.

My inference as to the effect of the shot upon the ear, as described in the report of Dr. Littlejohn and Dr. Macmillan, is that the shot practically perforated the ear, carrying away a considerable part of its substance. When I put the elongated pieces of skin, described as being attached to the superior and inferior extremities of the wound, in the proper natural position, the ear looked as if perforated. That was caused by the shot deflected from the skull. The measurement of the perforation as given by Dr. Littlejohn and Dr. Macmillan is 1½ inches vertically; the horizonal measurement is not given in the report, but I suppose Dr. Littlejohn will not object to my putting it at ¾ inch or thereby, so far as I can gather from the photograph. I think that this breach in the ear affords a fairly accurate measurement of the shot after it was deflected from the skull, showing that the shot had become deflected and flattened against the skull, and broadened out to the extent of 1½ inches in its vertical diameter, and narrowed, of course, correspondingly in its other diameter. Putrefaction does not interfere with a wound in the ear to the same extent that it does with a wound in the scalp. The reason for this is that there is little subcutaneous tissue, and gases are not formed as a rule underneath the skin of the ear, so that necessarily at the *post-mortem* the ear would have much its normal appearance. The diameter of the shot as it perforated the ear flap was, I take it, 1½ inches vertically, and perhaps half of that horizontally.

By the LORD JUSTICE-CLERK—I mean by that that the shot flattened against the skull, and fanned out vertically.

Examination continued—I explain the increase of diameter from 1 inch or thereby at the point of entrance of the shot to the skull to 1½ inches at the ear by the impact and spreading against the skull. The conclusion to which I am brought from an examination of the

233

Alfred John Monson.

Prof. M. Hay

wounds in the scalp, the skull, and the ear is that the shot as it entered the deceased's head had a diameter of not greater than 1 inch or thereby. I have no means of measuring the exact diameter of the shot.

The experiments which I made were conducted with the 12-bore and 20-bore guns—the 12-bore loaded with amberite cartridges and No. 5 shot, and the 20-bore with Schultze powder and No. 6 shot. I also made a few experiments with a gun exactly similar to the 12-bore in order to test the effect of black powder. We used for the experiments wooden boards. [Shown No. 3 of defence productions.] This shows a shot from the 12-bore gun fired at a distance of 1 foot with amberite at point-blank, and the wound is 1⅛ inches in diameter in one direction by 1 inch in another. I may state that the difference in the thickness of targets used is due to this, that we intended at first that the wood should be sufficiently thick to retain the shot and not allow it to pass through at all. Important deductions might have been obtained from such an experiment. But when we came to make our experiments the joiner who made the boards made them rather thin, and we had simply to take some rough blocks on the instant. No. 4 (one of the blocks described) shows a shot at 1½ feet, and gives a diameter very nearly the same as the first. It shows a mark of a wad on one side which adds to the diameter. The next, No. 5, is at 2 feet, and its diameter is 1¼ inches by 1⅛. I may call your attention to the fact that the edges are beginning to get rough and irregular. There is no irregularity in the others at 1 and 1½ feet. They are very cleanly cut. No. 6 is at 3 feet, and shows a wound 1½ inches in diameter. The ragged character is also pretty well observed in this case. No. 7 is at 4 feet, and the wound is 1⅝ inches by about 1¼ in diameter or thereby. No. 8, taken at 5 feet, shows a wound of 2 inches by 1¾ inches, with an exceedingly ragged margin. No. 9 is at 10 feet, also showing a very ragged wound. At 10 feet the wound is 1¾ inches by between 2 and 3 inches. No. 10 is at 20 feet, and now there is no central wound at all; the whole shot has become dispersed or scattered.

We made a similar series of experiments with the 20-bore gun. I can give you, if desired, the exact measurements. We got practically the same results, except that the wound is a shade smaller owing to the smaller bore of the gun. The targets show the raggedness as the wound increases, owing to the dispersion of the shot. We also made a series of experiments on a freshly killed horse, freshly killed for the reason that it is advisable to use such an animal because of the skin and underlying tissues being practically alive and showing retraction. The shots were fired into the head of the horse a minute after it had been destroyed. They were fired into the neck of the horse at its root, that is to say, close to the shoulder, partly upon the shoulder, and a few—only a few—were fired into the hind leg. The size of wound obtained in the case of the horse was—at 6 inches,

Evidence for Defence.

Prof. M. Hay

$1\frac{1}{8}$ inches by $\frac{11}{16}$ inches—that is point-blank. Then at 1 foot the wound was $1\frac{3}{16}$ by $\frac{3}{4}$ inch; at 2 feet, $1\frac{1}{2}$ inches by $1\frac{1}{4}$ inches; at 3 feet it was $1\frac{7}{16}$ inches by $1\frac{3}{8}$ inches; at $3\frac{1}{2}$ feet the wound was $2\frac{1}{4}$ inches by $1\frac{1}{4}$ inches; at 4 feet it was $2\frac{1}{8}$ inches by $1\frac{5}{8}$ inches; at $4\frac{1}{2}$ feet, $2\frac{3}{8}$ inches by $1\frac{7}{8}$ inches; at 5 feet, $2\frac{1}{4}$ inches by $2\frac{1}{8}$ inches; at 6 feet, $2\frac{3}{4}$ inches by $2\frac{3}{8}$ inches; at 7 feet, $1\frac{5}{8}$ inches by 1 inch; at 8 feet, $1\frac{1}{2}$ inches by $\frac{1}{2}$ inch; at 9 feet, $\frac{9}{16}$ inch by $\frac{9}{16}$ inch; at 10 feet, $\frac{1}{2}$ inch by $\frac{1}{2}$ inch. That is the central wound. The dispersion has begun comparatively early, and the centre of the wound gradually becomes less. The largest wound obtained was at 5 or 6 feet, and after that the central wound began to decrease, and was accompanied by a number of small pellet wounds—caused by an increasing dispersion of the pellets. It will be observed from the photographs that the wounds are of an oval shape, longer in one direction than another, although the shot fired into them was presumably round. This elasticity is due to the retraction of the skin acting more in one direction than another, as it usually does. These shots were all made point-blank. The shot which struck the deceased's head was of such a size as would have produced a wound about 1 inch in diameter, and that size of wound, with a 12-bore gun, would be got at 1 foot. Had wounds been similarly made (that is, perpendicular to the surface) in the position of the wound in the deceased's head, the longer diameter of the wound would, owing to the character of the tissues there, have been in line with the axis of the neck, or with the breadth of the wound actually observed. The breadth, therefore, of the actual wound in deceased's head ought to be compared with the longer diameter of the wound in the horse's shoulder. Making no allowance for the difference of retraction, I got a wound in the horse's head at 2 feet as great in diameter as the wound in the deceased's skull. In regard to the cardboard experiments, the distance is 1 foot.

I also made experiments with two models of a human head. Their value is of the same kind as that of the cardboard, but they show the effect of a shot fired at a surface of which the conformation is similar to that of the human head. They are superior to cardboard in respect that they show another aspect of the action of the shot. The shots were fired in at an angle and with an inclination corresponding as nearly as might be to those of the wound on the deceased's skull. At the model No. 1 the distance was 1 foot, at No. 2, 4 feet. The models were not modelled by myself, but they were modelled by my instructions to make them as nearly as possible like a man's head. The wounds are somewhat smaller than those in the human head, because here we have an inelastic substance which does not retract. As regards these wounds, they roughly correspond in shape and size to the wound in deceased's head. No. 1 is rather narrower, because the shot being fired at a distance of 1 foot did not spread so much as at 4 feet. The wounds in the horse's head

Alfred John Monson.

Prof. M. Hay

show the same thing as those in the human head. They show the effect of a shot fired obliquely, but the wounds are somewhat more elongated. Dr. Saunders was associated with me in these experiments with the horses' heads. When these shots were fired the flesh was physiologically alive although the animal was dead, but there is not so much retraction of a wound in the front of a horse's head on account of the close adherence of the skin to the bone.

Now I take you to the third point. You mentioned, as determining the distance of fire, the absence of stray pellet wounds around the main wound?—I regard that as of the very greatest importance. A charge of small shot leaves the gun almost in a body, having a cylindrical form, with the pellets in compact mass, but immediately after leaving the gun it begins to widen, and the pellets begin to disperse, the effect of which is that if the pellets or mass of lead enter a target at a distance of 2 or 3 feet it produces a somewhat larger wound than at a shorter distance, and the edges of the wound get ragged. As the distance increases the pellets become so much separated that the pellets around the circumference become quite detached from the general mass of pellets, and each takes a course of its own; and if you place in the front of the shot a target you get a number of small wounds round the central wound. Then at a still greater distance you have a greater dispersion of the pellets and no large central wound, but a great number of pellet wounds. This dispersion varies slightly with different guns. It varied with the guns in question. It is fairly constant with any particular gun. As to the point at which the scattering begins to show itself we made experiments with the Ardlamont guns. In the case of experiments with the 12-bore gun against wooden targets the dispersion began, or detached pellet marks were noticed, at 4 feet. There were separate pellet marks at some little distance from the margin; at 5 feet there were more of these detached pellet marks. There were eleven altogether at distances varying from $\frac{1}{8}$ inch to $\frac{1}{2}$ inch from the centre of the board. At 10 feet the dispersion was very considerable, and there was a large number of pellet marks all round the wound, the total area of dispersion being about 5 by $4\frac{1}{4}$ inches. We did not exactly ascertain at what distance there is no central wound at all, but we found that at 20 feet there was no central wound, and that complete dispersion had taken place. It must have begun somewhere between 10 and 20 feet. In the case of the 20-bore gun the dispersion was practically the same. That is to say, separate pellet wounds began at about 4 feet, and went on increasing in number at the greater distances. I may also mention that in making the experiments on horses we noted the amount of dispersion, and that we got practically the same results as with the wooden targets, except that the dispersion was a little greater and showed itself somewhat earlier. At $3\frac{1}{2}$ feet we got four distinctly detached pellet wounds. We made two experiments on the dummy heads, one at

236

Evidence for Defence.

Prof. M. Hay

1 foot and the other at 4 feet; the one at 4 feet shows a detached pellet mark some distance from the wound and a ragged entrance for the main wound.

As the result of these experiments, I conclude that it is quite impossible for a shot to be fired from either the 20-bore or the 12-bore gun at a distance of 9 feet without the production of numerous pellet marks, whether on a target or on the human head, and whether fired directly at the head or in an oblique direction. This opinion applies to all distances down to $3\frac{1}{2}$ to 4 feet. There would be detached pellet marks in the head from 4 feet upwards, and at 9 feet they would be very numerous. It is quite impossible for the separate pellet wounds to be eradicated or blurred over from the action of the central mass of shot, unless at the fag end of the wound. If the shot is fired obliquely to the head, it is conceivable that the central mass of shot following upon the action of the detached pellets forming a part of the shot might eradicate their marks—blot them out, so to speak—but those at the back and entering part would still remain, and also those at the sides—top and bottom.

I have examined the productions that were made by the Crown—cardboards, and so on. I hold in my hands Nos. 5, 9, and 21. These are the results of shots fired all at the distance of 9 feet, and show a large area of dispersion and a great number of pellet wounds around the central wound. They agree exactly with my own experiments. In the report of Dr. Littlejohn and Dr. Macmillan it is stated that no pellet mark was found around the wound in the head. My inference from this is that the distance from which the shot was fired must have been under 4 feet; that is to say, under a distance which would produce separate pellet marks. As regards the results of experiments made by the witnesses for the Crown upon the heads of dead human bodies, I think that the reliability of these experiments depends a great deal upon the angle of impact, and more particularly upon the amount of smashing. If the shot fired at 2 feet was so fired into the head that the whole body of pellets passed into the head, that would very materially affect the degree of dispersion. It might make a wound upon the near side of the head and blow out the remote side. Here there were only four pellets found, and that makes a great difference. I consider the bodies of persons dead for some time to a certain extent suitable for experiments, but they do not exhibit the exact effect of the shot fired at a living body.

What does the presence of the four pellets in the brain out of between two and three hundred show?—That the shot struck the head at a very acute angle—not point blank—and at an angle which would not result in a complete smashing of the head. The right half of Hambrough's skull was considerably fractured. Hambrough's skull was thicker than ordinary, and therefore was a little less liable to fracture.

I now come to another subject—the blackening and scorching

237

Alfred John Monson.

Prof. M. Hay

of the wound. Are these sometimes observed in connection with gunshot wounds?—Yes. I distinguish between scorching and blackening. Blackening is generally due to either smoke or perhaps fine dust; in some cases you may have blackening from black gunpowder where that is used. Blackening may be removed by washing, and it can even be removed by the finger. I have made experiments with the forms of powder used in the Ardlamont cartridges—amberite, Schultze, and black—in order to ascertain the results with regard to blackening and scorching. The experiments were performed by firing point blank at pieces of skin, the hair of which, of course, would become scorched if there had been any scorching. Blackening was obtained with all the kinds of powder—amberite, Schultze, and black —and, unexpectedly, rather more with the first and second than with the third. The blackening was got up to a distance of 4 or 5 feet. But it is very variable; even at the same distance you may almost miss it, and at other times have a great quantity. We never obtained scorching with amberite or with Schultze, although we fired down to a distance of 6 inches, but with black powder we obtained scorching up to a distance of 3 feet. These experiments confirmed my own experience of actual gunshot wounds.

So far as our experiments with amberite or Schultze powder went there was no scorching at 2 or 3 feet, but there might be blackening, which might be removed with the finger or with a sponge and water. Blood might, to some extent, have washed away any blackening. I am not sure that there is any incompleteness of the combustion of the grains of amberite or Schultze powders, but if it did occur the grains of the powders are of a light colour, and would not be readily seen, supposing that they were embedded in the skin. Even with black powder blackening and scorching are sometimes not seen. In my opinion the absence of blackening and scorching in the case of the deceased affords no safe indication of the gun having been fired from a considerable distance. The blackening, if originally present, was in any case removable.

I was present along with Dr. Littlejohn at Edinburgh University when the pellets which were found in the head were weighed. I am at one with Dr. Littlejohn as to the weight of the pellets, also of the pellet fragments or scrapings in the fractures. I am aware that three different kinds of cartridges were found at Ardlamont. The amberite cartridges were charged with No. 5 shot adapted for the 12-bore gun, the Schultze cartridges with No. 6 shot, and the black powder cartridges with No. 6 shot, the two latter kinds being for the 20-bore gun. Lead pellets are soft, and unless specially chilled can be cut with a knife or bruised by your teeth. They lose part of their weight by scraping, in passing through a hard substance like bone; the pellets found in the head must have lost weight in passing through the skull. It would be fair to assume that the four fragments of pellets found on the surface of the skull wound had been detached from

238

Evidence for Defence.

Prof. M. Hay

the pellets found in the head; they gave the same amount of lead that might have been expected to be detached in passing through the skull. Adding the weight of the four pellets found in the brain to the weight of the four fragments found in the wound, the total is 8·1 grains. I think that 8 grains or thereabouts may be taken as the full original weight of the four pellets found in the head. My conclusion as to the number of the shot is that I consider it would be No. 5 shot. No. 6 is a distinctly lighter shot. I weighed several samples of the different shot.

My only other point is in connection with the singeing. In the case of the clothes the productions are Nos. 35 and 36, and as to the experiments with dog-skins they are Nos. 37, 38, and 39. The amberite shot was fired from a 12-bore gun at a distance of 6 inches into a board on which there was a piece of dog's skin. You see that the result is that there is no scorching; the hair is cut by the shot, but not singed. Unfortunately, the skin is black, and prevents any alteration of colour being seen. But we made similar experiments afterwards with a white skin, and got the same results. It is easy to observe the cut ends of the hair. The ends are not singed. The odour of singed hair is easily perceived if present. I afterwards experimented on two pieces of tweed placed on boards; from these I found it possible to fire a gun along and very near to any surface covered by tweed—like a man's arm—without producing any blackening or scorching of the surface with amberite powder. The first piece of tweed shows the effect of a shot with a 12-bore gun charged with an amberite cartridge fired across the surface of the tweed, the muzzle of the gun resting upon the tweed, nothing intervening. It has got torn because of that, but it is not singed or discoloured. The gun was fired exactly on a level with the tweed across its surface. In another experiment a small object $\frac{1}{2}$ inch in diameter was placed between the muzzle of the gun and the tweed, and there was no scorching and no blackening. I exhibit here a glass jar containing a piece of the skin of the forehead of a person who shot himself there with a revolver, and therefore at a very close distance. It was a case of suicide. There was no scorching round the edges, although the distance was probably not more than 2 inches. There was blackening to the extent of $\frac{1}{2}$ inch round the wound. I saw the case immediately after death, but I removed the blackening at once by simply rubbing my finger across it. In my opinion a shot from Hambrough's own gun might have been fired very near to his clothing, say, along his arm as stretched out behind him, the barrel being held near the muzzle, without any signs of scorching of the coat sleeve.

As a result of the whole examination and the consideration of this case from a medical point of view, I consider that the death of Lieutenant Hambrough was more likely to be due to an accident from the gun he was carrying than to a shot from the gun of another person.

Alfred John Monson.

Prof. M. Hay

Tell us shortly the principal grounds on which you have arrived
at that opinion?—I have already said that I look upon the shot as
having been fired at a near distance, and near-distance injuries are
always strongly presumptive of suicide in the sense of being self-
inflicted, either suicidally or accidentally. The other ground is that
there is always a presumption—I am speaking again medically—in
any doubtful case of gun accident of its being accidental, because of
the greater frequency of gun accidents compared with homicide.
This is the view taken by medical jurists. Homicide by shot guns
is of very rare occurrence, so far as I know recorded cases, and we all
know that shooting accidents with a shot gun happen very often every
season. Apart from this presumption, and looking to the result of
my inquiries in this case, I think that all the probabilities are in
favour of this being an accidental shot by the man himself, with the
gun he was carrying.

Cross-examined by the SOLICITOR-GENERAL—I think, by the
express directions of the prisoner's legal advisers, you refused to give
any information to the Crown at all?—That is so.

[The SOLICITOR-GENERAL—It has been the practice, so far as I
know, in such cases, that witnesses on each side should be allowed to
be precognosced by the other side, for the express purpose of ascertaining what the witnesses have to say; and the witnesses on each
side being intimated, it has always been the practice hitherto that
orders were at once given to the Crown, and also to the advisers of
the defence, that they should be submitted to precognition. In this
case there was a correspondence on this subject, and the position was
deliberately taken by the advisers of the defence that no such precognition should be made. I think it very desirable that some
authoritative statement should be made with regard to what occurred
in this matter for future guidance.

Mr. COMRIE THOMSON—The Solicitor-General's statement is perfectly correct. We did not desire to precognosce the medical witnesses of the Crown, and did not attempt to do so. But on Friday of
the week before last Dr. Hay was asked to go late in the afternoon
to the Procurator-Fiscal in Aberdeen, an official who had no acquaintance with the case. He communicated with his advisers here by
telegraph, asking what he should do, and we took it upon ourselves
to say, as we did not wish a precognition of the Crown witnesses and
Dr. Hay was wanted in Edinburgh next day, in view of the trial
beginning on the Tuesday, that we did not think it desirable that
he should submit to precognition by the Crown.

The SOLICITOR-GENERAL—The same refusal applied to the doctor
who was resident in Edinburgh, and who was asked to attend the
Procurator-Fiscal's office in Edinburgh. In this case we are absolutely without precedent. I think that the Crown Office should know
the exact position for the future.

The LORD JUSTICE-CLERK—It seems to me that nothing could be

Evidence for Defence.

Prof. M. Hay

more prejudicial to either side than that the advisers of one side should direct their witnesses not to be precognosced. I think it is a grievous mistake. I express no ruling of law on the subject at all. There is no doubt about this, that in inquiries by the Crown for criminal prosecution, not only is a witness bound to submit to pre-cognition, but he is bound to submit to precognition upon oath, and may be imprisoned if he refuses to give his evidence, either with or without oath; and I think that the proper course for the witness was to submit to precognition. I do not know that the doctor was to blame. All I would say is, that I hope it will not touch the case prejudicially. I feel bound to say that it is a most unwise thing for any legal adviser to give such advice.

The SOLICITOR-GENERAL—I do not attach any blame to the witness, and I do not intend to make any use of the fact, but I feel bound to mention it because it affects the established rule of procedure.

The LORD JUSTICE-CLERK—I think the conduct of all criminal cases makes it a duty of every true citizen to give such information to the Crown as he may be asked to give with reference to the case he is to be called in; and also that every witness who is to be called for the Crown should give such information to the prisoner's counsel, if he is called upon and asked what he is going to say. I do not say that there is any blame attaching to anybody connected with this case, and the witness was quite right to do as he was told. I have no doubt that the legal advisers of the prisoner acted conscientiously. But I have been asked to express my view, and it is that every good citizen should give his aid, either to the Crown or to the defence, in every case where the interests of the public or the interests of the prisoner are involved.]

Cross-examination resumed—My visit to Ardlamont was on 14th September. I went there as a medical man in the interests of the defence, but I went with a perfectly open mind. I was taken there by the person conducting the prisoner's defence. In forming an opinion as between murder and accident in a case of death from a gunshot wound, the exact position of the body as first found is in most cases a most material point. If I had to advise in such a case I should undoubtedly make inquiry about the position of the body. That is an important point, but I consider the nearness of fire quite as important. The position in which the weapon was found relatively to the body is also important, but I consider the nearness of fire equally important. I admit that the nearness of fire to a foot or so may be a matter difficult of determination, but, as I have already said, I am fairly clear as to the distance in this case being within arm's length. I have no doubt as regards the position of the body and of the weapon from what I found in connection with the case.

Being there with the advisers of the defence, what place were you told to assume as that in which the body was first seen by human

R   241

Alfred John Monson.

Prof. M. Hay

eye after the shot?—I was told that the body was found lying on the top of the dyke on its back, with its head towards the rowan tree, and its feet more or less towards a gap in the whins. I was told by the prisoner's advisers that he had stated, in writing, shortly after the event, that he saw the body lying at the bottom of the sunk fence on its left side. I looked upon that as possible; I have not made any assumption either way, so far as I am concerned. I do not think that I was asked to assume anything as to where the body was first found. I placed myself entirely in the hands of Mr. Steven, the factor. I knew at the time that the prisoner had informed Mr. Steven that the body was found lying at the side of the ditch. Dr. Saunders and Mr. John Wilson, advocate, were with me.

What I want to get at is this. You went to Ardlamont, I understand, to see the place where the body was found, as being an important aid to you in making up your mind about the case?—That is so.

If so, did you satisfy yourself where the body was found?—I had no means of obtaining evidence in regard to it beyond Steven's information.

Is your opinion of this case based upon this view, that you do not know where the body was found, and make no assumption as to where it was found?—That is so. I considered the possibility of its being found by the ditch, and I also considered the possibility of its having fallen where it was lying on the top of the dyke. I looked for traces of the body at the bottom of the sunk fence. Of course, I looked at it a considerable time after the accident, and I could not form a proper opinion, because the place had been a good deal visited, and the grass all around trampled down.

The question is, did you see anything at the bottom of the ditch in any way to indicate that a dead body had been there?—I could form no opinion.

By the Lord Justice-Clerk—You are not asked to form an opinion. Did you see anything tending to indicate that a dead body had been lying in the ditch?—No.

Cross-examination continued—Having looked at the ditch and seen nothing, did you then assume that the body had been found on the top of the dyke?—I made no assumption at the time. I measured the height of the wall and the levels generally in relation to the trees and other points. We made experiments from the exact bottom of the ditch. The dyke at this point was quite narrow, and the height from the opposite side of the ditch in the young plantation was measured, and was found to be 4 feet above the level of the ditch. Everything else that I did there had reference to the position in which Mr. Steven saw the body lying, and not with any reference to the bottom of the sunk fence. The reason why I made experiments with reference to this position, and did not make any with reference to the bottom of the sunk fence, is that there were certain pellet marks

242

Evidence for Defence.

Prof. M. Hay

upon certain trees, and I thought it necessary to consider whether those trees had any connection with the dead body found lying on the top of the dyke.

The trees were not so situated with relation to the bottom of the sunk fence that they required investigation?—Quite so.

Why did they require investigation with reference to the one point and not to the other?—Because if the deceased had been shot at the bottom of the dyke the shot would not, in my opinion, have gone through these trees in the direction in which it was found; whereas if he had been shot on the top of the dyke it might have passed. I could not say that it would have passed; it depends how you stand. From the gap in the whins through which it is assumed that the shot was fired to the rowan and lime trees a straight line can be drawn which would indicate the supposed line of fire. Assuming that the body fell where Steven saw it lie, then if you put it upright the head would be so situated relatively to the pellet marks that it might have been shot in that position, but that would depend upon the position of the person who fired. I made no assumption as to where the body fell, but just investigated the circumstances. The amount of blood from the wound would depend upon the vessels that were injured. There are most important veins inside the bone of the head. The sinus vein is the largest in the head. It was situated underneath the fractured substances, and was ruptured by the shot. Blood would flow from the shot; it would begin to come at the time the wound was inflicted, and would continue up to the time of death, and perhaps for some time after, but chiefly before death.

Suppose it was found that " all the cavities of the heart were empty, and their internal lining showed no staining. The great vessels were empty, and generally throughout the body there was an absence of blood.'' That is taken from the medical report. And then the sinus vein was ruptured. What inference would you draw as to the extent of bleeding?—If I could draw any inference twenty-five days after death I should say that the bleeding had been considerable before death. But, of course, the blood tends to disappear from the vessels in the course of putrefaction. Eventually it disappears altogether. The appearances described in the report are consistent with bleeding. Supposing that people came to the spot immediately after the event and saw no blood at all at the bottom of the sunk fence, and at the place where the body was lying the head was found lying in a pool of blood, and if I was satisfied that the men had carefully examined the surrounding ground and had found no trace of blood, I should naturally conclude that the man fell where he was found lying. I admit the probability that the body fell where the blood was seen; but I nevertheless state, as I have stated before, that I look upon it as a possibility that persons not accustomed to make accurate observations had omitted to see traces of blood.

243

Alfred John Monson.

Prof. M. Hay

Suppose that there was no blood upon his own clothes, except a speck on the collar, what would that indicate?—That he had fallen immediately after he was shot. It does not necessarily indicate that he lay where he fell. I can form no conclusion as to whether it would be more likely that he lay where he fell or whether he had been lifted from a lower elevation and carried to another place, because the body would be carried with the head more or less dependent without the blood touching the coat. Suppose it had been carried with the head dependent to prevent the blood from running on to the clothes, the blood would have run on to the ground and left its marks. I think the probability is that he was not moved after he fell; that is to say, on the assumption that there was no blood anywhere except under the head. I have already stated that it was possible that the body may have been transferred from one place to another by two persons without their staining their own clothes with blood. It would require moderate care to do so.

Suppose an affectionate friend found a man shot, and was lifting him, would you expect blood upon the affectionate friend's clothes or hands?—I have no experience of that. Supposing a wad was found lying near the pool of blood, my inference as to the place where the man was shot is that the body had fallen where it was found lying, on the assumption I have already stated; and supposing that, in addition to the wad, two pieces of bone forming part of the deceased's skull were found near the pool of blood, I should say, with the same qualification, that it would point to the same conclusion.

When you were investigating did you find anything pointing to the body having been found elsewhere than at the top of the wall where it was found?—No. Coming to the place on the top of the wall where I was shown that the body had been lying, the head was close to the rowan tree about 6 or 7 feet distant. The body was lying on a sloping piece of ground covered with grass. There were no trees near the feet—I mean quite close to them. It was on a bit of open ground. I saw an opening in the whins a little way behind it. Between the whins and the top of the wall I observed there was an open space for walking along on the way to the south. I walked along the wall for a considerable distance going southwards. There were two openings in the whins. I went through them. They led down to the plantation behind, to which they formed an easy means of access. I examined them because I considered the question of any one firing at the deceased from one or other of these parts.

I examined the rowan, beech, and lime trees when I was at Ardlamont; they were so situated that, standing in the opening mentioned, and firing, the shot would have struck each of the three trees if it went straight. On examining these trees it was quite manifest that they had been struck by shot. The direction of the grooving was almost horizontal, with a slight inclination upwards. The injuries in the beech and lime were a little higher from the ground

244

Evidence for Defenee.

Prof. M. Hay

than those in the rowan. I am quite satisfied that deceased was killed by a shot from behind, and I am also satisfied that the line of fire into his head was a little up from horizontal if he were standing upright. So that anything which struck beyond him would be a little higher than his head if no deflection took place. On the whole, the line was a slightly rising one, taking all the pellet marks together. I cannot say I am quite sure that it rose in the same way and direction as the line of the wound through the deceased's head, but I do not think it is very important, because a very slight inclination of the head would cause deflection. I saw two gaps in the whins; one of them, the one nearer the plantation, did not at all suit the assumed line of fire, but the other came nearer to it. A six-foot man standing near where the deceased was assumed to be standing would be in a line between the gap and the damage done to the rowan, lime, and beech trees.

You say that the damage to the man's head and the damage to the lime, beech, and rowan trees were all in one line. Suppose you projected that line to your own body when you were standing at the gaps, where would it strike you?—In the case of the gap nearer to the plantation, it would have struck a point somewhere about the top of my own head, and at the other a point nearer to my own eye.

At that place your eye, the head, and the injury to the three trees would have been in a line?—Roughly speaking.

Did that fact strike you? It is a striking fact, is it not?—I do not think so; it is an important consideration in the case, in so far as affording a certain support to the theory of the Crown by getting those marks in the trees, the head of the deceased, and the supposed gun in the hands of an assailant in that particular spot all in a line. I admit that, if you want to determine a particular line of fire, the way to do is to get a series of points the one behind the other, but all that would have regard to the fact that you know you have secured all these points. In this case that is not by any means certain. If you get three or four points sufficiently distant from each other, that enables you to project a straight line beyond these points, but there were only a few stray pellets here.

If you diminish the distance between the point at which you were standing and the place the dead man is supposed to have been standing, that would not in any way affect the line, provided you kept at the proper angle?—It would not.

So that the line would be the same supposing the point where the shot was assumed to be fired was 9 feet, or 4 feet, or 1 foot from the man?—That is only considering the line in one aspect—in the vertical plane; in the horizontal plane by the moving forwards I should have passed to an elevated from a depressed point. I should have gone distinctly higher, and the position would have been affected by the man holding his head up or down; but that would not alter the other conditions to which I have referred. The step up is very

Alfred John Monson.

Prof. M. Hay

considerable. Supposing the angle was horizontal towards the head, the line of rise would be from 10 to 20 degrees. In the case of 20 degrees the line reached the ground at 15 to 16 feet from the person; at 10 degrees it reached the ground at 30 to 32 feet. With regard to the precise angle through the head, the points to be determined were the point of the original impact and the point of leaving the head. I assume that none of the shot passed the ear at a lower level than the injury to the flesh of the ear. I saw, in the photograph of the head, an injury in the front of the ear at a lower level than the injury to the flap of the ear. [Shown No. 239 B.] It is difficult from the photograph to see whether this is an injury in front of the ear penetrating the skin or an elevated cuticle through *post-mortem* decomposition. I cannot say from examination what it is. I want to refer to the doctor's report. [Shown No. 238.] On page 10 of this report this passage occurs—"Immediately in front of the right ear the skin exhibited a laceration fully ¼ inch long from above downwards, which communicated with a larger wound behind the ear." That is quite correct; there is apparently a wound behind and one in front of the ear. I imagine that was caused by the projection of the broken bone of the head, or perhaps by the passage of the pellets— more likely the bone.

I understood you to say that a man holding his gun in his own hand could do that injury to himself. Will you show us how that could be done?—It would be difficult to do so myself; I should prefer to show on some one else. With the hand at any distance from 2 feet 8 inches to 2 feet 10 inches from the head, a man grasping the gun by the muzzle with the stock behind could put it at such an angle at the back of the ear that the shot would come through the flap of the ear. This is not possible without the stock being supported. In addition to his own hands something must have been supporting the stock, so as to keep it at the proper angle, unless deceased had fallen and the stock was supported on the ground.

So that you require two things—a man holding his gun in that position relative to the back of his head, and something supporting the stock at that angle?—Yes; or the gun thrown away, and the man's head at the moment it goes off being in the particular position in relation to his gun. Supposing the wound were inflicted upon a man standing where I was told the body was lying and that the shot which caused the wound went through the rowan, beech, and lime trees, I should say that it was the whin bushes on which the gun was supported.

Suppose that a man 6 feet high standing there holds the muzzle of his gun at the back of his ear, what is the distance of the nearest whin at that elevation?—I do not think more than 7 to 9 feet. Assume the length of the arm to be 2 feet 10 inches, then you have the length of the gun to the trigger, 3 feet 10¼ inches; that gives 6 feet 8¾ inches. When we made the photograph we did not consider

246

Evidence for Defence.

Prof. M. Hay

the question of the left arm being used for holding the gun, but merely the right arm. Everything depends upon how the gun is being held; if it was supported by the whins he could hold it close to the muzzle end, leaving only enough of the end to keep his hand clear of the shot. Assuming that the man was standing and that the gun was at such a level as to be nearly horizontal, his hand would not necessarily be near his head. We have no photograph showing a man standing erect and holding a gun at such an angle that the shot would pass through the man's head and go on to the rowan tree; but you can alter the elevation; by elevating the gun in my photograph then you will get the angle horizontal. At the place in question at such a height as to send the shot horizontally through a man's head and on into the rowan, beech, and lime trees, the butt of the gun would be resting on the whins. They are about 10 feet high, and are about 6 feet or 7 feet from the deceased's feet; a good deal depends, however, upon where you place the feet. I confess I did not get from Mr. Steven the exact position of Hambrough's feet; he simply told me the way in which the body lay, indicating the exact position of the head and showing that the feet lay in a certain direction. There are whin bushes 10 feet high within a gun's length from the feet. I know that there are some whins high and some low.

A shot fired as shown in photograph No. 4 would have taken effect upon the ear and then gone away afterwards; it was a glancing shot and deflected from the skull. If the shot passed in a perfectly straight line, according to that photograph, it would, I believe, glance off the head. If a shot were fired directly at the head it would not necessarily enter it; a shot frequently glances off; common experience shows that. I do not suggest that the whole charge could not have struck the head. I have already said that the whole charge struck the head and deflected. One might as well say that a bullet fired point-blank would penetrate the head. I have known three cases where this has not happened and the bullet has glanced off. In one case, a homicidal one, the shot was fired point-blank at a distance of 2 or 3 feet at the outside. I explain the fact that only four pellets were found in the deceased's brain by saying that the shot struck at an angle upon a certain spot in the skull represented by an area of considerable comminution. That bone was partly carried in by the impact of the shot. The main body of the shot went on its way, and a pellet or two might have been caught on the edge of the bone and carried into the skull. In one case where the gun was fired point-blank at 2 feet the shot glanced off, taking the superficial parts with it. In the wooden block which I have here—[No. 2 of defence productions]—the shot entered in one direction and then glanced off in another. It is possible that a shot might be fired which would so glance past the head that the whole of the charge would not strike the head. Suppose that happened at such an angle that the edge of the charge would strike, the rest of the shot that did not strike

247

Alfred John Monson.

Prof. M. Hay

would pass on; it might be slightly deflected by the shot which had caught the head and which was deflected and thrown out on the main mass. Except for that, the shot would pass on undeflected. I express that merely as an opinion, and not as the result of any experiment. The diameter of the point of impact of a glancing shot would vary as to the angle of impact; if the angle were great the shot would naturally produce a smaller area of impact with the skull, and if it were small it would produce more.

Suppose you had two cases, one where a shot is fired from behind at such an angle that only a part of the mass of shot strikes the head. That is one case. Suppose you have another—a shot fired from behind in such a position that the whole mass strikes the head in passing. Would you expect the size of the wound to be the same in both cases?—If they were fired at exactly the same angle the wound where the whole shot strikes the head would be greater. If in this case the head was not struck by the whole mass of the charge, but only by the edge in passing, that fact would not necessarily account for the smallness of the wound. It is quite conceivable that if half of the cylinder of the shot mass—taking its long diameter—strikes the skull, it may leave as broad an impression as if the whole of the cylinder had entered, the diameter in both cases being the same. Of course, if the mere edge of the charge struck in passing the head, the wound must be smaller than if the whole mass struck. In making my calculations, I have assumed that the whole charge struck the head. Looking at the direction of the wound, beginning at the back of the head and glancing out at the ear, I think that the shot nearly missed the head in so far as 1 inch or 2 inches more to the right would have missed; but, as I have already said, I think the whole of the shot struck the head. The shot would be properly described as a glancing shot.

If you found after a glancing shot four pellets in the head, how do you account for their being separated from the rest of the charge? —Quite easily. The shot struck at an angle at a certain point of the skull represented by an area of considerable comminution. The bone was partly carried in by the impact of the shot. The main body of the shot went on its way, and a pellet or two might have been caught against the edge of the bone and carried into the skull. They did not get out again, because, apparently, they had not sufficient momentum; but I do not think that anything with regard to distance can be inferred from that fact. The rest of the shot had sufficient momentum to carry it away. Going through the barrel the shot is practically a ball, composed of a number of loose pellets, and it is possible that that loose mass may have had one or two pellets rubbed off the edge of it. If the wound was more ragged at the front side than at the back, that would indicate that the shot was spreading to some extent against the skull; the triangular shape also shows that. In my experiments I found the shot appear to begin to spread

248

Evidence for Defence.

Prof. M. Hay

at $3\frac{1}{2}$ feet in the case of the 12-bore gun, and at 4 feet in the case of the 20-bore gun. I made experiments with wood and also with cardboard; I think the cardboard on the whole better, the wood splitting more readily. As regards blackening, I found discoloration up to 5 or 6 feet with Schultze and amberite. With these powders it is apparently smoke or dust which causes discoloration; I really cannot say which, but there is blackening. With black powder you get both blackening and scorching. Firing at skin, for example, you can see the blackening and scorching distinctly. I do not think that *post-mortem* swelling would tend to displace marks upon the edge of the wound to any material extent.

May I take it that in every case where you have represented men having shot themselves, you assumed some support for the butt of the gun and some agent pulling the trigger?—I admit that in every case I assumed a support for the gun and an agent of some kind pulling the trigger. Of course, the gun could have gone off from hitting the trigger or from a blow upon the hammer. In regard to marks upon the trees, we searched for marks only in the trees which were along the dyke. The marks were all distinctly pellet marks, but they were not all grooved marks, because some were marks in broken twigs, and it was easy to see that when replaced there was an absence of tissue, which could only have been caused by a gunshot. We excluded any marks upon leaves. I have no means of stating with perfect certainty how old the marks were, but I am satisfied that they could not have attained their appearance within a month. I say that they were not more than four months old, because certain of the twigs showed weather marks which must have been made when they were fully grown. I am satisfied that the marks were older than two months, but how much older I cannot say.

You spoke of a man probably falling backward when shot. What do you mean?—I said that if he was standing it is possible that he would fall backwards, but he might have fallen forwards. I cannot say which is the more probable; I have not enough experience. I do not think that the effect of the shot carrying him forward would be anything at all, because the force of the shot was very slight considering the inertia of the body of the deceased.

You said that under certain conditions you think it more probable that the shot came from the direction of the rowan tree than went towards the direction of the rowan tree?—The body was found lying on its back with the head towards the rowan tree, and on the assumption that Cecil Hambrough fell backwards and was killed, and that the shot passed from behind forward, I arrived at the opinion that the shot would, in such a case, come from the direction of the rowan tree rather than from the other direction. I assumed that his back was toward the direction from which he was shot.

Re-examined by Mr. COMRIE THOMSON—The evidence I have given as to the line of fire proceeded upon the assumption that the

249

Alfred John Monson.

Prof. M. Hay

place pointed out to me as the place where the body was found was the place where Mr. Hambrough had been shot. The appearance of the pellet marks on the trees was considered upon the same assumption. I knew at the time that the Crown were founding upon the appearance of the pellets in the rowan and other trees, and that their theory was that the man had been shot where he was found lying. The rest of my evidence, as to the position of the wound, is not affected at all by the place where the man was found. If Hambrough had been walking from the south towards the rowan tree and fell forwards, he could not have been in the position in which he was said to have been found; he would have been found on his face; and if he had fallen backwards his feet would have been pointing towards the rowan tree. On the theory that he had fallen either backwards or forwards he could not have been in the position in which he was found on the top of the dyke unless the body had been subsequently moved. If it is conceded or maintained that he was shot from the south as he was proceeding towards the rowan tree, it follows that his body must have been lifted before it was found lying on its back with the head towards the rowan tree. The only theory upon which it can be maintained that the body lay as it fell, and excluding interference with the body, proceeds upon the assumption that he was walking from the rowan tree and fell upon his back. Interference with the body would explain the whole thing.

When I was at Ardlamont Steven told me that Monson had said to him that he found the body lying on the bank beyond the ditch, away from the brackens upon the grass. If there was blood and it fell upon the grass, I think that, considering the weather and one thing and another, it might very well have disappeared; it would have trickled down the blades of grass, and as the grass was long it would have become invisible. If the body had been lifted with the right side of the head pretty well upwards there would not necessarily have been much flow of blood. I have already said that gunshot wounds do not bleed very freely. Although in this case there was a sinus ruptured, I am not satisfied as to the condition of the sinus immediately after death. The wound was lacerated, and it is quite possible that a portion of the bone may have been forced into the skull and upon the sinus, and have acted temporarily to some extent as a plug to the opening on the surface. If the body was moved frequently afterwards the plug might fall out so as to let the blood clear. If I had been told that there had been a good deal of bleeding in the removal of the body in a cart to the house, and that subsequently it was placed on a bed, that, coupled with the processes of decomposition, would, in my opinion, account for the bloodlessness referred to in the report of the *post-mortem* examination. It might also show that the bleeding at the beginning had been very profuse.

In determining the line of fire the dispersion and deflection must both be taken into account. On the Crown's assumption there

250

Evidence for Defence.

Prof. M. Hay

would be a deflection from the head. As regards the deflection from the tree, the pellets which struck the twigs would be deflected, but there would be pellets going on which would not be deflected. In the case in my photographs, the positions involved that the butt of the gun should be resting on something. The momentary contact of the gun with something coincident with the act of stumbling would account for the accident. Supposing that a man had a gun behind him, and it got in contact with a fence, that would account for the accident if the gun was in the line of fire, and that without any momentary resting of the gun. The cardboard experiments of the Crown are almost identical with my own. If the shot had struck the back of the ear at a distance of 9 feet stray pellet marks would have been seen over the back of the head.

By the LORD JUSTICE-CLERK—There was blood found on the wad. The wad might have adhered to the head, and have been carried with it for a distance of several feet, and then fallen. The wad is made of spongy material, and by means of the blood might adhere to the wound for some time before dropping out. Blood is a rather adhesive material.

When a man is shot, can you predict how he will fall, whether on his face, or partially on his side, or on his back?—He might fall on one side. He might roll a bit over. That would carry him out of the line of fire if he were on a sloping bank.

Might he not turn round to a certain extent in the act of falling? —He might then be found more or less on his back. If any one went up to him as he was lying, to see whether he was alive or dead, that would account for his being on his side. I do not think the body could be turned over without altering the position of the head; the body is not turned upon the head as a pivot. The head would be lying limp at the time, with nothing supporting it. It would lie forward, and, if turned over, it would be moved according to the extent of the movement of the body. If a man carried a gun in his hand in the ordinary way, and he fell forward, I do not think it likely that he would fire the shot into the back of his head. If he fell backwards, he would fall on the back of his head.

8. WILLIAM GORDON WOODROW SAUNDERS, M.B., C.M., examined by Mr. WILSON—I am twenty-eight years of age, and am at present assistant to the Professor of Clinical Medicine of Edinburgh University. Formerly I was resident pathologist at Rainhill Asylum, near Liverpool, and while there had extensive opportunities in making autopsies. I got instructions from Messrs. Davidson & Syme to go to Ventnor to attend the examination of the body of the late Mr. Hambrough, and, as a matter of courtesy, I was present at the examination made by Dr. Littlejohn and Dr. Macmillan on behalf of the Crown. I concur generally in the report of these doctors. At that time and afterwards I made examinations of the scalp and skull

251

Alfred John Monson.

Dr. W. G. W. Saunders

for the purpose of ascertaining the answers to certain questions raised in this case.

From the appearance of the wound on the scalp, I inferred that the shot had passed from behind and below, forwards and upwards in the direction of the right ear, and the reason for this inference is that the hind part of the wound is lower down, that is, nearer the neck, than the front part. The point of entrance was the narrowest part of the wound; the edges were sharp and almost bevelled, and that leads me to believe that the shot had struck the skull in such a mass as to cause a wound of that diameter. From the fracture of the skull one could also say that the shot was from behind, forwards and upwards.

In determining the distance from which the shot is fired there are a number of points which are of importance. First of all, the size of the wound at the point of entrance. In this case the size of the wound was not accurately measured at the Ventnor examination. In the medical report it is stated to taper off posteriorly. Taking the size of the wound at the point where the shot is supposed to have entered, I consider that certainly consistent with a near shot, and only with a near shot. Another important consideration is the presence or absence of pellet marks round the wound. In this case there were no such marks visible when the hair was removed from the whole scalp. I did not expect to see evidence of blackening or scorching because of putrefaction, and because blood would have been diffused round the wound, and would have washed it away, and, as a matter of fact, I found none. Another important element in determining the distance is the extent of the shattering of the bone. In this case the considerable shattering which had taken place at the base and side of the skull is consistent with the shot having been fired at a very near distance. Taking these considerations into account, in my opinion the shot was fired within an arm's length or thereby, roughly speaking.

On the instruction of the agents for the defence, I visited Ardlamont and the *locus* of the accident on 14th September along with Professor Hay, and I there met Mr. Steven, the factor of the estate, who pointed out the spot where the head of the deceased was lying when the men came to remove it. He told me that he had been informed that before the body was put in that position it had been lying on the sward beyond the bracken on the other side of the ditch from the sunk fence. Mr. Steven lay down on the east side of the ditch in the young plantation to show the position described as that in which the body originally lay. He also showed us the place where the body had been seen on the top of the dyke. He said that there had been a pool of blood, and I saw a dark mark on the ground with some stones about it. He said that was the place where he found the body lying. I examined the marks on the surrounding parts to see if I could gather anything as to how the accident happened. We

252

Evidence for Defence.

Dr. W. G. W. Saunders

examined carefully the marks on the rowan, lime, and beech trees with a spirit-level and a tape, and made a minute examination of the character of the wounds on the trees. From notes we took at the time we laid down the different marks to scale, taking every possible care to be accurate. We came to the conclusion that the pellet marks were older than a month, or probably beyond two months old, and our reason for putting the age of the pellet marks at that was the amount of new growth in the wood and in the woody tissue in the track of the pellet marks. In the case of a pellet striking a twig, a portion of the woody fibre is excised or cut out; in course of time there is growth and vital reaction, filling up, to a certain extent, the part that has been excised; just like a cut finger, it tends to heal. Two months is making a liberal estimate against our own view. As regards the colour of the different marks, some were more tinged with brown or green than others, and that is consistent with the view that they were older than a month.

I do not consider that any safe inference could be drawn as to the direction or distance of the shot which did the injury to young Hambrough from the appearance of the marks on the trees, because the data were too few to give reliable information. Supposing that the body was found lying on its back on the top of the dyke at the spot at which I saw blood marks, and supposing that the feet were stretched to the south or south-west, my inference would be that the shot probably came from the north. The effect of such a wound as I saw on the scalp and the skull would be instantaneous death; Mr. Hambrough would have fallen at the place, and would have been incapable of making any movement after receiving the injury.

Along with Professor Hay I made a long series of experiments in order to corroborate the view we formed as to the direction and distance of the shot. Experiments were first made for the purpose of showing the size and the shape and the character of a wound made by the guns in question in this case with shot, point-blank, at various distances. I have seen and examined Nos. 3 to 17 of the productions for the defence. The experiments on the wooden boards were made to determine the character and size of the hole and the various surrounding parts as the result of shots at various distances. They were also made to show the scattering and the extent of blackening and singeing, and, incidentally, the size of the central hole made by the shot. From these experiments I inferred that the shot which killed Mr. Hambrough was fired from such a distance that there were no scattered pellet marks, and that the central hole or opening was of the diameter which I have shown on the diagram hanging here in Court. I put the muzzle of the gun at a distance from the head of probably under 3 feet, and certainly not over 4.

We made several experiments upon dummy wooden heads in order to test the difference of the obliquity of the direction of the shot. [Shown Nos. 1 and 2.] In two of these experiments, instead

Alfred John Monson.

Dr. W. G. W. Saunders

of there being a circular hole, as through a flat target, there is an elongated wound along the side of the target. The entrance of the shot, as shown on the wooden head, corresponds in appearance, as far as one can have a resemblance between wood and an ordinary head, with the wound on Mr. Hambrough's head; it is perfectly and sharply punched out. We also made experiments upon dead animals, in which the tissues were apparently living. They would still show vital reaction for two or three hours after death. We first fired point-blank into these, with the result of confirming generally the results derived from the wooden targets, but showing muscular and vital action. The vital action tended to enlarge the wound, but the aperture remained, at a short distance, clear and well defined. We also had oblique firing at horses' heads, and in this case the character of the wound which we got was distinct from the character of the wound produced on the flat surface; it was more elongated and laid bare the bone, showing that it was shattered by the shot. The results of these experiments were consistent with the view that the wound on Mr. Hambrough's head was the result of an oblique shot at a distance of 3 feet. I have had experience of the effect of a gunshot wound upon a man, when the shot was fired obliquely, at a distance of 9 or 10 feet. It was a gun accident which occurred in a fishing boat. One man was stooping down near the mast attending to a rope, and the other was standing in the sternsheets with a gun loosely held in his hand. The boat gave a lurch and the gun went off, lodging its contents in the left flank of the man and producing a glancing wound. When the wounded man's clothes were taken off it was observed that there was a series of furrows across the flank, with a breadth of about 6 inches, and a small central grazing of about 1 inch in diameter, where the pellets had been closer together. The gun was a 12-bore, with No. 5 shot, fired obliquely. As a result of my experience in that case, my opinion here is that the shot which killed Mr. Hambrough was oblique and fired at a distance of about 3 feet.

Cross-examined by the SOLICITOR-GENERAL—I have not had much experience of gunshot wounds, except the one mentioned. I was not present when it happened. I know, however, what distance the muzzle of the gun was from the man who was shot, because it was limited by the two thwarts of the boat. When I went to Ardlamont Professor Hay was with me and, I think, saw everything that I saw. We were there together on one occasion only. I went to a place near the rowan tree along with Professor Hay, Mr. Steven, and one or two others. Mr. Steven was the only person there who knew anything about the original position of the body. When we were there I saw Steven lie down on the sward in the young plantation beyond the ditch. I think that his feet would be about 3 feet from the wall. He lay down there because we were getting data on which to start our examination; we were trying to find out what was known about the position of the body. We asked Mr. Steven, so far as I can

Evidence for Defence.

Dr. W. G. W. Saunders

remember, if he had gathered what was the original position of the body, and in consequence of that he gave us that position as his impression. I think that he pointed out with his hand two different places below the fence, and said that he did not know which was the right one. I do not remember any definite spot. He stood upon the wall and described what his impression was; it was then that he pointed roughly to the other side of the wall. The object of his lying down was to show the position in which the body lay, and the object of his waving his hand was to show that he did not know the exact place. The place where he lay down was upon the bank which slopes down to the ditch and sunk fence. I gathered that it was in consequence of the general impression he had got from what he had been told that he was lying down, and that neither he nor any one else had any definite information as to where the body was found. The place he pointed out was not just under the wall, but on the bank between the sunk fence and the young wood. Mr. Steven did not point out anything more, except the mark of blood on the top of the dyke, where he said the body had been found by himself and others. As regards the place on the east side of the sunk fence, where Mr. Steven lay down, we examined the ground generally and also the sunk fence and the brackens, but that examination resulted in nothing that we thought had any bearing on this case, except a general survey of the ground.

We then transferred our attention to a place on a higher level above the sunk fence. I saw a dark mark on the ground, and was told that that was where the body had lain. The discoloration which I saw seemed to confirm what I was told, because it was a dark mark such as must have been produced by blood. I saw no similar discoloured mark in the locality at all. My inference was that the head of the deceased had rested at this place for a considerable time. It was impossible to draw any inference as to whether it had rested anywhere else after five weeks, because the ground had been walked over frequently, especially the day before. If there had been discoloration of the ground to a similar extent at a different place I think we would have seen it.

Would there be more discoloration by blood at the place where the man was shot and died than at the place where he was laid?— I should expect that would depend upon the length of time he had lain in another place. Supposing that he had bled to death, there would have been blood where he had been lying. I concur generally in the medical report of Dr. Littlejohn and Dr. Macmillan, and I concur in the part which says, "All the cavities of the heart were empty, and their internal lining showed no staining. The great vessels were empty, and generally throughout the body there was an absence of blood." That would indicate nothing as to the actual amount of bleeding at the time of death, but would show that the blood had all passed out of the body subsequently. It is the heart and

255

Alfred John Monson.

Dr. W. G. W. Saunders

vessels which drive the blood through the body. When a man is dead the heart does not go on driving the blood through the body.

Well, would the blood have circulated through the body after death if one of the vessels had been opened?—There may be some considerable discharge of blood even after death, because although the individual is dead the blood vessels are not. If the man were alive the action of the heart would tend to cause external bleeding if a vessel were opened.

And does not death and the stoppage of the heart tend in the direction of stopping the flow of blood?—By no means. May I explain? If a man or a body dies instantaneously blood may continue to flow for some considerable time. That is to say, that at the actual act of death there may be no blood flowing at all. I agree to what is said in the concluding portion of the medical report, namely, " From the foregoing examination we are of opinion that the deceased died from shock, the result of a gunshot injury of the skull and brain, and of subsequent loss of blood." One would expect blood to be found within a few minutes at the place where a man was shot, but blood would not necessarily come; it might be blocked by a bone. If it were not blocked it would flow. I was not shown the places where the wad and the two pieces of bone were found. Supposing they were found at a place where a pool of blood was, I do not think that I could draw any definite inference as to where death occurred, because it would depend on what position they were found in. Supposing, just for an instant, that a bone had come from far within the skull, I should be extremely surprised that it would give us any indication as to where death occurred.

But suppose you had been told that there were two pieces of bone found on the sward near the man's head, would you have attached any importance to that?—Certainly; it would entirely depend upon the subsequent examination and the answers I got. Suppose I was told that they were pieces of a man's head, and that they were lying there, I would attach importance to that, because it might suggest that the body had been moved after it was shot, as it is extremely likely that in being carried the head would hang down, and if it came in contact with the ground some pieces of the fractured part might be dislodged. My reason for thinking that it does not suggest that the pieces of bone were knocked out at the time when the man was shot is that one of the pieces of bone, so far as I have examined them, comes more from towards the front of the skull than the rest of the wound; it would therefore have to come in the reverse direction of the shot. There was no opening in front by which the bone came out. One of the portions of the bone comes from within the skull, and if it were sent out by a shot, to come out from behind, it must have come in the reverse direction from the shot which dislodged it.

Then, if you find a man shot from behind, and a bit of his

Evidence for Defence.

Dr. W. G. W. Saunders

skull lying a little bit in front of him, you think that that would imply that the shot had been fired the other way?—No; it would only show how careful one must be in drawing deductions in such a case. The same applies to the wad. I expect that it also would have some relation to the wound caused in the head. If it had stains upon it, I would suggest that that would prove that the shot had been fired from a near distance. I draw a different inference with regard to the wad from that with regard to the piece of bone; I cannot reconcile the occurrence of the bone with the shot which produced the death. It does not follow that I must necessarily be wrong about either the wad or the bone. When I spoke about insufficient data, I meant this, that we had very few pellet marks upon the rowan tree compared with the number of pellets in a cartridge. It would therefore depend to a large extent how the missing pellets were placed, as to what direction the shot was travelling in, and where it was discharged. We had the blood at the place where the man's head was shown to us, and we found out the pellet marks in the trees. We ascertained that the head of a man standing up, and the injury to the rowan, lime, and beech trees were all in one line.

What more data did you want?—In the first place, proof that the results were produced by the same shot; secondly, that the age of the pellet marks corresponded with the date of accident; thirdly, some explanation of how there were so few pellet marks present in the trees; and, also, the position of the remaining pellets that were present in the cartridge. If these points were explainable or explained, then the data would be fairly complete as pointing to the direction of the shot which caused the accident. Judging from the wound in the head, the hole at the back, and the injury to the ear, and assuming the deceased to have been standing with his head straight forward, and to have been shot from behind where he was standing, then I should think that the shot came from the middle line behind. I think so because of the position of the head. It depends upon the position in which the gun was held whether the shot would or would not have gone straight through the man's head in the line in which it struck him. Supposing that the gun was held straight, the shot would be delivered from the left rear, the point of impact being at the back of the skull, and the shot passing away about the middle of the flap of the right ear.

What means, if any, had you for ascertaining whether the skull was struck by the whole mass of the shot or only by the fringe?— I should say that the whole mass of shot struck, judging from the amount of the shattering of bone and tearing up of soft tissues. I did not find that a hole was furrowed through the head, such as would have been caused by the whole mass passing through. If the whole mass was fired against the head within a short distance, it depends upon the character of the bone struck whether the shot was deflected, or whether the shot would furrow its way right through.

s

Alfred John Monson.

Dr. W. G. W. Saunders

You were present at the *post-mortem* examination, and saw four pellets found in the brain; how did they get separated from the mass? —If pellets were deflected outwards towards the trees they could easily be deflected inwards towards the brain. I think that the four pellets in the brain were separated from the mass by striking the bone.

But I thought your idea was that the whole charge struck the head?—I said that in this thing one can only draw inferences.

Would it not be a more probable view that a small part of the charge struck the head and knocked in the bone, and went in themselves?—No; I do not think so, because I do not think that four pellets could possibly have done that damage to the skull.

Can you give us any explanation, if the whole charge struck the skull, and if the breaking of the bone caused four pellets to go in, why all the rest of the charge did not go in?—That depends upon how the skull was struck. It is impossible to argue as to the direction pellets will take after once striking a bone. I think that the four pellets struck the bone, and were deflected into the skull, and that their course was arrested by the breaking of the bone, so that they had no residual force to carry them out.

Would that point to a near or a far distance of the shot?—To neither; but the nearer the head the greater the force of impact. With regard to the age of the pellet marks upon the trees, that was a matter upon which I formed a definite opinion. I do not profess by examining a tree which has been struck by pellets to be able to tell the precise time that has elapsed since it was so struck; but I can estimate a marginal time beyond which it could not have been done. I find this margin by the general law of growth applicable to trees. I have no special knowledge of the matter, but I have studied botany as incidental to my profession, and have also attended separate botany classes. I have never been in practical charge of any forest or woods.

Re-examined by Mr. WILSON—When Mr. Steven pointed to the east side of the dyke he pointed to the green sward on the other side of the ditch; he did not point into the ditch.

If it were the case that the head was first lying, on a wet morning, on the grass on the other side of the ditch, where the grass is fairly long, I would not expect blood to be visible on the grass, because it would be easily washed out. Some particular blade of grass would act as a pipe or conduit for leading the blood down to the ground by capillary attraction.

One of the pieces of bone referred to formed part of the petrous bone. If that piece of bone had been shot from behind, it must have been a very heavy and forcible impact which caused it to be broken; the petrous bone is one of the hardest in the body, and is so called because of its hardness. If that bone had been driven out by a shot it would probably have been driven out in the direction of the eye.

258

Evidence for Defence.

Dr. W. G. W. Saunders

If the body were lifted and deposited on the ground it is possible that the piece of bone might have fallen out. That is what I meant when I said that the position of the bone or bones when found would not give any certain indication as to where the body actually had been when it first fell. There was a piece of bone fractured forming part of the skull adjacent to the sinus, and bleeding might quite easily have been stopped by the pressure of that bone.

As regards the question how the four pellets could be found in the head, my view is that when the body of the shot strikes a hard substance, like a skull, at an oblique angle, the whole, or almost the whole of it, may probably be deflected. But inasmuch as the pellets do not adhere closely together, two or three of them might find their way into the brain at some point where there was less resistance. That is what I think occurred in the present case.

By the LORD JUSTICE-CLERK—One of the pieces of bone would be likely to remain in the head after the shot was fired. I think that they would be likely to fall out when the body struck the ground. I could not say whether they would be more likely to fall out from the shock or fall of the body than from some one carrying the body head downwards. The petrous bone required some shock to throw it out. If the body fell upon its face the petrous bone could not get out, because it was more forward than the wound. If a man fell straight forward on his face I should expect as an ordinary thing that there would be signs of it on his face; and if he fell on his face the blood would flow down the front. I think that it would require some strong knock to cause the petrous bone to fall out; merely turning the body round would not be sufficient; supposing he struck the wall in his fall it would fall out.

The fact, as we had it, was that the bone was found 8 or 9 inches from the edge of the wall?—I cannot understand how it came to be found there, unless it was thrown out by some violent shock, either in the original fall of the head or by some one moving the body with a bump.

9. ARTHUR LOGAN TURNER, F.R.C.S., examined by Mr. WILSON— I hold the qualification of M.B., C.M., of Edinburgh University. On 21st and 22nd November I was present at The Inch, Liberton, along with Mr. Speedy, Professor Hay, and Dr. Saunders, when certain experiments were made and certain attitudes were photographed. [Shown Nos. 23 to 34 of defence productions.] This photograph was prepared by me, and is an exact representation of what took place.

10. J. HUME PATERSON, examined by Mr. WILSON—I am laboratory assistant in the Royal College of Physicians, Edinburgh. [Shown Nos. 23-24 of defence productions.] I made these photographs of horses' heads some time ago, having received the heads from Dr. Saunders.

Alfred John Monson.

James M. Bain

11. JAMES M. BAIN, examined by Mr. WILSON—I am a photographer, and on 2nd inst. I photographed Dr. Fowler holding a gun in different positions. I also photographed a horse's head.

12. TOM SPEEDY, examined by Mr. COMRIE THOMSON—I am factor on the estate of Craigmillar, and a partner of the firm of Tom & James Speedy, shooting agents, Edinburgh. I was a gamekeeper for twenty years, and during that time I cultivated a habit of observation in sport and in natural history. In my book, published in 1884, called "Sport in the Highlands and Lowlands of Scotland with Rod and Gun," I devoted a chapter on "Guns and how to use them." I have always taken a special interest in the subject of gun accidents.

On 17th October I visited Ardlamont and went over the shooting generally, accompanied by Lamont, the gamekeeper. He showed me the spot in the wood where Mr. Hambrough's body had been found. We entered the wood from the offices, and before I had gone 30 yards in the wood I saw marks of pellets in the trees. The very first tree I came to was marked with pellets, and so were many others. The marks were on the trunks. When I was taken to the place where the body had been found I was shown a stob driven into the ground where the rowan tree had been uprooted. I walked along the dyke southwards for some distance in the direction of the schoolhouse, and I observed the condition of the trees south from the place where the accident occurred; they were marked with shot, and in the big wood a very great many were so marked. It is just what I should have expected in a wood where there was game. I afterwards walked with the factor in the wood and noticed similar marks on the trees. I looked at them minutely, and cut a branch or two with marks on them, which I showed to the prisoner's agents.

I was asked to go back to Ardlamont, and went on 2nd November, when I made a more minute examination. I selected some bits of twigs. [Shown Nos. 148, 150, 151, 152 of defence productions.] No. 148 is a small twig of a birch which was growing on the top of the wall, 17 yards in a southerly direction from the rowan. I did not measure the distance except by stepping it. I cut this twig about 5 feet from the ground. The next one is a twig of a larch, which was also got on the top of the dyke, 76 yards from the rowan, going into the young wood on the other side of the sunk fence. The branch was taken from a height of 4½ feet from the ground. The next is a plane tree twig, which was taken 114 yards from the rowan, and the pellet marks in it were 5 feet from the ground. The next is a rowan tree down in the wood opposite the lodge gate nearer the road to the west of the dyke. It was 20 yards to the right of the road, and the road was a bit beyond it. There was another rowan tree 50 yards from the road, nearly opposite the lodge, 30 yards nearer the dyke than the one I have just spoken of. In many cases I could have brought larger pieces of wood, but I did not think it

Evidence for Defence.

Tom Speedy

was of much moment. The next tree was an ash, 40 yards from the road and 40 yards south of the lodge gate. This got almost the whole charge of the shot. The last is a plane tree. That was 13 yards from the sunk fence and 176 yards from the rowan tree. It also got the whole charge of the shot at about 5 feet in height. The trunks of the trees were mostly marked, but I could not bring them. All over the wood I found such marks. I was shown the place where the body was found. It was higher than the wood to the west of it up on the bank. There is one whin bush growing close to the place, and a few dwarf willows well into the wood. I do not think that the whin bush would be sufficient to prevent Hambrough from seeing any one approaching him with a gun. The willows would, but they are too far away.

In my gamekeeper days I had charge of a kennel of dogs. They were fed largely on horseflesh, and it was my duty to slaughter the horses. I have shot a great many horses in my day, probably over five hundred. The method I adopted was to shoot them chiefly on the forehead and sometimes behind the ear. The extreme distance from which I fired was 4 feet, but it was usually 1 foot to 2½ feet. My observation and experience enabled me to tell very closely how far the muzzle was from the head when the shot was fired. I shot them with an ordinary cartridge. If shot point-blank against the forehead at 1 foot the shot went clean through. At 2 feet it went in much the same manner, but very frequently you got a stray pellet outside the edge of the main hole. This was found frequently in skinning the body. At 3 feet and over still more stray pellet marks were seen; but shots vary, they are not always the same.

If it be the case that no shot marks were visible outside the wound on Mr. Hambrough's head, would you conclude that he was shot at a very near distance?—Not more than 2 feet. That is the result of my long experience, and I think it is demonstrated beyond all doubt. Even at 1 foot from the muzzle one of the wads might quite easily strike on one side of the wound and another on the other; we often see that in shooting. In shooting at an angle the wound is much larger than when the shot is point-blank. I remember shooting a nervous horse that would not stand still, and at last I had to fire at it when it had its head as high as it could get it, with the result that the wound was much larger than it otherwise would have been, because it was shot at an angle. The wound was an elongated one. I demonstrated this in presence of Professor Hay and Dr. Saunders by shooting at a horse's head, with the distances carefully measured. According to my experience, accidents with guns happen in the most inconceivable ways. I remember the case of a gentleman who was out shooting a year or two ago, and who met with an accident. He felt himself falling and flung the gun from him. Accidents happen in the most unexplainable ways, and the shot, when the gun goes off accidentally, enters the body, to my

261

Alfred John Monson.

Tom Speedy

knowledge, in the most unaccountable manner by the crown of the head, the back of the neck, or the sole of the foot. The last-mentioned case was one which came under my own personal knowledge. An Edinburgh gentleman let his gun fall, both barrels went off and one of the shots went through the sole of his foot horizontally. There was another man, whom I knew, who shot himself in the palm of his hand and the shot went up his arm. I did not see him just when it happened.

All that I have gathered in this case is not inconsistent with the wound having been caused accidentally by a gun in Mr. Hambrough's own hand. I think, however, it quite possible that Mr. Hambrough threw the gun from him, that it caught on something when it was falling, and that the occurrence might have been accidental.

Cross-examined by the SOLICITOR-GENERAL—My visit to Ardlamont was on 17th October. I was requested to go by Messrs. Davidson & Syme, the agents for the defence. I went for a special purpose. I brought back a birch branch, No. 148, together with No. 149, which I have since understood as having been shot at by way of experiment, and also No. 151.

That would rather suggest that you went to look for shot marks on the branches near the place where Hambrough was shot?—Well, no; these were not my instructions. I brought these productions back because I thought they would be of interest and to demonstrate that I had seen a number of pellet marks. I was at the place where the body had been, and I looked for shot marks, but I did not go there specially for shot marks. Of the specimens which I brought back, No. 148 was 17 yards from where I was told that the rowan tree had stood, and therefore south of the place where the body was said to have been. It was growing on the top of the bank, due south along the wall from the rowan tree. It was about my own height. No. 151 was 114 yards south of the rowan tree. I saw plenty more branches that I could not cut. I do not think that I took any measurements with regard to those near the rowan tree.

As the result of your visit, the only injury by shot to a tree near the rowan tree which you took note of was the one 17 yards south?—Yes; but I saw big trees with shot marks.

But you saw nothing in relation to the place where the body was lying to lead you to take measurements?—That is so; but I saw plenty trees marked. When I went back to Ardlamont on 2nd November I went to see and take note of trees with shot marks on them all over the wood. No. 155 was 52 yards distant from the rowan tree, and No. 152 was 172 yards off, and was on the top of the dyke. No. 152 and No. 155 could have no connection with each other.

Did any two of your specimens have any connection with each other?—Oh, no; they could not.

Evidence for Defence.

At the height of your own head, accessible to your hand if you had wished to take them, did you find twigs upon separate trees so injured as to indicate that they were the result of one shot?—I did not think of that; I should not like to swear dogmatically to that. I did not bring away any such specimens. Suppose I saw the branches of three trees, one behind the other, injured in a particular line by shot marks, it might be that the injuries were caused by one shot. If the shot marks were in a line that would be useful in determining the line of the shot.

If you put a tape along the line of the injury to the trees, would not that give you the line of shot?—If it was a straight line, of course. Supposing I had determined a line in that way by finding a series of trees injured in the same line, and I found a man lying dead near them, and by setting him up on end found that his head was in the same line, any inference that that shot was the true cause of death would depend upon whether the pellet marks were all newly done. If you got all the circumstances to suit it would be my belief that the shot which injured the trees was the shot which killed the man.

Assume that you had three trees, the one behind the other, with a shot through them at 6 or 7 feet from the ground, and a man 6 feet off found dead, and you stand him up, and his head is in a line with the shot, and assume that the wound through his head is horizontal and inflicted from behind, could it have happened by his falling with the gun in his hand?—Well, not having seen the trees, I am not disposed to answer that question as you have put it. Taking it as you have put it, I cannot suggest any result that could be produced by his falling. I do not know that I can suggest any method by which this result could be produced by a man not falling but letting his gun fall; I should not like to enter into that atmosphere of uncertainty.

You told us that you had great experience of shooting and of the direction of shot. Taking my conditions, could it happen by his falling himself and not letting his gun fall?—Well, I have seen people carrying their gun so carelessly that it is quite possible it might be done by falling, but I would hardly think it could happen except in the bushes. If the gun fell to the ground I would hardly expect that, if the man were standing, a horizontal wound on the same line as the marks on the trees beyond would be inflicted. The rowan tree was pointed out to me as the place where the body was found. There was one bush close by, and a great deal of willow in the wood. The undergrowth in the wood was thicker on the south-west side of where the body was lying than elsewhere; that is, into the wood a bit. Where the body was lying it was pretty clear, with no tree immediately near it.

In shooting horses I did not make any specific measurements as to distance. The spread of shot is precisely similar when you fire

Alfred John Monson.

at metal or paper or any other substance; it is not affected by the substance you fire at. A horse's head is not nearly so thick as the skull of a man; I have measured one before. I think that the bone of a horse's head is decidedly thinner than the skull at the back of a man's ear. The effect of the shot would differ according as the one was stronger or thinner, but there would be no difference in the breadth of the shot. When a shot is beginning to spread, that means that there are pellets getting away from the bulk of the charge. If I was firing past an object, not point-blank, but so as to give it the edge of the charge, the spreading pellets would go into the object, and the rest of the charge would go past.

Take the case of a shot fired at such a distance that it is beginning to spread when it reaches the object fired at, and at such an angle as to make the edge of the shot strike the head, would the pellets enter the head?—I do not believe that the outside pellets, assuming they were separated, would break the skull of the head. If you fired one pellet at a man's head 3 or 4 feet off it would glance off. With the ordinary force of the charge of a gun I suppose that it would indent the head. I do not think that it would do so at 9 feet. I should not like to say at what distance it would be safe to fire a pellet point-blank at a man's head with a full charge of powder so as not to make the pellet enter the head. It would be difficult to hit with one pellet, which might fly anywhere. The centre of a charge of shot has the greatest force. If I found a few pellets remaining in the head from a shot-charge fired at a comparatively near distance, that would indicate that the pellets which remain were part of the shot having least force; they would likely be the outside pellets, I should think, the centre pellets going on. I would not like to say that the whole charge struck the head, but I would certainly say that half of it did. Taking 9 feet as the distance, I do not think that more than half struck, for if that happened the stray pellets would have run to the very centre of the head.

Do you think the head was struck by the whole body of the charge at 4 feet?—I would not like to answer that, because the bone at the back of the head is so strong that it would make the shot glance off. Some of the pellets went into the head and stayed there, because they would strike the edge of the bone and get away round; some of the pellets would strike the sharp bone and not go in. My theory is that the great bulk of the charge struck the head, and only a few pellets remained. The reason why all those which struck the bone did not go into the head is that they glanced off.

By the LORD JUSTICE-CLERK—Whatever mass of the shot struck, that mass glanced off outwards again.

Cross-examination continued—If only part of the charge struck the head, the rest of the charge would go on its natural line. I assume the size of the wound in the bone caused by the direct

264

Evidence for Defence.

Tom Speedy

impact of the shot to be about the size of a half-crown, irrespective of stray pellets.

Re-examined by Mr. COMRIE THOMSON—I have seen this unfortunate man's skull. I noticed the size of the opening, and the fact that there had been a considerable amount of smashing, and also that there were openings in the fissures or sutures, both in the lower and upper parts of the head.

Do you think it possible that four pellets and nothing else striking the head could have produced all that?—Downright balderdash; it could never do it. But if the mass of the shot, either the whole or half of it, struck the head behind the right ear and deflected that would account for the condition in which the skull is; it would also account for four pellets, and no more, being found inside. I saw from the photographs that there was also a considerable flesh wound. The four pellets found inside the brain could not alone account for that. It would not be at all difficult to find three trees in that old plantation marked with shot on the trunks or in branches in a line with each other. I could go there, shut my eyes, and fire a shot and do it. So far as I could judge, all the trees were riddled with shot; in the centre of the wood you could not fire a shot without hitting a tree. Wood pigeons sometimes feed on the ground, and are very often shot when they are rising from the ground. Wood pigeons might be shot 3 or 4 feet from the ground. It is inaccurate to say that they are always shot up among the trees.

I made some experiments in order to see whether there was singeing with amberite powder fired from a short distance. I bought some human hair, and at 2 feet, and in the presence of others, I fired at it point-blank with amberite, and with different powders, but there was not a bit of singeing. My wife came out and took down her hair, and I fired a shot at 2 feet distance through her hair with a full cartridge of amberite powder, and it did not singe it; it did not even leave a smell in it.

The top of the dyke near where the accident happened is a likely place for a man looking for game to walk on; it is good enough walking, but one would require to walk carefully. Assuming that a man was standing with the rowan tree behind him, another tree 6 feet behind him, and another tree beyond, all the trees being in a line, if the shot hit the man's head, and did not enter, except to the extent of three or four pellets, I think it would deflect from the line of the trees. The extent of the deflection would depend upon the angle at which it was fired.

Re-cross-examined by the SOLICITOR-GENERAL—If part of the shot struck the man's head and was deflected, the other part of it would go straight on.

By the LORD JUSTICE-CLERK—I was shown the place where the body was said to be found. It was on the dyke, and it was there that Mr. Steven first saw it. I believe that Mr. Steven spoke about

Alfred John Monson.

Tom Speedy

another place on the other side of the dyke. Wood pigeon would be very likely to feed on the ground in a wood like that.

13. ARTHUR SEBRIGHT, examined by Mr. COMRIE THOMSON—I was cited as a witness for the Crown. I am a mortgage and insurance broker in London. Mr. Monson was introduced to me in the early part of this year by Captain King, the representative of the Royal Insurance Company. In January there was a meeting in my house, at which Monson and Cecil Hambrough were present. Both of them joined in making a proposition to me. It is not my business to enter into transactions with minors on the chance of getting a good thing out of them when they come of age. I told Mr. Hambrough and Mr. Monson that I would not go into any transaction with Cecil Hambrough unless he was separately advised. There were two propositions. One was that I should buy from the Eagle Insurance Company the life interest of Major Hambrough, and that I should execute a deed of trust and hold it on behalf of young Cecil Hambrough. There were two objects in that. One was that when Cecil Hambrough came of age he should join his father in cutting off the entail, and the provision out of the money so obtained should be given to Hambrough, senior, the rest, of course, going to Cecil Hambrough. In the event of Hambrough, senior, not agreeing to this, the terms not being arranged, it would have this effect, that it would give Cecil Hambrough an income to live upon when he came of age, whereas without that he would have none whatever. Being a minor, Cecil could not purchase, but I was to purchase on his behalf the life interest of the father, and new policies were to be issued on Cecil's life for £50,000. It was an absolutely necessary part of the scheme that Cecil's life should be insured. I discovered from what passed in connection with that that Monson was well aware that a minor could not assign a policy; I should say that he was as well aware of it as any man in England. The question was referred to frequently. The policy was to be taken out by Monson. I would like to explain that by the proposition that was offered me the income that he would have derived—that is, the difference between the premiums of the £50,000 policy and the old policy—would give him £1375 a year. The proposal was not carried out; it was, however, seriously entertained as a matter of business.

Cross-examined by the SOLICITOR-GENERAL—After the proposal was made to me I saw my solicitors about it, and they pointed out to me that if I went into this transaction I would have to lie out of the money that I was to find for a much longer period than I expected. The second reason was this, that my inducement for going into the transaction was that Cecil Hambrough came to me, and I told him I could not lend him money as a money-lending transaction. At that time I wanted a partner in my own business, and he was very anxious to put a certain amount of money into my business. On

266

Evidence for Defence.

Arthur Sebright

my instructions he took the advice of his solicitor on the subject—
Mr. Jones. Mr. Jones advised him that he would not be justified in
putting so large a sum as I wished for in my business, having regard
to the amount he had at his disposal. It was too large a proportion,
and that was one of the reasons. I think it was £30,000 originally,
and Mr. Jones told him that he ought not to put more than £10,000.
The business was mortgage and insurance broking. Cecil Hambrough
was to join me when he came of age, if his father should co-operate
with him in cutting off the entail. Cecil was very anxious to do
that. Mr. Monson was not always with Cecil when I saw him; I
think he was there two or three times. It was I who suggested the
£30,000, and I told Cecil to get independent advice on the subject.
He made inquiries, but I cannot tell you their scope. I showed him
books which showed the kind of business I was doing, but he did not
look at them very much, and that is the reason why I asked him to
have legal advice on the subject. Mr. Jones knew my business well.

And Cecil was referred to Mr. Jones, your own agent, to advise
him as to whether he should put money into the business?—Yes; he
temporarily ceased to be my agent in order that he might advise
Cecil. Monson did not advise that. I dealt with Cecil directly in
regard to the proposition. He came first of all simply to ask me to
buy the life interest. Mr. Monson brought him, and introduced him
to me. Any proposals that were made were made first of all by
Monson and afterwards by Cecil. I should not say that Cecil appeared
to be a thoroughly good business man. I think he understood what
his position was, and what his father's position was, but I should
not say that he had any knowledge, or experience, or skill to enable
him to know whether he should enter my business or not. I think
that Cecil was dealing more with me than Monson, and I do not
think that he took Monson's advice very much in the matter. He
had an inducement to enter my business, for he said, " If I do this,
you must make me an allowance and advance me certain moneys I
want now." When Monson and Cecil came to me they did not appear
to be very hard up for ready money; they seemed to be able to go
about in cabs and to stay at hotels. I should say that Cecil was most
hard up. Altogether I saw him about four or five times. That was
in the end of December or the first week of January. I broke off the
negotiations. They said that they came to me because Captain King,
of the Royal Insurance Company, had told them of me. I cannot
say that they told me they had been trying in other quarters before
they came to me. They did not tell me they had been negotiating
before 1892 to manage this through Mr. Carter, and that he had
abandoned it. I should think the thing was before me about a
month, and then I abandoned it. Cecil Hambrough had said that if
I would allow him £20 a month and lend him £250 he would be
prepared to go into partnership with me. This request was made to
me with the knowledge and approval of Monson.

Alfred John Monson.

Arthur Sebright

Did you receive this letter?—"Hotel Metropole, London, January 11, 1893.—My dear Sebright,—I have this day received an advance from you of £300, which I promise to repay you when I come of age. It is also agreed between us that you shall continue to allow me £20 a month till I attain my majority, which money I also agree to repay you at that time. In consideration of your doing this for me, I promise to become partner with you in your business as financial agent and bill discounter, and to put £100,000 into the business, you paying me 10 per cent. per annum upon all money used. I am fully aware you could not recover any money from me by action at law, but the only security I can offer you is my word of honour as a gentleman that I will carry out the terms of this letter.—Yours sincerely, D. W. C. Hambrough." I never received that letter from Cecil Hambrough; I have never seen it before. I do not think that at that time Monson could have lent Cecil the money. I gave him the first month's money, £20; I got no receipt from him. I really cannot say in whose handwriting that letter is. I cannot say if it is from Major Hambrough, because I am not sure if I ever had a letter from him in my life. [Shown No. 232.] That is an acknowledgment, dated 10th January, 1893, as follows:—" I hereby acknowledge having received this day £20 from Mr. A. A. Sebright, on account of £300 to be lent by him to me." I think this is a mistake; that money was on account of his month's allowance. Cecil never received an advance of £300 from me. He did not agree to put £100,000 into my business. I can give no explanation of the letter of 11th January, 1893. The only thing I can suggest is that they had written this letter beforehand, before they got the money, and had it ready as a copy of the letter they would write when they got the money.

By the LORD JUSTICE-CLERK—It might be an adjustment of the terms in which a receipt was to be given. The letter is in the same writing as the receipt. The suggestion of the partnership came from me.

Was that not a curious suggestion to make to a lad of twenty whom you had never seen before?—They wanted me to lend money to Cecil Hambrough, but I did not want to go into any lending transaction with a lad like that, and therefore I told him I would not lend him money as a money-lender, but that I would do so as a friend. I would take no receipt from him, but gave the money to him on his word of honour that if he liked he was to enter into a business arrangement with me when he came of age. It was the only way in which I could go into the transaction, but it was not a thing I had ever done before. The idea was that I was to lend money to Cecil, £300 down and £20 a month, and that he was to consider whether when he came of age he was to enter the business and put £100,000 into it.

268

Evidence for Defence.

14. EDWARD LANG, examined by Mr. COMRIE THOMSON—I am sole partner of the firm of Joseph Lang & Son, gunmakers, 10 Pall Mall, London. I was introduced to Monson early in this year by a customer. Monson introduced Lieutenant Hambrough on 19th April. I took his order for a rook rifle. On that occasion I put a gun into his hand. He informed me he had not been in the habit of using hammerless guns. I showed him how he was to put the " safety " forward before he took a shot, and after getting the gun full-cock he put it up opposite my foreman and snapped it. After he left the shop I remarked to my foreman, " Did you ever see a fellow handle a gun in that way before? He will shoot himself or some of his friends."

Cross-examined by the SOLICITOR-GENERAL—There was more risk to my assistant than to Hambrough himself. It was a hammerless gun, and he was trying the fit of it in the line of my assistant; he handled the gun generally carelessly. He said he had not been accustomed to hammerless guns. He was experimenting with a gun the action of which he was not familiar with. He told me it was a gun with hammers he was accustomed to. I gathered he had no gun of his own. He gave me an order for a gun to cost £90. He did not get it, because I was not satisfied with his reference. He referred to Mr. Monson. I supplied him with fishing tackle to the amount of £18, but that was before I had ascertained that the £90 would be a rather dangerously large amount. I have not received payment for the fishing tackle.

Re-examined by Mr. COMRIE THOMSON—Besides taking up the gun and levelling it at my manager, his general mode of handling the gun was dangerous.

By the LORD JUSTICE-CLERK—I consider it dangerous to snap any gun, loaded or unloaded. In my shop guns are very often put up to the shoulder, but they are not snapped.

Re-examination continued—Hambrough might have known that opening the lever cocked the gun, but I do not think he knew that so slight a touch of the trigger would pull it off; but it did, and snapped.

The Court adjourned.

Ninth Day—Thursday, 21st December, 1893.

15. GEORGE G. ANDRE, examined by Mr. COMRIE THOMSON—I am manager of the Clyde Mills Company, Sandbank, Argyllshire. I am a Fellow of the Geological Society of London and a member of the Institution of Civil Engineers. For nearly twenty years I have been connected with the firm of Curtis & Harvey. The gunpowder manufactured at the Clyde Mills is amberite powder. We manufacture no other kind. We are the sole patentees of amberite. The primary object sought to be obtained by amberite is the absence of smoke. It gives slightly less smoke than Schultze. After shooting with amberite the shot is clean and dry inside, and the quantity of solid products is very small. Fired in the dark, a flame is seen about an inch from the muzzle. The whole charge is converted into gases. I have made experiments with amberite with a 12-bore cylinder gun at various distances. I also fired two shots with ordinary black powder. I fired at a moderately thin cardboard. The cardboard was set at a right angle. At any other angle the portion of the card struck by the shot would be larger. At a distance of 1 foot from the muzzle of the gun the diameter of the hole made was $\frac{7}{8}$ inch to $\frac{3}{4}$ inch. It was clean cut. At 2 feet 6 inches the diameter was $1\frac{1}{4}$ inches to $1\frac{3}{8}$ inches, and the edges were still fairly clean. At 5 feet the diameter was $1\frac{1}{2}$ inches to $1\frac{3}{4}$ inches. At that distance it was very ragged, and the pellet perforations began to appear outside. At 7 feet, the hole made in the cardboard was very irregular. It was more torn at the edges, and the pellet perforations were a good deal more scattered. Then at 10 feet it was very irregular in form. The hole then gets less in area. The scattered pellets scatter much wider. At about 12 feet there begin to be more separate perforations without a central hole. In these experiments I found that the black powder, so far as the scatter was concerned, produced the same results as amberite. At a distance of 5 feet there was no discoloration with amberite. At a distance of 2 feet 6 inches I found a slight discoloration on the white surface of the card, but no singeing. At the distance of 1 foot I found also a slight discoloration. At that distance black powder generally blackens, but with amberite at that distance there is a slight brown discoloration— not singeing. I made another set of experiments with flannel to ascertain whether there was really singeing or not. The flannel represented a surface covered with hair. In these experiments I found a difference between amberite and black powder in the matter

270

Evidence for Defence.

G. G. Andre

of discoloration, which was greater than when a smooth card was used, because the texture of the flannel retains the black powder and shows more blackening. There was the same difference with amberite, but much less in degree. I also made experiments with rabbit skins with the furry side out. There is no singeing at all from a flash from a gun upon flannel or rabbit skins with amberite, but there is much singeing with black powder at a distance of 1 foot. At a distance of 6 inches there is no singeing of human hair with amberite.

The distance a wad will travel depends upon the air. If you are under cover, and it is calm, the greatest distance a heavy wad travels is 20 yards. A wad over a shot might be driven into a wound at close quarters if it struck full on. I should not expect to find the thick wad in a wound caused by a gun fired at 9 feet, but this would depend a good deal upon the nature of the wound.

It is quite possible that a man 6 feet high might accidentally shoot himself at a distance of nearly 6 feet, inflicting a wound in the head from behind forwards. In the case of a novice, who is very apt to carry a gun carelessly, he might carry it in a position in which an accident might very well happen. Suppose he were carrying it 2 or 3 inches from the hammer, and were to catch his foot in a rut or in a little hole, and fall forwards, in all probability he would drop the gun. He would then fall forward, and instinctively raise his head, as every one does when falling, to prevent his face from striking the ground. In that position the head would be more or less erect, and with the gun he might be shot from behind forward horizontally. The gun might be made to go off by coming in contact with the ground, or by the shock of the fall. This is especially the case where there is no rebounding lock in the gun. That supposition commends itself to my mind as a reasonable possibility.

Cross-examined by the SOLICITOR-GENERAL—In the case which I have supposed the butt of the gun when it went off would be on the ground, more or less flat, according to the nature of the ground. I also assume that the man would be lying on the ground when he was shot. In such a case I should expect the line of the shot to be nearly parallel with the surface of the ground—not very high from the ground, and I should expect to find that the shot had gone into the root of some adjacent tree. The case which I have mentioned appears to me to be the most probable way in which a man could be shot from behind. My illustration would not apply to a case where there were the following conditions to be dealt with :—A distinctly marked line, and shot marks through trees at about 5 or 6 feet from the ground, extending onwards and rising to about 7 feet. Accepting as an assumption that the shot which killed the man injured the tree in the line mentioned, at a point 6 feet from the ground at the nearest tree, rising to about 7 feet on the trees beyond, and passing through the head almost horizontally but slightly upward, I cannot

271

Alfred John Monson.

G. G. Andre

suggest any mode in which that could have occurred as an accident. Of course, in the case I have assumed the line of shot would be nearer the surface of the ground.

Accepting my conditions, can you, as a man of skill, suggest any mode by which death could have been produced by an accident to the man from a gun carried by himself?—I understand the conditions you have given me; I am quite sure that I considered them before I came here, and I know their importance with reference to this inquiry. As a result of my inquiry, I have not discovered any method by which the conditions which you have put before me could be produced accidentally. It is not impossible; accidents have happened in so many unsuspected ways.

But may I take it that you are a man of large experience in these matters, and that it surpasses your ingenuity to suggest any mode by which that could be produced?—Yes. The chances are against the thick wad travelling in a straight line for 9 feet; it might do so, but it is very erratic. I know that from many experiments. It is impossible to say how far a wad would travel in a straight line. It is not likely to go in a straight line at all, because the wads are left behind, and do not travel so far as the shot, and the resistance of the air very soon deflects them. No one can say with precision that when a wad is propelled out of the gun it necessarily deviates from the straight line, but it is not likely that it would travel 9 feet in a straight line. My experience shows that it would deviate long before that. One day I was firing into a door, only one-half of which was shut. I stood back, with the muzzle of the gun about 2 feet away from the door, and fired past the closed half of the door at a distance of 6 inches. One of the wads stuck on the door. I repeated the experiment about a hundred times, and I succeeded in putting nearly a dozen wads into that door. That was at a distance of 2 feet. The result depends upon many varied conditions. I do not think that it would much depend upon the gun and the way in which the cartridge is built. The extent to which a wad would travel in the line of the shot depends on the friction of the air. So long as a wad continues flat it will go in a straight line, but when it turns on one side it flies away. There are certain conditions connected with the precise line a wad takes with which I do not profess to be acquainted.

As regards the spreading of a charge, the shot leaves the gun in the form of a cylinder, but it immediately assumes a spherical form, and from that moment begins to expand. It is in the act of spreading all the way. At the distance of about 4 feet you get pellets detached from the mass, and if pellets are found detached from the mass, then you know that the shot has been fired at least 4 feet off.

With regard to the character of the wound produced, it depends very much upon whether the shot was straight on or oblique, and also whether the thing struck received the whole charge

272

Evidence for Defence.

or only a part of the passing charge. In the case of a grazing shot, if half the charge struck, it would make a wound of the same size probably as the whole. In that case you have the whole diameter of the charge.

Is it your opinion that a shot which nearly misses, but hits, produces the same effect as a shot straight on?—Oh no.

Well, that is what I want to know. Take the case where the whole body of the shot takes effect, and another case where a shot nearly misses, and only a small part of it strikes, would the effect in the two cases be practically the same?—No.

Would not the effect of the passing shot, when it takes effect only to a small extent, be much less than where it received the whole charge?—Yes. Up to 5 feet I found change of colour perceptible to the eye with black powder. In the case of amberite I found such change up to 3 feet. I did not experiment with Schultze.

Re-examined by Mr. COMRIE THOMSON—It is quite possible that the whole body of the pellets might hit a hard bone behind the ear at such an angle as to smash it to some extent, and then glance off.

16. PHILIP R. DAY, examined by Mr. COMRIE THOMSON—I am Mrs. Monson's brother, and live at 3 Bath Street, Dewsbury. I knew the late Lieutenant Hambrough very well, and went out shooting with him on several occasions when he was residing at Riseley Hall. That was in the autumn of 1891—October, November, and December. I have noticed the way in which he carried his gun. He generally carried it at full-cock when loaded, even when going through fences and plantations. I have remarked this to various people on several occasions. It struck me as peculiar. It made me uncomfortable and diffident about going out with him. I knew Mr. Walters, and I have seen him when in company with Lieutenant Hambrough. Mr. Walters did not shoot, but he spoke to Lieutenant Hambrough about his carelessness. On one occasion Hambrough accidentally shot a fox-terrier of mine.

Cross-examined by the SOLICITOR-GENERAL—In the autumn of 1891 I was out shooting with Mr. Hambrough several times at Riseley. I never shot with him after that.

17. JOHN BASIL WALTERS, examined by Mr. COMRIE THOMSON —I am a medical student. I remember in the autumn of 1891 being at Riseley Hall with Mr. Monson and Cecil Hambrough. Day, the last witness, was also there, and I heard him say that Hambrough was careless in handling his gun, and that he thought there would be an accident some day if he were not spoken to.

18. WILLIAM DONALD, examined by Mr. COMRIE THOMSON—I am a partner of the firm of Hanna, Donald & Wilson, engineers and boatbuilders, Paisley. My father was examined here a few days ago. The launch " Alert," was sold under the conditions

T

Alfred John Monson.

already stated. I remember being on the South-Western steamer coming up from the Kyles of Bute, along with my father, and meeting Hambrough. I had a conversation with Hambrough about an accident he had had with a rook rifle he was carrying. He showed it to me. He said he had been holding the gun in his usual way on the previous night, that the lock snapped, and the gun went off past the side of his head. He showed me how it was done. I know something of shooting, but I am not an expert. I considered the way in which Hambrough carried his gun to be very dangerous.

Cross-examined by the SOLICITOR-GENERAL—Hambrough's hand, when he showed me how he carried the gun at the time of its accidental discharge, was 12 inches from the muzzle, and the butt was near the ground. He said that the shot went past his head.

19. ROBERT HANNA DONALD, examined by Mr. COMRIE THOMSON —I am a partner of Messrs. Hanna, Donald & Wilson, engineers and boatbuilders, Paisley. I was preparing to deliver the launch, the " Alert," at Ardlamont on 10th August when I heard of Hambrough's death. In consequence of that I did not get up steam. I was on the road when I heard the news; I met Monson between Kames and Ardlamont, and he told me that he was going to meet the steamer from Glasgow to break the news to his wife. He came back to my house after the steamer came in, and said he had not yet broken the news. He hurried on to Ardlamont, and asked me to follow him on foot. I did so, and met him in the dining-room at Ardlamont. He was very excited and greatly distressed about the accident.

Mr. Monson once told me that they were trying to get Hambrough's life insured for £50,000, but I cannot recollect whether that was before the accident or not. He said they had been trying to effect an insurance for £50,000 to enable them to buy Ardlamont and to buy the life interest of Major Hambrough and allow him so much a year, but that Major Hambrough had refused. When he made the explanation I expressed surprise at the largeness of the sum.

I remember about 5th August being on board the yacht along with him at the Burnt Islands, in the Kyles. Hambrough was carrying an ordinary shot gun—12-bore, I think. We were shooting at herons, and I noticed him address himself and fire at a heron. The gun was half-cock, and he put it up to his shoulder and pulled the trigger. The gun did not go off, and he brought the gun down again and cocked it and fired it, but the bird was too far away, and he missed it. He told me he had been shooting wild fowl at Ardlamont on the previous day, and that he had fallen on the stock of his gun and shattered it, but that it did not go off. When I was shooting with him at the Burnt Islands I observed

Evidence for Defence.

that he carried his gun by the barrel with his right hand, and I thought it was dangerous at the time. The danger would be increased if the ground on which he was walking in that position was uneven or slippery. I remember being out with Hambrough fishing with a splash net, and I have landed him two or three times from the yacht at Ardlamont Bay. He conducted himself in a small boat in an awkward way. I checked him several times for not keeping his seat, and to prevent him from capsizing. I also noticed that he was careless in getting in and out of the small boat; he stepped on the seats or gunwale of the boat. I was glad to get rid of him.

Cross-examined by the SOLICITOR-GENERAL—As near as I can remember, the conversation about the insurance was on the night of the 10th, after the death. The amount Mr. Monson spoke about was £50,000. He told me that the insurance had not been effected, and that Major Hambrough would have nothing to do with it. It was in answer to a direct question from me whether Hambrough was insured that Monson told me that £50,000 had been proposed, but had not been effected. He did not tell me that he had effected an insurance for £20,000. It was my brother and I combined who sold the yacht to Mr. Monson. That was about 22nd July. The yacht was lying at Kames from that time till the death. The purchaser was Mr. Monson, on behalf of Mr. Hambrough. The price was £1200, and it was settled on 22nd July that the price was to be paid on 10th August. I did not go to Ardlamont on the 10th for the purpose of being paid, but in order to hear about the sad occurrence. Mr. Monson was at Ardlamont till 30th August. I applied for payment between 10th and 30th August, but did not get it.

Why?—Monson said that would be arranged when the insurance——. He said young Hambrough had left enough money to satisfy all his debts.

The price was due on the 10th. I asked you why you did not get the price, and in your answer you stopped in the middle of a sentence which contained the word " insurance "; would you be kind enough to complete that sentence?—A week or eight days after the death we were told that Mr. Hambrough was insured. My brother told me of it; Monson had told him that there was enough left to pay all Hambrough's creditors in full.

You mean in consequence of the insurance?—Well, I would understand so. My brother and I are partners. There was no transaction between Monson and our firm except about the yacht; we were not creditors to Monson and Hambrough except for the price of the yacht. My brother met Monson going down to the steamer, and Monson showed him a policy he had just effected in New York.

What was your understanding with regard to the insurance and the creditors being paid in full?—I understood on the night of the

Alfred John Monson.

10th, from what Mr. Monson told me, that young Hambrough had left as much money as would pay his creditors, but that there would be very little over. It was only through my brother that I heard about the insurance. We twice applied for payment of the yacht unsuccessfully. We have not been paid yet. I have seen Mr. Hambrough carrying his gun; his hand grasped it about the middle of the barrel. He held the gun vertically, straight up, and if it had gone off in that position the shot would have gone up in the air.

Re-examined by Mr. COMRIE THOMSON—Monson said that Hambrough had left enough money to pay his creditors, but whether it was to come from the next-of-kin or elsewhere I did not know. We did not deliver the yacht; we still have it.

20. GEORGE HENRY TILLARD, examined by Mr. COMRIE THOMSON—I am a retired colonel of the Madras Staff Corps and live at Wayside, Harrow. It was suggested to me by a former brother-officer, Colonel Kilgour, that it was my duty to give information as to an experience I had in connection with a shooting accident. I was given to understand that it was maintained by the prosecution that Lieut. Hambrough could not have shot himself by accident, as in that case the direction of the shot would have been more upwards and not so horizontal. I was twenty-eight years in India. I had a gun accident in March, 1871. I was just starting out for snipe shooting, and was carrying a small double-barrelled covert gun. It was at half-cock. I turned round to call my servant, who was loitering behind. As I turned round my foot slipped on some rocks I was walking over, and I fell backwards. I have no recollection of what happened after that for some minutes. My last sensation was feeling myself going backward. On coming to myself I found my servant standing at the same place where he was before, and called for him to assist me. I got back to my tent about five minutes afterwards, and found both barrels of the gun had gone off. The gunshot blew away a portion of my ear, and dug a trench in behind the ear in a horizontal direction. The shot scraped the periosteum of the skull. It was a glancing shot through the flap of the ear, furrowing the flesh and scraping the bone, but no part of the shot entered the skull. The shot came from the front. That was my idea. The doctor said so. The direction of the shot was as nearly as possible horizontal. I cannot say how I was carrying my gun.

Cross-examined by the SOLICITOR-GENERAL—I cannot say how the gun went off. The shot went past the ear, cutting off the flap of the ear, and scraping the periosteum.

I suppose it is a very simple matter for a man to fall forward on his gun and shoot himself from the front backwards?—I cannot understand it. I fell backwards, not forwards. My eyebrows and eyelashes were scorched—the eyebrows slightly. My ear was

Evidence for Defence.

G. H. Tillard

blackened, and the blackening lasted two months. It was not such a blackening as could be washed off with soap and water.

Re-examined by Mr. COMRIE THOMSON—It was ordinary black powder, and there were some grains of powder in my head.

21. JOHN WILLIAM BRODIE INNES, examined by Mr. COMRIE THOMSON—I am a member of the English and Scottish bars. I was called to the English bar in 1875 and to the Scottish bar in 1888. I have been in practice at the English bar as a conveyancer. It has been explained to me that there was a policy on the life of Cecil Hambrough for £20,000, and I have seen the letter under his own hand to the manager of that company at Glasgow. Then there is another letter to Mrs. Monson, dated 7th August, 1893. It says— " If you will pay the premiums on the two policies of assurance on my life of £10,000 each with the Mutual Insurance Company of New York, I am willing that you should hold the policies as security for all moneys due to you from me, and as security against all liabilities incurred by you on my behalf; and in the event of my death occurring before the repayment of these moneys you will be sole beneficiary of these policies, and I have given notice to the Mutual Insurance Company of New York that you are the person to whom the insurance is payable, and they have accepted my notice.—Yours sincerely (signed) W. D. C. Hambrough."

The assignment of the mandate to deliver is not a valid document, as it was written by a minor; it is voluntary and to the infant's detriment. Premiums cannot be recovered against an infant, and the covenant to pay is no consideration at all. The second letter would not be a valid will, as in England they have nothing like a Scots law holograph will. It is invalid in respect that it is deficient in the solemnities of execution and as being the will of a minor. A minor cannot make a will by English law.

Cross-examined by the SOLICITOR-GENERAL—The first letter is dated 7th August, and is signed by Cecil Hambrough; it intimates to the insurance company that the policies had been assigned. My evidence relates to the legal effect of the assignation. I can suggest no object whatever in making such an assignation.

Except that the person who made it believed it to be effective?— Oh, there might be a great many other possible objects. For instance, it might be an honourable understanding as to what you would do when you came of age, but I am not here to suggest possibilities. · I cannot suggest any object in writing that letter to the insurance company but that the writer thought it would be effectual. I cannot explain why Cecil Hambrough wrote that letter. The second letter is a very unusual document; I have never seen anything like it before. In the first place, it is not an assignation. I do not think it would be a valid assignation even if it were made by a person of full age. The first half of it seems to me to be inconsistent with

277

Alfred John Monson.

J. W. B. Innes

the second half; and the whole document, being written by a minor, would be void by English law. I cannot put any interpretation upon it at all; I know that it is void by English law, and that people often attempt to do things that are void. Interpreting it as an English lawyer, I do not think that it bears to have the intention to assign. It says—"I am willing that you should hold the policies as security for all moneys due to you from me," and I think these words would not amount to even an intention to assign. I do not see anything to connect the two documents. I do not think that their both being signed by the same man entitles them to be read together, unless there was something actually to connect them. Assuming that they refer to the same policy, there are cases, I think, which tend against it being legitimate by English law to read them together in order to get at their meaning.

In the second half of the second letter he says—"And in the event of my death occurring before the repayment of these moneys, you will be sole beneficiary of these policies, and I have given notice to the Mutual Insurance Company of New York that you are the person to whom the insurance is payable, and they have accepted my notice." How would you interpret these words as to their intention? I do not speak of their legal effect?—That would be a question not for an English counsel, but for an English jury; I might perhaps advise a client which view the jury would probably take, but that would not be as a lawyer. According to English law, the meaning of the document falls to be ascertained by legal construction. According to the rules of English interpretation the document is absolutely void. In my view the two halves of it are inconsistent with each other; and there is one rule of English law applicable to wills, that when you find two halves or two clauses of a will inconsistent with each other you take the latter one. I do not think that it is plain from looking at that document that the person who constructed it was not acquainted with the English law applicable to such a matter. He constructed a document which, as I think, is ineffectual in English law.

Would that imply that he understood the law?—I do not think that it implies ignorance. Minors very frequently make presents or make bargains, but it does not follow that they do not know that these are void legally. I do not suggest that he meant it to be ineffectual.

If he meant it to be effectual, and it is not, does that not show that he did not know the law?—I think not.

Re-examined by Mr. COMRIE THOMSON—If a minor executed the document the law of England would regulate it. That document would not be made effectual if the consent of the legal guardian was obtained to it. Nothing could make it effectual. Suppose he survived majority and adopted it, it would need a fresh consideration.

22. JOHN BLAIR, examined by Mr. COMRIE THOMSON—I am a Writer

Evidence for Defence.

John Blair

to the Signet and a partner of the firm of Davidson & Syme. My firm were retained by the Hon. Mrs. Monson, the mother of the prisoner, to conduct the defence. I first saw the prisoner on 25th or 26th August last at Ardlamont. He communicated to me his desires with reference to the man Scott. He said he was very anxious that Scott should be found, and he told me he had sent an advertisement to the *Glasgow Herald*, which advertisement, however, was not inserted. He asked me to advertise widely for Scott, and I did so in these terms —" Edward Scott, engineer, who was at Ardlamont, Argyllshire, on 9th and 10th August, 1893, is urgently requested to communicate with Messrs. Davidson & Syme, Writers to the Signet, 22 Castle Street, Edinburgh."

That advertisement appeared in three issues of each of the following newspapers :—The *Montreal Herald*, the *Toronto Globe*, the *New York Herald*, the *Boston Herald*, the *Chicago Tribune*, the *San Francisco Chronicle*, the *Charleston News*, the *New Orleans Picayune*, the London *Times*, the London *Daily Telegraph*, the *Shipping Gazette*, the *Liverpool Mercury*, the *Hull Morning News*, the *Newcastle Chronicle*, the *Bristol Times*, the Dublin *Irish Times*, the Edinburgh *Scotsman*, the *Glasgow Herald*, *Glasgow Daily Mail*, the *Dundee Advertiser*, the *Aberdeen Free Press*, and the Edinburgh *Scottish Leader*. I produce copies of the newspapers. It occurred to me to insert the advertisement in Australian papers, but I thought there was no chance of getting a reply in time. I got two replies—one anonymous, the other from a lady in New Orleans. One referred to a person who was not the person wanted. The other one I did not think it worth while to pay any attention to. I also applied to the father and brother of Davis, because it had been suggested by the Crown that Davis was Scott. I had the brother here. I cited the father, but I got a letter, and afterwards a telegram, that he was in bed ill and could not come. I have faithfully carried out the instruction to do my best to find Scott.

The usual way in which a man having only a life interest borrows money is by means of insurance policies. As the only security that he can find may terminate at any moment, he insures his life and assigns the policy on his life interest. That is constantly done, and is a transaction familiar to the most respectable insurance companies. The proposal spoken to by the witness Carter to insure the son's life and the son's life interest commends itself to me also as a perfectly reasonable one for an insurance company to go into; that is, supposing that the father's life interest, as well as the son's, is validly assigned.

Cross-examined by the Solicitor-General—I never went to 35 Sutherland Street. I sent for George Sweeney to come to me. The precognitions for the defence were under my care. One of my clerks went to 35 Sutherland Street to find out what could be found out about Scott. I saw Mr. Sweeney, senior, myself. I saw him about

Alfred John Monson.

three weeks ago. He gave me the same information as came out from his son in the witness-box. His son Edward was in bad health, and he thought it was likely he had gone abroad again. I did not search for a certain well-known engineer of the name of Scott in Greenock. I think that if there had been a well-known engineer of that name in Greenock I should have known him. Mr. Monson authorised me to endeavour to find Scott. No one of that name turned up in answer to the advertisements.

I see by a holograph writing by Mr. Monson, dated 22nd August, he said—" I am informed that Edward Scott started business as an engineer in Glasgow, and that he failed. That he was afterwards working in connection with yachts, and was well known in Greenock.'' When, if ever, was there any communication made to you with the view of your making a search?—I had a conversation with Monson. It could not have been at the date of the letter referred to, for the first time I saw Monson was on 25th August. I had no communication with him before that letter, if the date of the letter be 22nd August. He told me he knew very little about Scott.

You said that you assented generally to what Mr. Carter had said about the subject of insurance. Did you hear him say that all the time he was negotiating as Monson's agent for the purchase of Major Hambrough's life interest it was no part of the scheme that Cecil should be insured?—That was the scheme Mr. Carter was dealing with, but I thought the question referred to was a later proposal for insuring Cecil's life. The proposals for insurance on Cecil's life were solely in connection with the purchase of the life interest of his father.

Re-examined by Mr. COMRIE THOMSON—I knew of a Scott, a shipbuilder in Greenock. I do not think his name was Edward, but he had a brother of that name. I was satisfied that he could not be the man who was at Ardlamont.

This concluded the evidence for the defence.

Speech for the Crown.

The SOLICITOR-GENERAL then addressed the jury as follows:—Gentlemen of the jury, this prolonged and important trial has now reached the stage in which it becomes my duty to address you on behalf of the prosecution, and, after the evidence you have heard in the course of the case, I have no alternative in the discharge of my duty except to ask you to find a verdict of guilty against the prisoner on both charges in the indictment. In the indictment he is charged, first, with an attempt to murder Lieutenant Hambrough late on the night of the 9th or early on the morning of the 10th August by drowning, and, secondly, he is charged with murdering Lieutenant Ham-

The Solicitor=General (Asher).

Speech for the Crown.

Solicitor-General

brough on the morning of the 10th by shooting.   Gentlemen, it would be difficult to exaggerate the gravity, even the atrocity, of these crimes.   Lieutenant Hambrough had been living in the house of Mr. Monson, under his protection, and subject to his care, and the crimes charged against him, if they were committed, were committed at a time when he was continuing to express warm, even affectionate friendship for this young lad.   Under these circumstances it is undoubtedly necessary that evidence of a convincing character should be put before you, before you can find those charges proved.   The prisoner is quite entitled to say that he has no duty in the matter whatever, that the burden of proving the charges made against him rests upon the Crown, and that unless the Crown has proved these charges against him, he is entitled to be acquitted. Gentlemen, in telling you that I consider it my duty to ask you to find a verdict of guilty, I accept the full burden, the full duty, of establishing before you, from the evidence which has been led, that the charges in this indictment are both established, and, gentlemen, they must be established exclusively by the evidence which has been led in this Court.   In consequence of one of the questions put in cross-examination by my learned friend, some reference appeared to impressions or rumours outside of this Court.   I need scarcely tell you that such impressions or rumours must be put aside.   The prisoner must be tried by the evidence proved in this Court, and on nothing else, and the ground upon which I am to ask this verdict at your hands will rest on testimony which has been adduced before you.

You will observe that no statement has been made to you on the part either of the prosecution or of the defence up to the present time, as, by the humane arrangement of our procedure in criminal trials, no statement is made to the jury at all on either side until the whole evidence has been led.   I daresay you cannot but have felt that in a case of this magnitude, with so many details involved in it, it would have been for your convenience if you had had some preliminary statement which would have formed a guide to you in the due appreciation of the various points in the evidence put before you.   But that was against our established procedure, and no such statement can legitimately be made.   But I am sure you will appreciate what my statement is when I say, looking to the length of the case, its magnitude, and its importance, the mass of details which were involved in it, that it becomes all the more necessary now at this stage that I should give you a clear, concise account of the various stages of the case; and the facts, proved in evidence, which I am to submit to you will form a complete chain, establishing link by link the connection of the prisoner with both of the grave crimes with which he is charged.   I need scarcely tell you, gentlemen, that I appear here solely in my official capacity.   I represent the interests only of public justice.   It is my duty to put fully before you every fact in the case.   It will be my effort not to press one fact too far, not to press

Alfred John Monson.

unduly upon the wretched man who now sits at the bar; and it is a great satisfaction to me to feel that if I, through inadvertence, should by any possibility press any point of the case one iota beyond its legitimate sphere, the great capacity of my learned friend who is to follow me will not fail to put right any such mistake.

Now, gentlemen, I have said to you that the prisoner is charged with two crimes. I shall have to ask your attention, I am afraid, in great detail to the circumstances connected with both, but I think it will be convenient for you, before I approach these details, that I should explain to you those other portions of the case which have a very close bearing upon it, but which precede in point of time the two crimes which are charged, and which bring clearly before you the precise circumstances under which the accused and Cecil Hambrough were related at the time when this tragic event occurred.

You are aware from evidence which has been submitted to you that Cecil Hambrough was the eldest son of Major Hambrough. You are also aware that Major Hambrough was what is termed in England a life tenant—an heir of entail as we would call it in Scotland—of large estates known as the Hambrough estates, estates the precise rental of which does not enter very closely into the present case, but which undoubtedly requires to be taken note of in reference to some portions of it; and, accordingly, it was proved before you that the rental of the Hambrough estates was something like a little under £4000 a year, and that Major Hambrough had also a prospective interest in certain Pipewell estates dependent upon his surviving his uncle Oscar, and Oscar dying without leaving any children. Cecil Hambrough was in this position, that, being the eldest son of his father, if he survived his father he became tenant in tail of these estates. And during his father's life he might, after coming of age, with the consent of his father, do what was termed " barring the entail "—that is to say, get rid of the entail and convert the estates into fee simple. If he survived his father, then, even without having procured his father's consent, he would be in a position to bar the entail alone. Major Hambrough had undoubtedly in the year 1890 got into an extremely impecunious condition. In 1885 he had mortgaged his life interest with the Eagle Insurance Company for a sum something like £37,000, and by 1890, as he had failed to pay the interest upon his mortgage, the Eagle Company had foreclosed the mortgage, which, in popular language, means that they had taken the necessary steps to make themselves the absolute owners of Major Hambrough's life interest in the Hambrough estates.

In these circumstances, Major Hambrough appears to have gone to a person you saw in the witness-box of the name of Tottenham, a gentleman who flits across the stage of this extraordinary drama at several points, a gentleman of a somewhat variegated career. He told us he was thirty-three years of age, and he had during that comparatively short period of life been a lieutenant in the 11th Hussars,

Speech for the Crown.

served in the Turkish army under Baker Pasha, served in the Greek insurrection, and now finally developed into a financial agent in London, on what capital we do not know. And this gentleman, having in vain endeavoured to finance Major Hambrough and to effect a rearrangement of the foreclosed mortgage on the Hambrough estates, appears to have been in such relationship with Mr. Monson that he introduced Monson to Major Hambrough in the capacity of an army tutor. Gentlemen, that disastrous introduction took place in the autumn of 1890. Major Hambrough told you that the arrangement was made that Cecil Hambrough was to reside with Mr. Monson, who was to be his tutor, and the rate of remuneration was to be at £300 a year, to be paid at such time as Major Hambrough's finances became rearranged sufficiently to admit of his having the means to make that payment. But, gentlemen, in addition to that, Mr. Monson appears to have taken up the scheme which Tottenham had been unable to carry into effect, the purchase of the life interest of Major Hambrough from the Eagle Insurance Company. I think it must have struck you in watching the evidence in the case that Mr. Monson figures much more largely in this case as a financial agent than as an army tutor. Mr. Monson had had full opportunity of placing any evidence his advisers thought proper before you. We have had startlingly little information with regard to these phases of his life, which it might be suggested were connected with the occupation of an army tutor. Testimonials were presented to Major Hambrough. Where are the gentlemen who gave the testimonials? Where are the pupils? Where are the names of the pupils who have had the benefit of his tuition? We have had glimpses of Monson's life, in certain spheres of social life and in certain spheres of London life. These are, I should hope, rarely, if ever, closely associated with the profession of tutor to the young, and beyond such instances as have come out here and there in the course of the evidence we have no detailed information on the subject, and therefore I feel myself bound to record that, in so far as we have acquaintance with the history of the prisoner, he discloses much more of the financial agent than of the army tutor.

In 1890 Cecil Hambrough goes to the place where Mr. Monson was residing at the time. I am not sure whether he went to Riseley Hall at that time, but he went shortly afterwards there, and was virtually resident with Monson from that time until his death in August, 1893. It was an arrangement which might have been intelligible and reasonable in certain circumstances that a tutor should take a young man under his care, and postpone all claim of payment until a later day. I might have thought that a person entering upon a scheme of that kind would have been in such an established position that the addition of one pupil might have been not material to him from a financial point of view, and that a person

283

Alfred John Monson.

would not at least have taken a youth on terms of that kind if he was to be all but his only pupil. For, I think, it must have struck you how rapidly the introduction of Monson to Cecil Hambrough developed into all these labyrinths of financial scheming which were disclosed to you by the witnesses in the witness-box, and how that continued virtually to within a comparatively short period of the end.

What was Monson's financial position at this time as far as we can judge? His position, as far as we can see, was this—he takes from the father and the son mortgages to a large amount. I am unwilling to stop and consider how far these mortgages were genuine or not. You have evidence relating to them. I do not think it is essential to the case which I am to put before you. If they were genuine the amounts were stupendous—£16,000. If they were not genuine, that is, perhaps, a more disastrous alternative still. Bills were said to have been granted for £5000, manifestly granted by the person who signed them, Major Hambrough, for the purpose of producing pecuniary resources for himself. He told you that he found that these mortgages were utilised in the financial world—I do not fancy they were worth very much per £—they were certainly to some extent deposited with a bank which was giving an over-draft. Major Hambrough was receiving an unknown part of the money being raised upon them, and he began at once to distrust Monson, as he was manifestly using the mortgages and bills for a different purpose than that for which they were given, and he at once took steps to recover his son from the custody of the person to whom he had been entrusted. We find at this time there were financial operations involving something like £700 got from the York City and County Banking Company, £550 got from the London and Yorkshire Bank, and £600 upon a bond of Mrs. Monson over her interest in her father's and grandfather's estate. There, again, gentlemen, I do not dwell much upon the circumstances of that, but I cannot pass by without referring to the position in which that matter stands. A mortgage was granted by Monson and Mrs. Monson, and professedly by Mrs. Day, over Mrs. Monson's interest in her father's and grandfather's estate, such as it was—a mort-gage bearing to be signed by her mother as a guarantor of the loan. All we know about it is this, that the reversionary com-pany who lent the money sued Mrs. Day for the amount, and that she defended the action, and has been successful. So that from these sources apparently—money borrowed from the banks, partly raised on mortgages, and money given by Major Hambrough—Monson is able to pull along somehow. And then he begins to try and negotiate the purchase of the life interests. Gentlemen, if he was going to purchase the life interests and carry through a large financial transaction by which the life interest of Major Hambrough was to be bought at £40,000 from an insurance company; and that

284

Speech for the Crown.

was going to be held for the benefit of Cecil Hambrough or any other body, I think that you would expect that the person who proposed to negotiate such an arrangement, if his intentions were such as they ought to have been, would have been a person at least possessed of some means by which he could undertake such a negotiation.

Well, gentlemen, in the beginning of 1892 Major Hambrough, retaining the affection for his son which, notwithstanding all his spendthrift habits, was manifestly strong in him as disclosed in the correspondence, losing confidence in Monson and anxious to recover his son, put his affairs into the hands of Mr. Fuller; and, treating the case chronologically, you have that episode which, so far as it relates to this matter, is involved in the Fuller-Carter negotiations, by which I mean negotiations on the part of Fuller as representing Major Hambrough with Carter as representing Monson. These appear to have gone on for a considerable period of time, and the importance of the matter is this, that these negotiations, according to the view of Mr. Carter, who, on behalf of Monson, was trying to negotiate the purchase of Major Hambrough's life interest, did not involve, as a part of the transaction, any life insurance upon Cecil Hambrough at all, the only allusion in connection with the matter of life insurance being that, in certain contingencies, or if some special mode, not seriously entertained, were adopted, it might become expedient to take a policy on Cecil Hambrough's life. But the maximum suggested by anybody was £17,000. Why did these negotiations break down? There may have been many reasons, but there was one of which, I think, you are bound to take note. The reason was this, that Monson, or Monson's agent on his behalf, as instructed by him, said to Fuller, " I will be a party to no arrangement which does not make me personally the absolute owner of Major Hambrough's life interest." Gentlemen, what would have been the natural mode of carrying out negotiations of that kind if the negotiator was thinking of the interests of others and not of himself? Why, of course, the natural way would be, if Major Hambrough's spendthrift habits were such that it was expedient that the title should not be taken to himself, that it should be taken to some one as a trustee for Major Hambrough, according to the scheme which is now being carried out by Dr. Hambleton along with the solicitor, Mr. Prince, on behalf of Major Hambrough. Monson made it an absolute condition of the transaction being carried out, so far as he was concerned, that he should be the absolute owner; and I daresay you may remember that in cross-examining Mr. Carter I put the question to him, " Suppose that had been done, what position would Monson have occupied when Cecil Hambrough came of age? " I daresay you will remember that he, the solicitor of Monson, called as a witness on his behalf, was obliged to admit that " it would have made Monson master of

285

Alfred John Monson.

the situation." Gentlemen, it is very plain how that would have been so. At Cecil Hambrough's majority, no doubt, the joint act of father and son would have secured the immediate command of a large sum of money by disentail and re-settlement, but without the joint act of the two nothing could be done. Monson knew well from the letters which were received during 1892 that Major Hambrough had finally resolved to have nothing more to do with him, and, accordingly, if Cecil had lived to be twenty-one, and if Major Hambrough did not consent to place himself at the disposal of Monson, nothing would have been done. But if Monson had been the absolute owner of the life interest he would then have been in a position to say to Major Hambrough, " I have forfeited your confidence; you object to your son being with me, but my consent can place funds at your disposal, and if you will consent to break the entail, Cecil is in my hands, and I, by purchasing your consent, will set free the capital of the estate." Gentlemen, probably under these circumstances the £100,000 mentioned in the letter which you heard last night, which was found in the possession of Monson, might have found its way into a financial business selected by Monson. Now, gentlemen, fortunately for the financial interests of all concerned, Mr. Fuller absolutely repudiated that transaction. Monson did not like the idea of these matters going into the hands of an independent solicitor; I have so much to refer to that I cannot stop to read the letter to you. You heard it read in the evidence. As soon as he heard that Major Hambrough's interests were going to be put into the hands of Fuller, he wrote a long letter in February, 1892, bringing under Fuller's notice, the solicitor whom Major Hambrough had employed, every point and every threat that he could imagine and devise. I cannot tell whether they were all true or whether they were all false, but the object of the letter is demonstrated by its concluding words, which were to the effect that " I have endeavoured to explain matters fully to you, so that you may be aware of the responsibility you incur by taking up Major Hambrough's affairs." Gentlemen, Mr. Fuller was not deterred by any of the threats in that letter. He took up the agency in discharge of his duty to his client, and he absolutely refused to be a party to any arrangement under which Major Hambrough would facilitate the acquisition of this life interest by Monson under a title which would have made him absolute owner of it.

Gentlemen, I shall not dwell longe· upon this phase, except for the purpose of saying that in the course of Mr. Carter's evidence you had a pretty accurate statement of the precise extent of the benefit contemplated by Monson as the result of that transaction. When I say benefit, I mean direct pecuniary benefit, and on the supposition that he did not use his power as master of the situation. I have no doubt you will hear, most legitimately hear, from my learned friend who follows me a great deal about the interest

Speech for the Crown.

Solicitor-General

of Monson in this matter—the benefits which he might have obtained under various contingencies. So far as I can see, the most direct and the most distinct, and, indeed, the only accurate specification of the pecuniary benefit we have is ₐ sum of £11,000, which Carter contemplated, had this arrangement been carried out, would have been set free when Cec'l came of age as Monson's share. I ask you, gentlemen, what would be the consideration given by Monson for that £11,000? Why should an army tutor, who took a lad and educated him for three years under an arrangement that he was to be paid £300 a year—why should he put £11,000 into his pocket? He was apparently to advance nothing. He had nothing to advance. He employed law agents. I suppose the law agents must have seen their way to have their bills paid. The money for these must have come apparently from some other source than the resources of Monson, except in as fɐr as there had passed into Carter's hands the £600 overdrawn from the Yorkshire Bank on the security of part of Major Hambrough's mortgage. But, so far as one can see, the whole of these negotiations on the part of Monson with a view to the purchase of this life interest, had nothing to do with the education of Cecil Hambrough at all, but to his prospect of £11,000 if all went smoothly and Cecil Hambrough became of age.

Well, gentlemen, I had intended at this stage to ɪead to you some of the letters written by Major Hambrough to his son, urging him to return. It was a startling incident that Major Hambrough, who undoubtedly appeared to have friends in a good position, acquaintances in the Hants Militia, into which he had arranged that his son should enter, so that he should have the benefit of associating with persons known to the family in that regiment—it is a very striking circumstance that, such was the domination being exercised by Monson over this youth, that, absolutely against his father's express command, he put him into the Yorkshire Militia, which was near the place where he himself was living, and would not allow him to go into the regiment for which his father had arranged he should enter. Gentlemen, there are some letters at that stage which very graphically describe the anxiety of Major Hambrough and the boy's mother that he should leave the place where he was, and return to them. I daresay, gentlemen, it will be said to you that the home then occupied by Major Hambrough was not an attractive home for a youth to enter. I think that is extremely likely. But can you wonder, looking to what had preceded that time—mortgages taken on promises not fulfilled, suspicion generated in the father's mind by his past experience, and, I am afraid, a too true forecast of the evil effect of Monson's continued relations with his son—that, humble and poor as his home may have been, he was actuated by a genuine parental anxiety that his son should leave the place where he was, and at least be within the influence,

287

Alfred John Monson.

all the beneficial influences, of his own parental home? In answer to all these applications, pressed by Major Hambrough, to allow his son to come back, the response received from Monson was, to give you a single illustration—" Sir,—In reply to your letter, I beg to say that I am not your son's keeper. I have not seen him for ten days or more, but, so far as I know, he is staying at Riseley Hall " —written apparently from the chambers of Monson's friend, Mr. Tottenham, in Delahaye Street, in London, with reference to the youth who was entrusted to his care for the purpose of receiving the tuition of an army tutor. Well, gentlemen, apparently finances were getting low; and we see from the correspondence, and from the evidence which you heard in the box, a violent endeavour was made by the Monsons to raise £2000 upon Cecil's interest in the Hambrough estates. In November, 1892, they applied to a reversionary company, which was managed by Mr. Kidson, who was examined before you, and they proposed that money should be raised by a process under which the Court of Chancery would sanction advances being made on behalf of a youth under age, to be paid out of the money into the enjoyment of which he should come at some period subsequent to his majority. All this, however, fell through because the sanction of the Court of Chancery was not only not obtained, but was not even applied for—I presume for the reason that it was perfectly well known that it could not be obtained.

And, accordingly, at the beginning of 1893 we find the Monsons in so impecunious a position that they are obliged to have recourse to Tottenham, who from that time forward—as proved not only by his evidence, but by the letters which are in this case—financed the Monsons by doling out pittances of a few pounds weekly, which seems to have been the means by which they were enabled to keep their establishment going. They had recourse even to an extraordinary expedient at that time for getting a small sum of ready money. Mr. Tottenham, I imagine, is a gentleman, who, when he advances any money, has an eye upon some benefit to himself in exchange. I do not know that we have got entirely to the bottom of the precise benefit he expected to receive from all these particular advances, but we do see that one of the expedients for raising money was this— that in the beginning of 1893 Mrs. Monson brings an action—a suit as they would term it in England—against young Cecil Hambrough, the boy under age, who was residing with them—suing him in a Court of law for £800, as the amount of money due to them for his maintenance up to that date. Gentlemen, imagine the absurdity of such an expedient! The solicitor in London is instructed to issue the writ. It is served on the boy living in the house with the person who ordered it to be issued. I need scarcely tell you judgment went by default, and then the judgment in that action for £800 against Cecil is utilised in this manner—it is sold by Mrs. Monson to Tottenham for £240 cash down, and Tottenham writes a letter to Cecil to tell him that it was part of the transaction that he

288

Speech for the Crown.

Solicitor-General

should give his word of honour that this £800 should be paid at the earliest period when he became possessed of any finances out of which it could be paid. Now, gentlemen, at this stage—I omitted to mention it in stating these facts chronologically—in August, 1892, Monson had become a bankrupt. All the necessary steps for making him a bankrupt had been carried through. You heard what was the state of his affairs. An English official, corresponding to the Scottish trustee in bankruptcy, discovered assets to the value of 25 guineas, and found debts consisting of tradesmen's debts—debts which had been incurred in connection with household expenses amounting to—I do not remember the exact sum, but something like £2300. Gentlemen, you had proved before you pawn tickets taken out for sums amounting to a few shillings, and Mrs. Monson's estate mortgaged to the utmost point which it could carry—mortgaged to such an extent that, when it turned out that Mrs. Day was not liable as a guarantor, the reversionary company who had lent the money did not even endeavour to recover any part of the estate. They were absolutely exhausted so far as resources were concerned.

Gentlemen, these were the conditions—these were the circumstances—under which that fateful step was taken of deciding, to do what?—to become tenants of Ardlamont House and a Scottish shooting with a liability to pay a rent of £450, as the price of a year's occupancy, from Whitsunday, 1893. The lease was negotiated with a firm—I daresay you know them well—by the name of Messrs. J. & F. Anderson, Writers to the Signet, Edinburgh. Who were the parties to the lease? It could not be Monson. He was a bankrupt. It could not be Mrs. Monson, for her estate was gone. Cecil Hambrough and Mr. Jerningham are the persons who signed the lease, and I am not entitled to go further than to say that Jerningham in the witness-box before you told you that until he came to Edinburgh he never saw the documents at all, while the agents for the landlord told you that they instituted proceedings to recover the rent, and they have abandoned them as absolutely hopeless. These were the conditions, I say, under which the lease of Ardlamont was taken, which, I suppose, will be represented to you as a genuine, honest, *bona fide* method of arranging for spending the autumn in the interests of Cecil Hambrough. Well, gentlemen, they had to be transported from Riseley Hall to Ardlamont, and it is my duty, my painful duty, to give you a glimpse into the difficulty which attended that matter. We have the letters passing between Monson and Tottenham, at the time they were going to Ardlamont, and I find that Monson is writing to Tottenham with regard to the money required to enable them to get away from the one place to the other.

In the month of May, about the time they were going, Monson writes to Tottenham in the affectionate terms in which he always

Alfred John Monson.

addressed him—"Dear Tot,—I have been waiting in Harrogate all day, and only just got your wire at 3.33—too late to leave to-day. We shall be obliged to wait here until we get your cheque cleared to-morrow. We have left Riseley, and all the furniture has gone to Leeds, four vans and a truck load, stored in the name of John Kempton." That was the name under which the gentleman with the variegated career carried on his business as a financial agent. "Unfortunately, we cannot get away from here in time in the morning to get right through in one day. We have got rooms here for the night for all the family and servants, including board, for two guineas, so that is not out of the way. We could not get rid of the servants until we received proceeds of the cheque for their wages. Will you send off the enclosed wire the very first thing in the morning, as this will enable me to draw the money by showing the wire to the bank here? We shall stay in Glasgow to-morrow night, and arrive at Ardlamont on Thursday. I hope you have completed your settlement. Will write you on Thursday." I cannot possibly detain you by reading the whole of these letters, but if my learned friend will accompany my reading, and suggest to me any additional words which I should add, I shall be too happy to comply with any such request. Then a day or two afterwards Monson writes—"We shall be in quite a fix if we don't get your cheque to-morrow, because we are obliged to take possession of Ardlamont on Tuesday." Then on the same page he writes—"We can only just manage on the £40, because Hambrough wants £10 out of that, and we are leaving all the household linen, &c., at the laundry at Harrogate until we receive a further remittance this week, so I hope you will be able to manage this. Hambrough arrived back here with just 1s. out of the £15 you gave him. Of course he had to get his watch out and sundry other things from the custody of his uncle. Have you got the guarantor against the contract? I have written to Browne in case you had forgotten, and asked him to remind you, as it is most important. Hambrough is writing you to send him some money, but please don't send him more than a fiver. He is getting an idea that the supply is unlimited, and simply throwing away the money in consequence. He has no expense whatever until he goes out at training for a fortnight. He goes to-morrow for a fortnight to Strensall camp, and then does his three weeks' training, and comes on to us." Then I find the extremities to which they are reduced are such that, a cheque apparently not having come, Monson writes—"I have borrowed £5 from the chemist for Cecil this morning so as to enable him to join the regiment this afternoon, and I shall have to repay this to-morrow. They marched out to Strensall at 4.30." Then, again, he writes—"As to my resources, they are almost exhausted, and therefore I shall be glad if you will send me £25. There are, of course, many things to get at first." Then a little further down he says—"I am writing to Richards. I think it will

Speech for the Crown.

Solicitor-General

be a good idea to ask him to come up here in September or August. I do not know if he shoots, but he is awfully gone on golf, and I have no doubt he would be delighted to come up here to join in the golf tournament."

Mr. COMRIE THOMSON—Will you read a portion omitted at page 74?

The SOLICITOR-GENERAL—This is written from Ardlamont— " They are all thoroughly satisfied with the place, and I am sure this will keep Hambrough well in hand until the momentous time arrives when he comes of age. Please remember what I said about not lending him too much money." Is that the point?

Mr. COMRIE THOMSON—Yes.

The SOLICITOR-GENERAL—Then he writes further a number of similar letters, but I think what I have read are a sufficient illustration of the great extremities to which they had been reduced at the time that they went to Ardlamont. Now, gentlemen, I think it will naturally occur to your minds—and I hope my learned friend will pay attention to the remarks which I am making—it will naturally occur to you—what is the explanation of people in this wretchedly impecunious condition living from hand to mouth, unable to discharge their servants until they got a cheque from a London moneylender, leaving their household linen at the laundry because they had not the means of paying the washerwoman in whose hands it is—what is the explanation of people in that condition entering on a scheme such as the taking of Ardlamont House, an expensive place with a large rent, and, as far as we can see, for the purpose simply of being occupied by these impecunious people themselves, with one or two gentlemen as shooting boarders paying a rent of something like £100? Poor Cecil Hambrough may not have known much about business matters, but undoubtedly he knew something about the difficulties of this positon, because I see he says, in writing to Tottenham, with whom he also was on terms of such affectionate intimacy that he addressed him as dear Tot—" I have heard from Monson this morning. Try and send him the cash if you can, because you see if they start straight there "—that is, at Ardlamont —" they will be able to get credit afterwards in the shooting season, which will be very useful."

Well, gentlemen, having gone to Ardlamont, Monson appears to have re-entered upon the same wild notion of again trying to be the purchaser of this life interest of Major Hambrough. It seemed to have an attraction to him which he could not shake off. He felt that that was the medium through which the capital value of the Hambrough estates might, under certain circumstances, be virtually placed in his control, and, accordingly, in 1893, negotiations are resumed, and I think I must deal with these somewhat in detail, because I have no doubt they will be brought specially under your notice on the part of the defence. We have letters both from Cecil

Alfred John Monson.

Hambrough and from Monson at that time dealing with this matter of the proposed purchase. You will remember that the persons connected with this matter were Mr. Richards, whom you saw examined, who was the solicitor of the Eagle Insurance Company, and there was Mr. Prince, the solicitor in London, acting on behalf of Major Hambrough. Now, early in 1893, the correspondence which had been going on before they went to Ardlamont was continued after they went there. Lieutenant Hambrough writes to Messrs. Richards —" I have seen Mr. Jerningham since his interview with you on Friday last, and I understand that the proposition of his purchase has to be placed before your directors to-morrow. The question appears to be as to whether the directors will accept Mr. Jerningham's offer or that of Mr. Prince " (Jerningham's offer, of course, being on behalf of Monson, and Prince's being on behalf of Major Hambrough). " I hope, however, that the directors will take my position into consideration, and accept Mr. Jerningham's offer in preference to Mr. Prince's, and that they will distinguish what a great difference is between the *bona fides* of the two offers. The one made by Jerningham with a deposit of £500 is a substantial offer made by a gentleman of considerable position, and one from which I shall benefit; whilst the offer made through Mr. Prince with a small deposit is merely a speculation in the name of a person of no position whatever "—that is, the gentleman whom you saw in the witness-box—" with a view to making money out of me when I come of age, ostensibly for the benefit of my father, but really for the benefit of others. If the directors accept the offer made by Mr. Prince, I should be deprived absolutely of any further interest in the estates of which I am the tenant in tail, because when I come of age I shall have either to disentail or take the consequences, which might be very serious. My father has had the benefit of his life estate, besides which he has recently charged the estate with an annuity of £400 per annum to my mother, which has been already mortgaged with a policy on her life. He has also charged the estate with £5000 for the benefit of my sisters and brother, and thus I am left quite unprovided for, and have to suffer in consequence." Gentlemen, that letter is written and signed by Cecil Hambrough. You will judge whose views are embodied in that letter. It is a letter strongly urging the directors of the Eagle office to give the purchase to Mr. Jerningham, who told you in the witness-box that he had not a shilling which he could invest in any such purchase, that he was the mere friend and nominee of Monson; and, gentlemen, I ask you to refuse to accept the view that that letter is the spontaneous expression of any intelligent view of the subject on the part of Cecil Hambrough at all. It is the outcome of the absolute, predominating control which at that time prevailed on the part of Monson with regard to this unfortunate young man. Well, gentlemen, Monson writes a letter on 11th April, which, I think, was read to one of the

292

Speech for the Crown.

Solicitor-General

witnesses. I cannot bring everything before you, and I therefore do not read it all. But, in writing as he does a letter of his own, also to the directors, strongly urging that a purchase should be made by him, how does he represent the manner of his financial position at the time? He says, " Mr. Cecil Hambrough has continued to reside with me. He has passed his first examination for the army, and I have obtained him a commission in the 3rd West Yorks Regiment. He has now an allowance of £5 a week, a considerable portion of which he sends to his mother, and therefore I am indirectly supporting the family at the present moment. I ask you, in justice to myself, that this letter should be read at the meeting of your co-directors to-morrow." Supporting the family, gentlemen! He could not. This letter, which is written on 11th April, is at a time two or three months after Tottenham had begun to finance the family because they are stopped of all their resources. Therefore he goes to the directors and says, I am allowing Cecil £5 a week, and as Cecil is giving part of it to his own family, I am indirectly supporting the family. Therefore, pray consider me in the matter of selling his life interest. Gentlemen, does not that show the determination with which this idea was being followed out by Monson manifestly for the purpose of acquiring that position of command which he would have enjoyed if he had only succeeded in getting it.

But, unfortunately, the directors of the Eagle Insurance Company knew with whom they were dealing, and on 6th April, as proved to you by the witnesses Prince and Richards—Prince, the agent of Major Hambrough, and Richards, the agent of the Eagle Insurance Company—and I ask you to take special note of this important date and most important fact—on 6th April, 1893, finally and for ever it was settled that Monson was not to get the purchase of the life interest of Major Hambrough. It was to go to Mr. Prince, as the solicitor for Major Hambrough, taken in the name of Dr. Hambleton, as trustee for Major Hambrough, Dr. Hambleton being simply trustee, and with no personal interest in the matter whatever. You will see the importance of that date. I have no doubt you will be told that certain insurance negotiations which afterwards took place had some direct relation to a financial operation connected with the acquisition of this life interest; but keep your minds fixed steadily upon the fact that the contract was concluded on 6th April, 1893, under which this was to go to another person altogether, and that Monson knew it, because in the letter I am now reading, dated 11th April, he says, in writing to the directors, " A great mistake has been made in giving the contract for the purchase of the estates to Mr. Hambleton." No doubt, gentlemen, letters passed for the purpose of getting that, if possible, undone, and it is necessary for me to show you that that which was settled on 11th April never was undone, and that at the time when those important insurance transactions followed, there was no right on the part of Monson to this

Alfred John Monson.

Solicitor-General

life interest in the estates which could possibly have justified the insurances proposed to be effected.

Gentlemen, the letters which followed upon that are several, and I find that upon 13th April, in answer to the long letter from Monson to which I have referred, strongly urging the directors to give him the contract, expressing his regret that they had given it to Dr. Hambleton, and pressing strongly that it should be given to him, the agents of the Eagle Insurance Company wrote in reply— " Your letter of the 11th was received and considered by the directors at their meeting yesterday. It is unnecessary for the directors to go into any of the dealings between yourself and Mr. Hambrough; and having informed Dr. Hambleton's solicitor that they are prepared to sell to him, that transaction must go on. But if your views as to Dr. Hambleton's position are correct, then the negotiations with Mr. Jerningham are postponed until August." That was in consequence of the suggestions of Monson that, although the contract had been given to Hambleton, it could not be carried out by those who were acting upon his behalf by the beginning of August, at which date it was intended that the documents should be completed. Then there is another letter from Cecil Hambrough, again pressing the acquisition in the name of Jerningham, and one letter is written from the Infantry Barracks at York, and I think it was put to the witness—accompanied by the suggestion that, if written from the Infantry Barracks at York, it might be assumed to be the spontaneous, voluntary letter of Cecil Hambrough. Gentlemen, you will judge from its import whether there is any ground for so thinking. The letter says—" Dear Sir,—I am told that you have not yet given the contract to my father, and that they have not paid the deposit." Who told this youth at the barracks at York that the negotiations, which had been going on up to that time, had not been completed by the delivery of the deeds? Have you any doubt that the information was derived from Monson? The letter goes on— " I understand that my father is trying to raise the money to complete this contract by disentailing the Pipewell estate, and thus deprive me of my present contingent reversion to it. If money can be so raised, it will only benefit my father's creditors, and therefore it is very hard upon me that for such a purpose I should lose all prospect of inheriting this property. I understand that by the deed which my father and I signed, Mr. Monson undertook to provide for me until I came of age, and that my father agreed in the deed not to alter the entail of the Pipewell estate. I do not know if this is binding, but I am writing to Mr. Monson on the subject. I am quite sure that the only way in which my father and mother can derive any benefit from the life estates is by my being in a position to deal direct with you when I come of age. My father has had the full value of his life interest, and a great deal more besides, which he has borrowed from so many quarters, beyond which he is so heavily in debt that almost the whole value in the estates will be swamped

294

Speech for the Crown.

Solicitor-General

if he had them in possession when I come of age, before they could be redeemed, whereas in my case I owe nothing beyond the money agreed to be paid to Mr. and Mrs. Monson for my maintenance. I should be in a position to make such provision as would quite satisfy my father and mother. May I beg you to again put my appeal before the directors, and ask if they will accept the deposit on my behalf as before suggested? I am stationed here with my regiment until the end of June." Gentlemen, do you think that that is the letter of a young lieutenant of nineteen or twenty, or is it the letter of the financier Monson, who had been pressing throughout persistently for the acquisition of this life interest? Then, gentlemen, at this date there comes a letter from Dr. Hambleton to Monson, and I bring that under your notice because it will, no doubt, be commented upon by my learned friend in his speech, and I want to show you exactly the position which it occupies in the correspondence, and how far it is from founding any inference that the policies which followed had anything to do with Cecil Hambrough's interest. Dr. Hambleton was in the box when it was read to him. There had been proposals of some sort pressed by Monson upon Mr. Prince at the time that he was communicating with the Eagle Insurance Company through Hammond & Richards; and Hambleton, who had apparently been anxious to get into communication with Monson and Cecil, so that they should come to London, especially for the purpose of trying to get Cecil to leave Monson at this time, on 17th July writes the letter to which my learned friend so frequently referred. He writes from Seaford, Sussex—" I shall be down here for another week on account of my little boy. The suggestion you make can be made the basis of an arrangement if Cecil can pass life assurance for the required amount. If the figures we have are correct, and I believe they are, as things look better than they did, it will be all the better. Cecil would tell you I had expected to have heard before from you. Now, the question is, can Cecil pass the insurance? If you are satisfied of that, arrange to come to town to me, so that we may know for a certainty that a good office will give a policy. Will you agree to this? Please let me know immediately." Now, that letter is sent by Dr. Hambleton to Monson. You will observe the point of the letter is to request that they should come to town and get into communication, principally with the view of Cecil being taken away, but in any view it was with the view of discussion, or suggestion, or arrangement in regard to dealing with Monson. Now, we have at the time a record of the precise view which Monson took of that letter. We have a letter from him to Hammond & Richards, written on 31st July, and making specific references to that letter. You will observe that all the proposals up to that time had been on the basis of Jerningham being the man in whose name these are to be taken, as the friend of Monson, and Dr. Hambleton told you that the letter

295

Alfred John Monson.

of 17th July produced no result so far as he was aware. They had never come together from that day to this, and he had had no further communication with Monson. The reason why it is brushed aside, as a suggestion which Monson would have nothing to do with, becomes quite apparent, I think, from Monson's own letter to Hammond & Richards of 31st July. He writes thus—" I understand from a letter received from Dr. Hambleton that nothing has been done by them regarding the purchase of the Hambrough life estates. Therefore, I assume your clients will be open to negotiate otherwise for the sale, as the limit of time mentioned was August." He is referring to the contract which had been made in April, and which he had ascertained was to be fulfilled in August. "The proposal made by Mr. Cecil Hambrough for Mr. Jerningham to purchase on his behalf "—that is, the proposal referred to in Dr. Hambleton's letter—" cannot now be proceeded with, but Mr. Monson will be quite willing to enter into a contract for the purchase, provided the limit of time for completion was made June, 1894. Mrs. Monson would pay a deposit of 5 per cent. upon the agreed on purchase money. Mr. Cecil Hambrough is staying here with us, but I do not see that it concerns your clients what arrangements Mrs. Monson may enter into with Cecil Hambrough, so long as there is a *bona fide* purchase from your clients, with such a substantial deposit as suggested. The above is our permanent address, as we have taken a shooting for the season." To that there is a postscript—" Dr. Hambleton has written "—that is, the letter of 17th July—" asking me to join in with them in some arrangement, but I think it is far better that I should not do so. There is no reason why you should not know the proposed arrangement between Cecil Hambrough and Mrs. Monson."

Now, gentlemen, I ask you to be good enough to receive a clear and distinct apprehension of the situation of matters at this point, especially with reference to Dr. Hambleton's letter; and the points I desire to emphasise, and to press upon you, as, I would suggest to you, established beyond all doubt—because they are contained in a letter written by Monson hurriedly at the time, which I have read to you—are, first, that Dr. Hambleton's suggestion was put aside as one which he said in his letter he would not go into; second, that the proposal which Hambleton referred to, that Jerningham should acquire this contract, had been finally dropped, and a perfectly new, distinct proposal started, which had never been heard of by anybody before, namely, that Mrs. Monson should become the purchaser of this life interest, under some arrangement by which its fulfilment should be postponed until a date in 1894, when Cecil Hambrough would come of age. How Mr. Monson saw his way to make the deposit he then referred to is impossible for us, I think, to conjecture. I asked a witness in the witness-box, Mr. Richards—" Suppose you had assented to that, what would have been the deposit Mrs. Monson would have had to pay to make 5 per cent. upon something like

Speech for the Crown.

Solicitor-General

£40,000?" And I have shown you the pecuniary straits to which they were reduced at this time. At Ardlamont, the day before a rent of £450 becomes due, without a shilling in their pockets to meet it, Monson positively suggests a purchase by Mrs. Monson, without a shilling to bless herself with, under which a deposit of £2500 would have fallen to be made. Well, how did the Eagle Insurance Company receive that proposal? They wrote back—"In reply to yours of the 31st, so far as we are aware the arrangements are still going on with Dr. Hambleton, but they have rested with us, for we have been very much pressed with other matters, and have not yet submitted a draft contract. We shall, however, be doing so in the course of a few days." So you see that the agent for the Eagle Insurance Company, explaining to Monson in reply, took the trouble to deal specifically with this new suggestion as to Mrs. Monson. He says—"I have been busy. I have not been able to take up the preparation of the draft documents which Dr. Hambleton and the Eagle Company have to sign, because of pressure from other business, but I am going to take it up immediately." The transaction with Dr. Hambleton is still going on, and, accordingly, he does not pay the slightest attention to the counter proposal of Monson, and from that date the matter stops, and there is not the slightest ground for supposing that at any time Monson had any ground for believing that the transaction with Dr. Hambleton was not to be completed, or that he had any concluded arrangements for acquiring the life interest of Major Hambrough.

Gentlemen, Monson's own solicitor, Mr. Blair, Writer to the Signet, told you that, so far as he could see, he could not imagine any circumstances under which Cecil Hambrough's life would fall to be insured for the sum of £50,000, unless by somebody who had purchased the father's life interest and was trying to negotiate the matter upon some such lines as that. I showed you that Monson's own solicitor, Carter, did not contemplate such an insurance even if it had been carried out as he proposed. But it is not necessary to stop at that. Surely the first thing for any man to do was to secure the purchase of the life interest before he took any steps to effect an insurance—an insurance effected without any knowledge that the purchaser of the life interest to be secured would be a policy effected of an enormous amount, and imposing a waste of money which could not be kept up, and which would be absolutely useless except as an adjunct of the acquisition of the life interest. And on this part of the case—of which I have no doubt you will hear more from my learned friend—I ask you to accept as the facts, established conclusively by both parole and written evidence, that the life interest of Major Hambrough was sold to Dr. Hambleton on the 11th of April. Nothing ever afterwards occurred to interfere with the contract. It is still subsisting, has been subsisting all along, is at this moment in course of

Alfred John Monson.

execution. Monson negotiated, but never acquired any interest whatever, at any period of the negotiations, in Major Hambrough's life interest.

I have now stated to you what I thought it my duty to bring before you, relating to the position of Major Hambrough's life interest in these estates, and the position which the prisoner Monson occupied with regard to them, the result of the matter being, I submit, that the evidence which I have led had dissociated him from that matter—dissociated him from it because the contract was made with another, and that fact was known to him; and, accordingly, all efforts on his part necessarily came to an end.

Now, I propose in the next place, to ask your attention to what was done by Monson in the way of effecting life insurances upon the life of Cecil Hambrough, and I now propose to ask your attention to that matter in relation to three separate insurance offices. They are all closely related in point of time, but as far as I can discover, the one of the three which has the earliest commencement is the negotiations with the Scottish Provident Institution. So far as parole evidence is concerned, the details of that matter were put before you by the witness Mr. Wisely, who is the Glasgow agent of the Scottish Provident Institution, and it appears that about the 10th of July there was sent to the Edinburgh office a proposal by Monson for a £50,000 insurance on the life of Cecil Hambrough, to be taken out in the name of Mrs. Monson. That is to say, Mrs. Monson was to have a policy payable to herself for £50,000 upon the life of Cecil Hambrough. That proposal having gone to the Edinburgh office was transmitted to the Glasgow office. Mr. Wisely was absent, he said, at the time, but in his absence a proposal form had been sent on to Monson at Ardlamont, and, the proposed transaction being of a very large amount, he himself went to Ardlamont for the purpose of communicating with Monson on the subject. Then you will remember that he told you that he found a proposal filled up when he went there, but the proposal which had been sent was a proposal in the usual form for a person who is assuring his own life, which is, of course, the form of policy we are all most familiar with, and, accordingly, finding that that was so, he got the appropriate proposal form sent to Ardlamont. There was a letter written in connection with the matter by Monson, which he had written before Mr. Wisely arrived, but had not been despatched, dated 9th August, beginning thus—" I enclose a form proposal, duly filled up, and signed by Cecil Hambrough. The policy will have to be issued in favour of Agnes Maud Monson, and is to be effected for the purpose of covering certain advances made to Mr. Cecil Hambrough, extending over the last four years, and also to cover certain liabilities by Mrs. Monson in connection with the Hambrough settled estates," and you may remember that Mr. Wisely, refreshing his memory by reference to the letter which

298

Speech for the Crown.

Solicitor-General

he wrote at the time to the head office of the Provident Institution in Edinburgh, told you what had passed between Monson and himself. In the course of conversation Monson had told him that there had been expenditure by Mrs. Monson on these estates, and made some other explanations with reference to the nature of Mrs. Monson's interest. Then Monson wrote—" Since writing above I have received new form, which has been filled up as required." That is a form which puts the specific question to the proposer—" What is your interest in the life that you are going to insure? " You quite understand, gentlemen, the necessity of providing that. If a man is going to insure his own life he is held to have a sufficient interest in his own life. But no man can insure the life of another unless he has some interest in some degree in the life to be insured. In the case of you and me, with no relations between us of any description, it would be a most extraordinary thing if I were to propose to take out a policy in my own name on the life of any of you. What possible reason could I have for taking such a step? By proving that we are related in such a way that I may have a legitimate pecuniary interest in your surviving, I should have a clear interest in the life of such of you, which would entitle me to take out a policy on the life of such one. But in the absence of any such interest, properly instructed, no respectable insurance company would issue a policy by A on the life of B. And, accordingly, a new proposal was submitted by answering the question in this way, " To cover advances made and liabilities in connection with the Hambrough estates."

But, gentlemen, at that moment there were no liabilities or advances made, or liabilities in connection with the Hambrough estate. Mrs. Monson had no more interest in the Hambrough estates than I have. There had been certain expenditure made on behalf of Cecil Hambrough. These are not advances upon, or in connection with, the Hambrough estates. Well, this proposal came, and it resulted in this, that the office told him—" You must establish the interest. You can get the policy." The doctors examined young Hambrough. They were satisfied with his life— a strong, young man—and they said—" We accept your proposal, such as it is, but you must satisfy us that you have an interest in Hambrough's life to the value of £50,000." Of course, gentlemen, that could not possibly be done by Monson. And what he did was this. He limited the proposal to £10,000—down at a jump from £50,000 to £10,000. He got a letter saying—" We accept your proposal for the £50,000 on condition that you satisfy us that you have such an interest." In reply he wrote—" Dear sir,—I have received your letter accepting the proposal on the life of Mr. Cecil Hambrough. Since I saw you last I have been in communication with the solicitor acting in this matter, and he has suggested a method of insuring the mortgage with a security insurance com-

Alfred John Monson.

pany at ¼ per cent. This appears to be so much more reasonable that I have decided to follow his suggestion, so that under this scheme we shall only require a policy of £10,000 to cover money actually due by Mr. Cecil Hambrough on his attaining twenty-one." What solicitor had he been communicating with? What was the thing that was to be protected by a method of insuring the mortgage in the insurance company? What was the scheme that was to require a policy of £10,000 instead of £50,000? What had occurred between 21st July and 3rd August which should make it expedient only to insure for £10,000 as against £50,000? What was the change in the scheme?

These are questions which you will naturally put to yourselves, and to which you will expect some answer to be given. I can give you no answer. The facts given in the evidence supply no means of answering those questions, except upon the view that they were falsehoods to deceive the insurance company. Then there was to be a premium of £181 5s. to cover the £10,000, so that the Scottish Provident was in this position on 3rd August—they had agreed to insure Hambrough's life for £10,000, subject to the paying of a premium of £181 down, and that " you must satisfy us that you have an interest in his life to the extent of £10,000." But until both of these conditions are fulfilled there is no policy at all; and that is the policy which you have heard referred to occasionally by the prisoner shortly after young Hambrough's death as a policy which he missed having in consequence of his death on 10th August, implying that if he had lived a day or two longer it would have been completed. Gentlemen, it never could have been completed until the Scottish Provident Company had it demonstrated to them that Mrs. Monson had interests in the Hambrough estates to the value of £10,000.

The second insurance company with which negotiations were going on was the Liverpool and London and Globe, and the extra-ordinary thing, gentlemen, is that at the same time, and before getting a complete and conclusive answer as to whether the one was to be accepted or not, Monson has fired off another proposal to the Liverpool and London and Globe Company for a policy for £50,000, also on the life of Cecil Hambrough and in the name of Mrs. Monson. That seems to have begun somewhere about 17th or 18th July. The correspondence takes place with a gentleman of the name of Wardle. Monson encounters precisely the same difficulty there as in the case of the Scottish Provident. They say—" While we are quite willing to go on with this, of course, if you are going to take the policy in Mrs. Monson's name, you must show that Mrs. Monson has an interest to the extent of £50,000 over Cecil Hambrough's life." There, again, that was a poser, that was a difficulty that could not be faced; but there is a reduction made in the amount proposed. The interest is stated in the letter written by Monson on 18th July

Speech for the Crown.

Solicitor-General

to the Liverpool and London and Globe Insurance Company—" I promised you that you should have the offer of the policy for Cecil Hambrough. The policy for £50,000 will be required before or by the 5th of August. I think you had a form filled up, but perhaps you had better send another. The policy has to be in favour of Agnes Maud Monson, and is to cover advances made to, and at the request of, Mr. Cecil Hambrough, and to cover money due for his maintenance, &c., extending over four years; and also to cover certain liabilities incurred in connection with the Hambrough estates." Not one particle of liability had been incurred either by Mr. or Mrs. Monson in connection with the Hambrough estates.

Then the insurance company replied—" A form of proposal is sent herewith, and on the margin thereof you will find a place wherein to state the value of Mrs. Monson's insurable interest. Perhaps, however, it would be better in that place to refer to a separate document, and to give us, in as great detail as you can, particulars of this interest. If I remember rightly, when I last conversed with you on this matter the interest was your own. By what process has it been transferred to your wife? How comes it that you have a present insurable interest in Cecil's life, seeing that he is yet under age?" And further down—" It will be absolutely necessary for us to have the fullest details of the interest, otherwise we should stand no chance of dealing with the amount " (that is, to get another insurance company to take part of the risk with them). " I expect this will reach you on Tuesday morning, and I shall be glad if you will have the proposal filled up, and draw up the particulars of the interest, taking Cecil with you to Glasgow, telegraphing on your way to ' Globe, Glasgow,' the time at which you will call at the office." Then he says— " The papers will then be submitted to the directors as soon as possible, but you must not be surprised if the policy is not in your hands by 1st August. By the way, are you expecting some special settling up on that day that makes you so anxious for it? " That letter is dated 20th July. Monson, in answer to this, writes to the secretary upon 26th July—" Ardlamont House, Argyllshire, 26th July, 1893. Dear Sir,—I am instructed by Mr. Wardle, of your Leeds office, to send you particulars of Mrs. Monson's interest in the life of Mr. Cecil Hambrough; therefore I beg to inform you that the insurance is to cover advances made by request of Mr. Cecil Hambrough, and for his maintenance, &c., extending over four years; also to cover liabilities incurred under an agreement with the Hambrough estates."

Now, gentlemen, that is just what he said before, except that he introduced the words " under an agreement," which was simply emphasising the untruth, for there were no advances, and certainly no agreement. Mr. Wardle, the agent of the insurance company, not unnaturally replied, " This information is really nothing

301

Alfred John Monson.

further than you gave me in the first instance, and, as I said in the letter I wrote from Liverpool, is not nearly sufficient. It is far too vague for our directors to say whether Mrs. Monson has a legal insurable interest in Mr. Hambrough's life, particularly seeing that he is a minor." Then Monson, apparently in concern about that, writes this extraordinary letter to the secretary on 31st July— "Dear Sir,—I received a letter from Mr. Wardle to-day, saying that you require further particulars of Mrs. Monson's interest in the life of Mr. Cecil Hambrough. I had, however, just written a letter to you saying that the policy of £50,000 is not now required, as we had arranged to secure Mrs. Monson's liability under the agreement by other means which are less costly." That was the same line taken with the other company—all pure fiction. Nothing had occurred between the dates of the letters to make him reduce the amount, by protecting Mrs. Monson's interest otherwise. It was simply a mode of trying to evade the difficulty of showing the insurable interest. He goes on—"We shall, however, require a policy for £26,000, and this will have to be increased to £52,000 next year, when he attains twenty-one. Thus, you will require to know that the extent of Mrs. Monson's interest in Mr. Cecil Hambrough's life amounts to £26,000. Mr. Wardle seemed to think that a minor could not incur a liability beyond one for maintenance, education, and necessaries. This, however, does not concern us. A minor can undertake to make certain payments on his attaining his majority if he should so long live. There would obviously be an interest in the life of a minor after such an undertaking. This is the position in the present case. Mrs. Monson incurs liabilities on behalf of a minor, and makes him advances, and provides him with education extending over four years. Mr. Cecil Hambrough, in consideration therefor, gives an undertaking in writing, whereby he agrees to pay her the sum of £26,000 upon his attaining twenty-one, and, since he succeeds to estates under the will of his great-grandfather to the value of £200,000 or thereby, there can be no question as to whether Mrs. Monson has not an interest in his life to the extent mentioned, and it cannot concern you to enter into the details of how the £26,000 is made up, so long as you have evidence of the fact. I therefore enclose you a letter, signed by Mr. Cecil Hambrough, which I assume will be sufficient evidence." Now, what was the letter accompanying that? I will read it—"Ardlamont House, 31st July, 1893. To the Manager of the Liverpool and London and Globe Insurance Company. Dear Sir,—I am requested by Mrs. Agnes Monson to write and inform you that she has an interest in my life to the extent of £26,000. I have given her an undertaking, under which I agreed to pay to her this sum after my attaining twenty-one." And, gentlemen, there is a melancholy sound about the words following—"if I should live until then."

Speech for the Crown.

Solicitor-General

That was the mode in which, being cornered with regard to the insurable interest of Mrs. Monson in this life, put forward at first as an interest under an agreement in the Hambrough estates, driven from that by the pressing questions of the insurance company, and feeling that £50,000 was out of the question, Monson reduces it to £26,000, substitutes for the alleged interest under agreement in the Hambrough estates this boy's letter expressing an indebtedness to Mrs. Monson to the extent of £26,000—in other words, stating that he had been resident in her family, and was indebted to her to the extent of a few hundred pounds. I need scarcely tell you that the insurance company saw through the wretched flimsiness of these pretensions, and, accordingly, on the 2nd August, they telegraphed at once to him to say, " Hambrough's proposal declined." And he, therefore, at this stage was in this position, that the Globe Company had refused his proposal altogether, and that the Scottish Provident Company were willing to give him £10,000 subject to the condition, which he never could fulfil, to satisfy them as business men that Mrs. Monson had an interest in Cecil Hambrough's life. A change of tactics then ensued. These efforts to secure a policy in the name of Mrs. Monson, which would have made Mrs. Monson, in the event of the boy's death, the direct creditor for the sum insured, having failed —finding that that could not be accomplished without instructing an interest on her part, which, in fact, did not exist, and therefore never could be proved—their tactics were changed, and they adopted an expedient which would obviate the necessity for proving any interest at all, and applied for policies directly upon the life of Cecil Hambrough for themselves.

I now come to deal with those policies which were effected, the existence of which was persistently concealed, but which did exist at the date of the boy's death, and formed the subject of the claim afterwards put forward by Mrs. Monson with the view of recovering the money. On 2nd August Monson goes to the Glasgow office of the Mutual Assurance Company of New York, has an interview with Mr. M'Lean, who was examined as a witness, the manager of that company in Scotland, and proposes an insurance to the extent of £20,000, divided into two policies of £10,000 each. There is not much time to spare. He visits the insurance company alone, ascertains the payments, and arranges that he and Hambrough shall return at two in the afternoon. A doctor was to be there. The medical examination is made. The first stage is started for the completion of these policies. They are told that despatch is necessary, and that the arrangements must be completed not later than 8th August. And what is the reason assigned for effecting this insurance? All the misrepresentations about interest in the Hambrough estates had been tried and failed. This impecunious occupant of Ardlamont has the boldness to go to M'Lean's office and

303

Alfred John Monson.

say that he is about to purchase the estate of Ardlamont; that Mrs. Monson, who had not two shillings in her pocket, was to pay £20,000 towards the price, and that the purchase was to be made in the interest of young Hambrough. A policy was to be taken out to secure Mrs. Monson's interests. Well, there was not the same difficulty about such an insurance as this. All difficulties about the interest on the part of a third party had been displaced; and, accordingly, the proposal is entertained, an examination is made, and the policies are completed. A premium has to be paid. There is no time to wait till the policy is got from New York, and the expedient is adopted of taking a temporary policy, subsisting in any event for sixty days, and upon the cheap terms of payment of a premium only for half a year. A policy is effected, but the money has to be found. And I am bound to ask your close and careful attention to the circumstances under which that money was found. We are coming perilously close to the tragic event of 10th August. The acts of Monson, the motives of Monson, the objects he had in view, you must carefully scrutinise, watch, and observe at and about the same time which I have now reached. I have told you the misrepresentations under which this policy was obtained. I must now ask your attention to the flagrant misrepresentations under which the premiums were paid. The prisoner had reached a stage at which, apparently, even the bonds of that alliance which had subsisted between him and Tottenham, upon whom they were depending at the time for their daily bread, even these bonds were to be broken, and treachery had to be employed towards the friend who had provided them with daily bread, for the purpose of obtaining the necessary money. The idea of the purchase of Ardlamont had been ventilated, and the expedient evidently occurred to the ingenious and tortuous mind of Monson that, by devising some idea of the purchase of Ardlamont, and the necessity for a sum to be paid by way of deposit, he would secure the necessary amount to enable him to complete the insurance which he had got the New York office to accept; and, gentlemen, upon 23rd July he wrote a letter to his friend Tottenham for the purpose of procuring the necessary sum. He wrote from " Ardlamont," and the date is proved by Tottenham's answer, which was put to him in the witness-box. On 23rd July Monson wrote—" Dear Tot,—I have just returned home, and have seen the agents to-day, and have fully discussed the question of the purchase here. The existing mortgage on the property (that is, upon Ardlamont) is £37,000 at 4 per cent. The interest has always been paid regularly. The mortgagees are an insurance company, and the Lamonts (the owners of the estate), having policies with them, they had not wished to disturb the investment. I was asked to make an offer. I therefore said I thought £45,000 a good price, as I was sure the rentals would have to be reduced, &c. They would not, or pretended not (that is, the

Speech for the Crown.

Solicitor-General

agents, J. & F. Anderson), to consider such an offer. However, eventually they agreed to accept £48,000. They say that they only do this because Major Lamont is so anxious to be rid of the property before he starts for India, and their instructions from him are to close with the best offer they can get, and it appears they have spent a lot of money on advertising and trying to sell, but they never had a single offer. They are willing to accept £250 as a deposit, on the contract being signed by Mrs. Monson, to be limited to June, 1894. The contract is now being drawn, and will be ready in the course of a week or so."

Gentlemen, he wrote that letter to Tottenham on 23rd of July. You heard Mr. Murray, of Messrs. J. & F. Anderson, give his evidence in the witness-box. He told you that at that date and up to 8th August he never saw Mr. Monson or had communication with him with regard to this purchase; that Monson was never asked to make an offer; that he never received an offer; and never communicated with him about an offer. He would never have thought of £48,000 as the price of the estate. I am bound to say that if testimony from human lips that are the most reliable is to be believed, the letter shows a tissue of the grossest falsehoods that ever were put upon paper by a human being, and all palpably for the purpose of securing command of £250, which he was sorely wanting at that time. I cannot leave the letter without displacing a comment which was ingeniously suggested by my learned friend in the cross-examination of Mr. Murray. He suggested that the sum would be £85,000. Mr. Murray said—" £85,000 was my price. I never thought of looking at an offer of £48,000. I had no authority to do so. I have sold the estate since for £70,000 and to say that I accepted an offer of £48,000 is simply and absolutely absurd." My learned friend tried to interpret the letter as if it could possibly have been read in this way, that putting together £48,000 and £37,000, that would make £85,000, and that therefore the letter was intended to represent that the estate had been purchased at £85,000, and not at £48,000. No ingenuity, I think, can put that meaning on the words, seeing that it is said—" I purchased the estate for £48,000," even if it stopped there. But if my learned friend will read with me that passage at the bottom of the page, it contains within itself words which absolutely displace any possibilities of such an interpretation as has been suggested, because it goes on to say—" I have told Cecil that the price is £50,000— £1000 each for division—thus he will have to raise £13,000 to complete next year "; that is, he says, " I have told Cecil that it is £50,000, and that will enable you (i.e., Tottenham) and me to take £1000 each for division, without his knowing it." The £13,000 deducted from the £50,000 leaves £37,000, the amount of the burden on the property. It was £50,000 that he told Cecil he had paid for it. This makes it absolutely impossible to suggest

X

305

Alfred John Monson.

that that letter by any method of human ingenuity could be represented as conveying the idea that £85,000 was the price referred to and not £50,000. You are in this position. A letter absolutely false is written by Monson to his friend Tottenham in order to procure £250 on the false representations that he had purchased the estate without ever having been in communication with the owner of the estate or the agent who had charge of the sale. Gentlemen, I think you will have to ask yourselves and find an answer to the question why that was done. If it can be explained, my learned friend who follows me will, I am certain, be able to do so. If it is not explained—if that false letter is not explained—then you are bound to carry that with you into consideration of those portions of the case with which I have yet to deal. The fact is that nine days before this wretched boy's death, money to pay the premiums on a £20,000 policy is secured by the nefarious means which I have explained to you. Well, gentlemen, Mr. Tottenham swallows the bait. He sends the £250. A bank account had apparently been opened a few days before, and a wretched sum of £5, or something of that sort, put into it on the representation that it was required for household purposes. Tottenham's cheque is applied for, and he wishes it to be sent on the request of Cecil. Tottenham replies—
" Yours to hand. You seem to have made a good bargain re Ardlamont. Cecil had better write me a letter requesting me to pay the £250 deposit." Monson's letter, you will observe, had been full of falsehoods. The poor boy writes—well, we do not have his letter, but here is that of Beresford Loftus Tottenham, beginning "My Dear Cecil,—Enclosed you will find cheque for £250 to enable you to pay for the purchase of Ardlamont estate." On 3rd August there could not have been any communications about the estate at all with Messrs. J. & F. Anderson. Well, the £250 cheque comes. It is placed to the credit of Mrs. Monson, who lodged the amount with the bank at Tighnabruaich.

Monson seems to have perceived that the step he had taken was pretty strong, and, accordingly, he arranges for a visit to Edinburgh on 8th August, in order that there might be at least something in existence of the nature of negotiations for the purchase of Ardlamont. He says to the insurance company, " Have my policy ready; it must be ready by 8th August." He got the money to pay the policy on the representation that he had purchased Ardlamont. He goes through the form of a visit to Edinburgh and a verbal communication with the Ardlamont agent on 8th August—words and nothing more. How could he purchase Ardlamont? He negotiated in such a way as to make it appear that an interview took place—that something had taken place, but he took very good care that the margin between them was such that anything of the nature of a transaction was hopeless. Having in that way done his best to cover up the falsehoods in his letter of 23rd July, he returns

Speech for the Crown.

to Glasgow, and gives a cheque to the insurance company on the Tighnabruaich branch, which he knows will be honoured in respect of the £250 cheque of Tottenham, which had been paid into the account. He gets the policy, and hands to the insurance company the letter which the boy Cecil had been got to write on 7th August, preparatory to the visit to Glasgow, when the policy was to be delivered, in which he says, " Will you kindly deliver my two insurance policies of £10,000 each to Mr. and Mrs. Monson, as I have assigned the policies to Mrs. Agnes Maud Monson for proper considerations received. Mrs. Monson will, therefore, be the person to whom the insurance is payable in the event of my death." This is taken and handed to the insurance company at the time when the policy is taken out. My friend Mr. Brodie Innes came into the witness-box to-day to tell in Court what was the legal effect of that document according to law. But that is not a question for you. The question for you is, what did Monson think he had accomplished when he got that policy and that letter from Cecil Hambrough and delivered it to the insurance company? Can you accept any other view than this, that the man who took the letter from Cecil Hambrough to the insurance company, expressly directing the insurance company to deliver the policies to him—if a minor can give authority to deliver the policy—that the man who took this letter thought he could do that, must he not have thought he could also have an equal power to cause it to be assigned? And the document itself is conclusive evidence against Monson, who took it from the boy, and delivered it to the insurance company, that whatever may be the legal effect of such an instrument in the judgment of an accomplished barrister like my friend Mr. Brodie Innes, in the judgment of Monson himself he believed he had got for Mrs. Monson a legal title to demand payment from the insurance company.

But, gentlemen, Mr. Monson had had some experience of finance, and he was resolved to have all the strings to his bow which his ingenuity could suggest. Not satisfied with the letter which had been delivered to the insurance company on the same date, he takes from the boy a letter addressed to Mrs. Monson, in which the boy says—" Dear Mrs. Monson,—If you will pay the premiums on the two policies of insurance of my life of £10,000 each with the Mutual Life Insurance Company of New York, I am willing that you should hold the policies as security for all moneys due to you from me, and as security against all liabilities incurred by you on my behalf, and in the event of my death occurring before the repayment of these moneys you will be the sole beneficiary of these policies, and I have given notice to the Mutual Insurance Company of New York that you are the person to whom the insurance is payable, and they have accepted that notice." Gentlemen, so far as the insurance was concerned, in the judgment of Mr. Monson, by the delivery of one

307

Alfred John Monson.

letter to the insurance company, and the second letter of 7th August to Mrs. Monson, which was framed on the lines of combining within itself the assignation of the policy and a will in the name of the man in whose name the policy was, Mr. Monson manifestly thought he was armed with the necessary means of securing the total amount of both of the policies, in the event of anything afterwards happening to Cecil Hambrough.

Gentlemen, the 8th was an eventful day. Having the policies so completed and delivered, Monson returned to Ardlamont. Miss Hiron did not know where he had been. I am not surprised. The errand was of a kind as to which I should think even the most hardened person would hesitate to say more than he was obliged to do. He returned to Ardlamont with the policy in his pocket, and accompanied by his mysterious friend Scott. He had told the insurance company that the policies must be completed by 8th August. On 11th August several gentlemen were coming to Ardlamont. If the thing was to be done it must be before the 11th. He returns to Ardlamont accompanied by Scott. Scott is on the boat, and totally unacquainted with the region in which he finds himself. Monson is accompanied by Donald, with whom he had transactions about the yacht. He speaks to him about Scott, and tells him he is a person from the estate office. At Tighnabruaich—Monson not being on deck at Tighnabruaich—Scott, manifestly having heard of Tighnabruaich in connection with Ardlamont, by mistake leaves the boat at that point. He is seen by the witness M'Phee, the boots from the neighbouring hotel, who, having a conveyance there, ascertains the position in which he is, and proposes to drive him in his conveyance to the next pier, at which probably his friend might leave the boat. In the course of the drive he asked Scott where he was going, and having some doubts about the name he takes out a paper on which the boots sees Ardlamont written, and he then knows that he is going to the house at which Monson is residing. They ultimately meet the conveyance which had met Monson at the proper pier for his disembarking. He disembarked there and turned his conveyance to Tighnabruaich, knowing that his friend must have disembarked at Tighnabruaich, and, accordingly, they met, and thereafter went to Ardlamont House. Gentlemen, that is upon the 8th. Mrs. Monson appears to have known of Scott's arrival, because instructions were given to the servants to prepare a bedroom. Miss Hiron did not know he was expected to arrive. He arrives, and is treated as a member of the family, and we come to the morning of the 9th.

I now approach those details connected with the two crimes which lead us to ask you to find the prisoner guilty of both of them. Now, gentlemen, the first crime charged is that, late upon the night of the 9th, or early on the morning of the 10th, Monson attempted to murder Cecil Hambrough by drowning. Certain facts connected

Speech for the Crown.

Solicitor-General

with that night cannot possibly be disputed. It cannot be disputed that that night, somewhere between eleven and one in the morning, Cecil Hambrough and Monson were out in a boat fishing, or in a boat in Ardlamont Bay. That boat was immersed or upset, with the result that both were thrown into deep water, and the boat when seen immediately after the event had in it a hole of a kind altogether unusual in such boats, manifestly made by a person other than the builder of the boat, or a person skilled and competent to make a plug hole in the usual way. Therefore up to that time you have facts about which there can be no dispute—two men out in a boat in Ardlamont Bay late that night, one able to swim, the other not, and with a hole in the boat of this unprecedented character, covered over by a plank moveable, and made moveable presumably in the act of making the hole, because the corresponding plank on the other side of the boat is fixed, and when the boat is upset the plank over the hole disappears.

Well, now, gentlemen, the question you have to consider is this, are the facts which I have mentioned, combined with the further circumstances of that day which I have submitted to you as proved, reasonably reconcilable with any other result than an attempt upon the part of Monson to drown Cecil Hambrough that night? I shall afterwards have to deal with who Scott was, why he was there, and what is to be inferred from his disappearance. Scott is represented by Monson as a person of whom he knew nothing, not engaged by him, but engaged by young Hambrough in connection with the yacht—a yacht bought by Monson in his own name, not by Hambrough. These statements are made on the part of Monson with regard to Scott for the purpose of suggesting that he was a mechanical engineer, present at Ardlamont for the hinted purpose of making an examination of the yacht, Scott having dined and slept as a member of the family in a part of the house similar to that occupied by the rest of the family. He was treated as a guest in the usual way, and breakfasted in the morning with the family in the usual way.

The first incident we have about him is that he goes with Monson to bathe. I have to submit that this engineer, if absolutely unacquainted with the family, must have found himself rather uncomfortably situated in being transported into a family with which he was not familiar, and would have no reason to remain an hour longer than was necessary to perform the duty for which he had been brought there. I think one would have expected that Wednesday, 9th August, would have been spent in going over to Kames, where the yacht " Alert " was lying, to enable this engineer to perform the duty which he had been brought there to discharge, by making an examination of the boilers of the " Alert." Well, gentlemen, you know that he did nothing of the kind. They go out to Ardlamont Bay after breakfast to amuse themselves by having a bathe. Miss

309

Alfred John Monson.

Hiron did not know what they were doing. But we know. They went to pay a visit to M'Nicol, who had a boat. Splash fishing seemed to be one of the amusements connected with the occupation of Ardlamont. Accordingly there was a boat there adapted for the purpose, selected for the purpose, hired for the purpose—for a whole season M'Kellar's boat had been used for the purpose—and was now used by Hambrough along with Lamont, Douglas, and the other keepers, not one of whom had any complaint to make against the boat, who had never heard there was anything in the least unsatisfactory about the boat, and who were certain it was a boat which had no plug hole in it, who never heard Hambrough say that there was any inconvenience connected with the use of that boat without a plug hole. The forenoon of the 9th is spent by Monson and Scott in company going to M'Nicol. They ask M'Nicol for the loan of his boat, and they want it for two nights, and the reason assigned for the necessity for the boat is that the one that they had is dangerous and not fit to be used. M'Nicol assents to the proposal, and they immediately go and fetch round the boat, and it is brought to Ardlamont Bay. They return to lunch, and they are present at family luncheon in the usual way. They go out in the afternoon again—one would have thought a convenient time for the examination of the boilers of the " Alert "—but this engineer, of whom Monson knew nothing, and who was there to examine the " Alert " at Kames accompanies Monson down to the shore for the purpose of having a sail. Two of Monson's children are taken into the boat. Which boat did they use? They used M'Kellar's boat, which had been represented to M'Nicol to be dangerous, and necessitating, therefore, the use of Mr. M'Nicol's boat. They got into the boat, and they sailed about the bay. The children leave them, and then Monson is seen walking up from the boat across the shore, Scott still remaining in the boat. He remains in the boat for a little time, and ultimately he is seen dragging it up to somewhere about high-water mark. Why was Scott remaining in the boat? Somebody was in that boat with a knife, because we have found the knife washed up upon the shore. My learned friend in the cross-examination of one of the witnesses, who identified the knife, said, " Probably you do not know that was Hambrough's knife." I am not surprised the witness did not know, and I fully believed my learned friend had evidence to prove it. But it turns out now that there is no evidence in any way connecting Hambrough with that knife; but there is evidence absolutely disconnecting him with it, because the only other witness to whom the question was put was a witness who had always accompanied Hambrough. He was asked, " Is that knife like Hambrough's? " —a knife, gentlemen, quite common, which any man might have, and the witness says, " It resembles it," but it has this conclusive point of distinction, that Hambrough's knife, which resembled it,

310

Speech for the Crown.

Solicitor-General

had a ring by which he attached it to his chain, whereas the knife in question has not the slightest trace of ever having had anything of the kind. So that you have the facts of Scott remaining in the boat and a knife found upon the shore, and a hole in the boat which every expert says is a hole manifestly made by a knife. What stronger testimony can there be as to a hole having been intentionally made in that boat that afternoon? Now, if so, who did it? The only persons who were there were the persons who afterwards participated in the later occurrences of that night. After these performances, dinner takes place, and in the course of dinner something is said about a fishing expedition for the night. M'Intyre, the keeper, is said to have sent a message to the dining-room in connection with this. M'Intyre has not been examined; no such fact has been proved. The inference, I should say, is this, if M'Intyre was there in connection with the fishing, the natural thing would have been that he should have been retained to accompany those who went to fish in the usual way. He certainly did not accompany them, and if he was there making any communication in connection with the fishing, the message he must have got was such as to send him from the scene, with the result that the fishing party consisted exclusively of Cecil Hambrough, Monson, and Scott. Well, gentlemen, it appears that they left the house some time—it is not specifically fixed, I admit—but apparently it was about ten o'clock at night, later probably than earlier. They go to the shore, they are going to fish—which boat do they take for fishing? M'Kellar's boat had been pronounced to be dangerous, and they had therefore gone and borrowed M'Nicol's boat for two nights. Would you not have expected that with the safe boat there —if they had got it for the purpose, and because of that which they had represented—three men there and a boat borrowed specially for its being safe for the purpose of fishing—would you not have expected that they would all have gone into the safe boat for the purpose of going to fish? But what do you find? You find two out of three enter the boat, not the safe boat, but M'Kellar's boat, which up till that afternoon had been perfectly safe, but which was deadly unsafe at this time in respect of the hole that certainly had been made in it.

You, gentlemen, will have to pause at that point in making up your minds, and calmly consider the circumstances which I am now narrating. Put to yourselves the question—hear everything with patience, and attention, and deliberation which my learned friend can possibly say on the point, give every weight which it is possible to give to what he urges—put to yourselves the question—What is the explanation of these men on the shore that night, if there on an ordinary fishing expedition, selecting the dangerous boat, the boat alleged to M'Nicol to be dangerous, and which had been tampered with and made dangerous by the hole which

311

Alfred John Monson.

was cut in it, and going out to fish in that unsafe boat, leaving the sound and safe boat there into which they did not enter—and one of their number not in the boat, but standing on the beach? Gentlemen, the explanation which I am bound to suggest with reference to these facts is this—the visit to Ardlamont Bay that night was made for the deadly purpose of drowning the poor youth Cecil Hambrough, whose policies had been completed, and were at that time in Monson's pocket. It was to be done by the use of a boat in which a hole had been cut; at such a point distant from the shore as, through the medium of the hole, would result in the boat becoming filled with water, and thus sinking. Monson was a swimmer, no doubt; but no sane man, regardful of his safety, would trust to the accident of being thrown into the sea late at night without any assistance at hand. He, a swimmer, no doubt, was safe with his friend Scott, and another boat on the beach ready to go to his assistance if required. The poor boy Hambrough, who could not swim, could not take the slightest benefit of such assistance, because, before Scott with the other boat could arrive in the bay at the point where the accident may have been supposed to have taken place, a man who was unable to swim, according to every reasonable computation, would have disappeared underneath the waters of Ardlamont Bay for ever. If you find any explanation satisfactory to your mind more favourable to the prisoner than the one I have suggested, consistent with reason and propriety, adopt it, and discard what I have said. But if you cannot find it for yourself, or if my learned friend cannot group these facts together in a manner convincing you that the hole in the boat that night, the use of the dangerous instead of the safe boat, the placing of a member of the party on the shore at hand for rescue if required—if these facts cannot be surveyed consistently with anything except the intention to drown Cecil Hambrough, then the first charge in this indictment is established. You will not fail to take note of the fact that all the men in and about Ardlamont in any way associated with Hambrough in the matter of fishing have been examined. It was the duty of those representing the Crown in a case of this kind to bring forward every man connected with the place and put him into the box, and every one of them directly negatives the suggestion made by the prisoner in his formal declaration emitted before the Sheriff with the assistance of his law agent, and in the knowledge that what he said would be used against him—that the hole was cut by Cecil Hambrough himself, because he found it inconvenient not to have a hole in the boat, by means of which it could be emptied when lying on the beach! Do you believe that Cecil Hambrough would have sailed it day after day on a fishing expedition, and have found inconvenience from the want of a hole in the boat, and made it, without that matter coming up between him and those who had been accompanying him? Gentlemen, if you think not, then the prisoner's declaration on the subject is false, and if he has given a false explanation with reference to

312

Speech for the Crown.

the reason of that hole being there, then I am afraid you must add that fact to the rest to be taken note of in deducing the inferences, which you will have to do, as to whether these coincidences to which I have referred are casual, accidental occurrences unconnected with crime, or whether they are not parts of a well-devised scheme by which this boy was to be removed altogether and the insurances on his life obtained.

The prisoner also says, gentlemen, that the upsetting of the boat was due to contact with a rock, some 200 or 300 yards from the shore. Where is the evidence of the existence of any such rock? The seamen frequenting the bay, the splash fishermen who have fished there for three-and-twenty years, never saw or heard of anything of the kind. The prisoner says that, so far from attempting to murder Cecil Hambrough that night, he saved his life by swimming for and fetching a boat. Gentlemen, the story is an odd one. A youth is said to have been sunk. He could not swim. He is thrown into deep water, in the dead of night, and the prisoner says the first thing he saw, amid the darkness, was the youth laughing on the rock. Gentlemen, the boat providentially filled with water manifestly much earlier than was expected. Both were cast from the boat and immersed in the water, but at a distance which enabled Cecil Hambrough perfectly easily to scramble to the shore, and they returned, accordingly, that night saturated with water, without the scheme which had been devised being effectually accomplished. One would have thought that was sufficiently exciting and startling for one period of four-and-twenty hours; but you must take what followed along with you.

They returned home that night; they slept there during the night; they got up early in the morning, having returned home at one o'clock. It is startling to hear that at six o'clock in the morning the next day, after an expedition of the kind I have described, the same party were active and out for the purpose of undertaking a sporting expedition. On that morning Mrs. Monson, Miss Hiron, and some of the children leave the scene. Their expedition, at least so far as the nurse was concerned, had been previously unknown to her. It was not a morning which one would have thought calculated to invite those who had gone through the experiences of the night before, and with no further motive than amusement, to have entered upon a shooting expedition at seven o'clock in the morning. It seemed to be a tempestuous morning, there being both wind and rain. Now, I shall treat this part of the case as I have treated the other, I mean in this way, that I shall first bring under your notice facts about which, I think, there cannot possibly be dispute.

About nine o'clock on the morning of the 10th, in a secluded part of the wood near the mansion-house of Ardlamont, Cecil Hambrough was found shot dead. There can be no doubt that he died

313

Alfred John Monson.

of a gunshot wound. There were only three persons there—Cecil Hambrough, Monson, and the man whom we have hitherto been describing as Scott. There were only two guns—a 12-bore gun and a 20-bore gun. One gun was carried by Hambrough, the other one was carried by Monson. I class that, gentlemen, amongst the facts which cannot be disputed; because, shortly after the event, on the same day, in an explanation given in writing by the prisoner himself, he recorded, for the purpose of being communicated to the police, the fact—" I and Hambrough alone had guns "—the third person being there, apparently, for the purpose of carrying the rabbits, his natural duty, according to Monson's representation of what he was.

Well, gentlemen, on these facts I think you will be of opinion that there are only two possible alternatives with regard to what occurred. The alternatives inevitably are that Cecil Hambrough died in consequence of a gunshot accident from his own gun, or that he was murdered by Monson. Well now, gentlemen, alternatives may occur to your mind of suicide by Hambrough, or accidental shooting by Monson. These, gentlemen, are not within the case, because they are excluded, the one by the total absence of suggestions, from beginning to end, of any suicidal tendency or intention on the part of Hambrough, and the other, because every word that the prisoner uttered with regard to the event, or put in writing with regard to the event, is absolutely exclusive of the idea of the injury being caused accidentally by him. So that on this part of the case you are face to face with two alternatives, between which you must elect; and it is your duty carefully to consider the whole evidence on both sides with regard to what I am saying to you, and what my learned friend is to say after me, for the purpose of coming to a conclusion whether the facts established in this case can, by any reasonable construction, be reconciled with any other result than the murder of Hambrough by Monson.

Well, gentlemen, I must now call your attention to the established facts on which it is my duty to suggest to you that only one course is open. On the morning of that day the incidents are of a striking character. Mrs. Monson, as I explained to you, leaves the scene for the purpose of an expedition to Glasgow. The gamekeeper Lamont, the natural attendant of the gentlemen on a shooting expedition, is got rid of for the time. He is sent on a message—sent to Mr. M'Intyre upon some message of an apparently trivial character. At least M'Intyre has not been called to suggest that he had anything to say or anything to do which would naturally explain Lamont being despatched at that early hour of the morning to fetch him to Ardlamont for the purpose of an interview; and in these circumstances—the keeper away—Monson and Hambrough, accompanied by this unknown mechanical engineer, sally forth on this tempestuous morning for a shooting expedition in the adjacent woods.

314

Speech for the Crown.

Solicitor-General

Gentlemen, I should like you to have a very clear and distinct conception of the precise locality near which this event occurred. You may remember that at the very beginning of the case an engineer of the name of Brand was examined, and that he proved and explained a plan showing the details of the locality. [The Solicitor-General then showed and explained the plan.] The sunk fence, he said, divides what have been called the old and the young wood, the old wood being situated between the point where the event occurred and the mansion-house. The offices are situated half-way between the mansion-house and the place in question. As regards the particular spot where Cecil Hambrough met his death, it has been spoken of sometimes as a sunk fence and sometimes as a ditch. I suppose both are virtually applicable. The sunk fence means simply a perpendicular wall of about 4 feet, with a ditch containing a run of water at the bottom of the fence, covered over with ferns and brackens, and long grass, immediately to the east of the fence, with the new wood beyond. I can illustrate it, I think, by means of this table. The sunk fence consisted of a wall, which would be represented by the distance from the floor to the top of the table, if it were 4 feet, the front of the table would represent the face of the wall running up between the old and the new wood. Then at the bottom of the wall towards the new wood there was a ditch—a small run of water, with ferns and grass covering the surface of the ground all the way along at the bottom of the wall. Then at the bottom of the wall the whole of the ground behind had been made up so that it seems to have been very much like the ground entering any ordinary wood of the age of the one in question, with grass, some whins, here and there loose stones, I have no doubt—it would be a most extraordinary wood if there were not. When the top of the dyke is spoken of that does not mean that a man standing on the top of the dyke was free from the land. It means that he was standing on the highest level in the old wood on the land made up at the back of the stone wall. Accordingly, I do not know if my learned friend will make any point of this, but there seemed early in the case a good deal said about the dangerous character of the place along which Cecil Hambrough would be walking as he was going along there for the purpose of shooting. Mr. Speedie, when in the box last night, having that question put to him, could not support that view, and said that it was like any other wood through which a sportsman would be walking in pursuit of game. If you wish more accurate information about that you have only to look at the sections prepared by Mr. Brand, and which are taken at intervals of a few feet for a considerable space southward from where the body was found. The reason why these sections were taken was this—Assuming that the body was found in the position which I now mark, going northward Cecil Hambrough would be walking along on the ground to the

315

Alfred John Monson.

westward of the sunk wall, and if you have sections taken at intervals of a foot or two for some distance behind the spot where he was found, these sections will show exactly whether the ground here is level, or whether there are variations in the level which would make a man stumble. These sections, according to close engineering measurement, show the precise line of the surface of the ground for a considerable distance back from Cecil Hambrough's feet, and enable you to know with certainty the character of the surface of the ground over which he was passing immediately before he dropped dead. These sections show that the ground for a considerable distance back was practically level. In addition, we have Mr. Speedie's evidence that the ground was of the usual character that would be found in such a wood that any sportsman frequented.

That being the character of the ground, I have now to ask your attention to a question which I think you will require to answer before you can come to a determination with reference to this part of the case. It goes very deep into it. I would suggest to you in dealing with this part of the case—much the more important because it is the capital charge—I would advise you, having made you familiar, as I hope I have done, with the precise nature of the locality, to begin by putting to yourselves the question and finding an answer satisfactory to your own minds, Where was the body first found? In a question as to suicide or accidental death or murder, the precise situation of the body, and the precise position of the weapon, every one is agreed, are vital points for consideration. Therefore, let me ask your attention in the first instance to the question—Was the body first found on the top of the wall where the witnesses saw it, or was it at the bottom of the ditch, and if it was on the top of the wall, how does the suggestion that it was found at the bottom of the ditch come within the present case? Well, the last question it is my duty to enable you to answer first. The prisoner, within a few hours of the fatal event, was asked by the constable if he had any explanation to give. He could not avoid giving an explanation. The police constable, most properly, said—"I am a subordinate officer; if you have anything to say and communicate through me, express it in writing, and deliver it to me." And, voluntarily, before a shadow of suspicion of crime was in the mind of anybody, unless it was in the mind of Monson himself, he wrote the holograph statement you have heard referred to, and in which he said—"Just as we got to the end of the cover I heard a shot fired. I waited a minute or two, and called out to ask what he had shot. There was no reply. I walked towards the corner of the cover in the direction of the shot in company with Mr. Scott." Gentlemen, he told the factor, Steven, that Scott and he met at the spot, that he went round the top of the wood, and that Scott approached the spot on the south. "I called Hambrough

316

Speech for the Crown.

several times, but there was no reply. I then saw "—I beg your special attention to these words, written, observe, by Monson on the 10th, the day of the event—" I then saw Hambrough lying at the bottom of the sunk fence on his left side with the gun beside him. We lifted him up, but he was quite dead. I then called out to the men at the stables. Three or four of the men came, and Mr. Hambrough was conveyed to the house. I think the time would be about 7.30." Gentlemen, he did nothing of the kind. He deliberately walked past the stables, with the witness Carmichael standing looking at him, straight to the house, not communicating with anybody at the stables at all. But, gentlemen, you have got to deal with that written explanation by Monson as to where the body was found. That was not a casual statement. It was a statement deliberately made with his pen in his hand for the purpose of being communicated to the authorities to enable them to decide whether it was accident or crime. Dr. Macmillan came on the spot shortly afterwards and communicated with Monson, and it appears from his report—the report which he made at the time—that the same statement was communicated verbally by him to the doctor, because the doctor reports, as the result of his communication with him on the same day, that Monson told him they had not gone more than a dozen yards along the turf dyke until they found the body beside the wall in a ditch, quite dead, and the gun beside it, but not grasped. Then, on the same day, Steven goes to the place, accompanied by Monson, with whom he seemed to be on friendly terms, and with Steven there alone, he pointed Steven to the ditch as the place where he had found the body. Dr. Macmillan went to the place to make an official inquiry, as a surgeon, to report to the authorities. He goes to the place, accompanied by Steven and by Monson, and being there, Steven, in the presence of Monson, and with Monson's consent, points to the ditch as the place where the body was found. You have, therefore, Monson, during the whole of the proceedings immediately following this event, persistently adhering to the statement that the ditch was the place ·where the body was found. He gave some account inconsistent with that in the first place to the man Jeffrey, who came from Ventnor, connected with the cemetery there. He said to him that Hambrough had fallen getting over the wall, but that might perhaps be consistent with the view that he was found in the ditch, and he also told Major Hambrough, when he came, that he had fallen getting over the wall, and that he was found in the ditch; and he led Major Hambrough to believe that he was not himself present at the time. Well, I think, with that body of evidence before you, there can be no doubt at all as to what had been the representations of the accused with reference to the place where that body was first found. Well, gentlemen, the first question you have to ask yourselves is this— Did Monson deliberately and persistently state that the body was in

Alfred John Monson.

the ditch? The next question you have to put to yourselves and answer is this—Is that statement true? and I am afraid that if you find that it is not, you will have to ask yourselves the further question—Why was it made by Monson if it was not true? Now, gentlemen, with regard to the question whether the body was found in the ditch, I think I am bound to say there is no difference among the witnesses. Every man who was in that neighbourhood at any time on that day absolutely negatives the possibility of it. It had got rumoured about that the body had been found in the ditch, because Monson had pointed that out to Steven, and Steven had told the doctor, and these things were spoken of; and it immediately became suggested among the people there that this man had been found in the ditch, and they, having found him on the top of the wall, went there for the express purpose of satisfying themselves after the event.

Every person who was there is perfectly clear that there was not the shadow of a trace of any person having fallen into the ditch at all, or of the removal of any person from it, and that the character of the ground and of the vegetation upon it was such that anything of that kind was impossible without marks being left perfectly perceptible to the human eye. But, gentlemen, it does not stop there. This man was shot in such a way that one of the largest veins of the head was ruptured by the shot, involving an immediate discharge of blood, which the doctors in their report describe as " causing him to bleed to death," and, accordingly, blood was found in a large quantity on the bank where the body was found. An examination was made, not merely to see whether the ferns were trodden or pressed down, but whether blood of any kind was to be found either in the ditch or along any part of the intermediate ground. Not a single trace of blood was found by a single person who was very anxiously looking for it. But, gentlemen, it does not stop there. The doctors who made the examination for the Crown tell you that the body could not have fallen in the ditch and died there without a quantity of blood being there, perfectly perceptible to any one who looked. He could not have been carried from there to the top of the wall without either of two things happening—blood on his own clothes if he was held at a certain angle, or, if he were not held at the particular angle, on the clothes of those who carried him, and blood on the ground. There would have been blood upon the clothes of the men who lifted him and placed him on the bank. Not a shadow or a trace of anything of the kind was found. But, gentlemen, I think I am only pressing the matter to the extent which the evidence necessarily suggests when I say to you that, looking to what was the evidence of the first skilled witness for the defence yesterday, the defence themselves do not believe that the body was ever in the ditch.

Dr. Hay was taken to Ardlamont to form an opinion as to

318

Speech for the Crown.

Solicitor-General

whether the death was due to accident or to design. No reasonable man can reject the view that the original position of the body is one of the most important factors in the determination of that question. You heard this witness asked as to how far his examination had been directed and guided from the point of view of the body having been lying in the ditch. Gentlemen, I do not think he liked the suggestion. He seemed to be compelled to acknowledge that, if mentioned at all, it was mentioned so trivially and slightly that he treated it as of no moment. All his investigations on the spot were regulated and directed on the assumption that the body was on the bank, and not in the ditch. If he had believed—if he had been told that there were reasonable grounds for believing—that the body had been found in the ditch, why did he not construct a theory which, starting from that basis, would have shown that the event was an accident, and not due to design? Guided by the instructions received from the advisers of the prisoner, all Dr. Hay's investigations proceeded on the hypothesis that the body was originally on the bank and not in the ditch.

Well, gentlemen, what I have said is all the assistance I can give you in determining that vital question, but you will make little way in threading your path through the intricacies of this case until you have solved it for yourselves. It is so crucial, cuts so deep into the whole case, that I say again, as I said before, give every attention and patience to my learned friend when he addresses himself to that point. He will undoubtedly have to consider and speak to you upon the issue I am now discussing. Every one must see that it is at the core of the case; and if my learned friend is unable to displace from your minds the conviction that the body was upon the bank, and not in the ditch, then I am afraid he has the great task before him of giving some satisfactory explanation to you as to why the prisoner falsely, knowing the falsehood, made a representation with regard to the spot where he found the body, absolutely inconsistent with the facts of the case.

Gentlemen, the next question I think you will have to consider is a much more simple one than the one I have dealt with, or, at least, a much less serious one, and it is, Which gun was he shot with? Now, with regard to this, I doubt whether there is any serious dispute. The evidence, I submit, establishes conclusively that he was shot with a discharge from a 12-bore gun, and that the cartridge which killed him contained No. 5 shot. The weights spoken to by the doctor in regard to the pellets in the brain, weighed against the subsequent pellets purchased from Macnaughton, seemed absolutely to demonstrate that. I do not trouble you with the specific figures of the weight of the four pellets found in the brain, but they weighed more than No. 6, and came nearly up to No. 5. No doubt a pellet entering the brain through the skull may undergo attrition from contact with the skull, and consequently may lose

Alfred John Monson.

weight, but by no possible process can it increase in weight. And, therefore, finding them in the skull after undergoing any process of attrition to which they may have been subjected and weighing more than four pellets of No. 6 shot, we are inevitably led to the conclusion, whatever may be the effect of it, that the shot which killed Cecil Hambrough was No. 5 shot, and discharged from a 12-bore gun.

The next question which you will have to consider, if you could answer it, would afford a complete solution of the case. There being practical agreement, I imagine, that the death was caused by a discharge from a 12-bore gun with a No. 5 cartridge, and the two guns being a 20-bore and a 12-bore gun, of course you will see, if you have conclusive evidence as to who carried the 12-bore gun, that will show whether it was an accident or a shot from another. Now, gentlemen, I have to call your attention to the somewhat peculiar state of facts with regard to the two guns. About this, as far as I can see, there can be no dispute, that the 12-bore gun, as a rule, was Monson's gun, and the 20-bore gun was Hambrough's gun. Therefore, if things were normal, if Monson was using what may be called, for the purposes of the case, his own gun, his usual gun, and Hambrough was using his own or usual gun, then the 12-bore gun, with No. 5 cartridge, was in the hands of Monson, and not of Hambrough. Well, gentlemen, with that curious coincidence of circumstances connected with this case, doubt has been cast upon whether each man was carrying his own gun. It is an extraordinary coincidence, the upsetting in the bay of the boat on the night of the 9th, with the early expedition on the morning of the 10th—the man that was tumbled out of the boat with the hole in it, shot dead next morning—and, according to the case for the defence, the men having for that morning changed guns—a curious coincidence not likely to be accepted. It may be so, and if you are satisfied that it is so, it would solve the case. But I think you will be of opinion that careful and attentive consideration of the facts bearing on this matter is required before you will accept the explanation that this curious coincidence should have happened, that an exchange of guns had taken place immediately before one of the men was shot dead.

Now, it is my duty to put before you as minutely, and certainly with a desire to make it as accurate as I can, what is the evidence bearing on this matter. The first thing, I think, you probably would like to know in a matter of that kind is this—If the defence now is that there was a change of guns, when was it first suggested? When was the body in the ditch? The explanations about that could not be postponed. If the body was not to be admitted as having been at the place where it was found, of course, there could be no denial of that. Any suggestion about it being elsewhere must be made at once. With regard to the gun, it might be different. There was no actual evidence present to anybody for

Speech for the Crown.

Solicitor-General

determining that, and you must keep that fact in view. If the body had been found where it was lying, and if the gun that shot the man was his own gun, and was lying beside him, and had been left there, then the pellets in the head and the gun beside it, and the No. 5 shot, only available for the 12-bore gun, would have supplied facts which, in the course of an inquiry extending over an hour, would have conclusively determined whether the man was shot by his own gun or not. I should have thought—but you will judge—I should have thought that two friends shooting—one shot dead by an accident, the other anxious about his friend—with the possibility of restoration to life, perhaps the possibility of mistake as to life being extinct—would have rushed to the nearest point of assistance. The prisoner seems to have thought that too. In his written statement on the same day he says he immediately called for assistance to the nearest place—the offices. He did nothing of the kind. He left his friend, carefully taking with him not only his own gun, but the gun of his friend. Why this anxiety to remove the gun? What damage would it have done to have left the gun there till assistance had been got to see whether anything could be done? Not only were the guns lifted and carried away; they were carried past the offices into the mansion-house, carefully deposited in the smoking-room, and the cartridges of both removed. And after that process for the extinction of evidence, then for the first time it is communicated to the servants in the house that a catastrophe has occurred to one of its inmates, which had left him lying dead in the neighbourhood of the house. Gentlemen, you must note these particulars. You are men, and you will judge for yourselves how far it is within the range of reasonable probability that the innocent friend would have acted as I have described in connection with the ghastly circumstances in which he was placed. But if he had changed guns with his friend, would he not bitterly regret in that by any possibility the difference in the guns could have caused the mishap? Would it not have been the most natural thing for him to say, " I wish to God I had kept my own gun this morning! Possibly if Cecil had been using his own this never would have occurred." Not one word was said suggesting that any change of guns had taken place. He met the doctor, who was entitled to obtain the most minute information with reference to the circumstances under which the occurrence had taken place, and we have a record at the time of the effect produced upon the doctor's mind. The doctor, in coming as he did at the time to the conclusion that this was due to accident, and not to design, seems largely to have been influenced by the fact that the gun the lad was carrying was of unusually short dimensions in the barrel, and therefore might have got in a position relatively to his head which a gun of the ordinary length of barrel might not. And, accordingly, in his report he says, " the information above given "—referring to the information he had got at the time from Lamont, the keeper, from Monson,

Y

Alfred John Monson.

the prisoner, and from Scott, the fugitive associate—summarising
that information in his report, he says, "the information above
given makes it probable that the deceased was going along the wall
with a gun, a short 20-bore gun, under his arm and his finger on
the trigger, when his foot caught on something, and he plunged forward, put down his hand to save himself, thus lowering the breech,
raising the muzzle, and pressing the trigger." Then he says, in a
subsequent report, on the 25th of August—having by this time seen
that he had been misled in coming to the conclusion that it was
innocence and not guilt—"I implicitly accepted the statements of
the witnesses Monson and Scott that the injuries to Hambrough were
due to an accidental shot from his own gun, a short-barrelled 20-bore
boy's weapon, charged with amberite." Then, gentlemen, he again
recurs to the same matter in a document which he wrote to the insurance company, because part of the process was that, by a certificate
from Dr. Macmillan to the effect that death was accidental, the
insurance people were to be satisfied and the policies were to be
paid. In the original letter which Dr. Macmillan wrote to that
effect, and which he afterwards recalled, he says—"It seems to me
highly probable that he was going along here with a short-barrelled
20-bore gun, with his finger on the trigger," and so on. Well,
gentlemen, there is not merely silence on the part of Monson, not
merely failure to express his sorrow that a change of guns might
have taken place, causing the accident—there is direct misrepre-
sentation, direct misstatement to the medical man, whose report
would undoubtedly be submitted to the Procurator-Fiscal as the
report of the first doctor on the spot, and whose report was to be
submitted to the insurance men for the purpose of securing payment of the policy. The representation to the doctor, on which he
acted, and on which he wrote and delivered these official documents,
was that Cecil Hambrough was shot with his own gun—in short,
that things were in their normal condition in so far as the guns
were concerned, each man carrying his own gun. When, gentlemen, did this suggestion of a change of guns come into the case?
You can have no doubt upon that matter at all. On the 23rd of
August an interview of a most striking character took place at
Inveraray. The Procurator-Fiscal was resident at Inveraray. He
had received Dr. Macmillan's report to the effect that, in his opinion,
the accident might have been caused by Cecil Hambrough using
his short-barrelled boy's gun, and consequently, regarding the occu-
pants of Ardlamont as people against whom no suspicion of murder
could reasonably be entertained, he had taken no active step in
the direction of investigating crime.

Monson, believing that the danger was passed, that the time
had arrived when the fruits of villainy might be reaped, invited an
interview at Inveraray with the Procurator-Fiscal, accompanied by
the two agents of the insurance company and his friend Mr. Tottenham, for the purpose of securing what, placed side by side with the

Speech for the Crown.

Solicitor-General

doctor's report, would have the effect of the fulfilment of this dastardly design, namely, the payment of the sum in the £20,000 policies. The Procurator-Fiscal met the prisoner at the pier. The prisoner told him that he had two friends there. The Procurator-Fiscal naturally asked who his friends were who desired to see him. He then told him they were persons connected with the insurance. These are Monson's words to a public official in connection with such a death as this. He immediately replied, " What has insurance to do with this case—the man was not insured? " The secret could not be longer kept, because the Procurator-Fiscal's certificate had to be got as a condition of the policy being paid. Monson replied, " Oh, yes, there is an insurance which has been effected by his father on the boy's life." " What is the amount? " " £15,000." And, having got the information asked for, the Procurator-Fiscal naturally asked him about the gun by which the accident had happened, and was told that it happened with the boy's own gun. Knowing quite well that, with this new fact brought into the case, investigation was essential, he told Monson " the first thing to do is to send to me to-morrow morning the 20-bore gun you say caused the death, along with the amberite cartridges which are said to have been used," this being specifically mentioned in Dr. Macmillan's report as being one of the reasons, along with the 20-bore gun, which led him to come to the conclusion that the death might be accidental. Monson promised that both would be sent. Gentlemen, the next morning arrived, and neither was there. The Procurator-Fiscal instituted his official inquiry, and, having examined Lamont, the keeper, from whom he received no indication that any change of guns had taken place, he told him at once to go to Monson and fetch the 20-bore gun and the amberite cartridges by which he had, up to that time, said the death had been caused. And in response to that demand—it could not any longer be parried—Lamont returned, bringing with him the 12-bore gun, and stating that Monson's explanation was that up to that time it had been all a mistake—that the gun which had done the deed was the 12-bore gun, and not the boy's 20-bore gun at all. Gentlemen, these are facts which you must consider. The inconsistencies of Monson's statement about the guns do not stop there. On the morning of the death he went to Lamont, asked for the 20-bore gun, and told Lamont at the time that he was asking it for Cecil. Lamont never heard of the suggestion as to a change until the time which I have just mentioned. Steven, the factor, at that time the associate and friend of Monson, had been there, and in communication with Monson about it he never heard any suggestion at that time of any change of guns. And, gentlemen, these matters are so important and decisive that I ask you not to accept my description of the evidence on this matter from my recollection, but I ask you to bear with me for a very few minutes in order that I may make

Alfred John Monson.

the point perfectly clear. I shall read to you from the shorthand notes what was said both by Steven and Lamont respectively with regard to the matter of the change of guns. This is a matter of vital importance, because, as you solve it, you put the question at issue absolutely beyond doubt. If the 12-bore gun, Monson's own gun, with No. 5 cartridges, was in his hand that morning, then it is not a question of opinion, it is a matter of downright certainty that his gun shot Cecil Hambrough. Now, Steven says about this—" I remember an occasion when Monson showed me the remains of a rabbit. That was some time after the accident. It was the day Mr. Blair was at Ardlamont." The death occurred on the 10th, and this on the 25th, sixteen days after the event. " I went to the place on that occasion with Mr. Monson. On going there, did he tell you anything about the gun?—No; I was not in company with them; I was a little behind, and I overtook them when they reached the spot where the rabbit was found. Did you hear anything about going to the keepers on the morning of the death for a gun?—Not at that particular time; but he told me at another time he went to the gamekeeper's for a gun. It was on the morning of the death that he had gone to the gamekeeper's for a gun. Do you know when it was that he spoke to you about that?—I think it was the night he was under police surveillance in Ardlamont House. It would be a week after the death, or more." Mr. Steven is mistaken about that, because the police surveillance had not begun until towards the end of August. " He said he went over to the keeper's for the 20-bore gun. That was the gun Hambrough was in the habit of using. He left Hambrough and Scott in the house, intending to find them there, I suppose, when he came back from the keeper's. But when he came back he found that they had gone out. Hambrough had lifted Monson's gun—a 12-bore—and taken it with him. He had kept that gun all that morning, and Monson kept the gun—the 20-bore gun—he got from the keeper. He had kept the 20-bore gun?—Yes, the gun he got from the keeper. He had fired one shot, killing one rabbit, intending to pick it up on his way home; but they did not come that way, and it got leave to lie. About the two guns I have spoken about; there was a 20-bore gun and a 12-bore gun; the 20-bore gun is the smaller of the two. What was it that Monson said to you in regard to the 20-bore gun on the morning of the accident?—He went over to the gamekeeper (Lamont) and got that gun—the 20-bore gun. Did he say that that was the gun that Hambrough usually shot with?—Yes. He did not say why he got it that morning from Lamont. He said Hambrough had left the house with the 12-bore gun, and that he himself had kept the 20-bore gun. But I understood, if he had been back at the house before Hambrough and Scott had left, he would have given Hambrough his own gun?—He said that they were using some new powder, which I now know is

324

Speech for the Crown.

amberite. He did not say what powder Hambrough was using?—
No. Did he say who was using the amberite?—No; he just said
they were trying a new powder." Now, gentlemen, you will
observe that what Mr. Steven says about the guns was this—On the
day of the accident, Monson told him that he had gone to Lamont,
the keeper, and asked for a 20-bore gun for Hambrough. But
when he came back he found that Hambrough and Scott had started,
and that consequently he had no opportunity of giving to Hambrough, as he had intended to do, the 20-bore gun, nor of himself
taking the 12-bore gun. He says he went down the wood alone, and
shot a rabbit, which he did not pick up; it was to be picked up
at a future time. It was after the police were watching him at
Ardlamont that he first suggested any change of gun. Now,
gentlemen, if you will allow me I will now bring to your notice
what Lamont, the keeper, says on the same matter. " [Shown
No. 8.] That is a 12-bore gun. It is the gun which Monson was in
the habit of shooting with. Labels 7 and 8 were the two guns—
20-bore and 12-bore respectively—which Hambrough and Monson
were in the habit of using. These were the only guns they had,
with the exception of an estate gun they had before they got the
20-bore gun. When they got the 20-bore gun they ceased to use the
estate gun. The estate gun was the one I used. It was in my
possession. The 20-bore and the 12-bore, which have been shown
me, were the only guns which were at the mansion-house at that
time." I think it may be convenient that I should dispose of the
statement made by M'Ewan, the innkeeper—the burly, good-
natured innkeeper you saw the other day—who told you that
Monson had told him that the gun Hambrough was shooting with
was Mrs. Campbell Lamont's gun. That is an additional and
gratuitous falsehood apparently, because Lamont tells you plainly
that the only guns about the place that day were Monson's own
12-bore and the 20-bore. It just illustrates how Monson was
prevaricating on the subject of the guns which were out that
morning.

[At this stage the prisoner leant forward somewhat excitedly,
and was understood to intimate to his counsel that Mrs. Campbell
Lamont's gun was one of the productions.]

Mr. COMRIE THOMSON—I think it has been proved that the
12-bore gun here, and the 12-bore gun spoken of is Mrs. Campbell
Lamont's.

The SOLICITOR-GENERAL—I am sorry if I have made any mistake. There can be no doubt of the materiality of this. I suggest
to my learned friend that if what I am now reading is in any
aspect inaccurate—

Mr. COMRIE THOMSON—Oh, no.

The SOLICITOR-GENERAL—I should not say inaccurate, but if
it is incomplete, so far as the guns are concerned, I am sure my

Alfred John Monson.

learned friend will think it right to get an extract of the notes of the particular evidence which establishes that the guns in use that day were labelled 7 and 8, which were Monson's and Hambrough's, and which they were respectively in the habit of using.

The LORD JUSTICE-CLERK—M'Ewan said that Hambrough was carrying a 12-bore gun he had got a loan of from Mrs. Campbell Lamont.

The SOLICITOR-GENERAL—In a case of this voluminous character it is quite unjustifiable to rely absolutely on one's own memory, but I am bound to say that I have no recollection of any evidence of the kind to which my learned friend refers, and as I have no opportunity of commenting upon it, if it is produced I am bound to take the evidence we have heard, and I may point out that not one word was spoken to Lamont, the gamekeeper, in the way of shaking his clear and absolutely direct testimony, that the only two guns at the mansion-house, and in use that day were the guns labelled 7 and 8, which were Monson's and Hambrough's own guns respectively, which they had regularly used. I am very glad, if I have made any mistake, that it has been pointed out to me, but I must say that I am merely repeating to you what was said in the witness-box by Lamont.

Mr. COMRIE THOMSON—I accept every word that you have said. My point here is simply this, that the 12-bore gun referred to here is Mrs. Campbell Lamont's.

The SOLICITOR-GENERAL—It is the gun which Monson was in the habit of shooting with.

Mr. COMRIE THOMSON—Yes, but it was Mrs. Campbell Lamont's.

The SOLICITOR-GENERAL—Labels 7 and 8, the witness Lamont said, "were the two guns that Monson and Hambrough were in the habit of using. These were the only guns they had, with the exception of the estate gun that was used before the 20-bore gun came. When they got the 20-bore gun they ceased to use the estate gun. It was the one I used. It was in my possession at this time. The 20- and the 12-bore guns shown me were the only guns in the mansion-house at this time." Now, will my learned friend tell me that the witness who was examined said that the label No. 8 was Mrs. Campbell Lamont's gun and not Monson's?

Mr. COMRIE THOMSON—I take that as you read it as quite accurate, that labels No. 7 and 8 are respectively the 20-bore and the 12-bore guns. My point is that the 12-bore gun is Mrs. Campbell Lamont's, and the witness Lamont says, "Besides that there is another gun, the estate gun, which is in my possession."

The SOLICITOR-GENERAL—Would you refer me to any statement by any witness that the 12-bore gun is Mrs. Campbell Lamont's gun?

Mr. COMRIE THOMSON—Not at this moment. I will show it you as soon as possible.

Speech for the Crown.

Solicitor-General

The SOLICITOR-GENERAL (resuming his address to the jury)—I think I see what my learned friend points to, and I should be sorry to cause him any unnecessary anxiety or trouble. I fancy that his anxiety to assume that label No. 8 is Mrs. Campbell Lamont's gun is to get rid of the implication from the witness M'Ewan's statement.

Mr. COMRIE THOMSON—You put it that this was a gratuitous falsehood on the part of the accused?

The SOLICITOR-GENERAL—Yes.

Mr. COMRIE THOMSON—My point is this, that in talking of the 12-bore gun and Mrs. Campbell Lamont's gun the same gun is being spoken of, and I rather think if the Procurator-Fiscal is in the Court he could inform us that that is so.

The SOLICITOR-GENERAL—That would be most irregular. You will understand that upon the question which gun Hambrough was carrying and which gun Monson was carrying, it is perfectly immaterial whether the 12-bore gun was Monson's own or was Mrs. Campbell Lamont's. Therefore, upon the direct question of whether the gun that fired the shot was in Monson's hands or not, this is a side question of who owned the gun, and it cannot affect the matter. If my learned friend can point to any passage in the evidence that any witness gave in the witness-box to the effect that label No. 8 was not Monson's gun, but Mrs. Campbell Lamont's gun, then what I have said in regard to Monson's statement to M'Ewan being a " gratuitous falsehood " must be withdrawn. I say that on the question whether Monson or Hambrough carried a 12-bore gun it is immaterial to whom it belonged, but if the 12-bore [No. 8] is Monson's gun, he must have known it, and if he told M'Ewan that Hambrough was carrying Mrs. Campbell Lamont's gun, when there was no such gun about the place, I think you will agree with me, and my learned friend will agree, that it was a gratuitous falsehood. On the other hand, if my learned friend quotes from the evidence any statement by any witness that No. 8 is not Monson's gun, but Mrs. Campbell Lamont's gun, then what I have said about a gratuitously false statement to M'Ewan undoubtedly is displaced, and you will strike that out of your minds as an observation which has been made. The important point is this, whoever they belonged to, there was a 20 and a 12-bore gun on the scene that morning, and the point is, when did Monson say to anybody that he had exchanged guns, and the 12-bore he knew well had done the deed was in Hambrough's hands, and not his? I will read you what Lamont, the gamekeeper, further says about this—" After the death I first saw the two guns in the smoking-room in the afternoon. When I went to offer my assistance they were lying on the sofa. I took them away for the purpose of cleaning them. He made no remark. There were no cartridges in either of the guns. The 12-bore gun was in their possession that morning; I do not know when they had it, but it was down at the house anyway."

Alfred John Monson.

Solicitor-General

We are agreed that on the morning of 10th August the only guns in use were the 12-bore and the 20-bore; it is of no consequence to whom they respectively belonged. The point is, who had the 12-bore gun that morning? Confine your attention to the question, Was the 12-bore gun in Monson's hand or in Hambrough's hand, it being clear on the evidence that that was the usual arrangement; or had the exchange, which was put into the case after the police came upon the scene, been effected?

The point we now put to you is that that idea of the exchange of guns was an afterthought on the part of Monson. Now, Lamont goes on to say that the 12-bore gun and the 20-bore gun were out on the morning of the accident. After giving Monson the 20-bore gun, he says—" I did not know further about it. When I saw Monson in the smoking-room he seemed excited, distressed, and he at first was scarcely able to speak to me. I asked him **how it** happened, and he gave me his account of it." Then he says— "Monson said that Hambrough had invited some friends for the Twelfth, and he would like to stop their coming. The guns were breech-loaders. When a man has done shooting it is not unusual to draw the cartridges. I was not surprised to find them unloaded. I just put the cleaning rod through them in the ordinary way. I had known previously of Hambrough shooting with the 12-bore gun before the 20-bore gun came. Monson and Mr. Hambrough frequently went out shooting with no attendant at all. The wad found was the thick wad usually placed between the powder and the shot, and was a 12-bore wad."

Gentlemen, the wad makes it even clearer that it was a 12-bore gun that shot Hambrough, so that you have not only the shot but the wad necessarily associated with the 12-bore gun. I want you to observe not merely that this suggestion of the change of guns is made for the first time after the police inquiry is begun, but after the directly inconsistent accounts made to Steven and Lamont are given. Monson says to Steven that he asked the gun from Lamont for Hambrough, intending to take it back to Hambrough. Finding, however, that Scott and Hambrough had left the house, he followed them alone, and shot a rabbit, which he left to be lifted afterwards. When he tells Lamont about the exchange he says, " I got the gun from him and came back and found Hambrough standing on the lawn with a 12-bore gun for the purpose of trying the amberite cartridges." Which of these stories is true, or are they not both made under circumstances which compel you, from their contradictory character, to assume that they are both false? Why should Monson, if he had changed the gun for a particular reason, not have given the same reason to both men? When you find contradictions of that character combined with the fact that the accused carried off the guns after the fatality and removed the cartridges, what are you to think? The gamekeeper says quite naturally that it is usual and proper in every sportsman, when he stops shooting,

Speech for the Crown.

to remove the cartridges, but does the usual practice of sportsmanship apply in the case where a man's friend is found dead on the ground? I think the most natural thing would have been that Monson, shocked by what had occurred, if he had been innocent, would have left the gun on the ground, and the men who had gone there would have seen it. Then there would have been the gamekeeper to tell you how he found the gun, the condition of the hammers, and to show you the very cartridges which he found in the gun beside the body. Gentlemen, this whole matter connected with the exchange of guns—the fact that it was contrary to the usual custom that the 12-bore gun should be in Hambrough's hands, and the circumstances under which the idea of exchange was first ventilated, and the contradictory reasons which were given as the cause of the exchange—guides you, I am afraid, to draw the inference that this idea of exchange of guns was developed as an answer to what on reflection Monson must have known was standing as an indelible record against him. The pellets in the brain would be the pellets in the cartridges of the 12-bore gun, and by the removal of the guns and this theory of exchange, and the mixing up of the facts, that indelible record of evidence must in some way be displaced.

The next point you have to consider is this—If Hambrough had the 12-bore gun in his hand he would have 12-bore cartridges in his pocket, and cartridges with No. 5 shot. What is the state of matters with regard to the cartridges? You have heard the evidence about that. There is found hanging on the back of the door of the cupboard for clothes in the room in which Hambrough slept, found hanging where it was placed by those who undressed the dead man, his jacket, identified by a small speck of blood on the collar. It is examined, and there are found in the pockets of the coat nineteen cartridges. They are the only cartridges in the coat, and you have thus the means of knowing what cartridges he was carrying. What were the cartridges? There were eighteen cartridges for the 20-bore gun, and with No. 6 shot. There was just one cartridge for the 12-bore gun, but it had also No. 6 shot. Gentlemen, you see the importance of that vital fact. You are considering whether the man was killed by an accident from his own gun—the gun he was carrying—or whether he was shot by a gun carried by another. What better evidence could you have of the gun the man was carrying than finding out the cartridges in his pocket? He would have cartridges for the gun he was carrying, not cartridges for a different gun. Every cartridge in his pocket, but one, was a cartridge that would not have fitted the 12-bore gun, and the only cartridge in his pocket for a 12-bore gun, and which, no doubt, had got mixed up with the rest, could not have been taken from the lot from which the cartridge that shot the man was drawn, because that one also contained No. 6 shot. Now, gentlemen, you have to consider that, while I am treating these matters each one by one—the exigencies of argument compel me so to do—you will have to take

329

Alfred John Monson.

Solicitor-General

them in the lump; you must take them all, not only separately, but together.   You will have to take the removal of the gun—not a word said about the fact that the man was shot by a 12-bore gun and a No. 5 cartridge, and that that was the gun usually carried by Monson; not a suggestion made as to the exchange of guns till the police were on the spot; and in the pockets of the man cartridges found for the 20-bore gun with the exception of one, and that with No. 6 shot.

I come now to a part of the case to which I think you will attach grave importance; one would almost have said, if I had stopped where I am, the chain would be nearly, if not altogether, complete.   But, gentlemen, we come now to facts about which there can be no doubt, facts, the tendency and import of which it is for you to determine, but which I submit to you are eloquent, and eloquent only in one direction.   I refer to the position of the body and the character and direction of the wound.   It has been explained to you that the body was found lying on the ground a little way to the west of the top of the sunk wall, and in close proximity to certain trees.   Now, it is creditable, I think, to the medical men in the case that they seem to have, by virtue of the accuracy of their scientific investigations, determined with certainty two most important points in the case.   The medical men on both sides are agreed that this man died from a shot delivered from behind, and they are agreed, or nearly agreed, I think, as to the precise angle or direction of the course of the shot as it passed Hambrough's head.   Therefore you may start with this—that in forming an opinion from the facts as proved before you, you will probably, I think—but it is for you to judge, you heard the evidence—assume that he was shot from behind, and by a shot passing his head in a nearly horizontal direction, and, in so far as it was off the horizontal, tending upwards towards the front.   Then with regard to the precise portion of the head which was struck, that appears to me not to be disputed.   The shot struck the head a little way behind the back of the ear, passing away by the ear, or rather through the ear to a certain extent, carrying away a portion of the middle of the ear. By means of these two factors—the point of original impact on the skull, and the portion of the ear which was damaged, and furrowing of the skin between these two points, and the slighter injury of the skin in front of the ear at the point where the shot left the head —the direction of the wound is virtually determined.

The next question is, Where was the body immediately after it was shot?   I have already said to you what I have to say on that specific branch, and, therefore, for the purpose of this part of my argument I assume that you will arrive at the conclusion—as one of the doctors said—'' he fell where he was shot, and there he lay.'' He was found, as you remember, with the back of his head in a pool of blood, and a piece of wad and pieces of bone of the skull in close proximity.   I do not think any witness has been examined

330

Speech for the Crown.

Solicitor-General

before you who has been able to give any intelligent explanation of these various indisputable facts consistent with any other view than that the man was shot standing near the place where he was found. There is another fact which apparently is not disputed, and that is, that in the immediate vicinity of the place where the body was found certain trees were found with indisputable marks of injury from shot. Something has been said about this being a wood in which shot marks are to be found in various parts of it—in branches at various places. I think you will probably have come to the conclusion as the result of the evidence that no place could be found near where the body lay with any marks upon the trees in the least suggesting that they had been caused by the shot that killed Hambrough other than the marks in the rowan, beech, and lime trees, or you would have had from the witnesses for the defence some suggestion of that character on the part either of the doctor, or of Speedy, or of some of the persons who visited the place in the discharge, doubtless, of their duty to the prisoner ; and I think you will agree with me that their first duty, and all they had to do, was to find some other appearance of shot in the neighbourhood of where he lay which it could be suggested was associated with the fact of his death. Speedy made a very minute examination. He could only find one branch marked with shot about 17 yards off on the side of the dyke, and another about 174 yards off, and he was so anxious to find traces of shot that he wandered over to the opposite side of the wood and gleaned certain branches there.

You will see that in determining how a man is shot, the next best evidence to the position of the body and the relative position of the weapon, which we have not here—for, if Monson's story is correct in regard to either, both the body and the weapons were taken away—the next best evidence you can have at all is the ascertainment of the line in which the shot went that killed the man. Well, gentlemen, the body is found lying in an open space, between 6 and 7 feet from the stem of a rowan tree. The head is towards the rowan tree ; the feet away from it, towards the south. If you put the body erect, and take a tape and draw a line which passes the head and, extended northwards, goes through that part of the rowan tree and the beech and the lime which, by general consent, show the marks of the shot as it passed through them, have you any doubt, gentlemen, what that means ? Can any person have any doubt that, on these facts, the man being shot there, and on minute and careful examination of that continuous line between his head and the points of impact of the shot beyond being distinctly established—is there room for any doubt that the shot which caused the injury to the trees was the shot which caused the injury to the dead man's head ?

It has been suggested to you that the marks upon the trees are indicative of the shot having passed through them at a time

Alfred John Monson.

anterior to the death of Hambrough. It is said that they looked as if they might be two months old at the time when they were examined, which was only five weeks after the accident. I think the witnesses had to admit that it is impossible to gauge with such minute accuracy, from an examination of a twig, weeks after it has been injured, the precise date at which the injury was inflicted, as to determine that it was five weeks as against two months or any such minute period as that. Everybody seems to have agreed that these branches had been injured within some weeks of the time when they were being examined, and, in the absence of any other explanation, when you find the precise line passing through these various points, is it possible to doubt that they were all due to the same shot and the same cause, viz., a single shot?

Well, gentlemen, the next question you have to determine is this, How did this wound occur in this man's head? Now, if you are of opinion that the shot through the trees was the shot which killed the man, then I am afraid the testimony is all one way, that that shot could not have been delivered by the man's own hand. I put that directly to the witness Speedy, who made suggestions to you as to possible methods by which accidents can occur. Of course we all know, without the aid of witnesses at all, that accidents with guns may occur in an infinite variety of ways. That is not the question. The question is, finding the conditions you have here, a man admittedly shot from behind at the extremely peculiar angle at which this shot traverses the head, and marks of the shot found at the same height from the ground immediately in front of him and within a few feet, not a witness in the witness-box has suggested—with all the ingenuity he has been able to apply—not one can devise any theory by which the accidental discharge of Hambrough's own gun, carried by himself, could produce the injury to the head, and the shot passing through the trees at the same time. You have Dr. Hay suggesting to you that at a certain angle, or by the gun falling to the ground, or by some such causes, the accidental discharge of the gun might take place. But which of any of these would produce the discharge of the gun through the man's head from behind almost horizontally, at a height from the ground corresponding with the line of shot through the adjacent trees? Until you ascertain, or until my learned friend puts before you, what none of his witnesses has been able to suggest, some rational explanation of how that could be effected by a gun carried in the man's own hand, or falling from his hand, you must accept as true what the medical witnesses for the prosecution stated to you, namely, that, with all the efforts they have applied, they have been unable to imagine how these known, determined, and ascertained results could possibly be accomplished by anything else than the discharge of a gun in the hand of another. All the suggestions of the dropping of the gun are out of the case, because you must

332

Speech for the Crown.

Solicitor-General

have the butt of the gun upon the ground, and then you have a discharge either in a vertical line or along the ground, or at an angle altogether inconsistent with the horizontal line through the head and through the trees. Gentlemen, consider for a moment for yourselves the extreme difficulty of bringing the muzzle of a gun into the direction of the wound which has been found in this man's head. He has got to take his gun in his hand in such a position that he must bring the muzzle of it opposite the original point of impact where the hole is in his skull, and at such an angle that the shot will pass almost horizontally his head. That means, gentlemen, that the barrel must be almost horizontal, and the butt horizontal, and at that height from, the ground. If any of you can discover any process by which that can be accomplished without the artificial aids which the witnesses for the defence have had to call in, for example, the artificial erection lifting up the butt of the gun to the level appropriate for the discharge from the proper angle, and if any of you can discover any method by which a gun can be held in a man's hand with the muzzle of it in such a position that it will discharge in a horizontal line across his head, then give the prisoner the benefit of the discovery. You will then have accomplished what all the men of skill who have been examined before you have conceded they could not find out.

Gentlemen, please look at some of the photographs; I do not intend to put many of them before you, but I show you this set, which Dr. Hay represented as being about the best that occurred to him in connection with these experiments. Able, accomplished, ingenious men have laboured to find out and to represent to you in a photograph some conceivable method by which this wound upon Hambrough's head could have been produced by an accidental discharge of his own gun. The photographs which have been produced, depend upon it, are the very best which their ingenuity could devise, and not one of them is of the slightest assistance in this case, unless it shows the gun in the hand of the man, not, I suppose, for suicidal purposes, but in the position in which it could be accidentally discharged through carelessness. In any suggestion of carelessness there must always be produced a discharge at such an angle to the head as to cause a horizontal wound upon the head and to reach the trees 6 feet from the ground. Gentlemen, in these photographs you will see a small mark indicating where the barrel of the gun stops, and a rod is attached to it in order to show what would be the precise point of impact of the shot. I ask you to observe the attitude of the man holding the gun. In the next place, look at the point at which, as shown by the rod, the shot could strike the head. Have you the slightest idea that Hambrough was shot in that position, or have you the slightest idea, looking at that photograph, that the shot going from the gun, even if discharged in that position, would have been a glancing shot across

333

Alfred John Monson.

Solicitor-General

the back of his head from left to right and cutting off the flip of the ear? You will judge. If my vision and yours is the same, it would appear to me that the charge from the gun would have gone through the man's head. It would not have been a glancing shot past the back of it at all, but straight into the man's head. Then, gentlemen, this was the other photograph, which Dr. Hay represented as being the next nearest, but could give nothing to show that there is any probability that Hambrough was shot in the way represented in that photograph. I could imagine a man with great difficulty getting himself into that position if he were going to commit suicide, with a fantastic idea of committing it in a way which would make it very difficult to discover how he had accomplished it. But do you not see that he places the gun upon an artificial erection, with a support for the stock? Why, no man could hold his gun at this point near the head. The weight of the butt would carry it down to the ground, and he certainly supports the gun upon these upturned stools in order to get the gun into that position. Then, when he has brought it into that position, instead of being a slanting shot across the back of the head, it points straight into the head, and goes through the head at an angle totally different from the shot in question, which passed into the adjacent rowan, beech, and lime trees.

The theory undoubtedly is that there is some erection at the place where the accident occurred. I believe the suggestion is that it was a wall, and that he was lying at the bottom of the ditch, and was shot there. Well, I have already stated to you how the evidence stands on that matter. There was nothing else as far as the evidence goes. I have heard nothing else in the evidence that can supply the place of the support, except the dyke relative to the ditch. The man could not be at that angle towards the dyke, represented by that stool, unless he was down in the ditch, and fell in the ditch, bleeding and dying there, instead of on the top of the bank. I have said at the commencement of this part of my statement to you, that the body was found where it was shot. If you are of opinion that the body was in the ditch, died there, leaving no blood and no marks of depression on the ground, or in the ferns, well, then, if that were so, no doubt there is a wall which might supply the place of the stool in the photograph, although one does not quite see how the trigger was to go off in the circumstances in which that gun was placed.

Now, gentlemen, this part of the case is of vital importance, because if these wounds could not have been self-inflicted at a height of nearly 6 feet from the ground, and human ingenuity has failed to discover any mode by which they could be, this man's head was traversed by shot in the line in which it was struck—the shot going on through the adjacent trees. That necessitates the barrel of the gun being horizontal at a height of from 5 to 6 feet

Speech for the Crown.

Solicitor-General

from the ground at a place where there are no trees, no bushes in close proximity to the head, at the place where it was lying. Well, then, gentlemen, that, like the fact connected with the gun, is not a matter of opinion. It is simply an irresistible inference from well-known and determined conditions, and leaves no choice with regard to the inference which is to be drawn from them. Then, gentlemen, you have heard a great deal about the distance of the muzzle of the gun from the head, and that unquestionably is a matter of importance, but of secondary importance compared to the ascertained line of fire, because opinions may differ with regard to the precise distance from the head at which certain effects are produced upon an object struck by shot, but opinions cannot differ as to where the gun is which fires the shot when you have once determined the line of fire by the traces left upon the adjacent trees. The line of fire is the same whether you are nearer or further away. If this gun was fired 4 feet behind the victim's head or 9 feet behind the victim's head, the line of fire would be the same, the elevation of the gun from the ground would be the same, the angle of the barrel to the head would be the same, and the relation of the injury to the adjacent trees would be the same.

But on this part of the case, also, I submit to you, by far the weightiest part of the evidence is in favour of the view that the weapon was discharged at a distance from the victim's head which makes it impossible that the weapon could have been held in the hand of the man who was shot. There again, gentlemen, you will consider that all these experiments in the photographs were made with a gun held in the right hand. The only way in which a gun can be held even at a distance of a foot or two from the head is, as represented in the photograph, by putting the right hand behind and holding the muzzle of the gun, with the inevitable result that you fail to get the horizontal position relatively to the head. To get the horizontal position relatively to the head, you have to take the muzzle of the gun and hold it up, and I do not believe that there is a man in the jury box who could put his hand at the back of his head and hold the gun, and place it at such an angle as to cause such a wound as was found in Hambrough's head; and unless you can devise in your own mind some idea by which the gun, through falling, or through flying through the air, explodes in some peculiar way and effects this, you are driven, in spite of yourselves, to the conclusion that the discharge of the gun, which caused the wound in Hambrough's head and left marks in the adjacent rowan and beech and lime trees, was discharged by another in the immediate vicinity, and at a place which, I submit, you have little difficulty in determining—at a point not far off, where the adjacent belt of wood, which shut off from public gaze the place where the body was found, has a certain line of access through it, making the place where the body was found more accessible than at any other point. And, gentlemen, you will not forget the striking evidence of the witness

335

Alfred John Monson.

Whyte, who, on the day that this occurred, struck by what had happened, but hesitating to allow suspicion to take hold of his mind, hesitating even for a time to speak about what he had seen, went to the spot, examined it by himself, and saw traces plainly left apparent on the ground behind the opening in question of the approach of two men from the southern side of the wood towards the opening in the adjacent whins, the tracks being separated for a time, but ultimately combining into one, and leading through to a point—a place which, I admit, is only to be inferred, and is not susceptible of accurate definition—where if you stand, and a gun is placed to the shoulder of the person standing there, and a body is erected to the height of Hambrough on the spot where he was found lying, you have a direct line along the muzzle of the gun through the man's head in the direction of the wound, on through the vista of damaged branches of the rowan, the lime, and the beech.

Gentlemen, with these facts before us, in the discharge of my duty, I have to ask you to find it proved that there is but one view possible, in these circumstances, of the manner in which that unfortunate young man met his death. Now, gentlemen, I ought, perhaps before parting from that to have alluded to one fact which was pointed out. No doubt it will be said to you that on the morning the three men entered the wood there was a person in the neighbourhood, and his presence on the spot made it improbable that a crime of this character would be perpetrated. The prisoner, in one of the papers which he wrote at the time, and which he handed to Police Constable Campbell on 27th August, says—" When we entered the wood in which the accident happened I remember seeing a man watching us. I am told that he mentioned to some person here that he saw us in the wood. I have ascertained that his name is Smeaton, and that his luggage was taken away by Mr. M'Ewan, and that he has Smeaton's address." Gentlemen, it will probably be said to you that if Monson knew that, is it likely that, having seen a man watching them, he committed this crime within the short period after he was seen to enter the wood? I am afraid, gentlemen, there is a very simple explanation of that statement. The man who saw them was the witness Dunn. Dunn was not outside the schoolhouse that morning at all. He saw them on the road a little way before they entered the wood, saw the rabbit shot, and young Hambrough jump from the road down into the field and pick up the rabbit. He then saw them enter the wood at the south end after crossing the fence—not by being on the road in their neighbourhood, but by transferring himself from the back window to the front, and seeing them from the window. And it was plainly pointed out to you by the witness Brand that the particular point at which they disappeared from Dunn's vision was a few yards after they had entered the wood—from that point onward the under brushwood and the trees making them absolutely beyond his vision. But the important point is this, that about the same time as Monson

336

Speech for the Crown.

Solicitor-General

delivers to the constable this written statement about a man having seen him, no doubt intending it to be recorded as a piece of evidence against the idea that he could have committed any such crime, a letter is written by him to the Procurator-Fiscal, in which he says— "Referring to what passed when I saw you at Tighnabruaich, I think it right to inform you that this morning my keeper told me that he had heard that a gentleman who was staying at the schoolhouse facing the southern end of the wood in which the accident happened saw the three of us—Mr. Hambrough, Scott, and myself— enter the wood. If this be so "—now, this was the 26th August— "if this be so, no doubt he would corroborate what I have told you as to our relative positions as we went through the wood." Gentlemen, that absolutely negatives the idea that Monson had, on the morning of the 10th, seen any person watch them at all. I do not see how he could have seen the man who was inside the schoolhouse. But it does not rest upon that. His own letter shows that, after he had been communicating with the Fiscal, he tells the Fiscal that he had afterwards learned this fact from his keeper, who, no doubt, had heard the rumour that Dunn had seen them enter the wood. And so utterly incorrect is it to say that he was aware of it on the 10th, that even when he was informed by the gamekeeper that some one had seen them, he proceeds in his letter to say—" If this be so, he will be able to confirm my statement as to how we entered the wood." If he had seen a man who had been there watching them, as Monson represented, why would he not have said to the Procurator-Fiscal at once—" I saw a man on the morning of the 10th observe us going into the wood," and go and see if he was some one connected with the schoolhouse?

Now, I am sorry to detain you so long, but I come to a point which, I am sure you will agree with me, I cannot possibly pass over. I come to the point that on the scene during the occurrences with which I have been dealing there were three persons, and not two. What has become of the third person? Scott arrived, according to the prisoner's account, all alone and for a definite purpose—for examining a yacht which had been purchased by letters of Monson, and not by letters of Hambrough. If he came to examine the yacht, why did he not examine it? Why did he leave without examining it? Hambrough's death did not affect the purchase of the yacht. The letters between Monson and Hambrough bind Monson as much after the death of Hambrough as they did during Hambrough's life, and why has the yacht never been examined?

But, gentlemen, that is but a secondary point. Why has a person who was present on the scene absolutely disappeared from all human ken? You have to ask yourselves that question. At the time these events occurred, on the afternoon of the day, he takes his departure. He is met by the constable at the pier, who naturally informs him that, having been there when an event of

Alfred John Monson.

this character occurred, surely he will wait until there is some investigation. He gives a false address at a hotel in Glasgow, which he never visited, and from that time forward he absolutely disappears. What is the reason of that? What is the explanation of it? What does it suggest to your mind? What are likely to have been the circumstances in which he was participating when at Ardlamont as deduced or inferred from the fact of his disappearance? I am not now dealing with any doubtful question as to his identity. I am dealing with a matter as to which there is no dispute. One of the men who was there has fled and hidden himself. Why has he done that?—He was at the spot; he was on the shore on the night of the 9th; he was in the wood on the morning of the 10th. If the proceedings of the night of the 9th were purely accidental, and consequent on the folly of a youth cutting a hole with his knife in the bottom of the boat; if the death of the same youth next morning in the plantation was due to the accidental discharge of his own gun, why did one of the men who was there fly the same afternoon and conceal himself from that moment forward? You have got to consider and find an answer to that question, and I say again, listen with attention to my learned friend when he explains to you that indisputable fact; if he can suggest to you a rational explanation of why a man should fly under circumstances like these, why, with reference to an alleged crime which has resounded throughout the world, that person should remain concealed up to the present hour, consistent with any other than this, that he was a participator in, or an eye-witness of, a flagrant crime—if you can get any rational explanation which will displace that inference, by all means accept it, and give the prisoner the benefit of it. But, if you cannot, then the result must be that this, like all the rest, like every incident from the beginning to the end, points conclusively in one direction, and you should place it in its proper class, and give it its proper weight in the deliberations which by and by it will be your duty to enter upon.

But, gentlemen, this part of the case does not rest there. What is the relation of the prisoner Monson to the disappearance of his associate Scott? Do you believe the account which he gave as to who that person and associate was? We know exactly what his deliberate statement upon that point was within a comparatively short period of the occurrence of the event, and made for the purpose of being communicated to the criminal authorities. He voluntarily placed upon record his statement as to who Scott was, by saying, "I am informed that Edward Scott started business as an engineer in Glasgow, and that he failed, and that he was afterwards working in connection with yachts, and that he was well known in Greenock." For what purpose was that statement made? Was it for the purpose of giving truthful information, or deceiving and misleading the authorities?

For the answer to that question I refer you to the statement

Speech for the Crown.

Solicitor-General

made by the prisoner's own agent in the witness-box to-day, how Monson told the criminal authorities that that was the only measure of his knowledge with regard to the identity of Scott, going through the farcical performance of telling his solicitor to take steps to discover the whereabouts of this unknown man, never telling him that he is a person of the character described in the communication to the Crown, never telling him that he was a person who had been connected with yachts, and was well known in Greenock, and instructing him to insert lots of advertisements in the newspapers, intended all along to be presented at the trial. The agent for the defence was in the humiliating position of having to confess that, whilst instructed to discover the identity and whereabouts of this unknown man, his own client never told him that he was a person connected with yachts, and well known in Greenock. Gentlemen, the prisoner was too sagacious to put his own solicitor on any such false scent. Have you any doubt as to who the person Scott was? It is true he has not been found; it is true no photograph has been presented to you, identified by the witnesses at Ardlamont, and the witnesses from London. I think it right to say that no reproach is due to the Crown for any want of opportunity of bringing that element into the case. It was explained to you that no photograph was available at such a period, as the Crown were bound finally to put the documents on which they founded in the hands of the Court. But, gentlemen, you need no photographs to decide this point. You have a minute description of the man at Ardlamont. Every detail of his appearance was described with the minutest accuracy. You have a minute description of the man Edward Sweeney, or Davis, or Scott, the London bookmaker, the associate of Monson and his friends. This description of the two men is absolutely identical; and you have the instantaneous disappearance from the scene of the London bookmaker and the engineer Edward Scott.

Gentlemen, many things are possible in this world, but do you think it is within the bounds of reasonable possibility that the engineer Edward Scott and the bookmaker Edward Davis simultaneously disappear from the scene—both become absolutely unknown to those with whom they were associated, except on the ground they are one and the same person, and disappearing for the same motive? You heard the witnesses examined with regard to the disappearance of Davis. He is traced to London. The last we hear of him is in London a few days after the occurrence of this event. Then, on 15th or 16th August, he disappears altogether from the social sphere which he was in the habit of frequenting, and you have his brother coming here and giving explanations, on which I do not waste your time by commenting, with reference to his disappearance from the family circle and the reasons which were suggested for that having occurred. You have coincidences, no doubt; there may be startling coincidences, no doubt, in human affairs. Surely, gentlemen, if you begin by assuming the innocence of the

Alfred John Monson.

prisoner in this case, you have to deal with a series of coincidences absolutely unprecedented within the range of human experience— the occurrence of these two events of 9th and 10th August, the simultaneous disappearance, from independent causes, of two different men. You cannot fail to draw the inference from all that you have heard that the alleged Edward Scott, the engineer, was, in fact, Edward Davis, the bookmaker. And, gentlemen, the next question you have to consider is this, Why did he fly? Why did the prisoner give a false statement as to his identity? Why did the prisoner put the Crown upon a false scent with regard to his pursuit, and abstain from giving his own solicitor the information which he had communicated to the Crown? Gentlemen, at his examination before the Sheriff a question was put to him, a direct question, '' Is the man Scott the same as Davis? '' One would have thought that put to an innocent man and speaking of an engineer who had been employed for examining a yacht, it needed no agent's advice or anything else to enable him to answer that question, but I daresay you will have observed that, in answer to that question, there was a simple declinature to give any information at all.

Well, gentlemen, I am glad to say that I am drawing nearly to a close with regard to the painful circumstances which I have had to bring under your notice. But there is one group of facts which I cannot pass over consistently with the duty I have to perform, and that is the gross misrepresentations made by the prisoner, after this event, with regard to the insurance which he had effected. You cannot fail to see how pregnant and important any facts bearing upon that matter were. The accounts of the Procurator-Fiscal showed how pertinent and closely associated they were with any question of accident or crime. What do you deduce from the statement made by the prisoner on that point? Gentlemen, on the day of the death, when the witness Steven was there, the prisoner showed him the papers of the Scottish Provident Institution for the purpose of leading him to understand that the proposal for the insurance had been accepted, and only, indeed, failed to be completed by the fact of the young man's death. For what purpose was that statement made? To give the impression that the death, taking place at that time, was most inopportune with reference to the recovery of any insurance. Why did he tell him of the insurances not effected, and which he said would have been effected soon but for the death, and did not tell him of the two insurances which had been effected with such rapidity, and under such extraordinary circumstances, shortly before through the Mutual office? Then, gentlemen, Dr. Macmillan was there, and being there in an official capacity would naturally have been the recipient of any information of this character connected with the deceased. Not one word was communicated to him suggestive of any insurances in the case. Dr. Macmillan knew nothing of it until it was proposed to bring him into the matter by a certificate being got from him of an

Speech for the Crown.

accidental death, to be made available by way of securing payment of the policy. Tottenham arrived, and if any one should have been a recipient of the confidence of the accused, one would have expected that he would have been the man, but even with him the system of deception appeared to prevail. Whether the accused thought that the discovery of that amount might necessitate a partition of the spoil is another matter; but according to Tottenham's own statement, he extracted by degrees information as to the fact, the first statement being that the insurance was only for £8000, then for £10,000, and ultimately for £20,000. Major Hambrough, the father of the dead boy, arrived, accompanied by his wife. Monson told him that there was no insurance, but that an insurance would have been effected if he had lived some time, and that the only policy in existence was one for £400 in Mrs. Monson's favour. The Procurator-Fiscal met him on 23rd August. He was manifestly afraid to tell the truth. His first statement was that a policy for £15,000 had been effected by the boy's father upon his son's life. Then Houston, the town-clerk of Ventnor, and Livesey, a gentleman who was at the funeral, and who had been one of the referees with regard to the policies of the Mutual office, asked the question at the time of the funeral whether the policies as to which he had been a referee, or either of them, had taken effect, and received for an answer a direct negative to the effect that no policies existed at all.

Gentlemen, that must be added to the rest. What is the explanation of this prevarication, of this system of concealment and prevarication, after the youth's death with reference to the fact of insurance or not? You have to put to yourselves the question, What inference do you deduce as to consciousness of guilt on the part of the man who displayed that tortuous series of misstatements on the matter of insurance? It will be said to you, I dare say, that the title to the insurance is of a somewhat shaky character. We have a record at the time of what the prisoner's estimate was of the validity of his title, and the chances of receiving payment. You have that in the fact of Monson's interview with the Procurator-Fiscal, accompanied by the insurance agents, for the purpose of receiving the appropriate documents for enabling him to substantiate his claim and satisfy the insurance agents in getting payment. The certificates from the doctor and the Procurator-Fiscal, according to Mr. M'Lean, were to be enough to satisfy them with regard to the circumstances of the death. You have a letter written at the time, or shortly after, in which the policies are placed in the hands of the banker at Tighnabruaich for the purpose of collection. You have a letter written by Mrs. Monson on 28th August, two days before Monson was apprehended, and, no doubt, in the name of Mrs. Monson, because the bank account was in her name, and accordingly everything connected with it was written by her. On 28th August she wrote to the banker at Tighnabruaich

Alfred John Monson.

Solicitor-General

—" I enclose a policy of insurance received to-day on the life of the late Cecil Hambrough. The policy is for £10,000, and the company have arranged for the payment being made in Glasgow, when the policy will have to be handed over and a receipt given in the usual manner. A settlement will probably take place in a week or so. I will intimate the date as soon as I hear, as the money can be paid into your bank in Glasgow, and the policy sent there. The policy is to recover money paid on behalf of the late Mr. Cecil Hambrough, but I regret to say I lose a considerable sum of money by the death, owing to there having been delay in taking out the further policy to cover guarantees given on his behalf in connection with some liabilities of his father's. Curiously, the acceptance for the further policy only arrived on the very day of his death, and was therefore useless." Gentlemen, you have in that a double representation—first, that it was intended to produce the idea that the death was a cause of loss, in the sense of preventing the completion of the policy which, you know quite well, would never have been proceeded with because of the necessity of proving Mrs. Monson's interest, which, you know, she could not do. But the more important representation is this, that you have on record in the hand of Mrs. Monson, manifestly speaking the mind of Monson, a communication that a £10,000 policy was sent to them for collection, and that it would be paid into Glasgow, amply demonstrating that the belief of the accused at the time was that he had so arranged matters, with reference to these policies, that through the fact of his victim's death the money was now to come into his hands.

I shall not detain you, gentlemen, by reviewing all the facts, all the various heads under which I have grouped the points on which I have thought it my duty to speak. But, gentlemen, whilst I have repeated them one by one—compelled to do so by the circumstances of the case—I say again to you that you must take them not only singly, but in the lump. You must take the features of this case as they occur, and make up your minds, I repeat, severally and separately. But when you have done that my wish is that you should place them side by side, look at them in their relationship to one another, and consider whether they do not establish the grave and serious chain to which I have referred—Whether the circumstances do not infallibly and inevitably lead to one result, connecting the prisoner with the crimes with which he is charged. If you can find serious, intelligible, and honest ground that will influence you in coming to the conclusion that these facts are quite consistent with the innocence of the prisoner, by all means acquit him. But, gentlemen, if on the consideration of these you come to the conclusion that they are reasonably consistent with one, and only one, result, then your duty to the public, your duty to the oath which you have taken, is to find the prisoner guilty of the crime with which he is charged.

The Court adjourned.

Mr. Comrie Thomson,
Senior Counsel for the Defence.

Tenth Day—Friday, 22nd December, 1893.

Mr. COMRIE THOMSON rose immediately the judge had taken his seat to address the jury on behalf of the prisoner as follows :—May it please your lordship, gentlemen of the jury—I rise to address you on behalf of the prisoner at the bar with a mingled feeling of confidence and anxiety. On the one hand, I take courage from the fact that you approach the threshold of this case with a great barrier of improbabilities which stands between you and an adverse verdict—improbabilities which arise from what I may call moral considerations. Antecedently, these crimes are in the highest degree improbable. What I mean is this—There are many wicked men in the world, no doubt, and every now and again—very rarely in this country—we are startled by the commission of a great crime ; but, as a rule, men are not criminals. At all events, as a rule, they are not guilty of acts of brutal violence ; and when you are told that one man has imbrued his hands in the blood of another, the first exclamation that arises to your lips is something of this kind, " Impossible ; it is hardly credible ! " And when, as in the present case, the charges are that a man attempted to drown and then, in cold blood, assassinated a young man with whom he had for years past been on terms of the most affectionate intercourse, then I say that I am justified in feeling confidence in this, that except upon the most undoubted evidence, your verdict will be one which will acquit the prisoner at the bar. I take confidence, gentlemen, also from the unflagging attention which you have devoted to the consideration of this case, and I feel certain that when you put to yourselves what must be the first question and the last question, " Is it proved ? " your answer will be in the negative. I further feel encouraged from having received an impression—it may be an erroneous one, but still a very distinct impression—which has been developed as the case proceeded, and which was not shaken by the very able and fervent speech to which we listened yesterday from the learned Solicitor-General, that, after a careful consideration of the facts, you will be driven, in the exercise of your conscientious duty, to the conclusion that the charges have not been substantiated. And further, gentlemen, I feel confident of this, that you must be satisfied that you have had in the box men of science, men of practical experience in such questions as that with which you have to deal, who have given their opinions with equal capacity for doing so, and with equal conscientiousness ; and the two sets of men arrived at totally different conclusions upon what, after all, is the leading question of the case. If these capable, intelligent, experienced,

343

Alfred John Monson.

Mr. Comrie Thomson

practical men honestly differ, is it for you to adopt an opinion which is adverse to the man charged with these crimes? On the other hand, I am not ashamed to say that the case has, even from my point of view, an anxious side. The issue which you have to determine is the most awful issue which one human being could settle with reference to another. You know, gentlemen, what is the inevitable result of a verdict of condemnation. Death—a disgraceful death to the man at the bar, an indelible stain upon his wife and his young family. Gentlemen, I remember more than five-and-thirty years ago sitting in one of these benches and hearing an advocate, who afterwards became a great judge, standing where I now stand, pleading for a woman who was sitting in that dock charged with the crime of murder. He opened his address to the jury in words which have since become historical, but I repeat them to you now because of their great truth and their wonderful simplicity. "Gentlemen," he said, "the charge against the prisoner is murder, and the punishment of murder is death; and that simple statement is sufficient to suggest to you the awful nature of the occasion which brings you and me face to face." I feel anxiety also, gentlemen, because, if your verdict is against this prisoner, I shall not be able to rid myself of the impression that to some extent such a result must be due to my own failure sufficiently to lay the facts of the case before you.

But all these elements of anxiety are as nothing compared with that which I now mention to you, namely, the fact that I see the greatest difficulty, acting as conscientiously as you may, in your disabusing your minds of the prejudice which has been excited against this man at the bar during the last three or four months. I impute no motives to the newspapers. I am sure they were not actuated by any base feeling of animosity, but I cannot help saying that they have, in many instances and with great persistency, attempted to gratify the curiosity of the public at the expense of the man who was suspected of the crime. No one in this country has been able, during the period I have mentioned, to lift a newspaper in which he did not find himself face to face with paragraphs headed "The Ardlamont Mystery" or "The Monson Case"; and in every instance the statements contained in these paragraphs were highly prejudicial to the prisoner. He was charged with a life of immorality; he was charged with crimes; he was said to exercise mesmeric influence. Every sort of circumstance was raked up against him, every sort of effort seems to have been made for the purpose of producing sensation, intentionally or unintentionally, I honestly believe the latter, with the result of necessarily and unavoidably impressing the minds of the readers of these paragraphs with a feeling of prejudice against the prisoner, which, I own, it must be exceedingly difficult to get rid of. You would notice that my learned friend yesterday was imbued with the same feeling,

344

Speech for the Defence.

Mr. Comrie Thomson

because, even as public prosecutor, he felt it necessary to give you the hint, at all events, that you were not to allow any previously conceived notions to affect your judgment to-day, that you were to be guided entirely by what you have heard sworn to in the witness-box; and if the public prosecutor gave you that hint, I do implore and adjure you to purge your minds of every preconceived sentiment adverse to this man, and to deal with him, as every citizen is entitled to be dealt with, as a man absolutely innocent of the crime with which he is charged until you are satisfied that you are driven by the force of the sworn testimony to a conclusion which is condemnatory of him.

Gentlemen, the case for the Crown admittedly could not be supported by any direct evidence of the crimes. Accordingly it is founded, in the first place, more upon what we have been calling motive than upon any direct or circumstantial evidence, including such circumstances as the disappearance of Scott and the conduct of the accused after the occurrence. Two very important elements in the nature of indirect evidence have bulked largely in the course of the case. One of them was the direction of the fatal shot, and the other was the proximity of the gun to the deceased. Let me lodge this idea in your mind at once, and in doing so I am justified by what my learned friend said yesterday. In regard to the first point and the evidence which bears upon it, namely, the direction of the shot, the prosecution have perilled their case upon that point upon the pellets, twelve in number, which were found in the three trees which have been mentioned. And in regard to the other branch of the case, that which refers to the distance between the gun and the dead man, the evidence upon that was discarded altogether yesterday. Upon these vital parts of the case I shall, when the time comes, venture to argue to you that, as regards the latter, the evidence that we have led, and which intentionally was not referred to by the Solicitor-General yesterday, because it was dead against him, is conclusively in our favour; and with regard to the former the evidence is so slender that it will fall very far short of inducing you to take the course which the Solicitor-General invited you to follow.

Gentlemen, with regard to the alleged motive, we heard a great deal about it yesterday, and you will hear a little more to-day, although not at such great length. Consider, in the first place, what bearing motive has upon a crime. I grant at once that motive has a place in considering the evidence in support of a charge of crime, but motive is not sufficient. You do not condemn a man because he had a motive to do a criminal act. Nay, if the evidence in regard to the act itself is scanty and insufficient, you cannot add motive to eke out the otherwise imperfect evidence. You will see the importance of keeping that prominently before your minds when I suggest to you that human society involves in every direction a motive on the part of one man that another

345

Alfred John Monson.

man should be removed. The heir has a motive or interest to remove the person who is in enjoyment of the property. The aspirant to an office has a motive to remove the office-holder, and so on through every condition of life. But it would be perfectly intolerable and absurd if, supposing two persons in the relation that I have just described—a son and a father, let us say, or a younger brother and an elder brother—to be together, and a catastrophe to happen to one of them, if you were to be taken a single inch in the direction of saying—" Oh, there was a distinct motive; this man did not die by accident, it was the other man who compassed his death." So that while I grant there is a certain weight to be attached to motive, it does not take you very far, and if that is all that you have, it takes you no length whatever.

Now, what is the evidence about motive in this case? And here I directly challenge and traverse the position that was taken up by the Solicitor-General yesterday, and I think I shall be able to show by reference to one or two letters that that position is not tenable. I admit at once that at times, and generally, Mr. Monson and his family were not well off, that they were reduced sometimes to straits which involved them in doing what is always indicative of impecuniousness, pawning ornaments and other small articles; but at the time that this occurrence happened there is nothing to show that they were in want of ready money, because as you know, Tottenham was able and willing to advance to them, in order to enable them to live and maintain their boarder and pupil, Cecil Hambrough, £10 a week, and he further handed them larger sums on special occasions, such as the removal from England to Scotland. He told you in the witness-box that he would have been willing for any special reason, such as a deposit necessary in connection with the contract of which we have heard so much, or for any other reason which commended itself to his own mind, to have gone the length of £1000, or £1500, or even more.

You will notice as a fair and obvious observation arising from that state of matters, that by killing Cecil Hambrough Mr. Monson at once deprived himself of his only fixed source of income. They were living upon Tottenham's bounty. They had no other means of income that we know of; but Tottenham's bounty depended upon Cecil's life, and, accordingly, so far as that branch of the case is concerned, you will observe that the motive is all the other way, because the charge amounts to this, that the prisoner killed a man upon whose life his income and subsistence depended. There's his motive! But then I should like to refer you, just to show I am speaking without any exaggeration upon that point, to two letters from Tottenham to Cecil. The one is dated 13th May, 1893, and the other is dated 18th May, 1893. The first is in these terms—" My dear Cecil,—Herewith cheque £40, just to go on with. I conclude the moving job can be financed on that, and until the

Speech for the Defence.

Mr. Comrie Thomson

next week am short, as have to keep a balance at the Bank of England, or they give you notice to close the account. Next week a further remittance shall be sent. I have made the cheque payable to you for facility in cashing, but naturally I don't debit you with this oof, but look on it as a payment made on general account of the show," and he explained that he meant by that that this £40 was not a part of the weekly allowance that he was making to Cecil, but that it was to go to the general expenses of the household in which Cecil was living. And then in the next letter he says— "I conclude you are at Ardlamont by now. I will continue you the oof required, and hope you will remember yours truly when you come into your kingdom." Now, gentlemen, these two letters bear out what I have said—and Tottenham in the witness-box confirmed it—that the Monsons were living entirely upon the condition that Cecil remained alive. If he left, if he died, they were without a single sixpence. So long as he was with them, so long as he lived, they had enough to live upon in comparative comfort. Their sustenance at that time depended upon his living.

I further traverse my learned friend's argument by maintaining to you that at the time when attempts were made to effect the life assurances which have been so frequently referred to, viz., with the Scottish Provident, the London and Liverpool and Globe Insurance Company, and with the New York Mutual, there was a perfectly reasonable prospect that the contract to obtain which an effort was being made with the Eagle Insurance Company, would be got by Monson; and I will demonstrate that to you. I refer you to a letter of 13th and another of 23rd April. Cecil Hambrough writes to Tottenham on the 23rd—"Thanks for the cheque you sent. I have to come to town to-morrow to see Richards"—(Richards is the agent of the Eagle Company)—"with Jerningham, and shall stay the night at the Metropole. I shall be much obliged if you could post me a cheque on receipt of this to the Metropole, as the journey will clear me clean out of cash. I have heard from Richards. He says his directors will be quite agreeable to the proposal. You may be sure I shall not forget your having helped me when I come of age." And then he also writes on 9th April to Tottenham— "Thanks for cheque, which I have just received. I have just had notice regarding my training. Would you be willing to increase the £5 to £10 a week during that period? If you could, and let me have a small sum down, say, £10, to settle up one or two small bills here, I could do all right. Will you let me know soon, by return if possible? I am sorry to hear that Prince has got the contract, but I do not think that he can possibly complete, and, I think, will be glad enough to come to terms when he finds out the true state of things."

Now, we know, gentlemen, that although these negotiations had been nearly closed with Prince at that time, he was not able

347

Alfred John Monson.

to complete the arrangement, and the contract was never completed. But from other letters it is clear that the arrangements with Prince on behalf of Major Hambrough were only open till 1st August, and that at that time the Eagle Company were prepared to treat with Monson. Cecil writes to Richards on 23rd April—"I am making a tour up here with Mr. Monson. In your last letter to him, which was forwarded, you say that if his views as to Dr. Hambleton's position are correct, then the negotiations with Mr. Jerningham are only postponed until August. I shall be glad to know if your directors would not enter into a provisional contract with Mr. Jerningham, to date from August, in the event of the purchase not being completed, because at the present time Mr. Jerningham is quite willing to enter into the contract, whereas he might not be willing to do so in August."

And, again, on 31st July, Monson writes to Hammond & Richards, agents for the Eagle Company—"I understand, from a letter received from Dr. Hambleton, that nothing has been done by them regarding the purchase of the Hambrough life estates. Therefore, I assume your clients will be open to negotiate otherwise for the sale, as the limit of time mentioned was August. The proposal made by Mr. Cecil Hambrough for Mr. Jerningham to purchase on his behalf cannot be now proceeded with, but Mrs. Monson would be quite willing to enter into a contract for the purchase, provided the limit of time for completion was made June, 1894." That is the date at which Cecil would become a major.

You see at 31st July the position taken up was this—We are now ready to take the contract. Major Hambrough and his friends have not been able to complete it. You told us that you would give them to 1st August—that is to-morrow—and they have not completed. It can now go in Mrs. Monson's name, as Mr. Jerningham is no longer available; but it is an essential part of the arrangement made that you must delay the final completion of it, subject to the deposit being arranged, till this young man, Cecil Hambrough, is of age, that also depending upon his survival. Then Mrs. Monson, he says, would "pay a deposit of 5 per cent. upon the agreed purchase money. Mr. Cecil Hambrough is staying here with us, but I do not see that it concerns your clients what arrangements Mrs. Monson may enter into with Cecil Hambrough, so long as there is a *bona fide* purchase from your clients with such a substantial deposit as suggested." Now there is another letter written by Hambleton to Monson, dated 17th July, which bears upon this—"I shall be down here for another week on account of my little boy. The suggestion you make can be made the basis of an arrangement if Cecil can pass life assurance for the required amount. If the figures we have are correct, and I believe they are, as things look better than they did, it will be all the better. Cecil would tell you I had expected to have heard from you. Now, the question is, can Cecil pass the insurance? If you

348

Speech for the Defence.

Mr. Comrie Thomson

are satisfied of that, then arrange to come to town with him so that we may know for a certainty that a good office will have him. Will you agree to this? Please let me know immediately." So that you see, gentlemen, just at the time when these policies that I have mentioned were being negotiated, there was a most legitimate purpose for that being done, because it was an essential part of the contract for which Monson had been striving for a very considerable time, and in which strife he had a competitor in the shape of Major Hambrough, represented by his friends—it was an essential part of that contract that they should be able to go to the Eagle with good life policies either upon the Major or Cecil.

Observe what is the history. The Solicitor-General detailed it to you yesterday, and I shall only recall it shortly to you. The position was this—During the whole of 1892 the negotiations for dropping the existing insurances upon the Major's life, and receiving the surrender value of them and reinsuring him and getting the money borrowed at a lower rate of interest, had been going on. These attempts had been promoted by Tottenham even as far back as the end of 1891, and then by others in the course of 1892, and the failure in the arrangement had arisen from this, apparently, that the Major's life was not insurable. They had made several attempts to get him insured, but the doctors would not pass him, and, accordingly, it was impossible for the arrangement, which had that in it as a necessary element, to be carried out. But then, gentlemen, the idea occurred to Monson, not apparently for the first time, or, at all events, it is not developed by him for the first time, that it would suit perfectly well, in some respects better, to insure the life of Cecil Hambrough, and, accordingly, that suggestion is carried out by him, although it was not finally completed. He proposed that the existing policies on the Major's life should remain, and that a new policy should be effected to the extent of £17,000 on Cecil's life. The notion of insuring Cecil's life was not a new one, and it was a necessary part of the arrangement that this contract with the Eagle was to be handed over to some one who should acquire the Major's life interest in the estates. Hambleton told you in his evidence that he and Monson had joined hands in this matter, and Monson agreed that if he got the contract he would make an allowance to the Major, and Hambleton told us that they were at one at that time. Monson and the Major both at that time desired to get Cecil's life insured, and Sebright had taken steps for the same purpose. Cecil writes to Hammond & Richards on the 29th March, that is, to the Eagle people—" I have seen Mr. Jerningham since his interview with you on Friday last, and understand that the proposition of his purchase is being placed before your directors to-morrow. The question appears to be as to whether the directors will accept Mr. Jerningham's offer or that of Mr. Prince. I hope,

Alfred John Monson.

however, that the directors will take my position into their consideration, and accept Mr. Jerningham's offer in preference to that of Mr. Prince, and that they will distinguish what a very great difference there is between the *bona fides* of the two offers.'' And then comes the passage which was read to you yesterday, in which he says that '' the one made by Mr. Jerningham with a deposit of £500 is a substantial offer made by a gentleman of considerable position, and one from which I shall benefit; while the offer made through Mr. Prince, with a small deposit, is merely a speculation in the name of a person of no position whatever, with the view of making money out of me when I come of age, ostensibly for the benefit of my father, but really for the benefit of others. If the directors accept Mr. Prince's offer I shall absolutely be deprived of any further interest in the estate of which I am the tenant-in-tail, because when I came of age I should have to disentail, or take the consequences, which may be very serious.'' And Hammond & Richards write to Monson on 13th April—'' It is unnecessary for the directors to go into any dealings between yourself and Hambrough, and, having informed Dr. Hambleton's solicitor that they are prepared to sell to him, that transaction must go on. But if your view of Dr. Hambleton's position is correct, then the negotiations with Mr. Jerningham are postponed till August.''

So you see that at that time, namely, when the negotiations with the Scottish Provident began, the position was this—The Major had an interest to get a lower rate of interest than the Eagle was charging. Monson had a legitimate interest to recoup himself for the advances and education that he had been giving for some time to young Hambrough; and Cecil, when he came of age, if the arrangement were entered into, could borrow on the expectancy, his life being insured. Now, if the father, you will observe, concurred, when Cecil came of age, in barring the entail, the result of the arrangement which was proposed, coupled with that fact, was that Cecil would step into £67,000—one-half of the £134,000 that was mentioned; and out of that Mr. Monson would be not only handsomely recouped for the expenditure to which he had been put, but—he makes no secret about it—he would receive in addition a very considerable bonus, and Tottenham, of course, would benefit in the same way. Where the motive to take the life of a man, on whose surviving till he was twenty-one years of age that result depended, comes in, I confess myself entirely unable to see. Their one interest, the one thing that was essential to the carrying out of this arrangement, was that the young man should live. If he died before June, 1894, the whole thing was in the air. If they had one strong motive in this world in connection with this matter, it was to keep this lad in life. If you are satisfied of that, there is an end of the motive, there is an end to the case. If I have demonstrated to you from the letters that there was no barrier

350

Speech for the Defence.

Mr. Comrie Thomson

to the contract being given to Monson—I do not require to put it higher than this, that he believed that he would get it, that he was under that impression—then the whole of his conduct in doing what I am about to refer to in the way of endeavouring to effect insurances is explained away on the most rational grounds; and, instead of raising a suggestion of guilt and guilty motive against him, the facts show that the whole success of his scheme depended upon the survivance of Cecil Hambrough. Now, of course, it is perfectly obvious that, knowing as he did that the failure of Prince and the Major to get the contract had arisen from their inability to get life insurances upon the Major's life, and from the circumstance that Cecil declined to go up to London and have his life insured in order to further Prince's scheme, and therefore was not available, nothing was more natural than that Monson should proceed to effect insurances the moment the 1st of August arrived, because he knew that that had been the difficulty in the way of the competing scheme, and that if he went to the Eagle Company with good policies of insurance in his hand, and said, " Here are the policies—this young man has consented that his life should be insured—here they are," he would have been certain to get the contract. And, accordingly, it was only fair and proper business that he should, as soon as the time arrived when the thing was open to him, take the initial and essential step to secure his being put in possession of the contract.

And, accordingly, gentlemen, what he does is, he approaches a highly respectable and well-known office, the Scottish Provident Institution. I have heard some surprise expressed that the insurance which is, perhaps, most in question here was one effected, not with a well-known Scottish office, but with a New York office. I have not a word to say against the New York Mutual Insurance Company. I know nothing about it except what is good; but I point out that if there had been anything nefarious or suspicious in this transaction Monson would not have resorted to the Scottish Provident and to the Liverpool and London and Globe. I am making no invidious distinction between the offices, but what must be known to all, or nearly all, of you is this, that these two offices, along with many other Scottish offices that might be named, confine themselves entirely to absolutely legitimate business. They hold their heads deservedly high, as, I may say, all our Scottish offices do. If there had been no approach to a regular, recognised, respectable office, and if this business had been attempted with some speculative, shadowy, unknown office, I could imagine some suspicion attaching to it; but it is important to notce that the two first offices which are approached—and one of them is willing to undertake the risk to the extent of £50,000, one condition being complied with—are, as I say, old, respectable. highly reputable offices. Now, what is the state of matters with the Scottish

Alfred John Monson.

Mr. Comrie Thomson

Provident? The proposal you have been referred to is quite frank. Monson writes on the 19th of July—" I enclose the form (proposal) duly filled up, and signed by Mr. Cecil Hambrough. The policy will have to be issued in favour of Agnes Maud Monson, and is to be effected for the purpose of covering certain advances made to Mr. Cecil Hambrough extending over the last four years, and also to cover certain liabilities incurred by Mrs. Monson in connection with the Hambrough settled estates. I may mention that Mr. Cecil Hambrough has a reversionary life interest in certain estates which bring in about £5000 per annum, and that he will be in possession of them when he comes of age. There is a remark I wish to make in answer to question 14. Mr. Cecil Hambrough was proposed some four years since to the Reliance office in London, and he was not accepted, but was requested to come up for examination again. Why? I know nothing of the circumstances myself except from information received from the Liverpool and London and Globe office."

My learned friend commented on one expression in this letter as containing an untruth. Now, I wish to clear that away. In the first place, let me point out that the statement " for the purpose of covering certain advances made to Mr. Cecil Hambrough extending over the last four years " is absolutely true, and that was really all that the insurance company needed to know, because all that they needed was an insurable interest, and that was quite sufficient. It was quite unnecessary to proceed to say anything about the Hambrough estates, but he does say, " also to cover certain liabilities incurred by Mrs. Monson in connection with the Hambrough settled estates." Now that, of course, is an inaccuracy, because the liabilities had not at that moment been incurred; but it was a very natural and a very pardonable inaccuracy, and all the more trivial in this case, because it does not affect the question in which alone the insurance company was interested. He expected that immediately after the writing of this letter, or by the time the insurance was completed, or, at all events, very soon after it had been in force, liabilities would be incurred by Mrs. Monson in connection with the Hambrough settled estates. He was proceeding to carry that very thing out, and accordingly it is straining the matter, I think, quite unduly to say that this was making a false representation to the insurance company; and it matters not, because they had a perfectly true representation in regard to the advances that had already been made. And then let me point out the perfect frankness with which he discloses a fact that might affect the manager of the insurance company in an adverse direction. He discloses the fact in a letter—" I think it right to tell you that some four years ago the young man's life was rejected because of a certain temporary ailment."

At first the proposal was by Cecil on his own life, but then it

352

Speech for the Defence.

Mr. Comrie Thomson

is arranged, with the consent and approval of the insurance company, that Mrs. Monson should insure Cecil's life, and that he should not insure it himself. The reason of that is given, and is obvious, and it is important, with reference to the future history of the case, that at that time, doubtless before, but at that time certainly, Monson was well aware that on account of the minority of Cecil it was not possible for him validly to assign the policy. He must either have the consent of his father, or if he makes the assignation during his minority he must adopt it, or, as we say, homologate it when he came of age, and, until that was done, until he came of age, it was useless. That is the first piece of evidence we have showing that that was the state of knowledge in which Monson was towards the end of July. Now the provisional acceptance of that proposal was sent to him, but the provision was never fulfilled, and accordingly no more came of these negotiations with the Scottish Provident office. Weeks before this young man lost his life there was an insurance arrangement in force with the Scottish Provident. You have no motive there. The second application was one to the Liverpool and London and Globe, one of the largest and most respectable offices in the kingdom. The company, however, did not get a satisfactory statement of the insurable interest, and accordingly the risk was not taken there either. But in the correspondence with them, gentlemen, the same disclosures are made with the same frankness as characterises the communications to the Scottish Provident. But that, as well as the Scottish Provident negotiations, is out of the case, because no risks were in existence at the time of the fatal occurrence.

Then we come to the Mutual Insurance Company of New York, and the insurances are taken, as you know, in the name of Cecil himself. The first is dated 4th August, 1893, and the provisional contract states that the company does insure the life of Windsor D. C. Hambrough for the sum of £10,000, in favour of himself, until October, 1893, subject to the usual terms of the said company's policies. Now, gentlemen, M'Lean, the manager of the Mutual Company, was in the box, and he told us that the proposal that the policies should be taken in the name of Cecil came from him and not from Monson, and there is in evidence from him and from some one else this statement, that it was a part of the arrangement. It was from Mr. M'Lean. He says that it was part of the arrangement that these policies should be properly assigned to Mrs. Monson. " What do you mean," he is asked, " by properly assigned ? " and he replied, " Hambrough wished them to be assigned to Mrs. Monson." Then he was asked, " You knew the young man would not be of age until the following year," and he replied, " I did." " You knew an assignation could not be given by a minor without consent ?—I did." So, gentlemen, the position was this, that in so far as the completion of the contract was concerned, even with the

Alfred John Monson.

Mr. Comrie Thomson

Mutual Company of New York, it had never been done. It was an essential condition of Monson's liability upon that proposal that there should be a proper assignation, and the manager told you so. He says in his evidence—" Of course we both knew that a minor could not assign." Another witness in the box, when I put the question, " Did Monson know that? " replied, " Everybody knows that," and Sebright tells us he had spoken on the subject to Monson at the time his proposal for insuring Cecil's life for £17,000 was being considered in the beginning of 1893.

Thus, gentlemen, I stand in this position with reference to these policies at the time of the death of Cecil Hambrough, that there was admittedly no risk either with the Scottish Provident or the Liverpool and London and Globe, and I have demonstrated to you that there was no risk, no available policy, no fund which could ever come into the prisoner's hands through the taking out of the policy, no valid assignation by the man who held it, namely, Cecil, to Mrs. Monson, or anybody else. It is quite true the Solicitor-General dwelt upon the fact that you have documents, one a mandate to deliver the policy signed by Cecil, and the other a sort of testamentary document, a sort of will which he made, but we put a professional witness in the box yesterday to tell us that, so far as the English law regulated a minor's action, these documents were not worth the paper they were written on. The Solicitor-General says Monson thought they were. I have demonstrated to you that he knew they were not. It may very well be that this young man, who, so far as one can see, was a very noble and high-minded young man, from a sense of duty, from a sense of common honesty, said, " I may die any day, and I shall leave evidence behind me to show what my intention was; I shall assign these policies to Mrs. Monson, because I know I am indebted to the Monsons. They have kept me; they have got me into the service; they have educated me and boarded me and given me a great deal of pleasure; at all events I will let those people who come after me know what my intentions are. At all events I shall assign the policies to them, and my father may give his consent and make that assignation good. Perhaps my father may make that assignation good for his son, or if I live ten or eleven months I shall be able myself to adopt these writings, and homologate them, and they will just be as good as if I had written them when I was of age." All these views may be quite sufficient to account for these documents being written. But, gentlemen, my point is this—I beg of you to let it enter your minds—that at the time this lad died there was no obligation by any insurance company in this world to pay money to Monson in respect of his death. So that the point that is made against me, that this man imbrued his hands in his friend's blood because he had insured his life, and so to keep the proceeds of the policy, is absolutely without

354

Speech for the Defence.

Mr. Comrie Thomson

foundation. It is a point in the same direction—it is not perhaps so important, but it is not without importance—that one of the conditions of this policy coming into effect was that the first premium should be paid. It was not paid, and I will tell you why. An attempt was made to pay it by sending a cheque on the 8th— a cheque by Monson. At the time that cheque was sent and reached the office of the insurance company there were no funds to meet that cheque in Monson's bank account. It is true that on the 8th a cheque had been handed to the banker at Tighnabruaich for £250, which would have been sufficient to meet the cheque; but that cheque represented nothing until 10th August. At the time the attempt to make payment was made there was no money. It was waste paper, and certainly I am not responsible, my client is not responsible for the good-natured, but somewhat loose, actings of the agent of the bank at Tighnabruaich. It was the bank that made this policy a valid one, and therefore so far as the payment of the premium was concerned it was not Monson. And notice, Monson knew that the cheque which he had handed to the bank did not represent cash until the 10th; and on the morning of the 10th, when this lad was killed, he had no reason whatever to believe that that premium had really been paid. So that you see on both grounds, on the ground that there was no valid assignation, no binding assignation of this policy, and on the ground that the other condition had not been fulfilled, and therefore, as there was no claim available to Monson against any insurance company in the world, I think the whole Crown case, based upon motive, crumbles into dust.

Now, I think I shall complete this part of the case by simply referring in a sentence to what is certainly of importance—the conduct of Monson subsequent to the death with reference to these policies, and the evidence about that is found in the evidence of M'Lean and the Procurator-Fiscal. You will observe that the death of this young man was a serious loss to Tottenham. Upon the assumption which I ask you to entertain, and which I have demonstrated to you to be proved, namely, that there was no valid obligation on any insurance company to pay, the death meant a serious loss both to Monson and Tottenham. As I have shown you, it was to their highest advantage, it was the only good they could get out of the young man, that he should live until he was twenty-one years of age.

I do not want to say hard words to you about a Crown witness, but I rather think Tottenham produced the impression upon you of being rather a queer fish. I do not think he is the kind of man that you and I—quiet-going Scottish folk—are in the habit of meeting, or even I do not know that any of us desire to make his more intimate acquaintance. But he told us quite distinctly, after a little hesitation and pressing, when asked why he

Alfred John Monson.

Mr. Comrie Thomson

made a claim when Monson knew, as he said, that the policy was worthless, because it was not a good assignation, he told us, what I have no doubt you believe to be absolute truth, that he was " trying it on " with the insurance company. " I was bluffing them," he said; and observe, it is well known that insurance companies—there being such great competition in the business—very often pay claims in order to save their credit, in order to keep them popular, which they know are not strictly and legally due by them. That is done every day, as any one connected with insurance companies knows, in connection with fires. Rather than have the scandal of inquiry as to whether there has been incendiarism or not an office pays, and in the same way I have no doubt there are many instances in which, rather than incur the unpopularity of refusing a claim, although they are not legally bound, they pay. Tottenham knew that. He was man of the world enough to know. He thinks he will " try it on "; that he will " bluff " them by saying in effect, " The young man was not of age, but I will blazon your name all through the United Kingdom, and America also, if you refuse to pay the legitimate claim just because of a slight legal flaw." But you were told by the insurance office people that Monson took no part in this demand. It was Tottenham who made it. Monson was giving him his countenance, but it was throughout patent to everybody connected with it that Monson felt that the legal claim was unfounded, that the policy was worthless to him. If Tottenham chose to fight the company about it and get the money he would be perfectly pleased, and, no doubt, he would share in the proceeds; but he himself took up the position, " I have no claim that I can enforce." My learned friend said the desire to get the money was much more distinct and much more manifest in the case of Tottenham than it was in the case of Monson. I think that concludes what I have to say on the question of motive.

There is one cognate point to which I desire to draw your attention, and that is what was said as to alleged influence by Monson over Cecil Hambrough. Well, gentlemen, there is no harm in influence. We are all influenced and influencing. The only point here is whether the influence is a sinister influence; or, being sinister, was it used for selfish and fraudulent purposes by Monson over the young man? Gentlemen, all I can say about that is that the letters which were written by the young man at the time do not bear it out, and that the only attempted evidence to support the father's view negatives it. It was the evidence of the solicitor, Mr. Fuller, who said, " I thought that the young man was not allowed to come to see his father, and I rather advised him when I saw him that he ought to come to see his father." But, then, Mr. Fuller admitted that it was no great treat for the young man to go to see his poor father, who had no home for him to go to—he was knocked about from lodging to lodging in London, pursued by creditors,

Speech for the Defence.

Mr. Comrie Thomson

sheriff-officers, and writs, and I cannot tell you all what. And it was plain, as I shall demonstrate, and, indeed, was admitted, that the one object they had in wanting Cecil to go to town was not to enjoy his company, was not to have an opportunity of cultivating his mind and manners, but was simply to get hold of him so as to make him go up for the insurance of his life, and make himself a party to their scheme, which he declined to be. Mr. Fuller admitted that that was the object of pressing him to come up to town.

Now, let me read some of the letters between Cecil and his father in connection with this matter. Notice, please, that he is writing to his father in March. He says—" I cannot very well come to town immediately, as Mr. Monson is away. I am afraid he would not like me going away just now, as it is in the middle of the term, because it would interfere with my work so much. He wants me to go for my exam. in June. Mr. Connell says if I work hard I shall have a very good chance of getting through, but that I have no time to lose. He also says I am getting on very well now, so you see it would be a pity to waste any time. I am glad you have made it up with Mr. Monson. I am sure he is doing his best. I believe he meant to have sent you some money last week, only he was disappointed in getting it. He expects to get it to-day, or, at the latest, to-morrow—so I believe."

Then in the same month he writes again to his father, who had evidently been writing to him to come up to town—" I cannot see any good in coming to town. I could not do any good, and should only be an extra expense to you, and goodness knows, money is scarce enough, and I should think it likely to remain so for the next two years." That was written in 1892. He knew, of course, that when 1894 came he would have money. And then he says—" Mr. Monson says he does not see what good it would do. I should only be losing valuable time, and every day is of consequence to me now, if I am ever to pass this exam. Besides which, my going away would upset everything. Rawstone would think, if I had a holiday in the middle of the term, that he ought to have one likewise. Mr. Monson has been good enough to provide me with clothes and pocket-money for the last year, and you can hardly wonder that I am grateful for it."

Then he wrote again to his mother in the same month—" I would sooner not accept the invitation just now, because I am most anxious to get on with my studies; and I think it would be most unfair to Mr. Monson that I should leave in the middle of the term, and particularly when he has just engaged such an expensive tutor for me and Rawstone to read with; besides that, I have all I want here, and am quite happy and content." Here I may say that my learned friend suggested yesterday that there were no other pupils of Mr. Monson's besides young Hambrough. From this letter you see that there was, at least, another pupil—Mr. Rawstone—and in the course of the evidence we also heard of a Mr. Jebb, who was

357

Alfred John Monson.

Mr. Comrie Thomson

also under Mr. Monson's tuition. I say that merely to show that the suggestion of my learned friend, that the establishment was kept up only for Cecil Hambrough, is not accurate. The letter goes on to say—" Mr. Monson has entered me for a militia regiment, and I shall soon be going for my training. I am old enough to understand my position perfectly well, and quite understand that when I come of age I shall have to cut off the entail, so as to pay my father's debts, which, of course, I shall do. I only wish I could do something to help him now, but I cannot do anything until I am twenty-one. I am sorry that I am not able to do what you ask me, but I have quite made up my mind to work hard for my exam. Give my best love to my father. I hope he will soon be feeling better."

Finally, there is another letter to his father—" I am truly sorry if I have added to your troubles, and can only say I had no intention of doing so. I think you greatly mistake Mr. Monson's intentions. I am sure he has not misrepresented things to me, and I cannot see what nefarious ends he has in view. He has always been straightforward to me. How has he attempted to defraud you? He has only tried to save the estates from being sold by the Eagle. If it had not been for him Hanrock would have bought them." And we know that that is the case, because Hanrock had to be taken to a Court of law before he would give up his hold on them. " I can assure you I mean no disrespect to you whatever. I am only doing what I am sure is for the best. I would sooner not leave my studies now, but in the holidays I should very much like to come and see you. The Eagle, as you are aware of, have foreclosed, and have got the foreclosure made good by the Court of Chancery, so it is impossible to upset it. Mr. Monson is going to pay the Eagle off so as to cut off the entail when I come of age. If he does not succeed, and it passes into other hands, even when I come of age, I do not see what could be done. I do not see how anything can be done at all except through him, so I think it is bad policy, if nothing else, to quarrel with him. I shall never forget how good both you and my mother have been to me. I am sure this grieves me very much. But you know I must have an education; I cannot go about utterly ignorant all my life."

Are these not the letters of a well-meaning, intelligent, dutiful son who has arrived at a time of life when he sees two things very plainly—in the first place, that he must not go on idling and fooling through the world; and in the second place, that he must get himself educated, and must try to get into the profession he had chosen? He recognised that but for the assistance he had received from Monson he would not have been in the position in which he was, and that, therefore, although entertaining feelings of respect, duty, and love towards his father and mother, he feels himself justified in resisting the pressure that they are bringing to bear upon him for the purpose of inducing him to leave Monson. But this, as you

358

Speech for the Defence.

Mr. Comrie Thomson

will see from the telegrams, was nothing else and nothing better than a desire to get this young man into their hands so that the arrangement with the Eagle Insurance Company might be carried out. "Business blocked through you," telegraphs the father to the son; "you are causing great inconvenience"; and Fuller, the solicitor, through whom these negotiations were going on, told us that the business being blocked meant that he was not going to aid his father in getting the arrangement made with the Eagle which he was carrying out, because he did not like Prince or the other man with whom he was associated, and as he had the greatest interest in the matter, because his father's life interest was gone for ever, he said, "I am of opinion that this is a foolish proposal," and accordingly he declines to go to town or to leave his studies. That is the whole evidence we have of undue or sinister influence practised by Monson on Cecil Hambrough.

Now, that brings me to the evidence in regard to what I may call the leading facts of the crime. I have disposed of the motive. I now come to consider the evidence as to the facts. Gentlemen, three persons almost certainly knew exactly what happened, and no other human being. They were the poor lad, who is dead; the prisoner at the bar, whose mouth is closed; and the man called Scott, whom we cannot get. Now, that being so, the first thing I purpose to deal with is the position which Scott, and the evidence about him, occupy in the case.

We know, in so far as his connection with Monson is concerned, that he came with him from Greenock, possibly from Glasgow. About that we are not certain, but he came with him from Greenock, in the steamer, upon 8th August. Monson certainly knew him, because they were seen together talking on board the steamer. But it is just as evident that they were not on terms of great intimacy, still less of professed friendship, because Mr. Donald told you that, although Monson introduced Scott to him, he ceased to talk with him, and he missed him altogether when the steamer arrived at the Tighnabruaich quay; it turned out that Scott had got out at Tighnabruaich by some mistake, and it was necessary, when Mr. Monson got to Kames, to go back for Scott and pick him up. It is said by Mr. Donald that when he asked Monson who Scott was, his recollection was that he was from the estate office. All I can say is, that Mr. Donald is a most truthful and trustworthy man, but that Mr. Donald must have been under a mistake about this; and it is not an unnatural mistake, because there was a conversation going on, and they were talking at that time about the purchase of Ardlamont, which was known to be in the market; and it was about that time—I think it was that very day—that Mr. Monson had been at Edinburgh on the subject. He had just come from the estate office, that is, from the office of J. & F. Anderson here, after an interview with the agents for the estate, and it is clear, I think,

Alfred John Monson.

that when Mr. Donald received the impression that this lad Scott
had come from the estate office, that he had mixed up the two
things. Something had been said about Monson's visit to the
estate office, and this young man was with him. At all events, it
is not of consequence, and although my learned friend, the Solicitor-
General, adverted to it, he did not put any great stress upon it.
Then we know from Miss Hiron, and the housemaid, and the butler,
that he was spoken of at the house as an engineer. We further
know that he was not in quite the same social position as the
Monsons. He was respectable and well enough dressed, but there
were various little pieces of manner, and so on, which suggested
to Miss Hiron that he was not what we call a gentleman. Beyond
that, really we know hardly anything for certain; except that he
was out in the evening—I shall have to speak of what he did then—
and that he was also out on the beach in the morning, and that he
left under circumstances which I shall afterwards explain.

Now, both sides, gentlemen, I submit to you, have done their
best to find him. You heard what the Crown had done, and you
heard to what a great extent the prisoner's agents have exerted
themselves in order to find this missing man. The Crown got the
same information that we did, and that is an answer to the
Solicitor-General's comments upon the statement made upon 22nd
August by Monson—" I am informed that Edward Scott started
business as an engineer in Glasgow, and that he failed; that he was
afterwards working in connection with yachts, and is well known in
Greenock." That information was communicated to us, but the
statement was made in the first place to the Crown; and therefore
any remarks that were made yesterday as to the information not
being followed up by search in the quarter mentioned apply equally
to both the Crown and the defence. But the explanation is a
perfectly plain one. The Donalds knew some people of that name
in Greenock, and Mr. Blair also knew that at one time there had
been a brother of an Edward Scott in Greenock; but, in point of
fact, that information was inaccurate, so neither the Crown nor the
defence followed it up. But there was every effort conceivable
made by the Crown and by us to discover this man. Was there
anything suspicious in the mode of his leaving? The suggestion
was made that he came there as an engineer to look after the boilers
of the yacht. This yacht had been taken for Hambrough. That is
demonstrated; for although Monson took up a certain responsibility
with reference to guaranteeing the payment, the yacht had been
taken for Hambrough. The statement was made, and it has not
been contradicted by anybody, that Scott came in order to act for
Hambrough in connection with the boilers of the yacht. Now, it
is said that already there was an engineer, but that was the
Donalds' engineer, and it was only natural that the hirer of the
yacht should desire that he should be represented by some one on
board who had practical knowledge. It was further said that he

360

Speech for the Defence.

Mr. Comrie Thomson

never went to the yacht, and that he left on the 10th; but they had no business to put a foot upon the yacht until the 10th, and they had no business to put a foot upon it until they had got their money, or the deposit of an amount of it, on the 10th. Accordingly Scott could not upon the 9th go to the yacht; he had no business to do so. The accident happened on the morning of the 10th, before there was any chance of taking delivery of the yacht.

After the accident Scott's position is this, that his occupation is gone, that the man who hired him is dead. There is to be no yacht now, because there is no owner of the yacht. He is very much shocked at what has happened, necessarily—I am assuming, of course, that it was an accident—but there is no reason for his remaining. He does not, however, go away at once. He waits till the afternoon before he leaves, and takes the fifth boat which left Tighnabruaich that day. He remains in the neighbourhood with those who are concerned with the moving and the dressing of the body. He remains to the sad and silent luncheon that they partook of in the middle of the day. Monson says himself, " It is a pity you should go away "; but he takes his own way and does go, leaving his temporary address, at all events, as the Central Station Hotel in Glasgow. My learned friend said yesterday—I suppose by a slip of the tongue—that he went away leaving a false address. There is no falsehood about the address, so far as we know. He said, " My address is the Central Station Hotel," and there has been no attempt to disprove that statement. He was at the Central Station Hotel, so far as we know, that night, at all events. No attempt had been made to search any hotel until three or four nights afterwards, when Major Hambrough says he asked for him in a hotel he had never mentioned, the North British Railway Hotel. So that you have him going away deliberately for a perfectly sufficient reason—going away leaving a temporary address behind him, which is communicated to the local policeman, who, if he had thought to detain him—of course he did not think of detaining him—could either have stopped him going, or at all events, telegraphed to Glasgow that night to have him stopped there. It is true that the local policeman said to him at the quay that there would be an inquiry, and that he should wait; but notice this, because it is important. The doctor had completed his inquiry, and had stated in Scott's hearing, " It is true, we have no coroner's inquest in Scotland, but the authorities are particular about a sudden death, but here, in this case, I am satisfied there will be no difficulty." Why should Scott, in the knowledge of that statement made to him by the doctor, who had completed his examination, remain an hour longer merely because the policeman asked him, in a vague sort of fashion, if he were not going to stay for the inquiry, the policeman not knowing that the doctor's inquiry had been completed, and that the doctor's opinion was such as rendered it quite unnecessary that Scott should stay?

361

Alfred John Monson.

Mr. Comrie Thomson

Gentlemen, that seems to me, apart from his position with reference to the accident, pretty nearly to exhaust the facts that we have with reference to Scott. If it be the case that Scott is Ted Davis—if that is so, and, of course, it is a remarkable coincidence —there is no shutting one's eyes to the fact that apparently Ted Davis or Scott disappears; it is to be borne in mind that although the man known as Scott has not been seen, as far as we are aware, since 10th August, Ted Davis was seen in London up to 15th September by his brother, as he told you. Yet, I say, suppose that these two men are the same, is it not demonstrated to you that Ted Davis—if he was Scott—was one of the gentlest, most amiable and quietest of men? A bookmaker he was, but he was a sick bookmaker, a dying bookmaker; and Sidney Russell and his brother both concurred in telling you that he was the last man that would be party to a cruel act—he would not harm a fly; and yet the suggestion is, the most preposterous I ever listened to, that, for some mysterious reason, Monson invites this mild, amiable man to come down and be an eye-witness to an attempt to murder, and then takes him along with him to be an eye-witness to an act of murder, and does not take means to detain him so that he may give evidence in his favour. Is not that a thing perfectly absurd on the face of it? If Monson was to drown this man, or shoot him, why does he bring Scott? He does not want any assistance; wants no third party to throw him out of the boat; wants no third party to shoot him. He brings down this man, the suggestion is, that he might aid and abet him. What earthly help could be got from him? Did he not bring down a man who could have deponed here, if there was foul play, " I saw it," or who, as I hinted to you a moment ago, could have been retained if there had been foul play, and if he was the unredeemed villain he was suggested to be, could have been retained, and gone into the witness-box and said, " I saw it; there was no murder; it was a pure accident "? Gentlemen, it is probably the greatest calamity that could befall my client that Scott is not here. I do not pretend to know what he would have said, but according to my information, according to the instructions by which I am guided—I go no further than that, but I am justified in going so far as that—I think it is the greatest calamity that ever befell mortal man that Scott has not been able to enter this witness-box.

The result of this is, that without the three men, one being dead and the other with a closed mouth, and the third not to be got, the Crown has got to rely, as I said to you before, upon indirect or circumstantial evidence. Now, gentlemen, it has often been said that, in a certain sense, you can never get better evidence than circumstantial evidence, because facts do not lie, as human beings sometimes do. But it is essential that you should realise exactly what is meant by circumstantial evidence, and what is necessary before circumstantial evidence can be taken as valuable at all, or

Speech for the Defence.

Mr. Comrie Thomson

as equivalent in value to direct evidence. In the first place, gentlemen, observe this—and I have suspected it is sometimes overlooked—that it is an essential part of the value of circumstantial evidence that each circumstance should be distinctly proved. Circumstantial evidence does not mean a lot of suspicious circumstances. That is not it at all. You must have each circumstance which is founded upon, those which are to be pieced together into one whole, and from which the conclusion is to be derived, clearly demonstrated by evidence. It will not do to say, " That is rather suspicious," unless it is proved, proved in the usual way, proved by direct evidence. Then, gentlemen, having got your full proof of each circumstance, it is necessary that the effect of each shall not be misapprehended, or misapplied, or misjudged. And it is only when you have got each circumstance established by evidence, and when you are satisfied not only of its full authentication, but also that the inferences drawn from it have been justifiable and true inferences, that you are in a position to determine when that body of evidence so established and so applied is sufficient to exclude every theory except that of guilt. You must have your facts proved; you must be satisfied that a sound use is made of them, and then, having arrived at that state of mind, you must say to yourself, " Are these facts consistent with anything except the man's guilt? " You must be driven, forced to that conclusion, before you are justified in being guided by circumstantial evidence. Now, my friend yesterday used an expression which I gladly adopt. He said it was a chain of circumstances, and that very fitly describes the sort of view you are to take of circumstantial evidence. It is a chain; but as no chain is stronger than its weakest link, so no circumstantial evidence is worth anything if any essential circumstance is not conclusively established.

Gentlemen, I now come to the first charge—the attempt to drown; and it is important that you should know what exactly the Crown says here. It says that " you two "—that is, Monson and Scott—"having formed the design of causing by drowning the death of Windsor Dudley Cecil Hambrough, did in execution thereof bore or caused to be bored in the side of a boat, the property of Donald M'Kellar, boathirer, a hole, and having plugged or closed said hole, you did, on 9th August, 1893, induce Cecil Hambrough to embark along with you, Alfred John Monson, in the said boat on the said date or on 10th August, 1893, you, Alfred John Monson, in execution of said design, did in Ardlamont Bay, in the Firth of Clyde, while the said boat was in deep water, remove, or caused to be removed, the plug from said hole, and admit the water into, and did sink the said boat, whereby the said Windsor Dudley Cecil Hambrough was thrown into the sea." Now, notice what the charge is. There is, in the first place, a design set forth as having been entered into between Monson and Scott. I have suggested to you whether there was any probability of that; but then the mode

363

Alfred John Monson.

Mr. Comrie Thomson

in which this design was executed is, that having got Cecil to go into a boat with a plug hole in it, he, Monson, when they were out in deep water, drew out the plug, and then the water came in, and by that means the boat was sunk. Now, gentlemen, it seems to me that that is about as improbable a way for a man to compass the death of another as can very well be imagined. Hambrough was accustomed to fishing, and he was accustomed to fish at night. He was accustomed to use a large net, a splash net, when fishing. He was a careless fellow in a boat. We were told that yesterday by Mr. Donald. Mr. Donald was often out with him, and was always frightened, and was rather glad when he left him. Cecil Hambrough had hired a boat for himself from M'Kellar for the season; but he had told Douglas before this day that he was going to get a new boat and a net; and accordingly we know that M'Nicol's boat was got round. The arrangement that he should go out that evening accompanied by Monson was made openly at dinner. My friend made a point of this that they were not accompanied by M'Intyre. M'Intyre was not put into the box, although on the Crown list; but the point there seems to me entirely to fail. Miss Hiron said that she thinks she heard a keeper—whether M'Intyre or not, she is not sure—come to the house just about the time they were starting. There is no evidence to show that M'Intyre ever accompanied Hambrough or Monson in the boat. But nothing could be more natural than that they should be accompanied by a keeper to the boat, carrying the net, hauling the boat up to where they were to embark, and giving general assistance. The boat was not a very large one, and, along with the net, two were quite enough for it, and it is not suggested—at least from the witness-box —that Hambrough was ever accompanied by a keeper or by any person when he was out fishing.

Now, you have the account given by the prisoner in his declaration of what was done on this occasion, and I think I should read it to you once more. What he says is this—" After dinner on the evening of 9th August, Cecil Hambrough, who was living in family with me at Ardlamont House, stated that he was going out fishing, and asked me to go with him. I agreed to do so, though I did not care for the kind of fishing intended, which was fishing with a splash net. Hambrough had hired from a man at Kames or Tighnabruaich a small boat, which he used on previous occasions for the same purpose. In this boat he and I started. We had on board a considerable length of net, probably about 300 yards, the width being about 14 feet. The nets were piled up in the boat, and were in themselves a considerable load. Hambrough took off his coat and rowed, while I busied myself preparing the nets. I did not steer the boat. There was, in fact, no rudder. While occupied with the nets, suddenly there was a bump, and the boat tilted, and I fell over the side. At the same time the boat capsized,

Speech for the Defence.

Mr. Comrie Thomson

and for a minute or two I was entangled in the nets. Immediately on getting clear I called out to Hambrough, and then saw him sitting on the rock laughing. The boat had struck the side of this rock and tilted over, which, with the load piled up as it was with the nets, she would easily do. Hambrough, I knew, could not swim, so I told him to wait while I swam ashore and fetched another boat which was there. The sea was a little rough, and the night was dark. The distance I had to swim would be between 200 and 300 yards. As I was working with the other boat to get her off, I observed Scott, a man who was staying in the house at the time, coming down, and called out to him to run to the house and fetch a lamp, as I could not find the plug or the plug hole in the boat. The tide, I understood, was then rising; so I deemed it wiser not to wait until Scott returned, and, accordingly, pushed off the boat. I knew that although the plug might be out there might be time, without danger, to row to where Hambrough was and back. I pulled off and picked up Hambrough. I told him that I thought the plug was out, but there was then only 2 inches of water in the boat, and we decided to pull out, and pick up the other boat and nets, which were floating about 20 yards or so away. I got out, and made fast a line to the capsized boat, and we then hauled the nets in, and proceeded to row ashore, but made no progress. Eventually we discovered that the anchor had fallen out of the capsized boat, and was securely fastened aground. We then got released, and rowed ashore. There we found Scott, who had meantime come down with a lamp. By the time we landed the boat we were in was nearly full of water. We made fast the boats and went to the house. We all went into the smoking-room, and a man-servant brought whisky and water. I immediately went up to bed, leaving Scott and Hambrough together. Their rooms were near the smoking-room, on the same floor. I do not know whether the plug was in the boat we first went out in; neither of us looked to see. The plug hole in the boat, however, was a homely affair. Hambrough complained that it had no plug hole, and that in consequence it was a bother to empty her after he had been out splash fishing, during which a lot of water gathered, and accordingly he himself cut a plug hole in the boat. I have no further answer to give to the charge now made against me. It is not true. On the contrary, so far from attempting on that evening to take young Hambrough's life, I consider that I saved it. The foregoing statement up to this point has been dictated by me word for word. Question by the Sheriff-Substitute—' Is Scott, to whom you have referred, really called Davis, and do you know him?' Answer—' I have already said that I have no further answer to give to this charge.' Question by the Sheriff-Substitute—' Were the nets used that night at all?' Answer—' I have no further answer to give.' All which I declare to be the truth."

365

Alfred John Monson.

Mr. Comrie Thomson

Now, that is what he said. That is the account he gives, and, gentlemen, I put it to you whether in many important respects that declaration is not corroborated, and whether it is not plain that the account given by the Crown of what happened is absolutely untrue. In the first place, he says in his declaration that Hambrough took off his coat and rowed, and Whyte and M'Nicol tell you that, on examining the boat in which he had been next morning, they found his coat. It had been stuck beneath one of the seats, and although the boat capsized there it was. Naturally when a man rows he takes off his coat, and the next morning this man's coat is found under the seat. He says that he called to a man to go to the house and get a lamp. The servants tell you that they heard a man come and ask one. All the other details that he gives in this declaration surely have the impress of truth upon them. They are circumstantial if you will. There is no reason why he should say a number of these things except that he was telling an unvarnished and true tale, but there is remarkable corroboration coming from a totally independent source, namely, the fishermen who were put into the box, and who told you that before they started for their evening's work, after having landed for their supper, they saw two boats in what they considered foolish or dangerous positions, just beginning to bump with the rise of the tide, that some time afterwards they heard a boat put off from the shore, and that a very little after that they heard what they called screams, but what, it was explained by both of them, were not screams in the ordinary sense of the word. They were shouts. There was no scream of distress or danger or anything of that kind. There was shouting, just exactly as you would expect, just exactly what Monson says happened. They are capsized, one gets on the rocks and the other makes for shore, and he shouts to Scott to go and get a lamp. Can you doubt for a moment that the fishermen would tell exactly the truth, and that the noises they heard came from Monson and Hambrough? If that be the case, then the suggestion of an attempt to drown is entirely out of the question.

But, then, it is said that it is a very suspicious circumstance that the plug hole in that boat was what Monson himself calls " a very homely affair." Why there should have been evidence led here to show that it was cut with a knife, and not bored with an auger, and was done by an amateur, and not by a tradesman, I do not quite understand, because from the very beginning Monson says, as I read, " It was a homely affair. Hambrough cut it with a knife." And he gives the reason why—" because that boat had no plug hole, and he wanted one." But if the design of Monson was to drown that man, why did he take that particular boat, and not that of M'Nicol's, which had a plug hole in it—why should he have taken this other one, with a suspicious-looking plug hole, if you will. Would it not be natural, if he meant that this man

Speech for the Defence.

Mr. Comrie Thomson

should be drowned by his removing the plug when in deep water, that he should take the boat that had the ordinary plug hole—that of M'Nicol's—instead of taking this other one? And then, gentlemen, you heard that there was a plank covering this plug hole; and, beyond all, you have this fact, that the coming in of water by a plug hole is a most gradual operation, and it would be a most senseless thing, if you were going to attempt to drown a man, to take him out in a narrow bay like this and remove the plug for the purpose of filling the boat with water—taking, I suppose, a very considerable time; certainly more than a quarter of an hour before it would fill by a hole with a diameter of only an inch—when, if he desired to drown him, he had every chance of simply tipping him over whenever he stood up in the boat. The suggestion is absurd on the face of it, and the whole circumstances are entirely consistent with the story that Monson himself gives you.

Now, there was no plank covering the plug hole. It had been removed, and there my learned friend was in error yesterday. The act of getting the hole cut led to Hambrough removing the plank, and it was not there, so that the hole was perfectly visible to him the moment he put foot in the boat, because it was not covered up by the foot plank. So that the suggestion is that he went on board this boat with a plug hole staring him in the face, which he must have seen—recently made, and made, too, by an amateur—surely the story which was told by the prisoner himself is far the more probable, and the charge made by the Crown is one that it is impossible to credit for one moment.

There is nothing in the fact that the plug was out, because the boats—we know from the fishermen—were bumping upon the shore, and that may easily have bumped the plug out. And besides that, if Monson's statement is correct to the effect that the boat was capsized by a bump upon a rock, it is plain enough that would be quite sufficient to jerk out the plug also. Now, gentlemen, it is suggested by the Crown that there was no rock so far out as Monson says. It would have been a little suspicious, I think, if Monson had been able just to put his finger upon the actual rock in a rocky bay like that, which is all over with rocks. But he does not pretend to know exactly the spot at which this happened. He was engaged arranging the splash net, and was not guiding the boat in any way, and it is certainly not in the Crown's mouth to say that they have proved that there was no rock, because they have not attempted a survey of the bay. Mr. Brand, their principal witness in matters of survey, says he never made any such survey —that he only walked along the shore; and we have several witnesses well acquainted with this place who say that there are many boulders in the bay, and that at the Craigmore end the reefs jut out a considerable way, and that there is no impossibility whatever—and I do not require to prove more than that—that this

367

Alfred John Monson.

Mr. Comrie Thomson

boat bumped upon a rock upon which it was possible at this stage of the tide for Hambrough to clamber. It is true that Monson in his declaration says that he thinks he had to swim 200 or 300 yards, but surely that is explainable in more ways than one. It does not involve that he would swim 200 or 300 yards, for a man cannot calculate the distance he swims in a dark night. Besides, as was suggested by one of the witnesses, it was not at all unlikely that he was swimming a great deal further than was necessary, owing to the darkness, and that he had gone along the shore instead of going straight in at once. It is very important, as further corroborating the statement of the accused in regard to this matter, that next morning these two boats are found tied together by a rope, as Monson says they were, and one of them capsized or turned over. Do you think that if an attempt at murder had been made in the way that the Crown suggests, the man who made the attempt would not have had wits enough to restore the plug in the boat? Do you think that he would have left things just as they were unless his own tale was true?

A point was made about the knife. Well, it is true that we have it proved that Hambrough had a knife of the same construction as that which was shown. The witness Douglas told us that Hambrough carried his knife attached to a chain from the waist, and the knife which was shown here plainly was not a knife which could have been subjected to that process, because it had no loop or hook to attach it to the chain. That goes for very little, however. It is likely that Hambrough carried attached to his chain a different knife, and that this large, rather coarse, knife was the one which he would naturally use for making the hole in the boat. At all events, there is no suggestion that that knife belonged to Monson, or that he ever used it for such a purpose. I was not astonished to find yesterday that my learned friend, the Solicitor-General, did not refer for one moment to the absurd evidence with regard to the rowlock, which, of course, has no bearing upon the case. With his usual good sense, he did not recall the matter to your minds.

If the Crown theory is correct that an attempt of this kind was made by Monson to murder Hambrough, could Hambrough have failed to be aware of it? Is it conceivable that this lad should have been taken out into deep water, that he should have seen the plug withdrawn from the boat, that he should have found the boat sinking, and that he should have been allowed, as my learned friend said yesterday, to scramble ashore, without his suspicions being aroused—without his being absolutely certain that a nefarious attempt had been made upon his life? But if he knew that, would he have gone home and drunk whisky and water with the man who had attempted to murder him? Still less would he next morning have gone out shooting with the man who he knew had

Speech for the Defence.

Mr. Comrie Thomson

tried to compass his death by drowning the previous night. That is a point which I urge you to keep in your minds. If an attempt was made to drown, it must have been seen and known by the intended victim, who next morning goes out with a gun in his hand, and with the man who made the attempt upon his life with another gun in his hand. Is that consistent with any possible theory? Does it not carry absurdity on the face of it? I say not merely that the Crown have failed to prove this attempt at murder, but that it has been absolutely disproved by the conduct of the parties interested.

But then, gentlemen, if the first charge fails, it takes you a long way in the direction of finding that the second and more serious charge has also not been established. Each of these charges is said to have been part of a design, but if the Crown failed to prove the first attempt to carry the design into execution, it makes it far more difficult for them to prove the second attempt to carry the design into execution. They only proposed to prove an attempt in the first instance. They propose to prove an act in the second instance. But if they failed in proving the attempt, it is more likely that they shall fail with the act; so that if the evidence which has been adduced for the attempt is worthless, that for the act must be very minutely and very severely scrutinised.

That brings me to the second charge. The second charge is the most serious known to the law; it is murder. In most cases of crime, the fact that a crime has been committed is easily demonstrated. If a house is broken into and goods are removed, you know that there has been a crime—housebreaking. If a man is found shattered, as with the blows of a sledge-hammer, you know that he has been murdered. But in the present case the question you have to determine is, Has there been a crime at all? My learned friend said yesterday, very truly, that the idea of suicide is excluded here; and the idea that Monson shot Hambrough accidentally is also excluded. But, then, the question—and the first question—that you have to determine is whether there has been any crime; and you will observe that that question is complicated by this circumstance, that both Monson and the deceased were in the ordinary and lawful use of deadly weapons. A man carries a pistol, and fires. You say he had no business having a pistol. But when two men are out shooting each of them necessarily has in his hand, and to be used for the destruction of game, that which is equally available for the destruction of human life. So you see the peculiarity of this case is that you have got to find evidence that a crime was committed, and you start with this, that the person alleged to have committed it by shooting was entitled to have a loaded gun, and to discharge it; and that, on the other hand, the person who was unfortunately shot had in his hand that with which his death might be very easily brought about accidentally.

1 B

Alfred John Monson.

Mr. Comrie Thomson

The presumption, the probability that always arises in the case of a gun fatality is, as you were told by some of the doctors, always in favour of accident. A shot gun is very rarely used homicidally —Dr. Littlejohn could only tell you of two cases—one a case of poachers in the district here—in which, in his experience—and he has the largest experience of any man in Scotland—a gun had been used for homicidal purposes; and no other witness, so far as I recollect, had ever remembered of a shot gun being used for homicidal purposes; whereas, unfortunately, there never is a shooting season in which we do not read weekly in the newspapers accounts of accidents to sportsmen—some fatal, all more or less injurious. So that you start, as I say, with this—lawful possession of a lethal weapon very apt to lead to the accidental destruction of the person carrying it.

And now, gentlemen, my learned friend rather hinted than stated that it was a fact worthy of your consideration that on this unfortunate morning the lady of the house and the governess and the children were away, the suggestion being, I suppose, that it was desired that if there was to be this terrible crime committed they should be spared the shock. That is plainly a far-fetched suggestion. You are told by the nurse and by Miss Hiron that the proposal to go to Glasgow some days before the 11th had been made some days previously—whether they were to go on the Tuesday, or the Wednesday, or the Thursday—had been quite settled on, and that the nurse had made out a list of things which were necessary for the household, for the nursery, and that the whole arrangement of their going to Glasgow was entirely independent of Scott's presence, and had been made some days previously.

Shots were heard which indicate that before entering the wood in which this poor lad was killed, some of the party—I think necessarily Hambrough, as far as we can judge—had been firing at something in the plantation nearer to the sea, and to the west of the plantation in question, and that the party had then come round across the road past the schoolhouse, and there had entered the wood. And it is very important to notice their position at that time. The witness to that is a man called Dunn; and my learned friend entirely misapprehended yesterday the use that it was proposed to make of Dunn's evidence when he suggested to you that I was to maintain that Monson in his statement suggested that Dunn was an eye-witness of the event. Not at all. No such suggestion was made. What he says is this—" I remember seeing a man watching us. I am told that he mentioned to some person that he saw us in the wood. I have ascertained that his name is Smeaton, and that his luggage was taken away by Mr. M'Ewan, and that he had Smeaton's address." Now, there is no doubt that a man was watching them, namely, Dunn, and that he saw them entering the wood. I do not suggest for a moment—it never was

370

Speech for the Defence.

Mr. Comrie Thomson

suggested—that any human being saw them at the time of the occurrence. But the important point is this, that these three men in the course of their morning's walk—in the course of their morning's shoot—have gone through the one wood and that they entered the other just exactly in the way in which men shooting a cover in line would proceed. And Dunn tells you—being an independent observer—they enter in this order—On the right hand, or east side, Hambrough; in the middle, Scott, without a gun, carrying some rabbits; and on the other side, Monson; and he says —for it is important to bear this in mind—" if they kept walking in that order they never could meet." The point is simply this, that they were walking as men would do who were wanting to get game in the cover. The wood, as you know, is comparatively narrow at the schoolhouse end, and widens out so that at the place where the accident happened the distance from it westwards to the dyke which bounds the road is about 192 yards, if I remember rightly.

It may as well be noticed, as was pointed out by my learned friend, that in this case we have not the advantage of a statement by the accused in regard to what actually occurred—I mean made judicially before the Sheriff; and I ought to explain to you, gentlemen, in case his silence may be construed against him prejudicially, what exactly is the position of matters with reference to that. You will observe that a declaration was taken before the Sheriff on 31st August, just the day after he was apprehended, and only two days after he had discovered that the authorities entertained suspicions about his connection with the crime. He summons naturally—as he was justified in doing—to his assistance his law agent, and the law agent, knowing nothing about the real circumstances of the case, does what is done in, I suppose, nine cases out of ten, and probably in a much larger number of cases where the charge is one of so serious nature as this. The law agent, not having had an opportunity of making inquiry, having had little opportunity of consulting with his client, takes the safe course—the prudent course, I suppose, most agents would regard it—and says, " Well, in the meantime, my advice to you is don't answer any questions. The law entitles you to take up that position, and I cannot advise in any other way, because I have not sufficient information to do so "; and, accordingly, as I suppose is done constantly, the merciful provision, for the prisoner having the advantage of his law agent's assistance, which came into existence in the Act which was passed mainly by means of his lordship who now presides, comes into operation, and I think I am not wrong in saying that the advice in question, in the great majority of cases, is the best piece of advice that can be given. But that accounts, and I only mention it for that reason, for the silence of the prisoner when brought before the Sheriff.

371

Alfred John Monson.

Mr. Comrie Thomson

It was suggested yesterday that it was strange that there should have been no keeper with them, and it was said that Lamont would naturally have been with them. But, gentlemen, there is evidence to show that even before Scott came these two men were in the habit of going out and shooting in the plantation and cover near the house without any keeper. It is quite a natural thing, as you can understand, for them when going out for a couple of hours before luncheon, not to trouble with a keeper, and he himself explained to you that just at that period he was fully occupied in attending to the rearing of the young pheasants, a considerable quantity of eggs having been laid down. And it was explained to you that there was nothing unusual or remarkable in their not being accompanied by a keeper, and still less need was there of a keeper on that occasion, seeing that they had Scott, who did not care to shoot, and was willing to carry any game that they shot.

Now, it was a point that was very much urged by a witness— who may be a perfectly honest and respectable man, but who struck me as the only witness in the case who was inclined to press matters —namely, the witness Whyte, who made a statement in regard to what he saw in that wood, which is of considerable importance, but which I think you will be satisfied he was not justified in making. He says that he saw a track, by which he led us to understand he meant the trail of a man—a trail that would be made upon the underwood by a man passing once or, at the outside, twice over the same line. And he suggested that this was the mark of Scott and Monson, going from the portion of the wood in which they were walking across eastwards towards the opening in the whins, near which the body was found. But, gentlemen, Whyte, when he was examined before the Procurator-Fiscal, denied that he had seen such trails, and it is proved that the only trails or tracks near that place were two tracks which had been long in existence, which were thoroughly well defined, and which had been trodden down by foot of man or beast for months previously. M'Nicol says so, and Carmichael, the ploughman, too. They both told you so, so that I think you must dismiss as disproved the statement which was made by Whyte to the effect that he saw traces as if these two men, Scott and Monson, had crossed from the lower part of the wood towards the gap, in the direction of Hambrough. Monson's own statement afterwards was that he had gone quite to the extreme end of the wood, and that, having heard a shot, he had called out to Hambrough, " What have you got? " and getting no answer he proceeded up to where the man was lying.

The next point that it is necessary to attend to, and it is a very grave one, is the state of the evidence in regard to the path which was followed by Hambrough. He was on the top of a sunk dyke. I quite agree with the Solicitor-General in saying that it does not follow that his feet were always on the top of the stone

Speech for the Defence.

Mr. Comrie Thomson

structure, but he was either there or upon the ground close to it, within an inch or two of it. If you regard the wooden border of the table before me as representing the dyke, then I say he was walking upon that wooden border or within an inch or two of it upon the turf. It was the natural place for a man to be, because you will observe that in that way he was, from the elevated position, able to command the young plantation on the right of him, and could see the rabbits going about there, and, on the other hand, he was able to command the old plantation to the left of him. He was walking upon that, and it is important to consider what is the nature of what he was walking upon. You had before you yesterday the plans and sections put in by Mr. Brand. Well, they have their use, but they are of no use in disclosing to you what was the nature of the ground upon which this man was walking; but then you have abundant evidence. Some of the witnesses, such as Whyte, and I think Mr. Brand also, were very slow and stiff in admitting it, but I put it to you whether it is not distinctly proved that it was a place the walking upon which demanded that there should be considerable care exercised by the man who was upon it. There were loose turfs, loose divots, and holes, and other inequalities into which, if a man put his foot, he was almost certain to stumble, and when a man was walking along there with his gun, looking for game from this side to that, or looking above for wood pigeons, the chance of making a stumble was exceedingly great. I think I have sufficiently described to you the points that it is necessary for you to bear in mind in regard to the wood in which these three men were; keeping this further consideration in view, about which there is no dispute, that the morning was a wet and tempestuous one, and that everything appears to have been soaking, and slippery, and damp with rain.

Now, the first point that was made yesterday upon this subject, and the Solicitor-General most justifiably described it as a vital and important point, was the question, Where was the body of Hambrough first struck down? We know where it was found by what I may call third persons. We know where it was lifted to by Monson and Scott. The question is—and the important point of it is mainly founded upon this—that it is from that position that certain lines have to be drawn, and which demonstrated, or are said to demonstrate, the direction of the fire. Now, I am in a certain sense tied down by what the accused is alleged to have stated more than once on the morning of the accident. There can be no question—I do not pretend to dispute it—that on the morning of the accident he, by what he said, conveyed to the mind of more than one person that when he went up to find Hambrough on the ground dead, he was not lying on the top of the dyke, but somewhere, not in the ditch. He never says that; he admitted he stated that he did not find the body lying upon the top of the dyke,

Alfred John Monson,

Mr. Comrie Thomson

but, subject to correction, neither did he say that it was lying in the ditch. But it was lying on the other side of the ditch, on the sloping ground rising up from it. His words are, in his holograph statement made on the day of the occurrence, " We called Hambrough several times, and there was no reply. I then saw him lying at the bottom of the sunk fence on his left side with the gun beside him. I lifted him up, and he was quite dead." That is, of course, susceptible, I grant you, of the interpretation that the body was lying in the ditch, but it is also susceptible of the other interpretation that it was lying at the foot of the sunk fence. There is just the ditch which is right below. It is only 2 feet wide, and just beyond that is the place which Monson pointed out to every other witness—to Steven particularly; it is sufficient to take Steven, who is a witness of truth. It was on that place that he said the body was found. You will observe that the point made against me is that there must have been traces of the body having been there had it lain there for ever so short a time. No traces are proved to have been found. The only traces are either traces of crushed vegetation upon which it lay, or traces of blood. If it was lying in the ditch, the ditch, as my learned friend said yesterday, has running water in it, and therefore traces of blood would not have remained. It was said it had brackens and ferns, and that there might have been signs of breaking among them ; but if the place that was pointed out to Steven and Tottenham— outside the ditch, as the latter said—was the place, there would be no signs of crushing, as the grass would rise the moment the weight was taken away. There was no vegetation to break, and there might have been traces of blood ; possibly that might have been expected ; but we were told by an experienced witness yesterday or the day before that there would not necessarily be much blood coming from the body. With a shot wound bleeding very slowly, any blood that did come just in the moment of lifting it from the low ground on to the top of the dyke would most probably be caught by the blades of grass in the wet morning, and instantly be absorbed in the ground. Dr. Littlejohn used the expression " oozing " ; and we know that the poor lad's body was laid down, and lay for a considerable time, and that the whole quantity of blood that came from it, although one of the largest veins in the head had been severed, was not more than would have filled, as one witness said, an ordinary kitchen bowl. Further, it is suggested, not by me, but by men who are accustomed to deal with such matters, and who know what they are talking about, that it is exceedingly likely— more likely than any other theory that can be formed—that when the shot was fired two pieces of bone which were fractured by the shot would be driven back into the head so as to plug this vein until the body began to be moved ; and we know that these bits of bone are found close to the head, outside of it, after it had been placed

Speech for the Defence.

Mr. Comrie Thomson

in the position in which it was ultimately put. So, you see, although it is only of importance with reference to subsequent measurements and calculations there is nothing to show that the statement made by Monson at the time is not a perfectly true one. At that time he could not realise that measurements were going to be taken, and he had no earthly object to serve in stating anything but what was absolutely true. He told Steven he was not sure which place he lifted the body from, but that they certainly lifted him. He had no reason to state that unless it had been true. It is common ground that Cecil was walking at the time of the accident from the south, and that the shot entered the head from behind. But, assuming that the place at which he was shot was the place from which he was ultimately removed, he was found lying upon his back, with his head towards the north, or towards the rowan tree. That is to say, he was walking, as it were, in the direction of the rowan tree. He is shot from behind, but he falls with his back towards the rowan tree. If he was walking in that direction, and was shot from behind, he would either, we are told, have fallen forwards or backwards. If he fell forwards he could not have been found in the position in which he was, because he was lying on his back. If he fell backwards, he could not have been found in the position in which he was, because his feet would have been pointing to the rowan tree. I think that is unanswerable. I hope I have made it clear. Admit that he is walking from the south. If he falls forward he is on his face, with his head to the rowan tree; if he falls backward he would be on his back, with his feet to the rowan tree. But in point of fact he is found lying on his back, with his head towards the rowan tree. So that we both agree, and we agree about it in holding that if he was shot when walking in that direction, that he must have been moved. It may be that he was only turned over, but why should you imagine that he must be wheeled right round and put into a position with his feet so, or that he should be touched at all, except that it be true what this man tells you? " He was shot in the ditch, near to the ditch, and, for the sake of reverence and respect, we lifted him out of that low position and put him quietly and decently upon the open, upper, smoother ground." Now, then, if I am right there, you will observe, if you think it is proved that he was moved, the whole foundation of the Crown case crumbles to pieces, because they have no data for which there is any justification on which their measurements and evidence as to direction shall depend. If you think that that was not the spot where the man fell—and I demonstrated to you beyond all question that his body had been moved— I see no reason why you should doubt that it was moved in that way. The prisoner—the only person who can say anything about it with certain knowledge—says it was. If that is so, then you must throw to the winds the whole of the evidence with reference

Alfred John Monson.

Mr Comrie Thomson

to pellets in the rowan tree and the beech tree and the lime. But before I come to speak about that, and following the order of the learned Solicitor-General yesterday, I desire to draw your attention to the question—With what gun was he shot? And here also, up to a certain point, my learned friend and I are, I think, at one. He was shot with a 12-bore gun, with No. 5 shot and amberite powder. I think that that is demonstrated by the evidence as to the pellets which were found in the brain. They are No. 5 shot, and we know, otherwise, that these cartridges were used in the 12-bore gun. Now, gentlemen, this is, of course, a vital part of the case, as it was represented to you yesterday, and it is very important that you should apprehend exactly what the evidence is about it.

I start with this, that Lamont proves—and there is nothing to contradict it—that he that morning put the 20-bore gun, which was generally known as Hambrough's gun, into the hands of Monson, and there is no evidence to show that it ever left his hands until after the accident. Now I challenge any one to contradict that. Lamont, who was the witness of truth, as you saw, having no interest in this matter, and curiously had apparently forgotten it at first, not realising the importance of it, says this—" I gave Monson the 20-bore gun that morning to take to Hambrough, because it was the one that Hambrough usually shot with.'' Then we find—although the evidence is indirect statements, made long before this question was raised, long before there was the slightest suspicion of a crime, long before Monson could have done anything in the direction of making any evidence in his own favour—Monson telling Steven and M'Ewan, the piermaster, on the day of the incident exactly what happened. Of course, he did not—could not —see the significance of it. Even if guilty, he could not have seen the significance of it—no person had suggested that there was foul play. He said to these two men, " It is remarkable that I got poor Hambrough's gun from Lamont this morning, and when I went out of the house to give it to him, I found that he had gone out with the 12-bore gun for the purpose of trying the new amberite powder.'' So that it is a mistake to suggest that this was an afterthought. My very strong impression is that Monson certainly said that to M'Ewan, and I believe he said it also to Steven, on the 10th. It was a curious fact, but you have the fact that it is proved that the gun was put into Monson's hands that morning when they started to shoot, and it is not proved ever to have left his hand; and beyond that, his statement was made at a time when there was no occasion for his making it except it were a true narrative. " Curiously enough,'' he said, " When I came out of the house with the 20-bore gun in my hand I found that Hambrough had gone off with the 12-bore gun.''

If you are satisfied of the truth of that, then there is an end

376

Speech for the Defence.

Mr Comrie Thomson

of the case. If, as is admitted, Hambrough was shot with No. 5 shot out of a 12-bore gun, if the circumstances I have detailed to you are true, then he could not have been shot by any hand but his own. I said, if this is true. I do not require to put it so far as that. If there is reasonable doubt, you must give the prisoner the benefit of it. If you believe Lamont, if you believe the statements made at the time, if you are inclined to believe them, if you think that they are susceptible of belief—that is all I need. If there is a reasonable doubt in your minds raised by the circumstances I have been detailing to you, if it might have happened, if it possibly was the case, that the 20-bore gun never left the hand of Monson, and that Hambrough retained possession of the 12-bore gun, then you must acquit. Some mistake seems to have been made, and I think it points in the direction of the veracity of the witness and of Monson. On a somewhat later date, when examined before the Fiscal, not seeing the importance of the circumstance of his handing the 20-bore gun to Monson, Lamont told the Fiscal that Monson used to shoot with the 12-bore and Hambrough with the 20-bore gun. He did not see through the import of it. He assumed, when being examined on 25th August before the Fiscal, that on that morning it had been as usual, but when he goes back and tells Monson what he had been saying to the Fiscal, and that the Fiscal wanted the 20-bore gun and the cartridges sent out to him next day, he immediately sees that is a mistake, and when Lamont recalls the circumstances, he hurries back to the Fiscal, and explains, " Ah, I thought they had been shooting just as usual, but I remember well enough I gave the 20-bore gun to Monson, and if he shot with it then, then, of course, my evidence in regard to that falls to be deleted." That is how the matter stands in regard to that.

My learned friend said yesterday, and made a considerable point of it, how easy it would have been if this man had been innocent for him to have left the gun lying beside the unfortunate lad's body. Well, I declare to you, it did occur to me—it may be a very wicked suggestion—it occurred to me that if Monson had been guilty that is exactly the thing he would have done in order to make evidence for himself. He just would have left in the hand of the dead man the 12-bore gun, and brought witnesses, and said, " There is the man; I found him with this in his hand." That is just what a blackguard would have done, just what a murderer would have done, but when a man is innocent no such devices occur to him. Gentlemen, what would you or I do—Heaven only knows—if we found ourselves beside the dead body of a companion with whom we had been talking a few minutes before? If Monson had been the guilty man who had been planning this for weeks, as is suggested by the Crown, he would have taken very good care to make evidence so easily obtained in

Alfred John Monson.

favour of himself. It was also suggested that it was suspicious that when Scott and he passed the offices they did not inform the people there, and my learned friend said—I am sure inadvertently, because it was a mistake—that Carmichael was then standing at the door, and that they said nothing to him. Unless my memory entirely fails me, and I am corroborated by my learned friends beside me, there was no one at the stable or offices when they passed down to the house, and it was only when they came up from the house subsequently, after they had informed the inmates of the house of what had occurred—it was only then that Carmichael or any one else appeared on the scene.

Gentlemen, this is what happened. Some one came out of the stables and saw Monson and Scott, but they did not see him, and no communications passed between them. They told the sad tale to the servants, and on their way back they found men about the stable door, and took them back with them to where the body was lying. This case depends much upon detail, and I am following the line of and replying to my learned friend's speech yesterday, and giving a narrative of the matter. A point was made to the effect that Monson told the Procurator-Fiscal that Cecil was shot with his own gun. Now, of course, that is an expression which I think very likely was used. I do not know—I am assuming that the Fiscal is accurate in his recollection—but is that not exactly what a man would say, that the gun which caused the accident was the gun that he had in his own hand? The 12-bore gun belonged to Mrs. Campbell Lamont, and there is nothing surely in the statement to the Fiscal that the lad was shot with his own gun. That is just what we would say if we meant to indicate that some one had accidentally shot himself.

Now, another point was that, in searching the lad's jacket, 20-bore cartridges were found. It is essential to bear in mind this, that that discovery was made on 30th August. That jacket had been hanging, or at least had been within the power of Monson, ever since the time of the accident. If he were addressing you now, instead of me, he would tell you this, that he had been instructed to send to Inveraray the jacket and certain cartridges in the house, without any distinction, and that the day before it was taken away, or about that time, he had, in order to facilitate matters, put a certain quantity of cartridges into this jacket for facility of carriage to Inveraray. That is not susceptible of proof. I am speaking as the mouthpiece of the accused in this matter. On the other hand, the Crown did not put any one into the box, did not put the Depute Fiscal into the box, and I have no reason to doubt the statement that was made that the cartridges that were there were 20-bore cartridges. That is the explanation that is given, one that is perfectly rational and natural; and even supposing there were no such explanation, what are you to assume

378

Speech for the Defence.

Mr Comrie Thomson

from the fact that cartridges of that kind were found in this jacket which had been open to the whole house—open to the police constables you will observe—because the police constables had been two or three nights in the house before this date? What are you to assume, after such an interval of time, and with the jacket hanging in this place, and cartridges of all denominations lying about in the smoking-room, from the circumstance that certain cartridges are found three weeks after in this jacket? It would have been a different story if, at the time when the jacket was removed, and when it was examined by the doctor, on the morning and afternoon of the 10th, it had been found heavy with cartridges in the pocket, and they had been proved to be cartridges that would not fit the 12-bore gun. That would have been a serious fact in the case; but it is not suggested by any one that in examining the jacket on that occasion there was any sign of cartridges, or, on the other hand, such a quantity as eighteen in the pocket. If there were, the doctor or any one lifting it would have noted the additional weight they gave to the article. The evidence on the matter is that Mr. Steven, on that morning, said he felt cartridges in the pocket, but there was no question asked as to quantity, and no investigation as to denomination. Of course, it is natural that if he usually shot with the 20-bore he should have 20-bore cartridges in his pocket; but our case is that on that morning he was going to try the new powder—the amberite—with the 12-bore gun.

Now that brings me to the question of the direction of the shot, and here also we have, to a certain extent, common ground between the prisoner and the Crown—I mean the angle of the shot. And there I notice a difference between what apparently was the theory of my learned friend two days ago, in cross-examining witnesses, and the theory which he advanced to you yesterday. In his cross-examination it was apparent to me that his view was at that time—and I suppose he would have so presented it to you yesterday if he had not seen it was an impossible one—that the mass of shot had scarcely touched the skull, and that all the injury that was done to it, the smashing, the fissures, the tearing away of the skin of the ear, and so on, was caused by the fire of the pellets which had entered the head, and a few more which, after perforating the ear, had found their way into the rowan tree and the other trees. But yesterday I did not find that theory advanced, and I think I may take it as demonstrated that the great smashing of the bone of the skull, the external bone of the skull, of some of the internal and very hard bones of the skull, the fissures that spread up to the top of the skull, and certain fissures that were also visible in the lower part of the skull, were the effect of the whole contents of the cartridge, as if it were a mass—or, as it is called, *en balle*, like a ball—striking in a very oblique direction against the place which is the centre of the injury, that they were then

379

Alfred John Monson.

immediately deflected, and must have been deflected to a very considerable extent—to a corresponding angle, probably, to that at which they struck the body—and that the four pellets which were found, providentially left there in order to afford distinct evidence of the innocence of this man, that the four pellets which were left there were just four that had been caught on the extreme outside of the cartridge and lodged in the brain.

It is said that the Crown case depends upon the pellets in the trees. But no one knows what kind of pellets they were. There are only twelve of them altogether, twelve pellet marks found in rowan and beech and lime by the Crown. They found twelve pellet marks, and we do not know whether they are No. 6 or No. 5. But we do know that a scientific man, who has paid great attention to such matters, depones upon oath that these pellet marks upon these trees were older by weeks and weeks than the date of the crime. Professor Hay and Dr. Sanders concur in that statement, and no one contradicts them. What significance are you to attach, in a trial for murder, to evidence such as that? We want to know if the pellets in these trees were fired at the time that the pellets were fired into this man's head. We know what the nature of the pellets in the head was. We can identify them; we have no identification of the pellets that passed through the trees. They were there till they got into the hands of the Procurator-Fiscal. Where are they now? I am suggesting nothing improper; but I do suggest this, that for a blunder of that kind this man is not to suffer. There were pellets found in the bone. We have not them either. You can draw no safe deduction—and I do not require to put it higher —you can draw no conclusion, no safe deduction, from the evidence in regard to these pellets.

Besides, the whole wood is riddled with pellets, and necessarily so; it is a good cover, there is winged game during the season; there were wood pigeons at the time in question, there are lots of rabbits; and Speedy told you that within a few yards, 17 yards, he found branches broken, and that he found trees he could not remove marked by pellets—and pellets all round, all over the wood. What kind of thing is that to hang a case of this kind upon? And my learned friend attaches vital importance to it, because he has not another leg to stand upon. But, then, more than that, gentlemen. In considering the effect of the pellets—of finding pellet marks upon trees which are said to be in the line of fire—you have got to be satisfied that I was wrong when I demonstrated to you— as I think I did—that this body had been moved, because, unless it be true that the fatal shot was fired from just behind, where the man was found lying by the third parties—and that is in the exact line of fire—then again the evidence is valueless. And further, if you are satisfied, as you must be, that when a great mass struck the head in the way that it did, and deflected, the line

Speech for the Defence.

Mr Comrie Thomson

of fire is not a straight one, but is necessarily a deflected one, you would not find pellets from it in the exact line of fire.

Now I am endeavouring to use words of truth and soberness, and not to press anything unduly, although I am certainly justified in pressing that you are asked to return an adverse verdict—one involving a sentence of death—upon such flimsy, slender things as these. But these things are demonstrated to you, and no evidence in the least of a reliable nature in all we heard has been led about the marks upon the trees and the line of fire, and these all depend upon circumstances that are much too doubtful to render them of any value. You were told that there were between 200 and 300 pellets in each cartridge, and you are asked to find against this man because the marks of twelve pellets, not discovered, are found in three trees in the neighbourhood? I think it is useless to labour this part of the case further. My learned friend admitted that it is a vital part of his case, and I gathered from his tone and from what he said that if he fails on that he does not expect you to take the view he first pressed upon you.

Then comes the question as to the proximity of the muzzle of the gun to the head of the deceased, and you will notice, as I have already hinted, that my learned friend, in the exceedingly exhaustive speech which he delivered, passed that over in a single sentence, making practically no reference to it. Why was that? It cannot be because it is of no importance. Everybody has attached the highest importance to it—in the witness-box, at the bar, on the bench. We have all been attaching the highest importance to it; but the prosecutor passes it over without notice, except in a single sentence—not a production referred to, not an experiment referred to, except what, as represented to you, is approaching the grotesque, viz., the photographs of persons in possible situations of accidental killing by a gun. Now you will observe that the Crown witnesses—and I am entitled to tie my learned friend to his witnesses—maintained that, to the best of their judgment and according to their deductions, the distance at which the muzzle of the gun was from the wound was 9 feet, and we have proved to demonstration that at 9 feet there is a very considerable scatter of stray pellets. And we have proved to demonstration—it is not disputed—that upon the head, or neck, or any part of the person of this dead man, there was not a single stray pellet. I fitted on— one of the doctors fitted on—the cardboard that shows the effect of the 9-feet shot—fitted it upon the wound on the skull. You saw me, under his eye, draw my pencil round the external part of the scatter; and if that is a test at all—and the test is made by the Crown, you will observe, although they now discard it—you will remember that there was a great scatter, a scatter of several inches on each side, showing stray pellets there; and there is not the least indication—there is an absolute absence of any such indication

381

Alfred John Monson.

Mr Comrie Thomson

on the skull of the deceased. So, gentlemen, I also claim that as the most vital part of the case, and if my learned friend founds upon his evidence, from his twelve pellets, as indicating the direction, I have shown you how, in so many respects, that is fallacious and inconsistent. As to this there can be no mistake. There never was a shot fired at 9 feet that did not contain a great scatter. You can see the scatter on this cardboard for yourselves against the gaslight, and there is nothing of the sort in the skull. Now, there is not, even according to Dr. Littlejohn, a commencement of scatter. The edges, according to Dr. Littlejohn, according to fact, are described by him as bevelled and regular, so that you do not have even the commencement of scatter which is indicated in some of these cards. The only thing that happened was that, as the mass passed, four pellets became detached and entered the aperture that has been made, and there is no trace of any other pellets. Now, gentlemen, there cannot be any doubt of that, and it is manifest that that distance is absurd, and that beyond 3 or 4 feet there always is a scatter demonstrated. The distance here is somewhere between 2 feet and 3 feet, and the probability may be that it was even nearer.

The next point is in regard to the blackening and scorching, and here also we put in the box yesterday Mr. André, who is at the head of one of the largest gunpowder works in the country, the firm of Messrs. Curtis & Harvey. He told you that with amberite powder there is no scorching. Of course the point here is that Dr. Macmillan said that there was no scorching upon the poor ·lad's head when he saw it. But then that is disposed of at once. Amberite powder was used, we know, and it is proved beyond suspicion that there is no scorching with amberite. There is some blackening, a browny discoloration was the expression used, and probably that is a proper discrimination. There was some browny discoloration. But then it is proved that that can be rubbed off with the finger, and it is further proved that before the doctor saw the body there had been a considerable quantity of blood round the part where you would expect to find blackening, and that it had been carefully sponged with soap and water by the man Carmichael. So that you see, gentlemen, it is demonstrated clearly enough that there can be no ground, arising from the absence of scorching or blackening, for suspecting that this shot was fired at any distance, except a very short one, from the deceased.

Now, finally, gentlemen, because I think I shall be able now to leave you without hearing much more from me, there is certain direct testimony in favour of the theory of accident. I think we had a little evidence, but quite sufficient, that the poor deceased lad was a careless fellow with his gun. We had two of the Donalds, who told you that he narrated to them what had very nearly proved a serious accident. He had stumbled while carrying his gun and

382

Speech for the Defence.

Mr Comrie Thomson

fallen, and had broken the butt of it; and I think he said something about one of the triggers going off. We had the evidence of a gunmaker in London, perhaps it was not very important, but he seemed impressed with the fact that it was a wrong thing, and I entirely agree with him, to present a gun which you have any reason to believe to be loaded at any one, and he had the general impression produced upon him that Cecil Hambrough was careless, so that when Cecil left his shop he said to his manager, " Did you ever see such a careless fellow? Did you see the way he was knocking the gun about? He will either shoot himself or somebody else." This impression was made upon a gunmaker, who is accustomed to handle guns. Then Walters, and Day, Mrs. Monson's brother, were examined yesterday, and Day said he shot with Cecil Hambrough two years ago, and he was always in a fright when he was shooting, Cecil was so exceedingly careless, and he reproved him for it, not only on account of the way he carried his gun, but because he went through brushwood and over fences with his gun at full-cock. The other lad, Walters, made the same observation, and said he heard Day one day finding fault with Hambrough for the way he carried his gun; and Donald says that when he showed him how he carried his gun he thought it was an exceedingly dangerous way, and very likely to lead to mischief; so that there is evidence uncontradicted that this poor lad was just the kind of fellow who was very likely to come by serious injury, and even death, through the careless fashion in which he handled his gun. Then it seems to me it is instructive to attend to the evidence given us by the old soldier who was in the box yesterday, Colonel Tillard; because it demonstrated the possibility of that happening which happened here—I mean in the circumstances which we for the defence maintain. You heard that gentleman tell you that he was out some years ago snipe shooting in India, when, turning round to call his servant to him, his foot slipped. He was carrying his gun by the barrels, and he was shot by it holding it in his right hand, and how? From the front through the ear horizontally, the skull at the back of the ear being ploughed up so deep as to expose the *periosteum*, the covering of the bone, and then the body of the shot deflected from the head. It is exactly the same as this, a man carrying a gun having his head wounded in a horizontal direction, and the shot deflected in the way it did here. Now, that was a pure accident, and it seems to me just as extraordinary that if a man carries his gun in that position he should have been shot from the front as that he should be shot from behind. We have as a bit of real evidence Dr. Macmillan's first report, and that is the report of an honest, competent observer. Dr. Macmillan, in describing what he saw, said—" The bone had been carried into the substance of the brain. The wound was exactly what I would expect to find from a charge of small shot fired from a distance of perhaps 12

Alfred John Monson.

Mr Comrie Thomson

inches." Now, that is Dr. Macmillan's deliberate opinion at the time. He saw the body when it was warm. "That is exactly what I would expect to find from a charge of small shot fired from a distance of 12 inches. The shot had not time to spread, as there were no separate pellet marks. I would expect blackening of the edges of the wound from the powder, but afterwards ascertained from Mr. Monson that they had been trying amberite, a nitro powder. That explains the absence of blackening." Here is an intelligent man who knows what to look for. He says, on soul and conscience, only wishing to do his duty, " it is exactly what I would expect from a shot at 12 inches "; and without any hesitation he says, when some one remarks that in England they would have a coroner's inquest, that here an official makes close inquiry, and that he would be able to satisfy him that it was nothing but a pure accident.

What are the grounds upon which Dr. Macmillan comes to change his mind? This is very important. Dr. Macmillan says on 25th August—" I now wish to make the following addenda. I implicitly accepted the statements of the witnesses Monson and Scott that the injuries to Hambrough were due to an accidental shot from his own gun, a short-barrelled, 20-bore boy's weapon charged with amberite. The (apparently) entire absence of motive made the bent of my inquiry not so much ' how would this injury most likely be produced? ' as ' how could deceased have done it accidentally? ' It now transpires that there were no ' amberite ' cartridges for this diameter of gun, and that I too hastily came to the conclusion or theory advanced at the end of my former report. Having handled and tried the gun now in the possession of the Procurator-Fiscal, I am convinced that the injuries were not caused in the way I thought possible." Exactly so. He was told by the Fiscal, " My good sir, there are certain circumstances of suspicion here ; it turns out that it was not amberite powder that shot Hambrough, and it turns out it was not the 20-bore gun." And naturally enough the doctor, having been informed that that was the case, and tried the 20-bore gun, says, " I have been rather rash." But it all proceeds upon a mistake again, because, if it had been the case, as I have demonstrated to you it was the case, and as my friend admits it was the case, that Hambrough was shot with No. 5 shot and with amberite powder, and as I have shown you that it was the 12-bore gun with which he was shot, and that it was the 12-bore gun which he carried, then Dr. Macmillan would have returned to his original opinion as to the distance. In the second paper he says, " The keeper Lamont, who cleaned the gun, says that one trigger was full-cock and the other down, but, as Mr. Monson had removed the cartridge cases, he could not tell if the cap of the empty one had been struck by the hammer." So that the whole change of opinion arises from Lamont's blunder. The

384

Speech for the Defence.

Mr Comrie Thomson

only witness in the case who seems not to be open to entertaining any view but that which involves the guilt of the prisoner is my respected friend, Dr. Littlejohn. I claim as witnesses in my favour both Dr. Heron Watson and Dr. Bell, and I will tell you why. Because they say that in the conclusions they arrived at, I do not doubt with perfect accuracy, they were in the region of conjecture, and that there were infinite possibilities by which Hambrough's life might have been lost besides that which involves guilt on the part of the accused. I claim these two gentlemen, from the Crown list. It is all I need. If you are in the region of conjecture you cannot convict. If there is a reasonable possibility you must give effect to it. Both of these men say that they are in the region of conjecture, and that the possibilities are infinite. And I add to these Professor Hay, whose evidence you heard given under great physical weakness, he having risen from his bed, to which he had been confined by a severe attack of influenza; and Dr. Sanders, whose evidence you also heard subjected to a most searching cross-examination by my learned friend the Solicitor-General; and without going into the details of their evidence, the conclusion at which these two men arrived—and I claim for them just as much consideration as I give to the medical witnesses for the Crown, I claim that you shall deal with them as conscientious, and as men with a knowledge of the subject of which they are talking, just as I grant that to Dr. Watson and Dr. Bell—they tell you that the result of their best consideration is that this man shot himself accidentally, and that the accused is guiltless of crime. Now, gentlemen, that surely puts you in a very serious position if it has ever entered your minds that you might be driven to pronounce a verdict of condemnation. Can you do it in the face of such evidence as I have been commenting upon? Can you do it in the face of that one fact that experienced, conscientious men have sworn—I add Mr. Tom Speedy to their number—that these three men have sworn that, after the best consideration they can give, they do not see how this fatal shot can have been fired by the accused? They have said on their consciences that the poor man shot himself by accident.

The only other point that I need deal with is a very trifling one, but I think I am bound to mention it. There is a general consensus of testimony to the effect that the conduct and demeanour of the accused after the occurrence was just such as you would expect if he had been almost an eye-witness of the death of his friend by mischance. Every one speaks to this, that he was terribly distressed and agitated. I am not going to elaborate that to you, gentlemen; you heard the evidence, it cannot be without its effect.

One little incident I wish to recall to you. We were told that when Monson went with the doctor on the afternoon of the occurrence to show him the place where the body had been lying,

1 c

385

Alfred John Monson.

Mr Comrie Thomson

he took with him his little boy. Can you conceive that, if that man had within recent hours been guilty of murdering his friend who had been living with him, and had been attached to him for years past, he would take probably the purest and the simplest being within his reach to show him the place at which that horrible crime had been committed by his own father? We know that there is almost no limit to the depths of human depravity; but the notion that a murderer, when his hand was still red with the blood of the victim, would take his little boy by the hand to show him the spot where he had committed the crime is, I think, absolutely incredible.

Gentlemen, that is all that I have to say to you. The sum of it comes to this, that I have disposed, to the best of my ability, of the question of motive; I have shown you that motive only enters to a small extent into the question that you really have to determine, and that you must be satisfied by independent evidence that this crime has been proved. Everything was uncertain and incomplete in regard to these insurance policies, and if this diabolical scheme was in the prisoner's mind, he certainly acted very foolishly, because if he had waited for a little while it might have been that the Scottish Provident policy would have been given effect to; he shot the poor lad too soon for any benefit that it possibly could be to him. On the other hand, the motive to preserve the lad in life—at all events, until he came of age—was ten times more definite and much stronger. I have also shown you, I think, that the circumstances in regard to the boat accident can only bear an innocent interpretation, and in regard to the shooting I would put it to you—can any one of you say, " I am certain of the prisoner's guilt; there is no reasonable room for doubting it "? Can you say that after you have heard the exposition of the evidence that I have been endeavouring to give you? Gentlemen, " moral impression, suspicion, feeling," to use my learned friend's expression repeatedly used yesterday, " that everything has not been fully explained," will not do. All that falls very far short of what is necessary. Before you can return an adverse verdict you must have formed a perfectly clear opinion that you are forced by the evidence to find that these crimes, or one or other of them, have been committed; and I put it to you—not appealing to you for mercy—but asking you to give me simple justice—I put it to you, have I not demonstrated that there is ample room for entertaining serious doubt? Gentlemen, we are all liable to make mistakes. I pray you make no mistake in this terribly serious matter. The result of your verdict is final, irreparable. What would any of you think if some day, it may be soon, this mystery is entirely unravelled, and it is demonstrated that that man was innocent, while your verdict has sent him to his death? He will not go unpunished if he is guilty. There is One in Whose hands he is, Who is Infallible and Omniscient. " I will repay, vengeance is mine, saith the Lord."

386

The Lord Justice-Clerk (Macdonald).

Charge to the Jury.

The Lord Justice-Clerk proceeded to charge the jury as follows :—Gentlemen of the jury, we have now reached the last stage of this long and anxious trial. The case is one purely of circumstantial evidence. It is not a case in which there is any direct evidence. Everything in it depends upon inferences to be drawn; and it is quite certain that, in a case where the evidence is purely circumstantial, if every link in it is a sound link, and is well welded into the next, there cannot be a stronger case than that. On the other hand, it is a kind of evidence which requires of a jury that they shall examine it with the most minute criticism in order to be sure that, in passing along the chain of links which make up that which has told against the prisoner, they do not pass by any flaw or break. That is a caution which it is advisable, I think, to give you at the commencement of what I have got to say; but that must not cause you to find anything to be a flaw, or a break, which does not reasonably present itself to you as being so. On the other hand, very small signs of a defect in such a chain may make all the difference as to whether it is safe for the jury to find a verdict adverse to the prisoner in the awful position in which he is now placed.

Gentlemen, you and I have the satisfaction of knowing, from what we have observed during the last nine days, that there has been no failure on the part of those entrusted with the duty of watching over the interests of the country's justice, or of those who have been employed in defending the interests of the prisoner. In the many cases I have seen from time to time, I have never seen a case in this Court in which one could feel more clearly that justice had been done to their work, both by those engaged in it in the interests of the public, and those engaged in it in the interests of the prisoner; and that to a certain extent lightens the task of a judge, and enables me in this case to make up my mind that, in what I have got to say to you, I must endeavour to hold an even balance, bringing before you what occurs to myself by way of comment upon the case. I said "hold the balance," because I do not propose to go over the whole of the evidence in detail; it has been done in the elaborate speeches of the counsel, which are fresh in your recollection.

Now, I wish to explain, before I go further, what the province of a judge is in such a matter. The purpose of such a charge as this is twofold. It is, in the first place, that the case may be, as it were, summed up to you from a legal point of view, so that you may understand the aspects of it, and how you ought to look at it; and, in the second place, that those features of it may be brought before you which are worthy of your consideration in

387

Alfred John Monson.

a more unbiassed and collected form than they can be in two controversial speeches addressed to the jury from the one side and the other. For, of course, it being the duty of a public prosecutor to state all that he can as against the prisoner, he does so with the utmost of his ability. On the other hand, the counsel for the defence states his case with the umost of his ability in the opposite direction; and it is not an unreasonable thing that at the conclusion of the case some words should be addressed to the jury from a more judicial and impartial point of view. I may tell you further that it is the practice of a judge to suggest to the jury things which occur to his own mind upon the evidence, and I shall certainly do so in the course of my observations; but I do it with this remark to you, that what I have to say as matter of observation is said not to dictate to you, but solely for your personal consideration. You may be inclined to give some weight to what is said as coming from a person the business of whose life it has been to study such cases, to see how they ought to be treated, and to notice the points of them, and to see which points tell for and against the prisoner. You may be inclined to do that, and doubtless you will be inclined to do it, but do it always with this impression upon your mind, that what is addressed to you by way of observation upon the evidence is addressed to you for your consideration, and that it is quite open to you to accept it, or to accept it in a modified form, or to reject it, according to your deliberative judgment. One other thing the judge has to do, and that is to guide you in the matter of law, to guide you as to how the case must be looked at with respect to the way in which it has been presented by the Crown; and, of course, the law you will accept from me as solely responsible in that department.

The indictment against the prisoner charges him with having, in concert with a certain other man named—who is also summoned to the bar, but who is not here—formed the design of causing by drowning the death of the late Cecil Hambrough, and with having attempted to carry that out; and also it charges them both with having, in pursuance of the said scheme, shot Cecil Hambrough. Now, the Solicitor-General in his argument to you yesterday—at the stage of the case at which he was called upon to state how he proposed to put it to you—presented it to you still as being a scheme between these two men. I may tell you this, that he would have been quite entitled, on an indictment of this kind, if he thought proper, to say that this indictment, although it charges those two with acting together, does, according to a rule of law, imply a separate charge against each. It is as if it had said that both and each or one or other did the acts stated. But it is important for you to keep in view throughout your deliberations in this case that the case as stated to you now is that they were both engaged in such a scheme, and both privy to its being carried

Charge to the Jury.

out. Of course, in the case of the shooting charge the injury would be caused by the hand of one, but the case of the Solicitor-General is that, though caused by the one hand, it was the act of both, because the other was privy to it at the time.

Now, gentlemen, it will be necessary for me to glance at the history of this case before the time at which these alleged acts are said to have taken place. It certainly unveils a very dark side of social life. We have Major Hambrough, who, at forty-four years of age, has gone through his means, these means being a very considerable income from large estates in the south of England. His life interest, which amounted to thousands a year, has been mortgaged away in order to raise money to pay his debts and keep him in subsistence. All that having been done, he is reduced in the years 1891-92 to the miserable position of living upon odd sums got from people who had their own schemes to serve in keeping him friendly by keeping him up. He was living in lodgings, occasionally unable to get his luggage removed through inability to pay the rent. He was an impecunious, broken-down gentleman, unable to find education for his son, except by arranging for a postponed payment, and this it was which brought him into contact with the prisoner. Mr. Tottenham, who is a gentleman belonging to a particular class in London whose business it is to lend money, apparently at high interest, and make his own income out of his loans, having come to know Major Hambrough, and knowing his circumstances, and knowing that he had a son who was the next heir-of-entail—as we would call it—of these large estates, introduces Major Hambrough to the prisoner. It appears that the prisoner had capacity as an army tutor, which capacity was shown by certificates from the parents of those whom he had educated for the army, and Major Hambrough, being satisfied with the testimonials received, transferred his son to the care of Mr. Monson.

Now, Tottenham's connection with Major Hambrough was a connection arising from the Major's impecunious condition, and Tottenham was endeavouring to effect some arrangement of his affairs, but he failed, and the prisoner took the matter up about a year after Cecil was placed in his charge. About the month of May, 1891, the mortgages had been executed by which the Major handed over his life interest in the estates to the Eagle Insurance Company, and the plan was—it certainly was a sensible and a reasonable plan—to make some arrangement by which the Eagle mortgages could be got rid of—the interest on the mortgages being very high—and money got on easier terms, thus freeing a certain amount of income to enable Major Hambrough to live.

These negotiations went on for some months, but in 1892 Major Hambrough broke off finally from his relations with Monson. Major Hambrough says that he had come to distrust Monson,

Alfred John Monson.

because he thought he was looking after his own interests in the matter, and, not being satisfied, he took himself out of his hands and employed a solicitor of his own; and it was his strong desire—expressed over and over again—to get his son Cecil out of the charge of Monson. And from that point a certain amount of estrangement, though not an unkind or bitter estrangement, arose between father and son in the summer of that year—1892. We find Cecil ignoring his parents and declining to go near them. Gentlemen, I think it right to say to you that the temptation to that boy was very great. He was just at that age when a boy is easily inflated with an idea of his own prospects, and had a very strong idea of his own wants—his want of money, of good things, of handsome clothing, of good guns—everything of that description. And it cannot be surprising that the prospect of returning from the place where he certainly seems to have been happy, and where there was something of the nature of external affluence, to live in squalid lodgings, shifting from one place to another in London, did not commend itself to the boy, and I have no doubt that his youthful companions, in the person of those who were with him in the militia, would strongly advise him to stick where he was, when, by the aid of moneylenders, he could get a loan of so many pounds, and where he would be living in substantial comfort. And, with reference to this matter, I have to refer you to some letters which passed between father and son about the summer or spring of 1892. It was the father's desire that his son should get into the army through the militia, and join the regiment at Winchester, in which he had numerous friends, and where he thought his son would be under the influence of those who knew him. On the other hand, Monson, who was living at Riseley Hall, in Yorkshire, preferred—and naturally preferred—that the young man should be near him, and made arrangements for his entering the Yorks Regiment. Major Hambrough bitterly complains that that was done at the time when Monson was assuring him that he was doing nothing further in the matter. And this was brought to a point by a letter on 1st May, 1892, in which Cecil informs his father that he is gazetted into the Yorkshire Militia, and that Monson had said there was nothing for it but to join it now and get a chance of transfer into the Hants next year. Now, the Major seems to have resented that keenly, and he wrote on 20th June complaining " of the gross and unpardonable deception practised upon us " in regard to his son joining the Yorkshire Regiment, and wishing him to return to his own family. And he states that at that time he had obtained an insurance from the office, that is to say, that he had been informed he had been passed by the doctors, an insurance which, unfortunately, afterwards fell through owing to the examination by the doctors of another office. When all the doctors were brought into consultation, they found the Major's life unsatisfactory.

390

Charge to the Jury.

Lord Justice-Clerk

The correspondence went on for some time. The Major was very strong in his letters as to the conduct of Mr. Monson in taking his son out of his hands, but Cecil seems to have been convinced in his own mind that he was better in Monson's charge, for reasons which I have already explained to you, and he wrote back to his father—" I do not know what you have further found out against him, but after he has done everything he possibly can for me I think it would be extremely mean of me to leave him "; and he then mentioned that he is " sorry to hear his mother had been unwell," and " trusts she is now much better." I have no doubt that the boy thought he was getting great favours from Mr. Monson. He was happy, and apparently there is no reason to doubt the genuineness of his happiness, because at that time a kind of affection had sprung up between him and Monson. Then the Major writes to Monson complaining, and there are a number of telegrams which were referred to, some of them to-day, in which he urges his son to return, but all in vain, and Mr. Monson in rather strong terms latterly writes, and it was this letter that was referred to yesterday—" In reply to your letter, I beg to say that I am not your son's keeper. I have not seen him for ten days or more; but, as far as I know, he is staying at Riseley Hall." There is, no doubt, an expression in that letter which, if used as a quotation, would be full of meaning, and about which I think it necessary to give you a word of caution. I think people often write words which they do not intend to bear the double meaning which people may put upon them, and it may be that Mr. Monson did not mean to suggest anything else than to say in firm terms that if Cecil meant to return to his father's house he had no power over him. I suppose there can be little doubt he said that, in perfect confidence. Looking to the comfortable position Major Hambrough's son was in with him, he did not think Cecil would become a consenting party to going back to the poor lodgings in which his father was living. From that time on it appears that, except at rare intervals, he did not see his parents.

In August of that year the prisoner's affairs had become so embarrassed that he was adjudicated a bankrupt, and some idea of his position may be derived from what the result of that bankruptcy was. There was recovered a sum of twenty-five guineas which was due to him as tutor of another pupil he had before. There was £15 recovered upon furniture that was sold, and the net proceeds of that part of the estate realised a sum of 14s. 6d. At that time we find him and his wife pawning knives and forks, and spoons and silver watches and jewellery, for sums varying from about 10s. to £8. Mrs. Monson, who had some interest under a deceased relative's will, and also through her mother, had mortgaged her interest for all that could be raised upon it, and in the autumn of 1892 the interest upon these mortgages was in arrear

391

Alfred John Monson.

to the extent of £64 11s. 1d., and a cheque which was sent for the interest in the end of 1891 was dishonoured. And in a suit which has been raised, we are told, for payment of the mortgage itself, Mrs. Day—that is, Mrs. Monson's mother—has been set free by the judgment of a jury, and there do not seem to be any means to recover the amount of that mortgage from Mrs. Monson. You may take it as a fact that Mr. and Mrs. Monson were without means of their own in the latter part of 1892. It seems that Monson did raise some money, which carried them on for some time, by giving a mortgage which he had in his hands as a security to a Yorkshire bank, and at this time the prisoner was in close relations with Mr. Tottenham, from whom he hoped to get financial assistance which would enable him to carry on. Now, in January, 1893, a very extraordinary episode took place. Mr. Monson and the lad Cecil go to a man who calls himself a mortgage and insurance broker, a Mr. Sebright, and Cecil is introduced to him as a young man with some prospects who wants some immediate cash—£250 to pay debts and an allowance of £20 a month for his living and expenses. At that meeting the matter in connection with the Eagle Insurance Company is brought forward; a proposal is suggested for buying out the Eagle Company—the same thing that had been proposed before—and Mr. Sebright seems to have assumed a lofty financial agent's virtue, and did not see how he could negotiate with Mr. Cecil Hambrough alone. Sebright suggested that he should consult a solicitor, and he commended him to a solicitor, a Mr. Jones, who turns out upon investigation to be his own solicitor, and he took away his business from Mr. Jones in order to place Mr. Cecil Hambrough in his hands. To finish this history, on the conclusion having been come to that business cannot be done, Mr. Sebright replaces all his legal papers with Mr. Jones, and at that first meeting, and in Monson's presence, the proposal is made, and apparently assented to, that upon Cecil Hambrough's coming of age he is to pay—this lad of nineteen years of age agrees to pay—£20,000 into Mr. Sebright's business to become a partner. And there is a curious letter, which was found in Monson's possession, written by Cecil, but which apparently never was sent, in which the matter is more magnified. It is dated 11th July, 1893, and is in the following terms :—" I have this day received an advance from you of £300, which I promise to repay to you when I come of age. It is also agreed between us that you shall continue to allow me £20 a month till I attain my majority, which money I also agree to repay you at that time. In consideration of your doing this for me, I promise to become partner with you in your business as financial agent and bill discounter, and to put £100,000 in the business, you to pay me 10 per cent. per annum upon all money used."

Then follows a sentence which is of importance in favour of

Charge to the Jury.

the views maintained by the prisoner's counsel to a certain extent—
" I am fully aware that you could not recover any money from me
by action at law, but the only security I can offer you is my word
of honour as a gentleman that I will carry out the promises made
in this letter."

Now, certainly that was a most extraordinary proposal, but
it only indicates one thing which is of any consequence in this
case. It has very little bearing on the real gist of the case, but
it indicates the grandiose and absurd notions Cecil had as to the
magnificence of the estate into which he was coming, and that
the prospect before that poor lad was that when he came to the
age of twenty-one he would tumble into the hands of moneylenders. What the result of that would be it is not difficult to
conceive. These negotiations having broken down in February,
1893, it was arranged to make an advance of £5 per week. Tottenham was quite aware at that time that Monson had no resources
at his own disposal, and it was a fact, and doubtless Tottenham
was aware of that very well, too, that he was doing no business
as a tutor, except in so far as he was getting young Hambrough
brought forward for the army. He was not getting other pupils
into his charge. His whole employment, except looking after Cecil
Hambrough, seems to have been trying to work out the financing
of the Hambrough business, by which, of course, he expected to get
a handsome sum for himself.

The next episode which occurs is this—that in February Mrs.
Monson had a judgment in absence against Cecil Hambrough for
£800 for the amount that was due for maintenance and education
and board in the establishment which she kept, and that she sold
the judgment to Tottenham for £200, to get £200 of cash to be
going on with. And then the scheme was formed to take a shooting
in Scotland to which Cecil could go, and by which, I suppose,
the idea was, as one of the letters say, he could be " kept well in
hand " until he came of age. So the prisoner and Cecil came to
Ardlamont. Negotiations as to Ardlamont were carried on by
Monson with Paton & Son, and they were informed that Mr.
Jerningham was acting as trustee and guardian for young Cecil,
and would guarantee the rent. Jerningham declares that he never
had anything to do with Ardlamont, and that he had never sent
any telegram guaranteeing the rent. However that may be, we
have this fact, that, practically for Cecil—Mr. Monson going
with him nominally as his tutor—Ardlamont was taken on lease
for a year at £450 of rent, one-half of which was to be paid on
1st August, subject to an irritancy if not paid within a certain
number of days. The question has been mooted, but I told you
it is not a question for your consideration in a ruling I have
given—and you may therefore dismiss it from your minds—
whether Jerningham signed the lease at all; but it is of no very

Alfred John Monson.

great consequence in this case. Under that lease Monson and his family and Cecil went to Ardlamont, Cecil following after he had finished his training at York. They had the greatest difficulty in getting there, owing to their position as regards cash, and letters and telegrams have been referred to showing how straitened they were with regard to their means of getting forward to the place. Tottenham sent forward the sum of £40 in a letter to Cecil, which has been referred to. In that letter he says—" Herewith cheque for £40, just to go on with. I conclude the moving job can be financed on that. Until next week am short, so have to keep balance at the Bank of England, or they will give notice to close account. I have made the cheque payable to you for facility in cashing, but, naturally, I do not debit you with this oof, but look upon it as payment on the general account of the show."

In passing, let it be remarked that this is so far favourable to the prisoner, because, while it is suggested, and suggested with considerable force, that the Monsons were in pretty considerable straits for money, it seems to be at the same time clear that Tottenham, in the hope and belief that some satisfactory arrangement would be made about the Hambrough mortgages and estates, was prepared to advance money from time to time, to use his expression, " on the general account of the show." And, therefore, while it is quite true that while at Ardlamont Mrs. Monson was writing and sending sums of interest and renewing pledges on certain articles referred to before, it is also true that they had an expectation that Mr. Tottenham would carry them on under the scheme which they were carrying out. Now, it is in these circumstances that the prisoner began the negotiations for the purchase of Ardlamont, which was then in the market, and which the other day sold for £70,000. Mr. Tottenham tells us in his evidence that he would have been prepared to get that transaction financed. I do not know exactly how he would have proceeded. I suppose they would combine together and get people with means, who were not very particular what they did with their money as long as they got a large interest, to carry through the transaction, with the object of making ultimately a good interest and bonus out of it. Certainly at that time Tottenham was representing that he saw his way to finance them through that transaction.

Now, gentlemen, there is a curious letter which I think it necessary to call your attention to. Monson writes to Messrs. J. & F. Anderson—" Mr. Hambrough and I purpose coming over to see you on Monday, August the 7th, in Edinburgh. The object of our visit is to discuss with you the terms of a sale of this estate, and, if we can come to any satisfactory arrangement, we shall be prepared to enter into a contract for the purchase, in which case we should propose paying a deposit on the purchase in lieu of the rent due for this year's tenancy. The limit of time

Charge to the Jury.

for the completion of the contract would have to be fixed for June 1st, 1894, when Mr. Hambrough would have attained his majority. We have been fully into the details of rentals, &c." and so on.

That letter was written so as to fix a meeting for the 7th of August. In point of fact, the only meeting held was upon 8th August, and here comes in one of the most extraordinary episodes of this extraordinary case. Having arranged for this meeting on 7th August with Messrs. J. & F. Anderson, Monson writes to Tottenham on 22nd or 23rd July a letter, in which he describes at length the meeting which he had had with Messrs. J. & F. Anderson, the agents for the property—" Dear Tot,—I have just returned home and have seen the agents to-day, and fully discussed the question of the purchase here. The existing mortgage on the property is £37,000 at 4 per cent. The interest has always been paid regularly. The mortgagees are an insurance company, and the Lamonts having policies with them, they do not wish to disturb the investment. I was asked to make an offer. I therefore said I thought £45,000 a good price, as I was sure the rentals would have to be reduced, &c. They would not, or pretended not, to consider such an offer. However, eventually they agreed to accept £48,000. They say that they only do this because Major Lamont is so anxious to be rid of the property before he starts for India, and their instructions from him are to close with the best offer they can get, and it appears they have spent a lot of money in advertising and trying to sell, but they never had a single offer. They are willing to accept £250 as a deposit on the contract being signed by Mrs. M. to be limited to June, 1894. The contract is now being drawn, and will be ready in the course of a week or so. They have a power of attorney to act for Major Lamont, and the contract will be drawn in their name as attorney. I have told C. that the price is £50,000—£1000 each for division; thus he will have to raise £13,000 to enable him to complete next year."

Now, gentlemen, no such meeting ever took place at all. Mr. Murray, who is a member of the firm, and who had charge of this business, says that no such meeting ever took place—that the price which was proposed was a price that they would not have looked at. Mr. Thomson very ingeniously suggested that if you put the £48,000 and the £37,000 mortgage together, they would make £85,000 as the price they were standing out for. The Solicitor-General pointed out to you that that was inconsistent with what was proposed to be raised in the latter part of the letter, in order to complete the transaction; but there is another answer to it which I think is conclusive, and that is, that Mr. Monson says in the letter that Major Lamont is agreeing to take that money only because he is anxious to get the matter settled before he leaves for India, and is therefore taking a small price; and if Mr. Thomson's view is correct, it would have been the full price asked,

Alfred John Monson.

and there would be no difference about it. Now, what is the purpose of that letter? One purpose has been suggested, and that is, to get £250 from Mr. Tottenham then and there. On the other hand, it is to be said here that Tottenham had undertaken to find the rent, which was more than that—£450—and, therefore, that sum would have been coming, because there is no reason to doubt that Mr. Tottenham would not have allowed his pigeon to escape out of his hand for £250. He would be prepared to advance that for the larger transaction.

But here comes in a new phase. At that time Monson was at work to obtain policies upon Cecil's life, and these policies were to be in favour of Mrs. Monson, she being the person nominally through whom these transactions were to be carried out. He makes his statement to the London and Liverpool and Globe that he would be a loser to the extent of £49,000 by Cecil's death, and he states also to the insurance people that Mrs. Monson was interested in the life to the extent of £50,000. That, of course, it has been said—with such force as you will judge—was in view of the future transaction being carried out, and the obligations being undertaken.

But, gentlemen, there is one point in connection with this letter which I think it is necessary and right to point out to you, which has not yet been noticed. The Solicitor-General founded very strongly upon this letter, but there is another part of it which I think ought not to be allowed to escape observation, and that is, that in the subsequent part of the letter Monson, still writing to Tottenham, suggests to him that if he thinks proper he may make the cheque payable to J. & F. Anderson. Now, of course, if the cheque was payable to J. & F. Anderson, and if, in the subsequent meeting upon the 8th, he succeeded in getting them to negotiate, and to accept a deposit of £250 as a mark of binding in reference to a contract—a thing, of course, I do not think they ever would have done for such a small sum as that—still, if he had this cheque, if Tottenham had happened to send it in favour of J. & F. Anderson, that cheque could only have been got payment of through them, and, therefore, that, to a certain extent, takes the sting out of the observation that the £250 which he asked for on that occasion was got for a totally different purpose. It so happens that Tottenham did not take the course which it was suggested to him by the prisoner that he might take, and sent him the £250 by cheque payable to Monson. And then, having that £250 by cheque, a new complication arose. The premium upon the policy of the Mutual of New York was £194, and, having regard to the position of the Monsons at that moment, it is plain that if the premium was to be paid then and there, Tottenham's cheque for £250 was essential, because they had not money in their bank account at Tighnabruaich to enable them to pay the premium.

396

Charge to the Jury.

And, accordingly, Mrs. Monson wrote to the agent at Tighna-bruaich, stating to him what was certainly not correct, that the cheque had been dated 10th August, because the agent had been instructed to send the money on that date, and asked the agent at Tighnabruaich to pay that cheque into their account and give them credit for it, and the agent did so. Now, Mr. Thomson said that that cheque could not be made available till the 10th, that it was illegal to do so; and he pressed, therefore, strongly, that in point of fact the premium for the policy was not paid by the time that Cecil was dead. Gentlemen, that is a question of law which it is quite unnecessary to decide here. The question for you to consider in reference to that cheque is, did Monson believe that he had got the policy on the payment of the money?

But another complication arose; Tottenham stopped the cheque. He had got some idea that there was something unsatisfactory, that he was running out money too quickly, and he stopped the cheque, and, on intimation from the bank on the day on which Monson was to depart for Ventnor with the dead body of Cecil, Monson wrote the letter to the agent at Tighnabruaich, in which he said—" I received your kind note this morning at starting, also the wire as to the cheque, which is only a matter of proof of signature."

It is suggested by the prosecution that that was not true. It is just possible that at that moment Monson did not know what the cause of the cheque not being paid at the Bank of England was, and that this may have been a fair suggestion to make. But there is this against Monson, that by this time he and Tottenham had met at Ardlamont. Tottenham came down to Ardlamont—he was deeply interested in Cecil Hambrough, because he had made considerable advances for him already—and Monson told him first that he had got a policy for £8000, then that he had got a policy for £10,000, and then, ultimately, that he had got a policy for £20,000. Now, of course, these statements were not satisfactory, and could not have been satisfactory. I am bound to say that if he was ultimately to tell him of £20,000, there was no need for making the previous statements at all. On 23rd August, a considerable time after the death, Mrs. Monson writes to say that " she has arranged with Mr. Tottenham to have a cheque for £250, paid on presentation any day after Monday. It will be necessary to call at the Bank of England to verify the signature as a matter of form "; and then, on the 28th, she sends a policy of insurance to the manager of the bank at Tighnabruaich, stating that they had arranged for payment to be made at Glasgow. Now, these things were all just the expedients that people fall upon to put off the evil day—falsehoods of a very marked kind, and which were sure in a very short time to be discovered. All this story—certainly up to this stage—is a

Alfred John Monson.

very sad story of untruthfulness and fraud—for the purpose of putting off the evil day, and the discovery of impecuniosity by these expedients—and I am afraid that in other parts of the case similar instances of lying could be found.

With reference to that matter I am to give you a word of caution. It is always a very dreadful thing to find out that people are liars, and possibly consistent liars. It gives one a very bad impression of their general character, and one cannot trust such people after making such discoveries in the ordinary transactions of life, and to a certain extent it shows a serious moral breakdown. There are some people to whom it has become so natural to state what is untrue that, without any object at all—as was apparent in this case—on various occasions statements were made in matters of business by the prisoner and by his wife which were not true, without any conceivable object. I would caution you not to deduce too much from that. It is a long way from being dishonest to being murderers, and I think the only element which you can consider in connection with these lying episodes—the only connection in which you can consider these with reference to this case—is in so far as they are directly connected with the motive which is alleged by the prosecutor. Otherwise I think you ought to give little, if any, weight to them.

That leads me now to say a few words to you on the question of motive. It is true that the affairs of Mr. and Mrs. Monson as such were practically desperate. They had failed at that time in obtaining the contract with the Eagle, which would have placed them in possession, had they been able to finance the matter, of a considerable sum of money; and they had obtained these policies for £20,000. Now, that is the motive suggested by the Crown— these policies which had been granted by the New York Mutual Insurance Company were, with mutual consent, transferred by Cecil Hambrough to Mrs. Monson. Upon 7th August he writes to the manager of the company—" Will you kindly deliver my two insurance policies of £10,000 each to Mr. and Mrs. Monson, as I have assigned the policies to Agnes Maud Monson, for proper consideration received. Mrs. Monson will therefore be the person to whom the insurance is payable in the event of my death. Kindly acknowledge receipt of this notice, and oblige.—Yours truly, W. D. C. Hambrough." And there also was a letter, which is not apparently now in existence, but which the prisoner showed to Mr. Tottenham when they were on their way from Tighnabruaich to Glasgow on the day after Mr. Tottenham came from London. He showed it to Mr. Tottenham on the steamer, and of that letter Mr. Tottenham made a copy on the steamer. That copy was handed to Mr. M'Lean, one of the representatives of the Mutual of New York, and through some inadvertence it got lost, and was afterwards found in the papers connected with the insurance after

Charge to the Jury.

Cecil's death. It is dated " The Royal Route Steamer ' Iona,' " but that only means this, that the person who copied it had got possession of the steamer paper. The date to which it refers is 7th August, 1893, and it reads—" If you will pay the premiums on the two policies of assurance on my life of £10,000 each with the Mutual Insurance Company of New York, I am willing that you should hold the policies as security for all moneys due to you from me, and as security for all liabilities incurred by you on my behalf; and in the event of my death occurring before the repayment of these moneys, you will be the sole beneficiary of these policies, and I have given notice to the Mutual Insurance Company of New York that you are the person to whom the insurance is payable, and they have accepted my notice.—Yours sincerely, W. D. C. Hambrough."

Now, these policies, the Crown say, were the temptation to do this act. The prisoner's counsel, on the other hand, maintains that, while it had been suggested that the proper course would be to take out the policies in Mrs. Monson's own name, the policies were taken out in Cecil's own name; and that he knew this is shown by his letter, which I referred to formerly as a letter to Tottenham; and that Monson knew is shown by the evidence that these policies were unassignable by Cecil until he came of age. The case put to you on that matter is this, that they were a declaration on his part, which could be referred to as a matter of honour when he came of age, and possibly as a matter of honour by others to whom advances had been made, so that these advances might be repaid after his death took place. And it certainly is proved by the evidence led by the Crown itself that, as regards any power by Cecil to assign before he was twenty-one, or any power to recover if he died before twenty-one, Monson was quite aware that there was none.

And, gentlemen, in this matter I think it necessary to read to you a few words of Mr. Tottenham's evidence. Mr. Tottenham is a gentleman for whom we have not very much estimation. He is called by the Crown, and this is the evidence which he gives upon that letter—" Was there something said about Mrs. Monson making a proposal for an insurance on the life of Cecil—that the proposal be made by Mrs. Monson, and that the policy be made out in her favour?—No; Monson seemed to be under the impression that the assignment which he had would not operate. From Cecil?—Yes. That it was worthless?—Yes. That was after your arrival at Ardlamont on the 11th?—Yes. Then, after the funeral, was a claim made to the insurance office?—Yes. Did you make that claim?—Yes, I made that claim. Why was that?—I made the claim on behalf of Mrs. Monson." No doubt he had seen it to his advantage, having made the arrangement with Mrs. Monson to pay him a quarter of the money. " And why

Alfred John Monson.

Lord Justice-Clerk

was it you made the claim when Monson told you he did not think the assignment was good?—I had an arrangement with Monson that if I could get the money paid I was to have my £4000 out of it, and I thought it possible I might get it paid. May I put it that you were rather thinking of bluffing the insurance office?—Yes, that is just it.'' Now, this is the evidence of Mr. Tottenham. You can give it such weight as you may think proper. He also said to the representatives of the insurance company on the 14th, I think, the Monday after the death, or later than that, that he could not get a penny. It is quite true that, as I pointed out to you already, Monson made believe that this was going to be a fund from which the account might be replenished, when he went with Tottenham about the making of a claim; and that also Tottenham, having made this assignation, says to him that he is going to try what he could do, he having some information in regard to Scots law in this case which he hopes may lead to an effectual attack on the company. But as far as our information goes, the law of England provides that a claim on an assignation by a minor is absolutely worthless; and as regards this matter, if you consider that Monson went with Tottenham and backed him up in reference to this claim, it is only fair to him to keep in mind that he was dependent on Tottenham, and he could not afford to quarrel with Tottenham. Tottenham had thought the '' show '' worth carrying on. He was willing to purchase the life interest of Major Hambrough in the belief that when Cecil came of age it would repay him. Now, nothing would be got from Tottenham after the death unless he had hope of getting something out of these policies. I suppose you can have no doubt whatever that Mr. Tottenham was not going to advance one single sixpence to any one unless he could make his own out of it.

It is certainly clear that, if the prisoner Monson knew that the assignations of these policies were not worth the paper they were written on, then he could do nothing worse for his own interests than kill young Hambrough, because young Hambrough, as long as he lived, was—if I may use a vulgar expression—the decoy-duck by which money was to be got out of Tottenham '' to carry on the show '' until he should come of age, in the hope that, by some arrangement or other with reference to the Eagle Company mortgage, the source of a fund might be obtained through which Tottenham and the prisoner might get their own out of him. Now, what they were after in this is obvious. In a letter on their arrival at Ardlamont, the prisoner writes to Tottenham, saying—'' We are all thoroughly satisfied with the place, and I am sure this will keep Hambrough well in hand until the momentous time arrives when he comes of age.'' There was nothing wrong in that—I mean nothing criminal. The object was to keep Cecil as a friend of the prisoner and Tottenham until he should come of

400

Charge to the Jury.

Lord Justice-Clerk

age, in the belief which they both entertained that something could be worked out by which they would get their profit; and then a scheme seems to have been suggested, either by Hambrough himself or one of his brother officers, or, possibly, by Monson, for Monson writes to Tottenham to say—" His (this lad's) latest proposal is that Whiteley (one of his brother officers), myself, and himself should start on a tour through South Africa about February, and leave you to look after his affairs until his return." And Tottenham writes back in effect to say that, if he succeeded while they were away in making some arrangement—whether good or bad for the young man we do not know—but such arrangement as would carry on matters and enable the prisoner and Tottenham to get this bonus, these documents were to reach Natal just when he came of age. The shooting party out there were to be at Natal at the time in order to sign them. Now, that was what was before the parties, and it comes to this, that, if you are satisfied that Monson was in the sure and certain belief that the assignations of these policies were worth nothing, or, rather, to take it the other way, if you cannot with safety say that you are not satisfied of the contrary, that goes a long way to answer the question whether there was actual motive for the murder or not. I leave that matter with you. I do not know that there is in the documents that are before us, or in the evidence, anything which shows as matter of fact that he did believe that these assignations were good. If he did not believe them to be good, then a great deal of the superstructure built upon the foundation of motive would necessarily fall. But you are the judges whether that is so or not.

But I must tell you this, that the law of the land does not require any proof from the prosecutor of motive at all. If it is clear and certain that a crime has been committed, it is not an essential part of the public prosecutor's case to prove that there was motive for the crime. If he can prove the case without any motive, he is entitled to a verdict. But, then, another thing. Where the evidence is circumstantial only, and the guilt of a prisoner is only inferential and is not proved as a matter of fact by the evidence of witnesses who saw the crime, then the question of motive becomes of vital importance. If there is motive clearly and distinctly proved, then it is of enormous importance to the prosecution. If motive is displaced, or even made reasonably doubtful, it is enormously in favour of the prisoner.

Now, gentlemen, let us go back to 8th August. This brings us at once face to face with the arrival of the man called Scott, who, it is said by the prosecution, through the Solicitor-General, was a party to a plot for murder. He arrives by boat, and gets out by mistake at Tighnabruaich. He does not know very well where he is going to. He has a piece of paper in his possession marked " Ardlamont," and the boots of the hotel knows that he

Alfred John Monson.

is going there. He drives along towards Kames Pier, and is picked up by Monson in a trap which had gone to Kames to meet Monson.

And here comes in the great mystery of the case, and I think you will agree with me that the mystery has not been in the least cleared up. The Solicitor-General made a strong point of his allegation that this man Scott came there as a party to a plot for murder. Can you come to any conclusion in your own minds why he should be there as a co-conspirator for any such purpose? In regard to either of the crimes charged in the indictment, the drowning attempt or the successful shooting, I must say I have a difficulty in seeing what he was there for. I listened with considerable anxiety and care to the Solicitor-General in his speech upon this part of the case to see what he suggested, and all he suggested as regards the drowning incident was this, that it was important to Monson to have some one by him who might aid him, after he had succeeded in drowning Hambrough, in getting to the shore. I do not quite understand of what use a man would be upon the shore to a man in reference to whom it was a fact in the case that he was a swimmer. If you see any grounds for holding that, in the incidents of that night, Scott was there for the purpose of assisting in a determined criminal plot, then, of course, you will give effect to them. But, in watching this case, I have paid great attention to see whether there was anything to support that suggestion. At the present moment I am unable to see it. The idea of his being there to give assistance to Monson seems out of the question, and, if the suggestion be that he was there to give assistance in the drowning, it is very difficult to see how such assistance could be given by a party on the shore and not in the boat. Further than that, I do not quite see where the inducement was for him to take part in an attempted murder, as the Crown hold this was. So far as we know, Scott had nothing to do with Cecil Hambrough. He had no transaction with him. So far as we know, he only met him casually in London. Possibly he is the man who is suggested. Even then, the Crown have no theory even to show that he had any interest to murder young Hambrough. Assume him to have been, as he is alleged to have been, a low-class bookmaker from London, and that he was personally known to Monson in London, is there any theory put forward as to why he was brought there except the fact—as the Crown hold—that there was an attempted murder one night and a murder next day? It has not been shown that this man Scott had any connection with the affairs of Hambrough and Monson; and, so far as I can see, if the drowning or the shooting was to be carried out, there was no need for the presence of this stranger at all. Therefore, if there was no interest on the part of this third party, it must have been as a hired assassin to assist that he was there, if the

402

Charge to the Jury.

Crown's theory be correct; but for this view, too, there is no basis that I can see.

No doubt his presence there is mysterious in many ways, but, gentlemen, it is for the Crown to solve that mystery. If there be anything to make the matter one involving a criminal charge, it is for the Crown to solve the mystery. It will not do for the Crown just to point into the dark and say, "Unless you, the prisoner, throw light into that darkness, you must be held to have been engaged in a crime." The business of the Crown in such a case as this is to throw the light which will enable us to see. Now, the Solicitor-General says that there can be no doubt that this man Scott is Davis, that he answers to the description of Edward Davis. But that does not establish the identity of the man. To say that these men had a certain colour of eyes, certain kind of hair, and so on will not establish their identity. I wonder how many people in this country have within the last two or three months been under police surveillance, and some actually apprehended, because they so much resembled the description given of this man. There is no more frequent thing in this country than mistaken identity. When a description is given of a man, and we see a man something like him, we wonder whether he is the man or not; but, merely because he is like the description, he is not to be held to be the man and punished accordingly. It seems to me that the suggestion that, because the man who was at Ardlamont bears a description very simlar to the description of the man Edward'Davis, whom Monson knew in London, does not take you any way whatever towards settling that question.

The Solicitor-General referred to the prisoner's declaration given upon the charge of drowning. Just in passing, I may say that I entirely concur in the observations of the prisoner's counsel upon that matter. Mr. Monson was at first brought up solely on the shooting. He had an opportunity of meeting his agents a short time before that declaration was emitted, and, if he states in that declaration that he does not wish to make any further statement except that he is innocent of the charge, that is not a declaration which can be founded on against him. Observe, what is put to the prisoner is this—"You are now going to be asked some questions, and you may answer them or not as you please. Whatever is taken down may be used in evidence against you, but cannot be evidence in your favour." Is it strange that, in these circumstances, on many occasions, and particularly on occasions when undoubtedly the person who is charged was at the scene of the alleged crime, he should be advised by his agents to say— "I am not going to answer any questions just now; I reserve my defence"? I have from this very chair heard the Lord Justice-General, Lord Colonsay, even before the law was passed which gives an accused person the right to consult his agent, rebuke the Crown

Alfred John Monson.

for referring, as against the prisoner, to the declaration in which the prisoner had declined to answer questions. You will accept that from me as being the law on that matter. In this case the Solicitor-General very fairly did not make any comment of that kind, but the declaration, most properly, was read to you, in which he maintained his innocence, and that declaration does not in the least prejudice the prisoner. The declaration to which the Solicitor-General referred was the second declaration. It appears that it did not enter the minds of the authorities for a very considerable time to make this charge of attempted drowning, and it was only upon 30th October—that is to say, more than two months and a half after the events had happened—that the prisoner was removed from Greenock and taken over to Argyllshire to be examined on this new charge. Now, by that time he and his advisers had had ample opportunities of knowing the whole case against him and of examining what the witnesses had to say, and the prisoner, on being brought up, then made a statement which he dictated at the time, word for word, doubtless, what he and his agents had carefully revised as being the proper statement for him to make. At the close of that statement, and upon that charge, he was asked—" Is Scott, to whom you have referred, really called Davis, and do you know him? " And he, having given this statement which he and his agents had arranged, did not allow himself to be drawn into saying anything else, declined to answer the question. All he says is—" I have already said that I have no further answer to give to this charge." In doing so he was quite within his right, and I have to tell you that nothing can be urged to his prejudice because of that answer.

Now, as regards this man Scott, the prisoner's advisers have proved to you that they used the only means they had to find him, upon the prisoner's personal instructions, and the Crown have also used their best endeavours to find him. He has disappeared; we do not know where he is. It is not to be said that he has disappeared at the instance of the prisoner, because there is no such evidence before you. It is for the public prosecutor, with all the power of money which the country places at his disposal for the investigation of crime, to find this man. His absence is certainly not charged against the prisoner, or made a point against him by the Crown. It must be kept in view, in this case, that no prosecution was thought of for a considerable time after the event, and the traces of a man may disappear in those circumstances which would not have disappeared if the Crown had instituted their inquiries at once. The absence of this man, who was at Ardlamont on those two days, may be an unfortunate thing for the prisoner. He cannot be held responsible for it. If the view of the Crown is that he could have been a witness, could have given evidence, then, again, the Crown cannot prove his

404

Charge to the Jury.

Lord Justice-Clerk

absence as telling against the prisoner, because it is their duty
to put him into the box to give evidence. The prisoner is under
no such obligation. The day on which the death took place Monson
was heard to say to Scott, " It is a pity you cannot stay." And
what happened? The doctor turned round, as told by Steven,
the factor, and said there was no need for him to stay, because
he had made his investigation, and was quite satisfied.

I think it my duty to say all these things to you, because it
necessarily happens that prejudice arises against a prisoner at
the bar if an alleged accomplice disappears. I have told you
what I think the sound view to take of the matter, that you
must consider this case apart altogether from that disappearance.
If, immediately after the perpetration of a crime, a man, who is
in association with one of the criminals at the bar, is found actually
escaping from justice, disguised, using means to elude the police,
and so on, and if the prisoner who is under trial is proved to have
been privy to that, that would be a very important factor. Of
that there is no evidence here whatever, so far as I can see.
Monson, we are told, when they were taking this place, Ardlamont,
was most profuse in his invitation to all and sundry to come and
visit them there. It is a case of a man taking a shooting, and
in a grandiose way giving a kind of invitation—what we call a
French invitation—" Oh, come and see us at Ardlamont and take
a day's shooting." It is meant for nothing; it is just the high
talk of people who are wanting to show off that they have got a
fine place. Scott was a fairly presentable man. The servants
thought he was in the position of a clerk, although we have the
opinion of the governess concerning him that he was not quite a
gentleman and dropped his " h's." From the evidence of Mr.
George Sweeney—who was very unwilling to let it out, although
I do not see why—it appeared that they had some relatives at
Helensburgh. It is just possible that Mr. Edward Davis, who had
taken a trip northwards to see those relatives, and having an
invitation from Monson in his mind, just thought he would pack
a bag, take a run down in the steamer, and see Monson at Ardlamont, accepting his drinking-bar invitation to come up. If that
was so, I think it would be quite natural in Monson not to wish
his wife or his children, or his governess, or even Cecil Hambrough,
to know that he had got a bookmaker's clerk as a companion. He
might very well say that he was a Mr. Scott come to look at the
boilers, in order to pass him off. Then, having committed himself
to that, he would have to stick to it. Now, you will form your own
opinion upon all that. It has occurred to me as a suggestion that
might be made in the case.

Form your own opinion whether you have ground for thinking
that that is conclusive proof that that man came there for a joint
plot. You have no evidence of that whatever; nor have you

405

Alfred John Monson.

anything to suggest it, except that he was present on the shore and was present in the wood. There may be suspicion; but we are dealing here with what is substantially and fully made out. I only suggest these things for your consideration. If you consider it safe on the meagre evidence you have heard—and which, to my mind, amounts to nothing more than that the man was there—then you will hold accordingly. I submit what I have said for your consideration, and it is for you to accept it or reject it. As I said before, it is suspicious in many ways, but it is nothing more. It is quite clear that there had been no inspection of boilers either by Scott or Monson; they seem to have spent a pleasant day bathing and boating in open view. No one saw them doing to the boat anything that was suspicious. It is all right when the children are in it, and it is hauled up while the nurse, Mrs. Monson, and Cecil are there.

That leads me up to the evidence in support of the first charge—the charge which was made upon the 30th, when the prisoner was taken in Argyllshire and accused of this attempted drowning. Now, the prosecutor says in his indictment that these two men induced Hambrough to go in the boat that night. Is there any evidence of that? So far as we can learn, this lad was very fond of fishing, and liked to go at night "splash" fishing. I see no evidence that there was any inducement here to go on that night at all, and that he did not go in the ordinary course to fish. Now, the boat in which they went out was the boat in which the net was. It is said there was another boat brought round and another net put into it. They went out in the boat which had been hired from M'Kellar. It is said that there was a plug hole cut with a knife in the bottom of the boat, which had not been there before.

Now, gentlemen, there is no proof who did that. The prisoner's statement that it was cut by Cecil himself is not evidence, but there is no proof who did it at all. It is a bad plug hole, badly shaped, and difficult to keep the plug in. It is at the wrong place. A board has been taken away to make it. A boat like that has a flat bottom to enable you to stand without slipping, and there is a guard board put above that again. That, of course, prevented a plug hole of an ordinary kind being made, which is made in the low part of the boat, whereby any water might be readily run off. This was a boat in reference to which we are told it had no need for a plug hole. It was a light, varnished boat, which, when you got it upon the shore, could be easily overturned and the water run out. In point of fact, it had been so used, and M'Kellar tells us that he never had a plug hole in such a boat. There is no place for it. The board was taken away, and the object of the removal was to get as low down as possible in order to make this hole, and so let off the water. If

Charge to the Jury.

Lord Justice-Clerk

that piece of board had been replaced in its position, the hole would not have been seen from the inside of the boat at all. There is no evidence who made that plug hole; but, whoever made it, the prisoner's counsel says that that is not the way that a man would go about drowning another man in a small boat in the bay. If he got him into the bay—he being an expert swimmer, and the other not being a swimmer—he would simply just make the boat upset and throw his friend into the water. That is matter for your consideration, to consider whether that is reasonable. No doubt, in a plug hole like this—roughly made—the plug might easily come out; but it is for you to consider whether you have evidence before you to prove that Monson and Scott together, or that Monson, made that hole, and that, if he did it, he did it that the boat should fill with water, and so drown young Hambrough. Then another point arises. The evidence shows that when the boat upset it naturally filled with water, and that young Hambrough got on to a rock, and, of course, the rock saved him in deep water. I must say that, if the case was to be presented to you on the footing that if there was deep water there was no rock on which Hambrough could rest, I should have expected from the Crown much more satisfactory evidence than they have here. a very simple survey—a very simple examination of the water in the bay—would have proved that fact conclusively. Even the Admiralty charts have not been produced. In point of fact, Cecil Hambrough and Mr. Monson got into the water that night; in point of fact, Cecil Hambrough and Monson got to shore; and in point of fact, it is plain it never entered Cecil's mind that anything of the kind suggested had been done for the purpose of murdering him. Just take the case that might have occurred. If, when the boat was upset, Cecil had not got hold of the rock, but had kept his head above water, then he was either in shallow water, or it is not easy to see why any one who was attempting to drown him did not just leave him to drown. If he was upon a rock, what rock is it proved that he could have been on? From the evidence there is nothing from which it could be deduced that Monson could have taken him out to a place where he could drown him. It is said that Scott was there to save Monson, who was a swimmer, by bringing out another boat, and taking him out of the deep water. We have no proof where the boat was. Apparently the deceased did not know, and there is no proof that Scott knew where it was. It is said that Mr. Monson was telling a falsehood when he says he swam about 200 yards, but when you are swimming to the shore on a dark night—a night with no moon—when you are swimming to the shore in order to get another man in, who is rather unhappily sitting or standing upon a rock, you can have little idea of distance. In a case of this kind scraps and shreds of ideas of fact are, to my mind, not satisfactory. If Cecil Hambrough was out in deep

Alfred John Monson.

water and was thrown out of the boat, why was he not left there to die, if the intention was to drown him? We never heard before of an attempted murder or drowning in which the person against whom the attempt was made never had the slightest idea of anything of the kind, but came home with his companions, had his whisky and water, and laughed and joked, and was on perfectly friendly terms. Now, you must consider this case of the boat alone. Subsequent events can hardly throw light upon it. Is it proved to your satisfaction that that plug hole was criminally made by the prisoner, or by his suggestion, or with his knowledge; and that with the aid of that plug hole he tried to drown Cecil Hambrough? If it is proved to your satisfaction it would throw a strong light on what happened next day; but if it is not proved, if there is no ground for holding it proved, then it can throw no light on the events of the next day at all, none whatever.

Now, gentlemen, I come to what is the weightiest charge against the prisoner—what is really the true issue that you have to consider. And that issue has been grappled with in such a masterly manner on both sides of the bar, that I think you are well possessed with arguments on the subject. Everything, I think, that human skill can do to expiscate the facts of this case from the prosecution and defence points of view has been done. Cecil Hambrough did meet with his death on the 10th of August, and the events which lead up to it are these. The prisoner Monson rose in the morning and went to get Hambrough's gun from the keeper at the office. His case is that Hambrough had started off shortly before he got out with the 12-bore gun, and that he followed up with the 20-bore gun, and that might be so. There is nothing inconsistent with the Crown evidence in that, because Hambrough had on previous occasions carried the 12-bore gun. And now, gentlemen, the first time they are seen is by Mr. Dunn, who was in the school-house at the bottom of the wood in which the injury took place. Mr. Dunn was at one window, and saw them come along the road and go into the field adjoining the wood. He then transferred himself to the other side of the house, and from the window there saw them enter the wood at a certain distance up, and they did so exactly as you would expect three men to enter who were going to take a snapshot at rabbits in that way. One shooter went to the right side, the other shooter went to the left side, and the man who was carrying the game went as a sort of beater in the middle. And in that position they disappeared from Dunn's view. The Solicitor-General made some comments on the statement made by Monson with reference to this matter. Monson said—" I remember seeing a man watching us. I am told that he mentioned to some person here that he saw us in the wood." He says in another communication—" He saw three of us, Mr. Hambrough, Scott, and myself, enter the wood. If this be so, no doubt he would cor-

Charge to the Jury.

roborate what I have told you as to our relative positions as we went through the wood."

The Solicitor-General made some rather severe comments upon this, for which I do not think there is much foundation. You must assume that when the prisoner made this statement he did so as an innocent man, because we cannot find him guilty until we are satisfied of it. He saw a man at the window in the morning; and he hears also from somebody else that this man had told him he had seen them go into the wood, and he let the authorities know. All he said was, " This is the man that saw us enter the wood, and he can confirm the statement that I made as to the order in which we entered the wood." That is all he said, and I think it is very natural.

Now, Hambrough is shot, and I leave the place where he was shot in the meantime. The next thing that happens is that the prisoner and Scott return alone. Some suggestion was made early in the case that they returned by a circuitous route. I do not think that is the case, because they took the natural way by the pathway at the north end of the wood, and then past the offices. One, however, would have expected that they would have tried to alarm some one at the place, and to get some one at the place to come to their assistance. They did not do that, but different men are actuated by different motives in moments of agitation, and although this circumstance is somewhat strange, it is not a circumstance that goes very far. They reach the house, and inform Wright, the butler, that Mr. Hambrough had been killed. I may make this remark, that if before they left they were perfectly satisfied that the man was really dead, it may be that they did not think it necessary to rush for assistance, as men usually do rush for assistance at moments of accident. Another point that was made against the prisoner was that before bringing the guns into the house he took the cartridges out. I do not think that much, if anything, can be founded upon that. I think it is almost a mechanical action on the part of people who are accustomed to handle guns, and to handle them carefully, especially in these days of breech-loaders, not to bring them into the house loaded, but to take out the cartridges and close the breeches. They go back to the spot, accompanied by others, and they find Cecil lying on the top of the wall, a pool of blood at his head. His feet are inclined diagonally towards the wood. There are two pieces of bone, which are proved to have been pieces out of the head, a few inches off. There is a 12-bore wad with blood on it upon one side of it. There is a little blood on part of the collar. He is carried to the house, and the wounds are washed, and the doctor called in. At this stage we come to a phase of the case which is an unfortunate one—just as unfortunate for the Crown as for the prisoner. I refer to the first report of Dr. Macmillan. The doctor seems to have taken it for

Alfred John Monson.

granted that this was a shot which had gone off and lodged the charge inside Cecil Hambrough's head, and he certified accidental death. And it was he who said to Scott that there was no need for him to wait, because his examination and report to the authorities would be quite satisfactory.

No suspicion was aroused. Then a little later the insurance officials appear upon the scene in the person of M'Lean and his secretary. Monson takes them to the Procurator-Fiscal, and it is said by the Procurator-Fiscal that in walking up from the steamer to his office Monson had said it was a 20-bore gun with which Hambrough was shot, and he says he is quite sure of this because he gives as his reason of being quite sure of it that the idea of a 20-bore gun was, when Monson stated it, an entirely novel idea to him. He said, " I had never seen one, and I thought it would be very important to see it; therefore," he says, " I cannot be mistaken." Now, gentlemen, if it were thoroughly and securely fixed that he could not be mistaken upon that, it certainly would be a very strong element in this case. But, gentlemen, looking at the papers, I find that the Procurator-Fiscal, if he thought it his duty, as I have no doubt he did, to study with care the report first handed to him by his own doctor, who made the investigation, would have known that it was a 20-bore gun that was said to have been used at the time. That was stated to him in writing, because I find at page 7 of this print, " Information above given makes it probable that the deceased was going along the wall with the gun— a short 20-bore—under his arm "; and that is in a medical report which the Procurator-Fiscal got on 16th August. Therefore, the reason that he gives for his certainty that it was told to him by Monson entirely falls. He knew that fact from the report of the doctor. But, however that was, naturally on finding out there were considerable insurances made on Hambrough's life a few days before, he set to work to make some inquiry. It struck me as a very extraordinary thing in making the inquiries that he should ask the prisoner to go back to the house and pick out the gun and some cartridges and send them to him. However, that is what was done. He instituted inquiries, with the result that the prisoner was apprehended on 29th August. Now, the prisoner's account of what happened is this—that he and Scott found Hambrough below the wall, with the gun beside him. They tried to rouse him, and could not, and, realising that he was dead, they lifted him up and placed him on the top of the bank. Now, there is some difference of opinion as to whether that can be so, looking to the state of the ground. The ground immediately below the wall has a ditch in it, and that ditch had water in it at the time of the occurrence, and brackens growing over it. Beyond that there is a grass sward. It seems to have been mooted that Hambrough had fallen, and had been found on the other side of that ditch, and

410

Charge to the Jury.

had been lifted to the place on the top of the dyke where he was seen by the witnesses.

This is a very important point. The case put for the prisoner is that the body was lying in the ditch just below the wall, and, if you believe that, it is not very easy to see that there would not be some signs of it left on the ground. If he was in a ditch which had water in it, one would also have expected to find that there would be some water about his clothes. But even had his clothes been wet, that, of course, might have been accounted for in this case by the fact that it was a wet and stormy morning. Nothing was told to us about the quality of the water in the ditch; if it was just a clear, running rill the water would, of course, have had the same effect on his clothes as rain would have. Curiously, we cannot get any distinct evidence as to this point—in regard to the original place where the body lay. Mr. Steven, apparently, on a recent occasion when he was asked to show the place where the body was said to have lain, showed a place where there were no brackens at all, and himself lay down on the grass at a part where there were no brackens. At this stage of the case you will have to consider very carefully—as I have no doubt you have done already—the evidence given upon both sides in reference to blood. The witnesses for the prosecution say that if Hambrough fell outside the dyke they would expect to find blood upon the ground, and possibly tracks or drops of blood from the place where he was said to have fallen to the place where he was ultimately lying. On the other hand, the witnesses for the defence, with equal skill, say that it depended entirely upon circumstances. Loose pieces of bone, they point out, were driven into the head, and their view is that the pressure of these pieces of bone possibly held the ruptured vessel. Hæmorrhage might not in that case, they say, take place to any extent until, the body being moved, the broken bones were shaken and so dropped out, and this, in their opinion, accounts for the marks of blood being found at the place where the body ultimately lay. Further, they say if there was slight bleeding from the edges of the wound, marks of blood on such grass as there was on the top of the dyke, on a wet morning like that, might perhaps not be found unless minute and careful inspection was made immediately. It is for you to judge of these different points of the evidence.

The next and very important question is with regard to the gun with which the shooting took place. That it was a 12-bore gun there is no doubt. Both sides agree upon that matter. That is proved by the comparative weight of the pellets, which were pellets of No. 5 cartridges as distinguished from No. 6, and there were no No. 5 cartridges for the 20-bore gun. Gentlemen, here again we come across a sad want of care, I think, in investigating an important case of this kind at the outset. Mr. Steven says that

411

Alfred John Monson.

at the time he felt some cartridges in Cecil's pocket, but nothing was done about them. His coat is carried in and is afterwards carefully brushed and hung up, and one would have expected that any cartridges would have been taken out of the pockets. The curious thing is this : one of the strong points made by the Crown against the prisoner is that on 28th or 29th August, three weeks afterwards, certain cartridges are found in the pockets of this coat. If you are satisfied that the Crown have with sufficient care traced that coat, and have shown that it was never interfered with, and that no alteration was made of the cartridges in it, then that will be matter for your consideration. On the other hand, if this coat, from the time of the death down to the time when it was taken possession of, was treated just as a coat hanging up on a peg in a room where a number of cartridges were lying about, one would have liked to have heard the evidence of all the persons who were in that room. With these observations you have this fact, that in the pockets of the coat were found eighteen 20-bore cartridges and one 12-bore cartridge of No. 6 shot. Gentlemen, you heard the observations that Mr. Thomson made upon that matter, which are well worthy of your consideration. Of course, they are only matter of explanation ; they are not evidence. They are explanations addressed to you as reasonable to accept in the circumstances.

One thing about these cartridges indicates plainly, as clear evidence, that it is proved that Cecil did sometimes use the 12-bore gun, because one of these cartridges which were found in his pocket was a 12-bore cartridge with Schultze powder ; and I think the suggestion of the defence is this : this lad, going out for a turn round the woods, where he would get two or three shots, going round the wood in the morning, if he took the prisoner's gun, had picked up three or four amberite 12-bore cartridges with No. 5 shot and put them in his pocket along with others. That is the suggestion. Now, gentlemen, these two points about the cartridges and the guns are very important points for your consideration in regard to the question before you on this charge of shooting ; and I think these points are all the points of clear evidence which it will be necessary for me to refer to.

But now we come to what I may call the theoretical evidence of the case—that is to say, the evidence of persons of skill, drawing inferences from their skill for the purpose of aiding you in your decision. In such a case as this the evidence of gunmakers, the evidence of persons skilled in the use and carrying of guns, the evidence of doctors skilled in wounds and their effects, are all of great importance. Such evidence is always of the greatest importance, if it is recent after the event. It may be a misfortune of the prosecution, but it is not, certainly, the fault of the prisoner, that all these investigations in this case are of a comparatively late

412

Charge to the Jury.

Lord Justice-Clerk

date; and in so far as the case of the prosecution is weakened by their being of late date, so far the prosecution has to suffer in the consideration of that evidence.

Now, the first matter to which I think it necessary to refer in this particular branch of the case is the question of these paths which diverge from the body backward into the wood. These are spoken to by one of the witnesses—I think the witness Whyte—as going from where the body was, down through between some trees and a quantity of willows, in a backward direction down the wood. Gentlemen, the evidence of this witness is contradictory in this way, that he denied having seen anything of the kind, I think, at first; but, assuming that he did see such paths, there are many observations to be made upon it. It would have been very important, and a matter which should have been carefully investigated by more than one eye before any conclusion should be drawn from it. I do not know if any of you have had any experience or skill in going through woods; but it is quite certain that the position of things in a wood—trees and brushwood and the small growth that occurs upon the ground in such woods—almost instinctively leads people in particular directions which are not straight through the wood, and if you have a number of willow sallows growing up at one place, and whins at another, instinctively you direct yourself where you can readily pass through; and if people have been in the habit of frequenting the wood, as apparently was the case here—and I think there is evidence distinctly that that wood had been shot through on more than one occasion—you will not be surprised to find such marks of people having passed through the wood in a certain direction. It is founded on, so far as I can see, for the purpose of bringing the prisoner through the the wood up to this place, and I feel bound to say that I consider it unsatisfactory. All I have said to you, however, is just suggested for your consideration. Are you safe in holding that the fact that there were some marks—which there has never been any opportunity of testing on behalf of the prisoner—gives you a sufficient guide on this part of the case?

The next question is a very important one, and that is the question of the shot-marks on the trees; and I think it may fairly be said that the public prosecutor has perilled his case as to how this part of it is to be treated on those marks upon the trees. You have heard the observations made on both sides as to this matter—weighty and pregnant observations. The prisoner says, through his counsel—" I have proved that many, many shots have been fired in that wood in all directions. I have proved that wood-pigeons frequent it, rising from the ground just at the edge of the wood, that might very well be shot just at the level of 6 feet from the ground." But here, again, comes in a very important part of the evidence, which results entirely from the delay. Every one,

413

Alfred John Monson.

Lord Justice-Clerk

I think, will be satisfied that if you are going to found any strong
and decided opinion upon the position of a number of pellet marks
on two or three trees, one behind the other, you would like to have
them examined within a short time of the alleged firing of the shot.
Unfortunately, that could not be done here, because the authorities
not having taken up the case till very late, it was five weeks after
the event had happened that anybody went to examine those trees.
And all the witnesses for the prosecution who were examined before
you said candidly that when they saw them they were not fresh,
but showed signs of age, and that the twigs that were broken had
withered away, although from Mr. Macnaughton the important fact
was brought out that the breaks on them were breaks of this year.
The prisoner could only meet this matter of the trees by going
to examine them through skilled persons when he was warned of
these charges against him, and sending such persons to examine
them, who state that they have made that a matter of special study.
Now they declare that the state of the pellet marks upon those trees
is a state inconsistent with their having been made at the time
at which this alleged murder took place.   That, of course, is
evidence of inference from observation, but it is based upon their
sworn experience, and there is no evidence to the contrary.   All
the Crown witnesses say is this—" We admit that they are not
recent.   We are able from our skill to testify that they could not
have been of great age.''   If it is not proved by the Crown that these
marks on the trees were made by the shot that killed Hambrough,
then all their theory of a horizontal shot fired from behind at a
distance of about 9 feet is gone.   The shot may have gone in
another direction from the position he was in, and if what they saw
on these trees is not proved—reasonably proved, of course—then
their whole theory upon that matter falls to the ground.

Then, gentlemen, the next thing is that two pieces of bone are
found near the head.   That, the prosecutor says, shows that they
were blown out by the shot.   On the other hand, one very remarkable thing about one of these pieces of bone is deponed to by both
the doctors in the defence—Dr. Hay and Dr. Sanders, particularly
Dr. Sanders—namely, that one of these pieces of bone was a piece
of bone belonging to the inside of the skull, chipped off in the inside
of the skull at a very hard part, and which, if chipped off at the
time of the injury, could only go forward and could not go backwards, and that, therefore, it must have fallen out from the body
being put down on the ground in the place where it was through
some shock or other.   That, at any rate, as far as it goes, confirms
the theory of the body having been lifted from the place where it
was, because if the shot went into the inside of the head and chipped
off a piece of the petrous bone it could only chip it off by driving
it forward, and, therefore, it must have been from some shock that
the body got afterwards that that piece of bone, along with the

414

Charge to the Jury.

Lord Justice-Clerk

other, fell away. And the same doctors say that the wad which struck the wound may also have fallen out on the head being laid down. You will take along with that that while the prisoner and Scott came up to the body, it is not natural to suppose that, if there was innocence, they, in ascertaining whether the man was alive or dead, would not turn him over at least. They would try to rouse him, and in doing that they would necessarily move him more or less round, and if the position is altered in any substantial degree, then the line to which the Crown pledge themselves as regards the firing of the shot is deviated from more or less.

The idea of all the theoretical witnesses is that this was a glancing shot—that is to say, a shot which, while doing damage, was at the same time deflected off at an angle. Here, again, we have some difficulty, because we do not know what the angle is. But if it was to go through and make the measured spots or marks which Mr. Macnaughton ascertained to be on the trees, then it must have gone practically in a straight direction, according to him. Some of them think that only part of the shot flying *en balle* —that is, in the mass—struck the head. But in point of fact this skilled evidence must be accepted with this modification, that, fortunately, there is not a very vast experience of such shots of this kind, homicidal or otherwise. Dr. Littlejohn said he had known three cases, only one of them a murder case; I was counsel in it myself. And he said that homicidal shooting by a shot-gun was of rare occurrence. The sort of case is generally that of an enraged poacher, who, on a moonlit night, is tempted, having a gun in his hand, to use it against the keepers who are endeavouring to capture him, not deliberately, but in the excitement of the moment, in order to allow him to get away from his captors.

Then, gentlemen, we come to a very important part of the case, indeed, a part of the case which is crucial. The theory of the Crown is that the man's head was struck by a shot fired 9 feet from the wall, or at such a distance from his head that he could not have been holding his gun himself. The whole theory is based upon that. Then that brings the muzzle back a certain distance from the head, and their own theory of the distance is 9 feet. Now, gentlemen, if that shot struck Hambrough's head *en balle*, as it is said, on the right-hand side, then there was an area above and an area below, and an area upon the left side of it, in which any pellets detaching themselves from the main mass must lodge themselves. The direction of the shot was rather more towards the head than its actual effect. It was directed towards the head at an angle, and at that angle it glanced off, and, therefore, did not take the effect it would have had had it gone on straight. If it had gone on straight, without glancing, it would have gone into the head—that is to say, it would have gone in rather to the left of the right-hand side of the head. If so, the area round that shot,

415

Alfred John Monson.

which the shot going *en balle* passed, must have exposed itself to any circulating pellets which were spreading out. Now, in this case, as I say, there is no evidence of any spreading out of the pellets at all. There are only four pellets found in the head; but these pellets, I take it, were part of the mass which was flying *en balle*, but from the way in which these pellets struck the bone they were diverted into the head instead of glancing off. The suggestion of the Solicitor-General yesterday was that the whole injury was done by these four pellets. On that suggestion I shall just take one witness from my own recollection, Dr. Joseph Bell, who said quite distinctly that in his opinion the mass of shot—taking the distance at which he assumed the shot was fired as 9 feet—would have a diameter of 1½ inches, and that one-half of that struck the head. Now, gentlemen, if it was 9 feet, what would be the area of the pellets going on to the head to the left of the place where it struck? Have you materials for determining that? You have the Crown card at 9 feet; you have the prisoner's board at 9 feet; you have this diagram on behalf of the prisoner, with reference to which the witness who made it was not cross-examined.

Look at the spread of the shot at 9 feet, and, if you judge with your own eye—place in imagination a circle the size of a head at 9 feet—you will see there how much of that head is covered by the spreading shot. Now, in this case, neither in the neck nor in the head, nor at the side, nor upon the head above the wound, nor in the collar of the coat is there any trace of the pellets— not one; and that is a very important matter for your consideration. Dealing here with inference upon evidence, there are men skilled in that matter who have made experiments, who tell you if that shot was fired at 8 or 9 feet there must have been a circle of considerable size in which a number of pellet marks must be found. Gentlemen, that is all I have to say to you upon the direction and distance of the shot. If the absence of any spread of pellets indicates to you that it would not be safe to hold that the Crown theory is right, that the shot was fired at a distance of 8 or 9 feet, that will have a bearing on the case in two aspects. First, it will bear upon it in this aspect, that the shot was not nearly so likely to be fired by another in that case, because, from the character of the wound, the assailant would have had to come up quite close; but, second, it is of importance in this aspect that if, taking, of course, the most favourable and reasonable inference for the prisoner, as, of course, we are bound to do, the absence of any pellet marks indicates that the shot had not begun to spread, and if the shot had not begun to spread, then the injury must have been inflicted at a much less distance, and then you are at once outside of the theory set up by the Crown. You see the great importance to the Crown case of that 8 or 9 feet. The gun must be got out of the reach of the deceased himself. If it be the fact

416

Charge to the Jury.

that there was any spread of shot indicating a greater distance than 2 feet, then the prisoner, of course, would be entitled to the benefit of the doubt as regards the possibility of accident. Now, the prisoner has produced sets of photographs illustrative of the supposed ways in which such a shot might be fired. The comment made upon these is that in some cases the butt of the gun is supported artificially, in order to get the gun into the particular position, and that is an observation that you will give such weight to as you think proper. Then, I think it proper to point out to you that while these photographs are necessarily taken in relation to a fixed man—a man not moving—the idea they are meant to depict to you is that of a man moving, a man carrying a gun in a careless manner, so that something, perhaps a whin bush, catches the trigger, with the result that the shot is driven into his head. You will give the weight you think proper to that consideration. And in regard to this we have a very curious incident, and I think it is right that I should mention it. It was very proper that Colonel Tillard should have come to aid us in this inquiry. A most extraordinary incident happened to him while out shooting in India. He was carrying his gun by the barrel, and something caused him to fall backward, with this extraordinary result, that the gun in his hands got into such a position that it shot him in the head, the shot striking the skull and passing through the ear. And, I suppose, if any doctor of experience had been asked before that accident happened to Colonel Tillard whether it was likely to happen in such a way, he would have had no hesitation in saying that such a thing could not possibly happen. But accidents do happen in very extraordinary ways.

One thing you must take along with you on this matter is that Cecil was proved to be very careless with his gun. He was a young lad, and probably had not much experience, and he was rash in his way of handling guns, so much so that one gentleman ceased to go out with him, so alarmed was he. Mr. Donald gave evidence to the same effect also.

There is one other point to which I think it necessary to call attention. It is suggested—at least it suggested itself to me, and I have no doubt it occurred to you—that if the accident happened by the man holding his gun along his arm, and its being caught by something, you would have singeing of the coat. That seems to me disproved, because this amberite powder, which only throws out a flame from the muzzle for an inch or so, does not produce singeing; and Mr. Tom Speedy, who experimented by firing a shot through his wife's hair—rather an alarming experiment—found that at the distance of an inch there was no singeing with amberite powder.

Now, gentlemen, I do not know that I have much more to say to you, and I think I had better now leave the case with you.

1 E   417

Alfred John Monson.

Lord Justice-Clerk

You have, as I said before, to consider the delay which took place in making the examinations. So far as that is unfavourable to the prisoner, he is not to suffer; in so far as it is unfavourable to the prosecution—I do not say they are to blame—they must take the consequences; at least, they can blame no one but themselves. But in so far as it is unfavourable to the prisoner, he cannot be allowed to suffer—indeed, it must not be allowed to be unfavourable to him. Lastly, just a word about the bearing of the prisoner. You have heard all I have to say about him. No one can approve of his proceedings in many respects, but I am satisfied that in this particular case every one who saw him believed him to be perfectly genuine in his grief at the occurrence. That is in his favour, but you must not put too much upon that. At the same time it would have been a striking circumstance if the fact had been otherwise. I think that the witnesses were justified in coming to the conclusion that his grief was genuine.

Now, gentlemen, you must consider how this case is to be disposed of. You have got a path to go on in this case in which you must see your way. You must neither walk through darkness at any point of it, nor leap over anything that you meet in it. It must be a straight path, and a path on which you have light. If you have light which takes you to the end of that path, so that you can give a verdict for the prosecution, then you must do it manfully, and you must not allow yourselves to be stopped, though Pity, with uplifted hands, stands pleading and entreating that you shall not go on. On the other hand, if there is any darkness or dimness on that path which you cannot clear away, you cannot go on to the end. If there is any obstruction on that path you have to stop there. The prisoner is entitled to that. And, lastly, if you yourselves do not see your way along that path without passing through darkness or dimness or other obstruction, you must not allow yourselves to be urged forward along that path blindly by any demon pushing you from behind, telling you that the prisoner is a bad man, a liar, and a cheat, and that, therefore, you should send him to his doom. You must keep yourselves free from that. These things have a bearing on the case if you can go on, but you must not allow them to push you on. I am quite sure whatever verdict you arrive at will meet the justice of the case, so far as Providence has allowed its mysteries to be revealed. Do your duty. Think of nothing that people may say. Do your duty manfully, either in convicting the prisoner, if you must convict him, or in acquitting him, if you are not tied up to the conclusion on the evidence that you must convict. Gentlemen, that is all I have to say to you. You have listened attentively to this case, and know it in all its bearings. And now you have to do your duty by the Crown and by the prisoner.

Verdict of the Jury.

Lord Justice-Clerk

The jury retired at seven minutes to four to consider the verdict, and after an absence of seventy-three minutes returned into Court.

The CLERK OF COURT—Gentlemen, what is your verdict?

The FOREMAN OF THE JURY—My Lord, the verdict of the jury is one of not proven on both charges.

The verdict having been recorded,

The LORD JUSTICE-CLERK addressed the jury as follows :— Gentlemen of the jury, I have to thank you for the great attention you have given to this very serious case, and hope that you have not suffered in health. I have to intimate to you that, on account of the time you have been here, none of you will be again summoned on a jury. I have now to discharge you.

The prisoner was then released from the dock, and left the Court.
